THE FREE SOCIETY

Books by Laurence M. Vance

The Other Side of Calvinism
A Brief History of English Bible Translations
The Angel of the Lord
Archaic Words and the Authorized Version
A Practical Grammar of Basic Biblical Hebrew
Double Jeopardy: The NASB Update
Christianity and War and Other Essays Against the Warfare State
King James, His Bible, and Its Translators
Greek Verbs in the New Testament and Their Principal Parts
War, Foreign Policy, and the Church
Guide to Prepositions in the Greek New Testament
The Myth of the Just Price and the Biblical Case for Laissez Faire
Guide to Nouns in the Greek New Testament
Guide to Adjectives in the Greek New Testament
Guide to Pronouns in the Greek New Testament
The Revolution that Wasn't
Rethinking the Good War
Galatians 1 & 2: Exposition, Commentary, Application
The Quatercentenary of the King James Bible
The War on Drugs Is a War on Freedom
War, Christianity, and the State: Essays on the Follies of
        Christian Militarism
Social Insecurity
War, Empire, and the Military: Essays on the Follies of War and
        U.S. Foreign Policy
The Making of the King James Bible—New Testament
Gun Control and the Second Amendment
Free Trade or Protectionism?
The Free Society

THE FREE SOCIETY

by

Laurence M. Vance

Vance Publications
www.vancepublications.com

ISBN: 978-0-9967869-3-5

Published and Distributed by: Vance Publications
P.O. Box 780671, Orlando, FL 32878
E-mail: vancepub@vancepublications.com
Website: www.vancepublications.com

Printed in the United States of America

TABLE OF CONTENTS

CHAPTER THREE
LIBERTARIANISM vs. LIBERALISM/CONSERVATISM

CHAPTER FOUR
DISCRIMINATION AND FREE ASSOCIATION

CHAPTER FIVE
VICTIMLESS CRIMES

CHAPTER SIX
THE FREE MARKET

CHAPTER SEVEN
THE FREE SOCIETY

FOR FURTHER READING

Bergland, David. *Libertarianism in One Lesson*. 9th ed. Cartersville: Advocates for Self-Government, 2005.

Block, Walter E. *Defending the Undefendable*. San Francisco: Fox & Wilkes, 1991.

_____. *Defending the Undefendable II: Freedom in All Realms*. East Sussex: Terra Libertas Publishing House, 2013.

_____. *The Case for Discrimination*. Auburn: Ludwig von Mises Institute, 2010.

DiLorenzo, Thomas J. *Organized Crime: The Unvarnished Truth about Government*. Auburn: Ludwig von Mises Institute, 2012.

Harsanyi, David. *Nanny State*. New York: Broadway Books, 2007.

Higgs, Robert. *Against Leviathan: Government Power and a Free Society*. Oakland: Independent Institute, 2004.

Huebert, Jacob H. *Libertarianism Today*. Santa Barbara: Praeger, 2010.

McWilliams, Peter. *Ain't Nobody's Business If You Do: The Absurdity of Consensual Crimes in a Free Society*. Los Angeles: Prelude Press, 1993.

Murphy, Robert P. *The Politically Incorrect Guide to Capitalism*. Washington, D.C.: Regnery Publishing, 2007.

Napolitano, Andrew P. *It Is Dangerous to Be Right When the Government Is Wrong: The Case for Personal Freedom*. Nashville: Thomas Nelson, 2011.

Paul, Ron. *Liberty Defined: 50 Central Issues that Affect Our Freedom*. New York: Grand Central Publishing, 2011.

Rockwell, Llewellyn H. *The Left, the Right, and the State*. Auburn: Ludwig von Mises Institute, 2008.

_____., ed. *The Economics of Liberty*. Auburn: Ludwig von Mises Institute, 1990.

_____., ed. *The Free Market Reader*. Auburn: Ludwig von Mises Institute, 1988.

Rothbard, Murray N. *Egalitarianism As a Revolt against Nature and Other Essays*. 2nd ed. Auburn: Ludwig von Mises Institute, 2000.

_____. *For a New Liberty: The Libertarian Manifesto*. Rev. ed. San Francisco: Fox & Wilkes, 1978.

_____. *Making Economic Sense*. Auburn: Ludwig von Mises Institute, 1995.

Sirico, Robert. *Defending the Free Market: The Moral Case for a Free Economy*. Washington, D.C.: Regnery Publishing, 2012.

Stossel, John. *No, They Can't: Why Government Fails—but Individuals Succeed*. New York: Threshold Editions, 2012.

INTRODUCTION

Most Americans think they live in a free society. They think that because they can find fifty varieties of salad dressing at the grocery store, choose from among a hundred types of wine at the liquor store, select a television channel from over 1,000 choices, download any movie or song they want from the Internet, and sit at home for hours playing the latest video game that they live in a free society. They are oblivious to the extent of government encroachment on their freedoms. They are complacent when it comes to government edicts. And they are ignorant as to what a free society really means.

Oh sure, Americans are free compared with the people of North Korea, Sudan, Myanmar, Yemen, Saudi Arabia, and Venezuela, but there are 190 other countries in the world. The truth is, Americans live in a relatively free society, not an absolutely free society. The American people are relatively free when compared with people in Thailand, Egypt, the Republic of the Congo, Turkmenistan, Cuba, Nepal, Vietnam, and Pakistan.

And on top of all that, Americans live in a nanny state. We have a government full of politicians, bureaucrats, and regulators, and a society full of statists, authoritarians, and busybodies, who all want to use the force of government to impose their values, hinder personal freedom, remake society in their own image, destroy personal and financial privacy, restrict economic activity, compel people to associate with people they may not want to associate with, define and enforce morality, tell you how to live your life, and limit the size of soft drinks you can purchase at a convenience store.

I much prefer a genuinely free society, as I make clear in the 127 essays in this book.

The essays were all written as articles or columns during the years 2005–2017. With just two exceptions, they were all originally written for either LewRockwell.com or the Future of Freedom Foundation. The essays are arranged in chronological order within the sections of each chapter (explained below), and each one can be read independently. They are reprinted verbatim, with the exception of the correction of any typographical errors. Because most of the essays initially appeared online, there will occasionally be found references to websites that originally contained links. There is some overlap between the essays in each chapter, between chapters 1 through 3, and between chapters 4 through 7. Although some of the figures given and events described in the essays are dated, the defense of a free society is timeless.

Chapter one, "Libertarianism: Theory," begins with three essays that introduce libertarianism followed by eight essays that supplement and amplify the first three.

Chapter two, "Libertarianism: Practice," begins with five general essays on the libertarian perspective on a broad range of issues, continues with six specific essays on the libertarian perspective on certain issues, and concludes with three essays on libertarianism and education and two on libertarianism and taxes.

Chapter three, "Libertarianism vs. Liberalism/Conservatism," begins with two general essays on the relationship between libertarianism and liberalism/conservatism followed by six specific essays on the relationship between libertarianism and conservatism/Republicans.

Chapter four, "Discrimination and Free Association," contains sixteen essays on the libertarian perspective on discrimination (some general and some specific) and concludes with two essays on the related topic of free association.

Chapter five, "Victimless Crimes," begins with two essays on victimless crimes in general followed by specific essays regarding prostitution, pornography, gambling, adultery, ticket scalping, and drugs. Although I have written scores of essays on the evils of the government's war on drugs, some of which are collected in my book *The War on Drugs Is a War on Freedom*, I have selected just one, "The Libertarian Sticking Point," for inclusion in this collection of essays because of how it directly relates to libertarianism.

Chapter six, "The Free Market," begins with nine essays relating to market prices (including the price of labor) and concludes with thirteen essays in defense of the free market and in opposition to government intervention and regulation. My essays on free trade that one would expect to find here, are collected in my small book *Free Trade or Protectionism?*

Chapter seven, "The Free Society," begins with four essays relating to alcohol, continues with three on tobacco, and concludes with a wide variety of essays on the nature of a free society.

The mention of any book in the essays and the inclusion of any book in the above list of books for further reading should not be taken as a blanket endorsement of everything contained in the book or anything else written by the author.

1

LIBERTARIANISM: THEORY

THE SIMPLICITY OF LIBERTARIANISM

Libertarianism has been defined as an ethical system that seeks to preserve the liberty of individuals and as a political philosophy concerned with the permissible use of force or violence. These are two sides of the same coin.

As libertarianism's greatest theorist, Murray Rothbard, explained,

> Libertarianism is not and does not pretend to be a complete moral, or aesthetic theory; it is only a political theory, that is, the important subset of moral theory that deals with the proper role of violence in social life. Political theory deals with what is proper or improper for government to do, and government is distinguished from every other group in society as being the institution of organized violence. Libertarianism holds that the only proper role of violence is to defend person and property against violence, that any use of violence that goes beyond such just defense is itself aggressive, unjust, and criminal. Libertarianism, therefore, is a theory which states that everyone should be free of violent invasion, should be free to do as he sees fit except invade the person or property of another. What a person does with his or her life is vital and important, but is simply irrelevant to libertarianism.

It is that simple.

Libertarianism is not ...

Yet, some people still just don't get it. The simplicity of libertarianism is a stumbling block to them. And because some have made libertarianism more complex by confusing it with certain elements of liberalism or conservatism, reading into it what they think it means, expanding it beyond what it professes to be, blaming it for market "failures," ascribing to it what its critics have falsely said about it, or equating it with the absence of morality, myths regarding libertarianism abound. It should be therefore noted that —

• Libertarianism is not libertinism.
• Libertarianism is not amoral.
• Libertarianism is not indifference to the plight of the poor or less fortunate.
• Libertarianism is not just about economics.

1

- Libertarianism is not a lifestyle.
- Libertarianism is not utopian.
- Libertarianism is not about greed and selfishness.
- Libertarianism is not pacifism.
- Libertarianism is not "dog eat dog."
- Libertarianism is not about making the government more efficient.
- Libertarianism is not hedonism or licentiousness.
- Libertarianism is not being naive about human nature.
- Libertarianism is not atheistic or materialistic.
- Libertarianism is not some particular school of aesthetics.
- Libertarianism is not "every man for himself."
- Libertarianism is not privatization.
- Libertarianism is not being a social liberal and an economic conservative.
- Libertarianism is not egalitarianism.
- Libertarianism is not antinomian.
- Libertarianism is not inimical to tradition or religion.
- Libertarianism is not "survival of the fittest."
- Libertarianism is not "the free market."
- Libertarianism is not "low-tax liberalism."
- Libertarianism is not anarchy.
- Libertarianism is not "unfettered capitalism."
- Libertarianism is not limited government.
- Libertarianism is not a social attitude.
- Libertarianism is not rebellion against all authority.
- Libertarianism is not acceptance of alternative lifestyles.

Libertarianism celebrates individual liberty, private property, peaceful activity, voluntary interaction, laissez faire, personal freedom, financial privacy, individual responsibility, free markets, free thought, and a free society.

It is that simple.

The principle undergirding the libertarian philosophy is what is known as the nonaggression principle. Again, as Rothbard explains,

> The fundamental axiom of libertarian theory is that no one may threaten or commit violence ("aggress") against another man's person or property. Violence may be employed only against the man who commits such violence; that is, only defensively against the aggressive violence of another. In short, no violence may be employed against a non-aggressor. Here is the fundamental rule from which can be deduced the entire corpus of libertarian theory.

The nonaggression principle is designed to prohibit someone from infringing upon the liberty of another. It is the core premise and linchpin of the philosophy of libertarianism. Aggression is the initiation of nonconsensual violence, the threat of nonconsensual violence, or fraud. The initiation of aggression against the person or property of others is always wrong. Force is justified only in defense or retaliation, but is neither essential nor required.

It is that simple.

A libertarian society

In a libertarian society, people are free to live and let live.

In a libertarian society, it is legal for anyone to do anything he wants, provided that he not threaten or initiate violence against the person or property of others.

In a libertarian society, every individual is free to pursue happiness in his own way—even if his choices are deemed by others as harmful, unhealthy, unsafe, immoral, unwise, stupid, or irresponsible.

In a libertarian society, people are free to live their lives any way they choose as long as their conduct is peaceful.

In a libertarian society, people are free to participate in any activity with anyone else as long as their behavior is consensual.

In a libertarian society, people are free to associate with, discriminate against, do business with, and interact with anyone (or no one) as long as their association and business are voluntary and their discrimination and interaction are peaceful.

In a libertarian society, individuals, groups, and businesses are perfectly free to associate, discriminate, interact, and conduct business for any reason and on any basis—regardless of how illogical, irrational, or unreasonable the reasons are perceived to be or how stereotypical, prejudicial, or biased the bases are perceived to be.

In a libertarian society, people are free to engage in any economic enterprise or activity of their choosing without license, permission, restriction, interference, or regulation from government as long as they don't commit violence against others, violate their property rights, or defraud them.

In a libertarian society, people have the right to keep the fruits of their labor and decide for themselves what to do with their money—whether that means save it, spend it, invest it, donate it, hoard it, or waste it.

In a libertarian society, people are free to accumulate as much wealth as they can as long as they do it peaceably and without committing fraud.

In a libertarian society, buyers and sellers are free to exchange with each other for mutual gain any product of their choosing for any price.

In a libertarian society, charity, relief, and philanthropy are entirely voluntary activities.

In a libertarian society, individuals, organizations, and businesses are responsible for their actions that negatively affect others.

It is that simple.

One major difference between libertarians and libertarian-leaning liberals, conservatives, and fellow travelers is that libertarians extend the nonaggression principle to government. Libertarians oppose or otherwise seek to limit the intervention, regulation, and control of governments, which, after all, are the greatest violators of the non-aggression principle, personal liberty, and property rights. Those who are not libertarians believe that it is appropriate for government to punish people for engaging in entirely peaceful, voluntary, and consensual actions that do not aggress against the person or property of others. But as Rothbard also stated, "Libertarians simply apply a universal human ethic to government in the same way as almost everyone would apply such an ethic to every other person or institution in society." They "make no exceptions to the golden rule and provide no moral loophole, no double standard, for government."

It is that simple.

In a libertarian society, the only legitimate purpose of government is to prosecute and punish those who initiate violence against others, commit fraud against them, or violate their property rights.

In a libertarian society, government actions beyond judicial and policing functions to keep the peace are themselves unpeaceful and in violation of the nonaggression principle.

In a libertarian society, vices are not crimes and incarceration is limited to violent criminals only.

In a libertarian society, the government leaves those alone who don't threaten or initiate violence against the person or property of others.

In a libertarian society, the government doesn't legislate morality.

In a libertarian society, every crime needs a victim.

In a libertarian society, freedom is not the absence of morality, the rule of law, or tradition; it is the absence of government paternalism.

In a libertarian society, actions are prohibited that involve the initiation of violence against persons (murder, manslaughter, rape, assault) or property (burglary, robbery, embezzlement, shoplifting, vandalism, trespassing, arson) and permitted that don't.

In a libertarian society, behavior that some consider to be immoral, unsafe, addictive, unhealthy, risky, sinful, or destructive (drug use, alcohol use, skydiving, smoking, using pornography, bungee jumping, adultery, sodomy, boxing, gambling, prostitution, et cetera) is none of the government's business.

In a libertarian society, what is considered immoral, unethical, or sinful is the domain of conscience, family, and religion, not puritanical busybodies, nanny-statists, or government bureaucrats.

It is that simple.

A libertarian society is a free society.

*****

THE CONSISTENCY OF LIBERTARIANISM

The essence of libertarianism is that a person should be free to live his life in any manner he chooses as long as his activities are peaceful, his interactions are consensual, and his associations are voluntary.

Conservative godfather Russell Kirk (1918–1994) was right, at least on this point, when he said that a man who calls himself a libertarian because he "believes in an enduring moral order, the Constitution of the United States, established American way of life, and a free economy" is actually "a conservative, even if he labors under an imperfect understanding of the general terms of politics." That is because to the libertarian, liberty is the chief end: freedom from aggression and violence against person and property as long as one respects the person and property of others.

Now, I don't know of anyone who wouldn't want such freedom and wouldn't readily assent to this "nonaggression principle"—until you bring government into the picture. I don't know of anyone (except perhaps a criminal) who wouldn't say that acts of aggression and violence against one's person (like murder or assault) or against one's property (like burglary or arson) are wrong and should be prosecuted and punished. But libertarians go a step further and consistently extend their nonaggression principle to actions of government.

Libertarians believe that as long as a man doesn't infringe upon the liberty of others by committing, or threatening to commit, acts of fraud, theft, aggression, or violence against their person or property, the government should leave him alone to pursue his own happiness, engage in commerce, make his own choices, take part in economic enterprises, enjoy the fruits of his labor, and accumulate wealth—all without license, permission, regulation, or interference from the state.

Most conservatives, however—including those who believe in the Constitution and the enduring moral order, established American way of life, and free economy described by Kirk—deem it completely appropriate for government

(1) to punish people for engaging in entirely peaceful, voluntary, and consensual actions that do not aggress against the person or property of others; or

(2) to take people's resources against their will, by force if necessary, and transfer or redistribute them to other citizens or foreigners as the government sees fit.

In a libertarian society, that is, a free society, the only possible legitimate functions of government are defense, judicial, and policing activities. That does not require anything like a monolithic, authoritarian, intrusive, nanny state such as the U.S. government has become. In a libertarian society, there is simply no justification for any government action beyond keeping the peace, prosecuting and punishing those who initiate violence against person or property, providing a forum for dispute resolution, and constraining those who would attempt to interfere with people's peaceful actions—and the case has even been made that elements of those could be handled privately. In a free society, there would be no such thing as nebulous crimes against nature, society, or the state. Every crime would have to have a tangible and identifiable victim.

But if there is one thing aside from its simplicity that makes libertarianism the ideal political philosophy it is its consistency.

The aforementioned Russell Kirk bemoaned, "The ruinous failing of the ideologues who call themselves libertarians is their fanatic attachment to a simple solitary principle—that is, to the notion of personal freedom as the whole end of the civil social order, and indeed of human existence." Some conservatives, when writing about libertarianism, are fond of quoting a line from Ralph Waldo Emerson's essay "Self-Reliance"—without regard to context or meaning—"A foolish consistency is the hobgoblin of little minds, adored by little statesmen and philosophers and divines." And it's not just conservatives who bewail libertarianism's consistency. Tony Greco, writing against libertarianism for the leftist Daily Kos, says that libertarians can never achieve mass appeal because they are "hobbled by their principled consistency."

But libertarianism is anything but foolish or provincial, and its consistency is its strength. Unlike liberalism and conservatism, libertarianism consistently applies the nonaggression principle, and consistently applies to government actions the same standard. This is because libertarians consider the nonaggression principle to be both absolute in scope and universal in application.

We can see the consistency of libertarianism in operation by contrasting it with the liberal and conservative responses to some concrete examples of government actions that occur on a regular basis that violate some aspect of the non-aggression principle.

We can look first at an example of how the government punishes people for engaging in entirely peaceful, voluntary, and consensual actions that do not aggress against the person or property of others.

Drug use

Liberals and conservatives are united in their belief that the federal and state governments should classify drugs on a schedule, have a drug-enforcement agency, have drug-abuse prevention programs, and decree that certain drugs are legal for anyone to purchase, to be kept behind the counter, available for purchase only in limited quantities, to be used only by physicians administering medical treatment, available only if prescribed by a licensed physician, or illegal for anyone to purchase.

However, liberals and conservatives differ among themselves and each other on the type and amount of drugs that should be restricted or prohibited. Should marijuana use be legal for medical purposes? Should the possession of small amounts of marijuana be decriminalized? If so, then how many joints or how many grams should be allowed? Should the recreational use of marijuana be permitted? Should users of crack cocaine do more prison time than users of powder cocaine? Should stores keep certain legal drugs behind the counter? Should drug policy be left entirely up to the states? Should the United States help other countries to wage war on drugs? Should drug "traffickers" receive stiffer sentences? Should some drug dealers not be eligible for parole? Should drug possession be a felony or a misdemeanor? Should there be mandatory minimum prison sentences for possessing certain amounts of illegal drugs?

Libertarianism considers those questions to be irrelevant. It consistently maintains that there should be no laws, restrictions, or regulations of any kind regarding the buying, selling, growing, processing, manufacturing, advertising, using, or possessing of any drug for any reason. The war on drugs has failed to reduce drug abuse, drug smuggling, drug availability, and drug overdoses. The financial and human costs of the drug war far exceed any of its supposed benefits. The war on drugs has needlessly clogged the judicial system, swelled prison populations, fostered violence, hindered legitimate pain treatment, corrupted law enforcement, eroded civil liberties, and destroyed financial privacy.

But even if none of those things were true, since it is neither the proper role of government nor the business of any individual to regulate or prohibit what a man desires to inhale or ingest into his own body, the war on drugs is really a war on personal freedom, private property, personal responsibility, individual liberty, personal and financial privacy, and the free market. The solution to the problem of drug abuse is to be found in family, friends, acquaintances, co-workers, physicians, psychologists, psychiatrists, social workers, religion, treatment centers, and ministers—not in the government. A free society includes the freedom to use or abuse drugs just as a free society includes the freedom to use or abuse alcohol.

Almost exactly the same thing could be said regarding other victimless crimes such as gambling and prostitution. Vices are not crimes.

We can next look at some examples of how the government violates the nonaggression principle by taking people's resources against their will, by force if necessary, and transferring or redistributing them to other citizens or foreigners as the government sees fit.

Welfare

Liberals and conservatives are united in their belief that the federal and state governments should provide public assistance, have entitlement programs, maintain a safety net, and guarantee income security. Liberals and conservatives both believe that government should take money from some Americans and redistribute it to other Americans in the form of cash benefits and job training to the unemployed; cash assistance to those who are disabled (SSI) or have a temporary need (TANF); food aid to low-income women who are pregnant or have small children (WIC); Social Security and Medicare to the elderly; refundable tax credits to the working poor (EITC); and Medicaid, subsidized health insurance (SCHIP), food stamps (SNAP), free or reduced-price school breakfasts and lunches (NSLP), rent subsidies (Section 8), and heating assistance (LIHEAP) to those below some arbitrary poverty line.

However, liberals and conservatives differ among themselves and each other as to the type of, amount of, work requirements of, eligibility for, frequency of, permanency of, and cost-of-living increases of the welfare. Should unemployment benefits be extended? If so then for how long and in what amount? Should Medicaid pay for abortions or birth control? How much should doctors be paid for procedures covered by Medicare? Should food- stamp and SSI benefits have annual increases? Should WIC benefits be increased if a woman has a child out of wedlock? Should cash benefits have a work requirement or a time limit? Should passing a drug test be required before one can receive welfare benefits? Some conservatives object to cash payments of any kind but have no problem with other forms of welfare—except when it comes to Social Security. In that case, both liberals and conservatives think Social Security should be "saved" so that future generations of the elderly can be supported by the young.

Libertarianism considers those questions to be irrelevant. It consistently maintains that providing welfare of any kind is an illegitimate and unconstitutional function of government. And it is always wrong to take money from those who work and give it to those who don't. Therefore, no American—not men, not women, not single mothers, not pregnant women, not children, not the hungry, not the disabled, not the sick, not the elderly, not the unemployed, not the poor—should receive any welfare benefits from the government of any kind or for any reason. The government has no resources of its own. Everything it has to give to some Americans has first been involuntarily transferred out of the pockets of other Americans. Generosity is a hallmark of Americans. But government charity crowds out genuine charity. All Americans should therefore be able to keep the entirety of the fruits of their labors and give or not give to those in need—individually or through charities—as they see fit. But charity must be voluntary. A free society includes the freedom to be generous or stingy, benevolent or miserly, charitable or uncharitable. But that is up to each individual American to decide.

Education

Liberals and conservatives are united in their belief that the federal government should have a Department of Education, give grants and loans to college students, and help fund the states' elementary and secondary education programs. However, liberals and conservatives differ among themselves and each other regarding the amount of funding schools should receive, testing requirements, teacher qualifications, the extent of federal control, admission requirements, student-loan interest rates, the role of religion, and an assortment of school policies. Should Head Start be expanded to help more "at risk" children? Should students at public schools be required to wear uniforms? What should the interest rate be on federal student loans? What should the maximum Pell Grant be? Should Pell Grants have annual increases? Should vouchers be provided so that children can escape failing public schools and attend "the school of their choice"? How much control should the federal government have over state and local education policies? Should "No Child Left Behind" and "Common Core" be reformed or repealed? Should the power of the teachers' unions be curtailed? Should there be higher standards for teachers? Should there be more technology in the classroom? Should prayer and Bible reading be restored to public schools? Should schools have health clinics? If so, should they provide contraception information and devices to students? Should the Ten Commandments be posted in schools? Should teachers be allowed to carry guns?

Libertarianism considers those questions to be irrelevant. It consistently maintains that it is an illegitimate purpose of the U.S. government to have anything to do with the education of anyone's children. And it is immoral to force some Americans to pay for the education of other Americans' children. That means that there should be no federal Head Start program; student loans; Pell Grants; Department of Education, vouchers; Elementary and Secondary Education Act; Higher Education Act; teacher education or certification requirements; school accreditation; math and science initiatives; or Title IX, special-education, diversity, or bilingual-education mandates. The education of children is the responsibility of parents, not the state. How they choose to do that should be entirely up to them. In a free society, education would be a service offered on the free market just like haircuts, tanning, car repair, or any other service.

Foreign aid

Liberals and conservatives are united in their belief that the federal government should take money from American taxpayers and give it to foreign governments and organizations as foreign aid. However, liberals and conservatives differ among themselves and each other as to the nature and amount of the aid. Should the aid take the form of cash, food, construction projects, or technology? How much aid should be given? For how long should the aid be given? Should a country's foreign aid be tied to its human-rights record, its free-speech and free-press laws, its voting pattern in the United Nations, its poverty rate, its GDP, its economic growth, or its actions in fighting the drug war? Should aid in the form of weapons systems and military assistance be prohibited? Should aid be given only to countries that are U.S. allies, friendly to Israel, or have overseas U.S. military bases?

Libertarianism considers those questions to be irrelevant. It consistently maintains that no country should receive foreign aid from the U.S. government in any amount, at any time, or for any reason. Like domestic charity, foreign charity should be entirely voluntary. And like the decision to aid one's friends, neighbors, or family, the decision to aid foreigners is a decision for each American to make. A free society includes the freedom to be unconcerned or insensitive to the plight of foreigners who are less fortunate.

Disaster relief

Liberals and conservatives are united in their belief that the federal government should take money from American taxpayers and use it to provide relief in foreign countries whenever there is a major earthquake, flood, typhoon, mudslide, tsunami, or other natural disaster. Even the few conservatives who object on principle to foreign aid are usually willing to support disaster relief. However, as with the subject of foreign aid, liberals and conservatives differ among themselves and each other about the nature and amount of the disaster relief. Should the relief take the form of medicine, food, equipment, generators, blankets, rebuilding infrastructure, and the erection of temporary shelters, or just providing engineering or technical assistance? How much relief should be given? For how long should the relief be given? Should there be any strings attached to receiving the relief? How much of a role, if any, should the U.S. military play in disaster relief?

Libertarianism considers those questions to be irrelevant. It consistently maintains that no country should be given disaster relief by the U.S. government at any time or for any reason. Just as taking resources from one's neighbor to give to those in need is not distributing relief but engaging in theft, so U.S. government relief to foreigners in need instead of relief provided voluntarily through the generosity of American individuals and organizations is likewise theft. A free society includes the freedom to be unconcerned about the plight of refugees, insensitive to starving children, apathetic toward human suffering, and indifferent concerning natural disasters. If it is neither constitutional nor a proper function of the U.S. government to provide disaster relief to its own citizens, then it is certainly inappropriate to provide it to foreigners in other countries.

Libertarianism is simply consistent. Unlike all varieties of liberalism and conservatism, there is no hesitation in libertarianism, no apprehension, no compromise, no situation ethics, and no exceptions. Liberty is the chief political end. The free market is not really free unless it is completely free of government regulation and interference. Property rights are inviolable. Laissez faire is just and right, natural and inherent, moral and ethical. That means that government agents should leave alone the person and property of those who don't threaten or initiate violence against the person or property of others.

The consistency of libertarianism is a bulwark of liberty, property, and peace.

*****

THE MORALITY OF LIBERTARIANISM

Libertarianism is a political philosophy that says that people should be free from government interference to live their life any way they desire and engage in any economic activity they choose as long as their actions are peaceful and consensual and they don't violate the personal or property rights of others. It is that simple. Violence is justified only in defense of person or property against violence. Nonaggression—that is the libertarian creed. And that is the essence of libertarianism. One's lifestyle has nothing to do with it.

Liberal and conservative smears of libertarianism are legion. Libertarians are said to be naive, utopian, idealistic, materialistic, and nihilistic. They disdain religion and reject tradition. They are disciples of Rousseau. They are too individualistic. They have nostalgia for a fictional past. They have no compassion for the poor. They don't believe in social justice. They are weak on national security. They are pacifists and isolationists. Libertarianism aspires, like Marxism, to reduce social life to economics. It treats children like adults. It believes that man is inherently good. "Libertarianism," according to conservative Jonah Goldberg, "is an ideology best suited for young folks. It compellingly tells kids everything they want to be told." Libertarians "fetishize change, assuming it to be always and everywhere good."

But above all, liberals and conservatives like to characterize libertarians as libertines and hedonists who celebrate alternative life-styles and don't believe in moral principles or absolutes. The trump card they play has two sides: libertarians are all moral relativists and libertarianism is immoral.

Nothing could be further from the truth.

Libertarianism celebrates things such as individual liberty, private property, peaceful activity, voluntary interaction, laissez faire, personal freedom, financial privacy, individual responsibility, free enterprise, free markets, free speech, free thought, and a free society. There is nothing inherently immoral about any of those things.

There are two things generally cited by opponents of libertarianism to "prove" that libertarianism is immoral: the attitude of libertarians toward prostitution and their stand on drug use. Those are always the two sticking points, not because libertarians promote, endorse, defend, or practice them, but because they don't believe the government should interfere with the voluntary, private, peaceful activity of consenting adults.

Regarding prostitution, libertarians reason that it if it is legal for a woman to provide free sexual services as often as she wants and to as many people as she wants, then it shouldn't be illegal for her to charge for performing the same services. Especially since someone's indirectly paying for sex by paying for dinner and a movie is not a crime.

Regarding drug use, libertarians reason that it makes no sense for the government to wage war on illegal drugs, when tobacco, alcohol, and prescription drugs kill far more people every year. Tobacco use costs the U.S. economy billions of dollars every year in medical costs and lost productivity and causes hundreds of thousands of premature deaths every year from heart disease, stroke, cancer, and smoking-related diseases. Alcohol is also one of the leading causes of premature deaths in the United States. Alcohol abuse is a factor in many drownings; suicides; fires; violent crimes; child-abuse cases; sex crimes; and home, pedestrian, car, and boating accidents. More than 100,000 people die every year from drugs prescribed and administered by physicians. More than two million Americans a year have in-hospital adverse drug reactions. And thousands of people die every year from reactions to aspirin.

But the main reasons libertarians have their attitude toward prostitution and drug use are simply that vices are not crimes and that every crime needs to have a victim. That doesn't mean that libertarians don't think the practices are immoral. It just means that they believe that it is not the proper function of government to arrest people for them or seek to limit them.

The vice list used against libertarians used to also regularly include gambling and pornography, but since now almost every state has a lottery, there are casinos scattered all across the country, pornography is available for sale on newsstands, and porn is freely available on the Internet, libertarianism's detractors don't much mention those two vices anymore. And how can they? All the gambling and pornography viewing that takes place cannot be laid solely at the feet of libertarians any more than soliciting prostitutes and taking illegal drugs can. No political ideology has a monopoly on vice and bad habits.

Lifestyle libertarians

Some of the criticism of libertarianism is deserved: a small, but vocal, minority of libertarians have unfortunately given liberals and conservatives the impression that libertarianism is a social attitude or lifestyle.

Those libertarians say or imply that libertarians should celebrate change for change's sake; live an alternative lifestyle; partake of illegal drugs; embrace the feminist movement; support abortion on demand; defend same-sex marriage; celebrate hedonism, licentiousness, and libertinism even if they don't live that way; do something illegal; view pornography; own a gun; enjoy a particular kind of art; have a particular musical taste; and celebrate diversity for diversity's sake.

And, at the same time, they also say or imply that libertarians should reject organized religion, not work for a large corporation, not be socially conservative, disdain tradition, and never discriminate.

Whether any of those things is right, wrong, moral, immoral, good, or bad is irrelevant. Libertarians who say or imply them are improperly expanding libertarianism beyond its core nonaggression principle. Libertarianism has nothing to do with anyone's lifestyle, tastes, vices, sex life, traditions, religion, aesthetics, sensibilities, outlook, or cultural norms. An individual libertarian might be a moral relativist—as might an individual liberal or conservative—but libertarianism as a political philosophy cannot be said to be immoral.

That being said, libertarianism, even narrowly defined, does not oppose the educational efforts, debate, argumentation, media campaigns, organized boycotts, social ostracism, or other nonviolent, noncoercive methods of persuasion of others—libertarians or otherwise—to effect changes in their public and private behavior. It is liberals and conservatives who advocate government aggression and violence against peaceful people's person or property to achieve some desired end.

Is it moral?

Although they accuse libertarians of being moral relativists, it is liberals and conservatives alike who support the immoral actions of government.

• Is it moral to charge someone with the commission of a crime when there is no victim?
• Is it moral to force some Americans to pay for the health care of other Americans?
• Is it moral to make someone get a license or permission from the government before he can open a business?
• Is it moral to treat vices as crimes?

• Is it moral to incarcerate anyone but violent criminals?
• Is it moral to commit someone to an institution against his will?
• Is it moral to send a soldier to fight an unnecessary and unjust war?
• Is it moral to force people to pay for the education of other people's children?
• Is it moral to arrest, fine, or imprison someone for using drugs, when alcohol is readily available?
• Is it moral to take money from people without their consent and give it away to foreign governments?
• Is it moral to charge someone with the commission of a crime when no one's personal or property rights are violated?
• Is it moral for one person to live at the expense of another?
• Is it moral to criminalize marijuana, when tobacco kills tens of thousands every year?
• Is it moral for an immoral government to legislate morality?
• Is it moral to take money from some people and redistribute it to others?
• Is it moral to initiate force against someone who hasn't himself initiated force against another?
• Is it moral to demand that "the poor" have a right to the earnings of "the rich"?
• Is it moral to lock someone in a cage for years for possessing a plant the government doesn't approve of?
• Is it moral to sentence someone to life in prison for a drug "crime," when rapists don't serve that long?
• Is it moral to force people to contribute to a retirement program?
• Is it moral to force people to be charitable?

I think the answers are obvious.

Is it immoral?

Conservatives and liberals have it backwards; it is violating the tenets of libertarianism that is immoral.

• Is it immoral to let someone keep the fruits of his labor?
• Is it immoral to let someone live and let live?
• Is it immoral for charity, relief, and philanthropy to be voluntary activities?
• Is it immoral to let Americans spend their money however they choose?
• Is it immoral to permit buyers and sellers to freely exchange with each other for mutual gain?
• Is it immoral to allow people to engage in commerce with whomever they choose?
• Is it immoral to let every individual be free to pursue happiness in his own way?

• Is it immoral to believe that the initiation of force to achieve a political, or other goal, is wrong?

• Is it immoral to believe that acts of theft and violence are still wrong when committed by government?

• Is it immoral to allow people to live their lives any way they choose as long as their conduct is peaceful?

• Is it immoral for the government to just leave people alone who are not threatening or aggressing against the person or property of others?

• Is it immoral to allow people to participate in any activity with anyone else as long as their behavior is consensual?

• Is it immoral to want everyone—including government—to live by the nonaggression principle?

• Is it immoral to allow people to engage in any economic enterprise or activity of their choosing without getting permission from the government?

• Is it immoral for people to just mind their own business?

• Is it immoral to allow people to associate or not associate with whomever they choose as long as their associations are mutually voluntary?

• Is it immoral to want the government to stay out of people's bedrooms?

• Is it immoral to allow people to accumulate wealth as long as they don't defraud anyone?

• Is it immoral to allow people to do business or not do business with whomever they choose?

• Is it immoral to let someone do what he wants with his own property?

• Is it immoral to want to live in a free society?

Again, I think the answers are obvious.

It is liberalism and conservatism that have a morality problem, not libertarianism. It is liberals and conservatives who support the immoral actions of government and demonize genuinely moral impulses. "Libertarians," as economist Robert Higgs has said, "should never concede the moral high ground to those who insist on coercively interfering with freedom."

*****

IS LIBERTARIANISM COMPATIBLE WITH RELIGION?

This talk was given at the 2011 Austrian Scholars Conference at the Mises Institute.

I never met Murray Rothbard. I still remember the day when I received a postcard in the mail announcing that he had died. I think that he, an agnostic Jew, and I, a devout Christian, would have gotten along just fine since we shared a common enemy—the state. I still have the postcard and the admiration for Rothbard that I had sixteen years ago.

I think that libertarianism has reached the point where we can safely say that more than at any time in the last fifty years a great number of libertarians are religious people. It was twenty-three years ago—a time when many of us still identified ourselves as liberals or conservatives, and some of you were not old enough to know the difference—when Rothbard opined that "the libertarian movement, and the Libertarian Party, will get nowhere in America—or throughout the world—so long as it is perceived, as it generally is, as a movement dedicated to atheism." "Nock, Morley, Chodorov, Flynn et al. were not atheists," he continued, "but for various accidental reasons of history, the libertarian movement after the 1950's consisted almost exclusively of atheists." "There is nothing inherently of wrong with this," explained Rothbard, "except that many libertarians have habitually and wrongly acted as if religious people in general and Christians in particular are pariahs and equivalent to statists." Just a few months before this, Rothbard had lamented that he was "getting tired of the off-handed smearing of religion that has long been endemic to the libertarian movement." "Religion," he said "is generally dismissed as imbecilic at best, inherently evil at worst."

Although I think that things have greatly improved, many libertarians today are no more accommodating of religion than those in Rothbard's day. Even though many religious people perhaps deserve the disdain of libertarians because of their faith-based statism, religion itself certainly doesn't. It was the nonreligious Rothbard who acknowledged that "the greatest and most creative minds in the history of mankind have been deeply and profoundly religious, most of them Christian."

The question I want to address today is simply this: Is libertarianism compatible with religion? Many libertarians say no, the two are not compatible. Some of them even consider religion to be a greater enemy of human liberty than the state, a proposition that Walter Block has debunked. Many religious people also say no, the two are not compatible. In the minds of some of them, libertarianism is just a synonym for libertinism, an erroneous idea that has also been debunked by Walter Block. (Is there any false notion about libertarianism that Walter Block hasn't debunked?) Even some conservatives say no, the two are not compatible. Thomas Fleming, the editor of *Chronicles* magazine, considers the phrase "Christian libertarians" to be "as oxymoronic as Christian *socialists*."

Now, although I have some strong opinions about religion—and enough degrees in theology to make sure I offend the greatest number of people—what I personally believe about religion is totally irrelevant. The question of "Is libertarianism compatible with religion?" is a question that Walter Block or the most militant Randian could ask and answer without changing the content of this talk. What you personally believe about religion is also completely immaterial. Whether you think that a particular religion is the absolute truth that you would be willing to die for or that all religions are just a collection of myths and stories mixed with history doesn't affect the importance of the question. In the end, people are going to side with their religion over the ideas of dead Austrian economists. It is therefore imperative that the question be answered.

Libertarians who ignore the question do so at their peril. If libertarianism is *not* compatible with religion, then we who believe that the principles of libertarianism are true, just, and right must engage in the futile task of trying to get people to abandon their religion to accept libertarianism. We would face the impossible task of destroying someone's faith in his God and/or scripture before we could convince him of the truth of libertarianism. Now, you may be both a hard-core atheist *and* a libertarian, but as Rothbard warned: "We libertarians will never win the hearts and minds of Americans or of the rest of the world if we persist in wrongly identifying libertarianism with atheism. If even Stalin couldn't stamp out religion, libertarians are not going to succeed with a few Randian syllogisms."

The title of my paper is no accident. I think religious people have more of a problem with libertarianism than libertarians have with religion. I think it is harder to convince a religious person that libertarianism doesn't violate the tenets of his religion than to convince a libertarian that religion doesn't violate the tenets of libertarianism. Although some libertarians deserve the disdain of religious people for their libertinism, I put most of the blame for the need for this talk on religious people because of their ignorance of both libertarianism *and* religion.

So, all that being said, my short answer to the question of whether libertarianism is compatible with is religion yes. But since it would not be enough just to say "I am religious, I am libertarian, so the answer to the question has to be yes, thank you and good day," my long answer is what follows.

In order to determine if libertarianism is compatible with religion we must first understand what libertarianism is. The world is full of mistaken notions about libertarianism. It is often misunderstood and mischaracterized by its opponents as discounting human nature and disdaining morality while being grossly naïve and overly utopian. We have all heard the standard clichés, usually out of the mouth of conservatives, religious or otherwise:

• Libertarians are for abortion.
• Libertarians are for drug use.
• Libertarians are against religion.
• Libertarians are against traditional values.

True, some libertarians might be *for* and *against* these things, but so might someone who is not a libertarian.

To get a proper perspective of what libertarianism really is, I turn to two of its greatest proponents: Murray Rothbard and Walter Block.

As described by Rothbard:

> Libertarianism is not and does not pretend to be a complete moral, or aesthetic theory; it is only a *political* theory, that is, the important subset of moral theory that deals with the proper role of violence in social life. . . . Libertarianism holds that the only proper role of violence is to defend person and property *against* violence, that any use of violence that goes beyond such just defense is itself aggressive, unjust, and criminal. Libertarianism, therefore, is a theory which states that everyone should be free of violent invasion, should be free to do as he sees fit except invade the person or property of another. What a person *does* with his or her life is vital and important, but is simply irrelevant to libertarianism.

And as explained by Block:

> The non-aggression axiom is the lynchpin of the philosophy of libertarianism. It states, simply, that it shall be legal for anyone to do anything he wants, provided only that he not initiate (or threaten) violence against the person or legitimately owned property of another. That is, in the free society, one has the right to manufacture, buy or sell any good or service at any mutually agreeable terms.

In his seminal article "Libertarianism or Libertinism," Block compactly states the essence of libertarianism:

> Libertarianism is a political philosophy. It [is] concerned solely with the proper use of force. Its core premise is that it should be illegal to threaten or initiate violence against a person or his property without his permission; force is justified only in defense or retaliation. That is it, in a nutshell. The rest is mere explanation, elaboration, and qualification – and answering misconceived objections.

And in an article on plumb-line libertarianism, Block simply says: "Libertarianism is *solely* a political philosophy. It asks one and only one question: Under what conditions is the use of violence justified? And it gives one and only one answer: Violence can be used only in response, or in reaction to, a prior violation of private property rights." Clearly, libertarianism cannot be simplistically defined, like some Cato guys recently did, as "fiscally conservative, socially liberal." And I should also say that libertarianism is a way of life, not a lifestyle.

Now that we know what libertarianism is, in order to determine if it is compatible with religion it we must next look at what we mean by religion. Christianity, Judaism, Islam, Buddhism, Hinduism—these are all considered to be the world's great religions. That, however, is where their similarity begins and ends. Although they do have some common tenets, the constraints of my talent and your time mean that we are going to have to narrow our scope.

The focus of my talk will therefore be on Christianity—but not just because I am a Christian. I suspect that most of the people listening to me right now, or who will listen to a recording or read a transcript of this talk in the future, would identify themselves as Christians. This is not surprising since a majority of Americans still identify themselves as Christians. This does not mean that America is a Christian nation—regardless of what Islamic countries and God and country Red-State Christian fascists think (who would have thought those two groups would be in agreement on anything). It does mean that if we are to reach the majority of Americans with the message of liberty that we should know whether libertarianism is compatible with their religion.

This is a significant year in the history of Christianity. The year 2011 is the four-hundredth anniversary of the publication of the Authorized Version, better known as the King James Version of the Bible because it was translated under the authority of King James I of England, beginning in 1604.

But regardless of which version of Bible is used, to the Christian, the Bible is the supreme authority, not the works of Mises or Rothbard, however highly we may regard them.

The Bible is not only the book that has had the greatest impact on Western Civilization; it is the foundation of Christianity. Christians may differ on certain aspects of their religion, but they are all united in their belief that the Bible is some kind of an authority. For a Christian to say otherwise is to reveal that his religion is really meaningless.

For a Christian to respect the Bible as some kind of an authority to the extent that he might reject libertarianism because of it generally means that such an individual holds to a high view of Scripture or a literal view of the Bible. Obviously, not everything in the Bible is meant to be taken literally. The Bible contains idioms and figures of speech just like any other form of writing. And clearly, Christians have genuine differences of interpretation on certain portions of Scripture. A literal view of the Bible simply means that one accepts literally things in the Bible unless it is clear that they are not to be taken so. Miracles and other supernatural events actually happened. The virgin birth was an actual virgin birth. The resurrection of Christ is a real historical event. And most relevant to the question at hand, the precepts of Christ and the Apostles are meant to be obeyed and followed; they are not just opinions or suggestions to be accepted or rejected at will.

I only mention all this because some people wrongly believe that a literal view of the Bible is just a tenet of fundamentalist Christians. True, it is usually those who are the most ardent Bible literalists that are the toughest nuts to crack when it comes to libertarianism. It shouldn't be that way, as I will argue in this talk, but that's the reality. But if those who believe the Bible most literally can be persuaded of the compatibility of libertarianism with their version of Christianity, then those who take a somewhat less literal view of the Bible will not be far behind.

Let me reiterate that what you or I personally believe about the Bible is irrelevant. At issue is simply this: If libertarianism *is* compatible with a Christianity grounded on the authority of the Bible, then we have many possible "converts" to the cause of liberty and a free society. But on the other hand, if libertarianism *is not* compatible with a Christianity grounded on the authority of the Bible, then many Christian Americans, *if they take their religion seriously*, will be forever hostile or indifferent to liberty and a free society since the primary objections to libertarianism are moral.

So, why do I think that religion—in this case the Christian religion—is compatible with libertarianism? Let me give you two verses of Scripture, one from the Old Testament and one from the New, since Christians accept the authority of both:

> Proverbs 3:30—"Strive not with a man without cause, if he have done thee no harm."

> 1 Peter 4:15—"But let none of you suffer as a murderer, or as a thief, or as an evildoer, or as a busybody in other men's matters."

These verses, my friends, embody the essence of libertarianism. Don't kill anyone, don't take what's not yours, don't do anyone wrong, don't stick your nose in someone else's business, and don't bother anyone if he hasn't bothered you. Other than that do whatever you want—"Anything that's peaceful," as Leonard Read says, for "ye have been called unto liberty," as the Apostle Paul says. The only caveats for Christians when it comes to liberty are to not let their liberty become a stumbling block to weaker brothers and to not use their liberty for an occasion to the flesh; that is, don't be a libertine.

And you thought I was going to give you some complicated theological or philosophical argument. The Bible commands the Christian to devise not evil against his neighbor (Proverbs 3:29), love his neighbor as himself (Romans 13:9), show meekness unto all men (Titus 3:2), do good unto all men (Galatians 6:10), provide things honest in the sight of all men (Romans 12:21), and live peaceably with all men (Romans 12:18). If libertarianism is not compatible with these things then it is not compatible with anything.

The Christian is also told in the Bible:

> And whatsoever ye do in word or deed, do all in the name of the Lord Jesus, giving thanks to God and the Father by him. (Colossians 3:17)

And whatsoever ye do, do it heartily, as to the Lord, and not unto men. (Colossians 3:23)

Whether therefore ye eat, or drink, or whatsoever ye do, do all to the glory of God. (1 Corinthians 10:31)

Can a Christian assault someone in the name of the Lord Jesus? Can a Christian steal from someone heartily, as to the Lord? Can a Christian kill someone to the glory of God? I think the answer to these questions is obvious. And I also think it is apparent that libertarianism is compatible with the Christian religion.

But I would go a step further. Not only is libertarianism *compatible* with the most strict, most biblically literal form of Christianity, it is *demanded* by it. The Christian is enjoined in Scripture to go even beyond the non-aggression principle.

He is told, not to just turn the other cheek, but to "endure hardness" (2 Timothy 2:3), "endure afflictions" (2 Timothy 4:5), and "endure grief" (1 Peter 2:19). Revenge and retaliation for the Christian are not options. Some Christians get hung up on Romans 13 and end up making apologies for the state and its wars. It's too bad they skipped over Romans 12:

Bless them which persecute you: bless, and curse not. (Romans 12:14)

Recompense to no man evil for evil. (Romans 12:17)

Dearly beloved, avenge not yourselves, but rather give place unto wrath: for it is written, Vengeance is mine; I will repay, saith the Lord. (Romans 12:19)

Overcome evil with good. (Romans 12:21)

So, if libertarianism is more than compatible with the Christian religion, why do religious people—Christians—reject libertarianism? Why aren't the majority of Christians libertarians instead of liberals, conservatives, Democrats, Republicans, and other assorted statists? Let me briefly give you some reasons. One, misconstruing libertarianism as a hedonistic philosophy instead of a political philosophy. Two, the poor presentation of libertarianism by libertarians. Three, wrongly thinking that libertarianism demands that one be pro-abortion. Four, morality; the two-fold failure to make a distinction between vices and crimes and crimes and sins. And five, social justice; wrongly applying to the government admonitions given to individuals.

I have developed these latter three points elsewhere. On abortion, see my LRC article "Is Ron Paul Wrong on Abortion?" On morality, see my *Liberty* magazine article "An Open Letter to My Fellow Christians," which

is based on my 2006 ASC lecture "Christianity and Victimless Crimes."
And on social justice, see my little book *The Myth of the Just Price*, which
is the text of my 2008 Lou Church lecture of the same name in which I
argue that there should be no government intervention in society or the
economy.

I have tried in this talk to show why I believe libertarianism is scriptur-
ally compatible with religion. Is everything that has been done in the name
of libertarianism compatible with religion? Of course not. But neither is
everything that has been done in the name of religion compatible with libertarianism or even with religion. I think it is possible that it might someday be said not only that the greatest and most creative minds in the history of religion have been deeply and profoundly libertarian, but that the
greatest and most creative minds in the history of libertarianism have been
deeply and profoundly religious.

*****

I AM A LIBERTARIAN

I am a libertarian. I am not Democrat or Republican. I am not liberal or
conservative. I am not left or right. I am not moderate or progressive. I am
not a Libertarian. I am not a fusionist. I am not a constitutionalist.

I am a libertarian. I am not thin or thick. I am not brutalist or humanitarian. I am not holist or solipsist. I am not moralist or consequentialist. I
am not open or closed. I am not a modal, cosmopolitan, cultural, theo-
cratic, regime, sophisticated, or Beltway libertarian. I do not have a bleeding heart. I am not a neo, second wave, or millennial libertarian. I am a
plain old libertarian, one who needs no labels, issues no caveats, and
makes no apologies.

I am a libertarian. Libertarianism is a political philosophy concerned
with the permissible use of force or violence. It is not a political philosophy that says limited government is the best kind of government. It is not a
political philosophy that is socially liberal and economically conservative.
It is not a political philosophy that says government is less efficient than
the private sector. It is not a political philosophy that says freedom can be
achieved by promoting some government policies over others. It is not a
political philosophy that is low-tax liberalism. Libertarianism is not the
absence of racism, sexism, homophobism, xenophobism, nationalism, na-
tivism, classism, authoritarianism, patriarchy, inequality, or hierarchy.
Libertarianism is not diversity or activism. Libertarianism is not egalitarianism. Libertarianism is not toleration or respect. Libertarianism is not a
social attitude, lifestyle, or aesthetic sensibility.

I am a libertarian. I subscribe to the non-aggression principle that says,
in the words of Murray Rothbard: "The only proper role of violence is to
defend person and property against violence, that any use of violence that

goes beyond such just defense is itself aggressive, unjust, and criminal. Libertarianism, therefore, is a theory which states that everyone should be free of violent invasion, should be free to do as he sees fit except invade the person or property of another." I am concerned with actions; I am not concerned with thoughts: I am concerned only with the negative consequences of thoughts. I believe that the non-aggression principle extends to government. Libertarians should therefore oppose or otherwise seek to limit the domestic and foreign meddling and intervention of governments, which are the greatest violators of the non-aggression principle.

I am a libertarian. I believe in the golden rule. I believe in live and let live. I believe that a person should be free to do anything he wants, as long as his conduct is peaceful. I believe that vices are not crimes.

I am a libertarian. Our enemy is the state. Our enemy is not religion, corporations, institutions, foundations, or organizations. These only have power to do us harm because of their connection with the state. And since war is the health of the state, the state's military, wars, and foreign interventions must be opposed root and branch.

I am a libertarian. I believe in laissez faire. Anyone should be free to engage in any economic activity without license, permission, prohibition, or interference from the state. The government should not intervene in the economy in any way. Free trade agreements, educational vouchers, privatizing Social Security, etc., are not the least bit libertarian ideas.

I am a libertarian. The best government is no government. That government that governs least is the next best government. Government, as Voltaire said, at its best state is a necessary evil and at its worst state is an intolerable one. The best thing any government could do would be to simply leave us alone.

I am a libertarian. Taxation is government theft. The government doesn't have a claim to a certain percentage of one's income. The tax code doesn't need to be simplified, shortened, fairer, or less intrusive. The tax rates don't need to be made lower, flatter, fairer, equal, or less progressive. The income tax doesn't need more or larger deductions, loopholes, shelters, credits, or exemptions. The whole rotten system needs to be abolished. People have the right to keep what they earn and decide for themselves what to do with their money: spend it, waste it, squander it, donate it, bequeath it, hoard it, invest it, burn it, gamble it.

I am a libertarian. I am not a libertine. I am not a hedonist. I am not a moral relativist. I am not a devotee of some alternative lifestyle. I am not a revolutionary. I am not a nihilist. I neither wish to associate with nor aggress against those who are. I believe in the absolute freedom of association and discrimination.

I am a libertarian.

*****

SHALL WE ABANDON THE NON-AGGRESSION PRINCIPLE?

It has been fashionable of late for some libertarians to broaden the libertarian non-aggression principle in their attempts to make libertarianism less thin and brutal and more cosmopolitan and humanitarian.

I will not address this controversy here. I recently made very clear my views on libertarianism.

What I do want to address is an older libertarian attack on the non-aggression principle that has recently reared its ugly head.

Some libertarians, way back when (*Liberty*, May 1988) and more recently (here and here), have actually called for abandoning the non-aggression principle altogether. (See replies to the recent cases here and here).

I think it would be important before continuing to revisit exactly what it is that libertarians mean when they talk about the non-aggression principle being foundational to libertarianism. For this I turn to two of the greatest libertarian theorists and proponents: Murray Rothbard and his longtime friend and disciple (in the good sense) Walter Block.

Says Rothbard:

> The libertarian creed rests upon one central axiom: that no man or group of men may aggress against the person or property of anyone else. This may be called the "nonaggression axiom." "Aggression" is defined as the initiation of the use or threat of physical violence against the person or property of anyone else. Aggression is therefore synonymous with invasion (*For a New Liberty*).

> Libertarianism holds that the only proper role of violence is to defend person and property against violence, that any use of violence that goes beyond such just defense is itself aggressive, unjust, and criminal ("Myth and Truth About Libertarianism").

> The fundamental axiom of libertarian theory is that no one may threaten or commit violence ("aggress") against another man's person or property. Violence may be employed only against the man who commits such violence; that is, only defensively against the aggressive violence of another. In short, no violence may be employed against a non-aggressor. Here is the fundamental rule from which can be deduced the entire corpus of libertarian theory ("War, Peace, and the State").

And explains Block:

> The non-aggression axiom is the lynchpin of the philosophy of libertarianism. It states, simply, that it shall be legal for anyone to do anything he wants, provided only that he not initiate (or threaten) violence against the person or legitimately owned property of another ("The Non-Aggression Axiom of Libertarianism").

> Libertarianism is a political philosophy. It [is] concerned solely with the proper use of force. Its core premise is that it should be illegal to threaten or initiate violence against a person or his property without his permission; force is justified only in defense or retaliation. That is it, in a nutshell. The rest is mere explanation, elaboration, and qualification—and answering misconceived objections. ("Libertarianism or Libertinism").

Clearly, Rothbard and Block are saying that it is the *initiation* of aggression against the person or property of others that is always wrong.

But if we are to abandon the principle that the initiation of aggression against the person or property of others is *always* wrong, then what are the alternatives? I see only two:

> The initiation of aggression against the person or property of others is *never* wrong.

> The initiation of aggression against the person or property of others is *sometimes* wrong.

No civilized person, libertarian or not, would accept the first alternative. This leaves us with the second. The can of worms that this opens up should be quite evident. This is why most would then try to postulate a third alternative—that the initiation of aggression against the person or property of others is *basically* wrong. But this still leaves the door open for the initiation of aggression against the person or property of others to only *sometimes* be wrong.

The real problem comes in when the non-aggression principle is applied to the state. Many people who say that they subscribe to the non-aggression principle on a personal level have no problem supporting government aggression against certain peaceful activities.

What separates genuine libertarians from imposters and those who shun the name but likewise claim that they accept the non-aggression axiom in principle is the axiom's application. As Rothbard elaborates:

> Libertarians simply apply a universal human ethic to *government* in the same way as almost everyone would apply such an ethic to every other person or institution in society. In particular, as I have noted earlier, libertarianism as a political philosophy dealing with the proper role of violence takes the universal ethic that most of us hold toward violence and applies it fearlessly to government.

Libertarians "make no exceptions to the golden rule and provide no moral loophole, no double standard, for government."

It is government that is the greatest violator of the non-aggression principle. It is generally not neighbors, coworkers, gang members, muggers, rapists, and thieves that we have to worry about. The aggressions they commit against the person or property of others pales in comparison to state aggression. Fanatical right-wing ideologues who want to lock drug users in cages and throw away the key have no power to do so except by the power of government.

So, if we are to abandon the principle that the initiation of aggression by government against the person or property of others is *always* wrong, then we are once again left with two alternatives:

> The initiation of aggression by government against the person or property of others is *never* wrong.

> The initiation of aggression by government against the person or property of others is *sometimes* wrong.

The first alternative is the view of Lenin, Stalin, and Sarah Palin. The second is the view of conservative pundits and Republican politicians.

Again, the implications of this second view should be obvious. And again, to try and retreat to the position that the initiation of aggression by government against the person or property of others is *basically* wrong still leaves the door open for the initiation of aggression by government against the person or property of others to only *sometimes* being wrong.

Shall we abandon the non-aggression principle? Of course not. It is what separates men from beasts. To do so is to legitimize personal and state aggression.

In this article I have merely sought to show what the unsatisfactory alternatives are to the non-aggression principle. If libertarians who have disparaged the non-aggression principle really don't want to abandon it then they shouldn't say that they do.

The non-aggression principle can and should be applied, clarified, explained, built upon, have implications derived from it, and made the basis of logical deductions, but it should certainly not be abandoned.

*****

DRUGS, LIBERTARIANISM, AND ROSS ULBRICHT

Does facilitating the buying and selling of drugs make one a libertarian?

Of course it doesn't. But that hasn't stopped some libertarians from making Ross Ulbricht a libertarian hero.

Ulbricht was the creator of the Silk Road website, an online marketplace for the sale of heroin, cocaine, and other illegal drugs. As all libertarians are painfully aware, Ulbricht, was earlier this year found guilty by a federal court of narcotics trafficking, money laundering, and other dubious federal crimes, and was recently sentenced to life in prison without parole.

This is an outrageous and unjust sentence for a victimless crime. Too bad he just didn't commit rape or murder. Even Charles Manson comes up for parole every so often.

Libertarians have focused on whether Ulbricht is a hero (see, for example, here, here, and here). This is all well and good. What I want to focus on is whether he was a libertarian.

There is no doubt whatsoever, at least in the minds of libertarians, that Ulbricht or anyone else should be perfectly free to buy drugs, sell drugs, "traffick" in drugs, manufacture drugs, cultivate drugs, use drugs, abuse drugs, and/or facilitate the doing of any of these things.

But doing these things doesn't make one a libertarian.

The only evidence I have ever come across that Ulbricht was a libertarian is the fact that he operated the Silk Road website that facilitated the sale of illegal drugs.

But this does not make him a libertarian.

Perhaps I am mistaken. Perhaps Ulbricht is/was a libertarian in every sense of the word. Fine. That doesn't negate the point of this article since what I have to say relates to libertarianism and drugs in general.

For years I have noticed a disturbing trend among libertarians, and especially as it relates to drugs. I think some libertarians are too quick to identify certain individuals as libertarians based on one thing that said individuals say or do. For example, just because some liberal Hollywood actor gets caught with marijuana at an airport or says that pot smoking should be legal doesn't mean that he is a libertarian. I have observed the same thing when it comes to politics. Just because a Republican candidate for office says that marijuana legislation should be left up to the states because of the Tenth Amendment doesn't mean that he is "libertarian-leaning." He is more than likely just dodging the issue of the drug war and would never say that cocaine and heroin should be legal, not just because it would be political suicide to make such a statement, but also because he believes the government should lock people in cages for possessing substances the government doesn't approve of.

Growing your own marijuana does not make you a libertarian; it makes you an entrepreneur. Snorting coke does not make you a libertarian; it makes you a coke addict. Injecting heroin does not make you a libertarian; it makes you high. Smoking crack does not make you a libertarian; it makes you a crackhead. Manufacturing crystal meth does not make you a libertarian; it makes you an idiot. Drug trafficking does not make you a libertarian; it makes you a criminal. Facilitating the buying and selling of drugs does not make you a libertarian; it makes you a facilitator of the buying and selling of drugs.

Many people, some libertarians included, have other erroneous ideas about what it means to be a libertarian. Just as using or selling drugs does not make one a libertarian, so

- being a pimp does not make one a libertarian,
- being an exotic dancer does not make one a libertarian,
- being a prostitute does not make one a libertarian,
- engaging in illegal gambling does not make one a libertarian,
- engaging in premarital sex does not make one a libertarian,
- cohabiting does not make one a libertarian,
- having an affair does not make one a libertarian,
- watching porn does not make one a libertarian,
- making porn does not make one a libertarian,
- getting drunk as a skunk does not make one a libertarian,
- living an alternative lifestyle does not make one a libertarian,
- practicing discrimination does not make one a libertarian,
- buying alcohol for minors does not make one a libertarian,
- giving alcohol to one's minor children does not make one a libertarian,
- breastfeeding in public does not make one a libertarian,
- listening to alternative rock does not make one a libertarian,
- not paying one's taxes does not make one a libertarian,
- criticizing the government does not make one a libertarian,
- criticizing the police does not make one a libertarian,
- criticizing the NSA does not make one a libertarian,
- violating bad laws does not make one a libertarian,
- committing victimless crimes does not make one a libertarian,
- being a hedonist does not make one a libertarian,
- being a libertine does not make one a libertarian,
- engaging in civil disobedience does not make one a libertarian,
- working in the underground economy does not make one a libertarian,
- living off the grid does not make one a libertarian,
- owning a lot of guns does not make one a libertarian,
- paying with Bitcoin does not make one a libertarian,
- being eccentric does not make one a libertarian,
- owning an "illegal" gun does not make one a libertarian,
- voting Libertarian does not make one a libertarian, and
- saying one is a libertarian does not make one a libertarian.

I am waiting for some libertarian to say that Bruce Jenner is "heroic," and that it is "libertarian" to change one's gender.

No one is a libertarian because of something he does. Libertarianism celebrates individual liberty, private property, peaceful activity, voluntary interaction, laissez faire, personal freedom, financial privacy, individual responsibility, free markets, free thought, and a free society. This, of course, includes the freedom to buy, sell, and use drugs. But doing so does not make one a libertarian.

In addition to my writings on libertarianism, let me recommend to you two things: an article by Murray Rothbard titled "Six Myths about Libertarianism," and Jacob Huebert's book *Libertarianism Today*, which I reviewed here and recommended as "the best introduction to libertarianism."

*****

DO YOU OWN YOUR OWN BODY?

If there is one thing that the smelliest, most down-and-out, most destitute, most forsaken homeless guy who sleeps under a bridge has in common with Donald Trump it is that they both own their own bodies. That may be all the homeless guy owns, but he owns it free and clear and should be able to do what he wants with it.

And so should we—as long as our activities are peaceful, our interactions are consensual, and our associations are voluntary.

Your body belongs to you—not the state, not some government agency, not some puritanical busybody, not some government bureaucrat, and not some nanny statist.

So why can't we do what we want with our own bodies?

If a man owns his own body then surely he can ingest any drug he chooses? He can get high on marijuana. He can smoke crack. He can take PCP. He can snort cocaine. He can shoot up with heroin. He can drop acid. He can swallow an ecstasy pill. He can inject himself with crystal meth. He can eat psychedelic mushrooms.

Not so says the government. We have a war on drugs. We will lock you in a cage where you can be raped, beaten, humiliated, and suffer the loss of your job, your money, and your family.

If a man owns his body then surely he can use it to brew his own beer and distill his own alcohol on his own property? He can invite his friends over to watch football and serve them his concoctions. He can sell some of it to his friends to take home.

Not so says the government. It is a federal crime for an individual to brew more than 100 gallons of beer at home. A household with two or more adults can brew up to 200 gallons. However, none of the home-brewed beer can be sold. Then there are state laws that one must comply with. And don't even think about distilling any amount of your own alcohol.

If a man owns his own body then surely he can sell part of it? He can sell one of his kidneys while he is still alive to save the life of a dying man who is willing to pay him. He can sell his entire body to a hospital upon his death so that he can provide for his widow and save lives after his own has expired.

Not so says the government. You are forbidden from selling your organs, whether you are alive or dead, even though they are so much a part of you that they are inside your body.

If a man owns his own body then surely he can eat and drink whatever he wants to? He can drink huge sugary soft drinks. He can eat sweets laden with trans fat. He can eat junk food to his heart's content. He can eat processed food loaded in salt.

Not so says the government. We will issue nutrition guidelines, wage war on fat, demonize certain foods, regulate school lunches, and, on the local level, restrict the size of soft drinks, monitor salt content, and ban trans fat.

If a man owns his own body then surely he can rent out his body for sexual purposes? A man can be a male prostitute or a gigolo. A woman can be a female prostitute or an escort. They can all advertise their services on Craigslist.

Not so says the government. Even though men and women can provide free sexual services as often as they want, to as many willing people as they can find, we will arrest them if they charge for it.

If a man owns his own body then surely he can gamble with some of his money? He can run a blackjack tournament in his neighborhood. He can have his friends over to play poker for money while they all watch the World Series of Poker on television and take a rake for doing so. He can run his own lottery.

Not so says the government. There are a myriad of federal and state laws that restrict, regulate, or prohibit gambling. We have to fine and/or imprison you if you violate one of these laws.

If a man owns his own body then surely he can get any weapon he wants to defend himself against those who would aggress against him and do him bodily harm.

Not so says the government. In spite of the Second Amendment, there are many federal gun laws that you have to comply with. We will restrict what guns and ammo you are allowed to own. We will do a background check and if we don't like what we see, then you will be forbidden to purchase a gun. And state governments have waiting periods that you have to comply with.

If a man owns his own body then surely he can travel wherever he wants to go that is willing to allow him? While there he can spend any amount of his money that he chooses and bring back any amount of merchandise he chooses.

Not so says the government. If you decide to go to Cuba, even now with some restrictions eliminated, you have to give the State Department a reason why you are going. And we reserve the right to restrict what you can bring with you and bring back.

If a man owns his own body then surely he can work for any wage that is offered to him? He may be unemployed, never graduated from high school, and be unskilled. Any money he can make will help him feed himself, stay off welfare, and learn a skill.

Not so says the government. You cannot work for less than the federal minimum wage. And in some states and cities, there is an even higher minimum wage that you cannot make less than. We will fine any employer who tries to help you become a productive member of society.

If a man owns his own body then surely he can keep the fruit of your labor? If he makes $500 a week then he can put all of it in the bank, stash all of it under his mattress, or spend all of it.

Not so says the government. We are entitled to a cut of the fruits of your labor. And the more successful you are, the more we will take from you. We are in the business of spending money on boondoggles and redistributing money from those who work to those who don't, filtered, of course, through our large and inefficient bureaucracy.

If a man owns his own body then surely he can take his own life if he wishes? He can buy a quantity of pills to swallow that will render him unconscious and stop his heart in order to end his suffering from pain, disability, disease, depression, or anguish.

Not so says the government. If you try to commit suicide and fail, we will involuntarily commit you to the mental ward of your local hospital. We will limit your ability to purchase drugs by requiring a doctor to write you a prescription.

I can't help but concluding that, as far as the state is concerned, we don't really own our own bodies at all. We live, move, and have our being at the behest of the state.

*****

WHO SHOULD DECIDE?

Who are the real libertarians? Conservative Republicans who want to sucker libertarians to get their votes often describe themselves as libertarians or libertarian-leaning. Hollywood actors who favor the legalization of marijuana are sometimes referred to as libertarians—no matter what else they believe.

Here are fifty questions about who should decide certain things that people, as individuals or as business owners, do or might want to do. The answers should make it abundantly clear who the real libertarians are.

1. Who should decide whether you sell one of your kidneys?
2. Who should decide whether you smoke marijuana?
3. Who should decide to whom you sell your house?
4. Who should decide for whom your business bakes a cake?
5. Who should decide the dress code for customers at your business?
6. Who should decide the dress code for employees at your business?
7. Who should decide whether you manufacture crystal meth?

8. Who should decide whether your business sells alcohol?
9. Who should decide what kind of plants you have in your house?
10. Who should decide what kind of wedding you photograph?
11. Who should decide how much cash you deposit at one time?
12. Who should decide how many cash withdrawals you make each month?
13. Who should decide to whom you rent an apartment?
14. Who should decide whom you pick up in your cab?
15. Who should decide whether you snort cocaine?
16. Who should decide whether you make moonshine?
17. Who should decide against whom and for what reason you discriminate?
18. Who should decide how much water the toilets flush that you manufacture?
19. Who should decide whether you open a gambling establishment?
20. Who should decide whether you gamble for money in your own home?
21. Who should decide whether you give your kids wine with meals?
22. Who should decide whether you sell drugs?
23. Who should decide whether you send your children to school?
24. Who should decide how much beer you are allowed to brew at home?
25. Who should decide what size soft drink you drink?
26. Who should decide at what age your child gets a job?
27. Who should decide whether you have a smoking section in your restaurant?
28. Who should decide how many handicapped parking spaces your business has?
29. Who should decide whether and how you commit suicide?
30. Who should decide whether your business's restrooms are handicap accessible?
31. Who should decide whom you hire and don't hire?
32. Who should decide whom you fire and don't fire?
33. Who should decide what you pay your employees?
34. Who should decide what vaccines to give your children?
35. Who should decide whether you vaccinate your children in the first place?
36. Who should decide whether you purchase health insurance?
37. Who should decide whether you smoke crack?
38. Who should decide whether your store sells beer on Sundays?
39. Who should decide at what hours your store sells beer on Sundays?
40. Who should decide whether you exchange sex for money?
41. Who should decide whether you exchange money for sex?
42. Who should decide whether your refinery mixes ethanol into its gasoline?
43. Who should decide whether your business offers health insurance?

44. Who should decide what kind of gas mileage the cars get that your company manufactures?
45. Who should decide whether you consume trans fats?
46. Who should decide to whom you sell a gun?
47. Who should decide whether you shoot up heroin?
48. Who should decide what hours your business is open?
49. Who should decide by how much your business increases its prices during a natural disaster?
50. Who should decide whether your business is open on Sundays?

If you answered that you should decide these questions then you are a libertarian—whether you call yourself a libertarian. If you answered that the government should decide these questions then you are a statist—whether you call yourself a Democrat, a Republican, a liberal, a conservative, a moderate, a progressive, a populist, a neoconservative, a democratic socialist, a centrist, an independent, or non-partisan. If you answered that the government should decide most of these questions then you are simply an inconsistent statist.

This does not mean that you decide these things in a vacuum. Just because you decide does not mean that you don't consult your family, friends, club, church, pastor, priest, minister, physician, psychologist, psychiatrist, coworkers, and/or acquaintances. Ultimately, however, the decision is yours to make. This does not mean that that things are all safe, healthy, moral, or a good idea. And this does not mean that anyone or everyone should do any or all of these things.

It simply means that in a free society, you decide. In an authoritarian society, the government decides. Libertarians believe in a free society. Statists believe in a society heavily controlled by legislation, laws, regulations, judges, bureaucrats, ordinances, prisons, violence, force, aggression, coercion, badges, and guns.

I will take the free society.

*****

LIBERTARIANISM AND RACISM

Because the most non-libertarian Libertarian Party, presidential ticket in history is vying for the presidency, it is imperative now more than ever that libertarianism, rightly defined and applied, be explained to the masses.

Whenever I speak or write about libertarianism, I invariably refer to libertarianism greatest philosopher and theorist, Murray Rothbard (1926-1995). Here is his classic statement on libertarianism:

Libertarianism is not and does not pretend to be a complete moral, or aesthetic theory; it is only a political theory, that is, the important subset of moral theory that deals with the proper role of violence in social life. Political theory deals with what is proper or improper for the government to do, and the government is distinguished from every other group in society as being the institution of organized violence. Libertarianism holds that the only proper role of violence is to defend person and property against violence, that any use of violence that goes beyond such just defense is itself aggressive, unjust, and criminal. Libertarianism, therefore, is a theory which states that everyone should be free of violent invasion, should be free to do as he sees fit except invade the person or property of another. What a person does with his or her life is vital and important, but is simply irrelevant to libertarianism.

And here is one of his classic statements on the nonaggression theory that underlies libertarianism:

The fundamental axiom of libertarian theory is that no one may threaten or commit violence ("aggress") against another man's person or property. Violence may be employed only against the man who commits such violence; that is, only defensively against the aggressive violence of another. In short, no violence may be employed against a non-aggressor. Here is the fundamental rule from which can be deduced the entire corpus of libertarian theory.

Libertarianism maintains that people should be free from individual, societal, or government interference to live life any way they desire, pursue happiness, accumulate wealth, assess risk, make choices, engage in commerce with anyone who is willing, participate in any economic activity for profit, and spend the fruits of their labor as they see fit as long as their actions are peaceful, their associations are voluntary, their interactions are consensual, and they don't violate the personal or property rights of others.

The nonconsensual initiation or real threat to initiate aggression against the person or property of others is always wrong. Aggression is justified only in defense of person or property or in retaliation against aggression but is not required.

Libertarianism is concerned only with actions, or the threat of actions, of aggression, not ideology. One's personal judgments about religion, morality, ethics, values, or sin are immaterial. One's private opinions about sex, aesthetics, culture, tradition, or the meaning of life are irrelevant. One's secret thoughts about any individual, group, class, nationality, or race are neither here nor there.

It is no wonder that some people just don't get it since it seems that even some libertarians just don't get it either.

The recent libertarian debate over "thin" and "thick" libertarianism has apparently fizzled out. Lew Rockwell has succinctly explained the difference between the two:

> The "thin" libertarian believes in the nonaggression principle, that one may not initiate physical force against anyone else. The thin libertarian thinks of himself simply as a libertarian, without labels. Most "thick" libertarians likewise believe in the nonaggression principle, but they believe that for the struggle for liberty to be coherent, libertarians must be committed to a slate of other views as well.

Now, although this slate might contain a variety of views, depending on the libertarian who is committed to it, there is one thing that is usually first on the list: the rejection of racism. The roots of this debate go back at least twenty years.

I first noticed this expansion of the libertarian creed in a popular libertarian book published about twenty years ago. There the author felt it necessary to express some moral sentiments that go beyond the bare description of the libertarian policy and called upon Americans to affirm their commitment to rise above racial prejudice and reject overt and hateful racism.

Then, about eight or so years ago, I saw where a libertarian writer pondered whether libertarianism should be seen as a "thin" commitment or one strand among others in a "thick" bundle of intertwined social commitments. There the writer expressed the opinion that certain beliefs or commitments could not be rejected without logically undermining the deeper reasons that justify the nonaggression principle. Although one could consistently accept libertarianism without accepting certain commitments or beliefs, one could not do so reasonably. Therefore, libertarians should endorse things that are conceptually independent of libertarian principles, be committed to opposing certain social practices or outcomes even though they are not themselves coercive, and incorporate certain social and cultural projects into libertarian theory and practice.

More recently, these two things have been put together, resulting in the following sentiments:

> The grounds of libertarianism imply other obligations. Libertarianism is not just concerned with the proper and improper use of force. The strongest case for libertarianism entails commitments to not only the nonaggression principle but to other values that don't directly relate to aggression, like racism that doesn't violate rights. There are clear libertarian grounds for disapproving of racism that does not involve aggression. Racism is a primitive form of collectivism, which, of course, libertarians should detest. Racism can eat away at the values conducive to libertarianism. Implicit in racism is a potential for violence.

In addition to its unwarranted expansion of the nonaggression principle that strikes at the very core of libertarianism, I see three problems with this undue concern about libertarianism and racism.

First, the term "racism" is never defined or explained. The term is thrown around by some libertarians much the same as liberals, progressives, and social justice warriors employ it to attack and neutralize conservative and libertarian opponents of various government programs and social movements.

Second, the mostly left-libertarians who want to make value judgments about racism are generally vehemently opposed to libertarians making value judgments about things like abortion, an action that many libertarians consider to be a real violation of the nonaggression principle. And instead of being indifferent as to whether a libertarian uses drugs, views pornography, or practices an alternative lifestyle, it seems at times as though some of these libertarians believe that libertarians should celebrate these things.

Third, the most insidious thing about all of this is that it is an attack on free thought. "Racism" that doesn't involve violence or aggression, or the threat of these things—just like love, hatred, infatuation, disgust, obsession, or revulsion that doesn't involve violence or aggression, or the threat of these things—is a thought, an opinion, an idea, a belief, an attitude, a judgment. Libertarianism is concerned with action, not thoughts. Thoughts, like motives and desires, are the realm of morality and religion.

Being a libertarian doesn't preclude one from making gender, ethnic, national, religious, or racial distinctions. It doesn't disqualify one from discriminating for or against a particular gender, ethnic group, nationality, religion, or race. And it doesn't prohibit one from judging that one gender, ethnic group, nationality, religion, or race is better or worse than another *in some aspect or respect* or more likely or less likely to do or not do something than another *in some aspect or respect*.

Doing these things doesn't mean that one wants to commit, or that it will lead to one wanting to commit, aggression or violence against members of some gender, ethnic, national, religious, or racial group.

Can a libertarian be a "racist"? That is, can a libertarian think, deduce, conclude, presume, suppose, assume, or believe something about a racial group? Of course he can. Just like a progressive, a centrist, a liberal, a Christian, an atheist, a moderate, or a conservative can. It doesn't matter if people disagree on whether his thoughts are right or wrong, rational or irrational, correct or incorrect, logical or illogical, reasonable or unreasonable. Whether someone is a "racist" or has "racist" thoughts is beyond the scope of libertarianism.

*****

OF COURSE I'M A LIBERTARIAN

Libertarians are usually on the defensive because their principles seem so extreme and some of their views so radical. This is true whether the opponent or critic of libertarianism is a liberal, a conservative, a Democrat, a Republican, a centrist, a populist, a socialist, a moderate, or a progressive. All are united in their attacks on libertarians in many areas.

But it is these groups who ought to be on the defensive. They all believe that it is appropriate for government at some level

(1) to arrest, fine, imprison, or otherwise punish people for engaging in entirely private, peaceful, voluntary, and consensual actions that do not aggress against the person or property of others,

(2) to fund education, research, cultural, and construction projects,

(3) to regulate, oversee, and sometimes prohibit commercial activity between willing buyers and willing sellers, and

(4) to take people's resources against their will, by force if necessary, and transfer or redistribute them to other citizens or foreigners as the government sees fit.

Libertarianism is a philosophy of liberty, property, and peace. As I have written elsewhere about libertarianism:

Libertarianism is the philosophy which says that people should be free from individual, societal, or government interference to live their lives any way they desire, pursue their own happiness, accumulate as much wealth as they can, assess their own risk, make their own choices, engage in commerce with anyone who is willing to reciprocate, participate in any economic activity for their profit, and spend the fruits of their labor as they see fit as long as their actions are peaceful, their associations are voluntary, their interactions are consensual, and they don't violate the personal or property rights of others.

Libertarianism respects personal privacy, financial privacy, free thought, individual responsibility, freedom of conscience, free exchange, free markets, and private property.

Libertarianism celebrates individual liberty, personal freedom, peaceful activity, voluntary interaction, laissez faire, free enterprise, free assembly, free association, free speech, and free expression.

The creed of libertarianism is the non-aggression axiom: everyone should be free from aggression against his person and property as long as he respects the person and property of others. As long as people don't infringe upon the rights of others by committing, or threatening to commit, acts of fraud, theft, aggression, or violence against their person or property, the government should just leave them alone. But because the government is the greatest violator of personal and property rights, libertarians oppose and seek to limit, by peaceful means, the intervention, regulation, and control of the government.

Instead of being on the defensive and making excuses for or backing away from libertarian principles (like the recent Libertarian Party presidential ticket), libertarians should boldly say: Of course I support this and that! Of course, I oppose thus and so! Of course, I'm a libertarian.

For example—

Of course, I support medical marijuana! It is not the business of government to decide what medical treatments are appropriate. The government should not have anything to do with the practice of medicine.

Of course, I oppose gun-control laws! If guns are outlawed, only outlaws will have guns. Criminals who want to commit armed robbery or murder are not deterred by gun-control laws. There should be a free market in guns just like any other product.

Of course, I oppose public education! It is not the job of the government to educate anyone's children or force anyone to pay for the education of anyone else's children. All schools, vouchers, grants, and loans should be private.

Of course, I support the legalization of all drugs! Vices are not crimes. Every crime needs a tangible victim with measurable damages. It is not the job of the government to prohibit or control what a man wants to smoke, snort, swallow, inject or otherwise ingest into his body.

Of course, I oppose Medicare and Medicaid! It is not the job of the government to provide or pay for health care or health insurance. And it is immoral to force some Americans to pay for the health care of other Americans.

Of course, I oppose all foreign aid! No country should receive foreign aid for any reason. What the government gives in foreign aid must first be taken from Americans. No American is ever asked if he wants a portion of his taxes to go to some particular country. If individual Americans want a particular country to be supported, then they should write a check.

Of course, I support all tax deductions and credits! Reducing tax deductions and credits increases government revenue just like raising tax rates. It is always better when Americans are allowed to keep more money in their pockets and out of the hands of Uncle Sam.

Of course, I oppose refundable tax credits like the Earned Income Credit! Refundable tax credits are a form of welfare. No one is entitled to receive a tax refund of money that someone else paid in.

Of course, I oppose the U.S. military providing disaster relief! It is the sole purpose of the military to defend the country. It is never the purpose of the military to provide disaster relief, even in the United States.

Of course, I support the right of people to sell their organs! If there is anything that a man owns free and clear it is his own body. Everyone has the natural right to sell his organs to the highest bidder while he is alive or after he is dead.

Of course, I oppose food stamps! It is not the job of government to feed anyone. All food aid should be undertaken by private organizations.

Of course, I oppose all minimum wage laws! It is not the job of the government to set a minimum price for labor any more than it is the job of the government to set a minimum price for bananas.

Of course, I support free trade! Government-managed trade is nothing but Soviet-style central planning. It is not the job of the government to "protect" industries at the expense of American consumers or calculate the "trade deficit." Individuals and businesses have the natural right to export goods to or import goods from any country they choose.

Of course, I oppose government unemployment compensation! It is not the job of the government to pay people to not work. Unemployment insurance should be provided by the private sector just like auto, life, and fire insurance.

Of course, I oppose all anti-discrimination laws! These laws are an attack on private property, freedom of association, freedom of contract, and freedom of thought. In a free society, any individual, business, employer, or organization would have the right to discriminate against anyone for any reason.

Of course, I support ticket scalping! Ticket scalpers perform a valuable service for event hosts and patrons. What could possibly be wrong with an exchange of tickets for cash between a willing buyer and a willing seller, as long as their activity does not violate the property rights of the owner of the ground where they make their exchange?

Of course, I oppose welfare payments! It is immoral to take money from those who work and give it to those who don't—even when the government does it. All charity should be private and voluntary.

Of course, I oppose occupational licensing! Why should anyone have to get permission from the government to open a business, engage in commerce, work in certain occupations, have a particular vocation, or provide a service to willing customers? Why does anyone need permission from the government to work? All occupational certification could and should be done by the private sector.

Of course, I support these things! Of course, I oppose these things! Of course, I'm a libertarian! "Libertarians," as economist Robert Higgs has said, "should never concede the moral high ground to those who insist on coercively interfering with freedom."

*****

2

LIBERTARIANISM: PRACTICE

THE LIBERTARIAN PLEDGE TO AMERICA

Just in time to bamboozle conservative voters before the election, House Republicans unveiled their "Pledge to America" at a hardware store in Virginia in late September. Although the Pledge contains libertarian rhetoric about promoting "greater liberty" and "smaller, more accountable government," the fact that Republicans promise to roll back spending only to the level it was during Bush's last year in office and "advance the cause of freedom and democracy around the world" means that the Pledge is stupid and evil.

We libertarians are often told that instead of tearing down the policies of liberals and conservatives we should offer some real solutions. Well, if I were a libertarian running for office, I would issue my own pledge. But instead of vague, empty, and false promises we find in the Republican "Pledge to America," I have come up with fifty specific, unambiguous promises that seem so radical to the average voter that I know I could never be elected. But these are not just my preferences and convictions; these are things that all libertarians should be consistently and unequivocally promising—if they are trying to be honest instead of trying to be elected.

Here is the Libertarian Pledge to America:

- I promise to end the war on drugs.
- I promise to abolish the Department of Energy.
- I promise to abolish *all* anti-trust laws.
- I promise to abolish the Federal Housing Administration.
- I promise to abolish the Federal National Mortgage Association (Fannie Mae).
- I promise to abolish the Federal Home Loan Mortgage Corporation (Freddy Mac).
- I promise to abolish the Government National Mortgage Association (Ginnie Mae).
- I promise to repeal the Fair Housing Act.
- I promise to abolish the Department of Housing and Urban Development.
- I promise to abolish the Federal Trade Commission.
- I promise to abolish the EPA.
- I promise to abolish the Corporation for Public Broadcasting.
- I promise to abolish the Department of Education.
- I promise to end federal funding and control of education.

40

- I promise to cease funding Head Start.
- I promise to cease funding the National School Lunch Program.
- I promise to repeal the federal minimum wage.
- I promise to repeal the National Labor Relations Act.
- I promise to repeal the PATRIOT ACT.
- I promise to abolish the Department of Homeland Security.
- I promise to abolish the TSA and return airport security to airports and airlines.
- I promise to repeal *all* federal gun regulations.
- I promise to abolish NASA.
- I promise to abolish the National Endowment for the Arts.
- I promise to abolish the National Endowment for the Humanities.
- I promise to end the wars in Iraq and Afghanistan.
- I promise to cease *all* drone attacks and covert activities.
- I promise to bring *all* U.S. troops home from foreign soil.
- I promise to close *all* foreign military bases.
- I promise to stop meddling in the affairs of other countries.
- I promise to limit the Department of Defense to actual defense.
- I promise to end *all* federal bailouts.
- I promise to stop funding the UN, World Bank, and IMF.
- I promise to end *all* foreign aid.
- I promise to end *all* farm subsidies.
- I promise to repeal *all* trade restrictions, import quotas, anti-dumping laws, and trade agreements.
- I promise to abolish the Equal Employment Opportunities Commission.
- I promise to repeal the Americans with Disabilities Act.
- I promise to repeal *all* Affirmative Action, minority set-asides, and public accommodations laws.
- I promise to repeal the Family and Medical Leave Act.
- I promise to cease funding Planned Parenthood.
- I promise to abolish the Department of Health and Human Services.
- I promise to repeal the Patient Protection and Affordable Care Act.
- I promise to end Medicare and Medicaid.
- I promise to end *all* federal funding and control of medicine and medical research.
- I promise to abolish the FDA.
- I promise to abolish NPR.
- I promise to abolish the Department of Labor.
- I promise to cease funding any scientific research on climate change.
- I promise to end the FED.

These are just things that are unconstitutional according to article I, section 8, of the Constitution and its Tenth Amendment that I just thought of off the top of my head. If I took the time, I could come up with an additional fifty. Then I could ask some libertarian friends of mine to help me come up with even more. Walter Block could certainly come up with fifty more, including abolishing the Department of Transportation. Tom DiLorenzo could also come up with another fifty more, including repealing the Community Reinvestment Act.

Republicans are so statist and so opposed to liberty that they would choke on the first item. To libertarians, ending the war on drugs is a no-brainer. Aside from the moral argument for personal liberty, which is compelling enough, the costs of drug prohibition far outweigh any possible benefits. It clogs the judicial system, swells prison populations, fosters violence, corrupts law enforcement, erodes civil liberties, destroys financial privacy, encourages illegal searches and seizures, ruins lives, wastes hundreds of billions of taxpayer dollars, hinders legitimate pain treatment, turns law-abiding people into criminals, inconveniences shopping, and has no impact on the use or availability of most drugs in the United States.

The libertarian pledge to America—outside of Ron Paul and a few libertarians are there any candidates who will take it?

*****

LIBERTARIAN ANSWERS

Echoing George Wallace, it has been said many times that there is not a dime's worth of difference between liberals and conservatives. This is even usually true when the focus is on the most liberal liberals and the most conservative conservatives. The similarity may not be apparent on the surface, but once you compare both groups to libertarians it becomes perfectly clear.

The answers that libertarians give to questions debated by liberals and conservatives are unexpected and not what either of those groups wants to hear. I list below 11 topics with 50 questions that might be debated by liberals and conservatives followed by the libertarian answer.

Foreign Aid

1. Should the United States give less foreign aid to Egypt because of its violent crackdowns on protestors?
Libertarian answer: No country should receive foreign aid for any reason.
2. Should the United States give more foreign aid to Israel because it is our ally in the Middle East?
Libertarian answer: No country should receive foreign aid for any reason.
3. Should a country's foreign aid be tied to its human rights record?
Libertarian answer: No country should receive foreign aid for any reason.

Disaster Relief

4. How much disaster relief should the United States government provide to the Philippines?

Libertarian answer: It is not the purpose of government to provide disaster relief to foreigners.

5. How much disaster relief should the United States government have provided to Americans after the tornadoes in Illinois last year?

Libertarian answer: It is not the purpose of government to provide disaster relief to Americans.

6. How much of a role should the U.S. military play in disaster relief?

Libertarian answer: It is not the purpose of the military to provide disaster relief.

Education

7. Should the U.S. Department of Education provide educational vouchers so low-income children can go to the school of their choice?

Libertarian answer: There should be no U.S. Department of Education in the first place.

8. Should students at public schools be required to wear uniforms?

Libertarian answer: There should be no public schools in the first place.

9. Should the federal government cap the student loan interest rate?

Libertarian answer: The federal government should not be in the student loan business.

10. Should students be required to say the Pledge of Allegiance?

Libertarian answer: There should be no Pledge of Allegiance for students to recite.

11. How much should children who qualify for the National School Lunch Program have to pay for their lunch?

Libertarian answer: There should be no children who qualify since it is not the business of government to provide anyone lunch.

12. Should Head Start be expanded?

Libertarian answer: There should be no Head Start to expand.

Taxes

13. Should the Earned Income Tax Credit be indexed to inflation?

Libertarian answer: All refundable tax credits should be eliminated.

14. Should welfare benefits be included in determining taxable income?

Libertarian answer: There shouldn't be any welfare benefits in the first place.

15. Should the income tax be changed to a flat tax?

Libertarian answer: The income tax should be abolished.

16. Should the income tax code be made fairer?

Libertarian answer: The income tax code should be eliminated.

17. Should the number of tax brackets be increased or decreased?

Libertarian answer: There should be no tax brackets in the first place.

18. How much more should the "rich" pay in income taxes than the "poor"?

Libertarian answer: Neither the "rich" nor the "poor" should pay any income tax.

19. Which tax loopholes should be closed?

Libertarian answer: None of them; they should be made larger so Americans can keep more of their money.

20. Which tax deductions should be extended and for how long?

Libertarian answer: All of them should be made permanent so Americans can keep more of their money.

Health Care

21. How much prescription drug coverage should be included with Medicare?

Libertarian answer: Medicare should not exist in the first place.

22. Should the FDA approve more drugs or at least approve drugs quicker?

Libertarian answer: The FDA should not exist in the first place.

23. If Obamacare is repealed, how should the government reform health care?

Libertarian answer: The federal government should have nothing at all to do with health care in the first place.

24. How much funding should the government devote to finding a cure for cancer?

Libertarian answer: It is not the purpose of government to fund medical research of any kind.

Social Security

25. How much of a COLA should Social Security recipients receive next year?

Libertarian answer: Social Security should not exist in the first place.

26. How quickly should the Social Security retirement age be raised?

Libertarian answer: Social Security should not exist in the first place.

27. By what percentage should the Social Security payroll tax cap be increased for 2014?

Libertarian answer: Social Security should not exist in the first place.

Government Agencies

28. Should NASA go back to the moon or go to Mars instead?

Libertarian answer: NASA should not exist in the first place.

29. Should NPR give equal time to conservatives?

Libertarian answer: NPR should not exist in the first place.

30. Should the NEA be prevented from funding pornographic art?

Libertarian answer: The NEA should not exist in the first place.

31. How much of a fine should the FCC levy on television networks for broadcasting profane speech or actions?

Libertarian answer: The FCC should not exist in the first place.

32. Should AMTRAK increase its fares in an attempt to be profitable?

Libertarian answer: AMTRAK should not exist in the first place.

33. Should the TSA use less invasive procedures?

Libertarian answer: The TSA should not exist in the first place.

34. What criteria should the SBA use in granting loans?

Libertarian answer: The SBA should not exist in the first place.

The Military

35. Should the U.S. intervene militarily in Syria if it can prove that chemical weapons were used?

Libertarian answer: The U.S. military should not intervene in any foreign country for any reason.

36. Which overseas U.S. bases should be consolidated or closed?

Libertarian answer: The United States should not have any overseas bases.

37. By what percentage should the defense budget be increased or decreased?

Libertarian answer: It should be cut to the bone.

38. How many U.S. troops should stay in Iraq and Afghanistan as advisers and peacekeepers?

Libertarian answer: The U.S. military should never have gone to Iraq and Afghanistan in the first place.

Economics

39. What should the minimum wage be?

Libertarian answer: There should be no minimum wage in the first place.

40. For how long should unemployment benefits be extended?

Libertarian answer: There should be no unemployment benefits to be extended.

41. Should food stamp benefits be adjusted every year depending on the state of the economy?

Libertarian answer: There should be no food stamp benefits to be adjusted.

42. By what percentage should a businessman be able to raise prices in the aftermath of a disaster and not be guilty of price gouging?

Libertarian answer: There should be no such thing as price gouging laws.

43. What is the maximum interest rate that should be allowed on a credit card or a payday loan?

Libertarian answer: There should be no government regulation of interest rates to being with.

The Drug War

44. Should marijuana use be legal under certain circumstances?

Libertarian answer: There should be no restrictions on marijuana use for any reason.

45. Should users of crack cocaine do more prison time than users of powder cocaine?

Libertarian answer: There should be no difference between the two; both should be perfectly legal.

46. Should drug traffickers be eligible for parole?

Libertarian answer: No, they should be pardoned and immediately released as long as they have not also committed any real crimes.

Miscellaneous

47. Should public libraries be allowed to make available risqué books?

Libertarian answer: There should be no public libraries to begin with.

48. Should funding for Planned Parenthood be cut since the organization performs abortions?

Libertarian answer: There should not be any government funding of any private organization in the first place.

49. What should the CAFE standards for cars be for the 2014 model year?

Libertarian answer: There should be no CAFE standards to begin with.

50. Should sexual orientation and gender identity be added to anti-discrimination laws?

Libertarian answer: There should be no anti-discrimination laws in the first place.

Conservative and liberal debates over public policy are utterly meaningless. Not only do they not have the right answers; they don't even ask the right questions.

*****

LIBERTARIAN PRIORITIES

"I am getting more and more convinced that the war-peace question is the key to the whole libertarian business." ~ Murray Rothbard

That our enemy is the state, there is no question. As Rothbard explains:

Briefly, the State is that organization in society which attempts to maintain a monopoly of the use of force and violence in a given territorial area; in particular, it is the only organization in society that obtains its revenue not by voluntary contribution or payment for services rendered but by coercion. While other individuals or institutions obtain their income by production of goods and services and by the peaceful and voluntary sale of these goods and services to others, the State obtains its revenue by the use of compulsion; that is, by the use and the threat of the jailhouse and the bayonet. Having used force and violence to obtain its revenue, the State generally goes on to regulate and dictate the other actions of its individual subjects.

The libertarian goal is ultimately a free society where the non-aggression principle is the foundational principle and individual liberty, laissez-faire, and property rights reign supreme. Standing in the way of that goal is the state. And if that weren't already a formidable enough obstacle, the state is also actively seeking to increase and expand its power and its interventions into the economy and society.

What, then, should the priorities of individual libertarians and libertarian organizations be as they seek to stop the advances of, chip away at, and roll back the state?

It is only natural that liberals and conservatives since they seek to use the power of the state for their own ends, not only have the wrong priorities, but also many dreadful priorities that are destructive to liberty and property.

Liberals generally want to increase the minimum wage, provide every working mother with free day care, institute a national health care system, increase poor women's access to abortion, provide free contraception devices to any woman that wants them, expand Medicaid, remove "under God" from the Pledge of Allegiance, provide every child with a free college education, increase funding for mass transit, pass stricter gun control laws, make "the rich" pay their "fair share," increase the number of groups protected under anti-discrimination laws, grant special rights to LGBT individuals, increase funding for public education and maintain the welfare state.

Conservatives generally want to simplify the tax code, reduce government waste and fraud, amend the Constitution with a balanced budget amendment, restore prayer and Bible reading in public schools, repost the Ten Commandments in public schools, increase funding for abstinence education, force all school children to recite the Pledge of Allegiance, reform welfare, reform immigration, slow the rate of increase of certain federal programs while calling it a cut, make flag burning a crime, provide low-income children with educational vouchers to attend the school of their choice, prevent people from using marijuana for medical purposes, strictly enforce drug laws, increase defense spending, and maintain the warfare state.

Oh, and both groups want to "save" Social Security and Medicare for our seniors.

Contrary to some of their liberal and conservative critics, libertarians are neither naïve nor intransigent. They know there will never be any magic buttons to push to immediately and completely eliminate this or that government agency or program. They are willing to accept a gradual gain or step in the right direction, as long as doing so doesn't compromise their basic principles or detract from their ultimate goal of a free society.

But some libertarians are plainly headed in the wrong direction. There is nothing wrong with a gradual step toward liberty, but it has to be a step in the right direction. Other libertarians are indeed headed in the right direction but have the wrong priorities. It is this latter error that I want to focus on.

It is neither constitutional on the federal level nor the proper role of government at any level to take money from some and transfer it to others, fund medical or scientific research, monitor the weather, fund education, make or guarantee loans, provide medical care or insurance, fund welfare, provide airport security, collect economic statistics, provide flood insurance, operate a railroad, provide electricity, fight poverty, institute vehicle gas mileage standards, build public housing, operate a retirement program, promote home ownership or a college education, control prices, be involved in television or radio broadcasting, fight obesity, regulate or subsidize business or industry, collect garbage, ban substances, support the arts, explore space, or regulate voluntary, consensual, peaceful activities that take place on private property.

The "sum of good government," said Thomas Jefferson in his first inaugural address, is "a wise and frugal Government, which shall restrain men from injuring one another, shall leave them otherwise free to regulate their own pursuits of industry and improvement, and shall not take from the mouth of labor the bread it has earned."

Although the following agencies of the federal government are neither constitutional nor legitimate, they are not high on my list of federal agencies that I think libertarians should spend a lot of time trying to eliminate:

- United States Geological Survey
- National Weather Service
- National Park Service
- National Oceanic and Atmospheric Administration
- Army Corp of Engineers
- National Marine Fisheries Service
- Centers for Disease Control and Prevention
- National Institutes of Health

In the case of the National Institutes of Health (NIH), I myself have written about the need to abolish it. Others have written about the politicization of the National Park Service and the blunders of the Army Corp of Engineers. But I don't think libertarians should lose much sleep over the existence of these agencies.

Regular welfare programs like food stamps, free school lunches, subsidized housing, WIC, and Medicaid are clearly unconstitutional and illegitimate. They redistribute wealth and transfer income from "taxpayers" to "tax eaters." Now, while welfare programs that hand out cash payments like TANF, SSI, and refundable tax credits like the EITC should and could be immediately abolished, I will be the first to admit—even though I have written extensively against the welfare state and oppose it root and branch—that, rightly or wrongly, these regular welfare programs do help a great number of people and many families are now dependent upon them. Medicare and Social Security, while both welfare programs, are a little different since they are partly (in the case of Medicare) and mostly (in the case of Social Security) funded by payroll taxes. And these are programs that have fostered dependency like none other. All welfare programs should, of course, be eliminated, but there are other things more insidious that should have a higher priority.

There are some federal agencies that benefit a select group of Americans. Three immediately come to mind, but there are certainly many more:

• National Endowment of the Arts
• National Endowment of the Humanities
• Corporation for Public Broadcasting

I have made the case against funding for the arts and for broadcasting. Since programs like these, by their very nature, benefit not just a few, but a select few who would fail a means test should one be concocted, they should be eliminated immediately or, in the case of NPR, which is funded by the CPB, sold to the highest bidder.

We have not yet reached the top of the priority ladder, but we are getting close.

Some government agencies and programs are pure evil.

Federal and state Drug Enforcement Administrations, the war on drugs, and all of the other federal and state agencies involved in carrying out the war on drugs have got to be at the top of this list. They should be eradicated and suppressed like the government's Domestic Cannabis Eradication/Suppression Program destroys marijuana plants.

Another agency with an evil mission is the Transportation Security Agency (TSA). Not only is it unconstitutional and illegitimate for the federal government to provide security for airports and airlines, the TSA commits great evils in doing so. Things like unnecessarily inconveniencing and delaying air travel, humiliating travelers, sexually abusing passengers, operating a very expensive security theater, and forcing people to throw out tubes of toothpaste over 3.4 ounces before they can board an airplane.

The federal Department of Education must also be included at the top of the evil list. Federal interference in what is a state and local matter has been the cause of great evils. Not to mention that it is also both unconstitutional and illegitimate. Every state has a Department of Education and every county operates a school system. They, of course, have their own set of problems, but it is absolutely unnecessary for the federal government to have anything whatsoever to do with any state's educational system.

What, then, could possibly be a higher priority for libertarians than these evil triplets?

How about war, empire, and the military? How about the Army, the Navy, and the Air Force? How about the warfare/police/national security state? How about intervention, invasion, and occupation? How about foreign aid, foreign bases, and foreign wars? How about bombs, bullets, and missiles? How about innocents injured, maimed, and killed? How about an aggressive, belligerent, and meddling foreign policy?

And don't forget about the widow and orphan twins.

Rothbard early on recognized what libertarianism's priority should be: "I am getting more and more convinced that the war-peace question is the key to the whole libertarian business."

Until such time as the United States returns to the foreign policy articulated by Jefferson in his first inaugural address—"Peace, commerce, and honest friendship with all nations, entangling alliances with none"—the top priority of libertarians must be to expose the evils of the warfare state.

I didn't say the only priority, I said the top priority. Food stamps don't kill Americans or foreigners. Foreign interventions kill both. Working to privatize local garbage collection is certainly a good thing, but libertarians need to never lose sight of the insidious nature of the warfare state and U.S. foreign policy.

Nevertheless, some libertarians seem like they are more concerned about expanding gay rights than the evils of the warfare state and U.S. foreign policy.

Don't be one of them.

*****

THE CHANGE AMERICA NEEDS IS LIBERTARIANISM

The French writer Jean-Baptiste Alphonse Karr (1808–1890) famously said that "the more things change, the more they stay the same." This epigram is a perfect description of the American electoral process.

Americans elect a new president every four years. Members of the U.S. House of Representatives have a two-year term. U.S. senators are elected for six years. That means that every two years all House seats and one-third of the Senate seats are up for grabs. Although the president is limited by the Twenty-Second Amendment to just two terms, there are no term limits for U.S. representatives and senators. Over the past fifty years, the reelection rate for House incumbents has not dropped below 85 percent. And only six times has it even fallen below 90 percent. The percentages are lower in the Senate, but Senate races still overwhelmingly favor the incumbent. Since the election of 1982, the reelection rate for Senate incumbents has ranged from 75 to 96 percent.

Over the last twenty-odd years, it seems, on the surface, as though some radical changes on the national level have taken place. In the election of 1994—for the first time in fifty years—the Republicans gained control of both houses of Congress. They have held on to control of the House ever since, except for the last two years of George W. Bush's presidency and the first two years of Barack Obama's presidency. Republicans likewise controlled the Senate until the election of 2006, except for a brief interruption in 2001 and 2002 because Sen. Jim Jeffords switched his party affiliation from Republican to Independent. They regained control of the Senate in the 2014 election. For more than four years during George W. Bush's presidency, the Republicans had absolute control of the Congress and the White House. For the first two years of Obama's presidency, Democrats held the same.

On paper, Bush and Obama couldn't be more different. But after enduring eight years of each one, it is evident that nothing has really changed under their respective administrations as far as the federal government is concerned. Certainly nothing for the better. In fact, almost every one of Bush's bad policies was continued by Obama. Republicans and Democrats likewise appear to be different animals, but during this same period, what has really changed? The national debt has continued to increase. Federal regulation of almost every area of commerce and life has not abated. Tens of thousands of Americans are still incarcerated for nonviolent crimes. The United States still has the world's largest prison population per capita. The federal budget continues to increase. Budget deficits are still the norm. Social Security and Medicare continue to be insolvent. The United States is still engaged in numerous overseas military interventions. Senseless foreign wars are still raging. Hundreds of U.S. military bases still encircle the globe. Hundreds of thousands of U.S. troops continue to garrison the planet. U.S. foreign policy continues to be reckless, belligerent, and meddling. The welfare state continues to redistribute wealth. The warfare state continues to bleed Americans dry in order to line the pockets of defense contractors. The war on poverty continues to impoverish those who have to pay for it. Americans increasingly live in a police state. The government continues to take from those who work and give to those who don't. Money is still being taken from American taxpayers and given to corrupt foreign governments. The size and scope of the federal government continues to increase.

Americans have now endured yet another election cycle. Many promises have been made; many assurances have been given; many changes
have been proposed. And many changes will undoubtedly take place. But
what kind of changes will they be? If they are not changes in the direction
of more liberty and less government, then they are the wrong kind of
changes. That is why the change America needs is libertarianism.

Libertarianism

Libertarianism is the philosophy that says that people should be free
from individual, societal, or government interference to live their lives any
way they desire, pursue their own happiness, accumulate as much wealth
as they can, assess their own risks, make their own choices, engage in
commerce with anyone who is willing to reciprocate, participate in any
economic activity for their profit, and spend the fruits of their labor as they
see fit as long as their actions are peaceful, their associations are voluntary,
their interactions are consensual, and they don't violate the personal or
property rights of others. As libertarianism's greatest theorist, Murray
Rothbard, puts it, "Libertarianism, therefore, is a theory which states that
everyone should be free of violent invasion, should be free to do as he sees
fit except invade the person or property of another. What a person does
with his or her life is vital and important, but is simply irrelevant to libertarianism."

The creed of libertarianism is nonaggression: freedom from aggression
and violence against person and property as long as one respects the person and property of others. The principle undergirding the libertarian philosophy is what is known as the nonaggression principle. As explained by
Rothbard, "The fundamental axiom of libertarian theory is that no one may
threaten or commit violence ('aggress') against another man's person or
property. Violence may be employed only against the man who commits
such violence; that is, only defensively against the aggressive violence of
another." It is the initiation of aggression or violence against the person or
property of others that is always wrong—unless, of course it is consensual.
Boxing and mixed martial arts are violent sports where the initiation of
aggression against one's opponent is the whole purpose of the event. But
the violence is consensual. By stepping into the ring one fighter is granting
the other fighter permission to use violence against him.

The nonaggression principle is designed to prohibit someone from infringing upon the liberty of another. It is the core premise of the philosophy of libertarianism. Aggression is theft, fraud, the initiation of nonconsensual violence, or the threat of nonconsensual violence. The initiation of
aggression against the person or property of others is always wrong. Violence is justified only against violence. No violence may be used against a
non-aggressor. Force is justified only in defense or retaliation, but is neither essential nor required: You can chase a burglar away instead of shoot-

ing him. Force must also be proportional: You may not kill someone just because he walks across your lawn.

Libertarianism is a political philosophy of liberty, property, and peace. It is not a government philosophy of efficiency, privatization, and deregulation. Libertarianism is not a composite of social liberalism and economic or fiscal conservatism. Libertarianism respects personal privacy, financial privacy, free thought, individual responsibility, freedom of conscience, free exchange, free markets, and private property. It should not be identified with "rugged individualism," "unrestrained freedom of speech," "survival of the fittest," "unfettered capitalism," "every man for himself," or "dog eat dog." Libertarianism celebrates individual liberty, personal freedom, peaceful activity, voluntary interaction, laissez faire, free enterprise, free assembly, free association, free speech, and free expression. It has nothing to do with hedonism, libertinism, moral relativism, licentiousness, pragmatism, utopianism, materialism, selfishness, anarchy, or nihilism. Libertarianism is silent about people's lifestyles, tastes, vices, sex life, sexual orientation, traditions, religion, aesthetics, cultural norms, or social attitudes. It makes no moral or ethical judgments about individual actions or behaviors as long as they don't violate the personal or property rights of others.

Because government is the greatest violator of the nonaggression principle, personal liberty, and property rights, libertarians oppose and seek to limit the intervention, regulation, and control of government. To the libertarian, the only possible legitimate functions of government are defense, judicial, and policing activities. All government actions, at any level of government, beyond those functions are illegitimate. Henry David Thoreau said he agreed with the motto, "That government is best which governs least." And libertarians would certainly agree with him.

In a libertarian society, there is simply no justification for any government action beyond keeping the peace; prosecuting, punishing, and exacting restitution from those who initiate violence against, commit fraud against, or otherwise violate the personal or property rights of others; providing a forum for dispute resolution; and constraining those who would attempt to interfere with people's peaceful actions. Actions would be prohibited only if they involve the initiation of violence or aggression against person (murder, rape, assault, et cetera), property (burglary, embezzlement, shoplifting, vandalism, arson, trespassing), or both (armed robbery). There would be no such thing as nebulous crimes against nature, society, or the state. Every crime would have to have a tangible victim and measurable damages. As long as people don't infringe upon the liberty of others by committing, or threatening to commit, acts of fraud, theft, aggression, or violence against their person or property, the government should just leave them alone.

Libertarian changes

As things stand now, the government regularly criminalizes victimless crimes; violates individual liberty; tramples property rights; provides services that the private sector could and should be providing; redistributes wealth from "the rich" to "the poor" after funneling it through a vast bureaucracy; incarcerates people for nonviolent activity; transfers income from taxpayers to foreigners, contractors, and cronies; and interferes in the free market with rules and regulations it has no business making.

Not in any particular order, what follows is an eclectic mix of libertarian changes that America needs.

America needs a change when it comes to the war on drugs. Using drugs may be addictive, dangerous, immoral, and destructive, but it is not the job of the government to decide what kinds of behaviors Americans are allowed to engage in. All drugs should be legal for medical or recreational use. The war on drugs should be ended and the DEA should be abolished.

America needs a change when it comes to gambling laws. It is not the job of government to monitor how Americans use their money. All Americans should be able to do with their money as they see fit, whether that means to save it, invest it, spend it, hoard it, donate it, burn it, or waste it on vices such as gambling. All laws that regulate existing legal gambling or prohibit illegal gambling should be repealed.

America needs a change when it comes to prostitution laws. It is not the job of government to curb prostitution, legislate morality, stamp out vice, help anyone avoid a life of prostitution, deter men from buying sexual services, or criminalize one party or both parties who engage in peaceful, private, voluntary, and consensual activity. And besides, why should a service that is legal to give away be illegal if one charges for it? All laws against prostitution should be repealed.

America needs a change when it comes to alcohol laws. About 10 percent of the United States contains "dry" counties where alcohol cannot be sold. In most areas of the country, alcohol sales are restricted in some way on Sundays. Throughout the country, drinking alcoholic beverages is illegal for legal adults who are under twenty-one. It is an illegitimate function of government to prohibit people from drinking alcohol or to prevent or restrict commerce in alcohol. All laws that concern alcoholic beverages should be repealed and the ATF should be abolished.

America needs a change when it comes to foreign aid. The government has no right to take money from Americans against their will and give it to foreigners or their governments. Any American who wants to help the poor, starving, or underprivileged in any country is welcome to do so on his own or through any number of private organizations—as long as he uses his own money. All foreign aid should be private and voluntary. All foreign aid supplied by the U.S. government should be eliminated.

America needs a change when it comes to disaster relief. Americans are a generous people. They regularly donate millions of dollars to charitable organizations to provide relief in foreign countries whenever there is some major natural disaster. Not only is it not the job of government to take money from American and use it to provide disaster relief—even within the United States—government relief crowds out private relief efforts. All relief should be private and voluntary. No country should be given disaster relief by the U.S. government regardless of the circumstances.

America needs a change when it comes to unemployment compensation. What is unemployment compensation but the government's taking money from those who work and giving it to those who don't? Unemployment insurance should be purchased on the free market just like fire, car, homeowners', and life insurance. All government unemployment programs should be ended.

America needs a change when it comes to entangling alliances. The United States has committed itself to coming to the defense of scores of countries. Those commitments are the epitome of the entangling alliances the Founding Fathers warned against making. The U.S. military should be used only for the defense of the United States. Each country should provide for its own defense. Any American who wants to take sides in a conflict between countries is welcome to do so as long as he does it on his own dime. No agreements to defend other countries are in the interests of the American people as a whole and should therefore be rescinded.

America needs a change when it comes to foreign policy. U.S. foreign policy is reckless, belligerent, and meddling. It creates enemies and terrorists. It makes America and Americans less safe. It is arrogant and immoral for the United States to be the self-appointed policeman of the world. U.S. foreign policy should return to the neutrality and nonintervention of the Founders.

America needs a change when it comes to the use of its military. The United States has hundreds of bases on foreign soil and many tens of thousands of troops stationed overseas. That results in the military's being used more for offense than for defense. All foreign bases should be closed and all U.S. troops brought home.

America needs a change when it comes to the minimum wage. Many states (and cities) have already increased their minimum wage above the federal level. There is much agitation around the country for the minimum wage to be increased to $15 per hour. But what is the minimum wage but the forbidding of workers from freely contracting with firms under mutually agreeable terms? If someone can offer to sell his goods for whatever amount he chooses, then it stands to reason that he should likewise be able to offer to sell his labor for whatever amount he chooses. It is not the job of government to set a minimum wage or regulate the labor market. So, rather than being increased, the minimum wage should be eliminated.

America needs a change when it comes to education. It is not the job of the government to educate anyone's children or subsidize anyone's education. All education should be private, and none of it should be funded by the taxpayers. No American should be forced to pay for the education of any other American. All government schools should be closed, all government funding of education should be ended, and all departments of education should be abolished.

America needs a change when it comes to student loans. Student-loan debt and defaults are at the highest levels in history. But it is simply not the job of government to lend students money or to help anyone obtain a college education. All student loans should come from private sources. All government student-loan programs should be eliminated.

America needs a change when it comes to welfare. The United States has roughly 80 means-tested programs that provide cash, food, housing, medical care, and social services to poor and lower-income Americans. But whether it is called SNAP, NSLP, LIEAP, EITC, WIC, SSI, TANF, or Section 8, it is still welfare. And before the government can provide a welfare benefit it must first take the monetary equivalent from American taxpayers. But it is not the job of government to fight poverty or provide a safety net. All charity should be private and voluntary. All welfare programs should be eliminated in their entirety.

America needs a change when it comes to Medicare and Medicaid. These programs are nothing but socialized medicine. The fact that they are for the poor and the elderly doesn't change the nature of the programs. It is not the job of the government to subsidize anyone's health insurance or health care, pay for anyone's prescription drugs, have health-care programs, or have anything whatsoever to do with health insurance, health care, or medicine. No one has the right to health care. And no American should be forced to pay for the health care of any other American. Medicare and Medicaid should be ended.

America needs a change when it comes to Social Security. With more than 10,000 Americans becoming eligible for benefits every month, the system is unsustainable, since there are now fewer than three workers funding the program per recipient of benefits. Although Social Security is mostly funded by payroll deductions, there is no connection between the taxes paid and the benefits received. There is also no contractual right even to receive benefits. Social Security is an intergenerational income transfer from the working population to retired workers, survivors of deceased workers, and disabled workers. Even so, it is not the job of the government to operate a retirement or disability plan. Social Security should be ended and the payroll taxes that fund it should be eliminated.

America needs a change when it comes to funding for research and the arts. It is not the job of the government to subsidize scientific or medical research or cultural activities of individuals or organizations. All grants for research or the arts should come from private sources. All government grants should be canceled and all governmental grant-making agencies abolished.

America needs a change when it comes to farm subsidies. It is not the job of the government to subsidize agriculture or any other sector of the economy. Farming should be treated just like any other business. All farm subsidies should be eliminated and the Department of Agriculture should be abolished.

America needs a change when it comes to anti-discrimination laws. These laws violate private-property rights, freedom of association, freedom of contract, and freedom of thought. All anti-discrimination laws should be repealed and the Equal Employment Opportunity Commission (EEOC) should be abolished.

America needs a change when it comes to organ sales. If you own your own body, then you also own the organs in your body. Right now it is illegal to sell any of your organs. The federal government also basically controls the procurement and transplantation of organs. This is an illegitimate function of government that could be handled entirely and more efficiently by the free market. The National Organ Transplant Act of 1984 should be repealed.

America needs a change when it comes to occupational licensing. It is not just professionals such as doctors and lawyers who must obtain a certificate of permission and approval from a government-sponsored board before they can work in a certain occupation, it is also (depending on the state) barbers, travel agents, locksmiths, auctioneers, and others who need permission from the government to work. But why should anyone have to get permission from the government to open a business, engage in commerce, work in certain occupations, have a particular vocation, or provide a service to willing customers? Occupational licensing is an illegitimate function of government. There is absolutely no reason why all occupations cannot be privately certified. All occupational-licensing laws should be repealed.

America needs a change when it comes to Amtrak. It is not the job of government to own or operate a rail service. All passenger rail traffic throughout the United States should be privately owned and operated. All of Amtrak's assets should be sold to the highest bidder.

America needs a change when it comes to the TSA. The abusive treatment given travelers by the TSA is widely known. But the real problem with the TSA is that it is not the job of government to provide security for private businesses. Airports and airlines should handle their own security just as banks, theme parks, jewelry stores, and any other business does if it feels the need to have security. The TSA should be abolished.

Yes, America needs a change. But the change America needs is libertarianism.

*****

A LIBERTARIAN PRIMER ON THE ISSUES

Although the Libertarian Party has virtually no chance of winning any presidential election, the presidential campaign of any of its candidates in any such election can and should be used to promote libertarian ideas and educate Americans about libertarianism.

This is not a hard thing to do. The usual Democratic and Republican candidates for president are always so bad on so many issues that it doesn't take much effort to stand out from them. The Libertarian Party just needs to write a good, brief platform that espouses the libertarian philosophy and then let its candidates for president and vice president apply this philosophy to the issues.

Although the Libertarian Party has a decent platform this election year, its presidential candidates—Gary Johnson and William Weld—are the most non-libertarian Libertarian Party candidates in history. The libertarianism they present to the American public—when they actually present something that can be considered libertarianism—is watered down, weak, and confusing. Don't look to them to present a principled and effective case for libertarianism.

So, since I am a traditional libertarian, just in time for the election, I present a libertarian primer on the issues, most of which no candidate from any party is talking about—including the Libertarian Party. To keep this primer brief, I am deliberately limiting it to fifty issues, although there are certainly much more that I could mention.

1. Taxes: since taxation is government theft and most of what the federal government spends is unconstitutional, taxation should be ended, but until such time as it is, taxes for all Americans should be lowered as much as possible.
2. Tax deductions: like tax credits, loopholes, shelters, and exemptions, they are always good and should be broadened and expanded as long as we have a tax code.
3. Refundable tax credits: although tax credits are always good, refundable tax credits that give people refunds of money they have not paid in are a form of welfare and should be eliminated.
4. The no-fly list: only airlines should be able to make a list of people not allowed to fly—just like any business should be able to make a list of people it will not serve.
5. The TSA: should be abolished since it is an illegitimate purpose of government to provide security for private businesses.
6. Trade: should be free from government tariffs, quotas, regulations, and management.
7. Trade agreements: totally unnecessary with the real free trade.
8. Federal land: all federal land owned outside of Washington, D.C. should be turned over to the states or sold to the highest bidder.

9. Social Security: since it is not the job of government to institute or operate a retirement program, a safety net, an investment account, or a disability plan, the Social Security program should be abolished and the payroll taxes that partially fund it should be eliminated.

10. Medicare: since it is not the job of government to have health-care programs, subsidize health insurance or health care, pay for prescription drugs, or have anything to do with insurance or medicine, Medicare should be eliminated.

11. Planned Parenthood: should not be funded by the government even if it performs no abortions since the government should not be funding any private organization.

12. Space exploration: should all be privately undertaken and funded since it is not the job of government to do either.

13. Occupational licensing: should not exist since no one should have to get permission from the government to open a business, engage in commerce, work in certain occupations, have a particular vocation, or provide a service to willing customers.

14. Cultural grants: should be ended since all museums, exhibits, writers, artists, and performers should be privately funded.

15. Prison overpopulation: everyone in prison for victimless or non-violent crimes should be released.

16. Food stamps: should be eliminated since it is not the job of the government to feed anyone.

17. Foreign aid: since the federal government cannot give money to foreigners without first taking it from Americans, all government foreign aid should be ended and left up to private individuals and organizations.

18. Disaster relief: since it is an illegitimate purpose of government to provide disaster relief—to citizens or foreigners—all disaster relief should be privately donated.

19. Welfare: since it is immoral to take money from those who work and give it to those who don't—even when the government does it—all welfare programs should be abolished.

20. Public housing: since it is an illegitimate function of government to provide anyone with housing, all public housing should be sold to the highest bidder.

21. Discrimination: since anti-discrimination laws violate property rights, freedom of association, freedom of contract, and freedom of thought, they should all be repealed and the Equal Employment Opportunity Commission (EEOC) should be abolished.

22. Scientific research grants: should be ended since all scientific research should be privately funded.

23. *Citizens United*: money is not speech, but individuals, groups, organizations, corporations, and unions should be free to spend any amount

of their own money in any way they choose, including spending money on political activities.

24. Foreign wars: should be ended immediately since no foreign war should ever be fought in the first place.

25. Minimum wage: since it is an illegitimate purpose of government to set maximum or minimum prices for anything, including labor, there should be no minimum wage on the federal or state level.

26. NATO: the United States should withdraw from NATO and let the Europeans handle their own security.

27. Military spending: the Pentagon's budget should be slashed and military spending limited to defense instead of offense.

28. Foreign policy: neutrality, non-intervention, and Jeffersonian: "Peace, commerce, and honest friendship with all nations—entangling alliances with none."

29. Medicaid: since no American should be forced to pay for the health care of any other American, Medicaid should be eliminated.

30. Education: since it is not the job of the government to educate anyone's children or subsidize anyone's education, all public schools should be closed and all educate handled privately.

31. Vouchers: all educational vouchers should be privately issued and funded.

32. Farm subsidies: should all be eliminated since it is not the job of government to subsidize anything and farming should be treated like any other business.

33. Medical research grants: should be ended since all medical research should be privately funded.

34. Affirmative Action: should never be practiced by government, but private institutions, businesses, and organizations should have the freedom to practice it.

35. The Drug War: since it is none of the government's business what anyone wants to smoke, snort, or inject, the Drug War should be ended, all drugs should be legalized (not just marijuana), and the DEA should be shuttered.

36. Department of Homeland Security: since we already have a Department of Defense to secure the homeland, the Department of Homeland Security should be abolished.

37. AMTRAK: should be abolished because all passenger rail traffic throughout the United States should be privately owned and operated since it is not the job of government to own or operate a rail service.

38. Organ sales: since every American owns his own body, the government should not prohibit him from selling any of his organs while he is alive or after his death.

39. Affordable housing: there should be no government involvement of any kind in the housing market via subsidies or loans or loan guarantees.

40. Family leave: should be negotiated between employers and employees with no government laws, mandates, or regulations concerning family leave.
41. Cuban embargo: should be ended immediately since the government should never restrict Americans' trade or travel.
42. Guantanamo Bay prison: should be closed along with the U.S. Naval Base there.
43. The Patriot Act: the original act along with all of its reauthorizations should be repealed.
44. Funding for the UN, World Bank, and IMF: should be ended for many reasons, but especially since only a handful of Americans would give them money if it came out of their own pocket.
45. Obamacare: should be repealed but not replaced with anything.
46. Unemployment benefits: should be eliminated since the government should never pay anyone for not working.
47. E-verify: should be eliminated since businesses should be allowed to hire whomever they choose.
48. The National School Lunch Program: should be ended since it is not the job of government to feed any child or be involved in schools in any way.
49. The Corporation for Public Broadcasting: should be abolished since it is not the job of government to fund radio or television broadcasting.
50. The FCC: should be eliminated since it is not the job of government to regulate communications.

Bonus: In addition to the Department of Homeland Security, the Departments of Education, Agriculture, Health and Human Services, Housing and Urban Development, Labor, Energy, and the Interior should be shuttered.

What a shame that the Libertarian Party presidential candidates aren't discussing these issues.

*****

A LIBERTARIAN PERSPECTIVE ON AIRLINE SECURITY

Could TSA-style irradiating porno scanners, digital strip searches, near-naked photos, genital gropes, breast feel-ups, and invasive pat-downs be found in airports in a libertarian—that is, a free—society as a condition of getting on a flight?

Surprisingly, the answer is yes. And so could body cavity searches and enhanced pat-down procedures that would make sexual assault a welcome relief.

No, I am not making a sick caricature of libertarianism. Not only am I a libertarian, I am a libertarian who vehemently objects to all of these things as gross invasions of liberty, privacy, decency, civil rights, and the Fourth Amendment.

Libertarians are sometimes accused of being utopian, having their head in the sand, and pointing out what's wrong without offering any real solutions. Clearly, the draconian rules and procedures relating to airport security have steadily grown worse since the creation of the TSA in 2001 and the federalization of airline security. Americans of every political persuasion are currently outraged over the new full-body scanners and enhanced pat-down procedures.

So what is the libertarian solution? And how could it possibly include invasive techniques?

The libertarian solution is not to reform the TSA, change the pat-down procedure, use less-revealing pictures on the porno scanners, let us keep our shoes on, and start permitting larger tubes of toothpaste in carry-on luggage. The libertarian solution is one based on liberty and private property.

The first thing that needs to be done is that the federal government needs to cease its control of airline security. No more TSA, no more federal rules, no more federal regulations, no more federal mandates, no more federal oversight, no more "September 11 security fee" of $2.50 per enplanement. This is already the solution to practically every other problem in the country, be it education, health care, or the economy—get the federal government out of it. Anything short of severing federal control over airline security is no real and lasting solution.

Turning airline security over to state and local governments is not a good option. Although we have a federal system of government where, in the words of the Tenth Amendment: "The powers not delegated to the United States by the Constitution, nor prohibited by it to the States, are reserved to the States respectively, or to the people, " airline security should not be one of those powers anymore than mall security should be one of those powers. And aside from the issue of the proper role of government, it should be pointed out that state and local governments can be just as bureaucratic, just as wasteful of resources, just as burdensome, and just as tyrannical as the federal government, they just don't have the money and the military that the federal government has. Airports that are owned and operated by municipalities should be sold to private concerns, but that is an unrelated topic beyond the scope of this article.

This leaves only one possibility for control of airline security: airports and airlines. Yes, the actual businesses that own and operate the airports we fly out of and the airlines we fly on. Airports and airlines have tremendous incentives to keep undesirable people and products off their flights to protect their passengers and preserve their multi-million dollar airplanes. Airports could provide security and passenger screening, leave these things up to each airline, or share responsibility with the airlines.

Some airports might allow family and friends to wait with you for your flight and/or meet you at the gate when you return. Others might restrict airport access to flyers. Some airports might require an extensive background check or an invasive pat-down as a condition of getting on a flight. Others might simply require a driver's license and a walk through a metal detector.

Some airlines might allow pilots and passengers to have weapons and station armed security guards on each flight. Others might prohibit any metal objects. Some airlines might have no restrictions on liquids brought onto flights. Others might have severe limitations on anything carried on the airplane.

The possibilities in a free society are endless.

Airlines that objected to security procedures at an airport would have the option of not flying out of that particular airport. Passengers that objected to security procedures at an airport or a particular airline would have the option of going to a different airport or using another airline.

Could the owner of an airport require anything he wanted of passengers before they boarded an airplane in his airport? In a libertarian society—that is, a free society—the answer is a resounding yes. However, TSA-style security procedures would likely and soon cause a backlash from the flying public and cause the owner to make changes or face the loss of patrons willing to fly out of his airport. With the federal TSA, passengers have no choice as to whether they want to be violated.

Airports and airlines should compete for customers, just like any other business. They could and should compete on the basis of ticket price, on-time departures, frequent-flyer program, comfort, safety record, service, baggage fees, carry-on requirements—and security procedures.

Homeland Security Secretary Janet Napolitano says the TSA is "doing what we need to do to protect the traveling public. " But short of the federal government ending its grip on airline security, what will protect the traveling public from the TSA?

*****

IS THERE A LIBERTARIAN POSITION ON SAME-SEX MARRIAGE?

The subjects of abortion and same-sex marriage are not just points of contention between liberals and conservatives and Democrats and Republicans. They are also a source of division among libertarians.

Of all the articles I have written for LewRockwell.com, the response I received regarding my recent article "Should Libertarians Be Conservatives?" is (I am still getting e-mails) probably in the top ten in terms of the volume of e-mails received. (Number one, in terms of volume, hate mail, and vile hate mail, was probably "Thank You for Your Service?")

I address here the subject of same-sex marriage.

Same-sex marriage is permitted in ten countries (Argentina, Belgium, Canada, Iceland, the Netherlands, Norway, Portugal, Spain, South Africa, & Sweden). It is recognized in Israel, Mexico, and a few other countries.

I think it is inevitable that as the twenty-first century progresses, more countries will permit or recognize same-sex marriages.

In the United States, same-sex marriage is legal in six states (Connecticut, Iowa, Massachusetts, New Hampshire, New York, and Vermont) and the District of Columbia. It was legal for a time in California. Same-sex marriage laws are pending in Washington and Maryland. New Jersey, Maryland, and Rhode Island recognize same-sex marriages performed in other states. The majority of the states have a constitutional provision or a law restricting marriage to one man and one woman, most recently North Carolina, where voters on May 8, 2012, approved a constitutional amendment banning same-sex marriage even though the state already prohibited same-sex marriage by law.

I likewise think that as the twenty-first century progresses, more states will permit or recognize same-sex marriages.

But is a same-sex marriage a marriage? And is there a libertarian position on same-sex marriage?

Although the first state did not recognize same-sex marriage until 2004, in 1996, after a 1993 Hawaii Supreme Court case raised concerns about the possibility of Hawaii legalizing same-sex marriage, Congress passed (342-67 in the House and 85-14 in the Senate), and President Clinton signed into law on September 21, 1996, the Defense of Marriage Act (DOMA). This inserted the federal government in a fundamental way into the institution of marriage.

Marriage is defined for federal purposes in section 3 of the Act:

> In determining the meaning of any Act of Congress, or of any ruling, regulation, or interpretation of the various administrative bureaus and agencies of the United States, the word "marriage" means only a legal union between one man and one woman as husband and wife, and the word "spouse" refers only to a person of the opposite sex who is a husband or a wife.

The Act, in section 2, also permitted states to not recognize same-sex marriages performed in other states:

> No State, territory, or possession of the United States, or Indian tribe, shall be required to give effect to any public act, record, or judicial proceeding of any other State, territory, possession, or tribe respecting a relationship between persons of the same sex that is treated as a marriage under the laws of such other State, territory, possession, or tribe, or a right or claim arising from such relationship.

The Defense of Marriage Act has survived numerous court challenges over the years, and several cases are still pending.

On March 16, 2011, bills to repeal DOMA were introduced by Democrats in both the House and Senate. The Respect for Marriage Act was introduced in the House (H.R.1116) by Jerrold Nadler. It has 146 cosponsors. It was introduced in the Senate by Dianne Feinstein (S.598). It has 32 cosponsors. The Respect for Marriage Act would repeal section 2 of the Defense of Marriage Act and amend title 1, chapter 1, section 7, of U.S. Code to read:

(a) For the purposes of any Federal law in which marital status is a factor, an individual shall be considered married if that individual's marriage is valid in the State where the marriage was entered into or, in the case of a marriage entered into outside any State, if the marriage is valid in the place where entered into and the marriage could have been entered into in a State.

(b) In this section, the term "State" means a State, the District of Columbia, the Commonwealth of Puerto Rico, or any other territory or possession of the United States.

But the Respect for Marriage Act may now be unnecessary, as section 3 of DOMA was just declared unconstitutional on May 31, 2012, when a three-judge panel of the U.S. Court of Appeals for the First Circuit unanimously affirmed the July 8, 2010, ruling of Judge Joseph L. Tauro of the U.S. District Court in Boston. In the cases of Gill v. Office of Personnel Management and Massachusetts v. United States Department of Health and Human Services, Judge Tauro ruled that section 3 of DOMA violated the Fifth and Tenth Amendments. The Appeals Court has stayed its ruling in anticipation of an appeal to the Supreme Court.

It is therefore entirely possible that the Supreme Court could take up the issue of federal recognition of same-sex marriage as early as its next term. And it is even conceivable that the whole of DOMA could be thrown out, paving the way not only for federal recognition of same-sex marriage, but also the requirement that all the states do likewise under the "full faith and credit" clause of Article IV of the Constitution, although the states that have banned same-sex marriage would certainly challenge this in court. The latter judgment would be "worse" than the former, not only because of its erosion of federalism, but because the federal government recognizing same-sex marriage is more fiduciary than philosophical, as it is in the states.

But would a same-sex marriage then be a marriage? And is there a libertarian position on same-sex marriage?

I said in my aforementioned article "Should Libertarians Be Conservatives?" that I agreed with the statement of conservative Jay Richards that "just as government may not redefine our rights as individuals, it has no authority to redefine marriage." It has been said that everyone is entitled to his own opinion, but not his own facts. This is why I also said, and here reiterate, that "marriage has always been and will forever be the union of a man and a woman" and that "anything else is just cohabitation, fornication, civil union, voluntary contract, or domestic partnership, whether it is called a marriage or not." Marriage predates the nation-state, the community, society, states and counties, cities and towns, governmental bodies of any kind, and even the church. If words and 6,000 years of human history mean anything, then there can be no denying the fact that marriage means only marriage in the traditional sense.

Even governments at all levels getting out of the marriage business—like they should—still wouldn't make a same-sex marriage a marriage.

Now, regarding libertarianism – the philosophy that says that violence is proper only in the defense of person or property and that people have the fundamental right to do anything that's peaceful without interference from government or society.

The 2012 Libertarian Party Platform doesn't expressly mention same-sex marriage, but reads in section 1.3, "Personal Relationships":

> Sexual orientation, preference, gender, or gender identity should have no impact on the government's treatment of individuals, such as in current marriage, child custody, adoption, immigration or military service laws. Government does not have the authority to define, license or restrict personal relationships. Consenting adults should be free to choose their own sexual practices and personal relationships.

The current Libertarian Party presidential nominee, Gary Johnson, is a strong supporter of same-sex marriage. In a recent interview with Robert Wenzel, Johnson said he would be the only candidate (aside from Romney and Obama) committed to marriage equality as a constitutionally guaranteed right.

But what really prompted me to delve into this subject is an e-mail I received from a libertarian who was not happy with what I said about abortion and marriage in my article "Should Libertarians Be Conservatives?":

> I say it's the not the government's job to say who gets married—it's their job to passively record it when it happens, just like these other things. And I'm not just talking about gay marriage—if a Mormon or Moslem man wants to marry three gals, that's their business. If thirteen Wiccan lesbians living in a commune all want to marry each other, the only thing the clerk should say is "sign here, sign here, initial here....Next!" That's the real libertarian position on marriage; although if the government just got out of the marriage business altogether as you advocate, it would also, I suppose, be acceptable.

But is that the libertarian position on same-sex marriage?

I believe that libertarians are unnecessarily divided over the issue of same-sex marriage. Based on what I said above about marriage, it is my contention that there is no more a libertarian position on same-sex marriage than there is on chocolate, toothpaste, or whether the sky is blue.

Same-sex couples should certainly have the right to form any kind of legal arrangement they choose whereby medical and financial decisions by one party on behalf of another could be made. But this right has nothing to do with them being a same-sex couple. It is only because any couple—gay, lesbian, straight, bisexual, transgendered, or undecided—or any group of people should have the right to form any kind of legal arrangement they choose. If they want to call their arrangement a marriage, have a ceremony, and go on a honeymoon—fine. They have the freedom to do so just like they have the freedom to replace their Chevy emblems with Ford emblems and call their Camaro a Mustang. They just shouldn't expect or demand everyone else to violate nature, language, tradition, and history and do likewise.

And if the federal government should recognize same-sex marriages, domestic partnerships, civil unions, consensual contracts, or voluntary agreements of homosexual couples for tax, Social Security, and other purposes, then it should likewise recognize similar legal arrangements of heterosexual couples, whether male/male, female/female, or male/female.

If a libertarian wants to redefine marriage—or call black white, up down, or right left—then he is perfectly free to do so, but he shouldn't term his personal preference or individual decision a libertarian position.

One's opinion of same-sex relationships—whether wonderful, wholesome, unnatural, or disgusting—has nothing to do with the issue.

Libertarians as individuals may support or oppose the "marriage" or legal arrangements of same-sex couples—just like they may support or oppose the health benefits of Vitamin C or the use of child safety locks—but that doesn't mean there is a libertarian position on it.

*****

LIBERTARIANISM AND ABORTION

My recent article "Should Libertarians Be Conservatives" elicited a huge response—most of it positive. Some libertarians, however, were quite annoyed because I expressed my opposition to abortion and same-sex marriage.

I promised my critics that I responded to (I didn't respond to profanity-laden missives or to statements like: "A libertarian is really a fascist SOB if he is pro-life.") that I would write about these two subjects individually, and sooner rather than later. I addressed the subject of same-sex marriage in an article published on June 8. There I argued that there is no libertarian position on same-sex marriage. I address here the subject of libertarianism and abortion.

Other than brief mentions in my article "Should Libertarians Be Conservatives" and in a couple of articles about Ron Paul's views on the matter, I have only written at length about abortion in the article "Is Ron Paul Wrong on Abortion?" I have actually written more that was critical of the pro-life movement than I have about abortion: I defended Ron Paul against the attacks of pro-lifers and took them to task for their hypocrisy and warmongering.

What I recently said about abortion in my article "Should Libertarians Be Conservatives" that ruffled the feathers of some libertarians was this:

> I have argued that because the non-aggression axiom is central to libertarianism, and because force is justified only in self-defense, and because it is wrong to threaten or initiate violence against a person or his property, and because killing is the ultimate form of aggression that, to be consistent, libertarians should be opposed to abortion.

The link I gave was to my article "Is Ron Paul Wrong on Abortion?" in which I said these things:

> Why should it be considered libertarian to kill a baby in the womb or unlibertarian to oppose such killing? And even worse, why would a libertarian say that it was unlibertarian to advocate killing foreigners in an aggressive war but not non-libertarian to kill a baby in the womb?

> Killing someone is the ultimate form of aggression. Especially a helpless, defenseless fetus that is only guilty of suddenly waking up in a womb. The fetus certainly had no control over being a parasite, aggressing against a woman, invading a woman's body, or adding unwanted pounds to his host—but its mother certainly did. If an unborn child is not entitled to protection of life, then to be consistent, libertarians should have no problem with the abortion of a fetus from one month old to nine months old. The nine-month old fetus is no more viable than the one-month old one. In fact, a one-month old baby has the same degree of viability. I hate to be so crude, but leave all three of them unattended on a table in a hospital and see what happens.

> Why should it be considered libertarian to kill a baby in the womb or unlibertarian to oppose such killing? This has nothing to do with giving the government greater control over a woman's body; it has everything to do with preventing aggression and protecting innocent life.

> If *Roe v. Wade* were overturned and abortion laws were once again made the provision of the states, there would be nothing unlibertarian about supporting state laws making abortion a crime just as laws against murder,

manslaughter, and wrongful death are considered legitimate actions of the states.

I'm not sure who bothered to click the link and read what I had previously written about abortion, but doing so would have answered some of the questions that I was asked.

I base my statements about abortion on the libertarian non-aggression principle, which I believe is also a biblical principle, or else I wouldn't hold to it.

According to the late Murray Rothbard here and here:

> The fundamental axiom of libertarian theory is that no one may threaten or commit violence ("aggress") against another man's person or property. Violence may be employed only against the man who commits such violence; that is, only defensively against the aggressive violence of another. In short, no violence may be employed against a non-aggressor. Here is the fundamental rule from which can be deduced the entire corpus of libertarian theory.

> Libertarianism holds that the *only* proper role of violence is to defend person and property *against* violence, that any use of violence that goes beyond such just defense is itself aggressive, unjust, and criminal. Libertarianism, therefore, is a theory which states that everyone should be free of violent invasion, should be free to do as he sees fit except invade the person or property of another.

And according to Rothbard's disciple Walter Block here and here:

> Libertarianism is a political philosophy. It [is] concerned solely with the proper use of force. Its core premise is that it should be illegal to threaten or initiate violence against a person or his property without his permission; force is justified only in defense or retaliation.

> The libertarian position on anything is based on the question of, Does it violate the non aggression principle (NAP) about initiating or threatening physical violence. If so, the libertarian position is that it should be illegal, and punished by the full force of the law. If not, the libertarian position is that it should be legal, and it would be unjustified to use physical violence against the person who engages in that act.

Because a child in the womb is helpless, not initiating violence, not committing aggression, and not there of its own accord, I believe that, to be consistent, libertarians should not only be opposed to abortion, but in favor of making it a criminal act just like murder, rape, kidnapping, theft, assault, and robbery would be in any libertarian society based on the non-aggression principle.

Now, what sort of penalty should be imposed, how criminality would be determined, how to divide culpability between the woman and her doctor, how to handle situations where pregnancy is the result of rape or incest, how to handle situations where parents force their pregnant teenage daughter to get an abortion, how far along the pregnancy has to be, etc., etc., etc. are things that would have to be determined that I don't profess to have precise answers to. But, aside from premeditated, witnessed, proven-beyond-a-doubt first degree murder, neither do I have precise answers as to what the penalty should be for manslaughter, rape, kidnapping, theft, assault, or robbery.

I reproduce below relevant portions of interaction regarding the subject of abortion that I had with five "pro-choice" libertarians. I only gave them brief responses because I knew from their comments and questions that it would be much better for all interested parties if I took the time to write something much more in depth than an e-mail. I appreciate them taking the time to write and hope they are reading. Judging from the whole of what they wrote to me, I don't expect to change their minds. Nevertheless, in addition to what I have said above regarding libertarianism and abortion, I offer my comments below.

> Try as I might, I can't reconcile a position favoring small, non-intrusive government, with support for the criminalization of abortion, which necessarily involves the government sticking its nose into doctors' examining rooms, and one could say, into the orifices of any woman being examined there.

> _____

> It cannot be denied that pregnancy is inherently dangerous, therefore any abortion can always be justified as defensive, not initiated force. It is an unpleasant fact that we all start our lives as parasites, and a potential mother has no more obligation to support such a parasite in her body than the body politic has to support "welfare parasites."

> I would kindly ask that you either: 1) Don't tell people that you're a libertarian if you're going to defend a "pro-life" position, or 2) Don't tell people you're pro-life if you're going to defend a libertarian position.

> People like you are "spoiling the brand name," and if folks hear you advocate both libertarianism and anti-abortionism, it may reinforce their false belief that we are far-right wingers.

> It occurs to me that I don't remember you saying in your article or your reply that you favor making abortion illegal. If what you mean when you call yourself a pro-life libertarian is that you would use peaceful persuasion to convince women not to get abortions, then any disagreement I may have thought we had was all in my head. If, however, my original assumption was correct, then I should point out that the right to life does not include the

right to live at the expense of another. If it does, then government wealth redistribution is OK, right? Making abortion illegal again would turn the gift of life into just another entitlement coerced by government force.

Also, I am given to understand that quite often a fertilized egg fails to implant in the lining of the uterus and is expelled during menstruation, making God, if you will, perhaps the biggest performer of abortions.

I would like to someday hear from the "Pro-lifers" how we would deal with a pregnant woman that does not want to carry her unborn fetus to the full term and give birth to a child. What does a "libertarian" society do with her? What does a "libertarian" society do with her...legally?

Tell us how to be libertarians and advocate criminal activity to abortion. Tell us what we SHOULD DO legally when a woman chooses to abort. Is it OK to put her in a straitjacket in a padded cell and force feed her to keep her and her fetus healthy?

How should the law deal with an unwanted pregnancy. And by the way to your question "Should abortion be legal at anytime before the child is born?" My answer is yes. You and I may not like the choice someone makes but as long as we have the "right to life" I can't see any other meaning to that than the right to our own life. The woman makes the choice and will have to live with it her entire life.

The bureaucratic apparatus that would be required to actually prevent and or punish even a fraction of abortions would be overarching, imposing, and by necessity invade the privacy of all women.

It would be a TSA of the vagina. Not a pleasant thought, at least not to me.

Or, less poetically, it would be but another tentacle of the already metastasized and gut-wrenchingly corrupt "justice" system that has – with little effect on crime – built a gulag system filled with more hopeless convicts than any other time in history or place in the world. And you'd like to add to this? Really? Should we not be focused on limiting, or better yet removing, state power?

Such an apparatus would necessarily impose force and coercion, and as such be the antithesis of "libertarian" (as you define it by NAP.) Frankly, I think this is why so many "conservative" politicians slobber over the issue, it would allow them more justification to spend more money on prisons and police while engendering a tumescent response from their latent sadism.

It really doesn't matter if abortion itself is "libertarian" or not, any attempt to stop it would require un-libertarian means. Just as there can never really be a libertarian war, since all war harms the innocent.

———————

I personally take the Rothbardian position that while regrettable that the fetus cannot live outside the mother's womb, it is slavery to force a woman to carry an unwanted child to term.

A woman's right to have an abortion has nothing to do with a woman's "right to privacy" and everything to do with her right of self ownership. You wouldn't allow anyone to forcibly insert any object into your body without your consent. By the same token, it would be well within your rights to remove an object consensually inserted into your body at any time. This is the most basic application of your inalienable right of self ownership.

I see perhaps nine things that I need to address.

First, opposition to abortion is not an exclusively far-right wing or conservative position. This was the whole point of my original article, "Should Libertarians Be Conservatives?" Libertarians who advocate "anti-abortionism" shouldn't abandon their position so they won't be mistaken for conservatives anymore than they should abandon their advocacy of lower taxes, the free market, and other things that liberals associate with the right wing. And if a libertarians advocate "pro-abortionism," won't it reinforce the false belief that libertarians are far left-wingers?

Second, although it is true that "often a fertilized egg fails to implant in the lining of the uterus and is expelled during menstruation," this doesn't necessarily make God the "biggest performer of abortions." Just because God allows something to happen doesn't mean he's the cause of it. Otherwise he would be responsible for all abortions. God "giveth to all life, and breath, and all things" (Acts 17:25) and "in him we live, and move, and have our being" (Acts 17:28). As the author of life, God can take life anytime he chooses in any manner he chooses.

Third, if an act violates the non-aggression principle, as I believe abortion does, then I think it inherently means that it should be punished in some way. Thus, to be consistent, pro-life libertarians should also support the criminalization of abortion just like they support the criminalization of other acts of aggression like murder and robbery. The fact that there may be no living victim to seek restitution and that all those who had knowledge of the victim (woman, boyfriend, doctor, nurse) preferred him dead is irrelevant just like it is in the case of the murder of someone who is already out of the womb.

Fourth, that the U.S. has a corrupt criminal justice system and a gulag filled with hopeless convicts there is no doubt. But abortion is not a victimless crime like drug use that should just be ignored. And just because the system is bad doesn't mean that genuine acts of aggression should go unpunished. I am in favor of *adding* to prison anyone guilty of real crimes (assuming that prison should be the punishment) and *removing* from prison anyone not guilty of real crimes. And I should also add that abortion should not be a federal crime anymore than murder, rape, or robbery should be federal crimes. Most federal crimes (the ones that are really crimes, not the ones like taking unlicensed dentures across state lines) should not be federal crimes at all.

Fifth, criminalizing abortion would not lead to a greater police state that increases the bureaucratic apparatus and violates privacy. The fact is, we already have a police state, and it's not because murder, robbery, and other real crimes are prosecuted. If abortion were illegal, it would no more entail the government sticking its nose in doctors' offices and women's wombs than murder being illegal means that the government stations agents in every home, bar, and alley waiting for a murder to take place.

Sixth, no pro-life libertarian believes in aggression to prevent possible or potential aggression. It would therefore not be okay to enslave a pregnant woman by forcing her "to carry an unwanted child to term" or put her "in a straitjacket in a padded cell and force feed her to keep her and her fetus healthy." It would not be permissible to use "un-libertarian means" to stop abortion. It's not the job of the government—whatever form it appears in—to prevent crime. A criminal act is not a criminal act until it is committed. Preventing abortion would be no different than preventing other crimes. The way to stop abortion is by persuading pregnant women to not undergo abortions or educating them sufficiently in the pro-life position before they get pregnant so they won't consider abortion an option should they get pregnant. People so inclined to kill, rape, or rob should be persuaded not to kill, rape, or rob or educated to the extent that they would never be so inclined.

Seventh, although a fetus is a parasite in the sense that it lives inside, is dependent upon, and obtains nutriments from a host, I hasten to point out that a newborn baby is totally dependent upon someone to feed and take care of it as well. Even a six-month-old baby left to itself will soon die. Is it okay to just throw parasitical children in the trash with aborted babies? A child in the womb a week before birth is just as much a parasite as a child in the womb six months before birth. Are libertarians who advocate abortion on demand ready to allow the procedure at any time before birth in the name of consistency? And what about the gruesome practice of partial-birth abortion?

Eighth, certainly it is equally true that no object should be forcibly inserted into one's body and that one would be well within his rights to remove, not only an object inserted without consent, but any object consensually inserted. But we are talking about a child here, not a choice. When a woman engages in an activity the natural consequence of which is pregnancy, she is obligating herself to bring to term a completely separate individual with uniquely different DNA that didn't choose to "invade" her body or "aggress" against her. To be consistent, pro-choice libertarians should limit their argument here to pregnancy in the case of rape, a very rare occurrence. But even in the case of pregnancy via rape, it is the result of the aggression of someone else that the woman is pregnant, not the child which has, through no fault of its own, been inserted into the woman's body. If someone owned a ship and discovered a child on board that someone had stowed away, would he be well within his rights to throw the child overboard for being a trespasser? Should he not rather give the child up safely at the end of his voyage?

And finally, based on everything I have said thus far, it should be obvious that if a pregnant woman doesn't want to keep her baby—for whatever reason—then I see no other alternative for her than to have her baby and then give it up for adoption. If money is an issue, there are pro-life organizations that will care for women during their pregnancy. But I think pro-lifers have dropped the ball here. If pro-lifers would pay women with unwanted pregnancies to not abort their child, carry it to term, and give it up for adoption, they would do more to prevent abortions than they are doing now. But would not some women get pregnant just for the cash? Certainly, but there have always been and always will be women that will do unusual things for money. Even now some women have more children just to get increased welfare benefits. But even if a small percentage of women became baby factories because they got paid to carry babies to term, it would still be better than having a million abortions every year like occurs now in the United States. And since I mentioned adoption, let me also say that the state should get completely out of the adoption business and leave it entirely up to the free market.

I have not undertaken here a systematic defense of the libertarian pro-life position. I have merely addressed the concerns of those who wrote me.

One of the people who wrote me said that libertarians are pro-choice on everything. I see nothing libertarian about a woman choosing to kill her unborn child for getting in the way of her lifestyle.

*****

DO LIBERTARIANS HATE THE POOR?

The U.S. Census Bureau has released its annual poverty report based on the 2012 Annual Social and Economic Supplement (ASEC) of the Current Population Survey (CPS).

The CPS ASEC is a sample survey of approximately 100,000 households nationwide conducted over a three-month period in February, March, and April. The data reflect conditions in calendar year 2011.

The press release accompanying the publication of *Income, Poverty, and Health Insurance Coverage in the United States: 2011* reports that "in

2011, median household income declined, the poverty rate was not statistically different from the previous year and the percentage of people without health insurance coverage decreased."

According to the Census Bureau's press release, in 2011:

• The official poverty rate was 15.0 percent.
• There were 46.2 million people in poverty.
• 13.7 percent of people 18 to 64 (26.5 million) were in poverty, compared with 8.7 percent of people 65 and older (3.6 million) and 21.9 percent of children under 18 (16.1 million).
• After three consecutive years of increases, neither the official poverty rate nor the number of people in poverty was statistically different from the 2010 estimates.
• Real median household income in the United States in 2011 was $50,054, a 1.5 percent decline from the 2010 median and the second consecutive annual drop.
• Real median household income was 8.1 percent lower than in 2007, the year before the most recent recession, and was 8.9 percent lower than the median household income peak that occurred in 1999.
• Income inequality increased by 1.6 percent between 2010 and 2011.
• 6.2 percent of married-couple families, 31.2 percent of families with a female householder and 16.1 percent of families with a male householder lived in poverty.

The press release also noted that in the spring of 2012, 9.7 million young adults age 25-34 (23.6 percent) were additional adults in someone else's household.

It is not surprising that Democrats and Republicans both tried to spin the numbers to their own advantage.

Rebecca M. Blank, the acting U.S. Commerce secretary, issued a statement supporting the Obama administration,

> It is clear that had President Obama not taken swift and aggressive action to grow our economy and create jobs, today's report would have shown much higher poverty rates, lower incomes, and a greater share of the population without health insurance. The Obama administration has also proposed a host of remedies that would help spur additional economic growth and job creation, but which are still awaiting congressional approval.

Speaking for the Romney campaign, Andrea Saul commented about the poverty report:

> Today's report confirms that the American Dream remains out of reach for too many families. Nearly 1 in 6 Americans are living in poverty, including a record number of women, and the middle class is struggling amid falling

incomes, rising prices, and persistently high unemployment. While this may be the best President Obama can do, it's not the best America can do. Mitt Romney's pro-growth agenda will revive our economy, spur job creation, lift families out of poverty, and create a better future for our country.

The Democratic and Republican positions on poverty and the poor can be seen in their recently adopted party platforms.

In the Democratic platform, poverty is mentioned 15 times and the poor are mentioned 3 times. The Democratic Party believes it is the job of the federal government to "make ending poverty a national priority" and "help lift people" out of poverty, and specifically "people with disabilities" and "communities of color." To this end, it is committed to the Neighborhood Revitalization Initiative, the Sustainable Communities Initiative, Growth Zone Initiatives, green-jobs training programs, community development, public and affordable housing, homelessness prevention, raising the minimum wage and indexing it to inflation, and refundable tax credits, the Child Tax credit, unemployment insurance benefits, and food stamps.

Democrats also think it is the business of the federal government to "reduce hunger and lift tens of millions of people from poverty across Africa." They will also invoke the poor to justify anything: "We understand that global climate change may disproportionately affect the poor, and we are committed to environmental justice."

In the Republican platform, poverty is mentioned six times and the poor are mentioned five times. The Republican Party likewise believes it is the job of the federal government to fight poverty. It is "committed to saving Medicare and Medicaid" because "absent reforms, these two programs are headed for bankruptcy that will endanger care for seniors and the poor." Medicaid should be "block-granted" to the states "with the flexibility to design programs that meet the needs of their low income citizens." The Republican platform suggests that "such reforms could be achieved through premium supports or a refundable tax credit, allowing non-disabled adults and children to be moved into private health insurance of their choice." Public assistance "should be reformed to ensure that it promotes work." Programs "like food stamps must ensure that those benefits are better targeted to those who need help the most."

Republicans are as wedded to the welfare state as Democrats. Although they talk about limited government and fiscal conservatism in their platform and elsewhere, they are firmly committed to Medicaid, food stamps, unemployment, WIC, SCHIP, the Earned Income credit, housing assistance, and every other so-called anti-poverty measure. Welfare programs just need to be reformed, redesigned, or revamped.

But what is it with the Libertarian Party? The only mention of the poor or poverty in their new platform is in this sentence: "The proper and most effective source of help for the poor is the voluntary efforts of private groups and individuals."

Do libertarians hate the poor?

First of all, government anti-poverty programs are doing a terrible job at alleviating poverty. According to Robert Rector, senior research fellow at the Heritage Foundation, "The federal government operates more than 80 means-tested welfare programs to provide cash, food, housing, medical care, and social services to poor and low-income people." Trillions of dollars have been spent on combating poverty since Lyndon Johnson declared a war on poverty in 1964. "Welfare spending amounts to $9,040 per year for each lower-income American," remarks Rector, "If converted to cash and simply given to the recipients, this spending would be more than sufficient to bring the income of every lower-income American household to 200 percent of the federal poverty level."

Second, there are a lot of misconceptions about poverty in the United States. According to a Heritage Foundation, analysis of the Census Bureau's poverty report,

• 80 percent of poor households have air conditioning. In 1970, only 36 percent of the entire U.S. population enjoyed air conditioning.
• 92 percent of poor households have a microwave.
• Nearly three-fourths have a car or truck, and 31 percent have two or more cars or trucks.
• Nearly two-thirds have cable or satellite TV.
• Two-thirds have at least one DVD player, and 70 percent have a VCR.
• Half have a personal computer, and one in seven have two or more computers.
• More than half of poor families with children have a video-game system, such as an Xbox or PlayStation.
• 43 percent have Internet access.
• One-third have a wide-screen plasma or LCD TV.
• One-fourth have a digital video-recorder system, such as a TiVo.
• 42 percent of poor households actually own their own homes.
• The average poor American has more living space than the typical non-poor person in Sweden, France, or the United Kingdom.
• 40 percent have an automatic dishwasher.
• More than half have a cell phone.

The scope and severity of poverty in the United States is certainly not what the raw numbers in the Census Bureau's poverty report lead us to believe.

Third, the poverty level figures are deceiving. According to the Census Bureau: "Currently, anyone earning less than $11,484 per year is considered to be living in poverty. For a family of four, the earnings threshold is $23,021 per year." However, that doesn't mean that individuals and families counted as making less than those amounts actually do so. Government assistance is not included when determining one's earnings. It is even stated by the Census Bureau: "The poverty estimates released today compare the official poverty thresholds to money income before taxes, not including the value of noncash benefits." A family of four "officially" earning less than $23,021 might be receiving $400 in food stamps every month and a $5,000 refundable earned income credit at the end of each year. That is the equivalent of almost $10,000 in additional income.

Fourth, the poor don't pay any federal income taxes. Although the Obama campaign and the Democrats in their platform talk about the "rich" paying their fair share, according to the IRS, the top 1 percent of taxpayers (in terms of adjusted gross income) paid 36.73 percent of all federal income taxes. The top 5 percent of taxpayers paid 58.66 percent. The top 10 percent of taxpayers paid 70.47. The top 25 percent of taxpayers paid 87.3 percent of the taxes, and the top 50 percent paid a whopping 97.75 percent. That doesn't mean that the poor should be forced to pay more; it just means that they don't have a federal income-tax bill to pay.

Fifth, the Constitution nowhere authorizes the federal government to fight poverty. The powers delegated to the federal government under Article I, Section 8, simply do not include the authority to set up anti-poverty programs or establish a safety net for Americans. But what about the "General Welfare" clause in the Preamble and in Article I, Section 8, Paragraph 1? The clause says "general welfare," not "specific welfare" for certain individuals. It is neither the grant of a general legislative power to the federal government nor an additional grant of power beyond what is specifically enumerated in the Constitution. As the "Father of the Constitution," James Madison, explained,

> With respect to the two words "general welfare," I have always regarded them as qualified by the detail of powers connected with them. To take them in a literal and unlimited sense would be a metamorphosis of the Constitution into a character which there is a host of proofs was not contemplated by its creators. If the words obtained so readily a place in the "Articles of Confederation," and received so little notice in their admission into the present Constitution, and retained for so long a time a silent place in both, the fairest explanation is, that the words, in the alternative of meaning nothing or meaning everything, had the former meaning taken for granted.

And although the census itself is constitutional, the Census Bureau's poverty report is not.

Finally, and most important, fighting poverty is simply not a legitimate purpose of government. The only legitimate purpose of government is to protect the life, liberty, and property of its citizens from the violence or fraud of others. No matter how noble the intentions, government goes astray when it attempts to "help" or "fix" or "remedy" the plight of some person. Government has no resources of its own. The only way it can spend money to help one person is by taking it by force from another.

The libertarian position on the poor and poverty is clear, consistent, and uncompromising: It is not a legitimate purpose of government to provide anti-poverty programs, safety nets, job training, welfare, income security, retirement security, medical care, premium supports, housing assistance, energy assistance, unemployment compensation, food stamps, or refundable tax credits.

That doesn't mean that libertarians hate the poor, are not bothered by malnourished children, don't care whether homeless people starve, or are not concerned about the plight of the poor.

It means that libertarians cherish the individual liberty, private property, personal responsibility, limited government, and free society that allow the actions of families, friends, philanthropists, humanitarian institutions, religious organizations, and charitable associations to flourish.

*****

LIBERTARIAN STATISM

It is the wackiest "libertarian" non-libertarian proposal I have ever seen. Or perhaps it is the wackiest non-libertarian "libertarian" proposal I have ever seen. I'm not sure yet. Either way, it is nothing short of libertarian statism.

For many years now, some libertarians have promoted educational vouchers in the name of "school choice." But as I have pointed out many times (see here, here, here, here, and here), since the state has no business funding any child's education, government-issued vouchers for education are just another income redistribution scheme like food stamps, WIC, TANF, and refundable tax credits.

But support for vouchers is a mild aberration compared to the latest wacky "libertarian" scheme.

Writing in "The Libertarian Case for a Basic Income," Matt Zwolinski argues not only that "guaranteeing a minimum income to the poor is better than our current system of welfare," but that "it can be justified by libertarian principles."

Zwolinski is Associate Professor of Philosophy at the University of San Diego and the founder of the Bleeding Heart Libertarians blog. He is also a libertarian statist.

Here is how he defines his proposed Basic Income Guarantee:

A Basic Income Guarantee involves something like an unconditional grant of income to every citizen. So, on most proposals, everybody gets a check each month. "Unconditional" here means mostly that the check is not conditional on one's wealth or poverty or willingness to work.

And who would guarantee this grant of income? Why, the state, of course.

This not only not libertarian; this is not even something that most Republicans and conservatives would ever propose.

Zwolinski has "three libertarian arguments in support of a Basic Income Guarantee":

1. A Basic Income Guarantee would be much better than the current welfare state.
2. A Basic Income Guarantee might be required on libertarian grounds as reparation for past injustice.
3. A Basic Income Guarantee might be required to meet the basic needs of the poor.

The answer to all of these arguments is a simple one: there is nothing even remotely libertarian about the state taking money from some and giving it to others.

Zwolinski also mentions three objections that one might raise: disincentives, effects on migration, and effects on economic growth. A Basic Income Guarantee "would create objectionably strong disincentives to employment," "would create pressures to restrict immigration even more than it already is" and because "even a modest slowdown of economic growth can have dramatic effects when compounded over a period of decades."

He doesn't even posit the most obvious and most important objection: there is nothing even remotely libertarian about the state taking money from some and giving it to others. And neither does David Friedman in his reply to Zwolinski.

Zwolinski's first argument is for an efficient welfare state. Whether it would be "much better" than the current welfare state is simply his opinion. Whether "eliminating bloated bureaucracies" would put "more money in the hands of the poor and lower costs to the taxpayer" is pure speculation. And what are libertarians doing advising the state on how to make its income transfer programs more efficient?

Zwolinski insinuates that because the guaranteed income counts as reparations, it is not taking money that belongs to some and giving it to others since the money properly belongs to the poor. But he has given us no reason to think that the poor are entitled to reparations just because they are poor. And it is the state is the greatest perpetrator of "past injustice." It would be a current injustice for one to be required to hand over his money to a criminal gang for it to remedy some past injustice.

For his third argument Zwolinski appeals to Friedman's father, Milton, and to Friedrich Hayek. He points out that the elder Friedman maintained: "Some 'governmental action to alleviate poverty' is justified. Specifically, government is justified in setting 'a floor under the standard of life of every person in the community.'" Hayek's "even more powerful" argument is that "the assurance of a certain minimum income for everyone, or a sort of floor below which nobody need fall even when he is unable to provide for himself, appears not only to be wholly legitimate protection against a risk common to all, but a necessary part of the Great Society in which the individual no longer has specific claims on the members of the particular small group into which he was born." Zwolinski went on to write an entire article on Hayek's view.

But as anyone familiar with libertarianism knows, Murray Rothbard demolished Friedman's decidedly unlibertarian ideas in "Milton Friedman Unraveled" and Hans-Hermann Hoppe showed Hayek to be just a moderate social democrat in "Why Mises (and not Hayek)?"

In a recent article of mine—"Shall We Abandon the Non-Aggression Principle?"—I pointed out that once you reject the libertarian non-aggression principle (see Zwolinski's rejection here and Michael Rozeff's reply here), you open the door to justifying state aggression. The state taking money from some and giving it to others is an act of naked aggression.

The federal government's welfare programs don't need to be reformed, simplified, better managed, made more efficient, block granted to the states, used as a form of reparations, or made less bureaucratic, they simply need to be abolished.

*****

A LIBERTARIAN PERSPECTIVE ON FAMILY LEAVE

Paid family leave is getting a lot of attention lately. And while there is certainly nothing wrong with paid family leave, and employers can benefit from it just as much as employees, there is everything wrong with it when government—at the federal, state, or local level—provides it or mandates that employers have to provide it.

Since the passage of the Family and Medical Leave Act (FMLA) in 1993—which mandated that eligible workers could take 12 weeks of unpaid leave—Democrats in Congress and liberal and progressive groups have been calling for the unpaid leave in the FMLA to be changed to paid leave. It is continually pointed out that the United States is the only industrialized nation that does not guarantee any type of paid family leave at the national level.

As one would expect, all three Democratic candidates for president announced their support for some kind of mandatory paid family leave program.

Donald Trump and Hillary Clinton both brought up the issue of paid family leave during their first presidential debate. Under the Trump plan, mothers who take leave would receive benefits from the unemployment insurance system for a period of six weeks. This would amount to about 46 percent of a worker's wages. It would be funded by reducing "waste and abuse" in the unemployment insurance system. Under the Clinton plan, new parents, caregivers, and others eligible to take leave, leave would be paid for a period of 12 weeks at a 66 percent wage replacement rate. It would be funded by "taxes on the wealthy."

There has been a bill (S.786) introduced in Congress called the Family and Medical Insurance Leave Act. It would establish "the Office of Paid Family and Medical Leave within the Social Security Administration (SSA), to be headed by the Deputy SSA Commissioner." This Act

> Entitles every individual to a family and medical leave insurance (FMLI) benefit payment for each month beginning on the first day of the first month in which the individual meets the criteria.
>
> Prescribes a formula for determination of an individual's monthly FMLI benefit payment, as well as for the maximum and the minimum monthly benefit amounts.
>
> Establishes the Federal Family and Medical Leave Insurance Trust Fund in the Treasury. Requires FMLI benefit payments to be made only from this Fund.
>
> Amends the Internal Revenue Code to impose a tax on every individual and employer, all self-employment income, and every railroad employee, employee representative, or railroad employer to finance the Federal Family and Medical Leave Insurance Trust Fund in the Treasury for FMLI benefits.

The bill is currently languishing in a Senate committee.

Four states (California, New Jersey, New York, & Rhode Island) have enacted paid family leave that is financed by employee contributions to a social insurance fund. Some cities and counties offer paid family leave as a benefit for municipal employees.

NPR's "All Things Considered" has had some stories recently devoted to the subject of paid family leave:

- "On Your Mark, Give Birth, Go Back To Work"
- "'I Wasn't There To Help': Dad With Newborn Struggles With Lack Of Leave"
- "How California's 'Paid Family Leave' Law Buys Time For New Parents"
- "State Laws Build Momentum For First National Paid Family Leave Program"

It is this last story in particular that really caught my attention. Kelly McEvers, the NPR host, interviewed Aparna Mathur, currently a resident scholar in economic policy studies at the American Enterprise Institute (AEI) in Washington, D.C. AEI is a "conservative" think tank.

NPR could have interviewed an economist from a liberal think tank and gotten the same result. Not once did Mathur propose a market solution or criticize government or government-mandated paid family leave programs.

Mathur has also written on the subject of paid family leave for *Forbes*:

• "The Problem With Paid Family Leave: Access Is Not The Same As Take-Up"
• "Trump and Clinton Miss The Mark On Paid Family Leave"

Again, more of the same. No market solutions. No criticism of government intervention in the workplace.

NPR should have interviewed a libertarian on the subject of paid family leave. But since I never received a call, I here offer a brief libertarian perspective on the subject.

1. Paid family leave obviously benefits newborn babies.

2. Paid family leave generally benefits mothers (and fathers if eligible) who take it. However, if the benefit pays less than 100 percent of the beneficiary's regular salary, then the mother (or the father) may want to go back to work before required to do so. Also, the beneficiary may not want to miss work for more than a certain period in order to maintain a certain skill set.

3. It is a blatantly unconstitutional for the federal government to have a paid family leave program, no matter how it is funded. Just like it is unconstitutional for the federal government to have Social Security, Medicare, and welfare programs.

4. It is just as unconstitutional for the federal government to mandate that employers must offer paid or unpaid family leave. Just like it is unconstitutional for the federal government to set a minimum wage, require that employers offer their employees health insurance, and establish overtime regulations.

5. It is an illegitimate function of government at any level to have anything to do with fringe benefits offered by employers.

6. There is no answer to the question of whether a company should offer paid family leave as a fringe benefit. Just like there is no answer to the question of whether a company should offer any number of other fringe benefits.

7. Offering paid family leave may benefit certain employers. It might help them to acquire and retain quality employees. It might be cheaper to pay a skilled employee to take time off after the birth of a child than to hire and train someone to take his or her place.

8. Once it is accepted that it is okay for the government to mandate that employers provide paid family leave, no reasonable and logical objection can be raised to the government mandating that employers provide any

other fringe benefit.

9. Paid family leave, vacation pay, holiday pay, sick leave, jury-duty pay, paid time off, and any other fringe benefit are matters to negotiate between employers and employees. The government shouldn't even know what fringe benefits companies offer.

10. Market solutions to problems are always to be preferred to government solutions.

These are the things that the economist from the American Enterprise Institute should have said.

*****

LIBERTARIAN WELFARE

Why do some libertarians continue to support an income transfer program that is just as much a welfare program as food stamps, SSI, and AFDC? I am speaking of vouchers for education.

Vouchers: Another Income Redistribution Scheme

The goal of all proponents of educational vouchers is a government-funded, universal voucher system that allows parents to choose the schools their children attend.

A government-funded (that is, a taxpayer-funded) educational voucher program is a libertarian welfare program. It is a welfare program because it takes money from one taxpayer and redistributes it to another; it is a libertarian welfare program because libertarians are some of the most vocal proponents of vouchers and at the same time the very people who vocally oppose federal income transfer programs.

Many conservatives, and especially devotees of President Bush, likewise support vouchers. In his brilliant analysis, "The Trouble with Conservatives," Ralph Raico remarks that "conservatives are known for their blind nationalism, their readiness to engage in military adventure throughout the world, their envious Puritanism." I would like to add to this their "selective interventionism." It is therefore no surprise that many conservatives support vouchers since most conservatives never met a federal program they didn't like—as long as it furthers their agenda. Thus, in the eyes of the typical conservative, spending millions of taxpayer dollars on the National Endowment for the Arts and the Legal Services Corporation is bad, but spending millions of taxpayer dollars on abstinence education and faith-based initiatives is good.

The fact that a voucher program is just another income transfer program has been pointed out before, so I want to extend my indictment of vouchers further than that. I have two additional propositions:

Instead of *most* schools being subject to the control of the federal government, the imposition of a universal voucher program will result in *all* schools being subject to the control of the federal government. *Partial* socialism of education will be replaced by *total* socialism of education.

Vouchers are not an intermediate step toward a free market in education. A voucher program ensures that a free market in education will never exist.

School Choice: A Myth

The whole concept of "school choice" is a myth.

Although it is true that all states have some sort of compulsory attendance law, no one is forced to send his children to a public (that is, a government) school. In my state (Florida) the compulsory attendance statute (sec. 232.01) basically states that all children between six and sixteen years of age "must attend school regularly during the entire school term." Florida law defines a "habitual truant" as a "student who has 15 or more unexcused absences within 90 calendar days." But nowhere in Florida law (or in the law of any state) does it require that school attendance be at a government school. (On the evils of compulsory education—see Murray Rothbard's *Education: Free & Compulsory*).

Since no parent in the United States has to send his child to a government school, it is a myth that we need "school choice" (meaning vouchers) so that children can get out of an unsafe, failing government school. Every parent right now has a choice as to where his child goes to school. If the government school in his area is "bad," he can move to some other part of town, move to another city, homeschool his children, or put his children in a private school.

When it comes to their children's education, parents have educational choice just like they have a choice when it comes to their children's food, clothing, shelter, and medical care. A child's basic needs are obviously more important than his education. Why, then, don't we hear libertarians and conservatives clamoring for vouchers for food, clothing, shelter, and medical care? What is so special about educational services? If the state is to provide vouchers for education, then what about vouchers for other services like vacations, haircuts, and recreation? And to be "fair" to everyone, why don't we just give the federal government every dollar we earn and leave it up to the state to dole out vouchers for every good and service that we desire.

Money: The Real Issue

If everyone has school choice right now, then what is the problem? The problem is a financial one; many parents don't have the resources to move to a location with a better school or put their children in a private school. Homeschooling is out in many cases as well since either both parents have to work to make ends meet or else there is only one parent in the home. The "rich" have the resources to move, to put their children in a private school, to have one parent stay home to homeschool the children, or, in some cases, to hire a private tutor to teach their children.

The lack of money keeps us from doing a lot of things. If they had the money, many people would buy a new Cadillac or an SUV. Others would take a cruise to the Caribbean or a trip to Europe. The state doesn't give vouchers for cars and vacations to those who can't afford them. Why, then, should it give parents vouchers for their children's education?

Participation in a voucher program, like the Cleveland program in the celebrated *Zelman v. Simmons-Harris* case, is generally based on financial need. Most schools are funded by property taxes. This means that the "rich," who pay the majority of the taxes, don't qualify; while the "poor," who pay little or no taxes, reap the benefits of vouchers. In this respect, how does an educational voucher differ from a welfare check?

But that is not all. Vouchers are both an income transfer program and a subsidy to private industry—all courtesy of the U.S. taxpayer.

Yet, I like vouchers. They are a great way to provide needy children with an education. Even if every state closed all of its "public" schools, the federal and state departments of education were abolished, and all governments got out of the education business altogether, vouchers would still be an option for educational funding.

The problem with vouchers is their funding. There is nothing stopping any small business or large corporation from issuing an educational voucher right now to any child. It would, in fact, be a great fringe benefit to offer employees. If libertarian voucher supporters want parents to receive a voucher for the education of their children, then let them put their money where their mouth is. Let them empty their own pockets. Why should they expect someone to pay for the education of someone else's children?

The cry is often made that "we must do something to 'rescue' children from unsafe, failing government schools." But "we" don't need to do anything. Parents need to do something. Grandparents need to do something. Concerned citizens need to do something. And if, as Milton Friedman says, "The business community has a major interest in expanding the pool of well-schooled potential employees," then let the business community do something. If parents, grandparents, concerned citizens, and potential employers of children do not want to do anything then so be it. Not only is it unlibertarian to expect someone to pay for the education of someone else's children, it grossly immoral and the height of arrogance. If a couple doesn't want their children in a public school, can't afford to hire a tutor or send them to a private school, and doesn't want to teach them at home— they shouldn't have any children. The problem is that most people spend more time deciding where to eat on Friday night or where to go on their next vacation than they spend planning their children's education.

Vouchers: Another Central Plan

Estate planning, so the government doesn't confiscate your hard-earned wealth when you die, is a good thing. On the other hand, *state* planning, where the government takes your money now and controls how it will be spent, is a bad thing—unless you are a socialist.

Vouchers are the ultimate in state planning and control.

Recall my proposition: Instead of *most* schools being subject to the control of the federal government, the imposition of a universal voucher program will result in *all* schools being subject to the control of the federal government. *Partial* socialism of education will be replaced by *total* socialism of education.

Under a government-managed voucher system, the state must calculate the amount of the voucher, it must come up with some kind of criterion to determine who is entitled to receive the voucher, and it must decide on certain standards that a school has to meet in order to be able to accept a voucher redeemable from the state in lieu of payment. Those familiar with economics will recognize that we have an incredible calculation problem here. Instead of father knows best we would have government knows best.

The government at present has control over the education of children in its schools. Under a universal voucher system, the government will have control over the education of all children. The only children who will be exempt are those whose parents homeschool or refuse to accept a voucher and pay their child's school tuition themselves. It is even conceivable that the state might not recognize schools that don't meet its requirements to accept vouchers. Vouchers would allow the state to take complete control of private schools that accepted voucher payments through regulation, hiring quotas, teacher certification, curriculum requirements, etc. Federal control of private schools would have the same disastrous results as federal control of airport security. All but the most prestigious private schools that cater to the rich will be forced to serve the one that pays the bills—the state—or go out of business.

Voucher advocate Charles Murray sides "with those who are prepared to accept government funding, though not government control, of education." But the two can't be separated. How can a libertarian be naïve enough to think that they can? And how can a libertarian countenance government funding of education? Instead of castigating "libertarian purists" for their intransigence, libertarian voucher proponents need to face the fact that their agitation for vouchers amounts to a call for more government control over education and more government spending on education.

So rather than making things better, vouchers would further cement the bond that the government has on the educational system.

Vouchers: Market Socialism

According to the "godfather" of the voucher movement, Milton Friedman, "Vouchers are not an end in themselves; they are a means to make a transition from a government to a market system."

Vouchers are another attempt to reach market ends by socialist means.

My other proposition was this: Vouchers are not an intermediate step toward a free market in education. A voucher program ensures that a free market in education will never exist.

Vouchers are not a step toward the free market. The imposition of a universal voucher program will merely give us an additional layer of government bureaucracy financed by taxes, inflation, or borrowing. Vouchers will also ensure the continued existence of the federal Department of Education.

Suppose that vouchers proponents get their heart's desire: The public schools are abolished, private schools flourish, total spending on education decreases, and the state gives a voucher to every parent to get education services for each one of his children, including parents who homeschool their children. Voucher proponents would be ecstatic. They would finally get what they have clamored for.

But then what?

Once this universal voucher scheme was instituted, voucher supporters would then (if they mean what they say about vouchers being an intermediate step toward a free market in education) say to the state: "Now we need to abolish the voucher system." The state would reply: "Now wait a minute, we just gave you everything you wanted. We closed our public schools, we cut spending on education, and we instituted a universal voucher system—just like you asked. And now you want to abolish the voucher system? Nothin' doin'."

The state will never relinquish its hold on the American educational system without a fight—even if it means embracing vouchers.

Vouchers: Just Say "No"

Just say "no" to vouchers.

Say "no" to state control of education. Say "no" to state funding of education. Say "no" to state central planning. Say "no" to compulsory education. Say "no" to parental irresponsibility. Say "no" to pseudo-free market schemes. Say "no" to income redistribution. And say "no" to libertarian welfare programs.

As I have pointed out before, libertarian voucher supporters should pay more attention to Ludwig von Mises than Milton Friedman: "There is, in fact, only one solution: the state, the government, the laws must not in any way concern themselves with schooling or education. Public funds must not be used for such purposes. The rearing and instruction of youth must be left entirely to parents and to private associations and institutions" (Mises, *Liberalism*, p. 115).

I am getting weary writing about vouchers. I have written my fill of articles, book reviews, comments, replies, and responses about vouchers. Nevertheless, after reading some of the comments by libertarian voucher supporters about my most recent article on vouchers, I felt compelled to pen yet another article.

*****

THE LIBERTARIAN CASE AGAINST PUBLIC SCHOOLS

Conservatives and libertarians have a precarious relationship. On the surface, they appear to agree on some issues, but once you dig a little deeper, vast philosophical differences quickly become evident.

To get votes and support, Conservatives sometimes spout libertarian rhetoric, claim they are "libertarian leaning," and—their favorite pastime—criticize liberals. The truth, however, is that conservatives are bitter opponents of libertarianism, lie incessantly, and are no better than liberals on most issues.

Yet, the case of public schooling is one where conservatives and libertarians appear to have some common concerns.

Liberals love public education. And especially when it promotes an agenda of diversity, environmentalism, political correctness, inclusivism, socialism, relativism, interventionism, statism, gun control, and LGBT causes. But like libertarians, most conservatives regularly criticize public education.

Conservatives cite the drop in SAT scores. They talk about the dumbing down of our kids. They vehemently express their opposition to Common Core. They talk about high schools graduating functional illiterates. They bewail the decline in discipline and standards. They bemoan the violence that occurs in schools. They are aghast at the increasing number of teachers caught having sexual relationships with students. They expose the anti-Christian bias that exists in many public schools. They express their opposition to the employment of gay teachers. They criticize the teaching of evolution as an established fact. They lament the elimination of prayer and Bible reading in schools. They denounce the power of the teachers' unions. They condemn school-based "health clinics" for being pro-abortion. They complain about the public schools pushing a liberal agenda. They denounce the bureaucracy in the federal Department of Education.

Although libertarians may point out some of these very things, they have nothing whatsoever to do with the libertarian case against public schools. The libertarian case is a simple one. Libertarians oppose public schools because they are government schools. It doesn't matter if none of the evils of public schools mentioned above even exist. It is simply not the proper role of government to educate children. Neither is it the proper role of government to force Americans to pay for the education of their children in a public school or to pay for the education of the children of other Americans. It is an illegitimate purpose of government to have anything to do with the education of anyone's children. It is the responsibility of parents to educate their children. How they choose to do that is entirely up to them, but public schooling shouldn't even be an option.

The solutions conservatives propose to "fix" public schools include school uniforms, vouchers to help children escape failing public schools, higher standards for students and teachers, streamlining the education bureaucracy, more accountability to parents, increased local control, restoration of prayer and Bible reading, a more conservative curriculum, classes on the Constitution, allowing teachers to be armed, year-round schooling, getting rid of Common Core, the posting of the Ten Commandments, more school resource officers, and, of course, various reforms. Some conservatives even talk of abolishing the federal Department of Education.

On this latter point, conservative Republicans used to call for this department's elimination. Ronald Reagan proposed abolishing the department while campaigning for president in 1980. The Republican Party platforms of 1980 and 1996 likewise called for the department's elimination. But during Reagan's first six years as president (when the Senate was controlled by the Republicans) the budget for the Department of Education increased by billions of dollars—just as it did when George H.W. Bush and Bill Clinton (with a Republican majority in the Congress for six years) were president. Under George W. Bush, when the Republicans controlled both Houses of Congress for over four years, the budget of the Department of Education ballooned to $100 billion.

The libertarian solution to the problems in the public school system is likewise a simple one: abolish not just the federal and state Departments of Education (not because they are too expensive, have too many bureaucrats, have failed to improve education, are beholden to the teachers' unions, and promote a liberal agenda—but because they are departments of *education*), but public; that is, government, education itself.

Conservatives have no problem with government-provided education and the forcing of Americans who object to public schools or keep their children out of public schools to pay for it.

This means, of course, that conservatives are enemies of the Constitution they claim to revere.

If there are to be any public schools; that is, government schools, they should be limited to state-government schools, fully supported and supervised by state governments. This is because while every state has provisions in its constitution for the operation of K-12 schools, colleges, and universities, the federal government has been given no such authority by its Constitution.

This means that the federal government should not be involved in any way, shape, or form with the education of anyone. No Pell Grants, student loans, federal regulations, research grants, Elementary and Secondary Education Act, teacher-education requirements, Department of Education, teacher-certification standards, school accreditation, Title IX mandates, educational vouchers, No Child Left Behind Act, school breakfast or lunch programs, Head Start funding, bilingual-education mandates, busing to achieve racial desegregation, Education for All Handicapped Children Act, diversity mandates, Common Core, presidential visits to schools, standardized-testing requirements, special-education mandates, math and science initiatives, Race to the Top funds, or Higher Education Act.

Since conservatives regularly support most of these things, there is a world of difference between their criticisms of public schools and the consistent and principled criticisms offered by libertarians.

*****

ARE ANY OF THEM LIBERTARIAN?

It's back to school time.

Time then to answer an important question. Vouchers, charter schools, education saving accounts, tuition tax deductions, and tuition tax credits: Are any of them libertarian?

Vouchers are continually touted by some libertarians as a way for parents to send children to the school of their choice instead of a dangerous and destructive public school. Government at some level provides a voucher worth a certain amount that parents can use to pay all or part of their child's tuition at a private school. The school would then redeem the voucher for payment from the government that issued it.

Vouchers are certainly not libertarian. The government forcibly takes money from people through compulsory taxation and uses it to pay for the education of other people's children. Vouchers are welfare just like food stamps. Giving one group of Americans the choice of where to spend other Americans' money to educate their children is immoral and unjust. If vouchers were used for anything but education, they would be denounced as an income-transfer program and a subsidy to private industry. Once government vouchers for education are deemed to be acceptable, no reasonable or logical argument can be made against the government's providing vouchers for other services.

Charter schools are also pushed by some libertarians. These are publicly funded, but privately managed, schools established by teachers, parents, or community groups under the terms of a contract or charter with a state or local authority. Charter operators may include local school districts, universities, non-profit corporations, or for-profit corporations. Charter school laws exist in 43 states and the District of Columbia. According to the National Alliance for Public Charter Schools: "There are now more than 6,800 charter public schools enrolling an estimated 2.9 million students throughout the country." Charter schools are subject to fewer rules and regulations than traditional public schools when it comes to staffing, curriculum, and instruction. But like public schools, education at charter schools is provided at no charge.

Charter schools are certainly not libertarian. Like traditional public schooling or vouchers, the government forcibly takes money from people through compulsory taxation and uses it to pay for the education of other people's children. Charter schools can also receive federal funding. The fact that a charter school can receive private grants and donations does not make it a private school. And of course, even when truly private schools receive government funds there are always strings attached. Charter schools must still adhere to all state and federal health, safety, and civil rights laws, as well as business regulations. None of this means that charter schools don't do a better job of educating children than traditional public schools. They may or they may not. But providing students a better education doesn't make charter schools libertarian.

Education saving accounts like a Coverdell or 529 plan allow parents or others to deposit money into an account for a child's future qualified education expenses. Proceeds can be withdrawn tax-free for qualified education expenses at a qualified institution. Distributions not used in this manner are subject to federal income tax and an early-withdrawal penalty on the gain, but not on the deposits since they are contributed on an after-tax basis. Although money deposited into an education saving account is not deductible on one's federal income tax, many states do provide a state income tax deduction for all or part of the donor contributions.

Education saving accounts are libertarian, but not because they are related to education. Money withdrawn from an education savings account and spent on a child's education is entirely private money since no government money (i.e., taxpayer dollars) is deposited into these accounts. And not requiring a taxpayer to pay income tax on gains earned in an education savings account as long as he spends the money a certain way is not a government subsidy and is always a good thing from the standpoint of the taxpayer's liberty and property.

Tuition tax deductions reduce one's income subject to tax. The tuition and fees deduction is found on line 34 of the 1040 tax form and is reported on form 8917. It can reduce the amount of income subject to tax by up to $4,000 as long as one's modified adjusted gross income (MAGI) is not over $80,000 ($160,000 if married filing jointly). Some states also allow a tax deduction for tuition expenses.

Tuition tax deductions are libertarian, but not because they are related to education. A tuition tax deduction does not mean that the government is paying any child's tuition. And not requiring a taxpayer to pay tax on all of his income, for whatever reason, is not a government subsidy and is always a good thing from the standpoint of the taxpayer's liberty and property.

Tuition tax credits are dollar-for-dollar reductions of the amount of tax owed on one's income. The credit for educational expenses is found on line 50 of the 1040 tax form. and is reported on form 8863. The lifetime learning credit can reduce one's tax owned by up to $2,000 for qualified education expenses as long as one's MAGI is not over $65,000 ($131,000 if married filling jointly). The American opportunity credit can reduce one's tax owned by up to $2,500 per qualified student for qualified education expenses as long as one's MAGI is not over $90,000 ($180,000 if married filing jointly). Some states also allow a tax credit for tuition expenses. A tax credit on the federal level for the full amount of tuition paid at a private school is an idea that has been around for years.

Tuition tax credits are libertarian, but not because they are related to education. A tuition tax credit does not mean that the government is paying any child's tuition. And not requiring a taxpayer to pay all of the tax owed on his income, for whatever reason, is not a government subsidy and is always a good thing from the standpoint of the taxpayer's liberty and property. The only other thing that needs to be said regarding tax credits is that refundable tax credits are not libertarian because they allow a "taxpayer" to receive a refund of money that he never paid in to the government. Forty percent of the American opportunity tax credit may be refundable.

The libertarian position on education is a simple one. Government should not operate public schools, fund anyone's education, or regulate education in any way.

This means no mandatory-attendance laws, no property taxes to pay for public schools, no public-school teachers, no Pell Grants, no student loans, no research grants to colleges, no teacher-education requirements, no government teacher-certification standards, no government school accreditation, no Title IX, special-education, desegregation, diversity, or bilingual-education mandates, no educational vouchers, no Higher Education, Elementary and Secondary Education, Education for All Handicapped Children, or No Child Left Behind Acts, no school breakfast or lunch programs, no Head Start funding, no Common Core, no standardized-testing requirements, no math and science initiatives, no Race to the Top funds, and no Department of Education.

Education of children is a service that parents should provide themselves or pay for just like when they need their car repaired or their lawn mowed.

As Ludwig von Mises wrote about education many years ago in his book *Liberalism*: "There is, in fact, only one solution: the state, the government, the laws must not in any way concern themselves with schooling or education. Public funds must not be used for such purposes. The rearing and instruction of youth must be left entirely to parents and to private associations and institutions."

If there is to be any state involvement in education, it must be limited to the state level. The federal government has been given no such authority by its Constitution. But this is only because every state has a provision in its constitution for the operation of K-12 schools, colleges, and universities, not because it is libertarian for the states to do so.

*****

WHAT IS THE LIBERTARIAN VIEW OF TAXES?

What is the libertarian view of taxes? Inquiring minds want to know. And some of them are libertarians.

In a recent article of mine, "Obama's Tax Proposals: A Libertarian Analysis," I subjected President Obama's proposals to raise taxes—by increasing rates or eliminating deductions—and lower taxes—by increasing tax credits or instituting new ones.

But like Republicans miss the point on tax cuts and conservatives just don't get it when it comes to taxes, some libertarians miss the point or don't get it either.

The libertarian view of taxes is not that taxes should be fair, adequate, sufficient, constitutional, uniform, flat, simple, efficient, apportioned equally, or low. It is not that the tax code *should* help the poor, benefit the middle class, and be business friendly, *should* not be used for social engineering purposes, income redistribution schemes, or have loopholes, and *should* ensure that everyone pays some arbitrary "fair share." And neither is it that most Americans are not legally required to pay income tax, filing your taxes is voluntary, paying your taxes is voluntary, the 16th Amendment was not properly ratified, etc., etc., etc. My final reply to those arguments is simply two words: Irwin Schiff.

The libertarian view of taxes is simply that taxes should not exist in the first place. There should be no tax code because taxation is theft and violates the non-aggression principle. I cannot improve upon the late, great Murray Rothbard, who wrote in *The Ethics of Liberty*:

> *All* other persons and groups in society (except for acknowledged and sporadic criminals such as thieves and bank robbers) obtain their income voluntarily: *either* by selling goods and services to the consuming public, or by voluntary gift (e.g., membership in a club or association, bequest, or inheri-

tance). *Only* the State obtains its revenue by coercion, by threatening dire penalties should the income not be forthcoming. That coercion is known as "taxation," although in less regularized epochs it was often known as "tribute." Taxation is theft, purely and simply, even though it is theft on a grand and colossal scale which no acknowledged criminals could hope to match. It is a compulsory seizure of the property of the State's inhabitants, or subjects.

It would be an instructive exercise for the skeptical reader to try to frame a definition of taxation which does not also include theft. Like the robber, the State demands money at the equivalent of gunpoint; if the taxpayer refuses to pay his assets are seized by force, and if he should resist such depredation, he will be arrested or shot if he should continue to resist.

Since the United States has a tax code, since the United States has an IRS, since the United States has an income tax—anything that *in and of itself* keeps more money in the pockets, purses, and bank accounts of Americans and out of the hands of Uncle Sam, the mouth of the federal leviathan, and the treasury of the U.S. government is a good thing that should be encouraged and supported.

Thus, tax *increases* of any kind, tax *reform* that is revenue neutral, tax base *broadening*, tax *replacement* of one tax with another, and tax *shifting* from one group of taxpayers to another are not in the least bit desirable or libertarian.

Depending on one's income, the income tax rates that Americans will pay in 2015 are 10, 15, 25, 28, 33, 35, and 39.6 percent. These rates correspond to seven brackets. For individual taxpayers, the 10 percent rate applies to income up to $9,225, the 15 percent rate applies to income between $9,226 and $37,450, the 25 percent rate applies to income between $37,451 and $90,750, the 28 percent rate applies to income between $90,751 and $189,300, the 33 percent rate applies to income between $189,301 and $411,500, the 35 percent rate applies to income between $411,501 and $413,200, and the 39.6 percent rate applies to all income over $413,200.

The brackets are *narrower* for married individuals filing separate returns, *wider* for heads of households, and *wider still* for married individuals filing jointly.

Clearly, it would be a good thing for taxpayers if any of the seven tax rates *decreased* or if any of the brackets *expanded*. The results would be the same: *more* money retained by taxpayers and *less* money taken by the government.

What is not so clear, however, are the results of tax exemptions, deductions, and credits.

Tax exemptions and tax deductions serve to reduce one's income subject to tax. Exemptions and deductions work the same way, but deductions are generally subject to more limitations, conditions, and exclusions. Both differ from tax credits in that tax credits serve to reduce the amount of tax owed on one's income. Either way, one will pay *less* in taxes the *greater the number*, and the *greater the amount*, of exemptions, deductions, and credits that he qualifies for.

For tax year 2015, each taxpayer is entitled to one personal exemption for himself, his spouse, and each of his dependents in the amount of $4,000. There are also various deductions that one might qualify for. But even if one doesn't qualify for any deductions, there is still available to all taxpayers the standard deduction of $6,300 ($12,600 for married filing jointly). And then there are tax credits—dollar-for-dollar reductions of the amount of income tax owed—like the child and dependent care credit, the adoption credit, the child tax credit, the earned income credit, and various education credits.

Lowering or eliminating tax exemptions, deductions, or credits has the same result as *raising* tax rates or *contracting* tax brackets: *less* money retained by taxpayers and *more* money taken by the government. *Raising* or *instituting* tax exemptions, deductions, or credits has the same result as *lowering* tax rates or *expanding* tax brackets: *more* money retained by taxpayers and *less* money taken by the government.

Any change to tax rates, tax brackets, tax exemptions, tax deductions, or tax credits that *in and of itself* results in *more money* retained by taxpayers and *less* money taken by the government is both desirable even if the change is not across-the-board and regardless of the government's reason for the change.

Take, for example, the child tax credit. It is worth up to $1,000 per qualifying child under the age of 17 depending upon your modified adjusted gross income. The credit is reduced by 5 percent for each $1,000, or part of that amount, above the income phase-out amount of $75,000 ($110,000 if married filing jointly).

It would be desirable if the amount of the credit *increased*, the age of children it applied to *increased*, the credit was *reduced* by a *lesser* amount or *not at all*, and/or the phase-out amount was *increased* or *eliminated*—as long as the credit was not *refundable* and taxes were not *shifted* to those without children to "pay" for the credit. A tax credit *in and of itself* is not a subsidy. The fact that the government may have instituted or changed the credit to encourage the production of children, make the tax code more "family friendly," help the poor, or benefit the middle class is immaterial. It is unfortunate that those without children don't get the same credits as those with children, but this doesn't mean that we should oppose out of hand tax credits that relate in some way to children.

If Congress—for whatever reason—decided to give a special tax deduction or credit to Americans named Bob, Americans who owed a horse, Americans with red hair, or Americans with green eyes it would be a good thing as long as Americans not named Bob, who didn't own a horse, who didn't have red hair, or didn't have green eyes didn't have to make up the difference.

The libertarian view of taxes merely mirrors the libertarian view of government regulations and government itself.

Government regulations are bad, but since we have them and since the chance that they will all be eliminated is nonexistent, libertarians should encourage and support action to have as many regulations eliminated as possible, the number of businesses the regulations apply to decreased, and/or the extent of the regulations reduced.

Government itself is bad, but since we have one and since the chance that it will be eliminated is nonexistent, libertarians should encourage and support action to have the government as limited as possible in size and scope. Really limited, not limited in the Republican sense of the government being limited to control by Republicans.

Taxes are bad; tax exemptions, deductions, and credits are good. Always and forever.

*****

WHY DO LIBERTARIANS PAY TAXES?

It never fails. Every time I write *anything* about taxes I get long, rambling e-mails from tax trolls who scour the Internet looking for articles about taxes so they can contact the writers and impress them with their knowledge of the tax code.

These tax trolls usually call themselves "non-taxpayers." They say things like: paying taxes is voluntary, the Sixteenth Amendment was not properly ratified, most Americans aren't required to pay income tax, many Americans have gotten refunds of all the money withheld from their paychecks, and the income tax is a classical liberal tax on federal employments, offices, and privileges. Sometimes they boast that they haven't paid taxes for 10, 15, or 20 years and the IRS hasn't done anything about it.

Let's review the libertarian view of taxes.

The libertarian view of taxes is *not* that taxes should be fair, adequate, sufficient, constitutional, uniform, flat, simple, efficient, apportioned equally, or low.

The libertarian view of taxes is *not* that the tax code should help the poor, benefit the middle class, and be business friendly.

The libertarian view of taxes is *not* that taxes should not be used for social engineering purposes and income redistribution schemes.

The libertarian view of taxes is *not* that the tax code should not have loopholes so that everyone pays their "fair share."

The libertarian view of taxes is simply that taxes should not exist in the first place. There should be no tax code because taxation is theft and violates the non-aggression principle.

The libertarian view of taxes is that tax increases of any kind, tax reform that is revenue neutral, tax base broadening, tax replacement of one tax with another, and tax shifting from one group of taxpayers to another are not in the least bit desirable.

The libertarian view of taxes is that the lower the taxes the better and the greater number of deductions, credits, exemptions, and loopholes the better.

This is all much ado about nothing, says the "non-taxpayer." Libertarians miss the point on the income tax because they are not enlightened like "non-taxpayers" are. Libertarians don't have a proper understand of the tax code.

These "non-taxpayer" tax trolls misunderstand why libertarians pay taxes. But so do liberals and conservatives. Some might reason that, on a philosophical level, if taxation is government theft, then why do libertarians pay taxes? And on a practical level, unless someone makes a lot of money, the chances of an IRS audit are low. So why do libertarians bother to pay taxes?

There are some important reasons why libertarians pay taxes. But before looking at them, perhaps it would be beneficial to look at reasons why libertarians *don't* pay taxes; that is, erroneous reasons why libertarians pay taxes.

Libertarians don't pay taxes because they believe it is just what Americans do.

Libertarians don't pay taxes because they are confused about the tax code.

Libertarians don't pay taxes because they believe the government is entitled to them for services provided.

Libertarians don't pay taxes because they don't understand that the U.S. income tax cannot tax earnings from the common, ordinary occupations of life.

Libertarians don't pay taxes because they believe paying taxes is the right thing to do.

Libertarians don't pay taxes because they believe taxes in the United States are lower than they are in other countries.

Libertarians don't pay taxes because they believe the Sixteenth Amendment was properly ratified.

Libertarians don't pay taxes because they believe taxes are the price we pay for civilization.

Libertarians don't pay taxes because they believe taxes are a necessary evil.

Libertarians don't pay taxes because they believe the tax code requires them to.

Libertarians don't pay taxes because they aren't aware that most Americans aren't legally required to pay income tax.

Libertarians don't pay taxes because they don't understand the tax code.

Libertarians don't pay taxes because millions of Americans are dependent on government handouts.

Libertarians don't pay taxes because they are not educated tax scholars.

Libertarians don't pay taxes because they believe the Constitution gives the government the power to tax.

Libertarians don't pay taxes because they don't know how to read the tax code.

Libertarians don't pay taxes because they think it is patriotic.

Libertarians don't pay taxes because they haven't yet figured out how to lay a proper factual evidentiary foundation on how not to pay the income tax.

Libertarians don't pay taxes because they don't understand that the federal government has no constitutional power to tax the wages of ordinary Americans.

Libertarians don't pay taxes because they think the government needs the money.

Libertarians don't pay taxes because they don't believe the income tax is part of the contract involved with acceptance of a government privilege.

Libertarians don't pay taxes because they don't know the history of the income tax.

Libertarians don't pay taxes because they never noticed in the withholding statute in Subchapter C of the tax code that the only people subject to withholding are government employees.

Libertarians don't pay taxes because they are not enlightened about the income tax.

Libertarians don't pay taxes because they believe the constitutional functions of government should be funded.

Libertarians don't pay taxes because they don't realize what an excise tax is.

Libertarians don't pay taxes because they would feel guilty if they didn't and other Americans did.

Libertarians don't pay taxes because they don't understand from Title 26, Subtitle A, that most Americans aren't engaged in engaged in ordinary occupations liable for the income tax.

Libertarians don't pay taxes because they don't understand the difference between a privilege and a right.

Libertarians don't pay taxes because they don't understand the difference between direct and indirect taxes.

Libertarians don't pay taxes because they have misinterpreted the Supreme Court tax cases.

Libertarians don't pay taxes because they don't realize that paying taxes is voluntary.

Libertarians don't pay taxes because they don't read the tax code with the understanding of the history of the tax.

Libertarians don't pay taxes because they believe they have engaged in an excise taxable activity.

Libertarians don't pay taxes because they don't understand that the income tax is a classical liberal tax on federal employments, offices, and privileges.

Libertarians don't pay taxes because they believe "non taxpayers" are screwballs.

Why, then, do libertarians pay taxes?

Libertarians pay taxes so they don't end up in a cage like Irwin Schiff.

Libertarians pay taxes so their property doesn't get seized by the IRS.

Libertarians pay taxes so the IRS doesn't garnish their wages.

Libertarians pay taxes so they are not ruined financially by the IRS.

Libertarians pay taxes so they don't get killed by an IRS agent for resisting arrest.

Libertarians pay taxes for the same reason you would hand over your wallet to someone who pointed a gun in your face and said: "Give me your money or else."

The Constitution, the Sixteenth Amendment, Supreme Court decisions, tax court rulings, and the tax code have nothing to do with it.

*****

3

LIBERTARIANISM vs. LIBERALISM/CONSERVATISM

THE LIBERTARIAN SOLUTION

The United States of America is facing some major issues in the twenty-first century. The national debt is $18.5 trillion. The budget deficit is $500 billion. Homelessness is widespread in most major cities. Student-loan debt is more than a trillion dollars. Social Security and Medicare are insolvent. Government spending continues to skyrocket. There are more than 45 million Americans receiving food stamps. Millions of Americans have stopped looking for work even as the number of government employees continues to grow. Real wages are stagnant. The United States is engaged in unending and expensive overseas military interventions. The nation's infrastructure is in need of massive repairs even as the American military destroys infrastructure in other countries. Racial tension is on the rise. More than 20 percent of the American population receives some kind of means-tested public assistance every month. Even families with two incomes are struggling to make ends meet. The United States has the world's largest prison population per capita. Tens of thousands of Americans are incarcerated for nonviolent crimes. Students are graduating from high school who are functionally illiterate. Americans are polarized politically as never before. The government increasingly regulates almost every area of commerce and life.

Liberals, Democrats, conservatives, and Republicans all agree with each other and with libertarians that the country has issues that need solutions. The trouble is that that is the only thing they agree on. Those on the Left have their solutions and those on the Right have their solutions. Sometimes their solutions are somewhat similar; some-times their solutions are completely different, but they are all united in their opposition to the solutions put forth by libertarians.

Libertarianism

Libertarianism is a political philosophy that says that people should be free from government interference to live their lives any way they desire and engage in any economic activity they choose as long as their actions are peaceful, their associations are voluntary, their interactions are consensual, and they don't violate the personal or property rights of others.

Libertarianism celebrates individual liberty, free speech, property rights, free expression, peaceful activity, free markets, voluntary interaction, free thought, personal freedom, free assembly, individual responsibility, and a free society.

The essence of libertarianism is its nonaggression principle. Aggression is theft, fraud, the initiation of nonconsensual violence, or the threat of nonconsensual violence. The initiation or threat of aggression against the person or property of others is always wrong. Aggression is justified only in defense of person or property or retaliation against the same, but is not required. Unlike liberalism and conservatism, libertarianism strictly and consistently applies the non-aggression principle to actions of government. After all, governments are the greatest violators of liberty, property, and the nonaggression principle.

Libertarians maintain that as long as people don't infringe upon the liberty of others by committing, or threatening to commit, acts of fraud, theft, aggression, or violence against their person or property, the government should leave them alone and not interfere with their pursuit of happiness, commerce, personal decisions, economic enterprises, or what they do on or with their property.

Libertarians hold that in a free society, the functions of government—in whatever form it exists—should be limited to prosecuting and exacting restitution from those who initiate violence against, commit fraud against, or violate the property rights of others. All government actions beyond judicial and policing functions are illegitimate. That is true at every level of government. And on the national level, it means that war and violence can only be strictly defensive in nature.

But in spite of the simplicity, consistency, and morality of libertarianism, liberals and conservatives have a problem with libertarians. When they are not smearing them as irreligious, uncompassionate, ignorant of human nature, moral relativists, and materialistic, or accusing them of being naive, utopian, impractical, individualistic, and idealistic, liberals and conservatives castigate libertarians for offering nothing but complaints, criticisms, and condemnations of government, while never offering any real solutions. That, of course, is simply not true. Libertarians have put forth as many solutions as there are issues. The problem is that liberals and conservatives just don't like the no-nonsense solutions offered by libertarians.

Wrong solutions

Liberals and Democrats believe that they have the solutions to all of the issues facing the country. The minimum wage should be increased. Taxes should be raised on "the rich" to make them pay their "fair share." Fighting climate change should be one of the top priorities of government. The use of coal and other fossil fuels should be phased out. The government should take steps to reduce income inequality. Companies should have to increase the family and medical leave they offer their employees. All companies should be required to offer sick leave. Federal job-training programs should be expanded. College education should be free so that no student has to take out student loans. Welfare should be expanded to protect the most vulnerable of America's children. Refundable tax credits should be expanded. Every American should have health insurance. "The poor" should have better access to free medical care, including contraception and abortions. Unemployment benefits should be extended. The *Citizens United* Supreme Court decision should be overturned. There should be more government intervention in the economy and more regulation of business. And of course, more Democrats should be elected to office.

Conservatives and Republicans likewise believe that they have the solutions to all of the issues facing the country. Americans need to elect Republican presidents so that they can appoint conservative Supreme Court justices. There should be a balanced-budget amendment to the Constitution. Stipulations should be put on a country receiving U.S. foreign aid. The states need to call a constitutional convention to institute necessary reforms to the federal government. The president should be given line-item veto power. The tax code should be simplified. The income tax should be changed to a flat income tax or a national sales tax such as the Fair Tax. Tax loopholes should be closed. Social Security and certain other government programs should be privatized with government oversight. Obamacare should be repealed and replaced with something else. Defense spending should be increased. The size of the military should be larger. The Navy needs more ships. The Air Force needs more planes. Congressmen should be subject to term limits. Welfare programs should have more work requirements. Vouchers should be given to parents so they can get their children out of failing public schools and send them to the school of their choice. Businesses employing illegals should be heavily fined. Congress should implement the suggestions in policy papers written by conservative think tanks. And of course, more Republicans should be elected to office.

Both Left and Right, Democrat and Republican, liberal and conservative believe that the solutions to all the issues facing the country are to be found in new legislation, reform measures, a fairer tax system, more government accountability, increasing government efficiency, eliminating waste, and rooting out fraud. Oh, and, Social Security and Medicare should be "saved" for future generations.

Libertarian solutions

It is libertarians who indeed have the solutions to all the issues facing the country. And not only that, their solutions are clear, simple, consistent, logical, and reasonable. Their solutions aren't found in some think tank's policy paper. Their solutions aren't found in some 500-page bill that members of Congress won't even read before voting on. Their solutions don't concern reform, gradualism, privatization, or making the government more efficient. Their solutions can be adopted immediately—no ridiculous ten-year plans to balance the budget. Their solutions won't cost anything to implement. Their solutions are permanent—they don't have to be renewed, revisited, or reevaluated every year. Their solutions are based on principle, not politics.

So, what are the libertarian solutions that both liberals and conservatives are so opposed to? In what follows, I will list fifteen wide-ranging issues of varying degrees of importance, along with typical questions asked about the issue by liberals and conservatives, followed by the no-nonsense libertarian solution.

1. Issue: unemployment benefits. Should unemployment benefits be extended? For how long should they be extended? Should payments be increased? By how much should payments be increased? Should any extension or increase be temporary or permanent? Solution: Since the government has no authority to take money from those who work and give it to those who don't, unemployment benefits should be ended as well as the taxes on employers that partially fund the program. Unemployment insurance should be purchased on the free market just like fire, car, homeowners', and life insurance.

2. Issue: the drug war. Should marijuana be legal for medical purposes? Should marijuana be legalized and taxed and regulated like tobacco? Should the possession of small amounts of drugs be criminalized? Should the sentences of those imprisoned for nonviolent drug crimes be reduced? Should the government focus more on prevention and treatment than probation and prison? Should sentencing disparities for crack and powder cocaine be reduced? Solution: Since the government has no authority to prohibit the manufacture, sale, possession, or use of any drug, the drug war should be ended immediately, the DEA should be shut down and all of its employees laid off, and all Americans imprisoned for nonviolent drug crimes should be pardoned and released. Drugs should be a commodity on the free market just like cigarettes, beer, wine, whiskey, and bananas.

3. Issue: food stamps. Should food stamps be made available to more low-income families? Should benefits be reduced? Should there be a work requirement to receive benefits? Should only wholesome foodstuffs be legal for purchase with food stamps? Solution: Since the government has no authority to take money from some Americans and give it to other Americans in the form of food assistance, the food-stamp program should be abolished. All food assistance to the poor should be provided by families, neighborhoods, civic clubs, restaurants, farms, charitable organizations, food drives, religious institutions, and concerned individuals, but all without funding of any kind from the government.

4. Issue: foreign aid. Should countries receiving U.S. foreign aid be

expected to vote with the United States at the United Nations? Should aid be tied to a country's human rights record? Should allies of the United States receive more aid? Should aid be limited to disaster relief? Should the military be used to provide disaster relief? Solution: Since the government has no authority to take money from Americans and give it to foreigners or their governments, all foreign aid in any form it is given should be eliminated immediately. Any American who wants to help the underprivileged or disaster-stricken in another country can do so at any time on his own or through any number of private organizations.

5. Issue: AMTRAK. Should AMTRAK increase its fares in an attempt to be profitable? Should more routes be added? Should speeds be lowered in some areas? Should more attention be devoted to safety? Solution: Since the government has authority to neither own nor operate a rail service, all of AMTRAK's assets should be sold to the highest bidder and all of its employees laid off. All passenger rail traffic in the United States—like freight traffic—should be privately owned and operated.

6. Issue: job training. Should job-training programs be expanded? Should existing programs be reformed? Should some be eliminated? Should some be consolidated? Solution: Since the government has authority to neither institute nor operate job-training programs, they should all be eliminated. All job-training programs should be private programs run by companies seeking skilled workers, charities wanting to help the unskilled and economically disadvantaged, or for-profit companies willing to offer a service that meets a need, but all without funding of any kind from the government.

7. Issue: Obamacare. Should Obamacare be replaced with some other program? Should insurance companies have to cover those with pre-existing conditions? Should insurance companies be required to eliminate annual and lifetime spending caps? Should the government subsidize the health-insurance premiums of low-income Americans? Solution: Since the government has no authority to dictate anything to insurance companies, subsidize anyone's health-insurance premiums, or mandate that employers provide a service to their employees or that individuals purchase a service, Obamacare should be abolished in its entirety and not be replaced with anything.

8. Issue: minimum wage. Should the government raise the minimum wage? How much should it be raised? Should future increases be tied to inflation? Should a lower minimum wage be instituted for students and teenagers? Solution: Since the government has no authority to institute a price floor for labor, there should be no federal minimum wage. All wages should be freely negotiated between employers and employees.

9. Issue: Medicare and Medicaid. Should doctors be paid more for seeing Medicare and Medicaid patients? Should the federal government provide more money to the states for Medicaid? Should the Medicare

payroll tax be increased? Should the age to begin receiving Medicare be increased? Should more low-income Americans be made eligible for Medicaid? Should more attempts be made to reduce the rampant fraud in these programs? Solution: Since the government has no authority to subsidize any American's health insurance or health care, pay for anyone's prescription drugs, or operate health-care programs, Medicare and Medicaid should be abolished. All health care and health insurance should be handled by the free market with no government regulation, mandates, or interference.

10. Issue: farm programs. Should farm subsidies be increased? Should farmers be guaranteed a price for their commodities at least equal to the cost of growing or raising that commodity? Solution: Since the government has no authority to take money from some Americans and give it to other Americans who work as farmers, all farm subsidies should be ended immediately. Farming should be treated just like any other business. If a farmer can't make a profit without government assistance, then he should sell his farm and find another line of work.

11. Issue: space exploration. Should NASA's budget be increased? By how much? Should astronauts go back to the moon? Should NASA undertake a mission to Mars? How much of the cost of the international space station should NASA pay for? Solution: Since the government has no authority to explore space or study space, NASA should be abolished and all of its assets sold to the highest bidder. All space exploration, study, and travel should be handled by the free market with no government direction, oversight, or funding.

12. Issue: the TSA. Should TSA agents be held more accountable for their thefts from travelers? Should pat-downs be less intrusive? Should all travelers have to remove their shoes? Should the size limit of allowable containers with liquids be increased? Solution: Since the government has no authority to provide security for private businesses, the TSA should be abolished. Airports and airlines should handle their own security just like banks, hospitals, and stores.

13. Issue: welfare. Should cash payments under the TANF program be reduced? Should the WIC program be expanded to more low-income women? Should the amount of housing vouchers be increased in high-rent cities? Should welfare benefits have a time limit for one to receive them? Should welfare recipients be required to take a drug test? Should welfare be reformed? Solution: Since the government has no authority to take money from some Americans and give it in any form to other Americans, all welfare programs should be eliminated. All charity and assistance should be provided voluntarily.

14. Issue: Social Security. What should be done to save Social Security? Should taxes be increased? Should COLAs be eliminated? Should benefits be reduced? Should it be means-tested like the government's regular welfare programs? Should it be privatized? Solution: Since the

government has no authority to manage a retirement or disability program, the Social Security program should be ended along with the taxes on employers and employees that partially fund the program. All retirement planning should be done by means of the free market.

15. Issue: grants. Should government grants for scientific or medical research be limited to important things that could benefit a large number of Americans? Should government cultural grants be withheld if some Americans deem what is funded to be blasphemous or pornographic? Solution: Since the government has no authority to take money from some Americans to subsidize the research or cultural activities of individuals or organizations, all grants should be canceled and all grant-making agencies abolished. It is on the free market that all grants should be sought.

These libertarian solutions have been available in books and articles, and on the Internet for years. They are exactly what is to be expected from libertarians because of their principled consistency. But these solutions have also been right under the noses of liberals and conservatives. Not only is the government instituting, operating, funding, mandating, and carrying out all of these illegitimate purposes of government, none of these government actions is authorized by the Constitution. That is why I continually pointed out that the government has no authority to do any of them. The fact that liberals and conservatives accept those government actions as legitimate—merely disagreeing on some details of the actions—when the Constitution they profess to follow doesn't authorize any of them, shows just how utterly devoid of any principles they are.

The libertarian solution is not just simple, consistent, and moral, it is also constitutional, and should therefore be embraced, wholeheartedly and immediately, by Americans of all political persuasions.

*****

WHAT LIBERTARIANS WANT FROM GOVERNMENT

Americans of all political persuasions want something from the government, including libertarians. But what libertarians want from the government is quite different from what liberals and conservatives want.

Liberals want much from government. To get an idea of just how much they want, just look at the new 2016 Democratic Party platform. Liberals, progressives, and socialists—all of whom always vote Democratic—want the government to:

• Raise workers' wages
• Support working families
• Help more workers share in near-record corporate profits
• Expand access to affordable housing and homeownership

• Protect and expand Social Security
• Ensure a secure and dignified retirement
• Revitalize our nation's Postal Service
• Build a 21st-century infrastructure
• Foster a manufacturing renaissance
• Create good-paying clean energy jobs
• Create jobs for America's young people
• Make the wealthy pay their fair share of taxes
• Promote trade that is fair and benefits American workers
• End systemic racism
• Close the racial wealth gap
• Institute non-discrimination protections for all LGBT Americans
• Invest in rural America
• End poverty and invest in communities left behind
• Promote arts and culture
• Combat climate change
• Build a clean energy economy
• Secure environmental and climate justice
• Be a strong advocate for the rights and opportunities of women and girls around the world
• Support sexual and reproductive health and rights around the globe
• Prevent drilling in the Arctic
• Continue to have the strongest military in the world
• Defeat ISIS, al Qaeda, and their affiliates
• Provide development assistance to foreign countries
• Make debt-free college a reality
• Support historically black colleges and universities and minority-serving institutions
• Guarantee universal preschool and good schools for every child
• Secure universal health care
• Support community health centers
• Reduce prescription drug costs
• Combat drug and alcohol addiction

Oh, and how could I forget, the government should protect a woman's right to "safe and legal abortion—regardless of where she lives, how much money she makes, or how she is insured."

There are a number of things that conservatives want from the government as well. It is a common misconception that conservatives favor limited government. The truth is, the only limited government that conservatives want is a government limited to one controlled by conservatives.

As usual, many things in the new Republican Party platform sound good and echo the conservative mantra of the Constitution, limited government, federalism, free enterprise, free trade, free markets, and individual freedom. Too bad that even the "conservative" Republicans neither believe nor follow the "good" parts of their party platform.

Not all is well with the Republican Party platform, however.

Instead of cutting taxes, Republicans want the government to "simplify" the tax code and "eliminate loopholes."

Instead of real free trade, Republicans want the government to negotiate "better trade agreements."

Instead of ending federal involvement in the housing market, Republicans want the government to "scale back the federal role in the housing market," institute "reforms," and "review" federal regulations.

Instead of abolishing the TSA, Republicans want the government to just abolish its union.

Instead of ending government space travel and exploration, Republicans want the government to create more "public-private partnerships between NASA, the Department of Defense, and commercial companies."

Instead of eliminating occupational licensing, Republicans want the government to "reduce the occupational licensing laws."

Instead of eliminating funding for Planned Parenthood, Republicans want the government to just withhold funds so long as organizations like Planned Parenthood "provide or refer for elective abortions or sell fetal body parts rather than provide healthcare."

Instead of eliminating the SNAP (food stamp program), Republicans want the government to "separate the administration of SNAP from the Department of Agriculture."

Instead of cutting the federal budget, Republicans want the government to balance the budget.

Instead of allowing businesses to hire whomever they choose, Republicans want the government to require them to use its E-verify program.

Instead of eliminating federal regulations, Republicans want the government to enact "sensible" regulations and "cap the costs federal agencies could impose on the economy in any given year."

Instead of abolishing Social Security, Republicans want the government to "preserve and modernize" the Social Security program.

Instead of abolishing Medicaid, Republicans want the government to "preserve the promise of Medicaid" by making the program "a vehicle for good health in an entirely new era."

Instead of abolishing Medicare, Republicans want the government to "save Medicare by modernizing it, empowering its participants, and putting it on a secure financial footing."

Instead of cutting the bloated budget of the strongest military on earth, Republicans want the government to "restore our nation's military might" and rebuild the military "into the strongest on earth."

Instead of ending all foreign aid, Republicans want the government to provide "a new model of foreign assistance that helps ensure taxpayer dollars are spent on projects that are effective, results-driven, transparent, and accountable."

What is remarkable about the Republican Party platform is what it doesn't say about things that conservatives generally support—like the federal government's war on drugs. And of course, one of the hallmarks of conservatives is that they want the government to incessantly meddle in the affairs of other countries, build military bases on every continent, police the world, and station troops all over the globe.

In contrast to the 55 pages of the Democratic Party platform and the 66 pages of the Republican Party platform, the platform of the Libertarian Party consists of just 7 pages. Here is what it says about the proper role of government:

> The prescribed role of government is to protect the rights of every individual including the right to life, liberty, and property.

> The protection of individual rights is the only proper purpose of government.

> The only proper role of government in the economic realm is to protect property rights, adjudicate disputes, and provide a legal framework in which voluntary trade is protected.

The military should be "sufficient" to "defend the United States against aggression," but "the United States should both avoid entangling alliances and abandon its attempts to act as policeman for the world." U.S. foreign policy "should emphasize defense against attack from abroad and enhance the likelihood of peace by avoiding foreign entanglements." The "current U.S. government policy of foreign intervention, including military and economic aid" should be ended. Criminal laws should be limited to those that actually violate "the rights of others through force or fraud, or to deliberate actions that place others involuntarily at significant risk of harm." The government should not interfere "in the areas of voluntary and contractual relations among individuals."

The difference between the Libertarian Party and all other political parties is a simple one: "All political parties other than our own grant to government the right to regulate the lives of individuals and seize the fruits of their labor without their consent." Indeed, this is the root of the difference between libertarians and everyone else. Most non-libertarians deem it completely appropriate for government:

> (1) to punish people for engaging in entirely peaceful, voluntary, and consensual actions that do not aggress against the person or property of others; or

(2) to take people's resources against their will, by force if necessary, and transfer or redistribute them to other citizens or foreigners as the government sees fit.

Libertarians maintain that people should be free from government interference to live their lives any way they desire and engage in any economic activity they choose as long as their actions are peaceful and consensual and they don't violate the personal or property rights of others.

It is too bad that the Libertarian Party candidates for president and vice president deviate significantly from both their party platform and libertarian theory.

What do libertarians want from government? If they haven't violated the personal or property rights of someone else, libertarians just want to be left alone.

*****

SHOULD LIBERTARIANS BE CONSERVATIVES?

In a recent article for the online journal *Public Discourse*, conservative Jay Richards asks the question: "Should Libertarians Be Conservatives?: The Tough Cases of Abortion and Marriage."

Richards is Director and Senior Fellow of the Center on Wealth, Poverty, and Morality at the Discovery Institute, a Visiting Scholar at the Institute for Faith, Work, and Economics, and co-author, with James Robison, of the New York Times bestselling book *Indivisible: Restoring Faith, Family, and Freedom Before It's Too Late* (FaithWords, 2012). Richards and I have many common interests: Christianity, theology, economics, politics. He sounds like my kind of guy—except that he's not.

Richards is your typical "criticize the welfare state while you support the warfare state conservative." I wasn't sure at first, but after looking at his new book *Indivisible*, and especially his remarks in chapter five ("Bearing the Sword") on pacifism, just war, the war on terror, the military, and defense spending, my suspicions were confirmed.

Richards maintains in his *Public Discourse* article that libertarians "tend to disagree with conservatives on social issues." He views the issues of abortion and marriage as "the two greatest sources of conflict between libertarians and conservatives." He believes that "there is a tacit if inarticulate conservative wisdom that recognizes that the libertarian commitment to free markets and limited government is best preserved within a broader conservative context." He posits that this "conservative wisdom" should appeal to the "'everyman libertarian' who values limited governments, individual rights, and free markets, but is not otherwise committed to a deeply libertarian philosophy." Richards concludes: "We conservatives need to strengthen our base without alienating our near allies. One way to do that is to show how the central convictions of 'everyman libertarians' can find a peaceful repose in a conservative home."

Baloney.

One does not have to be a conservative to oppose abortion and defend traditional marriage. And one should certainly not be a conservative when it comes to other important issues.

I have argued that because the non-aggression axiom is central to libertarianism, and because force is justified only in self-defense, and because it is wrong to threaten or initiate violence against a person or his property, and because killing is the ultimate form of aggression that, to be consistent, libertarians should be opposed to abortion.

If conservatives are so committed to pro-life principles, then why did they continue to fund Planned Parenthood during the Bush presidency? Why did John McCain and others vote to confirm pro-abortion judges like Stephen Breyer, Ruth Ginsburg, and David Souter to the Supreme Court? Why did George H. W. Bush even nominate Souter?

I agree with Richards that "just as government may not redefine our rights as individuals, it has no authority to redefine marriage." Marriage has always been and will forever be the union of a man and a woman. God created Adam and Eve, not Adam and Steve. Anything else is just cohabitation, fornication, civil union, voluntary contract, or domestic partnership, whether it is called a marriage or not. Same-sex marriage, which is not even supported by some homosexuals, is like a square circle, solid jello, or liquid steel.

But more importantly, and as I have also argued, the state should get out of the marriage business. Why do governments at every level require a license for people to engage in consensual, peaceful activity? And not only that, in some states there is not only a hefty fee to get a marriage license, but a required waiting period or recommended premarital counseling course. Why do two individuals need the state's permission to get married? Who knows better if two individuals are fit to be married than the two individuals? If they want advice regarding their union, they can consult their pastor, parents, co-workers, and/or friends. It is none of the state's business.

Marriage predated the state. It needs no protection, regulation, or monitoring by the state to continue its existence.

The real threat to the institution of marriage is not homosexuals wanting heterosexuals to recognize their same-sex marriages, it is Christians standing in a church and saying "for better for worse, for richer for poorer, in sickness and in health, to love and to cherish, till death us do part" and then getting divorced a few years later. The real assault on marriage is by serial adulterers who preach family values like the thrice-married Newt Gingrich. As Doug Bandow has recently said: "When it comes to sex the Republican Party is divided. A few members actually don't believe it is the government's business. However, the GOP is full of leaders with multiple marriages engaging in multiple affairs who lecture everyone else about the importance of sexual morality."

So, should libertarians be conservatives? Did not Ronald Reagan famously say: "The very heart and soul of conservatism is libertarianism"? The issues of abortion and same-sex marriage are used by conservatives to sucker pro-life, pro-family libertarians into believing that they should abandon libertarianism for conservatism. This would be a terrible mistake, for there is much more to conservatism than its emphasis on social issues.

There are four areas I would like to briefly mention that show the incontrovertible divide that exists between libertarians and conservatives.

First, the state. As concisely summed up by Mises Institute chairman Lew Rockwell:

> The problem with American conservatism is that it hates the left more than the state, loves the past more than liberty, feels a greater attachment to nationalism than to the idea of self-determination, believes brute force is the answer to all social problems, and thinks it is better to impose truth rather than risk losing one soul to heresy. It has never understood the idea of freedom as a self-ordering principle of society. It has never seen the state as the enemy of what conservatives purport to favor. It has always looked to presidential power as the saving grace of what is right and true about America.

Second, the welfare state. As recently explained by Future of Freedom Foundation president Jacob Hornberger:

> Conservatives are having a heyday calling President Obama a socialist. What they block out of their minds is that by their own measure, they are socialists too. . . . But while conservatives want to protect the assets of the rich from IRS confiscation and welfare-state redistribution, conservatives cannot deny that they themselves also favor the welfare-state concept of taxing people so that the state can redistribute the money to others. The only thing different between conservatives and liberals is the identity of the people they wish to tax and the identity of people they wish to receive the loot.

Third, war. I have said on more than one occasion that the very heart and soul of conservatism is war. Patriotism, Americanism, and being a real conservative are now equated with support for war, torture, and militarism. I firmly stand by this assertion that I first made in 2009, although it was true long before then.

And fourth, the drug war. Out of one side of their mouth conservatives talk about individual liberty, free markets, limited government, less intrusive government, cutting regulations, personal responsibility, and the Constitution, but at the same time they say out of the other side of their mouth that if you buy, sell, or possess a substance the government doesn't approve of then we will lock you up in a cage. And if you buy, sell, or possess too much, then we will throw away the key.

Should libertarians be conservatives? To be consistent, must pro-life, pro-family libertarians be conservatives? Absolutely not.

*****

CONSTITUTIONAL CONSERVATIVE OR LIBERTARIAN?

Libertarians—those who believe that violence is proper only in the defense of person or property and who believe that people have the fundamental right to do anything that's peaceful—have an image problem, according to some "libertarian-leaning" conservatives. Although those conservatives claim to espouse many libertarian viewpoints, they prefer to shy away from the term "libertarian" and instead call themselves "constitutional conservatives."

Now, the issue here is plainly a philosophical one, and not a matter of linguistics. Although the specific adjectives one uses to describe his political philosophy are irrelevant alongside what he actually believes, they do make a philosophical statement about one's political views.

Consider, first of all, conservatism. Although some libertarians may have said and done some things in the name of libertarianism that they had no business doing, I think it is conservatives who have not only an image problem, but a real philosophical problem as well.

I have written a few times that the very heart and soul of conservatism is war. Patriotism, Americanism, and being a real conservative are now equated with support for war, torture, and militarism. I stand by my assertion.

An amendment (no. 232) last year to H.R. 1, an appropriations bill that included spending for the Department of Defense, would have limited the use of funds for U.S. military operations in Afghanistan to $10 billion "to reduce the funding for Afghanistan sufficiently to leave enough funds to provide for the safe and orderly withdrawal of our troops but not funding for ongoing combat operations." Only 7 of 239 Republicans in the House voted for it. The ones who voted against the amendment are the same Republicans in the House who boast how conservative they are.

But it's not just Republicans in Congress who are war-crazy. The conservative faithful who listen to conservative talk-show hosts such as Sean Hannity and Rush Limbaugh, read conservative magazines such as *National Review* and the *Weekly Standard*, support conservative institutions such as the Heritage Foundation and the American Enterprise Institute, attend conservative meetings such as CPAC's in Washington, D.C., and generally support anything the Republicans in Congress do that is pro-war, pro-empire, or pro-militarism.

But the trouble with conservatism goes much deeper. As Lew Rockwell, chairman of the Ludwig von Mises Institute, has written,

> The problem with American conservatism is that it hates the left more than the state, loves the past more than liberty, feels a greater attachment to nationalism than to the idea of self-determination, believes brute force is the answer to all social problems, and thinks it is better to impose truth rather than risk losing one soul to heresy. It has never understood the idea of freedom as a self-ordering principle of society. It has never seen the state as the enemy of what conservatives purport to favor. It has always looked to presidential power as the saving grace of what is right and true about America.

It is indeed strange that "libertarian-leaning" conservatives think it is libertarians who have the image problem.

I recognize that there are some conservatives who love liberty, loathe Republicans such as George W. Bush and Newt Gingrich, and oppose the wars in Iraq and Afghanistan. Many of them call themselves "constitutional conservatives" because they are realize that mainstream conservatives have departed in great measure from the Constitution. Some might also say that they are "libertarian leaning," but—for whatever reason—shy away from the term "libertarian."

Unlibertarian Constitution

I'm all in favor of following the Constitution, but definitely not in every respect. There are some things in the Constitution that, while obviously constitutional, are certainly not libertarian. There have been things in the Constitution that were decidedly unlibertarian but have since been changed by an amendment, such as the protection of slavery and Prohibition. Those changes are a good thing. However, there yet remains the power of the federal government to tax with or without the Sixteenth Amendment, as Sheldon Richman has shown in a series of articles in *Freedom Daily* (August–October, 2006). The federal government, in the "takings clause" of the Fifth Amendment to the Constitution ("nor shall private property be taken for public use, without just compensation"), assumes that it has the legitimate power to take Americans' private property. The purpose of the taking and the payment for the taking are irrelevant if the owner doesn't want to sell.

Conservatives sometimes, and rightly so, criticize Congress and the president for going to war, as the United States has done many times since World War II, without a constitutionally required declaration of war. But would a declaration of war against Iraq and Afghanistan have made those unjust and unnecessary wars more just or more necessary?

And then there are the ambiguous clauses in the Constitution such as the "general welfare" clause, the "commerce" clause, and the "necessary and proper" clause. In the early years of American history, a national bank was said by some in Congress and by the Supreme Court to be justified because of the "necessary and proper" clause. And most recently, in 2009, House Speaker Nancy Pelosi claimed that the constitutional justification for Obamacare was the "commerce" clause.

A major problem with conservatives is that most of their talk about the Constitution is just a lot of hot air. Just look at the empty promises, grandiose claims, vain assurances, and blatant lies in the House Republican "Pledge to America." Does anyone actually take seriously anything the Republicans say about the Constitution in their pledge? Does anyone think for a minute that the statement in the pledge about requiring "each bill moving through Congress to include a clause citing specific constitutional authority upon which the bill is justified" will actually prevent any unconstitutional legislation from being passed? And who received the "Defender of the Constitution Award" at last year's CPAC conference? It was former Secretary of Defense Donald Rumsfeld.

Still another problem is that conservatives who claim to revere the Constitution generally hold not only to some nonlibertarian opinions, but to some unconstitutional ones as well. Constitutional conservatives should unequivocally oppose the war on drugs, Social Security, Medicare, Medicaid, federal aid to or control of education, all welfare programs, all federal regulations, and most federal departments and agencies. That would include not just the "liberal" CPB and NEA, but the whole alphabet soup of federal departments, agencies, commissions, corporations, administrations, and bureaus such as the EPA, NASA, CPSC, ATF, SEC, TVA, FEMA, and FCC. When was the last time a conservative congressman, politician, talk-show host, pundit, think-tank, magazine, or writer called for the wholesale elimination of any of those bureaucracies because it is unconstitutional?

Constitutional conservative or libertarian? When it comes to the questions of individual liberty, peace and nonintervention, free markets, personal freedom and responsibility, and limited government, only one philosophy really measures up.

*****

CAN CONSERVATIVES BE LIBERTARIANS?

Some libertarians are applauding the recent Supreme Court decisions relating to same-sex marriage, not because of anything to do with the

Constitution, limited government, federalism, individual liberty, the proper role of government, or separating marriage from the state, but because they just happen to like the idea of same-sex marriage. As I have argued elsewhere, they are entitled to their opinion, but there is no libertarian "position" on same-sex marriage.

On Tuesday, March 26, the Supreme Court heard oral arguments for and against California's Proposition 8, a ballot initiative passed in 2008 that eliminated the right of same-sex couples to marry that the California Supreme Court had recognized.

On Wednesday, March 27, the Supreme Court heard oral arguments on the merits and demerits of the Defense of Marriage Act (DOMA), federal legislation passed in 1996 that defined marriage as only "a legal union between one man and one woman as husband and wife" and that permits states to refuse to recognize same-sex marriages performed in other states.

On June 26, 2013, the Supreme Court ruled that the section of DOMA that defined marriage (sec. 3) was unconstitutional, thus ending the ban on same-sex married couples being recognized as married and eligible to receive federal benefits. The Court also let stand a 2010 federal district court ruling that declared Proposition 8 to be unconstitutional.

Conservatives who believe in traditional marriage and consider the term "same-sex marriage" to be an oxymoron are disturbed by the Supreme Court's rulings. This is not generally because they find fault with any legal or constitutional arguments, but because the Court did not, in their eyes, rule in favor of traditional marriage—legal and constitutional arguments be damned.

But conservatives are also disturbed by what they see as libertarian support for same-sex marriage. This is not generally because they find fault with any arguments about individual liberty and the proper role of government, but because libertarians are not, in their eyes, upholding traditional marriage—philosophical arguments be damned.

The issue of same-sex marriage is one of three, the other two being abortion and drug legalization, that I believe keeps some conservatives from becoming libertarians.

When I say conservatives, I don't mean political conservatives who blindly follow Ann Coulter, Rush Limbaugh, Sean Hannity, Bill O'Reilly, and Mark Levin, and watch Fox News. The only limited government they want is a government limited to one controlled by conservatives in the Republican Party.

When I say conservatives, I do mean social conservatives, many of whom are religious, mainly nominally Christian, but also theological conservatives. Their feelings about homosexuality, abortion, and drug use range from disapproval to disgust. They may "lean libertarian" on economic issues, have a healthy skepticism of the political process, loathe the size and scope of the federal government, and even espouse a noninterventionist foreign policy, or at least a healthy Buchanan-esque reserved foreign policy. They are good candidates for libertarians, and would be more interested in libertarianism were it not for some libertarians equating the agitation for same-sex marriage as a battle for human rights, terming abortion a woman's right to choose or expelling a trespasser or parasite, and/or and extolling the joys of the recreational use of marijuana.

When I say libertarians, I mean those who believe that a free, just, and peaceful society is grounded in the nonaggression principle—that it is always wrong to threaten or employ violence against someone except in defense of one's person or property. And it is just as wrong for the government to do it, and even worse, considering its vast resources and the incredible damage it can do. Libertarianism is a political philosophy that is concerned with the proper use of force. The only proper role of coercion or violence is to defend person and property against coercion or violence. These should not be used against anyone who has not himself deprived someone of life, liberty, or property. This does not mean that coercion or violence should actually be employed, just that it might rightly be. Coercion or violence that goes beyond just defense is unjust aggression. Peaceful and consensual activity should never be aggressed against. But, of course, this doesn't mean that all such activity is moral, wholesome, and beneficial.

It is no wonder that some conservatives have mischaracterized libertarianism—some libertarians have done the same thing. Libertarianism cannot be simplistically defined as "fiscally conservative, socially liberal." Libertarianism is a philosophy of life, not a lifestyle. Libertarians who view libertarianism as more of a social attitude than a political theory are making it something it is not. No one is more libertarian than someone else because he celebrates more alternative lifestyles rather than tolerates them.

Although some conservatives have mischaracterized libertarianism as depreciating tradition, rejecting religion, and disdaining morality, nothing could be further from the truth. I believe it is entirely possible to be a resolute social and theological conservative and at the same time be an uncompromising and hardcore libertarian.

Conservatives can and should be libertarians because there is nothing inherently libertarian about same-sex marriage, legalized abortion, or recreational drug use.

Same-Sex Marriage

Same-sex marriage is now legal in California, Connecticut, Delaware, Iowa, Maine, Maryland, Massachusetts, Minnesota, New Hampshire, New York, Rhode Island, Vermont, Washington, and the District of Columbia. Section 2 of DOMA, which was *not* ruled unconstitutional by the

Supreme Court (although I believe it eventually will be), allows the 37 other states to refuse to recognize same-sex marriages performed in these 13 states (and Washington D.C.). However, since the federal government now recognizes same-sex marriages performed in these states, it is only just a matter of time before Uncle Sam sticks his nose further into the institution of marriage and imposes uniformity on the entire country.

But even if every state in the union legalized same-sex marriage, that still wouldn't make it a marriage. Fulton J. Sheen, the Catholic television preacher of the 1950s, although not talking about marriage, said something profound that illustrates perfectly what I am saying: "I am free to draw a triangle if I give it three sides, but not, in a stroke of broadmindedness, fifty-seven sides." You are free to call your cat a dog, but that doesn't mean you have the right to enter your cat in dog shows.

Marriage has always been and will forever be the union of a man and a woman—anything else is just cohabitation and fornication.

Now, as a libertarian, I am for absolute freedom of contract: partnerships, unions, agreements, arrangements, pacts, compacts, conventions, relationships, associations, companionships, contracts—between anyone: homosexuals of the same sex, heterosexuals of the same sex, homosexuals of the opposite sex, heterosexuals of the opposite sex, a homosexual and a heterosexual, three or more people of any sex and sexual orientation—for any reason or purpose.

But as a libertarian, I never make unqualified, ambiguous statements like "I support same-sex marriage." That could mean just about anything:

• I support homosexuality.
• I believe in a free society.
• I see nothing unnatural about homosexual relationships.
• I believe in individual liberty.
• I don't believe in any moral restraints.
• I believe in live and let live.
• I see nothing wrong with homosexuals adopting children.
• I believe in the nonaggression principle
• I think gay sex is a wholesome activity.
• I don't believe in discrimination.
• I see nothing wrong with Heather having two mommies.
• I believe in personal freedom.
• I support the government redefining things to pacify a vocal minority.
• I believe in equality.
• I support the government intruding into the institution of marriage.
• I don't support the government intruding into the institution of marriage.

Same-sex couples are free to get "married" and call their relationship a "marriage," just like they are free to call red green, a circle a square, and chocolate vanilla. They just shouldn't expect the rest of us, and the government, to follow suit.

Unlike some libertarians, I am concerned that same-sex marriage, because of unlibertarian federal and state discrimination laws, will result in ministers being told that they have to marry same-sex couples, orphanages being told that they have to place children in same-sex households, and photographers being told that they have to photograph same-sex marriages—or suffer penalty of law.

Should the Supreme Court have ruled section 3 of DOMA unconstitutional? I could argue both ways. One thing is for sure: there should be no federal tax, health, retirement, marriage, or nonmarriage benefits for anyone to sue over. And not only should the federal government get out of marriage, it should also get out of everything else. State and local governments should get out of marriage as well.

Marriage predates the nation-state, society at large, countries, states, provinces, counties, cities, towns, local communities, jurisdictions, all government bodies and judicial systems, and the church. It doesn't need government protection or regulation.

Conservatives, and especially religious conservatives, sometimes argue that same-sex marriage will destroy traditional marriage. I've got some old news for them: traditional marriage has already been destroyed, but not by government or gays. It is Christians who have destroyed traditional marriage. Just look at the divorce rate, even among conservative Christians. Since Massachusetts became the first state to legalize same-sex marriage in 2003, how many professing Christians have stood at the altar and said "I do" only to say "I don't" a few years later?

Legalized Abortion

Social conservatives are particularly concerned about abortion. But so are many libertarians—as I believe they should be. They are just not as vocal as "pro-choice" libertarians.

I have argued here and here that because the non-aggression axiom is central to libertarianism, and because force is justified only in self-defense, and because it is wrong to threaten or initiate violence against a person or his property, and because killing is the ultimate form of aggression that, to be consistent, libertarians should be opposed to abortion. The fact that some of them are not is irrelevant to the question of whether conservatives can be libertarians.

Why should it be considered libertarian to kill a baby in the womb or unlibertarian to oppose such killing? There is nothing libertarian about a woman choosing to kill her unborn child for getting in the way of her lifestyle.

But the Libertarian Party says . . . . Who cares what the Libertarian Party says? A common mistake of conservatives is to identify libertarians and libertarianism with the Libertarian Party. The Libertarian Party does not, and does not profess to, speak for all or even a majority of libertarians. And why should a party named Libertarian that runs a nonlibertarian for president like Bob Barr be trusted to speak for libertarians?

Being pro-life and libertarian is not contradictory. However, being pro-life and conservative may very well be because of the conservative propensity to support acts of violence committed by the U.S. military. Because of their opposition to senseless foreign wars and an interventionist foreign policy, libertarians can actually be more consistently pro-life than conservatives.

Recreational Drug Use

I don't know of any social conservatives who use illicit psychoactive drugs or recommend that anyone else do so, at least they don't make it public. Many religious social conservatives not only don't use illegal drugs, they also abstain from or limit their use of alcohol. That is my choice; that is their choice. But none of this has anything to do with anyone else being freely and lawfully able to use or abuse whatever drugs—legal or otherwise—they choose.

The libertarian approach to drug use is a simple one: there isn't one. If you *don't* choose to cook meth, smoke marijuana, snort cocaine, or shoot up with heroin for moral, ethical, religious, health, safety, or any other reason then fine—Just Say No. But if you *do* choose to partake, then you are responsible for your actions while you are stoned, and your ambulance, hospital, and doctor bills if you overdose. To be a libertarian, there is no requirement that you use drugs or change your opinion about them or those who use them.

The libertarian approach to the legality of the manufacture of, "trafficking" in, and possession of drugs is also a simple one: yes. Nowhere does the Constitution authorize the federal government to have anything to do with what anyone smokes, snorts, injects, or swallows. Nowhere does the Constitution authorize the federal government to classify, prohibit, regulate, restrict, hamper, or monitor the manufacture, sale, possession, or use of any drug by anyone for any reason.

The libertarian approach to the morality of drug use is another simple one: legal doesn't necessarily mean moral. One may think that the recreational use of drugs is the most immoral thing anyone could possibly do, but that would still be no reason to look to the government to ban drugs. Furthermore, why should anyone's opinions about drug use be based on anything the government says? Today the federal government says that this drug is legal and this one is not, but tomorrow it may say just the opposite. And if you want to talk about morality, how can anyone with any sense of morality support the government arresting someone, seizing his property, ruining him financially, destroying his family, and locking him up in a cage for manufacturing or possessing certain quantities of a plant the government doesn't approve of?

Some libertarians share in the blame for this particular conservative aversion to libertarianism because of how they are so quick to call any Hollywood leftist a libertarian who calls for drug or marijuana legalization even though he may be just a dope-smoking statist.

I have written much on the evils of the drug war. See my book *The War on Drugs Is a War on Freedom*, and especially this essay titled "Should Christians Support the War on Drugs?"

The $64,000 Question

Can conservatives be libertarians? In spite of opposition from most conservatives and doubts from some libertarians, certainly they can.

*****

SHOULD LIBERTARIANS VOTE REPUBLICAN?

Constitutional conservatives, Reagan Republicans, and other conservative Republicans have no use for libertarians—except when it comes time for another election. Then they want the votes of libertarians. Although they shy away from the term "libertarian" in non-election years, they will describe themselves as libertarian-leaning when they want to sucker libertarians to vote for them on election day.

There are two things that these libertarian-leaning Republicans can't stand. The first is not voting and the second is voting for a third party.

Many libertarians simply don't vote. They know that the system is rigged. They know that you have a greater chance of being killed in a car accident on the way to the polls than of your vote making any difference. They know that there is not a dime's worth of difference between the two major parties. They know that most elections are simply contests between tweedledum and tweedledee, socialist A and national socialist B, or socialist A and fascist B. They know that even though Republicans use libertarian rhetoric, they are welfare/warfare statists just like Democrats. They know that voting for candidate D or R is like voting for Hitler to keep out Stalin or voting for Stalin to keep out Hitler. They know that voting for the lesser of two evils is still voting for evil. They agree with Noam Chomsky that "if voting could actually change anything, it would be illegal," with Mark Twain that "if voting made a difference, they wouldn't let us do it," with Charles Bukowski that "the difference between a democracy and a dictatorship is that in a democracy you vote first and take orders later; in a dictatorship you don't have to waste your time voting," with H. L. Mencken that "every election is a sort of advance auction sale of stolen goods," and with whoever said that voting just encourages the bastards. They know that only way to vote against crook A and crook B is to not vote. And libertarian Christians know that the Bible says: "Thou shalt not follow a multitude to do evil" (Exodus 23:2).

Many libertarians vote for a third party. Obviously, the Libertarian Party is their first choice. However, if no libertarian candidate is running for a particular office, they might vote for another third party, even if they don't agree with its platform, just to send a message to the Democratic and Republican Parties that they despise them. Democrats and Republicans both say that voting for a third party is wasting your vote since a third party has almost no chance of winning. But not only that, Democrats and Republicans both say or imply that you should never vote for a third party because it takes votes away from them. Republicans especially will point to particular elections that SJWs Always Lie: Takin... Vox Day they say Republicans would have won if the Libertarian Party candidate had not siphoned off votes from the Republican Party candidate. What they are really saying, of course, is that Republicans would have won these elections if they weren't indistinguishable from Democrats.

More than anything else, Republicans want libertarians to vote for them. They know that liberals, Democrats, progressives, and other socialists will never vote Republican. They would rather vote for an Obama or a Hillary than a Republican.

But why should libertarians vote Republican? Yes, it keeps those evil Democrats out of office. But then it just gives us evil Republicans. The Republican Party stands for everything libertarians oppose. Here are twenty-five things off the top of my head:

1. The Drug War
2. Gambling laws
3. Anti-discrimination laws
4. The National Instant Criminal Background Check System
5. The ATF and federal gun laws
6. Cuba sanctions
7. Indefinite detention at Guantanamo
8. Torture
9. Crony capitalism
10. Militarism
11. Foreign wars
12. The welfare state
13. The warfare state
14. The police state
15. The national security state
16. Food stamps
17. The CIA, FBI, DIA, DHS, TSA, and NSA

18. The Earned Income Tax Credit
19. Foreign aid
20. The U.S. global empire of troops and bases
21. Farm subsidies
22. Social Security
23. Medicare and Medicaid
24. The National School Lunch Program
25. Pell Grants and the Elementary and Secondary Education Act

And judging from the reaction of Republicans to the Iran deal, I don't think they would have a problem with killing Persians in Iran.

Are there individual Republicans who oppose some of these things? Certainly. But not many, and only a few things. But what about all the Republican talk about the Constitution, the free market, free enterprise, limited government, smaller government, less regulation, balanced budgets, lower taxes, property rights, and fiscal conservatism? Is it all just lies and hot air? In a word, yes.

Okay, okay, okay, say Republicans, enough already. But you libertarians should at least vote for a Republican for president so he can nominate conservative Supreme Court justices and Republicans in the Senate so they can confirm the nominations.

Is that so? Three of the most significant Supreme Court decisions in my lifetime that didn't turn out how Republicans wanted were:

Roe v. Wade (abortion)
National Federation of Independent Business v. Sebelius (Obamacare)
Obergefell v. Hodges (gay marriage)

The writer of the majority opinion in all three cases was a Republican appointee: Harry Blackmun, John Roberts, and Anthony Kennedy. And why did only three Republicans in the Senate back in 1993 vote against the confirmation of the most radical leftist on the Supreme Court, Ruth Bader Ginsburg?

Libertarians would have to be out of their mind to vote Republican.

*****

CONSERVATIVISM AND LIBERTARIANISM

When conservative politicians are trying to get the votes of libertarians and "libertarian-leaning" Republicans, they often tout the supposed affinity between conservatism and libertarianism. They claim that there is a conservative and libertarian confluence of thought on many issues. They maintain that because the real enemy of conservatism and libertarianism is liberalism, conservatives and libertarians stand on common ground. Conservatives are not averse to using libertarian rhetoric to portray themselves as advocates of libertarian principles. They often recite their mantra of the Constitution, private property, the free market, individual liberty, and limited government—as if they actually followed the Constitution, believed in the inviolability of private property, desired a free market in everything, believed in the freedom of individuals to do anything that's peaceful, and wanted a government limited to anything but one controlled by conservatives.

Reaganism

Ronald Reagan (1911–2004) is a conservative icon. Conservatives revere him as they revere the Constitution. They consider Reagan to be one of the greatest American presidents in history.   And   as   the   late president's son, Michael Reagan, has pointed out, "Conservatives love to drop my father's name and try to find candidates that act and think like he did." Conservative Republicans who want to sucker their fellow Republicans to get their votes often call themselves Reagan conservatives or Reagan Republicans. Even some libertarians romanticize Reagan.

In addition to using libertarian rhetoric and reciting their phony laissez-faire mantra, conservatives are also fond of quoting what Reagan said during an interview with *Reason* magazine back in 1975:

> If you analyze it I believe the very heart and soul of conservatism is libertarianism. I think conservatism is really a misnomer just as liberalism is a misnomer for the liberals—if we were back in the days of the Revolution, so-called conservatives today would be the Liberals and the liberals would be the Tories. The basis of conservatism is a desire for less government interference or less centralized authority or more individual freedom and this is a pretty general description also of what libertarianism is.

Reagan also said he believed that libertarianism and conservatism were traveling "the same path."

Yet, the path Reagan trod was anything but libertarian.

As a two-term governor of California, Reagan presided over a state budget increase from $5.7 to $10.8 billion. He was a tax cutter in some areas (property tax) but a tax raiser in others (sales tax). He introduced withholding to the state income-tax system. Under his administration, government funding for primary and secondary public education increased 105 percent, government support for junior colleges increased 323 percent, and government grants and loans to college students increased 900 percent. Reagan overhauled the state welfare system, reducing total welfare caseload, but also raised benefits by 30 percent and increased administrative costs. He vetoed legislation to reduce marijuana possession to a misdemeanor and signed legislation to sharply increase penalties for drug dealers.

As president, Reagan is famously remembered as a tax cutter. But, again, he was also a tax raiser. He supported the refundable Earned Income Tax Credit; eliminated "loopholes" that allowed taxpayers to hold on to more of their money; and increased corporate income taxes, Medicare taxes, Social Security taxes, and capital gains taxes. He also began the practice of taxing Social Security benefits.

The Reagan record is anything but fiscal conservatism. During his tenure, federal expenditures increased by more than 60 percent, spending on education increased by 68 percent, and health-care spending increased by 71 percent.

Reagan's deregulatory policies have been grossly overstated. During the 1980s, the Code of Federal Regulations increased in size by roughly 20 percent. Reagan also increased import barriers and quotas and expanded the agricultural subsidies.

And even though he said in a 1981 speech that "government's first duty is to protect people, not run their lives," he didn't practice what he preached when it came to drugs. Federal spending on law enforcement, prisons, and the war on drugs greatly increased, as did incarceration rates. Reagan signed legislation reinstating civil asset-forfeiture laws and mandatory minimum sentences for drug-related crimes.

His support for gun rights is mixed. And as Reagan's budget director David Stockman tells us, "Reagan tripled the size of the U.S. defense budget based on a totally phony neocon claim that the Soviet Union was on the verge of military superiority and nuclear first-strike capacity."

Doesn't sound like Reagan's conservatism was too libertarian.

Conservatism

What, then, is conservatism? Ask a hundred conservatives and you may get a hundred different answers. In his book The Conservative Mind, first published in 1953, conservative godfather Russell Kirk (1918–1994) listed and described "six canons of conservative thought" that he considered to be a summary of themes common to conservative thinkers:

1. Belief in a transcendent order, or body of natural law, which rules society as well as conscience.

2. Affection for the proliferating variety and mystery of human existence, as opposed to the narrowing uniformity, egalitarianism, and utilitarian aims of most radical systems.

3. Conviction that civilized society requires orders and classes, as against the notion of a "classless society."

4. Persuasion that freedom and property are closely linked: separate property from private possession, and Leviathan becomes master of all.

5. Faith in prescription and distrust of "sophisters, calculators, and economists" who would reconstruct society upon abstract designs.

6. Recognition that change may not be salutary reform: hasty innovation may be a devouring conflagration, rather than a torch of progress.

In the chapter "Ten Conservative Principles" in his 1993 and last book, The Politics of Prudence, Kirk said that the canons in *The Conservative Mind* differed "somewhat from edition to edition." He also mentioned that in his 1982 anthology, *The Portable Conservative Reader*, he offered "variations upon this theme" of his canons. In *The Politics of Prudence*, Kirk presented "a summary of conservative assumptions differing somewhat from my canons in those two books of mine." In introducing his new "ten articles of belief," he said that they "reflect the emphases of conservatives in America nowadays":

First, the conservative believes that there exists an enduring moral order.

Second, the conservative adheres to custom, convention, and continuity.

Third, conservatives believe in what may be called the principle of prescription.

Fourth, conservatives are guided by their principle of prudence.

Fifth, conservatives pay attention to the principle of variety.

Sixth, conservatives are chastened by their principle of imperfectability.

Seventh, conservatives are persuaded that freedom and property are closely linked.

Eighth, conservatives uphold voluntary community, quite as they oppose involuntary collectivism.

Ninth, the conservative perceives the need for prudent restraints upon power and upon human passions.

Tenth, the thinking conservative understands that permanence and change must be recognized and reconciled in a vigorous society.

For a more recent description of conservatism, we can consult the

2006 work *American Conservatism: An Encyclopedia.* Here are some brief excerpts from the entry on "conservatism":

> Conservatism is a philosophy that seeks to maintain and enrich societies characterized by respect for inherited institutions, beliefs and practices, in which individuals develop good character by cooperating with one another in primary, local associations such as families, churches and social groups aimed at furthering the common good in a manner pleasing to God.

> Conservatives are attached, not so much to any particular regime or form of government, as to what they believe are the requirements for a good life for all peoples. In the American context, conservatives defend the ordered liberty established by the Constitution and the traditions and practices on which that constitution was built.

> Conservatives' rejection of liberals' claims that they may, if only given the political power, reshape individuals into more caring, healthy members of richer communities rests in part on an appreciation of the importance of private property and free markets. These social institutions serve as important bulwarks of individual and group initiative against state planning.

> Conservatives believe that there is a natural order to the universe, governed by a natural law that gives mankind general rules concerning how to shape their lives in common as individuals. The natural law is not a detailed code, spelling out how men should act in every possible situation. But it provides general guidelines prohibiting acts such as murder and indicating the central importance of moral decency (best summed up in the Golden Rule) and of institutions, like the family, in which alone decent character can be formed.

One of the problems with conservatism is that it has no coherent, consistent (or concise) definition or description. In "Ten Conservative Principles," Kirk remarked, "The diversity of ways in which conservative views may find expression is itself proof that conservatism is no fixed ideology. What particular principles conservatives emphasize during any given time will vary with the circumstances and necessities of that era." That is why George W. Bush could say during a CNN interview in 2008, "I've abandoned free-market principles to save the free-market system." And that is why he could remark the next year at the unveiling of the George W. Bush Presidential Center at Southern Methodist University, "I went against my free-market instincts and approved a temporary government intervention."

The problem with "American conservatism," as concisely summed up by Ludwig von Mises Institute chairman, Lew Rockwell,

> is that it hates the left more than the state, loves the past more than liberty, feels a greater attachment to nationalism than to the idea of self-

determination, believes brute force is the answer to all social problems, and thinks it is better to impose truth rather than risk losing one soul to heresy. It has never understood the idea of freedom as a self-ordering principle of society. It has never seen the state as the enemy of what conservatives purport to favor. It has always looked to presidential power as the saving grace of what is right and true about America.

Libertarianism

Contrast conservatism with the simplicity of libertarianism. Libertarianism is a political philosophy which says that people should be free from government interference to live their lives any way they desire, pursue their own happiness, make their own choices, engage in any economic activity for their profit, and spend the fruits of their labor as they see fit as long as their actions are peaceful, their associations are voluntary, their interactions are consensual, and they don't violate the personal or property rights of others.

Libertarianism is the philosophy of nonaggression, whether that aggression be theft, fraud, the initiation of nonconsensual violence against person or property, or the threat of nonconsensual violence. The initiation or threat of aggression against the person or property of others is always wrong, even when done by government. Aggression is justified only in defense of one's person or property or in retaliation in response to aggression against them.

Libertarianism has nothing to do with one's lifestyle, tastes, vices, sexual orientation or practices, traditions, religion, aesthetics, sensibilities, social attitudes, or cultural norms. It has nothing to do with libertinism, greed, selfishness, hedonism, licentiousness, nihilism, moral relativism, egalitarianism, antinomianism, anarchy, materialism, or utopianism. It is neither naive about human nature nor inimical to organized religion. It neither disdains tradition nor rejects moral absolutes. Libertarianism is not low-tax liberalism, and a libertarian is not a conservative who is socially liberal.

Libertarianism has everything to do with individual liberty, private property, free markets, free enterprise, free exchange, individual responsibility, personal freedom, free association, voluntary interaction, freedom of conscience, free expression, and peaceful activity—as long as those things don't violate the personal or property rights of others.

Conservatism and libertarianism

So, is libertarianism "the very heart and soul of conservatism"? Is the basis of conservatism "a desire for less government interference or less centralized authority or more individual freedom"? Do conservatives have an "appreciation of the importance of private property and free markets"? Do "conservatives defend the ordered liberty established by the Constitution"? Are libertarianism and conservatism traveling "the same path"?

Perhaps the best way to see whether those things are true is by simply looking at what conservatism and libertarianism say about certain issues. Here are twenty-five of them, some general and some specific—enough to show beyond a shadow of a doubt that conservatism and libertarianism are not brothers, cousins, or related in any way.

Conservatism says that the government is entitled to a portion of every American's income through taxation. Libertarianism says that taxation is simply government theft, and that all Americans should be allowed to keep the fruits of their labor and spend their money as they see fit.

Conservatism says that Social Security should be "saved" so that future generations of the elderly can be supported by the young. Libertarianism says that Social Security is an intergenerational, income-transfer, wealth-redistribution welfare program that should be abolished.

Conservatism says that the defense budget should be increased and tied to the nation's GDP. Libertarianism says that the defense budget should be decreased and the military used for defensive purposes only.

Conservatism says that the government should prohibit people from selling their organs both while they are alive and after they are dead. Libertarianism says that your body is your own and, alive or dead, you should be able to do whatever you want with all or part of it.

Conservatism says that the government should take money out of the pockets of American taxpayers and put it in the hands of corrupt foreign governments and organizations in the form of foreign aid. Libertarianism says that because it is not the proper role of government to give out any foreign aid, the decision to give money to foreigners should be an individual one, and no country should receive foreign aid from the U.S. government in any amount, at any time, for any reason.

Conservatism says that the government should expend resources, arrest, fine, or imprison people for growing, manufacturing, buying, selling, using, or possessing drugs it has deemed to be illegal. Libertarianism says that the war on drugs is a war on freedom and that government has no business being concerned about the commercial, medical, or recreational use of drugs.

Conservatism says that most federal gun laws, including the National Instant Criminal Background Check System, should be retained. Libertarianism says that the federal government has no authority whatsoever to pass any laws that relate in any way to weapons, ammunition, waiting periods, or background checks.

Conservatism says that the government should take money from those who work and transfer it to those who don't by means of unemployment benefits. Libertarianism says that unemployment insurance should be private and that government has no business paying people for not working.

Conservatism says that laws prohibiting discrimination against someone because of his race, color, religion, sex, or national origin should be enforced and that no one should legally be able to refuse someone service, entrance, or membership on account of those things. Libertarianism says that all discrimination laws should be repealed because they destroy the rights of private property, freedom of assembly, freedom of association, free enterprise, and freedom of contract.

Conservatism says that the government should establish overtime rules and a minimum wage if it is not too high or burdensome to small businesses. Libertarianism says that those things should be negotiated between employers and employees on an individual or group basis without any government involvement whatsoever.

Conservatism says that the government should have refundable tax credits so that "the poor" can get a refund of taxes that were never withheld from their paychecks. Libertarianism says that refundable tax credits are a form of welfare and that the government should never issue a tax refund in excess of what is withheld from paychecks.

Conservatism says that government should take money out of the pockets of American taxpayers and use it to give out grants for scientific and medical research. Libertarianism says that all scientific and medical research should be privately funded and conducted.

Conservatism says that the government should take money from some Americans to feed other Americans by means of food stamps or school breakfasts and lunches. Libertarianism says that all food aid should be private and voluntary and that the government should have nothing to do with feeding students, the poor, or anyone else.

Conservatism says that the government should regulate some, and prohibit other, forms of gambling. Libertarianism says that all gambling laws should be repealed because they are gross violations of individual liberty and property rights.

Conservatism says that the government should take money from some Americans to educate the children of other Americans in public schools or by means of educational vouchers. Libertarianism says that the government should have nothing whatsoever to do with schools, education, teachers, student loans, testing, or standards.

Conservatism says that the United States should continue its military alliances with many countries around the world and come to their defense if necessary. Libertarianism says that the United States should not make entangling alliances and should observe a foreign policy of strict neutrality.

Conservatism says that the government should take money out of the pockets of American taxpayers to explore space and conduct experiments on a space station. Libertarianism says that all space exploration and experimentation should be privately funded and conducted.

Conservatism says that the government should take money out of the pockets of American taxpayers and use it to provide disaster relief in foreign countries. Libertarianism says that because it is not the proper role of government to provide disaster relief—even to its own citizens—the decision to provide disaster relief to foreigners should be an individual one, and no country should receive disaster relief from the U.S. government in any amount, at any time, for any reason.

Conservatism says that the United States should have an interventionist foreign policy and police the world. Libertarianism says that the United States should have a noninterventionist foreign policy and mind its own business.

Conservatism says that the government should provide the poor and farmers a safety net. Libertarianism says that the government should not give or lend money to, or subsidize the poor or any particular group.

Conservatism says that the United States should maintain an empire of troops and bases around the world. Libertarianism says that all foreign bases should be closed and all U.S. troops brought home.

Conservatism says that "the rich" should pay their "fair share" of taxes by paying a higher percentage of their income to the government than "the poor" or by forgoing certain deductions, exemptions, and credits that the government grants to them. Libertarianism says that a progressive tax system is Marxist and that neither "the rich" nor "the poor" should be taxed on their income.

Conservatism says that the government should take money out of the pockets of Americans who "have" and redistribute it to other Americans who "have not" by means of WIC, TANF, Section 8 rent subsidies, SSI, and the Low Income Home Energy Assistance Program. Libertarianism says that the welfare state is immoral because taking resources from people to give to those in need is not a noble act of charity but engaging in theft, and that all charity should be entirely private and voluntary.

Conservatism says that the government should make and enforce laws against victimless crimes. Libertarianism says that there is no such thing as nebulous crimes against nature, society, or the state, and that every crime should have a tangible and identifiable victim.

Conservatism says that the government should take money from some Americans to pay for the health care and health insurance of other Americans by means of SCHIP, Medicaid, and Medicare. Libertarianism says that the government shouldn't subsidize anyone's health care or health insurance and that the government should have absolutely nothing to do with either one.

What are we to conclude from this comparison between conservatism and libertarianism but that conservatism is merely one of many varieties of statism? Indeed, the very heart and soul of conservatism is statism. Conservatism deems it completely appropriate for government to punish people for engaging in peaceful, voluntary, and consensual actions it doesn't approve of and to take people's resources against their will and transfer or redistribute them to others as it sees fit. Ronald Reagan was wrong. There is an incontrovertible divide that exists between conservatism and libertarianism. The two are following opposite paths. It is libertarianism alone that desires less government interference, less centralized authority, and more individual freedom.

*****

ARE REPUBLICANS LIBERTARIANS?

Our two-party system makes it almost impossible for libertarians to get elected to office, especially on the national level. In order for libertarians to get elected to Congress, their best bet is to run as a Republican. Ron Paul is a perfect example of this. But libertarians should have no illusions about the Republican Party. And they shouldn't make the Republican Party out to be something it is not.

A former member of the Libertarian Party who is now running for office as a Republican recently said about the Republican Party:

> At its core, the Republican Party is supposed to be a liberty party—that's why it was the party of Abraham Lincoln and Ronald Reagan. For a Republican, so long as you are not violating the lives and liberties of other human beings—and that includes the lives of human beings in the womb—the government should give you the freedom to do as you see fit. The party strives to put the trust and the power back in the hands of the people instead of handing it over to unelected bureaucrats.

This almost makes Republicans sound like libertarians. Nothing could be further from the truth.

Let's first look at some principles of libertarianism followed by an analysis of the above statement.

Libertarianism is the philosophy that says that people should be free from individual, societal, or government interference to live their lives any way they desire, pursue their own happiness, accumulate as much wealth as they can, assess their own risks, make their own choices, engage in commerce with anyone who is willing to reciprocate, participate in any economic activity for their profit, and spend the fruits of their labor as they see fit as long as their actions are peaceful, their associations are voluntary, their interactions are consensual, and they don't violate the personal or property rights of others.

Libertarianism is the philosophy of nonaggression, whether that aggression be theft, fraud, the initiation of nonconsensual violence against person or property, or the threat of nonconsensual violence. The initiation or threat of aggression against the person or property of others is always wrong, even when done by government. Aggression is justified only in defense of one's person or property or in retaliation in response to aggression against them, but is neither essential nor required.

Libertarianism respects personal privacy, financial privacy, free thought, individual responsibility, freedom of conscience, free exchange, free markets, and private property.

Libertarianism celebrates individual liberty, personal freedom, peaceful activity, voluntary interaction, laissez faire, free enterprise, free assembly, free association, free speech, and free expression.

Libertarianism opposes the welfare state, the warfare state, the national security state, the deep state, the nanny state, the regulatory state, the administrative state, and the police state because they are inimical to human flourishing and the free society.

Libertarianism seeks to limit the intervention of government in the economy and society, the government regulation of business and commerce, and the control of government over private, consensual peaceful activity.

Are Republicans libertarians? Don't make me laugh.

I have five things to say about the aforementioned statement.

1. The Republican Party is only a liberty party in the mind of those who are suckered by the conservative mantra of the Constitution, limited government, individual freedom, private property, traditional values, free enterprise, and a strong national defense. Republicans, even the "conservative" ones, don't follow the Constitution in many areas. They prefer a government limited to one controlled by Republicans. They don't accept the freedom of individuals to do anything that's peaceful. They don't believe in the inviolability of private property. They think traditional values should be legislated by government. They don't yearn for free enterprise in everything. And they confound the idea of national defense with national offense.

2. The Republican Party is the party of Abraham Lincoln. But that is a terrible thing. Lincoln was one of the worst U.S. presidents. His legacy is one of mercantilism, income taxation, crony capitalism, protectionism, militarism, authoritarianism, and centralized government. Just spend a few minutes in Tom DiLorenzo's LRC article archive.

3. The Republican Party is the party of Ronald Reagan. But even this is a bad thing. Sure, Reagan was a tax cutter, but he was also a tax raiser. He increased Social Security taxes, corporate income taxes, Medicare taxes, and capital gains taxes. He instituted taxation of Social Security benefits, required the self-employed to pay the full payroll tax rate, and broadened the tax base. But that's not all. Reagan was an incorrigible drug warrior, signing legislation reinstating civil asset-forfeiture laws and mandatory minimum sentences for drug-related crimes. He also signed legislation forcing states to raise their drinking age to 21. During his ten-

ure as president, federal expenditures increased by more than 60 percent, spending on education increased by 68 percent, and health-care spending increased by 71 percent. He added over $1 trillion to the national debt by the end of his presidency. He increased import barriers and quotas and expanded the agricultural subsidies. And as Reagan's budget director David Stockman tells us: "Reagan tripled the size of the U.S. defense budget based on a totally phony neocon claim that the Soviet Union was on the verge of military superiority and nuclear first-strike capacity."

4. The Republican Party certainly does not believe that the government should give you the freedom to do as you see fit as long as you are not violating the lives and liberties of other human beings. Republicans want to lock people in cages for possessing too much of a plant that the government doesn't approve of. Need I say anything more?

5. The Republican Party certainly does not strive to put the trust and the power back in the hands of the people instead of handing it over to unelected bureaucrats. The federal government is full of hundreds of thousands of unelected bureaucrats in the EPA, FDA, SBA, TVA, DEA, ATF, NEA, NEH, GSA, NSF, SSA, USAID, SEC, FCC, EEOC, FEC, FTC, CFTC, CPSC; the Departments of Education, Health and Human Services, Housing and Urban Development, Homeland Security, Energy, the Interior, Commerce, State, Justice, Labor, Transportation, Veterans Affairs, Treasury, Defense, and Agriculture; and the National Council on Disability. What have Republicans ever done about eliminating the federal government's agencies, bureaus, commissions, departments, administrations, corporations, authorities, foundations, and services? The silence is deafening.

Republicans represent everything that libertarians are opposed to. How could a Republican ever be mistaken for a libertarian?

*****

4

DISCRIMINATION AND FREE ASSOCIATION

DISCRIMINATION AND A FREE SOCIETY

So, Rand Paul, the Kentucky Republican nominee for the U.S. Senate, is in hot water for disparaging remarks he has made about the Civil Rights Act of 1964.

Good for him.

Rand is merely echoing the sentiments of his father, Rep. Ron Paul (R-TX), who, on the fortieth anniversary of the Civil Rights Act, cast the lone nay vote against H. Res. 676 in which it was resolved that the House

(1) recognizes and honors the 40th anniversary of congressional passage of the Civil Rights Act of 1964; and

(2) encourages all Americans to recognize and celebrate the important historical milestone of the congressional passage of the Civil Rights Act of 1964.

The vote on June 24, 2004, was 414—1, with eighteen representatives not voting.

On a related note, the Civil Rights Act of 1964 Commemorative Coin Act (H.R. 2040) was passed via voice vote in the House and Senate in 2008. It was signed into law by President Bush on December 2, 2008.

Defenders of liberty and a free society should not be intimidated by enemies of liberty and a free society—liberal and conservative, Democrat and Republican, and even some libertarians—who label them as racists, bigots, or Neanderthals for objecting to certain provisions of the Civil Rights Act.

This is not to say that no congressmen who voted against the Civil Rights Act were racists, bigots, or Neanderthals. But the fact that some or all of them were doesn't mean that the Civil Rights Act—like most legislation passed by Congress for the past 100 years—wasn't an unconstitutional expansion of federal power that destroyed the rights of private property, freedom of assembly, freedom of association, free enterprise, and freedom of contract.

The Civil Rights Act of 1964 was introduced in the U.S. House of Representatives as H.R. 7152 by Emanuel Celler (D-NY) on June 20, 1963. It passed the House on February 10, 1964, by a vote of 290—130. It passed the U.S. Senate with revisions on June 19, 1964, by a vote of 73—27. The House agreed to the Senate's revised bill on June 30, 1964, by a

136

vote of 289—126. The Civil Rights Act was signed into law by President Johnson on July 2, 1964, thus becoming Public Law 88-352.

Unlike the gargantuan bills that Congress passes today (the recent health care bill was 2,409 pages), the Civil Rights Act is only 28 pages long, divided into 11 titles. The complete text can be viewed here.

The preamble reads as follows:

> To enforce the constitutional right to vote, to confer jurisdiction upon the district courts of the United States to provide injunctive relief against discrimination in public accommodations, to authorize the Attorney General to institute suits to protect constitutional rights in public facilities and public education, to extend the Commission on Civil Rights, to prevent discrimination in federally assisted programs, to establish a Commission on Equal Employment Opportunity, and for other purposes.

The second-longest and most far-reaching part of the Civil Rights Act is Title II: "Injunctive Relief against Discrimination in Places of Public Accommodation." The internal justification for this title is the ambiguous commerce clause in Article I, Section 8 of the Constitution that gives the Congress the power "To regulate Commerce with foreign Nations, and among the several States, and with the Indian Tribes." More evils have resulted from the federal government abusing the commerce clause than from any other part of the Constitution. But as Congressman Paul has said: "The framers of the Constitution intended the interstate commerce clause to create a free trade zone among the states, not to give the federal government regulatory power over every business that has any connection with interstate commerce."

The key part of Title II is the first section:

> SEC. 201. (a) All persons shall be entitled to the full and equal enjoyment of the goods, services, facilities, and privileges, advantages, and accommodations of any place of public accommodation, as defined in this section, without discrimination or segregation on the ground of race, color, religion, or national origin.

> (b) Each of the following establishments which serves the public is a place of public accommodation within the meaning of this title if its operations affect commerce, or if discrimination or segregation by it is supported by State action:

> (1) any inn, hotel, motel, or other establishment which provides lodging to transient guests, other than an establishment located within a building which contains not more than five rooms for rent or hire and which is actually occupied by the proprietor of such establishment as his residence;

> (2) any restaurant, cafeteria, lunchroom, lunch counter, soda fountain, or

other facility principally engaged in selling food for consumption on the premises, including, but not limited to, any such facility located on the premises of any retail establishment; or any gasoline station;

(3) any motion picture house, theater, concert hall, sports arena, stadium or other place of exhibition or entertainment; and

(4) any establishment (A) (i) which is physically located within the premises of any establishment otherwise covered by this subsection, or (ii) within the premises of which is physically located any such covered establishment, and (B) which holds itself out as serving patrons of such covered establishment.

(c) The operations of an establishment affect commerce within the meaning of this title if (1) it is one of the establishments described in paragraph (1) of subsection (b); (2) in the case of an establishment described in paragraph (2) of subsection (b), it serves or offers to serve interstate travelers or a substantial portion of the food which it serves, or gasoline or other products which it sells, has moved in commerce; (3) in the case of an establishment described in paragraph (3) of subsection (b), it customarily presents films, performances, athletic teams, exhibitions, or other sources of entertainment which move in commerce; and (4) in the case of an establishment described in paragraph (4) of subsection (b), it is physically located within the premises of, or there is physically located within its premises, an establishment the operations of which affect commerce within the meaning of this subsection. For purposes of this section, "commerce" means travel, trade, traffic, commerce, transportation, or communication among the several States, or between the District of Columbia and any State, or between any foreign country or any territory or possession and any State or the District of Columbia, or between points in the same State but through any other State or the District of Columbia or a foreign country.

(d) Discrimination or segregation by an establishment is supported by State action within the meaning of this title if such discrimination or segregation (1) is carried on under color of any law, statute, ordinance, or regulation; or (2) is carried on under color of any custom or usage required or enforced by officials of the State or political subdivision thereof; or (3) is required by action of the State or political subdivision thereof.

(e) The provisions of this title shall not apply to a private club or other establishment not in fact open to the public, except to the extent that the facilities of such establishment are made available to the customers or patrons of an establishment within the scope of subsection (b).

Because this part of the Civil Rights Act in particular was an unconstitutional expansion of federal power that destroyed the rights of private property, freedom of assembly, and freedom of association, free enterprise, and freedom of contract, it was opposed by members of Congress like Barry

Goldwater. Although it has been part of federal law for over 45 years, it should still be repudiated by all proponents of liberty and a free society just like the rest of Lyndon Johnson's Great Society programs.

Although the inns, hotels, motels, restaurants, cafeterias, lunchrooms, lunch counters, soda fountains, gas stations, movie theaters, concert halls, sports arenas, and stadiums referenced in Title II of the Civil Rights Act are all in business to offer goods and services to the public, they are all still private businesses (excepting certain halls, arenas, and stadiums that are owned by a municipality, in which case my comments would not apply).

Just as no one has a right to enter my home, so no one should have a right to stay at my inn, hotel, or motel; eat at my restaurant, cafeteria, lunchroom, or lunch counter; enjoy a beverage at my soda fountain; fill up at my gas station; view a movie at my theater; listen to a concert in my hall; or watch a sporting event at my arena or stadium.

There should be no distinction between a private home and a private business. In a free society, as Jacob Hornberger has recently pointed out, "a person has the fundamental right to associate with anyone he chooses and on any basis he chooses." In a free society, business owners, like homeowners, would have the right to run their businesses as they choose, including the right of exclusion. In a free society, everyone would have the right to discriminate in his place of business—yes, discriminate—against male or female, Blacks or Whites, Christians or Jews, Protestants or Catholics, heterosexuals or homosexuals, atheists or theists, natives or immigrants, smokers or nonsmokers, obese or anorexic.

The simple truth is that Americans don't live in a free society, although they may think they do. We live in a *relatively* free society compared to people in many other countries, but we do not live in a society that is *absolutely* free. We have a nanny state. We have a government full of politicians, bureaucrats, and regulators and a society full of statists, authoritarians, and busybodies who all want to use the force of government to impose their values, remake society in their own image, and compel others to associate with people of their choosing. It is futile to attempt to change human nature. Like attracts like, whether it is political preference, sexual orientation, religious piety, or skin color.

It's time to stop considering *discrimination* to be a dirty word.

I prefer Wal-Mart to K-Mart, ketchup to mustard, blue to pink, Chevy to Ford, blonds to brunettes, and Coke to Pepsi. Pepsi may be cheaper, healthier, and better tasting, but I still prefer Coke. Perhaps I just like the color, the smell, or the Coke logo on the can. My preference for Coke over Pepsi may be completely irrational, but in a free society it is my choice to discriminate against Pepsi as long as I don't violate the rights of Pepsi drinkers.

By the same token, if I prefer to rent my home to married couples instead of unmarried ones, serve in my restaurant Whites instead of Blacks, allow into my theater heterosexuals instead of homosexuals, put up in my hotel Democrats instead of Republicans, sell merchandise in my store to Christians instead of Jews, and permit to join my club men instead of women, then I have the natural and moral right to do so. The fact that I don't have the legal right to do any of these things means that the state is violating my rights instead of protecting them.

To say that proponents of liberty and a free society long for the return of Jim Crow laws is a gross misrepresentation. Jim Crow laws, which banned White businessmen from serving Black customers, are just as wrong as anti-discrimination laws. These government-mandated and government-enforced laws denied the fundamental right of Whites to associate and conduct business with Blacks. The real problem with segregation and discrimination is that they were de jure, not de facto; mandatory, not voluntary; public, not private.

In a free society, discrimination could serve as the mother of innovation and entrepreneurship. If a restaurant is for Whites only, someone can open a similar one for all races or for just Blacks. If a store is for Christians only, someone can open a similar one for all religions or for just Jews. But discrimination could also function as a death knell for any business due to bad publicity, boycotts, and too narrow of a market to generate sufficient profits.

In a free society the possibilities are endless. As much as some enemies of liberty and a free society don't want to hear it, and as much as some defenders of liberty and a free society have waffled on the issue, a truly free society means the freedom to discriminate—against any group for any reason.

*****

IS THERE A RIGHT TO LIVE WHERE YOU CHOOSE?

In addition to certain days being designated as holidays, the federal government and various organizations have also singled out certain days, weeks, and months as times to emphasize a particular issue or commemorate a group or event.

Some of these are well known, like Earth Day (April 22) and Black History Month (February); others are fairly obscure, like National Cancer Survivors Day (June 1) and National Missing Children's Day (May 1).

In addition to being Poetry Month, Dental Health Month, National Cancer Control Month, Parkinson Awareness Month, and Irritable Bowel Syndrome Awareness Month, the month of April is also National Fair Housing Month.

April is the month that the Fair Housing Act (FHA) was passed in 1968 as Title VIII of the Civil Rights Act of 1968. Along with Medicare,

Medicaid, and Head Start, the FHA was one of the key parts of Lyndon Johnson's Great Society.

The FHA prohibited discriminatory acts regarding the sale, rental, and financing of housing based on race, color, religion, and national origin. It has since been amended, adding to the prohibition list discrimination based on sex, disability, and familial status, and its enforcement mechanism strengthened. And although it is not part of the official list, housing discrimination based on sexual orientation and gender identity is now also being targeted.

The Office of Fair Housing and Equal Opportunity (FHEO) administers and enforces federal laws relating to housing discrimination. It maintains a housing discrimination hotline and a website where one can report housing discrimination in English, Spanish, Arabic, Cambodian, Chinese, Korean, Russian, and Vietnamese.

To commemorate National Fair Housing Month, the Department of Housing and Urban Development (HUD), which has the primary authority for enforcing the FHA, has launched a national media campaign using newspaper and magazine ads and social networking sites to "increase the Department's efforts to educate the public and housing providers about their fair housing rights and responsibilities."

The campaign is called "Live Free." One of its more controversial print advertisements features a Latino worker looking into the horizon with a caption reading: "You Have the Right to Live Where You Choose."

Is that so? Is there a right to live where you choose?

First of all, no sane person would take the Live Free campaign statement at face value. No one would say that there is a right to live in the White House, in the middle of an interstate highway, in the Sears Tower, or in the local public library. No one would say that there is a right to live in Bill Gates' mansion, Donald Trump's apartment, your house, or my house. And, of course, there is no right to live anywhere that you cannot pay for, although some liberals and progressives might think otherwise and want the federal government to subsidize housing.

What HUD and the Office of FHEO are concerned about is the practice of discrimination in the sale and rental of housing. One "Fair Housing" document on the HUD website, the front page of which reads: "You have the right to choose where to live!", says that in the sale and rental of housing, no one may take any of the following actions based on race, color, religion, gender, disability, familial status, or national origin:

- Refuse to rent or sell housing
- Refuse to negotiate for housing
- Make housing unavailable
- Deny a dwelling
- Set different terms, conditions or privileges for sale or rental of a dwell-

ing
• Provide different housing services or facilities
• Falsely deny that housing is available for inspection, sale or rental
• For profit, persuade, or try to persuade homeowners to sell or rent dwellings by suggesting that people of a particular race, etc. have moved, or are about to move into the neighborhood (blockbusting) or
• Deny any person access to, or membership or participation in, any organization, facility or service (such as a multiple listing service) related to the sale or rental of dwellings, or discriminate against any person in the terms or conditions of such access, membership or participation.

Second, although it is an established principle of our age that we must never discriminate, there is in fact nothing wrong with discriminating. Discrimination is not a dirty word. We used to laud a man for having discriminating taste. Discrimination involves choosing between or among options. When you eat a hamburger, fries, and a coke at a fast-food restaurant you discriminate—consciously or unconsciously—against chicken sandwiches, onion rings, and water. This doesn't necessarily mean that you hate chicken sandwiches, onion rings, and water. It just means that on that particular day and under a particular set of circumstances you prefer a hamburger, fries, and a coke. But, it is argued, people are not food. Agreed, but it works the same way, and usually on a larger scale. When a man proposes marriage to his sweetheart, he discriminates against every other woman in the world. When a couple adopts a child, they discriminate against every other child in world. When you pick your friends, you discriminate against the ones you reject. We can't go through the day without discriminating.

Third, how does the government know for sure that someone was denied housing because of discrimination due to his race, color, religion, national origin, sex, disability, or familial status instead of his credit score, income, debt-to-income ratio, criminal record, immigration status, employment history, or references? Can government bureaucrats and social workers read minds and judge motives? Recent cases investigated by HUD include a New Hampshire woman who was discriminated against and insulted by her landlord because she was married to a Hispanic man and Black and Latino tenants in the state of Washington being charged higher rents for the same units. But the state is not even sure of its own anti-discrimination laws. In the Live Free ad campaign, there are two print advertisements that feature a parent with a child. They both say: "Refusing to rent to persons because they have children is almost always against the law." Why is it "almost always" against the law? Does this mean that discrimination against people with children is sometimes okay? Apparently so. But I thought all discrimination was bad. Discrimination laws are based on the false notion that society rooted in conflict and that a central authority is necessary to bring about social peace and justice.

Fourth, there may in fact be good, reasonable, and rational reasons to discriminate in the sale or rental of housing. A religious person may not wish to rent his house or apartment to an unmarried or same-sex couple because he feels he would be providing the means for them to "live in sin." A landlord may want to charge college students a higher security deposit or not rent to them at all because of a well-founded fear that the students will disturb the neighbors with loud parties or damage the residence. The owner of an apartment complex may prefer a relatively homogeneous clientele to avoid potential racial or ethnic conflicts among the tenants.

Fifth, and most important, even if the housing discrimination is not deserved, reasonable, and rational, and is in fact undeserved, unreasonable, and irrational, as well as bigoted, racist, and xenophobic—there should be no federal laws against it. If I as a homeowner forbid another family—of any race, creed, color, or national origin—from moving into my house with my family—for any price—then no one bats an eye. And if I as a homeowner allow another family—even one that looks and speaks exactly like my family—to move into my house with my family—for a price or not—then there is still no objection. But if I vacate my house and decide to rent it—once again selectively deciding who shall live there—then I face potential lawsuits and fines for housing discrimination if—and only if—I rent to the family that looks and speaks like my family. This is ludicrous. Just as there is a right to live where you choose if you own the property, so there is no right to live where you choose if you don't own the property. Housing discrimination laws are an attack on private property, freedom of association, and a free society.

The other relevant point here concerns the very existence of not only laws like the FHA, but of HUD itself.

This federal Department was created in 1965. It now has over 10,000 employees and a budget of over $45 billion. Other agencies under the HUD umbrella include the Federal Housing Administration (FHA) and the Government National Mortgage Association (GNMA). HUD redistributes the income of taxpayers to over 4.5 million families through HUD's rental programs like Tenant-Based Rental Assistance (TBRA), Project-Based Rental Assistance (PBRA), and Public Housing. According to a HUD press release, HUD "recently awarded nearly $41 million to 108 fair housing organizations and non-profit agencies across the country to educate the public and combat housing and lending discrimination." According to another HUD press release, "$100 million in new grants was just awarded to 45 regional areas to "support more livable and sustainable communities across the country" and to "build economic competitiveness by connecting housing with good jobs, quality schools and transportation."

The stated mission of HUD is to

create strong, sustainable, inclusive communities and quality affordable homes for all. HUD is working to strengthen the housing market to bolster the economy and protect consumers; meet the need for quality affordable rental homes: utilize housing as a platform for improving quality of life; build inclusive and sustainable communities free from discrimination; and transform the way HUD does business.

However noble these goals are, there is one big problem. There is nothing in the Constitution that authorizes the existence of a government department—termed HUD or something else—to achieve them.

It is simply not the job of government to provide public housing, subsidize housing, ensure that housing is affordable, regulate the lending or housing market, strengthen the housing market, provide mortgages, guarantee mortgages, or stamp out discrimination.

Republicans in Congress who claim to want to cut the budget, rein in federal spending, and adhere to the Constitution should be calling for the wholesale elimination of HUD. Why aren't they?

*****

THE RIGHT TO REFUSE SERVICE

Back in 1994, the restaurant chain Denny's settled a class-action racial-discrimination lawsuit for $54.4 million. Although the restaurant is known for always being open and serving breakfast, lunch, and dinner at any time, day or night, black patrons alleged that they had been refused service, forced to wait longer than white customers, charged more than white customers, and asked to prepay for service.

The agreement resulted from separate lawsuits filed in California and Maryland that were then expanded to include claimants in 48 other states. In California, a black girl alleged that she had been refused the restaurant's customary free birthday meal. In Maryland, six black U.S. Secret Service agents alleged that they had been forced to wait an hour for service while white customers were served ahead of them.

In a strange twist of fate, Denny's restaurant parent company, Advantica, was chosen by *Fortune* magazine in 2001 as the "Best Company for Minorities."

More recently, Hands On Originals, a T-shirt company in Lexington, Kentucky, was picketed by Lexington's Gay and Lesbian Services Organization (GLSO) for refusing to produce T-shirts for the city's "gay pride" festival to be held on June 30. The design featured a number 5 on the front, with "Lexington Pride Festival" and the names of the event's sponsors appearing on the back.

Although the firm bid on producing the T-shirts, the owners declined to fill the order after they had been selected. The owners, who were not initially aware that they were bidding on a gay-themed T-shirt, explained to the GLSO that, as a Christian organization, producing the T-shirts would be against their conscience. The owners did locate another T-shirt business for GLSO that would honor their low bid.

Nevertheless, the GLSO fileda public-accommodation discrimination complaint with the Lexington-Fayette Urban County Human Rights Commission, alleging,

> On or about March 8, 2012, members of the GLSO were told that our Pride Festival t-shirt printing quote would not be honored due to the fact that the t-shirt company is a Christian organization. We were told that our t-shirts would not be printed. We believe that we have been discriminated against in violation of Local Ordinance 201-99, based on sexual orientation.

Last month, an organized demonstration with picketing by about 60 homosexual activists in front of Hands On Originals encouraged the public to boycott the business. The Lexington school district has already stopped purchasing merchandise from the company.

One of GLSO's officers who attended the demonstration, Aaron Baker, stated, "Ultimately the owners of Hands On Originals need to recognize that discrimination is not OK and need to make a commitment not to continue that." But he also said that "Hands on Originals does a lot of business in this town, and people should be aware of the situation, so they can make an informed decision about whether they want to buy from them."

Baker is wrong, but he is also right.

Discrimination is neither "not OK" nor something "not to continue." Every individual and business owner *should* have the right to refuse service. In a free society, every individual and business owner *would* have the right to refuse service. It is part and parcel of the inviolability of private property, the freedom of assembly, the freedom of association, the freedom of contract, free enterprise, and the free market. In a free society, as Future of Freedom Foundation president Jacob Hornberger maintains,

> A person has the fundamental right to associate with anyone he chooses and on any basis he chooses. He might be the biggest bigot in the world, choosing only to associate with white supremacists, but that's what freedom is all about—the right to make whatever choices one wants in his life, so long as his conduct is peaceful—i.e., no murder, rape, theft, fraud, or other violent assaults against others.

In a free society, business owners, like homeowners, would have the right to run their businesses as they choose, including the right to refuse service. And that's not all. In a free society, business owners would have the right to discriminate in their place of business on the basis of race, creed, color, religion, age, gender, height, weight, disability, attire, familial status, marital status, socioeconomic status, political preference, religious piety, national origin, appearance, odor, sexual orientation, or anything else, whether logical or illogical, reasonable or unreasonable, rational or irrational. It couldn't be any other way and really be a free society.

As it is now, although it is unlawful to refuse to serve certain classes of people, it is not unlawful to give senior citizen discounts (discrimination based on age) or free meals to groups such as children, people celebrating birthdays, and police officers even though doing so discriminates against adults, people not celebrating birthdays, and all occupations besides police officers.

Clearly, there is much confusion about discrimination in our relatively free (as opposed to absolutely free) society overseen by regulators, bureaucrats, and judges—authoritarians, statists, and busybodies who seek to use the force of government to compel others to associate or do business with people they don't want to. Currently, if the patron of a business or organization is not a member of a federally protected class, the legal right to refuse service generally depends on whether the refusal was arbitrary or whether there was a specific interest in refusing a patron service. That leaves everything up to the whim of government regulators, bureaucrats, and judges.

Lest there be any misunderstanding, I should say that a free society has nothing in common with the Jim Crow era. Jim Crow regulations, which prohibited white businessmen from serving black customers, were maintained by government force. They were the antithesis of the voluntary association found in a free society. And not only did they harm blacks, they denied the fundamental right of whites to associate and conduct business with them as they saw fit.

The basis of GLSO's public-accommodation discrimination complaint is the Civil Rights Act of 1964. Listed among the goals in the preamble of the Civil Rights Act is, in addition to enforcing "the constitutional right to vote," preventing "discrimination in federally assisted programs," and authorizing "the Attorney General to institute suits to protect constitutional rights in public facilities and public education," the government's intent "to provide injunctive relief against discrimination in public accommodations."

The government is using the word "public" in two different senses. As Title II, "Injunctive Relief against Discrimination in Places of Public Accommodation," section 201 states,

> (a) All persons shall be entitled to the full and equal enjoyment of the goods, services, facilities, and privileges, advantages, and accommodations of any place of public accommodation, as defined in this section, without discrimination or segregation on the ground of race, color, religion, or na-

tional origin.

(b) Each of the following establishments which serves the public is a place of public accommodation within the meaning of this title if its operations affect commerce, or if discrimination or segregation by it is supported by State action:

(1) any inn, hotel, motel, or other establishment which provides lodging to transient guests, other than an establishment located within a building which contains not more than five rooms for rent or hire and which is actually occupied by the proprietor of such establishment as his residence;

(2) any restaurant, cafeteria, lunchroom, lunch counter, soda fountain, or other facility principally engaged in selling food for consumption on the premises, including, but not limited to, any such facility located on the premises of any retail establishment; or any gasoline station;

(3) any motion picture house, theater, concert hall, sports arena, stadium or other place of exhibition or entertainment; and

(4) any establishment (A)(i) which is physically located within the premises of any establishment otherwise covered by this subsection, or (ii) within the premises of which is physically located any such covered establishment, and (B) which holds itself out as serving patrons of such covered establishment.

But there is a big difference between the government's protecting "constitutional rights in public facilities and public education," and the government's providing "injunctive relief against discrimination in public accommodations." The former is a legitimate purpose of government; the latter is an illegitimate purpose. One protects rights; the other violates rights. The first ensures that the government grants the public equal access and equal opportunity to what is public; the second dictates how a private business should operate.

The GLSO's Aaron Baker is right about one thing. People should be aware of the practices of any business "so they can make an informed decision about whether they want to buy from them."

In a free society, it is not just businesses that have the right to refuse service; customers have the right to investigate the practices of any place of business and boycott or give bad publicity to any business establishment that doesn't meet their standards. Discrimination is a two-edged sword. It could function as a death knell for any business because of boycotts, bad publicity, or too narrow a market to make a profit. But in a free society, the practice of discrimination must be an option for buyers and sellers.

Although conservatives may sound like libertarians when they talk about freedom, property rights, and limited government, they usually fall short of advocating a truly free society.

Typical is Richard Garnett, professor of law and associate dean at Notre Dame Law School. In his recent *Public Discourse* article "Confusion About Discrimination," he shows that it is conservatives who are confused about discrimination:

> We believe that "discrimination" is wrong. And, because "discrimination" is wrong, we believe that governments such as ours—secular, liberal, constitutional governments—should take steps to prevent, discourage, and denounce it. We are right to believe these things. The proposition that it is not only true, but "self-evidently" true, that all human persons are "created equal" is foundational for us. The principle of equal citizenship holds near-universal appeal, even though we often disagree about that principle's particular applications.

> At the same time, it is not true that "discrimination" is always or necessarily wrong. Nor is it the case that governments always or necessarily should or may regulate or discourage it—say, through its expression and spending—even when it is wrong. "Discrimination," after all, is just another word for decision-making, for choosing and acting in accord with or with reference to particular criteria. We do and should "discriminate"—we draw lines, identify limits, make judgments, act on the basis of preferences—all the time.

What Garnett really means is that "wrongful discrimination is wrong." It is this that governments should oppose, but only when "it makes sense, all things considered, and when it is within their constitutionally and morally limited powers, to do so" because "we do not believe that governments should or may prevent, correct, or even discourage every instance of wrongful discrimination." Some acts of wrongful discrimination "are beyond the authorized reach of government policy," some are "too difficult or costly to identify, let alone regulate," and others are "none of the government's business."

Many liberals could agree with exactly what the conservative Garnett is saying, but then both would argue endlessly about whether this case of discrimination is "wrong" and whether that case of wrongful discrimination should be corrected by government action.

Libertarians, on the other hand, would argue correctly and consistently that, by their very nature, the rights of private property, freedom of assembly, freedom of association, free enterprise, and freedom of contract include the right to refuse service and otherwise discriminate—for any reason.

*****

WOMEN, DISCRIMINATION, AND A FREE SOCIETY

For the first time in its history, South Korea has elevated a woman to the office of president. Newly elected Park Geun-hye is the daughter of the president and dictator Park Chung-hee, who ruled the country from 1961 until his assassination in 1979.

During her presidential campaign, she pledged to increase government aid to single parents, expand maternity and paternity benefits, and promote flexible work arrangements in order to get more women in the work force.

In an interview with NPR, Kim Eun-Ju, director of the Center for Korean Women and Politics, noted that the South Korean presidential campaign ignored what she sees as two big problems: "One is that Korean women get paid nearly 40 percent less than their male counterparts—the biggest such disparity among the world's developed economies. The other is that Korean women's representation in politics ranks 108th out of 132 countries."

Also interviewed was Kim Wan-hung, a researcher with the Korean Women's Development Institute. She spoke of how difficult it is for any government policy to undo centuries of cultural tradition: "Men work. Women stay at home. This idea is ingrained in people's minds. The salary differential has not been considered important. And less has been done to solve this problem in Korea than in other developed countries."

I suppose it might be the case in traditional male-dominated Korean society that women would be deliberately paid less than men for the same job. But such is certainly not the case in the United States, where record numbers of women hold political office, are on police forces, and work in what used to be considered male occupations.

So why do we in the United States still hear about the "glass ceiling"? Why do we still hear the cry of "equal pay for equal work"? Why do we still hear about the "wage gap" between men and women? What are we to make of reports from organizations such as the American Association of University Women that "among all full-time workers, women are paid about 77 cents for every dollar paid to men"?

The wage gap between the sexes was an issue in the recent presidential election. Democrats touted Barack Obama's signing of the Lily Ledbetter Fair Pay Act, while Republicans pointed out that, according to 2011 White House salary records, female employees of the Obama administration earned a median salary 18 percent less than men. Similar disparities have been found on the staffs of Democratic legislators, including Obama's former senate office.

There is no denying the fact that in the United States men, on average, earn more than women. Now, although it is true that women's productivity was lower than men's when physical strength and stamina were more important in the workplace, such is generally not the case nowadays. So what accounts for the "pay gap"? The main thing is marriage and children. Women who marry and leave the work force to raise children have less experience and seniority than men when they return to work. It's not that women are paid less; they earn less. When you compare not all men and women, but only men and women who have never been married (or had children), the wage gap disappears.

But that's not all. According to Warren Farrell in the book *Why Men Earn More: The Startling Truth Behind the Pay Gap—And What Women Can Do About It*, there are a number of things that account for a pay gap between the sexes:

• Men go into technology and hard sciences more than women.
• Men are more likely to take hazardous jobs.
• Men are more willing to expose themselves to inclement weather at work.
• Men tend to take more-stressful jobs.
• Men are more likely to work longer hours.
• Men work more weeks per year than women.
• Men have half the absenteeism rate of women.
• Men are more willing to commute long distances to work.
• Men are more willing to relocate to undesirable locations for higher-paying jobs.
• Men are more willing to take jobs that require extensive travel.
• Men are more likely to work on commission.

And as explained by Carrie Lukas of the Independent Women's Forum,

> In truth, I'm the cause of the wage gap—I and hundreds of thousands of women like me. I have a good education and have worked full time for 10 years. Yet throughout my career, I've made things other than money a priority. I chose to work in the nonprofit world because I find it fulfilling. I sought out a specialty and employer that seemed best suited to balancing my work and family life. When I had my daughter, I took time off and then opted to stay home full time and telecommute. I'm not making as much money as I could, but I'm compensated by having the best working arrangement I could hope for.
>
> Women make similar trade-offs all the time. Surveys have shown for years that women tend to place a higher priority on flexibility and personal fulfillment than do men, who focus more on pay. Women tend to avoid jobs that require travel or relocation, and they take more time off and spend fewer hours in the office than men do.

But now we are also told in reports such as *Graduating to a Pay Gap* from the American Association of University Women that "just one year out of college, millennial women are paid 82 cents for every dollar paid to their male peers." They are "paid less than men are even when they do the same work and major in the same field." The report finds that "women's choices—college major, occupation, hours at work—do account for part of the pay gap." However, "About one-third of the gap remains unexplained, suggesting that bias and discrimination are still problems in the workplace."

There are two problems with this alleged pay gap.

The first is that we almost never hear complaints about a pay gap when sex roles are reversed. Female fashion models get paid much more money than their male peers. As do female porn stars. Where is the outrage? Where are the charges of bias against men? Where are the cries of discrimination? Where are the calls for government intervention to rectify the problem?

And the second is that profit usually trumps bigotry. If women have the same productivity, skill-set, and availability as men, but are willing to work for less money than men, then there would be additional profits available for the taking to any firm that hired only women.

The alleged bias and discrimination in pay is also said to exist in hiring.

Following an investigation by the U.S. Department of Labor, Clougherty Packing Company, a subsidiary of Hormel Food Corp., has just settled allegations of discriminating against female job applicants.

Clougherty Packing sells more than 400 million pounds of pork a year, including the "Dodger Dogs" sold at the Los Angeles Dodgers' baseball stadium. But the company also holds a federal contract of $3.9 million with the U.S. Department of Agriculture, which distributes Clougherty products to food banks and other assistance programs. Federal compliance officers reviewed the company's hiring practices and determined that between 2007 and 2009 the company violated Executive Order 11246, Lyndon Johnson's directive that laid the foundation for a federal program that would later develop into what is known as Affirmative Action. This executive order reads in part,

Except in contracts exempted in accordance with Section 204 of this Order, all Government contracting agencies shall include in every Government contract hereafter entered into the following provisions:

During the performance of this contract, the contractor agrees as follows:

(1) The contractor will not discriminate against any employee or applicant for employment because of race, creed, color, or national origin. The contractor will take affirmative action to ensure that applicants are employed, and that employees are treated during employment, without regard to their race, creed, color, or national origin. Such action shall include, but not be limited to the following: employment, upgrading, demotion, or transfer; re-

cruitment or recruitment advertising; layoff or termination; rates of pay or other forms of compensation; and selection for training, including apprenticeship. The contractor agrees to post in conspicuous places, available to employees and applicants for employment, notices to be provided by the contracting officer setting forth the provisions of this nondiscrimination clause.

As part of its settlement with the Labor Department, Clougherty Packing has agreed to pay $439,538 in back wages, including interest, to 1,988 mostly Hispanic women who were rejected for entry-level positions at the company's meat-packing plant in Los Angeles. The company will also "make 700 job offers to affected women as positions become available. Furthermore, the company has agreed to undertake extensive self-monitoring measures to ensure that all of its hiring practices fully comply with the law."

Said Patricia Shiu, director of the Labor Department's Office of Federal Contract Compliance Programs,

So many Americans grew up eating Dodger Dogs and other Hormel products. These are uniquely American brands that ought to reflect American values, particularly when it comes to ensuring fairness in the workplace.

During this holiday season, I hope that this settlement can provide a little financial help and a whole lot of justice for the women who were denied a fair shot at employment. Moreover, I am glad we were able to work with Clougherty to make sure that there will be greater opportunities for women to get jobs going forward.

It should be noted that a company's agreeing to a settlement with the government doesn't necessarily imply an admission of guilt.

At the second presidential debate in October of last year, the question was asked of both candidates, "In what new ways do you intend to rectify the inequalities in the workplace, specifically regarding females making only 72 percent of what their male counterparts earn?"

Obama talked about his grandmother's becoming vice president of a bank but hitting "the glass ceiling" and training "people who would end up becoming her bosses during the course of her career." He then touted his signing of the Lily Ledbetter Fair Pay Act.

But Mitt Romney, instead of directly answering that question, focused on what he had done as governor of Massachusetts to rectify the alleged bias and discrimination against women in hiring. It was at that debate where Romney, after mentioning his "concerted effort to go out and find women who had backgrounds that could be qualified to become members of our cabinet," ignominiously said he went "to a number of women's groups" for help and "they brought us whole binders full of women."

Once again we have two problems.

The first is that we almost never hear complaints about discrimination in hiring when sex roles are reversed. The Hooters restaurant chain features waitresses in tight shirts and short shorts. Men need not apply. The 2013 Hooters calendar features only "Hooter Girls," not "Hooters Guys." A Texas man received a settlement in 2009 after filing a complaint against Hooters because the company's local Corpus Christi franchisee refused to hire him as a waiter because, he alleged, the position was being limited to females by an employer "who merely wishes to exploit female sexuality as a marketing tool to attract customers and insure profitability." But such lawsuits are seen as publicity stunts and the men who work at Hooters are still in positions such as cook, host, bartender, or manager.

And the second, again, is that profit usually trumps bigotry. If women have the same productivity, skill-set, and availability as men, any firm willing to hire women has a much larger pool of potential applicants to draw from and, consequently, a decided advantage when it comes to salary and benefit negotiations.

But let's assume for just a moment that some corporations, companies, and small businesses in the United States really do have a bias against women and discriminate against them in pay and hiring. Is that a problem? Is it a bad thing? Is it immoral? Should the government intervene to rectify the situation? Should discrimination be made a criminal offense?

To the libertarian the solution is a simple one: Because a free society must include the freedom to discriminate, there should be no government oversight of the workplace and no discrimination laws.

Discrimination is neither a dirty word nor an evil deed. When a man asks a woman to marry him he is discriminating against every other woman in the world. When a woman accepts a man's proposal of marriage, she is discriminating against every other man in the world.

Some people prefer Coke to Pepsi. Pepsi may be cheaper, healthier, and better tasting, but they still prefer Coke. Perhaps they just like the color, the smell, or the Coke logo on the can. Their preference for Coke over Pepsi may be completely irrational, but in a free society it is their choice to discriminate against Pepsi as long as they don't violate the rights of the sellers of Pepsi.

And yes, it is the same way with employment. Women may be more productive, have more skills, and have better availability, but if a firm chooses—for whatever reason—to pay women less or not hire them at all, then—in a free society—they have a right to make that choice.

The same goes for discrimination on the basis of religion, age, height, weight, sexual orientation, marital status, national origin, ethnicity, or color. No one has a right to employment in a particular job at a particular rate of pay.

In a free society it couldn't be any other way.

What proponents of discrimination laws are of necessity also proposing is that the government set hiring and salary standards, maintain an army of bureaucrats to enforce them, have access to all employment records, and monitor all workplaces.

In a controlled society it couldn't be any other way.

In a free society, discrimination could serve as the mother of innovation and entrepreneurship. But discrimination could also function as a death knell for any business because of bad publicity, boycotts, and a market that is too narrow to generate sufficient profits.

Those who object to a company's hiring or compensation practices can choose to not work there, to not patronize the company, or to petition the company to change its policies.

In a free society every person has the natural right to associate or not associate with anyone he chooses and on any basis he chooses. And that includes business owners. In a free society business owners have the fundamental right to run their businesses as they choose, including to exercise the rights of discrimination and exclusion—as it concerns both employees and customers. A free society worthy of the name *must* include the freedom to discriminate—against any group and for any reason.

*****

RELIGIOUS DISCRIMINATION

Do churches and other religious organizations have the right to discriminate? Even advocates of discrimination laws in general are usually willing to make an exception for churches and religious organizations to practice discrimination in employment based on religious creed, sex, marital status, or sexual orientation.

Thus, a church of a particular denomination is free to limit offers of employment to ministers of that particular denomination and discriminate against all others; a church that considers homosexuality to be a sin is free to hire only heterosexuals and discriminate against homosexuals; a church that believes in having only men in leadership positions is free to hire only men and discriminate against women; and a church that believes in having an unmarried priesthood is free to employ as priests only those who are unmarried and discriminate against those who are married.

Regardless of our personal feelings about religion and morality, that is what we expect. That is, we expect a Jewish community center to be staffed by Jews, we expect a Catholic mass to be said by an unmarried male priest; we expect the minister of a theologically conservative church to be a heterosexual; we expect a Baptist church to be pastored by a man who is a Baptist; and we expect a Christian school to have Christian teachers.

Yet a Christian school in Thousand Oaks, California, and two former teachers are fighting over that very point.

Calvary Chapel, a Christian church in Thousand Oaks, purchased the previously secular Little Oaks School in 2009. According to the *Ventura County Star*,

> While the vast majority of religious schools are nonprofit and tax-exempt, church leaders said they organized Little Oaks as a for-profit because they were on a tight deadline. They said forming a tax-exempt corporation is a lengthy process. They said the school is operated not as a profit-generating entity but as a spiritual arm of the church. Its students include about 130 children in preschool through fifth grade.

In 2012, the church requested from all employees a statement of faith and a reference from a pastor in order to have their contracts renewed. Two teachers, Lynda Serrano and Mary Ellen Guevara, refused to provide the documents and lost their jobs.

"We're a Christian school," said the Rev. Rob McCoy, pastor of the church and headmaster of the school. "We were coming to the point where we were establishing a Christian curriculum. We wanted to make sure teachers subscribed to that faith."

The teachers retained a law firm in Los Angeles and were prepared to sue, but asked for $150,000 apiece from the school to settle the case. "They did not believe they should be required to obtain a pastoral reference in order to continue their employment," their attorney wrote in a letter to the church.

The church and school say their right to hire teachers who share their beliefs is protected by civil rights laws, the U.S. Constitution, and the California Constitution, which says in its Declaration of Rights in Article I,

> SEC. 4. Free exercise and enjoyment of religion without discrimination or preference are guaranteed. This liberty of conscience does not excuse acts that are licentious or inconsistent with the peace or safety of the State. The Legislature shall make no law respecting an establishment of religion. A person is not incompetent to be a witness or juror because of his or her opinions on religious beliefs.

The teachers cite the California Fair Employment and Housing Act, which, although it has some religious discrimination exemptions, supposedly don't include for-profit religious groups.

But instead of settling, church and school leaders filed their own lawsuit in U.S. District Court seeking an injunction to prevent the teachers from filing their lawsuit in a different venue because they wanted to make sure litigation took place in federal court. Their suit alleges that the Fair Employment and Housing Act is unconstitutional when used to restrict a religious school's hiring practices, even if the group is for-profit.

The lawyers for the teachers maintain that the "Fair Employment and Housing Act has been upheld in hundreds of cases in state and federal courts." They described the school's lawsuit as a desperate attempt to "avoid the consequences of their illegal and discriminatory practices."

But the lawyer representing the church and its school believes "the question is ultimately, do the nondiscrimination rights of the teachers under state law trump the religious rights of the school under federal law?"

There is no question that California's Fair Employment and Housing Act outlaws discrimination in employment as a matter of public policy:

> 12920. It is hereby declared as the public policy of this state that it is necessary to protect and safeguard the right and opportunity of all persons to seek, obtain, and hold employment without discrimination or abridgment on account of race, religious creed, color, national origin, ancestry, physical disability, mental disability, medical condition, genetic information, marital status, sex, gender, gender identity, gender expression, age, or sexual orientation.
>
> It is recognized that the practice of denying employment opportunity and discriminating in the terms of employment for these reasons foments domestic strife and unrest, deprives the state of the fullest utilization of its capacities for development and advancement, and substantially and adversely affects the interests of employees, employers, and the public in general. Further, the practice of discrimination because of race, color, religion, sex, gender, gender identity, gender expression, sexual orientation, marital status, national origin, ancestry, familial status, source of income, disability, or genetic information in housing accommodations is declared to be against public policy.
>
> It is the purpose of this part to provide effective remedies that will eliminate these discriminatory practices.
>
> This part shall be deemed an exercise of the police power of the state for the protection of the welfare, health, and peace of the people of this state.

Therefore, according to section 12921(a), "The opportunity to seek, obtain, and hold employment without discrimination because of race, religious creed, color, national origin, ancestry, physical disability, mental disability, medical condition, genetic information, marital status, sex, gender, gender identity, gender expression, age, or sexual orientation is hereby recognized as and declared to be a civil right."

But there is also no question that the Fair Employment and Housing Act contains a religious exemption: "12922. Notwithstanding any other provision of this part, an employer that is a religious corporation may restrict eligibility for employment in any position involving the performance of religious duties to adherents of the religion for which the corporation is organized." And, as it states in section 12964(b)(5)(j)(4)(B), "Notwithstanding subparagraph (A), for purposes of this subdivision, 'employer' does not include a religious association or corporation not organized for private profit, except as provided in Section 12926.2" (which has to do with religious entities that operate health-care facilities that are not restricted to adherents of the religion that established the entity).

The problem is that a religious organization not organized for profit (Calvary Chapel) operating something as a for-profit entity (Little Oaks School) is not something that was envisioned by the writers of the California Fair Employment and Housing Act.

But there is an even bigger problem here: the folly of discrimination laws in the first place.

First of all, if discrimination is wrong; if discrimination is bad; if discrimination is mean-spirited; if discrimination is hateful; if discrimination is bigoted; if discrimination is immoral; if discrimination is racist, sexist, xenophobic, and homophobic; if discrimination "foments domestic strife and unrest, deprives the state of the fullest utilization of its capacities for development and advancement, and substantially and adversely affects the interests of employees, employers, and the public in general," then it doesn't suddenly cease to be or do those things because the entity doing the discriminating is religious instead of secular, or nonprofit instead of for-profit.

Second, it would be madness for employers not to discriminate in hiring. People with physical disabilities are discriminated against by owners of coal mines. People without accounting experience are discriminated against by owners of accounting firms. People without a driver's license are discriminated against by owners of taxi companies. People without typing skills are discriminated against by executives looking for secretaries. Any company that requires a college degree is discriminating against those without degrees.

Third, "discrimination" is not a dirty word. Discrimination is not necessarily something bad. Discrimination is not something inherently evil. To discriminate is simply to distinguish, differentiate, or make a distinction. Discrimination involves choosing between or among options. We used to say that a man had discriminating taste.

Fourth, to discriminate against someone is not an act of aggression against him. The underlying premise of libertarianism is the nonaggression principle; that is, it is wrong to threaten or employ violence against someone unless in defense of one's person or property. No one of any race, religion, sex, color, national origin, or sexual orientation has the right to be employed by anyone else. Not hiring or not promoting someone on the basis of any of those things—however undeserved or irrational it might be—is not aggressing against him.

And fifth, to outlaw discrimination is to outlaw freedom of thought and freedom of association. Every man has the natural right to think or not to think whatever he wants about any other man. Every man has the natural right to associate or not to associate with any other man who is willing to associate with him. It doesn't matter if those decisions are or are not based on someone's identification with a group. It doesn't matter if the decisions are unwise, unreasonable, or ridiculous. It doesn't matter if they are based on prejudice, bigotry, or racism. Every free man has the right to think or not think what he wants about anyone else and associate or not associate with anyone else on any basis and for any reason. At least in a free society he does.

A free society must be free of discrimination laws altogether, not just laws without exceptions for religious discrimination.

*****

WORKPLACE DISCRIMINATION AND A FREE SOCIETY

Lately, it seems as though everyone thinks he is being discriminated against in the workplace.

According to a national survey of employed American adults who were asked about their experiences with religious discrimination at work, "What American Workers Really Think about Religion: Tanenbaum's 2013 Survey of American Workers and Religion,"

• More than half of employed Americans agree that there is a lot of discrimination against Muslims in the United States;
• One in three American workers has actually experienced or personally seen incidents of religious bias when he goes to work;
• Six in ten white evangelical Protestants agree that discrimination against Christians has become as big a problem as discrimination against other religious minorities; and
• 60% of atheists believe that people look down on their beliefs, as do nearly one-third of non-Christian religious workers (31%) and white evangelical Protestants (32%).

The survey was conducted by the Tanenbaum Center for Interreligious Understanding and the Public Religion Research Institute.

But it's not just religious discrimination that people say is taking place in the workplace. The latest form of alleged discrimination is discrimination on the basis of sexual orientation or gender identity. In fact, the U.S. Senate has just passed a bill to address that very thing.

The Employment Non-Discrimination Act of 2013 (S.815), a bill "to prohibit employment discrimination on the basis of sexual orientation or gender identity," recently passed the Senate by a vote of 64-32. Ten Republicans voted for the bill. Three Republicans and one Democrat did not vote. The bill is not expected to pass the Republican-controlled House of

Representatives.

The Employment Non-Discrimination Act (ENDA), not to be confused with ADEA, the Age Discrimination in Employment Act, forbids an employer with 15 or more employees

(1) to fail or refuse to hire or to discharge any individual, or otherwise discriminate against any individual with respect to the compensation, terms, conditions, or privileges of employment of the individual, because of such individual's actual or perceived sexual orientation or gender identity; or

(2) to limit, segregate, or classify the employees or applicants for employment of the employer in any way that would deprive or tend to deprive any individual of employment or otherwise adversely affect the status of the individual as an employee, because of such individual's actual or perceived sexual orientation or gender identity.

However, the bill is careful to add that it neither requires nor permits employers to grant "preferential treatment" to "any individual or to any group because of the actual or perceived sexual orientation or gender identity" or to adopt "a quota on the basis of actual or perceived sexual orientation or gender identity."

But of course, even though the Civil Rights Act of 1964 said basically the same thing, it led both to Affirmative Action policies and to quota systems so that employers could demonstrate to the government that they were not practicing discrimination.

ENDA also contains a religious exemption: "This Act shall not apply to a corporation, association, educational institution or institution of learning, or society that is exempt from the religious discrimination provisions of title VII of the Civil Rights Act of 1964."

About half of the 50 states and the District of Columbia already prohibit discrimination on the basis of sexual orientation, with many of those states also prohibiting employment discrimination on the basis of gender identity.

The origins of ENDA can be traced back to the Equality Act of 1974, which sought to ban discrimination against gays and lesbians. It died in committee in the House and was never introduced in the Senate.

ENDA itself was actually first introduced in Congress in 1994 by Rep. Gerry Studds (1937–2006) of Massachusetts, the first openly gay member of Congress. It would have made it illegal for employers to discriminate on the basis of a person's actual or perceived sexual orientation. House and Senate versions died in committee. A version of ENDA has been introduced in almost every session of Congress since then. Discrimination based on gender identity was added in 2007.

It is no surprise that Lesbian, Gay, Bisexual, and Transgender (LGBT) groups are hailing the Senate's passage of ENDA. And according to a

"Monthly Religion News Survey" by the Public Religion Research Institute, "Roughly three-quarters (73%) of Americans favor laws that would protect gay and lesbian people from employment discrimination."

Former Minnesota Republican senator Norm Coleman, now a lobbyist in support of ENDA, argues that his counterparts in the House should "unite" on the bill. Says Coleman, "We are the party of Lincoln. Our roots are in anti-discrimination." This is an "economic issue." "This is a right for someone to get a job, and to get a job based on their ability to do the job."

Coleman faces an uphill battle in the House. A spokesman for House Speaker John Boehner said that "the Speaker believes this legislation will increase frivolous litigation and cost American jobs, especially small-business jobs." A spokesman for Majority Leader Eric Cantor "confirmed that the House has no plans to take up ENDA." The conservative Heritage Foundation is opposed to ENDA because "the legislation would severely undermine civil liberties, increase government interference in the labor market, and trample on religious liberty."

Republican and conservative opposition to ENDA is inconsistent. They fully support federal civil rights laws that ban workplace discrimination in hiring, firing, compensation, assignment, classification, transfer, promotion, layoff, recall, recruitment, testing, training and apprenticeship programs, benefits, or retirement plans on the basis of race, color, religion, sex, national origin, age, pregnancy, martial status, disability, genetic information, birthplace, ancestry, culture, or linguistic characteristics common to a specific ethnic group.

Like Democrats and liberals, they would reason that everyone should be entitled to a job he is qualified for and able to perform regardless of his physical, national, cultural, or religious characteristics. No attempt was made during the Bush years, when conservative Republicans controlled both Houses of Congress, to abolish the Equal Employment Opportunity Commission (EEOC) or repeal any so-called civil rights laws.

Although Republican and conservative opposition to ENDA is often couched in economic terms, it is no secret that much of their opposition is politically motivated. The Tea Party and conservative elements in the Republican base view any anti-discrimination laws that relate to sexual orientation or gender identity as accommodating the LGBT lobby.

And then there are the inconsistencies in ENDA itself. Why the exemption for employers with fewer than 15 employees? Why the religious exemption? If workplace discrimination is bad, unfair, wrong, immoral, bigoted, racist, sexist, xenophobic, or homophobic, then it is still bad, unfair, wrong, immoral, bigoted, racist, sexist, xenophobic, or homophobic if a company has fewer than 15 employees or is a religious institution.

Libertarians alone are consistent here. ENDA should be opposed, not because it outlaws discrimination on the basis of sexual orientation or gender identity, but because it outlaws discrimination in the first place. In a free society everyone would have the right to discriminate against anyone for any reason.

To ban discrimination is to ban freedom of thought and freedom of association, not aggression or violence. In a free society everyone has the right to think whatever he wants to think about everyone else and to choose to associate or not associate with anyone on the basis of those thoughts. That includes employers and business owners. His opinions may be erroneous; his opinions may be illogical; his opinions may be irrational; his opinions may be based on stereotypes, prejudice, bigotry, or racism— but he is entitled to them. In a free society it couldn't be any other way.

Those who object to a company's hiring, promotion, pay, or benefit practices can seek employment elsewhere, protest the company's policies, boycott the company, and try to persuade others to do likewise.

And of course, any business that practiced discrimination would have to pay a price in whatever negative consequences might come as a result of it: bad publicity, smaller labor pool, loss of market share, low employee morale, a decline in profits, et cetera.

None of that means that libertarians think discrimination is always a good thing. Indeed, they may deplore workplace discrimination as much as any liberal, conservative, progressive, or moderate and yet still vehemently oppose discrimination laws.

A free society is not free of discrimination, but a free society is free of discrimination laws.

*****

DISCRIMINATION MEANS FREEDOM

Liberal "gay rights" advocates of are foaming-at-the-mouth furious over the passage of a bill by the Kansas House of Representatives that would permit discrimination against gay couples based on one's religious beliefs and prohibit anti-discrimination lawsuits based on such activity.

Introduced on January 16, HB2453, "an act concerning religious freedoms with respect to marriage," passed on February 12 by a vote of 72-49. Three Democrats joined the Republican majority in voting for the measure. Nineteen Republicans voted against the bill.

Section 1 of the bill reads:

Notwithstanding any other provision of law, no individual or religious entity shall be required by any governmental entity to do any of the following, if it would be contrary to the sincerely held religious beliefs of the individual or religious entity regarding sex or gender:

(a) Provide any services, accommodations, advantages, facilities, goods, or privileges; provide counseling, adoption, foster care and other social services; or provide employment or employment benefits, related to, or related to the celebration of, any marriage, domestic partnership, civil union or similar arrangement;

(b) solemnize any marriage, domestic partnership, civil union or similar arrangement; or

(c) treat any marriage, domestic partnership, civil union or similar arrangement as valid.

The bill defines a "religious entity" as "an organization, regardless of its nonprofit or for-profit status, and regardless of whether its activities are deemed wholly or partly religious, that is:

(1) A religious corporation, association, educational institution or society;

(2) an entity operated, supervised or controlled by, or connected with, a religious corporation, association, educational institution or society; or

3) a privately-held business operating consistently with its sincerely held religious beliefs, with regard to any activity described in section 1, and amendments thereto."

The bill also contains this unusual provision:

If an individual employed by a governmental entity or other nonreligious entity invokes any of the protections provided by section 1, and amendments thereto, as a basis for declining to provide a lawful service that is otherwise consistent with the entity's duties or policies, the individual's employer, in directing the performance of such service, shall either promptly provide another employee to provide such service, or shall otherwise ensure that the requested service is provided, if it can be done without undue hardship to the employer.

A writer at *Slate* says the bill is an "abomination" that will "legalize segregation of gay and straight people in virtually every arena of life." Another calls it "grotesque."

Someone at the *Daily Beast* maintains that the "Kansas House of Representatives took a step back to the 1890s with a shameful bill that borrows from Jim Crow to legalize discrimination." It is "meant to isolate and stigmatize a despised minority, under of the guise of some higher priority ('religious liberty')."

A professed "life-long believer who has read the Bible cover-to-cover more than once" at the *Huffington Post* believes that "Kansas House Bill 2453 is not only immoral, it's unbiblical."

At *Politicususa*, home of "real liberal politics," a writer insists that

"Republican fascists" in Kansas "are passing legislation to violate the Constitution and other Americans' rights." The consequence of this "to gay and straight people in Kansas is that every area of their lives will be controlled by religious bigots."

My thoughts on the matter as a Christian and a libertarian are as follows.

1. The bill will never pass. The Republican president of the Kansas Senate, Susan Wagle, has issued a statement saying that "a majority of the Republicans in the upper house will not vote for the bill." And of course, the Democratic minority is solidly against the bill. "A strong majority of my members support laws that define traditional marriage, protect religious institutions and protect individuals from being forced to violate their personal moral values," said Wagle. "However, my members also don't condone discrimination," she added.

2. In as much as the bill legalizes—if only in a small degree—the freedom to discriminate, such provisions in it should be welcomed.

3. Individuals employed by government agencies should quit if they can't "provide a lawful service that is otherwise consistent with the entity's duties or policies."

4. A Christian's acceptance of the Bible's negative assessment of homosexuality does not *necessarily* preclude him from providing certain "services, accommodations, advantages, facilities, goods, or privileges; provide counseling, adoption, foster care and other social services" or providing "employment or employment benefits" to gays or "other perverts."

5. Same-sex or LGBT couples should be viewed by Christians the same as straight or regular couples *who are not married* when it comes to providing certain "services, accommodations, advantages, facilities, goods, or privileges; provide counseling, adoption, foster care and other social services" or providing "employment or employment benefits."

6. The bill doesn't go far enough. It merely opens up a small window of freedom. Why limit legal discrimination to just providing something "related to, or related to the celebration of, any marriage, domestic partnership, civil union or similar arrangement"? Why not expand it to include something "related to, or related to the celebration of," any birthday, business activity, or change in the weather?

7. What not just say what you mean? Although the bill doesn't mention homosexuality or LGBT individuals, it is perfectly clear that the purpose of the bill is to allow business owners to discriminate against homosexuals by refusing to provide them with a service that they would ordinarily provide to heterosexuals. Why not just come out and say that it shall henceforth be legal to discriminate based on sexual orientation or gender identity?

8. There is no right to service. In a free society, every individual and

business owner has the right to refuse service. It is part and parcel of the inviolability of private property, the freedom of assembly, the freedom of association, the freedom of contract, free enterprise, and the free market. In a free society, business owners, like homeowners, have the right to run their businesses as they choose, including the right to refuse service, and including the right to discriminate on any basis against anyone. I am speaking of a free society—a society that hasn't existed in the United States for quite some time.

9. The freedom to discriminate doesn't mean that discrimination will take place. This is the beauty of the free market. To take an extreme example, suppose someone decided to open "The Homophobic Café" and post a sign on the door that said "No LGBT Allowed." This might result in a lack of business from not only LGBT individuals, but their families, friends, and unrelated sympathetic souls who deplore bigotry in any form. Then again, it might attract customers who were paranoid about eating in a restaurant with homosexuals. But even those who considered homosexuality to be a great sin might also stay away because of the extremists who might be attracted to the eatery. The success or failure of such a café should be decided by consumers in the restaurant market.

10. Kansas Republicans don't have a clue what a free society really is. They have to cloak discrimination under the guise of religious freedom because they are scared of the word and misunderstand the concept. They would never pass legislation saying that businesses could discriminate against anyone on the basis of race, creed, color, religion, age, gender, height, weight, disability, familial status, marital status, socioeconomic status, political preference, religious piety, national origin, odor, or appearance. That is, they would never legalize freedom.

Discrimination means freedom. A free society includes the freedom to discriminate based on anything, not just religion, but a free society also includes the freedom to discriminate based on nothing. A free society includes the freedom to discriminate against all gays, not just gay couples, but a free society also includes the freedom to discriminate against anyone, not just gays. And a free society likewise includes the freedom to discriminate whether doing so is logical or illogical, reasonable or unreasonable, rational or irrational.

*****

PREGNANCY DISCRIMINATION

Lawmakers in the House and Senate in my state of Florida have proposed two bills (HB 717 & SB 774) that would amend the Florida Civil Rights Act (FCRA) to prohibit pregnancy discrimination. Penalties would include back pay and punitive damages up to $100,000.

"Some (of the pregnant women) are terminated from their jobs or they go into a hostile work environment because of their pregnancy so we want to make sure we eliminate those kinds of things," said State Sen. Geraldine Thompson (D-Orlando). "Let's not allow employers to prevent women from doing their jobs," added State Rep. Lori Berman (D-Lantana).

There are three major problems with this political grandstanding.

One, pregnancy discrimination is already illegal in Florida. Two, if there is any form of discrimination that should not be prohibited, it is pregnancy discrimination. And three, no discrimination should be prohibited in the first place.

Pregnancy discrimination is already illegal in Florida. Title VII of the Civil Rights Act of 1964 prohibited sex discrimination in employment. Employers with 15 or more employees are covered by Title VII. In 1976, in the case of *General Electric Co. v. Gilbert*, the U.S. Supreme Court ruled that Title VII did not prohibit pregnancy discrimination. In response to this, Congress in 1978 amended Title VII with the Pregnancy Discrimination Act to also prohibit discrimination on the basis of pregnancy. In 1969, the Florida legislature passed the Florida Human Relations Act (FHRA). This prohibited discrimination based on "race, color, religion, or national origin."

The FHRA was amended in 1972 to also prohibit "freedom from discrimination because of sex." Subsequent amendments to the FHRA (now called the Florida Civil Rights Act or FCRA) did not add a pregnancy clause. Thus, pregnancy discrimination appears to be legal in Florida—but it's not. Florida courts are divided, depending on whether decisions are based on the letter of the law or the original intent of Title VII of the Civil Rights Act. But either way, discrimination on the basis of pregnancy is prohibited under federal law, which means that it is prohibited in Florida.

If there is any form of discrimination that should not be prohibited, it is pregnancy discrimination. Even opponents of discrimination on the basis on sex might agree. Does anyone really think that coal mines and fire departments should be forced to hire pregnant women to work underground extracting coal or up on ladders fighting fires? But aside from safety issues, does anyone really think that Hooters should be prohibited from refusing to hire pregnant waitresses and *Sports Illustrated* should be prohibited from refusing to hire pregnant bikini models? And don't think that some pregnant women wouldn't bother applying for any of these jobs. Being pregnant does not automatically make a woman intelligent. Most men discriminate against pregnant women all the time and no one thinks anything of it—including pregnant women. When looking for a girlfriend or a wife most men immediately discriminate against any woman that is pregnant (unless, of course, she is pregnant with his child).

No discrimination should be prohibited in the first place. Discrimination is not a dirty word. We discriminate every day when we choose Coke over Pepsi, Chevy over Ford, chocolate over vanilla, Wal-Mart over K-mart, cake over pie, wheat bread over rye bread, etc., etc., etc. And like it or not, we also discriminate against people. Like attracts like, whether it is political preference, financial condition, sexual orientation, social standing, religious piety, or skin color. What bothers people is the reasons people discriminate against other people or on what basis they discriminate. Some people don't mind discrimination if *they think* it is rational, logical, and reasonable. But if *they think* it is irrational, illogical, and unreasonable, or based on race, color, religion, sex, national origin, age, sexual orientation, gender identity, disability, or pregnancy, and is therefore hateful, unfair, wrong, immoral, bigoted, insensitive, racist, sexist, xenophobic, or homophobic, then it should be prohibited. But in a free society, as Future of Freedom Foundation president Jacob Hornberger explains:

> A person has the fundamental right to associate with anyone he chooses and on any basis he chooses. He might be the biggest bigot in the world, choosing only to associate with white supremacists, but that's what freedom is all about—the right to make whatever choices one wants in his life, so long as his conduct is peaceful—i.e., no murder, rape, theft, fraud, or other violent assaults against others.

To ban discrimination is to ban freedom of thought and freedom of association. Everyone in a free society should have the right to think whatever he wants to think about anyone else and to choose to associate or not associate, in both personal or business relationships, with anyone on the basis of those thoughts. His thoughts may be erroneous, illogical, irrational, or unreasonable, his opinions may be based on stereotypes, prejudice, bigotry, or racism—but in a free society everyone is entitled to his own thoughts and opinions.

Even though opponents of individual liberty and a free society don't want to hear it, and even though some defenders of these things shy away from the issue, a truly free society must include the freedom to discriminate against any individual or group—including pregnant women—and on any basis and for any reason—including pregnancy.

*****

JEB BUSH: ENEMY OF A FREE SOCIETY

Jeb Bush, like his father and brother before him, and like all of the Republicans and conservatives who, although they may disagree with Jeb on Common Core and immigration, agree with him wholeheartedly on this issue, hasn't the slightest idea what a free society is.

Bush officially declared his candidacy for the Republican presidential nomination earlier this month in the small town of Derry, New Hampshire (the state that holds the first primary). Speaking at a small, historic opera house known for hosting political events, Bush promised that if elected he would create sustained national economic growth of 4 percent, simplify the tax code, and repeal Obamacare.

But when asked how he would balance religious and personal freedoms, Bush cited the Washington state flower shop that was sued for refusing to do business with a same-sex couple that was getting married.

In 2013, after florist Barronelle Stutzman refused to provide flowers for a gay friend's same-sex wedding, she was sued by the two men and the attorney general of Washington for violating the state's anti-discrimination law. She was ordered to pay a $1,000 fine.

Said Bush:

> If someone walks into a flower shop and says, I'd like to buy flowers, you shouldn't be able to discriminate against them because they are gay. But if you're asking someone to participate in a religious ceremony or a marriage, they should have the right of conscious to be able to say, I love you, but I can't do it because it goes against my religious teachings. Does that make sense?

No, as a matter of fact, it doesn't make any sense.

Is Bush saying that asking a florist to provide flowers for a same-sex wedding is "asking someone to participate in a religious ceremony or a marriage"?

If so, then he should choose his words more carefully because the two things are not necessarily the same. Buying something from someone ordinarily has nothing to do with asking someone to participate in an activity. One can buy flowers from a florist for a wedding or any other event and not have the florist do anything beyond handing over the flowers or delivering them to an address you provide.

If not, then he makes even less sense because his two statements would then not be related at all. Even the staunchest proponent of same-sex marriage would not say that someone should be forced to participate in a same-sex or any other kind of wedding.

Is Bush saying that if someone walks into a flower shop and wants to buy flowers, you should be able to discriminate against him for other reasons besides his sexual orientation?

If so, then why is it wrong to discriminate on the basis of sexual orientation but not to discriminate on the basis of race, gender, or religion?

If not, then does he believe that no business owner should ever be allowed to refuse to do business with anyone? I can remember when certain businesses used to post signs reading: "No shirt, no shoes: no service." Even now, some restaurants have a dress code. Heck, even prisons have a dress code for visitors. Would Bush allow these exceptions to his "no discrimination policy"?

For someone who has given countless numbers of speeches, press conferences, and interviews, Jeb Bush should be more clear when he speaks.

I want to say seven things about discrimination.

First, there is nothing inherently wrong with discrimination. Despite its demonization by the news media—and Jeb Bush—the word discrimination is not a dirty word. Discrimination involves choosing between or among options. To discriminate is to choose one thing and exclude others. Men used to be lauded for having discriminating taste.

Second, Bush is as guilty as anyone when it comes to discrimination. When he married his Mexican wife Columba in 1974, he discriminated against every American woman, every white woman, every blonde, and every other woman in the world. He discriminated against the Episcopalian church of his youth when he converted to Catholicism in 1995. He also discriminated against all other religions and denominations in the world when he did this. Bush discriminates every day of his life. He discriminates against one store when he shops at another. He discriminates against vanilla ice cream when he eats chocolate ice cream. He discriminates against one interviewer when he chooses to do an interview with another instead. He discriminates against Pepsi when he drinks Coke. He discriminates against Democrats when he votes Republican. He discriminates against English when he speaks Spanish. Bush can't get through the day without discriminating against something or someone.

Third, why is it that customers can legally discriminate against businesses but businesses cannot legally discriminate against customers? Why is it that customers can discriminate against merchants for whatever reason they want—no matter how irrational, illogical, or unreasonable—and on any basis they want—no matter how racist, sexist, or homophobic—but not the other way around? Does Jeb Bush have an answer for this? No one is ever charged with violating an anti-discrimination law if he publicly announces that he will never patronize a particular business—because there are no such laws. Not yet.

Fourth, there is no right to service. Not if the concept of private property has any meaning. Not if the concept of freedom of association has any meaning. Not if the concept of a free market has any meaning. Not if the concept of freedom of contract has any meaning. In a free society, business owners have the right to run their businesses as they choose. Just as homeowners have the right to exclude anyone they want from entering their house for any reason, so business owners should have the right to refuse service to anyone—including Jeb Bush—for any reason.

Fifth, discriminating against someone is not aggressing against him. Discriminating against Jeb Bush on election day and voting for someone else is not an act of aggression against him. No one is entitled to a particular job. No one is entitled to rent a particular apartment. No one is entitled to buy a particular house. No one is entitled to enter anyone else's property. Not hiring, renting, selling, or granting the right of entry to someone on the basis of his race, religion, sex, color, national origin, political views, or sexual orientation may be wrong, immoral, hatful, or nonsensical, it may be based on stereotypes, prejudice, bigotry, or racism, but since it is not committing an act of aggression or violence against him, it should not be prohibited by force of law.

Sixth, discrimination means freedom. A free society must include the freedom to discriminate, not only against someone because he is gay, but because he is straight—or obese, bulimic, attractive, ugly, handicapped, tall, short, black, white, Hispanic, Asian, Catholic, Jewish, Muslim, Protestant, agnostic, married, single, divorced, transgendered, Democrat, Republican, liberal, conservative, young, old, pregnant, or named Jeb Bush.

And seventh, to ban discrimination is to ban freedom of thought. In a free society, everyone has the right to think what he wants to think about anyone else—including Jeb Bush—and choose to discriminate or not discriminate against anyone on the basis of those thoughts. His thoughts may be erroneous, illogical, irrational, or unreasonable, but in a free society everyone is entitled to freedom of thought.

Jeb Bush and the Republicans and conservatives who want the government to criminalize discrimination are enemies of a free society just like the Democrats, liberals, and progressives they castigate for favoring more government intervention in society.

*****

DISCRIMINATION AND THE CONSTITUTION

"Nowhere does the Constitution allow businesses to discriminate against others for religious reasons" ~ The Rev. Dr. Chuck Currie

Today being Constitution Day means that any educational institution receiving federal funds must hold an educational program about the Constitution on this day. As a libertarian, I see it as the perfect day, not to pledge to, swear allegiance to, or honor the Constitution, but to point out some of the latest nonsense that is being said about the Constitution.

September 17th has been designated Constitution Day because it is the anniversary of the signing of the U.S. Constitution in 1787. The Constitution was written by delegates from twelve states to a convention held in Philadelphia from May 25 to September 17, 1787. The Constitution was sent to the states for ratification on September 28, 1787. On December 7, 1787, Delaware became the first state to ratify the Constitution. The ninth state needed for ratification was obtained on June 21, 1788, when New Hampshire ratified. After Virginia (June 25, 1788) and New York (July 26, 1788) ratified the Constitution, the Confederation Congress passed a resolution on September 13, 1788, to put the new Constitution into effect on March 4, 1789.

I have previously pointed out (here and here) how the Constitution was flawed from the very beginning, that conservatives don't follow the Constitution, that being a constitutionalist is not enough, that constitutionalists don't even follow the Constitution, what the worst part of the Constitution is, that a new constitutional convention is unnecessary, how the Constitution is against the executive branch departments, that a constitutionalist shouldn't support the drug war, that it is better to be a libertarian than a constitutional conservative, that Democrats and Republicans are enemies of the Constitution, and that our current government is about as far removed from the Constitution as it could ever be.

The Constitution is not a libertarian document. However, if the government would just follow its own Constitution, we would certainly be much better off than we are now. There would be no welfare, no drug war, no TSA, no ATF, no Social Security, no Medicare, no Medicaid, no federal laboratories, no farm subsidies, no foreign aid, no Pell grants, no federal restrictions on home brewing of beer, and no Departments of Education, Health and Human Services, Housing and Urban Development, and Homeland Security.

On the other side of the spectrum, we have people and groups who claim that the Constitution *provides* the right to engage in some activity or use a product or service—like the supposed constitutional rights to abortion, birth control, pornography, sodomy, welfare, health care, and same-sex marriage—or *proscribes*, by virtue of the fact that it doesn't provide it, the right to undertake some action, like discrimination.

That the Constitution doesn't allow businesses to discriminate is the latest nonsense that is being said about the Constitution.

What prompted someone to utter such nonsense was a recent development in the case of the well-known refusal of an Oregon bakery to bake a cake for a same-sex wedding. Back in 2013, Sweet Cakes by Melissa, a bakery in the Portland area—owned by Aaron and Melissa Klein—refused to bake a wedding cake for a lesbian couple—Laurel and Rachel Bowman-Cryer—because doing so would violate the religious convictions of the bakery's owners. The Oregon Bureau of Labor and Industries (BOLI), which enforces some of Oregon's civil rights laws, recently ruled that because "businesses cannot discriminate or refuse service based on sexual orientation, just as they cannot turn customers away because of race, sex, disability, age or religion," Sweet Cakes by Melissa must pay $135,000 in damages to the lesbian couple "for emotional suffering stemming directly from unlawful discrimination."

Writing in the *Huffington Post*, the Rev. Dr. Chuck Currie, a United Church of Christ minister, and the Director of the Center for Peace and Spirituality and University Chaplain at Pacific University, says "the decision was, in fact, perfectly appropriate." The civil rights of the lesbian couple were "violated" and therefore they were "entitled to appropriate compensation after being denied service at the bakery because of their sexual orientation." Currie finds "discrimination against gays and lesbians intolerable." He applauds a recent resolution adopted by the General Synod of the United Church of Christ that "called on our local churches to fight new discriminatory laws that target the LGBTQ community with the intent of robbing any 'persons of any sexual orientation, gender identity or gender expression of the security that they will not be denied services, employment or even a place to live on the basis of their sexual orientation, gender identity or expression, or marital relationship.'" Curry maintains that "no business owners have any right to use faith as a legal excuse for discrimination." Why? Because "nowhere does the Constitution allow businesses to discriminate against others for religious reasons."

Baloney. Nonsense. Gibberish. Gobbledygook.

Like the typical Republican and conservative, Currie (the quintessential liberal Democrat), is about as ignorant of the Constitution as the typical public high school student (or teacher). Not only does the Constitution not prohibit businesses from discriminating against others for religious reasons, it doesn't prohibit businesses from discriminating against others for sex, race, color, gender identify, sexual orientation, national origin, age, pregnancy, martial status, disability, birthplace, ancestry, culture, political affiliation, physical appearance, or any other reason. One can search the Constitution morning, noon, and night with an electron microscope, x-ray vision, and night-vision goggles and not even find the word discrimination. How does the Constitution prohibit businesses from discriminating if it doesn't even contain the word? Not to mention that there is nothing the Constitution allows or doesn't allow businesses to do. That is the role of federal, state, and local regulations, all of which shouldn't exist, of course, but that is the subject of another article. The Constitution provides a framework for the federal government to operate and sets limits (mostly ignored) on its power. The Constitution does not provide a framework for Sweet Cakes by Melissa or any other business to operate, and neither does it set limits on what a business can or cannot do.

The Rev. Dr. Chuck Currie is a stark, raving lunatic.

And so is former Pennsylvania senator and bottom-of-the-pack Republican presidential candidate Rick Santorum. After the Colorado Court of Appeals recently ruled that Masterpiece Cakeshop in the Denver suburbs could not refuse to bake a cake for a same-sex wedding, Santorum explained to CBS's "Fact the Nation" that there has to be a distinction between "discrimination of the person because of who they are" and "unwillingness to participate in actions that are inconsistent with your religious beliefs."

But no such distinction is necessary. As I have pointed out in my many articles on discrimination:

• Discrimination is neither a dirty word nor an evil deed.
• There is no right to service.
• Discriminating against someone is not aggressing against him.
• To outlaw discrimination is to outlaw freedom of thought and freedom of association.
• A free society is not free of discrimination, but a free society is free of discrimination laws.
 • A free society must include the freedom to discriminate against any individual or group, on any basis, for any reason.

The Rev. Dr. Chuck Currie is not only an enemy of a free society, he is also an enemy of the Constitution.

*****

REPUBLICANS JUST DON'T GET IT ON DISCRIMINATION

ENDA is dead, but the Equality Act yet lives.

The Employment Non-Discrimination Act (ENDA), first introduced in the 103rd Congress in 1994 and in every Congress since then, except the 109th and the current 114th, would have forbidden an employer with 15 or more employees:

> (1) to fail or refuse to hire or to discharge any individual, or otherwise discriminate against any individual with respect to the compensation, terms, conditions, or privileges of employment of the individual, because of such individual's actual or perceived sexual orientation or gender identity; or

> (2) to limit, segregate, or classify the employees or applicants for employment of the employer in any way that would deprive or tend to deprive any individual of employment or otherwise adversely affect the status of the individual as an employee, because of such individual's actual or perceived sexual orientation or gender identity.

The "gender identity" provision was added beginning in 2009. The bill generally died in committee, but most recently (Dec. 2013) passed the Senate by a vote of 64-32, only to die in the House.

In its place, the more onerous Equality Act was introduced on July 23, 2015, in both Houses of Congress. In the House, H.R.3185 has 172 co-sponsors (only 1 of them a Republican). In the Senate, S.1858 has 40 co-sponsors (only 1 of them a Republican).

The Equality Act is a bill "to prohibit discrimination on the basis of sex, gender identity, and sexual orientation, and for other purposes." It would amend the Civil Rights Act of 1964 "to include sex, sexual orientation, and gender identity among the prohibited categories of discrimination or segregation in places of public accommodation." It would also expand the categories of public accommodations to include places or establishments that provide:

• exhibitions, recreation, exercise, amusement, gatherings, or displays;
• goods, services, or programs, including a store, a shopping center, an online retailer or service provider, a salon, a bank, a gas station, a food bank, a service or care center, a shelter, a travel agency, a funeral parlor, or a health care, accounting, or legal service; or
• transportation services.

"Establishment" is prohibited "from being construed to be limited to a physical facility or place." The legislation authorizes the Department of Justice (DOJ) to bring a civil action if it receives a complaint from an individual who claims to be:

• denied equal utilization of a public facility owned, operated, or managed by a state (other than public schools or colleges) on account of sex, sexual orientation, or gender identity; or
• denied admission to, or not permitted to continue attending, a public college by reason of sexual orientation or gender identity, thereby expanding DOJ's existing authority to bring such actions for complaints based on race, color, religion, sex, or national origin.

The Equality Act also:

Revises public school desegregation standards to provide for the assignment of students without regard to sexual orientation or gender identity.

Prohibits programs or activities receiving federal financial assistance from denying benefits to, or discriminating against, persons based on sex, sexual orientation, or gender identity.

Prohibits employers with 15 or more employees from discriminating based on sexual orientation or gender identity, subject to the same exceptions and conditions that currently apply to unlawful employment practices based on race, color, religion, sex, or national origin. Requires employers to recognize individuals in accordance with their gender identity if sex is a bona fide occupational qualification that is reasonably necessary to the normal operation of that particular business or enterprise.

Provides government employees with protections against discrimination based on sexual orientation or gender identity.

Authorizes DOJ to intervene in equal protection actions in federal court on account of sexual orientation or gender identity.

Requires protections against discrimination based on race, color, religion, sex, sexual orientation, gender identity, or national origin to include protections against discrimination based on: (1) an association with another person who is a member of such a protected class; or (2) a perception or belief, even if inaccurate, that an individual is a member of such a protected class. Prohibits the Religious Freedom Restoration Act of 1993 from providing a claim, defense, or basis for challenging such protections.

Prohibits an individual from being denied access to a shared facility, including a restroom, a locker room, and a dressing room, that is in accordance with the individual's gender identity.

Amends the Fair Housing Act, the Equal Credit Opportunity Act, and jury selection standards to add sexual orientation and gender identity as classes protected against discrimination under such laws.

Major corporations like Apple, General Mills, Facebook, Nike, and American Airlines have expressed support for the legislation. This follows the signing by over 100 prominent leaders in the tech industry of the "Joint Statement from Tech Industry Leaders" calling on legislatures "to add sexual orientation and gender identity as protected classes to their civil rights laws and to explicitly forbid discrimination or denial of services to anyone."

Late last year, the Obama Administration endorsed the legislation after reviewing the bill "for several weeks." Said White House press secretary Josh Earnest: "Upon that review it is now clear that the administration strongly supports the Equality Act." The president's endorsement came on the same day that he became the first sitting U.S. president to be featured on the cover of an LGBT publication.

Naturally, all current and former Democratic presidential nominee aspirants have expressed their support for the Equality Act.

With the exception of Robert Dold and Mark Kirk, both moderates from Illinois and the lone Republicans in the House and Senate who are cosponsoring their chamber's respective bills, Republicans in and out of Congress are balking at the legislation. But not because they have any philosophical objection to federal anti-discrimination legislation or because of any commitment to the principles of individual liberty, free association, free assembly, voluntary interaction, and private property.

The Civil Rights Act of 1964—an unconstitutional expansion of federal power that destroyed the rights of private property, freedom of assembly, freedom of association, free enterprise, and freedom of contract—currently prohibits discrimination in public accommodations based on race, color, religion, sex, or national origin. The Fair Housing Act of 1968 adds to this list discrimination based on disability and familial status.

Republicans have been accepting of these things for at least forty years. Even when Republicans controlled the White House and both

Houses of Congress for over four years of Bush's presidency, there was never any attempt change federal anti-discrimination law or abolish the Equal Employment Opportunity Commission (EEOC). Republicans have no problem with government attempts to prevent individuals and businesses from discriminating against certain groups in the course of renting hotel rooms, serving food, leasing apartments, selling houses, hiring employees, admitting to clubs and organizations, or engaging in commerce.

The main objection Republicans have to the Equality Act is how it will adversely affect religious liberty. Here is Andrew Walker, Director of Policy Studies for the Ethics and Religious Liberty Commission of the Southern Baptist Convention:

> The Equality Act represents the most invasive threat to religious liberty ever proposed. Were it to pass, its sweeping effects on religious liberty, free speech, and freedom of conscience would be historic.
>
> Aside from the enumerated protections that give rise to conflict between sexual identity and religious liberty, by elevating sexual orientation and gender identity to the level of race, the law's effect would functionally equate those who don't agree with it with racists and label them perpetrators of irrational bigotry. Indeed, to favor the Equality Act is to oppose and actively stigmatize the moral convictions that millions of Americans adhere to with abiding sincerity and deep religious precedent.
>
> All public accommodations and programs would be prohibited from denying any good or service to persons on the basis of sexual orientation and gender identity. This sounds acceptable in theory, but it leaves no room for accommodating the viewpoints of those whose services, speech, or creativity are used to serve wedding ceremonies. Consider the cases of florists, photographers, and bakers who have had no problems serving gay customers for years, but have objected to providing their services for gay weddings. The Equality Act leaves these individuals defenseless by failing to accommodate their sincere religious beliefs and by failing to distinguish between the dignity of gay individuals and the particular conduct (such as wedding ceremonies) in which some cannot in good conscience participate.

What he says is, of course, absolutely true. As is this:

> The bill's stated intentions and its actual consequences are very different. While the bill purports to protect individuals from discrimination, the Equality Act would discriminate against those who do not agree with a regime of laws premised on sexually permissive understandings of human nature that deny sexual complementarity. It would thus create a new form of discrimination by socially isolating certain beliefs.

What this all comes down to is that Republicans (and most conservatives) believe that discrimination is perfectly okay if it concerns religion. Thus, churches, synagogues, and mosques should be free to hire as ministers, rabbis, and imams only men for leadership positions and discriminate against women. Christian, Jewish, and Muslim schools should be free to hire as teachers just Christians, Jews, and Muslims and discriminate against those of other religions. Religious organizations should be free to admit only heterosexual members and discriminate against homosexual, transgender, and gender fluid individuals. Religious florists, photographers, and bakers should be free to refuse to provide their services for same-sex weddings.

But do Republicans and conservatives really believe what they are saying? Do they actually believe that religious discrimination is okay? Not always. Consider the recent case of Kuwait Airways refusing to carry Israelis on its airplanes.

After thirty-five years of service, Kuwait Airways recently ended its flights between New York City and London rather than have to transport Israelis between the two cities. Kuwait, like sixteen other mostly Arab countries, does not recognize the state of Israel. And Kuwaiti law prohibits domestic companies from conducting business with Israeli citizens. Kuwait Airways does not allow Israelis on its nonstop flights between New York City and Kuwait City because Israelis are granted visas to visit Kuwait. At issue is just the flights from New York City that used to connect in London before going on to Kuwait City. After an Israeli citizen filed a complaint when his attempt to book a flight on Kuwait Airways from New York City to London was refused, the U.S. Department of Transportation (DOT) ruled that the airline's longstanding policy of prohibiting Israelis from traveling on those flights amounted to "unreasonable discrimination" because Israeli passport holders have the legal right to travel from the United States to the United Kingdom. "An airline does not have the right to refuse to sell tickets to and transport a person between the U.S. and any third country where they are allowed to disembark based on the laws of that country," said a spokeswoman for the DOT.

I don't know of a single Republican who has come to the defense of Kuwait Airways for its practice of discrimination against Israelis. Keep in mind that the Kuwaiti attitude toward Israel is ultimately a religious dispute.

Republicans just don't get it on discrimination.

If discrimination is bigoted, racist, sexist, xenophobic, homophobic, unjust, and just plain wrong, then it doesn't suddenly cease to be those things when the discrimination is based on some religious conviction.

But discrimination is not "wrong." In fact, there is nothing inherently "wrong" with discrimination. It is not a dirty word. No one has the right to work any job, be served in any restaurant, shop at any store, enter anyone's property, rent any hotel room, lease any apartment, buy any house, be admitted to any club or organization, or associate with someone who doesn't want to associate with him. Discrimination is not aggression—even if it is based on stereotypes, prejudice, bigotry, or racism, and even if it appears to be illogical, irrational, nonsensical, or unreasonable—and should not be prohibited by force of law.

Discrimination means freedom. All discrimination, not just religious discrimination.

A free society is a society free of discrimination laws.

*****

SOCIETY'S NEWEST VICTIMS OF DISCRIMINATION

The federal government has long been concerned about discrimination based on race, color, religion, sex, national origin, age, and disability. Although the Obama administration supports adding discrimination based on sexual orientation or gender identity to the list, they haven't been officially added yet. Meanwhile, the administration has come to the rescue of another group that it feels is being discriminated against: convicted felons.

Late last year, Barack Obama directed the federal government's Office of Personnel Management (OPM) to modify its hiring rules to delay inquiries into an applicant's criminal history until later in the hiring process for federal employment. The purpose of the change is to reduce discrimination against former convicts, thus making it easier for the federal government to hire people with criminal records. Said the president,

> Now, the federal government is a big employer, as you know, and like a lot of big employers, on many job applications there's a box that asks if you have a criminal record. If you answer yes, then a lot of times you're not getting a call back.

> We're going to do our part in changing this. The federal government, I believe, should not use criminal history to screen out applicants before we even look at their qualifications. We can't dismiss people out of hand simply because of a mistake that they made in the past.

This "ban the box" (the box next to the question asking whether the applicant has ever been convicted of a crime) directive applies only to federal employees, not federal contractors—at least not yet.

In the past few years, "ban the box" laws applicable to private-sector employers that do business with government agencies and private-sector employers in general have been passed on the state, county, and city level. These laws require employers to remove from employment applications questions about an applicant's having a criminal record and not to ask about an applicant's possible criminal history until later in the hiring process. Some of them also prohibit employers from ordering a criminal-background check on job applicants until after a conditional offer of employment has been made. There is also legislation in force that restricts the types of criminal records employers can consider in making hiring decisions.

But not only is the Obama administration wanting to help convicted felons get employment, the administration also wants to help them get housing.

New guidelines recently issued by the Department of Housing and Urban Development (HUD) will make it tougher for homesellers and landlords to discriminate against applicants who have criminal records.

According to HUD,

> As many as 100 million U.S. adults—or nearly one-third of the population—have a criminal record of some sort.

> Since 2004, an average of over 650,000 individuals have been released annually from federal and state prisons, and over 95 percent of current inmates will be released at some point.

And since "African Americans and Hispanics are arrested, convicted and incarcerated at rates disproportionate to their share of the general population" discriminating against applicants who have a criminal record is "likely to have a disproportionate impact on minority home seekers."

The Fair Housing Act already prohibits "discrimination in the sale, rental, or financing of dwellings and in other housing-related activities on the basis of race, color, religion, sex, disability, familial status or national origin." But now "policies that exclude persons based on criminal history must be tailored to serve the housing provider's substantial, legitimate, nondiscriminatory interest and take into consideration such factors as the type of the crime and the length of the time since conviction."

But even "where a policy or practice excludes individuals with only certain types of convictions, a housing provider will still bear the burden of proving that any discriminatory effect caused by such policy or practice is justified." And even though "a criminal record can constitute a legitimate, nondiscriminatory reason for a refusal to rent or other adverse action by a housing provider, a plaintiff or HUD may still prevail by showing that the criminal record was not the true reason for the adverse housing decision, and was instead a mere pretext for unlawful discrimination."

Now, it is true that when persons are released from prison, gaining adequate employment and having access to affordable housing is crucial to successful reentry into society. It is also true that many formerly incarcerated individuals encounter significant barriers to securing employment and housing.

The case can certainly be made that just because someone has a criminal record, it doesn't follow that he is not qualified for some particular job or wouldn't be a good employee. And the case can also certainly be made that just because someone has a criminal record it doesn't follow that he will be a bad tenant or not pay his rent.

That is especially true of those ensnared by drug laws. Libertarians would argue that vices are not crimes. Consequently, no one should ever have been arrested or imprisoned for the non-crime of drug possession, use, buying, selling, manufacturing, cultivating, or "trafficking," and no one's future options for employment and housing should be diminished on that account.

The problem is simply who decides what the consequences are of someone's having a criminal record. Who decides whether someone should not be hired because of his criminal record? Who decides whether a landlord should rent an apartment to someone with a criminal record? Who decides whether a homeowner should rent or sell his home to someone with a criminal record? Who decides what type of crimes will exclude someone from a particular job or place to live? Who decides how recently a crime has to be committed before it excludes someone from a particular job or apartment? Who decides whether someone who has served time in prison is sufficiently rehabilitated? Who decides at what point in the employment interview or housing application process that someone's criminal record should be disclosed? Who decides whether a criminal background check of an applicant for employment or housing is even conducted? Who decides whether the discrimination against someone with a criminal record is "reasonable" or "justifiable"?

In a free society, businesses, employers, homesellers, and landlords decide those questions, not the government. It doesn't matter if the discrimination against convicted felons is unreasonable, unjustifiable, illogical, irrational, nonsensical, or stupid. And it doesn't matter if the discrimination is based on stereotypes, partiality, assumptions, prejudice, bigotry, or racism.

Discrimination is not aggression. No one has the right to any particular job or place to live. To ban discrimination is to ban freedom of thought. And if a business owner cannot restrict whom he employs, and a property owner cannot restrict whom he rents or sells to, he has no property rights.

A free society must include the freedom to discriminate, not only against someone because of his criminal record, but for any reason and on any basis.

*****

RELIGIOUS LIBERTY BILLS MISS THE REAL ISSUE

Same-sex marriage was first legalized in the United States in Massachusetts in 2004. That came as no surprise. But then followed the states of

Connecticut (2008), Iowa (2009), Vermont (2009), and New Hampshire (2010), plus Washington, D.C. By the time of the Supreme Court's decision in *Obergefell v. Hodges* (June 26, 2015), which ruled that marriage between same-sex couples was a fundamental right guaranteed by the Fourteenth Amendment, same-sex marriage was already legal in thirty-two other states, many because of federal court decisions, not by state court decisions, legislative statutes, or popular votes.

But, as usually happens when it comes to government interference in the market or society, there were unintended consequences of these actions.

Over the course of the last ten or so years, there have been numerous high-profile cases of business owners—usually bakers, photographers, and florists—refusing, on religious grounds, to provide wedding-related services to same-sex couples. Most have lost their court battles to "freely exercise" their religion.

For example, Sweet Cakes by Melissa, a bakery in the Portland area, was ordered to pay $135,000 in damages to a lesbian couple "for emotional suffering stemming directly from unlawful discrimination" after the bakery refused to bake a cake for the couple's wedding.

It is on account of religious conviction, not bigotry, that Christian small business owners are refusing to provide wedding-related services to same-sex couples. Consider the case of Jack Phillips, owner of Masterpiece Cakeshop in Colorado. After refusing to bake a cake for a gay couple in 2012, Colorado's Civil Rights Commission ruled in 2013 that Phillips discriminated against the couple and ordered him to change his store policy or face fines. Explained Phillips: "I don't feel that I should participate in their wedding, and when I do a cake, I feel like I'm participating in the ceremony or the event or the celebration that the cake is for." In 2015, the Colorado Court of Appeals likewise ruled against him. Because of this, his shop no longer makes wedding cakes of any kind, although it used to make 200-250 wedding cakes per year. But Phillips has said that "he has no problem with lesbian, gay, bisexual or transgender (LGBT) customers or staff members." He has also maintained that "he has no problem serving gay people at his store," just that "making a wedding cake for a same-sex wedding would violate his Christian beliefs."

So, what we are dealing with here is just *certain* businesses discriminating for a *certain* reason against certain people who want them to provide a *certain* service. I have never heard of any case of a hardware store or grocery store refusing to sell merchandise to someone because he was a member of the "LGBT community." I have never heard of any case of a movie theater or amusement park refusing to admit same-sex couples.

Several state legislatures have introduced "religious liberty bills" in an attempt to protect the right of *certain* business owners to discriminate against *certain* people in certain instances for *certain* reasons. Some of the legislation has passed, like in Mississippi, and some have been vetoed by state governors, like in Georgia.

Since it did pass in Mississippi, let's look briefly at the law as it stands. House Bill 1523 basically allows private businesses and religious organizations to refuse wedding-related services to same-sex couples if such action is based on religious beliefs that oppose same-sex marriage. Although government entities in Mississippi cannot refuse service to anyone, individual government employees may opt out.

House Bill 1523, the Protecting Freedom of Conscience from Government Discrimination Act, is designed to protect the sincerely held religious beliefs or moral convictions that

(a) Marriage is or should be recognized as the union of one man and one woman;

(b) Sexual relations are properly reserved to such a marriage; and

(c) Male (man) or female (woman) refer to an individual's immutable biological sex as objectively determined by anatomy and genetics at time of birth.

As it relates specifically to denial of service, the bill states:

(4) The state government shall not take any discriminatory action against a person wholly or partially on the basis that the person declines to participate in the provision of treatments, counseling, or surgeries related to sex reassignment or gender identity transitioning or declines to participate in the provision of psychological, counseling, or fertility services based upon a sincerely held religious belief or moral conviction described in Section 2 of this act.

(5) The state government shall not take any discriminatory action against a person wholly or partially on the basis that the person has provided or declined to provide the following services, accommodations, facilities, goods, or privileges for a purpose related to the solemnization, formation, celebration, or recognition of any marriage, based upon or in a manner consistent with a sincerely held religious belief or moral conviction described in Section 2 of this act:

(a) Photography, poetry, videography, disc-jockey services, wedding planning, printing, publishing or similar marriage-related goods or services; or

(b) Floral arrangements, dress making, cake or pastry artistry, assembly-hall or other wedding-venue rentals, limousine or other car-service rentals, jewelry sales and services, or similar marriage-related services, accommodations, facilities or goods.

(6) The state government shall not take any discriminatory action against a

person wholly or partially on the basis that the person establishes sex-specific standards or policies concerning employee or student dress or grooming, or concerning access to restrooms, spas, baths, showers, dressing rooms, locker rooms, or other intimate facilities or settings, based upon or in a manner consistent with a sincerely held religious belief or moral conviction described in Section 2 of this act.

Governor Phil Bryant signed the bill into law on April 5 despite opposition from gay-rights groups and some in the business community. "This bill merely reinforces the rights which currently exist to the exercise of religious freedom as stated in the First Amendment to the U.S. Constitution," said the Republican governor. It does not "limit any constitutionally protected rights or actions of any citizen of this state under federal or state laws."

But, on the other hand, someone from the ACLU said the bill "flies in the face of the basic American principles of fairness, justice and equality and will not protect anyone's religious liberty." The bill is "an attack on the citizens of our state, and it will serve as the Magnolia State's badge of shame."

The new law takes effect on July 1.

Before looking at the problem with religious liberty bills, it should be said that *some* liberty is better than *no* liberty. The state allowing *certain* businesses to discriminate in *certain* areas against *certain* people for *certain* reasons is better than the state allowing *no* businesses to discriminate in *no* areas against *no* one for *no* reason.

It is also true that *more* liberty is better than *less* liberty. The state *sometimes* allowing *certain* businesses to discriminate in *certain* areas against *certain* people for *certain* reasons is better than the state *seldom* allowing *certain* businesses to discriminate in *certain* areas against *certain* people for *certain* reasons.

Just like tax deductions for *some* are better than tax deductions for *none*, and tax credits for *many* are better than tax credits for *few*.

So, what's wrong with religious liberty bills? Don't look to People for the American Way to tell you. Better look to libertarians who support individual liberty, private property, freedom of contract, and freedom of association and oppose political correctness, the nanny state, government regulation, and the police state.

Religious liberty bills miss the real issue.

The real issue is freedom. In a free society, business owners have the right to refuse service to anyone for any reason on any basis. Religion has nothing to do with it. It's not just a pizza delivery driver refusing to deliver pizza to certain neighborhoods. It's not just a taxi driver refusing to pick up or drop off patrons on certain streets. And it goes much deeper than "no shirt, no shoes, no service," as I can remember signs posted in some store windows.

In a free society, discrimination against a potential customer in any form and for any cause *must* be permissible. It doesn't matter if the denial of service is because of religion, race, creed, color, complexion, national origin, ancestry, gender, age, sexual orientation, gender identity, health condition, disability, mental state, IQ, height, weight, hair color, eye color, hair style, facial hair, tattoos, scars, pregnancy, marital status, criminal record, political ideology, or socio-economic status.

In a free society, business owners likewise have the absolute right to hire only certain people and give discounts to only certain people. Just like private clubs and organizations have the absolute right of inclusion and exclusion.

The fact that denying someone service, not hiring someone, and not admitting someone to your club might be based on stereotypes, prejudice, hate, sexism, xenophobism, homophobism, bigotry, or racism is immaterial.

The fact that denying someone service, not hiring someone, and not admitting someone to your club might be viewed as unfair, illogical, irrational, nonsensical, or unreasonable is also immaterial.

I don't hear any legislator in any state who supports a religious liberty bill making the case for freedom.

If an individual can discriminate against a business in any way, for any reason, and on any basis, then why can't a business discriminate against an individual? What is so unreasonable about that?

Discrimination is not aggression. It is freedom.

*****

I'M A DISCRIMINATOR

I plead guilty. I'm tired of the deception. I can't hide it anymore. The stress is killing me. I am coming out of the closet. May God have mercy on me. I have a confession to make. I'm a discriminator.

Consider the following—

I prefer to drive a Chevy and discriminate against all other makes of cars. This doesn't mean that I want to do anything to stop anyone from driving a Ford. This doesn't mean that I hope all Hondas and Toyotas crash. It just means that I prefer to drive a Chevy.

I prefer to drink regular Coke and discriminate against all other types of soft drinks. This doesn't mean that I hope all diet soft drinks make people sick. This doesn't mean that I want to keep people from drinking Pepsi. It just means that I prefer to drink Coke.

I prefer to put French dressing on my salad and discriminate against all other varieties of salad dressing. This doesn't mean that I want the government to ban Thousand Island dressing. This doesn't mean that I want restaurants to poison their supplies of Italian dressing. It just means that I prefer to eat French dressing.

I prefer to watch drag racing and discriminate against all other forms of racing. This doesn't mean that I hope all NASCAR races get rained out. This doesn't mean that I want to prevent people from attending Formula One races. It just means that I prefer to watch drag racing.

I prefer to eat apples and discriminate against all other types of fruit. This doesn't mean that I want the government to ban banana imports. This doesn't mean that I hope all peach trees get infected with blight. It just means that I prefer to eat apples.

I prefer to stay at a Hampton Inn and discriminate against all other hotels. This doesn't mean that I want to bomb all Holiday Inns. This doesn't mean that I hope all Quality Inns close down. It just means that I prefer to stay at Hampton Inn.

I prefer to order Domino's pizza and discriminate against all other pizza places. This doesn't mean that I hope all other pizza places go out of business. This doesn't mean that I will never eat pizza from Pizza Hut. It just means that I prefer Domino's.

I prefer to wear a blue suit and discriminate against all other suit colors. This doesn't mean that I think everyone else should wear a blue suit. This doesn't mean that I want the government to punish wearers of black suits. It just means that I prefer to wear a blue suit.

I prefer to eat beef and discriminate against all other types of meat. This doesn't mean that I hope that all chickens die of disease. This doesn't mean that I want farmers to slaughter all of their pigs. It just means that I prefer to eat beef.

I prefer to eat green beans and discriminate against all other green vegetables. This doesn't mean that I wish all heads of lettuce would get infected with E. coli. This doesn't mean that I want the government to mandate that everyone must purchase green beans. It just means that I prefer to eat green beans.

I prefer to read non-fiction books and discriminate against all other forms of literature. This doesn't mean that I want to burn magazines and comic books. This doesn't mean that I want to prevent anyone from reading novels. It just means that I prefer to read non-fiction.

I prefer to put ketchup on my French fries and discriminate against all other condiments. This doesn't mean that I think mayonnaise and barbecue sauce are disgusting. This doesn't mean that I want mustard producers to go out of business. It just means that I prefer to eat ketchup.

Three things should be noticed about my discrimination, other than the fact that it is real and not hypothetical.

First, in each of the above cases, my discrimination is not the result of any technical, scientific, controlled, or empirical study. My discrimination is simply the result of my own personal preferences, judgments, beliefs, and opinions.

Second, my discrimination against certain foods, beverages, colors, hotels, literature, and cars is not an act of aggression against any of these things. No book has the right to be read. Just because someone opens a hotel doesn't mean anyone has to stay there. No fruit, animal, or vegetable has the right to be eaten. Just because a store offers many varieties of an item doesn't mean that its customers have to purchase each one. No condiment or dressing has the right to be used.

Three, although some may consider my discrimination to be arbitrary, capricious, subjective, and based on ignorance or prejudice, and others may consider my discrimination to be irrational, nonsensical, groundless, and based on neither reason nor logic, no one would say that I should be fined, imprisoned, or forced to drive a car I don't want to drive, stay at a hotel I don't want to stay at, watch a race that I don't want to watch, or eat or drink something that I don't want to eat or drink.

But, some will say, these objects of discrimination are things; they are not people. It is one thing to discriminate against a car, a food, a beverage, a color, a hotel, or a book, but it is another thing to discriminate against individuals or groups of people. It is always wrong to discriminate against people.

Is it really? Is it always wrong to discriminate against people? Since when?

Consider the following—

I prefer to have my hair cut by a particular barber and discriminate against all other barbers. This doesn't mean that I want to kill all other barbers. This doesn't mean that I want all other barbers to go out of business. It just means that I prefer a certain barber.

I prefer to have my teeth cleaned by a particular dentist and discriminate against all other dentists. This doesn't mean that think everyone should see my dentist for dental care. This doesn't mean that I want the government to punish those who see other dentists. It just means that I prefer a certain dentist.

I prefer to have my car repaired by a particular mechanic and discriminate against all other mechanics. This doesn't mean that I think all other mechanics are bad. This doesn't mean that I hope all the cars repaired by other mechanics crash. It just means that I prefer a certain mechanic.

I prefer to listen to the music of a particular composer and discriminate against all other composers. This doesn't mean that I hate all other composers. This doesn't mean that I want to do anything to stop anyone from listening to some other composer. It just means that I prefer a certain composer.

I prefer to have my medical care performed by a particular doctor and discriminate against all other doctors. This doesn't mean that I hope the patients of all other doctors get sicker and die. This doesn't mean that I want other doctors to be sued for malpractice. It just means that I prefer a certain doctor.

Again, three things should be noticed about my discrimination: It is based on my own personal preferences, it is not an act of aggression against individuals or groups of people, and no one would say that I should be fined, imprisoned, or forced to stop discriminating against the barbers, dentists, mechanics, composers, or doctors I refuse to patronize.

Okay, okay, some will say. I get your point, but it is still mostly or usually or sometimes wrong to discriminate against people. It must be. It just has to be.

But is it? Why is it?

What opponents of discrimination; that is, supporters of laws against freedom of choice, will eventually say when pinned down is that it is not wrong to discriminate against individuals or groups as long as such discrimination is not based on stereotypes, prejudice, bigotry, sexism, racism, homophobia, or xenophobia.

But they don't actually believe this. If someone's discrimination against certain barbers, dentists, mechanics, composers, or doctors is in fact based on stereotypes, prejudice, bigotry, sexism, racism, homophobia, or xenophobia, then opponents of discrimination, although they might say that such discrimination is wrong or immoral, would not go so far as to say that such discrimination should result in fines, imprisonment, or being forced to patronize barbers, dentists, mechanics, composers, or doctors that someone doesn't want to.

What opponents of discrimination; that is, supporters of laws against freedom of choice, have done is create two standards: one for buyers, customers, and consumers and one for sellers, businesses, and producers.

But if it is not illegal for buyers, customers, and consumers to discriminate (for any reason and on any basis) against sellers, businesses, and producers, then neither should it be illegal for sellers, businesses, and producers to discriminate (for any reason and on any basis) against buyers, customers, and consumers.

No one has the right to have his hair cut by a particular barber, to have his teeth cleaned by a particular dentist, to have his car repaired by a particular mechanic, to hire a particular composer, or to be treated by a particular doctor. Just like no one has the right to be employed in a particular job, to be served in a particular restaurant, to buy a particular house, to lease a particular apartment, to be admitted to any club or organization, to have a wedding cake made by a particular baker, or to have a wedding photographed by a particular photographer.

To criminalize discrimination is to criminalize freedom of thought.

*****

DISCRIMINATION MISCONCEPTIONS

Back in 2013, Barronelle Stutzman, the owner of Arlene's Flowers in Richland, Washington, refused to provide flowers for a gay friend's same-sex wedding. The legal battle that ensued has now ended: The Washington State Supreme Court just unanimously ruled that the florist violated the state's anti-discrimination law.

The case has given rise to some misconceptions about discrimination. Here is the back story.

In 2012, the state of Washington enacted Senate Bill 6239, which recognized same-sex marriage. Gay men Robert Ingersoll and Curt Freed, who had been a couple since 2004, decided to get married in September of 2013. At the time of his engagement, Ingersoll had been a customer of Arlene's Flowers and Gifts for at least nine years. Stutzman, an active member of a Southern Baptist church who believed that marriage can exist only between a man and a woman, knew that Ingersoll was gay and in a relationship with Freed. When Ingersoll spoke with Stutzman about providing flowers for his wedding, she told him that she would be unable to do so because of her religious beliefs. She gave Ingersoll the names of other florists who might be willing to serve him and hugged Ingersoll before he left the store.

Stutzman said she "draws a distinction between creating floral arrangements—even those designed by someone else—and selling bulk flowers and 'raw materials,' which she would be happy to do for Ingersoll and Freed." But she said she believes that "to create floral arrangements is to use her 'imagination and artistic skill to intimately participate in a same-sex wedding ceremony.'"

Ingersoll maintains that he left "feeling very hurt and upset emotionally." His partner Freed posted something on Facebook about the incident and the story "drew the attention of numerous media outlets." Ingersoll and Freed then "lost enthusiasm for a large ceremony" and got married in July in "a modest ceremony at their home."

That, of course, should have been the end of it. But

> after the state became aware of Stutzman's refusal to sell flowers to Ingersoll and Freed, the Attorney General's Office sent Stutzman a letter. It sought her agreement to stop discriminating against customers on the basis of their sexual orientation and noted that doing so would prevent further formal action or costs against her. The letter asked her to sign an "Assurance of Discontinuance," which stated that she would no longer discriminate in the provision of wedding floral services.

Stutzman refused.

The state then filed a complaint about injunctive and other relief against both Stutzman and Arlene's Flowers under the Consumer Protection Act (CPA) and the Washington Law Against Discrimination (WLAD). Stutzman answered by "asserting, among other defenses, that her refusal to furnish Ingersoll with wedding services was protected by the state and federal constitutions' free exercise, free speech, and freedom of association guarantees." Ingersoll and Freed then filed a private lawsuit against Stutzman and Arlene's Flowers, which the trial court consolidated with the state's case.

The trial court ultimately decided against the defendant and awarded "permanent injunctive relief, as well as monetary damages for Ingersoll and Freed to cover actual damages, attorneys' fees, and costs." The court ruled not only that Stutzman violated the WLAD's "public accommodations" provision, violated the CPA by refusing to sell floral services, and was personally liable, but also made five constitutional rulings. It concluded that the application of the WLAD's "public accommodations" provision to Stutzman in this case:

(1) did not violate Stutzman's right to free speech under the First Amendment to the United States Constitution or article I, section 5 of the Washington Constitution,

(2) did not violate Stutzman's right to religious free exercise under the First Amendment,

(3) did not violate her right to free association under the First Amendment,

(4) did not violate First Amendment protections under the hybrid rights doctrine, and

(5) did not violate Stutzman's right to religious free exercise under article I, section 11 of the Washington Constitution.

Stutzman appealed to the Washington State Supreme Court, which affirmed the trial court's rulings last month.

There are a number of misconceptions that people have about discrimination, including Barronelle Stutzman, the attorneys who represented her, and the state's attorney general.

Stutzman contended that her floral arrangements were "artistic expressions protected by the state and federal constitutions and that the WLAD impermissibly compels her to speak in favor of same-sex marriage." She contended that her floral arrangements are "speech" for purposes of First Amendment protections "because they involve her artistic decisions." She argued that the WLAD violated her First Amendment protections against "compelled speech" because it "forces her to endorse same-sex marriage." She sought "an exemption permitting discrimination in public accommodations." She argued, "discrimination cannot be 'invidious'—and thus subject to governmental prohibition—if it is based on religious beliefs."

The Alliance Defending Freedom (ADF) attorneys who represented Stutzman argued: "It's wrong for the state to force any citizen to support a particular view about marriage or anything else against their will. Freedom of speech and religion aren't subject to the whim of a majority; they are constitutional guarantees."

Washington's attorney general, Bob Ferguson, said that "Arlene's Flowers in Richland doesn't have to sell wedding flowers at all." However, "if they choose to sell wedding flowers, they cannot choose to sell wedding flowers only for heterosexual couples and deny that same service to gay couples."

Let's clear up these and other misconceptions about discrimination from the libertarian perspectives of property rights, the non-aggression principle, and individual liberty.

Designing, making, selling, or not selling floral arrangements has nothing to do with free speech or speech. The U.S. Supreme Court has greatly erred by labeling certain actions as a form of speech in order to protect them instead of just recognizing property rights.

Refusing to sell a product has everything to do with property rights. Since no potential customer has a claim on the property of any business owner, he has no legal recourse if the owner of the property refuses to sell it to him.

Selling someone a product has nothing to do with endorsing the buyer's opinions or use of the product.

Discrimination is a crime in search of a victim. Every real crime needs a tangible victim with measurable damages. Discrimination is not aggression, force, or threat. It should never be a crime.

To outlaw discrimination is to outlaw freedom of thought.

Public accommodations are still private businesses. Just because they serve the public by offering to sell them goods and/or services doesn't mean that they should be regarded as public libraries, public parks, and public buildings that have to accept all members of the public.

If discrimination is wrong, immoral, unjust, hateful, and bigoted, then it doesn't suddenly cease to be these things because the entity doing the discriminating is religious in nature or the person doing the discriminating is doing it for religious reasons.

There is no "right to service." In a free society, business owners have the right to refuse service to anyone for any reason on any basis.

If a florist can choose not to sell a particular type of flower arrangement, then why can't it choose not to sell a flower arrangement to a particular person? If the government is so interested in stamping out discrimination, they why doesn't it mandate that florists sell every type of flower arrangement for every situation? Aren't florists who don't sell flower arrangements for weddings discriminating against customers who want to buy them and suppliers who want to provide the necessary raw products to the florists?

If an individual can discriminate against a business owner in any way, for any reason, and on any basis, then why can't a business owner likewise discriminate against an individual?

That discrimination may be based on based on stereotypes, prejudice, hate, sexism, xenophobism, homophobism, bigotry, or racism is immaterial.

That discrimination may be because of race, creed, religion, sex, color, age, national origin, political ideology, IQ, physical appearance, marital status, socio-economic status, disability, gender identity or sexual orientation is irrelevant.

That someone thinks an act of discrimination is unfair, illogical, irrational, nonsensical, unreasonable, or just plain stupid is of no consequence.

Barronelle Stutzman should be able to choose to whom she will sell flowers or floral arrangements. Discrimination is the exercise of freedom.

*****

DISCRIMINATION HYPOCRISY

Soon after Donald Trump won the presidential election in November, it was widely reported that a number of prominent fashion designers were refusing to work with his wife, Melania Trump, because they do not approve of her husband's politics.

In a word, they were practicing discrimination.

Designer Sophie Theallet, who dressed First Lady Michelle Obama, posted an open letter on her Twitter account stating,

> As an independent fashion brand, we consider our voice an expression of our artistic and philosophical ideas. The Sophie Theallet brand stands against all discrimination and prejudice. Our runway shows, ad campaigns, and celebrity dressing have always been a celebration of diversity and a reflection of the world we live in.

> As one who celebrates and strives for diversity, individual freedom, and respect for all lifestyles, I will not participate in dressing or associating in any way with the next First Lady. The rhetoric of racism, sexism, and xenophobia unleashed by her husband's presidential campaign are incompatible with the shared values we live by.

> I encourage my fellow designers to do the same.

Designer Derek Lam stated,

While I have incredible respect for our country's political institutions, I find it challenging to be personally involved in dressing the new first lady. I would rather concentrate my energies on efforts towards a more just, honorable, and a mutually respectful world. I don't know Melania Trump personally, so I don't wish my comments to seem I am prejudging her personal values, but I really don't see myself getting involved with the Trump presidency.

No liberals or progressives of note have criticized these blatant acts of discrimination based on the political beliefs held by these or other designers.

Recently, however, some other acts of discrimination have received a lot of media attention, especially in the LGBT community.

A gay man recently sued a funeral home in Mississippi for breach of contract and emotional distress, alleging that it refused to cremate his recently deceased partner because it did not "deal with their kind."

John Zawadski and Robert Huskey met in 1965 in California. They settled in Picayune, Mississippi, in 1997, and soon after took advantage of the Supreme Court's decision to legalize same-sex unions nationwide. Less than two months later, Huskey's health began to deteriorate and he moved into a nursing home. In 2016, his nephew made arrangements with a local funeral home to transport his uncle's body from the nursing home to the funeral home for cremation and related services. After his uncle's death, the nephew said "the nursing home contacted him and told him the funeral home 'adamantly' refused to provide services after learning through the paperwork that Huskey's spouse was male." Because the nursing home did not have a morgue on site, a frantic search ensued for another funeral home with an on-site crematorium. Although one was found about 90 miles away, the "turmoil and exigency" created by the funeral home "permanently marred the memory of Bob's otherwise peaceful passing," the lawsuit states. The lawsuit requests a jury trial and unspecified monetary damages.

A farmer in Michigan was recently banned from the East Lansing farmers' market because he refused to host same-sex weddings at his orchard.

In 2014, Steve Tennes, owner of the Country Mill Orchard—which hosts a corn maze, birthday parties, weddings, and other events—denied the request of two lesbians to hold their wedding at the orchard because of his religious opposition to same-sex marriage. He referred the women to an orchard that held same-sex weddings, and they followed up on his suggestion the next year. But in 2016, after one of the women wrote a Facebook post discouraging people from doing business with Country Mill, Tennes ceased hosting weddings. He later changed his mind and expressed his traditional view about marriage on his farm's Facebook page. East Lansing city officials then determined that his statements violated the city's 1972 human-relations ordinance prohibiting discrimination and banned the Country Mill from participating in its farmers' market. Tennes and his wife have in turn sued the city for religious discrimination in the U.S. District Court for the Western District of Michigan. The lawsuit says in part that the city "has no authority to enforce its ordinance based on Tennes' religious beliefs and their impact on how he operates Country Mill."

This is discrimination hypocrisy. When fashion designers refuse to serve Melania Trump because they don't want to appear that they endorse her husband's politics liberals are silent, but when others refuse to serve homosexuals because they don't want to appear that they endorse their behavior liberals are vocally upset.

But there is enough discrimination hypocrisy to go around.

Conservatives generally don't have a problem with religious people who discriminate against others on the basis of sexual orientation or sex identity, but at the same time they generally support laws against discrimination based on other things such as race, religion, national origin, color, sex, or age.

Here is a typical example. In the midst of a post regarding fashion designers and Melania Trump on *National Review*'s blog, The Corner, conservative Veronique de Rugy said,

> I guess this is my chance to say that I thought Gary Johnson was absolutely wrong during the campaign to argue that the government should force a Jewish baker to bake a Nazi cake. While I agree with Johnson that there is a role for government to address a widespread refusal of service for things that are central to human flourishing—such as a business refusing to provide everyday food, medical services, or housing to a person due to race, religion, sexual orientation, or political views—it is my impression, however, that in spite of what some are claiming, there is no such widespread discrimination against gay marriages that justifies the government's intervention.

Since both liberals and conservatives seem to have trouble with the concept of discrimination, and because even Libertarian Party presidential candidate Gary Johnson is confused about it, perhaps it is time to review the libertarian perspective on discrimination. Here are twelve maxims.

1. Discrimination is not a dirty word. It simply involves choosing between options.

2. Everyone discriminates all day every day. Ordering a coke instead of an iced tea, buying a Ford instead of a Chevy, wearing a black outfit instead of a blue one, or patronizing Wendy's instead of McDonalds are acts of discrimination.

3. Discrimination is a crime in search of a victim. Every real crime needs a tangible victim with measurable damages.

4. There is no "right to service." In a free society, business owners have the right to refuse service to anyone for any reason on any basis.

5. What the government terms "public accommodations" are still private businesses. Just because they serve the public by offering to sell them goods or services, it doesn't follow that they should have to accept all members of the public, as the post office does.

6. It doesn't matter why discrimination takes place. That discrimination might be due to someone's race, creed, religion, sex, color, age, national origin, political ideology, IQ, physical appearance, marital status, socio-economic status, disability, gender identity, or sexual orientation is irrelevant.

7. It doesn't matter what anyone thinks about acts of discrimination. That discrimination is thought to be unfair, illogical, irrational, subjective, capricious, nonsensical, unreasonable, sexist, homophobic, or stupid, or based on stereotypes, ignorance, prejudice, hate, bigotry, or racism is of no consequence.

8. If customers can legally discriminate against businesses for any reason and on any basis, then businesses ought to likewise be able to discriminate against customers.

9. Discriminating against someone is not aggressing against him. Since no one is entitled to any particular job, apartment, house, good, or service, he has no recourse if he is denied any of those things.

10. Refusing to sell a product or provide a service has everything to do with property rights. Since no potential customer has a claim on the property or the time of any business owner, he has no legal recourse if the owner of the property refuses to do business with him.

11. To outlaw discrimination is to outlaw freedom of thought. In a free society, everyone has the right to think what he wants to think about anyone else and choose to discriminate on the basis of those thoughts.

12. Discrimination means freedom. A free society must include the freedom to discriminate against any individual or group for any reason and on any basis.

It goes without saying that anyone should have the same right to refuse to cremate a dead body or host a wedding—or bake a cake, sell flowers, or provide photography for a same-sex wedding—as fashion designers have to refuse to serve Melania Trump.

*****

DOES THE FIRST AMENDMENT PROTECT THE FREEDOM OF ASSOCIATION?

The Augusta National Golf Club—where the Masters golf tournament has been played since 1933—is in the news again, and not because Tiger

Woods failed to earn a fifth green jacket.

The exclusive club has come under fire again because of its male-only membership policy. And although the club has traditionally extended membership to the CEOs of its corporate sponsors, one of its major sponsors—International Business Machines (IBM)—has a new female CEO, Virginia Rometty, who has not been asked to join. The past four CEOs of IBM have all been Augusta members.

"It's just an embarrassment that it's still all-male," said Debora Spar, president of Barnard College in New York—an all-women's college. Seeming oblivious to the irony, she added, "Any argument that can be made anymore for male-only recreational sites is just kind of past its day."

Soon after Bubba Watson won the Masters tournament at the all-male Augusta last month, Jennifer Tyrrell was removed as a leader of her local Tiger Scout troop in Ohio, not because she is a woman, but because she is a lesbian.

Tyrell, who lives with her partner and their four children, allowed her seven-year-old son to join the Scouts in Bridgeport, a small town across the Ohio River from Wheeling, West Virginia. After she was drafted to lead her son's pack, she told parents at their first meeting about her sexual orientation.

The Ohio River Valley Council of the Boy Scouts of America told her last month that she had to resign because of her sexuality. Founded in 1910, the Boy Scouts has about 2.7 million youth members and more than 1 million adult volunteers. The organization believes that homosexuality is incompatible with membership or leadership positions. A board member of the Ohio River Valley Council has now resigned to protest Tyrrell's ouster.

The Augusta National Golf Club and the Boy Scouts have one thing in common—they are both private organizations that practice freedom of association.

Does the First Amendment protect the freedom of association? The First Amendment reads as follows:

> Congress shall make no law respecting an establishment of religion, or prohibiting the free exercise thereof; or abridging the freedom of speech, or of the press; or the right of the people peaceably to assemble, and to petition the Government for a redress of grievances.

The answer is: technically, no; legally, yes; but practically, it doesn't matter.

Clearly, the First Amendment protects the individual rights to freely exercise one's religion, speak freely, publish freely, peaceably assemble, and petition the government. Technically, the freedom of association is not mentioned. It is sometimes subsumed under the freedom of assembly but usually by limiting it to things such as trade unions and collective bargaining.

Legally, the freedom of association is considered to be a fundamental right protected by the Constitution. In the Supreme Court case of *N.A.A.C.P. v. Alabama* (1958), a unanimous Court ruled that the NAACP did not have to reveal to the Alabama attorney general the names and addresses of the NAACP members in the state because it would violate the NAACP members' freedom of association. Writing for the Court, Justice John Marshall Harlan II said in the decision that

> immunity from state scrutiny of membership lists … is here so related to the right of members to pursue their lawful private interests privately and to associate freely with others in so doing as to come within the protection of the Fourteenth Amendment. [Alabama] has fallen short of showing a controlling justification for the deterrent effect on the free enjoyment of the right to associate which disclosure of membership lists is likely to have….

> Freedom to engage in association for the advancement of beliefs and ideas is an inseparable aspect of the "liberty" ensured by the Due Process Clause of the Fourteenth Amendment.

> In the circumstances of the NAACP case, compelled disclosure of the petitioner's membership lists was likely to constitute an effective restraint on its members' freedom of association.

> Inviolability of privacy in group association may in many circumstances be indispensable to the preservation of freedom of association, particularly where a group espouses dissident beliefs.

In a later case that directly relates to the woman recently dismissed from her leadership position in the Boy Scouts, the Supreme Court ruled in *Boy Scouts of America v. Dale* (2000) that the Boy Scouts could revoke the membership of a former Eagle Scout and assistant scoutmaster (James Dale) when it found out that Dale was a homosexual and a gay-rights activist. To force the Boy Scouts to do otherwise abridged the organization's right to freedom of association. As Chief Justice William Rehnquist wrote in the majority opinion,

> Applying New Jersey's public accommodations law to require the Boy Scouts to admit Dale violates the Boy Scouts' First Amendment right of expressive association. Government actions that unconstitutionally burden that right may take many forms, one of which is intrusion into a group's internal affairs by forcing it to accept a member it does not desire.

But practically speaking, whether the First Amendment, the Fourteenth Amendment, or any other part of the Constitution mentions the freedom of association is irrelevant. Likewise, whether the Supreme Court finds the freedom of association in the First Amendment, the Fourteenth Amendment, or any other part of the Constitution is irrelevant.

The Bill of Rights—of which the capstone is the First Amendment—was added to the Constitution in 1791 at the insistence of the Anti-Federalists. Contrary to what most Americans probably think, the Bill of Rights does not grant anyone rights. What the government grants, the government can take away. Since no power was granted to the federal government in the body of the Constitution to infringe what are commonly referred to as Americans' "First Amendment freedoms," the government has absolutely no authority to do so. That is why James Madison, who did not initially support adding a bill of rights to the Constitution, said that no "great and important power" could be exercised by Congress unless it was "evidently and necessarily involved in an express power." The First Amendment merely reinforces the idea that the federal government lacks the authority under the Constitution to abridge Americans' existing freedoms. The individual rights to freely exercise one's religion, speak freely, publish freely, peaceably assemble, and petition the government are natural rights independent of the Constitution—just like the right to freedom of association.

The freedom of association simply means that a person has the right to associate, not with whomever he chooses, but with whoever is willing to associate with him. Inherent in the right to associate is the right not to associate. Any person has the right not to associate with whomever he chooses.

In a free society, any person or group of persons has the right to associate with any other person or group of persons willing to associate with him or it on the basis of any standard and for any reason. And likewise, any person or group of persons has the right not to associate with any other person or group of persons on the basis of any standard and for any reason.

It doesn't matter whether a government bureaucrat or a person who was refused association believes that the actions of the refusing person or group are illogical, unreasonable, irrational, hateful, discriminatory, bigoted, or racist. What matters is freedom.

The freedom of association is just as important as any of the "First Amendment freedoms." Neither government nor society has the authority to force a person or group to associate with another person or group that they don't want to associate with. In a free society, it can't be any other way.

*****

THE WRONGS AND RIGHTS OF FREE EXERCISE AND FREE ASSOCIATION

The state of California has effectively banned its 2,000 state court judges from participating in the Boy Scouts. The California Supreme Court recently voted unanimously to eliminate an exception for nonprofit youth groups to a rule that prohibits California judges from belonging to groups that practice discrimination on the basis of sexual orientation. The judges have until January 21, 2016, to sever any connection they have with the Boy Scouts.

Although California judges have long been barred from membership in groups that discriminate on the basis of race, gender, religion, or sexual orientation, the state's Supreme Court approved an exemption in 1996 for "nonprofit youth organizations" to accommodate judges affiliated with the Boy Scouts.

In 2003, after the San Francisco Bar Association and other legal organizations sought to repeal the exemption, the California Supreme Court instructed judges to disclose their connections to the Boy Scouts when they heard gay-rights cases, and to recuse themselves for any conflicts of interest. In 2014, an ethics advisory committee recommended eliminating the exception altogether. The proposal was supported by the California Judges Association, which represents three-quarters of the state's judges.

So why the Boy Scouts?

Founded in 1910, the Boy Scouts has about 2.7 youth members and more than 1 million adult volunteers. It was always looked upon as an organization that stood for old-fashioned values and wholesomeness. Homosexuals were neither allowed to be scout leaders nor members. But in 2013, the Boy Scouts' approximate 1,400-member National Council agreed in a resolution to admit openly gay boys as members (effective January 1, 2014) after intense lobbying by gay-rights activists, and after 61 percent of local Scout leaders voted at their annual meeting to support the proposal. Nevertheless, even though the resolution still stated, "Scouting is a youth program, and any sexual conduct, whether homosexual or heterosexual, by youth of Scouting age is contrary to the virtues of Scouting," some conservative religious groups were saddened by the change in policy, even predicting a "mass exodus" from the Boy Scouts.

The ban on gay Scout leaders was left in place. It led Disney last year to "cut off funding" to the Boy Scouts "through its employee volunteer program." And now it has led to California's barring its judges from participating in the Boy Scouts.

Harvard Law professor Noah Feldman maintains that "the current state of the law allows judges to belong to religious groups that discriminate but not secular organizations that discriminate. 'So if the particular judicial code bans belonging to organizations that discriminate on the basis of sexual orientation, then it would make sense that the Boy Scouts would be included.'"

California judges are therefore free to belong to whatever religious organizations they want to, including ones that discriminate, not only on the basis of sexual orientation, but also on the basis of sexual identity, such as the prohibition against female clergy in the Catholic Church and many conservative Protestant groups. But the Boy Scouts is not a religious organization.

The decision of the California Supreme Court has drawn a mixed response from state judges. San Diego judge Julia Kelety disagreed with the ruling: "The issue is whether individual judges can choose in their private lives to be involved in an organization that has tremendous qualities and provides tremendous support for young people." Robert Glusman, a former president of the California Judges Association, which supports the ban, began his objection with a question: "Would a judge be able to join an organization where black men could not be part of the organization? I don't think that would be as close a question. Here we're dealing with gay men or LGBT. So we put it in a slightly different framework, but there is something that rankles many of the judges about that."

Professor Feldman believes that the U.S. Supreme Court will one day take up the question of judges' free association rights, and when it does, he thinks the Court will say that judges can participate in organizations such as the Boy Scouts, regardless of their discriminatory policies. The good professor is certainly welcome to his opinion on what the Court will eventually do, but he is not welcome to spread misinformation about Americans' free exercise and free association rights: "You have a free exercise right to pray where you wish. And you have a free association right to belong to whatever club you wish to belong to," he says. "And I don't actually think the distinction between the two is constitutionally justified."

But you don't right now have a free exercise right to pray where you wish in American society. And neither do you have a free association right to belong to whatever club you wish to belong to. You have never had these rights, you don't have them now, and neither would you have them in a libertarian, that is, a free society, should the United States ever become one.

How much ink has been spilled, and how many court cases have been tried, over the issue of children's praying in their public schools or at their school's sporting events? It is simply not allowed. Does a Muslim or a Jew have the right to pray out loud in the middle of a service at a Christian church? Does a Christian have the right to pray out loud in the name of Jesus at a Muslim mosque or a Jewish synagogue? Does any adherent of any religion have a free exercise right to pray out loud at the annual American Atheists National Convention? Does any adherent of any religion (including my own) have a free exercise right to pray in my living room if I don't want him to?

The same goes for the free association right to join a club. Just because you want to join a particular club, it doesn't follow that you have the right to join. Not unless members of a club that you want to belong to are forced to admit you. Should a woman's organization have to admit men?

Should the Masonic Lodge have to accept all comers? Should a black group have to admit white supremacists? Should a Jewish organization have to admit Neo-Nazis? Should a Christian group have to admit atheists? Should a heterosexual group have to admit homosexuals? Should a vegetarian group have to admit meat eaters? Should an environmentalist club have to admit those who don't recycle?

And looking at free association from another angle, can a group of whites, blacks, Jews, or Christians even get together and start an organization or open a business that excludes from membership or refuses service to all who are not like them? Of course not. Not in America.

In a free society, no one has the right to pray or otherwise exercise his religion anywhere but on his own property or on property to which he has been granted access.

In a free society, property ownership inherently includes the rights of exclusion and refusal of service.

In a free society, any individual or group has the right to associate with any other individual or group willing to associate with him or it.

In a free society, any individual or group has the right to *not* associate with any other individual or group willing to associate with him or it.

In a free society, any individual or group *does not* have the right to associate with any other individual or group *not* willing to associate with him or it.

In a free society, there is no distinction between discrimination as practiced by religious groups and discrimination as practiced by secular organizations.

In a free society, the rights of exclusion, refusal, discrimination, and nonassociation are absolute; they can be exercised on the basis of any standard and for any reason—regardless of whether a busybody or bureaucrat considers the standard or reason to be illogical, unreasonable, irrational, hateful, bigoted, or racist.

In a free society, it couldn't be any other way.

*****

5

VICTIMLESS CRIMES

AN OPEN LETTER TO MY FELLOW CHRISTIANS

Dear Friends,

We Christians are law and order types. We can generally be counted on to obey the laws of the land—federal, state, and local. And that's good. We are also a moral people. We don't generally frequent crackhouses, bathhouses, or whorehouses. And that's also a good thing.

These things are especially true of Christians who consider themselves to be conservatives, evangelicals, fundamentalists, independents, Bible-believers, or Bible-literalists. Since I fit into this general category, I write on this subject with some authority.

I would like to propose what is a radical proposition to most conservative Christians: there should be no laws against victimless crimes. None. Zero. That proposition may not sound too radical to most readers of this publication, but it would get me censured in some religious circles. And if there are laws against victimless crimes, Christians should not be supporters of them.

What kinds of victimless crimes am I referring to? There should be no laws against drug possession, drug use, drug importation, or drug sales. In fact, there should not be any such thing as an illegal substance. There should be no blue laws, no usury laws, no seatbelt laws, and no motorcycle helmet laws—including those ridiculous bicycle helmet laws. There should be no laws against price gouging, drunk driving, pornography, or gambling. Since there is no reason for me to shy away from the hard cases, I would even go so far as to say that no consensual acts between two individuals should be illegal. That would include escort services, lap dancing, peep shows, topless or nude dancing, and prostitution. Sodomy laws would fit in this category and so would that great crime against humanity—ticket scalping.

I am not suggesting for a minute that all or any victimless crimes or consensual acts are necessarily good things. Many of them are always bad—like smoking crack cocaine. Some of them might be bad some of the time, but not all the time—like the difference between smoking pot to get high and smoking pot to relieve the pain of glaucoma. Others are always good things—like a willing seller and a willing buyer exchanging a concert ticket for cash. And I am not suggesting that the participants in a victimless crime or a consensual act are not harming anyone. The participants might in fact be hurting or severely injuring each other or themselves. But as long as they are not harming or violating the rights of non-participants, what they do should not be a crime. What they do may be stupid, but stupidity should not be criminalized. If doing stupid things were a criminal offense, then most government officials would be in jail.

In any event, there are three reasons why Christians should oppose victimless crime legislation. First, not all crimes are sins, and not all sins are crimes. Second, contrary to popular belief, there is no support in the New Testament for the idea that Christians should seek legislation that would criminalize victimless behavior. Third, Christians are making a grave mistake by looking to the state to enforce their morality.

Crimes and Sin

We know that murder, robbery, and rape are both crimes and sins, but everything the state or the authorities brand a crime is not necessarily a sin. This has been true in all ages.

In the Old Testament, the Hebrew midwives were commanded by the state to kill any newborn sons (Exodus 1:16). But because "the midwives feared God," they "did not as the king of Egypt commanded them, but saved the men children alive" (Exodus 1:17). In the book of Daniel, we read that King Nebuchadnezzar "made an image of gold" and decreed that when the music started, everyone was to "fall down and worship the golden image that Nebuchadnezzar the king ha[d] set up." Three Hebrew children defied the king and refused to worship the golden image, for which they were cast into a burning fiery furnace (Daniel 3). Daniel himself got into trouble with King Darius when the king decreed that "whosoever shall ask a petition of any God or man for thirty days," except from the king, "shall be cast into the den of lions." Daniel, the Bible tells us, did not submit to the state, but rather "prayed, and gave thanks before his God, as he did aforetime" (Daniel 6).

In the New Testament, the apostles Peter and John were imprisoned by the authorities for preaching and then brought before them and commanded "not to speak at all nor teach in the name of Jesus." But instead of being in subjection, they replied: "Whether it be right in the sight of God to hearken unto you more than unto God, judge ye. For we cannot but speak the things which we have seen and heard" (Acts 4). After this incident, some apostles were again brought before the authorities and asked: "Did not we straitly command you that ye should not teach in this name? And, behold, ye have filled Jerusalem with your doctrine, and intend to bring this man's blood upon us." It was then that the apostles uttered the immortal line: "We ought to obey God rather than men" (Acts 5).

No Christian could read these accounts and say with a straight face that everything the state labels a crime is a sin. The Bible is very clear about what sin is. Sin is "whatsoever is not of faith" (Romans 14:23). Sin is transgressing the divine law (1 John 3:14). Sin is knowing to do good and doing it not (James 4:17). But if not all crimes are sins, then why are some Christians often so quick to nod in agreement when it comes to the enforcement of victimless crime laws? And why would Christians even think about wanting something to be made a crime that was not a sin? The only explanation is that some Christians think that disobeying the state is itself a crime. They have made the state into a god. They have violated the First Commandment.

The other side of this coin is the statement: not all sins are crimes. If they were, then everyone would be in trouble, Christians included, for the Bible says that "there is not a just man upon earth, that doeth good, and sinneth not" (Ecclesiastes 7:20). Saying that not all sins are crimes is just a Christian way of rephrasing the classical liberal political philosopher Lysander Spooner:

> Vices are those acts by which a man harms himself or his property. Crimes are those acts by which one man harms the per- son or property of another. Vices are simply the errors which a man makes in his search after his own happiness. Unlike crimes, they imply no malice toward others, and no interference with their persons or property. ("Vices Are Not Crimes," 1875)

No Christian would be in favor of criminalizing all sins. Not when the Bible says: "The thought of foolishness is sin" (Proverbs 24:9). Why, then, are some Christians so quick to applaud making some sins criminal just because the state happens to select them and not others? Spooner's wisdom is apropos here:

> It is a maxim of the law that there can be no crime without a criminal intent; that is, without the intent to invade the person or property of another. But no one ever prac- tises a vice with any such criminal intent. He practises his vice for his own happiness solely, and not from any malice toward others.

> Crimes are few, and easily distinguished from all other acts; and mankind are generally agreed as to what acts are crimes. Whereas vices are innumerable; and no two persons are agreed, except in comparatively few cases, as to what are vices. ("Vices Are Not Crimes")

But how many conservative, evangelical, or fundamentalist Christians have ever read or even heard of Lysander Spooner? Or Benjamin Tucker, Albert J. Nock, H.L. Mencken, Garet Garrett, or Murray Rothbard?

Victimless Crime Legislation

The Christian's ultimate rule of faith is the New Testament. There is no support in the New Testament for the idea that Christians should seek legislation that would criminalize victimless acts—whether they are sins or not. Specific sins are mentioned that are in fact crimes, such as murder (Romans 1:29), stealing (Ephesians 4:28), rioting (Romans 13:13), and extortion (1 Corinthians 6:10). But what we mainly see in the New Testament are admonitions about how Christians should behave:

Recompense to no man evil for evil. Provide things honest in the sight of all men. (Romans 12:17)

As we have therefore opportunity, let us do good unto all men. (Galatians 6:10)

Let no corrupt communication proceed out of your mouth. (Ephesians 4:29)

Abstain from all appearance of evil. (1 Thessalonians 5:22)

Then there are the lists of vices to avoid. But there are no indications anywhere in the New Testament that Christians should seek or support making these things crimes.

Where did the Apostle Paul, in his travels throughout the Roman Empire, ever express support for any type of legislation? When did he ever tell people who were not Christians how they should live their lives? Paul was himself a victim of a victimless crime law. He was beaten and imprisoned for teaching" customs, which are not lawful for us to receive, neither to observe, being Romans" (Acts 16:21). He was almost killed for teaching "all men every where against the people, the law, and this place" (Acts 21:28). I suspect that many Christians would support legislation against victimless crimes only as long as it stopped short of their particular vice.

It is not the purpose of Christianity to change society as a whole outwardly; it is the purpose of Christianity to change men as individuals inwardly. The Christian is in the world but not of the world. He is to "have no fellowship with the unfruitful works of darkness, but rather reprove them" (Ephesians 5:11), not legislate against them. The Christian is to "live peaceably with all men" (Romans 12:18). Christians are to pray for those in authority that they (the Christians) "may lead a quiet and peaceable life" (1 Timothy 2:2). The attitude of the Christian should be to mind his" own business" (1 Thessalonians 4:11) and not be "a busybody in other men's matters" (1 Timothy 4:15).

The Mistake of Looking to the State

Christians are making a grave mistake by looking to the state to legislate morality. The state is no friend of religion, and especially not of Christianity. Why do so many Christians defend, support, and make excuses for the state, its politicians, its legislation, and its wars? Why would

Christians even think of looking to the state to enforce their moral code? The actions of the state are the greatest examples of immoral behavior that one could possibly think of. The state exists only by stealing and killing, and then lying about it. It is not the purpose of Christianity to use force or the threat of force to keep people from sinning. Christians who are quick to criticize Islamic countries for prescribing and proscribing all manner of behavior are very inconsistent when they support the same thing here. A Christian theocracy is just as unscriptural as an Islamic theocracy.

I believe that Christians have for the most part failed to fulfill their calling. Instead of making converts and instructing them in the biblical precepts of Christian living, they turn to the state to criminalize what they consider immoral. Instead of changing people's minds about what is and what is not acceptable in society, they seek to use the state to change people's behavior. Instead of greeting with a healthy dose of skepticism the state's latest pronouncement about what substance needs to be banned, regulated, or taxed, they wholeheartedly embrace it. Instead of being an example to the world, they want to use the state to make the world conform to their example. Instead of educating themselves and other Christians about what is appropriate behavior, they rely on the state to make that determination. Instead of looking internally for funding, they look to the state to fund their faith-based initiatives. Instead of minding their own business, they mind everyone else's.

William Anderson has summed it up nicely: "Most conservative Christians abhor libertarianism because they see it as promoting a permissive lifestyle, from abortion to taking drugs. Yet, what they fail to understand is that the restrictive, prohibition-oriented state that they are trying to create (and also preserve) is much more likely to take away allliber- ties than a state that gives people permission to live as they wish" ("Libertarianism and Religious Freedom," 2003).

Cases in Point

Since we do in fact have an abundance of victimless crimes in this country, the question to be asked is simply this: what should the response of Christianity be to such things? Should Christians support seatbelt laws? What about helmet laws that govern not only the riders of motorcycles but also the riders of bicycles? Should Christians be in favor of laws that impose penalties for usury, price gouging, and ticket scalping? What about laws that prohibit gambling, drugs, and prostitution? Should church-going Christians support blue laws that regulate the sale of certain items on Sundays?

Seatbelt and helmet laws are predicated on the idea that we need the state to protect us from doing something stupid. Is it a good idea to wear a seatbelt? Probably. Is it a good idea for kids to be securely fastened into a car? Most definitely. Is it foolish to ride a motorcycle without a helmet? I think so. But it is families and friends who should be the ones persuading people to buckle up or wear a helmet, not the state. But they won't do it, some say, and therefore the state has to do it. This supposes, however, that the state cares more about an individual than do his family and friends—a very dubious proposition. It would be compatible with Christianity to uphold the ideas of individual responsibility and parental responsibility.

What about prices and interest rates that are too high? It might be immoral in some circumstances to charge above a certain price or a certain rate of interest, but it should certainly not be illegal. Economics knows nothing of a "just rate of interest" or a "just price"; these are the products of legislation. Christians who support usury laws and price gouging laws are violating the First Commandment by ascribing omniscience to the state. How else could the state determine what the maximum rate of interest should be and then apply that to every situation? How else could the state determine what the correct price of an item should be and then apply that to all circumstances? Christianity would take a common-sense approach: if you don't want to borrow money at what you believe is a usurious rate of interest, then don't borrow the money; if you don't want to pay what you think is an inflated price for an item, then don't buy it.

But, some will say, don't we need the state to regulate interest rates to protect consumers? Well, how do you help customers by preventing a willing lender from doing business with a willing borrower? From an economic standpoint, we know that what is called price gouging is nothing more than charging what the market will bear. Price-gouging laws violate the property rights of resource owners, they hinder the price system's signaling ability, they contribute to the misallocation of resources, and they cause shortages.

As for ticket scalping, this has got to be one of the most ridiculous examples of a victimless act labeled as a crime. There is no precept of Christianity that frowns on a willing seller and a willing buyer exchanging tickets for cash, as long as they do not violate the rights of the owner of the ground on which they make their exchange. Ticket scalpers should actually be applauded for the valuable service they perform.

But what about gambling, drugs, and prostitution? Christians have historically shied away from games of chance. But is it any of our business if people want to throw their money away? And anyhow, it isn't gambling that the state is concerned about, it's gambling in which the state doesn't take a cut. Christians should not be deceived into thinking that the state is concerned about the immorality of gambling. If a Christian is concerned about gambling, then the answer is persuasion, not prosecution.

When it comes to the attitude of the typical Christian toward drugs, two things are taboo: taking drugs to get high, and not supporting the war on drugs. But do the two things have to go hand in hand? There is no precept or principle in Christianity that would lead me to want the government to arrest and jail an individual who liked to smoke, snort, or shoot up in the privacy of his home. Proof that many Christians are simply not thinking when it comes to drugs is the subject of alcohol. Aside from a small minority of Christians who long for the days of Prohibition, Christians don't generally support making *private* drunkenness a crime. But why is getting high on drugs treated differently from getting high on alcohol?

As would be expected, Christianity is strongly against prostitution, if for no other reason than because it is adultery or fornication. Unfortunately, too many Christians equate a refusal to make prostitution a crime with support for prostitution itself. But if adultery or fornication should not be crimes, then why should prostitution be one? What is the difference between paying $50 directly for 15 minutes of a girl's time and paying $50 for dinner and a movie in order to get 15 minutes of a girl's time? True, both activities are sinful in the eyes of God, but why is one illegal and the other not?

Blue laws—laws that forbid the sale of all or certain goods at most stores on Sunday—are some of the silliest victimless crime legislation. (And they're not just concerned with Sunday. In Massachusetts, all stores except convenience stores and gas stations have to remain closed on Thanksgiving, Christmas, and New Year's Day.) But why should Christians who attend church on Sunday care whether people who don't attend church go shopping? I've noticed that Christians who have a problem with repealing a law that prevents beer from being sold on Sunday don't seem to mind restaurants being open so they have somewhere to eat after church.

Why?

There are five reasons why most Christians support victimless crime legislation.

The first can be seen in H.L. Mencken's famous definition of puritanism: "The haunting fear that someone, somewhere, may be happy" ("A Book of Burlesques," 1916). Some Christians simply don't enjoy their Christianity as they should because they focus on the negative. They don't drink, dance, smoke, chew, or go with girls that do—and they live their lives in misery because of it. These people want to spread the miser)', even if it means using the state to tell others how they should live.

The second reason appears in another passage from Mencken: "The urge to save humanity is almost always a false-face for the urge to rule it" ("Minority Report," 1956). Some Christians want to save humanity from every vice so they can have an outwardly Christian society—but without the work of evangelism and discipleship.

The third reason is that most Christians lack a proper appreciation of the sanctity of private property. Although the Bible defends private property, they do not appreciate the possibility that what a man buys, sells, manufactures, drinks, smokes, or looks at on his own property may be his own business.

The fourth reason is that most Christians have too lofty a view of the state. They are too quick to rely on the state, trust the state, and believe the state. Sure, they may criticize the state because it permits abortion, but they generally fail to discern the state's true nature, as Richard Ebeling has correctly described it: "There has been no greater threat to life, liberty, and property throughout the ages than government. Even the most violent and brutal private individuals have been able to inflict only a mere fraction of the harm and destruction that have been caused by the use of power by political authorities" (The Freeman, Jan.-Feb. 2005).

The fifth and final reason is just plain biblical ignorance. The spirit of New Testament Christianity can be seen in two statements by the great economist Ludwig von Mises:

A free man must be able to endure it when his fellow men act and live otherwise than he considers proper. He must free himself from the habit, just as soon as something does not please him, of calling for the police. ("Liberalism," 1927)

He who wants to reform his countrymen must take recourse to persuasion. This alone is the democratic way of bringing about changes. If a man fails in his endeavors to convince other people of the soundness of his ideas, he should blame his own disabilities. He should not ask for a law, that is, for compulsion and coercion by the police. ("Bureaucracy," 1945)

That is the spirit of New Testament Christianity. It is a sad day for Christianity when a nonreligious Jew like Mises has a better grasp on Christian principles than the average Christian in the pew.

Yours for better Christian thinking.

*****

EVERY CRIME NEEDS A VICTIM

Just as every husband needs a wife, every child needs a parent, and every teacher needs a pupil, so every crime needs a victim. Not a *potential* victim or *possible* victim or a *supposed* victim, but an actual victim.

There are a myriad of federal, state, and local laws on an incalculable number of subjects. The result of this is that the United States—the land of the free—has one of the highest per-capita prison populations in the world. With less than 5 percent of the world's population, the United States has almost a quarter of the world's prisoners.

The volume and scope of federal laws are especially distressing because very few of them are authorized by the Constitution. Congress and the federal agencies it has created have federalized a host of ordinary street crimes already covered by state criminal codes. Things like arson, carjacking, and gun possession by felons. The federal criminal code has over 4,000 separate offenses, including such violent crimes as transporting birds across state lines to engage in fights and interstate transport of unlicensed dentures.

Sometimes the federal government also pressures the states to enact laws. Thus, the National Minimum Drinking Age Act of 1984 required states to raise their drinking ages to twenty-one or lose 10 percent of their federal highway funds.

The most senseless category of what governments—federal, state, or local—have labeled crimes is victimless crimes. These are crimes like not wearing a seatbelt, not wearing a motorcycle or bicycle helmet, texting while driving, doing business on Sunday, charging an excessive interest rate, price gouging, and that great crime against humanity—ticket scalping.

New Hampshire is the only state that has no adult seat belt law. This makes me a law breaker in forty-nine states. Many of the same people who say that what you do or don't do in your own car is your business make an exception when it comes to seat belt laws. Is it a good idea to wear a seatbelt? Certainly. Is it a good idea for kids to be securely fastened in? Most definitely. But the idea that we need the state to protect us by forcing us to wear seatbelts is ludicrous. Whatever happened to the ideas of individual responsibility and parental responsibility? This is something that could easily be handled on the free market. Insurance companies could charge higher premiums to those drivers who forego wearing a seatbelt. Drivers should want to ensure that everyone in their car arrives at their destination safely, but they don't need the threat of a ticket to do so. And is there any doubt that governments are more interested in revenue than safety?

Only three states (Illinois, Iowa and New Hampshire) have absolutely no motorcycle helmet requirement. The other states require helmets for everyone or just for adults. Twenty-one states require bicyclists below a certain age to wear helmets. New Hampshire even requires a bicycle helmet for riders under sixteen even though no one who rides an obviously more dangerous motorcycle is required to wear one. Should advocates of liberty be in favor of state governments requiring riders of motorcycles and bicycles to wear helmets? Not if they want to be consistent. Is it foolish to ride a motorcycle without a helmet? I think so. But I think it's foolish to ride a motorcycle without a full suit of armor. The issue of motorcycle helmets is also something that could easily be handled on the free market in the form of higher insurance premiums to those motorcycle riders who forego wearing a helmet. Families and friends should be the ones persuading motorcycle riders to wear helmets—not the state.

Wisconsin just became the twenty-fifth state to ban texting while driving. The problem with these laws, in addition to the obvious—that they grossly infringe upon personal liberty and criminalize an otherwise harmless activity because it *might* cause a driver to be distracted and *perhaps* have an accident—is their selectiveness. What about eating and drinking while driving? What about women applying makeup while driving? What about men shaving with an electric razor while driving? What about people reading a map while driving? What about people glancing too long at billboards or blinking while driving? Drivers should be held accountable for *actual* accidents, not *potential* ones.

Seat belt, helmet, and texting laws are predicated on the idea that we need the state to protect us from doing something stupid. But it is families and friends that should be the ones persuading people to buckle up, wear a helmet, or turn off their cell phone, not the state. But they won't do it, some say, and therefore the state *has* to do it. But this presupposes that the state cares more about an individual than does his family and friends—a very dubious proposition.

Too many Americans are willing to surrender their liberty without a whimper at the slightest whisper by the state of "safety" or "children."

Blue laws—laws that forbid the sale of all or certain goods at most stores on Sunday—are some of the most laughable victimless crime legislation ever concocted. In some states it is illegal to not just purchase alcohol on Sunday, but to buy a car from a dealer. And it's not just Sunday. In Massachusetts, all stores (except convenience stores and gas stations) have to remain closed on Thanksgiving and Christmas Day. But why should those who attend church on Sunday (as I do, and as many of you do) care if those who don't attend church want to do their shopping? Church goers who have such a problem with the repeal of a blue law that prevents beer from being sold on Sunday don't seem to mind restaurants being open so they have somewhere to eat after church.

Some victimless crimes relate to economics. This would be things like usury laws, price gouging, and ticket scalping.

Ethically, usury is an exorbitant interest rate. Legally, usury is an illegal interest rate. But in what is now viewed as its archaic or obsolete sense, usury is simply the price of interest charged on a loan for the lack of use of the money and the risk of loss. So, based on this artificial distinction between usury and interest, we have the victimless crime of usury in all fifty states. Usurers—that is, moneylenders, have been despised throughout history. In Dante's *The Divine Comedy*, usurers are in the seventh circle of hell along with blasphemers and sodomites. But as the late economist Murray Rothbard pointed out, moneylending is a business in the market like any other business: "If the number of usurers multiplies, the price of money or interest will be driven down by the competition. So that if one doesn't like high interest rates, the more usurers the better!"

Although it might be immoral to charge above a certain rate of interest in some circumstances, it should certainly not be illegal. How could anyone possibly calculate what the maximum rate of interest should be and then apply that to every situation? And what should be the basis of the rate? Should it be the prime rate, the federal funds rate, the discount rate, or the LIBOR rate? The common-sense approach is simple: If you don't want to borrow a sum of money at what you believe is a usurious rate of interest, then don't borrow the money. But, some will say, we need the state to regulate interest rates to protect consumers. But how is preventing a willing lender and a willing borrower from doing business helping consumers?

Price-gouging laws are predicated on the fallacy that there is a just price for every good and service, and even more so during bad weather or some government-declared state of emergency. The U.S. Department of Energy even maintains a "Gas Price Watch Reporting Form" where people who know nothing about supply and demand, refinery capacity, gasoline futures, world surplus production capacity, and the price of a barrel of crude oil can report price gouging by gas stations. These laws are very similar to usury laws. In some circumstances, it might be immoral to charge above a particular price, but it should certainly not be illegal. There is no such thing as a just price. One cannot support price-gouging laws without ascribing omniscience to the state. How else could the state determine what the correct price should be? From an economic standpoint, we know that what is called price gouging is simply nothing more than charging what the market will bear. Price-gouging laws violate the property rights of resource owners, they hinder the price system's signaling ability, they contribute to the misallocation of resources, and they cause shortages. Once again, the common-sense approach is the simplest: If you don't like what you think is the inflated price of an item, then don't buy it.

The crime of ticket scalping has got to be one of the most ridiculous examples of a victimless act ever labeled as a crime. What precept of any ethical system would frown upon a willing seller and a willing buyer exchanging tickets for cash, as long as it was not violating the property rights of the owner of the ground where they made their exchange? Ticket scalpers perform a valuable service and should be applauded not condemned.

The nanny state is at its prime when it comes to monitoring illicit substances and consensual behavior that some people find objectionable, e.g., gambling, prostitution, and drug use. Thus, the most widely accepted victimless crimes are those that involve what is considered to be immoral activity. Here is where even believers in a free society acquiesce to the state. And religious people in particular look to the state to enforce their morality when it comes to these issues.

The problem with the moral crusades of the nanny state against gambling, prostitution, and drug use is that they fail to distinguish between vices and crimes. As the 19th-century classical-liberal political philosopher Lysander Spooner explained it:

> Vices are those acts by which a man harms himself or his property. Crimes are those acts by which one man harms the person or property of another. Vices are simply the errors which a man makes in his search after his own happiness. Unlike crimes, they imply no malice toward others, and no interference with their persons or property.

> Unless this clear distinction between vices and crimes be made and recognized by the laws, there can be on earth no such thing as individual right, liberty, or property—no such things as the right of one man to the control of his own person and property, and the corresponding and coequal rights of another man to the control of his own person and property.

To be a crime, adds Spooner, there must exist criminal intent to invade the person or property of another. But vices are not engaged in with criminal intent. A man practices a vice "for his own happiness solely, and not from any malice toward others." This reminds me of H. L. Mencken's famous definition of Puritanism: "The haunting fear that someone, somewhere, may be happy."

According to John Stossel: "Americans bet a hundred million dollars every day, and that's just at legal places like Las Vegas and Indian reservations. Much more is bet illegally." No one should be deceived into thinking that the state is really concerned about the immorality of gambling. It is only illegal gambling—gambling in which the government does not get a cut of the action—that the government is concerned about. State lotteries, which have odds worse than any casino, are marketed to the poor with tax dollars. If an individual is genuinely concerned about the negatives associated with gambling, then the answer is personal persuasion, not government prosecution. Is it anyone's business if people want to throw their money away?

Prostitution isn't just the world's oldest profession, it's also the world's oldest victimless crime. But if adultery or fornication should not be crimes, then why should prostitution be one? They are all consensual acts between two or more parties. Forced prostitution, of course, is a crime because it has a victim. And prostitutes who trespass by plying their trade without permission on private property are themselves committing a crime. But sex between two consenting adults without dinner and a movie should not be the business of government or anyone else. Again, if an individual is genuinely concerned about what he sees as the plight of prostitutes, then he should resort to persuasion or provide an employment alternative instead of looking to the government to outlaw immoral activity.

The state's war on drugs, like its war on poverty and its war on terrorism, is a failure, unless you consider turning hundreds of thousands of oth-

otherwise law-abiding people into criminals a success. Out of the 847,863 arrests for marijuana in 2008, 754,224 were for possession alone. According to the Sentencing Project, over half of the federal prison population is the result of drug charges. Twenty percent of the state prison population and 25 percent of the local jail population is due to drug charges. There are currently about half a million drug offenders in prison or jail, an increase of 1,100 percent since 1980. Not only has the unconstitutional drug war had virtually no impact on the use or availability of most drugs in the United States, it has destroyed civil liberties and financial privacy. The costs of drug prohibition far outweigh any possible benefits. Proof that people are not thinking when it comes to drugs is the subject of alcohol. There is no reason why getting high on drugs in the privacy of one's home should be treated differently from getting drunk on alcohol in the privacy of one's home. And not only is it simply not the purpose of government to protect people from abusing drugs, government intervention begats more government intervention. As the late economist Ludwig von Mises explained:

> Opium and morphine are certainly dangerous, habit-forming drugs. But once the principle is admitted that it is the duty of government to protect the individual against his own foolishness, no serious objections can be advanced against further encroachments. . . . And why limit the government's benevolent providence to the protection of the individual's body only?
>
> Is not the harm a man can inflict on his mind and soul even more disastrous than any bodily evils? Why not prevent him from reading bad books and seeing bad plays, from looking at bad paintings and statues and from hearing bad music? The mischief done by bad ideologies, surely, is much more pernicious, both for the individual and for the whole society, than that done by narcotic drugs.

There should be no DEA agents, no undercover sting operations, and no jail time for growing a plant.

Every crime needs a victim. Not wearing a seatbelt, not wearing helmet, texting while driving, doing business on Sunday, usurious lending practices, price gouging, ticket scalping, gambling without the state's permission, using the services of a prostitute, abusing drugs, and a host of other "crimes" that I have not mentioned are not crimes at all. They may be immoral, they may be vices, they may be bad habits, they may be dangerous, they may be foolish, they may be addictive, they may harm those who willingly participant in them, they may have no redeeming value whatsoever, but as long as those who engage in them are not harming or violating the personal or property rights of non-participants, they should not be crimes.

There are two reasons that no one should look to the government as a nanny to enforce morality and micro-manage the behavior of its citizens.

First, the purpose of government is supposed to be to protect life, liberty, and property from violence or fraud. It is simply not the business of government to prohibit the advertising, sale, and use of what it deems to be harmful substances. Likewise, the government should not be concerned with keeping people from vice or bad habits and regulating or prohibiting activities that take place between consenting adults. A government with the power to outlaw *harmful* substances and *immoral* practices is a government with the power to ban *any* substance and *any* practice. A nanny state is a perversion of government.

Second, all governments—the U.S. government included—eventually degenerate into the greatest violators of the life, liberty, and property they are supposed to protect. As former Foundation for Economic Education president Richard Ebeling has said:

> There has been no greater threat to life, liberty, and property throughout the ages than government. Even the most violent and brutal private individuals have been able to inflict only a mere fraction of the harm and destruction that have been caused by the use of power by political authorities.

And as C. S. Lewis remarked:

> Of all tyrannies a tyranny sincerely exercised for the good of its victims may be the most oppressive. It may be better to live under robber barons than under omnipotent moral busybodies. The robber baron's cruelty may sometimes sleep, his cupidity may at some point be satiated; but those who torment us for our own good will torment us without end for they do so with the approval of their own conscience.

Religious people in particular make a grave mistake when they look to the state to enforce their morality. The actions of the state are typically the greatest examples of immoral behavior that one could possibly think of. Yet, many religious people not only look to the state to enforce a moral code, they defend, support, and make excuses for the state, its politicians, its legislation, and its wars. Some victimless crimes may indeed be sins, but it is not the purpose of religion to use force or the threat of force to keep people from sinning. Rebuke, persuasion, and instruction are certainly more biblical methods than using the power of the state to change or restrict people's behavior. As Mises again explains:

> He who wants to reform his countrymen must take recourse to persuasion. This alone is the democratic way of bringing about changes. If a man fails in his endeavors to convince other people of the soundness of his ideas, he should blame his own disabilities. He should not ask for a law, that is, for compulsion and coercion by the police.

Many people support legislation against victimless crimes only as long as it stops short of their particular vice. But vice or no vice, no advocate of liberty and a free society should seek legislation that would criminalize any victimless crimes. Liberty means liberty for everyone, even those who use substances and engage in practices that others in society don't use or find offensive. Our liberty is compromised and society is made worse off when we deprive a select few of liberty who are not themselves violating anyone's liberty.

In closing, I refer first to Mises and then to John Stuart Mill:

> A free man must be able to endure it when his fellow men act and live otherwise than he considers proper. He must free himself from the habit, just as soon as something does not please him, of calling for the police.

> The only freedom which deserves the name is that of pursuing our own good in our own way, so long as we do not attempt to deprive others of theirs, or impede their efforts to obtain it. Each is the proper guardian of his own health, whether bodily, or mental and spiritual. Mankind are greater gainers by suffering each other to live as seems good to themselves, than by compelling each to live as seems good to the rest.

Victimless crime legislation requires a nanny state to enforce it. A nanny state must of necessity be a police state and therefore hostile to liberty. Real crimes that violate personal or property rights should be enforced to the fullest extent of the law; victimless crimes should be opposed root and branch.

*****

WHY ARE BROTHELS ILLEGAL?

In contrast to the boring and predictable presidential candidates, there are some unusually colorful candidates who somehow manage to get into office each time there is an election. Actor Arnold Schwarzenegger was twice elected to the California governorship. Professional wrestler Jesse Ventura was elected governor of Minnesota. Singer Sony Bono was a member of the U.S. House of Representatives until his life was tragically cut short in a skiing accident. Comedian Al Franken is currently the junior U.S. senator from Minnesota.

Sometimes a candidate who dies during an election campaign gets voted into office anyway. The most famous example is Melvin Carnahan (1934–2000), the former governor of Missouri who was elected posthumously to the U.S. Senate. In the county in Florida where I live, the deceased tax collector Earl K. Wood, who died from natural causes at age 96 just a few weeks before the election, was recently reelected to a 12th term as Orange County Tax Collector by a margin of 56 percent to 44 percent.

The most interesting person to be voted into office in the recent election has got to be brothel owner Lance Gilman. He won 62 percent of the vote for a seat on the county commission in Storey County, Nevada.

Gilman is the current owner of Nevada's infamous Mustang Ranch brothel in Storey County, east of Reno. Originally opened in 1971, it became Nevada's largest and most profitable brothel before being seized by the federal government in 1999 after its owner was convicted for tax fraud and racketeering. After the furniture, paintings, and accessories were auctioned off in 2002, the buildings were purchased by Gilman and reopened in a new location in 2005. He won the right to the name and branding in 2006.

Although brothels are illegal in most parts of the United States, it is obviously not the case in Storey County, Nevada. And it is not the case in other parts of Nevada either. Licensed, regulated brothel prostitution is permitted in 10 of Nevada's 17 counties, although brothels are currently operating in only 8 of them. Under state law, Nevada counties with a population of under 400,000 are allowed to license or prohibit brothels, but incorporated cities may prohibit brothels in counties where they are legal. Because prostitution is illegal in Nevada's more heavily populated counties (such as Clark County, home to Las Vegas), the brothels are generally located in rural areas.

But why are brothels illegal in Nevada's other counties and why are they illegal everywhere else in the United States?

Now, for the record, I don't patronize brothels, don't want to patronize brothels, don't want a brothel in my neighborhood, don't know anyone who patronizes brothels, don't recommend that anyone patronize brothels, and would not want any women I know to work in a brothel.

But neither do I believe in using the power of government to prohibit, regulate, or punish voluntary, consensual, peaceful behavior that my neighbors, friends, and I may not personally approve of. That is the difference between libertarians and statists of all varieties—Democrat, Republican, liberal, conservative, progressive, and moderate. Libertarians believe that consenting adults have the fundamental right to do anything that's peaceful as long as they don't aggress against someone else's person or property while they do it.

But if frequenting a brothel on private property with the owner's permission and paying for sex with a willing participant is engaging in a peaceful activity agreed to by all parties, then why are brothels other than the few operating in Nevada illegal?

The main objection from most people would be that patronizing brothels is immoral.

But there are serious problems with using the power of government to legislate and regulate morality and prohibit and crusade against immorality.

To begin with, many Americans, if not a majority of Americans, would unite in saying that adultery, fornication, homosexuality, and co-habitation are immoral—even if they themselves engage in any of these things. Yet what percentage of those Americans would call for government at any level to outlaw and punish any of them? Rather small I suspect. And what about other immoral things such as lying, gluttony, lust, greed, envy, pride, and drunkenness? Does anyone really think that the government should concern itself with them?

So why are brothels illegal?

Another objection raised is that, unlike adultery, fornication, homo-sexuality, and cohabitation, the immoral behavior in brothels involves the exchanging of money. But here we have another problem. Frequenting strip clubs, producing or purchasing pornographic magazines or movies, and gambling, which are all generally viewed as immoral, all involve money as well. Yet in most areas of the country, one can visit a strip club, view pornography, or gamble—all without interference from the government as long as certain guidelines are followed. In fact, in 43 states (and the District of Columbia) the state government runs a gambling enter-prise—the state lottery.

So why are brothels illegal?

It appears that the only reason that people and governments want brothels to be illegal is that they combine sexual immorality with the ex-changing of money. But here we run into another problem. There is little difference as far as morality is concerned between paying $50 to a brothel for 15 minutes of a woman's time and paying $50 for dinner and a movie for 15 minutes of a woman's time.

So why are brothels illegal?

The real reasons brothels are illegal have nothing to do with their be-ing a danger (supposedly) to public health, safety, or morals.

Brothels are illegal because government's attempts to legislate and regulate morality and prohibit and crusade against immorality are woe-fully inconsistent, arbitrary, and nonsensical.

Brothels are illegal because of the failure to distinguish between vices and crimes.

Brothels are illegal because of the failure to discern that every crime needs a victim.

Brothels are illegal because of the failure to recognize the right of consenting adults to do whatever they want on their property or with the owner's permission on someone else's property.

Brothels are illegal because of the failure to understand that it is not the purpose of government at any level—federal, state, or local—to regu-late or monitor Americans' sexual activities.

Brothels are illegal because of the failure to acknowledge that it is the business of families, friends, business associates, ministers, religious organizations, and social institutions to shape Americans' moral values and educate them about the nature of brothels—not that of the government.

Brothels are illegal because of the failure to adopt the freedom philosophy.

Brothels are illegal because puritanical busybodies, nanny-statists, and government bureaucrats think it is their business to mind everyone else's business.

It goes without saying that in questioning why brothels are illegal, no advocate of a free society is condoning or excusing in any way human trafficking, kidnapping, child prostitution, rape, forced prostitution, or the sexual exploitation of women. These things currently occur all over the world even where brothels are illegal.

Brothels need not exist in a free society, but their absence should not result from governments' having made them illegal.

*****

POLICE REJECT INTERNET SOLUTION TO SOLICITATION PROBLEM

Like any other large city, Washington, D.C., had, and to some extent still has, what is termed a red-light district. Home to a collection of seedy bars, strip clubs, peep shows, burlesque shows, massage parlors, sex shops, porno theaters, and, of course, prostitutes, a visit to these areas served as a rite of passage for young men, although they were a scourge to nearby residents.

Although 14th Street in Washington, D.C., is now lined with respectable office buildings, restaurants, and hotels, the world's oldest profession is still practiced in some areas.

D.C. police have been responding to complaints from local residents, business owners, and church pastors concerning prostitutes trolling along 14th Street and soliciting customers.

John Fanning, chairman of the Advisory Neighborhood Commission for Thomas Circle, a fashionable D.C. neighborhood, said that "street prostitutes still come out on the weekends, generally in the hours just before dawn, walking along the bike lanes." Adam Briddell, the associate pastor of the nearby Asbury United Methodist Church, said that "5 a.m. near his church 'is like a traffic jam' of women seeking the after-bar crowd."

But thanks to the Internet, the solicitation problem in Washington, D.C., and no doubt other large cities as well, is not what it used to be.

Prostitutes are now able to solicit business online. Indeed, as Pastor Briddell also stated, "The prostitutes seem to work three different markets to get clients—the Internet by day, the clubs at night, and the street after hours." And as John Fanning explained, "Making rendezvous on the Internet has largely moved the street action inside."

One would think that D.C. police would be glad that because the number of prostitutes walking the streets was greatly diminished they could turn their attention to fighting real crime. No more scantily clad women trolling up and down the street in broad daylight. No more seedy hotels to accommodate prostitutes and their clients. No more customers endlessly driving up and down streets and contributing to traffic congestion. No more complaints from business owners that the presence of prostitutes was negatively affecting their businesses.

But there is no joy in the nation's capital. Police there reject the Internet solution to the solicitation problem.

Since January, "D.C. police have run a string of stings at hotels near Thomas Circle, luring men with fake ads on the Internet and then waiting for them to knock on a hotel room door." It turns out that for years D.C. police have been placing ads on Backpage and Craigslist "to draw in men and make busts." The police have declined to reveal their ads.

The operation that started in January has resulted in more than "50 alleged customers" being put "in cuffs in the past several weeks in this one neighborhood alone." The high-profile arrest in January for "solicitation for the purpose of prostitution" of former NBA player turned CBS sports commentator Greg Anthony has not deterred customers. Anthony was arrested after police said "he answered a Backpage ad placed by detectives and offered an undercover officer $80 for sex." If convicted of the misdemeanor he could face up to 90 days in jail, but prosecutors said "they would consider dismissing the case if he completes 32 hours of community service."

Regardless of what one thinks about prostitution, the glaring question here is: Why are the police trying to cause people to commit crimes? Don't they have more than enough work to do preventing, stopping, investigating, and solving real crimes? Prostitution may be illegal, but there is no law that says police must set up sting operations to entrap prostitutes and their customers.

But there is an even more important question that very few people aside from libertarians are asking: Why is prostitution illegal in the first place? I would like to make seven observations about this.

1. How can something that is legal to give away be illegal if one charges for it? If it is legal for a woman to provide free sexual services as often as she wants and to as many people as she wants, then how can it be illegal for her to charge for her services?

2. Indirectly paying for sex is not a crime. Is there really any moral difference between a man's paying a prostitute for sex and a man's paying for dinner and a movie for sex? If adultery or fornication should not be crimes, then why should prostitution be one? Why is it only a crime if a woman accepts the cash directly and forgoes the dinner and movie?

3. Paying people to have sex is not a crime. A woman in a hotel bar who accepts money for sex is subject to arrest even though at the same time another woman in a hotel room who accepts money for sex is not because she is in front of a camera and a director.

4. Every crime needs a victim. Not a potential victim or possible victim or a supposed victim, but an actual victim. Prostitution isn't just the world's oldest profession, it's also the world's oldest victimless crime. Any crime is a victimless crime when it consists of a consensual act between two willing adults. Forced prostitution, human trafficking, child prostitution, assault, rape, trespassing, and kidnapping are, of course, real crimes, and no libertarian would defend or excuse them.

5. Vices are not crimes. No one has ever improved on the distinction between vices and crimes as explained by the 19th-century classical-liberal political philosopher Lysander Spooner:

> Vices are those acts by which a man harms himself or his property. Crimes are those acts by which one man harms the person or property of another. Vices are simply the errors which a man makes in his search after his own happiness. Unlike crimes, they imply no malice toward others, and no interference with their persons or property.

To be a crime, adds Spooner, there must exist criminal intent to invade the person or property of another. But vices are not engaged in with criminal intent. A man practices a vice "for his own happiness solely, and not from any malice toward others."

6. Other immoral acts are not crimes. Sexual acts that most Americans consider to be immoral—adultery, fornication, homosexuality, perversion, sadism, and cohabitation—are not crimes. And neither are the "seven deadly sins" of wrath, greed, sloth, pride, lust, envy, and gluttony. And of course, neither is drunkenness. Why single out prostitution?

7. In a free society, prostitution would be a choice not a crime. It may be an immoral choice, a sinful choice, an unhealthy choice, a dangerous choice, and an unwise choice, but in a free society, it is an individual choice that should not be the concern of government.

Legalize prostitution; legalize freedom.

*****

SHOULD CHRISTIANS SUPPORT LAWS AGAINST PROSTITUTION?

Poor Jimmy Carter. It must be tough for a life-long liberal Democrat to almost sound like a conservative Republican.

In a recent *Washington Post* op-ed, the former president argues that to curb prostitution, the government should punish those who buy sex rather than those who sell it. Carter's one-sided approach is why I say that he almost sounds like a conservative since the typical conservative is perfectly happy with both parties being locked in a cage for engaging in peaceful, private, voluntary, consensual activity.

Carter is disturbed that "some human rights and public health organizations are advocating the full legalization of the sex trade." He agrees with "Amnesty International, UNAIDS and other groups that say that those who sell sex acts should not be arrested or prosecuted," but "cannot support proposals to decriminalize buyers and pimps." He equates prostitution with "violence against women," "domination," "oppression," and "exploitation." Legalizing the act of paying money for sex "debases men by assuming that they are entitled to access women's bodies for sexual gratification" and teaches every young boy that "women and girls are commodities to be bought and sold." To be clear, Carter is arguing against prostitution itself, not just "the harm that accompanies it."

Carter feels that the "Nordic model" pioneered in Sweden is a "much better policy option" that advances "human rights and healthy societies." This strategy "involves decriminalizing prostituted women and offering them housing, job training and other services" but "treats purchasing and profiting from sex acts as serious crimes." Another key component is "public education about the inherent harms of prostitution for those whose bodies are sold."

Carter says that taking the approach that "mature adults should be free to exchange money for sex" ignores "the power imbalance that defines the vast majority of sex-for-cash transactions" and demeans "the beauty of sexual relations when both parties are respected."

Carter concludes that "it is better to help women and girls avoid a life of prostitution and to deter men from buying sex acts."

Carter has always claimed to be a religious man, a church goer, and a Sunday School teacher. Yet, not once in his op-ed does he appeal to Scripture to justify his call for arresting and prosecuting those who purchase sex for money but not those who provide sex for money.

How could he?

There is no biblical warrant for either.

Before proceeding I should say that, as a Bible-believing, theologically conservative Christian, I believe prostitution to be wrong, immoral, debauched, sinful, bad, evil, impure, shameful, dishonorable, wicked, depraved, lewd, unholy, lascivious, degenerate, unclean, licentious, filthy, indecent, and every other bad thing you could possibly say about it. Prostitution is not something anyone should want in their city or neighborhood. Prostitution is not something anyone should want their wife, daughter, aunt, mother, grandmother, mother-in-law, niece, or sister to be involved in.

I should also say that not supporting laws against prostitution does not mean that I don't support laws against forced prostitution, violence against women, exploitation of women, oppression of women, human trafficking, forced prostitution, child prostitution, trespassing, loitering, sexual abuse, assault, rape, public nudity, public sex, slavery, or kidnapping. Does the non-crime of prostitution sometimes involve one or more of the real crimes that I mentioned? Certainly. But that doesn't mean that prostitution itself should be a crime.

It is a shame that I have to be so tedious, monotonous, repetitive, and redundant in denouncing prostitution. But if I don't make my opposition perfectly clear, then some of my conservative Christian brethren will smear me as a liberal, a moderate, a compromiser, a freethinker, a libertine, a hedonist, a sellout, and/or an antinomian who approves of prostitution.

Just like my conservative Christian brethren, I approve of no such thing. But there is a big difference between not approving of something and thinking the government should arrest, fine, and imprison people for doing what you don't approve of.

Before turning to the Bible, I first want to make some practical and philosophical observations.

Does Carter not realize that it takes two to tango? He assumes that the woman offering her body for sale is always exploited, always dominated, always oppressed. In a word, she is always a victim. I don't know any prostitutes personally, but I suspect that many would disagree. The high-priced call girls that former New York governor Eliot Spitzer paid for were certainly not victims.

Is there any difference as far as morality is concerned between paying $50 cash for 15 minutes of a girl's time and paying $50 for dinner and a movie for 15 minutes of a girl's time? Why is it only a crime if a woman accepts the cash directly and forgoes the dinner and movie?

Most people who support laws against prostitution do not support laws against fornication and adultery. Why? Why does the introduction of money suddenly turn fornication and adultery into criminal offenses?

If it is legal for a woman to provide free sexual services as often as she wants and to as many people as she wants, then how can it be illegal for her to charge for her services? How can something that is legal to give away be illegal if one charges for it?

It is not the job of government to curb prostitution, come up with policy solutions regarding prostitution, legislate morality, provide prostitutes with housing, job training and other services, help women and girls avoid a life of prostitution, deter men from buying sexual services, or to criminalize one party or both parties who engage in peaceful, private, voluntary, consensual activity.

And besides, if the government really wanted to curb prostitution, it would make more sense to focus on the much smaller, and more easily identifiable, number of those who are selling services than the much larger, and more difficult to identify, number of those who are buying services.

My main concern, however, is whether Christians ought to support laws against prostitution.

The practical and philosophical observations I have made above should be reason enough for Christians not to support such laws. But let me make two additional observations.

One, there is no warrant in the New Testament for Christians to support laws against prostitution. There is no warrant in the New Testament for Christians to support the government arresting, fining, and/or imprisoning prostitutes, pimps, or johns—as long as they are not aggressing against anyone or violating someone's property rights.

And two, Christians are very inconsistent when they support laws against prostitution and not other immoral activities or sins. The immorality of prostitution is without question. The sinfulness of prostitution is without question. The question, then, is why don't Christians want the government to go after people for other immoral activities and sins? Are not wrath, greed, sloth, pride, lust, envy, and gluttony the "seven deadly sins"? Does not the Bible say: "These six things doth the LORD hate: yea, seven are an abomination unto him: a proud look, a lying tongue, and hands that shed innocent blood, An heart that deviseth wicked imaginations, feet that be swift in running to mischief, false witness that speaketh lies, and he that soweth discord among brethren" (Proverbs 6:16-19)? Why prostitution and not these things? Why prostitution and not the sins they commit? This is where I say: To ask the question is to answer it.

No, Christians shouldn't support laws against prostitution. Just like they shouldn't support laws against gambling, drug use, homosexuality, blasphemy, adultery, fornication, cohabitation, and transporting unlicensed dentures across state lines. Just like they shouldn't support laws against any victimless crime. Every crime needs a tangible victim and measurable damages.

Yes, Christians should support outreach ministries to prostitutes and other "sinners." Instead of looking to the government to curb prostitution, they should do something about it themselves.

What consenting adults do on their property or in the privacy of their homes, hotel rooms, and cars is their business as long as their actions don't infringe upon the rights of others. This is true even if Christians don't approve of the things they are doing.

*****

THE ABSURDITY OF LAWS AGAINST PROSTITUTION

Aside from voting for candidates for federal, state, and local offices, residents of California recently had the option of voting on a most unusual measure on their election ballots. There were seventeen initiatives on the general election ballot in California this year. Proposition 60, the Condoms in Pornographic Films Initiative, would have required "adult film producers to provide condoms and ensure that performers use them."

It failed by a vote of 53.94 to 46.06 percent.

California is a leading producer of pornographic films in the United States. The California Division of Occupational Safety and Health (Cal/OSHA) already requires condom use during sex in pornographic films, but "generally enforces these rules by responding to complaints." During the last two years, Cal/OSHA has cited only four production companies for violations of the condom rules. Moreover, in 2012, the Los Angeles City Council passed an ordinance that mandated the use of condoms by pornography actors on location. Los Angeles County voters then approved Measure B, which required pornography actors to wear condoms on set throughout the county, producers of adult films to pay an annual fee to the county's Department of Public Health, and all principals and management-level employees of adult-entertainment-producing companies to undergo blood-borne pathogen training.

The official ballot summary of Proposition 60 prepared by the California attorney general reads as follows:

• Requires performers in adult films to use condoms during filming of sexual intercourse.
• Requires producers of adult films to pay for performer vaccinations, testing, and medical examinations related to sexually transmitted infections.
• Requires producers of adult films to obtain a state health license, and to post condom requirement at film sites.
• Imposes liability on producers for violations, on certain distributors, on performers if they have a financial interest in the film involved, and on talent agents who knowingly refer performers to noncomplying producers.
• Permits state, performers, or any state resident to enforce violations.

This summary of Proposition 60 was "identical to the initial summary provided to initiative proponents for the purpose of circulating the initiative for signature collection."

The accompanying fiscal-impact statement expected that the passage of Proposition 60 would result in the

• likely reduction of state and local tax revenues of several million dollars per year; and increased state costs that could exceed $1 million annually to
• license and regulate adult-film production and to enforce workplace health and safety rules. The costs would be offset to some extent by new fee revenue.

The summary that appeared on the ballot to be read by California voters was as follows:

Requires adult film performers to use condoms during filming of sexual intercourse. Requires producers to pay for performer vaccinations, testing, and medical examinations. Requires producers to post condom requirement at film sites. Fiscal Impact: Likely reduction of state and local tax revenues of several million dollars annually. Increased state spending that could exceed $1 million annually on regulation, partially offset by new fees.

Spending in support of Proposition 60 by For Adult Industry Responsibility (FAIR), all of which was donated by the AIDS Healthcare Foundation, was more than nine times that spent by opponents of the initiative, organized as the Coalition Against Worker Harassment.

Naturally, the adult-film industry vehemently opposed the measure. But both the California Democratic and Republican parties opposed it as well.

Clearly, from a libertarian perspective, it is an illegitimate purpose of government to regulate the production of adult films or any other films. The use of condoms—or any other protective clothing, equipment, or devices—in the workplace is something to be negotiated between employers and employees. It should be out of the reach of government.

So what do laws requiring performers in adult films to wear condoms have to do with laws against prostitution?

Simple: How can engaging in sex for money be legal in the first instance but illegal in the second? How can the presence of lights, a camera, and a film crew turn an illegal act into a legal one?

To be logical and consistent, it seems abundantly clear that if prostitution should be outlawed, then so should the making of adult films, since both activities involve paying people to engage in sex acts. And even more so in the case of adult films, since acts of prostitution are done privately and in secret, while adult films are made in front of a crew and meant for public viewing by hundreds, if not thousands, of people. Yet most Americans who are not in favor of the government's outlawing pornographic movies or massage parlors are at the same time in favor of the government's outlawing prostitution.

There is, of course, one other glaring reason that laws against prostitution are so absurd. How can something that is *legal* to give away be *illegal* if one charges for it? If it is *legal* for consenting adults to have sex as often as they want and with as many different partners as they want, then why should it be *illegal* if one of the parties pays the other for it? Why does the introduction of money turn sex into a criminal offense? Again, most Americans who are not in favor of the government's outlawing fornication, adultery, cohabitation, communal living, and swinging are at the same time in favor of the government's outlawing prostitution.

Aside from those two considerations, the libertarian case against prostitution laws is straightforward.

It is not the job of government to concern itself with how people choose to make a living. There is a big difference between not approving of someone's actions and thinking the government should arrest, fine, and imprison people for doing something people don't approve of.

What consenting adults do on private property is none of the government's business as long as their actions don't infringe upon the rights of others. That is still true even if the majority of Americans don't approve of what they are doing.

Every crime needs a tangible victim with measurable damages. It is absurd to criminalize one party or both parties who engage in peaceful, private, voluntary, consensual activity.

Now, none of that means that libertarians favor prostitution or want their wives, sisters, or daughters to be prostitutes. None of this means that libertarians think that prostitution is not immoral, sinful, risky, or hazardous to one's physical health. None of it means that libertarians are ignorant of or ambivalent toward the plight of women who feel they are trapped in a life of prostitution. None of it means that libertarians don't support laws against kidnapping, human trafficking, slavery, rape, assault, child prostitution, or sexual abuse. None of it means that libertarians support trespassing, loitering, or other violations of property rights that might occur when prostitutes seek or service customers.

No, libertarians aren't fans of prostitution any more than they are fans of drug use, gambling, fornication, pornography, and other vices, but they are fans of freedom—the freedom of consenting adults to do anything that's peaceful as long as their actions are voluntary, don't aggress against others, and respect private property rights.

*****

DEFENDING THE REALLY UNDEFENDABLE

Back in 1976, economist Walter Block, now of Loyola University in New Orleans, wrote a provocative book titled *Defending the Undefendable*. In it he famously defended the "pimp, prostitute, scab, slumlord, libeler, moneylender, and other scapegoats in the rogues' gallery of American society." Now, Block was not recommending that anyone engage in those occupations or arguing that they are held by people you would want to have as neighbors. He was making the case for libertarianism, the basic premise of which he stated in his introduction: "It is illegitimate to engage in aggression against nonaggressors."

In libertarianism, Block goes on to say, "violence is justified only for purposes of defense, or in response to prior aggression, or in retaliation against it." Libertarianism "condemns only the *initiation of violence*—the use of violence against a non-violent person or his property." He therefore concludes that "government is not justified in fining, punishing, incarcerating, imposing death penalties on people who act in an immoral manner—as long as they refrain from threatening or initiating physical violence on the persons or property of others."

If Block's book had been written twenty years later there is no doubt that it would have included a chapter on someone that many consider to be really undefendable—the Internet pornographer.

When the infamous Ariel Castro pled guilty a few months ago to kidnapping three Cleveland women, imprisoning them in his home for a decade, beating them, and raping them, he blamed his problems on addiction to pornography. He described himself as a sex addict and said, "I'm not a monster. I'm sick." Yet millions of men who view Internet pornography don't kidnap, imprison, beat, or rape young girls. Nevertheless, conservative Morgan Bennett, in a pair of articles on Internet pornography written for *Public Discourse* ("an online publication of the Witherspoon Institute that seeks to enhance the public understanding of the moral foundations of free societies"), calls for government censorship of Internet pornography.

In "The New Narcotic," Bennett points out that new "neurological research has revealed that the effect of internet pornography on the human brain is just as potent—if not more so—than addictive chemical substances such as cocaine or heroin." In "Internet Pornography & the First Amendment," he argues that "current jurisprudence protecting pornography as 'artistic expression' contradicts the Founders' understanding and the underlying purposes of the First Amendment's protection of speech, and it fails to protect Americans from the social and personal trauma caused by pornography."

Although pornography has been around in various forms "for most of human history," there are three reasons that Bennett feels that Internet pornography is radically different: affordability, accessibility, and anonymity. In the scientific perspective he gives in his first article, Bennett explains that "while the addictive effects of internet pornography are similar to a combination of addictive chemical substances, internet pornography's effects go beyond those of chemical substances." Pornography reshapes and develops new maps in the brain. It "literally changes the physical matter within the brain so that new neurological pathways require pornographic material in order to trigger the desired reward sensation." A pornography user has "'unknowingly created a neurological circuit' that makes his or her default perspective toward sexual matters ruled by the norms and expectations of pornography." Pornography addiction surpasses drug use because of its permanence:

> While substances can be metabolized out of the body, pornographic images cannot be metabolized out of the brain because pornographic images are

stored in the brain's memory. While substance abusers may cause permanent harm to their bodies or brains from drug use, the substance itself does not remain in the body after it has metabolized out of the body. But with pornography, there is no timeframe of abstinence that can erase the pornographic "reels" of images in the brain that can continue to fuel the addictive cycle.

It is not until the end of his first article that he hints at his solution to the problem of Internet pornography: "More akin to cocaine than to books or public speeches, internet pornography is not the sort of 'speech' the First Amendment was meant to protect from government censorship."

In his second article, Bennett focuses on the "epidemic social harm" of Internet pornography. It is "a massive, paradigm-shifting social harm that undermines the family unit and causes abuse, life-long addictions, infidelity, and unhealthy perceptions and expectations among men, women, and children." It "certainly qualifies as speech injurious to society's health and moral foundations." It also qualifies as "speech used in the course of injurious conduct" because of its "power to addict and harm those who see it."

Bennett is careful to not focus on the morality of Internet pornography, although there is no doubt he would argue the inherent immorality of pornography in general in some other context. Saying that the government should ban an activity because it is immoral would not get him much of a hearing nowadays. It is for that reason that he cleverly focuses most of his attention on the scientific perspective and legal standpoint of Internet pornography.

I do think, however, that the author hurts his case when he makes the sensational and unproven claim that Internet pornography is "one of the greatest evils of our time" and "almost always" involves violence, rape, the exploitation of children, drugging of participants, kidnapping, sex trafficking, prostitution, forced performances, slavery, assault, or murder.

Acts of violence and coercion against women and children are real crimes of aggression that don't need to be committed in the context of the production of Internet pornography to be considered criminal offenses punishable under existing state laws.

In his first article, Bennett implies that because the negative consequences of Internet pornography are worse than those of hard drugs, it should be illegal just as drugs are; in his second article he is not so subtle.

Bennett finds it "absolutely baffling that the underlying acts required to make internet pornography are not prosecuted by way of prostitution laws" since pornography ("prostitution with a camera") "is almost always created by an act of prostitution (paying a human being to perform a sex act)."

Since prosecution for prostitution isn't likely to take place, he favors "prosecution and cultural engagement" followed by government censorship of Internet pornography:

> First, local, state, and federal governments should enforce the current obscenity-related laws already on the books. Nearly every state has anti-obscenity laws. The enforcement of those laws would send a message that the production and distribution of obscene material is unacceptable in a civilized society. Second, local and national groups should run billboard, TV, and internet advertising campaigns to expose the harms of internet pornography to the public.

> Looking beyond those "first steps," I would argue for the eventual enactment of new laws that would censor obscene internet pornography.

Bennett is not advocating government censorship of all pornography. He is careful to add that "censoring hardcore pornography on the internet would not affect the private viewing of pornographic material by way of a DVD or a downloaded file." His goal is to "strip two important elements from internet pornography: its affordability and its accessibility."

Bennett, of course, is not advocating anything new. Governments throughout history have sought to censor books, plays, movies, advertisements, radio and television broadcasts, speech, magazines, and newspapers that they considered to be obscene, subversive, immoral, harmful, or critical of government.

And he is not alone. According to a recent *Baptist Press* article, British Prime Minister David Cameron earlier this year called online pornography a "corroding influence" on British children and "pushed for new regulations on adult content delivered online." Petition efforts to block online pornography have been launched in Canada and India. Iceland and Saudi Arabia are also considering bans on online adult content.

Now, just consider what Bennett and other conservative advocates of Internet censorship are advocating. If the government were to censor readily accessible pornography on the Internet, it would first have to determine which websites featured adult content that was readily accessible and not just available for download or purchase on DVD. That would mean the creation of a new army of government bureaucrats to function as the purity police to certify that no new or existing website contained any readily accessible content that was obscene or sexually explicit.

And if "by 2017, access to pornography on smartphones and tablets will be available to 250 million people worldwide," as a new study from Juniper Research, a London-area analyst of the wireless sector, asserts, government attempts to censor the Internet would be doomed to fail because of the sheer volume of content online. And as is the case with most government failures, more taxpayer money would then be expended to hire even more bureaucrats to police the Internet.

Consider also what this government job would entail. The government would be paying people to view the very online content that it wants to prohibit people from seeing.

What it all comes down to is this: Proponents of Internet censorship are saying that because the *excessive* viewing of pornography on the Internet *may* cause certain biological changes in the viewer that *may* have a negative impact on culture and society, government should censor Internet pornography.

The problem with that is that the very same thing could be said about the excessive consumption of Red Bull, Big Gulps, alcohol, and high-fructose corn syrup.

I don't dispute Bennett's claim that "brain research confirms the critical fact that pornography is a drug delivery system that has a distinct and powerful effect upon the human brain and nervous system." In fact, I don't dispute any of the scientific evidence about the psychological, physiological, or neurological effects of Internet pornography that he presents. And I think that libertarians who attempted to argue the contrary would be wasting their time, since it has nothing to do with the real issue.

We can even go beyond Bennett and add that the majority of Americans probably find Internet pornography to be distasteful, unnatural, disgusting, obscene, degrading to women, or immoral.

But whether Internet pornography may be addictive and cause physical and spiritual harm to those who view it is not the real issue. The real issue is simply this: Is it the proper role of government to prevent people from becoming addicted to something or causing harm to themselves? If the answer is no, then the government should not censor the Internet. But if the answer is yes, then there is no logical argument against government censorship of anything.

The libertarian defense of pornographers is a very limited one. As Block says in the introduction to his *Defending the Undefendable*, "It consists solely of the claim that they do not initiate physical violence against non-aggressors. Hence, according to libertarian principles, none should be visited upon them. This means only that these activities should not be punished by jail sentences or other forms of violence. It decidedly does not mean that these activities are moral, proper, or good."

Viewing pornography should be a personal decision, not a government decision. Addiction to anything is a personal problem with a variety of remedies and treatment options. However, in a free society, government censorship is not one of them.

A government with the power to ban pornography on the Internet is a government with the power to ban *anything* on the Internet.

*****

PORONOGRAPHY AND THE FIRST AMENDMENT

Would the freedom of speech exist without the First Amendment? How about the freedom of the press? What about the right of the people to peaceably assemble or petition the government for a redress of grievances? Is it the First Amendment alone that prevents the federal government from making laws respecting an establishment of religion or prohibiting the free exercise thereof?

Many Americans misconstrue the nature of the First Amendment. They include the current and former justices of the Supreme Court, liberals who look to the First Amendment when it can be used to further some agenda, and conservatives who profess allegiance to the strict interpretation and original intent of the Constitution. That last case is especially baffling.

A case in point is a recent pair of articles for *Public Discourse* advocating government censorship of pornography on the Internet. Conservative Morgan Bennett argues that the First Amendment should not be used to protect Internet pornography and other "obscene" material. He finds that "current jurisprudence protecting pornography as 'artistic expression' contradicts the Framers' understanding and the underlying purposes of the First Amendment's protection of speech, and it fails to protect Americans from the social and personal trauma caused by pornography."

It is in the middle of his first article "The New Narcotic" that Bennett raises the question of the First Amendment:

> Yet many would argue that pornography is merely "speech," a form of sexual "expression" that should be protected as a constitutional right under the First Amendment.

> The question of First Amendment rights is undeniably the ultimate hurdle to clear from a legal standpoint.

And then he adds at the end of his first article, "Internet pornography is not the sort of 'speech' the First Amendment was meant to protect from government censorship."

In his second article, "Internet Pornography & the First Amendment," Bennett insists that Internet pornography "certainly qualifies as speech injurious to society's health and moral foundations." It also qualifies as "speech used in the course of injurious conduct" because of its "power to addict and harm those who see it." He points out that "while many assume that the First Amendment protects internet pornography as 'artistic expression,' that is largely not the case under current statutory and constitutional law." He explains that "under current First Amendment jurisprudence, any sexually explicit 'expression' (including images and videos) is protected under the First Amendment unless it is obscene or 'real' (non-virtual) child pornography." But he charges "current First Amendment jurisprudence, at least as it relates to sexually explicit material," with failure "to properly discern and apply the First Amendment's purposes." He believes that "an examination of prior and even current precedent reveals that speech or acts of a sexual nature are a historically unique category and thus require a unique analysis." Bennett concludes that "by considering the duties of good government and the intended purposes of the First Amendment, we can develop a just and principled interpretation of the First Amendment as it relates to internet pornography."

Bennett, a law student, misconstrues the nature of the First Amendment. He is correct only insofar as the "freedom of speech" clause of the First Amendment was never intended to "protect" pornography, Internet or otherwise. Obviously, there were no motion pictures, DVDs, Internet, or even photographs when the First Amendment was adopted. However, that does not mean that pornography is not "protected."

The First Amendment reads as follows:

> Congress shall make no law respecting an establishment of religion, or prohibiting the free exercise thereof; or abridging the freedom of speech or of the press; or the right of the people peaceably to assemble and to petition the Government for a redress of grievances.

In order to not "protect" certain forms of speech, the federal government has over the years come up with certain speech tests—bad tendency, clear and present danger, fighting words, imminent lawless action, balancing, preferred position—to limit speech.

But in order to "protect" certain activities, the federal government has defined things as forms of "speech" so they could be "protected" by the First Amendment. For example, flag burning.

Back in the 1980s, Gregory Johnson burned an American flag in Texas in protest against Reagan administration policies. He was tried and convicted under a Texas flag-desecration law. After the Texas Court of Appeals reversed the conviction, it went to the U.S. Supreme Court, in the case of *Texas v. Johnson* (1989), which ruled against the state of Texas. Congress then passed the Flag Protection Act of 1989. It criminalizes the conduct of anyone who "knowingly mutilates, defaces, physically defiles, burns, maintains on the floor or ground, or tramples upon" a U.S. flag. In 1989, Shawn Eichman burned a flag on the steps of the U.S. Capitol. He was charged with violating the Flag Protection Act, but the charges were dismissed by the U.S. District Court for the District of Columbia. The federal government appealed the case to the Supreme Court, which held the Act unconstitutional in the case of *United States v. Eichman* (1990). Flag burning was held to be "symbolic speech" and therefore subject to First Amendment "protection."

And as Bennett points out in his second article, "In 1952, the Supreme Court struck down a film censorship statute on First Amendment grounds and announced that motion pictures were 'expressions' and therefore protected as 'speech.'"

When it comes to obscenity, the Supreme Court, as Bennett also mentions, follows the standard it set down in *Miller v. California* (1973) when it ruled that "obscene material" was "not protected by the First Amendment." However, in order for something to be subject to state obscenity laws, it must first be proved "that the work in question, taken as a whole, appeals to the prurient interest, is patently offensive in light of community standards, and lacks serious literary, artistic, political, or scientific value."

Bennett, like many conservatives, believes that Internet pornography is in fact obscene and therefore is a form of "speech" or "expression" that should not be protected by the First Amendment.

His conclusion is correct, but not because Internet pornography is obscene or doesn't qualify as "protected" speech.

Let's just stick with the First Amendment. Congress shall make no law "abridging the freedom of speech or of the press."

Pornography is not speech any more than flag burning is, regardless of the tortured interpretations of the First Amendment by the Supreme Court over the years in an attempt to "protect" certain activities by classifying them as "speech." The First Amendment has nothing to do with "protecting" artistic expression.

Once you start defining things as speech in order to grant them First Amendment "protection" from government interference, you must forever argue over what is classified as speech and what kind of speech it is.

If Internet pornography is to be "protected" by the First Amendment, it seems that it would make better sense to do so under the rubric of freedom of the press. Proponents would argue that since pornography is published material, it should be treated no differently than any other book, magazine, or movie. Opponents would argue either that Internet pornography is different from traditional media so it doesn't qualify as "the press" or that pornography is obscene so it cannot be "protected" by the freedom of the press.

But if Internet pornography cannot be "protected" by the First Amendment by means of the speech or press clauses, does that mean that the federal government can censor it?

Absolutely not.

The First Amendment does not grant Americans any rights. That is an all-too-common, but erroneous, viewpoint. The First Amendment merely prohibits the federal government from infringing upon the natural rights that Americans already have.

In Article I, Section 8 of the Constitution, Congress is granted certain limited powers. Aside from six paragraphs related to war, the military, and the militia, Congress is granted the power to lay and collect taxes, duties, imposts, and excises; to borrow money; to regulate commerce; to establish rules and laws regarding naturalization and bankruptcies; to coin money and regulate its value; to fix the standard of weights and measures; to provide for the punishment of counterfeiting and piracies; to establish post offices and post roads; to secure to authors and inventors the exclusive right to their respective writings and discoveries; to constitute tribunals inferior to the Supreme Court; and to exercise authority over the District of Columbia. In Article III, Section 1, Congress is given the power to regulate the jurisdiction of the Supreme Court; in Article III, Section 2, to designate the location of certain trials; and in Article III, Section 3, to declare the punishment for treason.

The federal government has been granted no authority whatsoever to regulate, monitor, or censor any speech of any kind or any movie, magazine, newspaper, advertisement, television program, or website. The fact that any of those things might be pornographic doesn't change anything.

That doesn't mean that pornography is natural, wholesome, or harmless. And it doesn't mean that pornography is not obscene, immoral, or degrading to women.

It simply means that no power was granted to the federal government to abridge any of what are commonly referred to as First Amendment freedoms. The First Amendment merely reinforces this idea. The individual rights to freely exercise one's religion, speak freely, publish freely, peaceably assemble, and petition the government are natural rights independent of the Bill of Rights.

Although the Bill of Rights' being added to the Constitution is generally looked upon as a good thing, there are, unfortunately, two misunderstandings in American political thought that have developed because of it. First, the idea that natural rights are instead rights granted by government; and second, that if a right isn't listed, then it doesn't exist unless government says so.

The misconstruing of the First Amendment and the Bill of Rights has destroyed federalism, centralized power in the national government, clogged the federal judiciary with needless cases, and unnecessarily polarized Americans.

Pornography is an individual, personal, moral, and religious concern, not a political one.

*****

THE GAMBLING QUESTION

My state of Florida, like many other states, is facing a budget shortfall. Although our new Republican governor, Rick Scott, maintains that the budget gap is "nothing" compared with other large states, $3.6 billion is still a lot of money.

Although some states are turning to tax increases to make up their budget deficits—like Illinois, which just raised personal income tax rates by 66 percent—Florida, like only a handful of other states, has no personal income tax.

Florida, like some other states, is now asking the gambling question.

On the table in the Florida legislature is a major gaming expansion to help close the state's budget gap. Florida state senator Dennis Jones said he would "introduce legislation that would allow up to five casino resorts in various locations across the state." Governor Scott, who recently stopped in Las Vegas to meet with officials from a casino corporation on his way to a meeting of Republican governors in San Diego, said he is "open to casino proposals."

By state law, gambling is only permitted in Florida on Indian reservations, offshore cruises, and in pari-mutuel facilities. Betting on horse racing was legalized in Florida in 1931, followed by the more popular greyhound dog racing. Betting is also allowed on jai-alai, an extremely fast-paced game similar to racquetball but played on a three-walled court called a fronton by players with wicker basket devices attached to their right arms. Slot machines and poker tables can also be found at some pari-mutuel facilities. Offshore cruises must sail at least three miles from the coast into international waters before gambling operations can commence. The Seminole Indian tribe was permitted to offer high-stakes gambling when they opened a bingo hall in Hollywood, Florida, in 1979. There are currently seven Seminole casinos operating in Florida. The Miccosukee Indian tribe also operates a casino in Miami.

The problem with expanding gaming in Florida is four fold. As expected, some religious groups are opposed to expanded gaming operations because they are opposed to current gaming operations. Some in the pari-mutuel and casino industries are opposed because they see more gambling options as cutting into their business. There is also opposition from the family-friendly tourism industry, including the largest tourism magnet in Florida, Disney World. The other concern about gambling expansion is the agreement that the state of Florida recently made with the Seminole Indian tribe that guarantees the state $1 billion over five years. Legalizing other casinos would mean breaking the contract with the Seminoles and losing the money from the Seminole casinos.

It is obvious that any gambling that takes place in the state of Florida must be first approved by the state legislature. The state of Florida only allows gambling to take place when it can get a cut of the action. Private gambling not done under the regulatory eye of the state is illegal in any form according to Florida statutes, chapter 849, except for certain bingo games (s. 849.0931) and charity drawings (s. 849.0935).

It is a criminal act to maintain a gambling house:

Whoever by herself or himself, her or his servant, clerk or agent, or in any other manner has, keeps, exercises or maintains a gaming table or room, or gaming implements or apparatus, or house, booth, tent, shelter or other place for the purpose of gaming or gambling or in any place of which she or he may directly or indirectly have charge, control or management, either exclusively or with others, procures, suffers or permits any person to play for money or other valuable thing at any game whatever, whether heretofore prohibited or not, shall be guilty of a felony of the third degree, punishable as provided in s. 775.082, s. 775.083, or s. 775.084 (s. 849.01).

It is a criminal act to bet on the result of a contest of skill:

Whoever stakes, bets or wagers any money or other thing of value upon the result of any trial or contest of skill, speed or power or endurance of human or beast, or whoever receives in any manner whatsoever any money or other thing of value staked, bet or wagered, or offered for the purpose of being staked, bet or wagered, by or for any other person upon any such result, or whoever knowingly becomes the custodian or depositary of any money or other thing of value so staked, bet, or wagered upon any such result, or whoever aids, or assists, or abets in any manner in any of such acts all of which are hereby forbidden, shall be guilty of a misdemeanor of the second degree, punishable as provided in s. 775.082 or s. 775.083 (s. 849.14).

The only exception is for a bowling tournament (s. 849.141).
It is a criminal act to gamble:

Whoever plays or engages in any game at cards, keno, roulette, faro or other game of chance, at any place, by any device whatever, for money or other thing of value, shall be guilty of a misdemeanor of the second degree, punishable as provided in s. 775.082 or s. 775.083 (s. 849.08).

The only exception is for a penny-ante game of "poker, pinochle, bridge, rummy, canasta, hearts, dominoes, or mah-jongg in which the winnings of any player in a single round, hand, or game do not exceed $10 in value" (s. 849.085, 2, a) Provided, of course, that the game is conducted in a dwelling, that no one receives a commission for allowing the game in his dwelling, that admission to the game is not charged, that no advertising of the game is done, and that no one playing the game is under 18 (s. 849.085, 3, a-e).
It is a criminal act to posses any gambling device:

It shall be unlawful for any person to manufacture, sell, transport, offer for sale, purchase, own, or have in his or her possession any roulette wheel or table, faro layout, crap table or layout, chemin de fer table or layout, chuck-a-luck wheel, bird cage such as used for gambling, bolita balls, chips with house markings, or any other device, implement, apparatus, or paraphernalia ordinarily or commonly used or designed to be used in the operation of gambling houses or establishments, excepting ordinary dice and playing cards (s. 849.231).

And according to statute 849.232, there is no right of property in any gambling device. Anything seized will be destroyed after used as evidence against you.

And just in case you thought that chapter 849 of the Florida statutes was unnecessary, the last paragraph in the chapter is for you:

It is deemed by the Legislature that this chapter is necessary for the more efficient and proper enforcement of the statutes and laws of this state prohibiting lotteries and gambling, and a lawful exercise of the police power of the state for the protection of the public welfare, health, safety and morals of the people of the state. All the provisions of this chapter shall be liberally construed for the accomplishment of these purposes (s. 849.46).

So, the state of Florida has set itself up as a protector of the morals of Floridians. But if gambling is a vice, as most people in Florida—including gamblers—would acknowledge, then why does the state allow it at all? If gambling is immoral then it is immoral. Whether it is done in a state-approved and state-regulated gambling facility or done in secret in the privacy of one's home is irrelevant. And if the state thinks it needs to monitor gambling activities to protect people's morals then why does it levy a special tax on income from these activities? On the one hand, the state tries to discourage gambling, but on the other hand wants people to gamble so it can get revenue for its coffers.

And what about other vices? Here we see how inconsistent the state is. Prostitution and drugs are forbidden under any circumstances, and although alcohol and tobacco sellers are subject to strict regulations, consumers can purchase booze and cigarettes in any quantity and drink themselves knock down dead drunk in their home and smoke until they get cancer—and invite all their neighbors to join them and do likewise. They just better not dare set up a blackjack table in their living room while they are doing it.

But not only does the state of Florida sanction and regulate gambling, it has operated its own gambling racket—the Florida Lottery—since 1988, with odds far worse than blackjack or poker. Yet, according to the same Florida statutes, chapter 849, it is unlawful for any person in the state of Florida to set up a lottery, dispose of property by a lottery, conduct any lottery drawing, assist in conducting a lottery, attempt to operate, conduct, or advertise a lottery, possess any lottery implement, sell or offer for sale any lottery ticket, possess any lottery ticket, assist in the sale of a lottery ticket, possess any lottery advertisement, or possess any "papers, records, instruments, or paraphernalia designed for use, either directly or indirectly, in, or in connection with, the violation of the laws of this state prohibiting lotteries" (s. 849.09, 1, a-k)—unless, of course, he works for the Florida Lottery or buys a Florida Lottery ticket.

So, what about the gambling question? Should the state of Florida legalize more gambling options and tax them to help close the state's budget gap? Absolutely not. More forms of gambling should not be legalized just because doing so will help prevent a budget shortfall, because doing so will provide extra money for education, or because doing so will allow the state to regulate gambling in such a way as to protect "the public welfare, health, safety and morals of the people of the state." The state of Florida—and every other state—should legalize gambling simply because this activity should have never been criminalized in the first place. And the states should not just legalize more forms of gambling, but all forms of gambling, and for the same reason.

This does not mean that I'm a gambler (I'm not), that some people don't have a gambling problem (some do), or that some people won't blow their whole paycheck on lottery tickets or at a casino to the neglect of their families (some will).

The simple fact is, some people already gamble, some people already have a gambling problem, and some people already blow their whole paycheck on lottery tickets or at a casino to the neglect of their families. They always have and they always will, whether gambling is legal or illegal, regulated or unregulated, or treated as a vice or a crime.

The same is also true of using drugs, frequenting prostitutes, abusing alcohol, and smoking oneself to death.

There are four reasons why the state should not be involved in the gambling question: the nature of government, the nature of vice, the nature of man, and the nature of liberty.

First, it is simply not the business of government to prohibit people from engaging in immoral activities. It is in fact a perversion of government to do so. The purpose of government is supposed to be for the protection of life, liberty, and property from the violence or fraud of others. The government should not be concerned with banning or regulating any activity that takes place between consenting adults. It is a grave mistake to look to the state to enforce morality. A government with the power to outlaw an immoral practice is a government with the power to outlaw any practice.

The second reason is that vices are not crimes. As the 19th-century classical-liberal political philosopher Lysander Spooner explained it:

> Vices are those acts by which a man harms himself or his property. Crimes are those acts by which one man harms the person or property of another. Vices are simply the errors which a man makes in his search after his own

happiness. Unlike crimes, they imply no malice toward others, and no interference with their persons or property.

Unless this clear distinction between vices and crimes be made and recognized by the laws, there can be on earth no such thing as individual right, liberty, or property—no such things as the right of one man to the control of his own person and property, and the corresponding and coequal rights of another man to the control of his own person and property.

Third, legislation will never change human nature. The decision to gamble or not to gamble should be an individual decision, made on the basis of culture, morals, religion, family, risk aversion, financial status, or any other reason. The government should have nothing to do with it.

And finally, true liberty means liberty for everyone, even those who engage in practices that others in society find immoral or offensive. Why do some people want to use the force of the state to commit violence against others for engaging in peaceful, voluntary activity? "The only freedom which deserves the name," said political philosopher John Stuart Mill, "is that of pursuing our own good in our own way, so long as we do not attempt to deprive others of theirs, or impede their efforts to obtain it." "A free man," said economist Ludwig von Mises, "must be able to endure it when his fellow men act and live otherwise than he considers proper." Individuals, society, and the government—they should all be willing to tolerate, in the immortal words of Leonard Read, "anything that's peaceful."

*****

GAMBLING, FREEDOM, AND FEDERALISM

The United States Congress Joint Select Committee on Deficit Reduction, better known as the supercommittee, was created back in August by the Budget Control Act of 2011, which raised the debt limit. The committee consists of twelve members of Congress, evenly divided between the House and the Senate and between Democrats and Republicans.

By the day before Thanksgiving, the committee is supposed to come up with $1.5 trillion in deficit-reduction measures (to be applied over a ten-year period). These measures don't necessarily have to be in the form of spending cuts; they can also include real revenue increases and the elimination of tax deductions and loopholes.

One proposal being entertained by the supercommittee is to legalize Internet poker and other forms of online gambling currently illegal under federal law—not just legalize them, of course, but legalize them and then tax them like the government taxes alcohol, tobacco, and other "vices."

Maryland governor Martin O'Malley recently urged the leaders of the deficit-reduction supercommittee to reject any proposal to increase federal government revenue by legalizing Internet poker and gambling. In his October 20 letter to the supercommittee chairs, Sen. Patty Murray (D-WA) and Rep. Jeb Hensarling (R-TX), O'Malley said in part,

> I am writing to ask you to oppose proposals to federalize Internet poker and casino gambling. Such proposals would diminish significant sources of revenue for the states when we have already had to endure significant revenue reductions.
>
> Many of us in the states already face significant budget deficits. Federalizing internet poker and casino games would serve to widen these deficits—and therefore threaten our nation's fragile jobs recovery.

The federal government currently has a myriad of laws regarding gambling:

• The Transportation of Gambling Devices Act of 1951
• The Wire Act of 1961
• The Travel Act of 1961
• The Interstate Transportation of Wagering Paraphernalia Act of 1961
• The Gambling Devices Act of 1962
• The Illegal Gambling Business Act of 1970
• The Racketeer Influenced and Corrupt Organizations Act of 1970
• The Interstate Horseracing Act of 1978
• The Professional and Amateur Sports Protection Act of 1992
• The Illegal Money Transmitting Business Act of 1992
• The Interstate Wagering Amendment of 1994
• The Gambling Ship Act of 1994
• The Indian Gaming Regulatory Act of 1998
• The Unlawful Internet Gambling Enforcement Act of 2006

Basically, most forms of gambling are illegal except at Indian casinos, state-approved casinos like in Las Vegas and Atlantic City and along the Mississippi River, at horse-racing tracks, or on cruise ships in international waters.

How serious is the federal government about relaxing some of its gambling prohibitions?

Back when the Democrats controlled the House before the 2010 midterm elections, the House Financial Services Committee, under the leadership of then-chairman Barney Frank (D-MA) did approve a bill (H.R.2267) to legalize, license, and regulate online gambling. The Internet Gambling Regulation, Consumer Protection, and Enforcement Act was never voted on by the full House, and it died when the 111th Congress came to an end.

After the Obama administration cracked down on online poker sites in April of 2011, Representative Joe Barton (R-TX) introduced a bill (H.R.2366) in June to legalize and regulate online poker. The Internet Gambling Prohibition, Poker Consumer Protection, and Strengthening UIGEA Act of 2011 would establish an Office of Internet Poker Oversight in the Department of Commerce and allow "a licensee to accept an Internet poker bet or wager from U.S.-located individuals and offer related services so long as the license remains in good standing." The bill is presently under review in the House committees of the judiciary, energy and commerce, and financial services.

The House Energy and Commerce Committee's Subcommittee on Commerce, Manufacturing, and Trade held a hearing last month on October 25 entitled "Internet Gaming: Is There a Safe Bet?" The purpose of the hearing was "to examine the status of Internet gaming in the United States and to consider how consumers and other stakeholders would be affected if current legal restrictions were eased."

In her opening statement at the hearing, the subcommittee chair, Mary Bono Mack (R-CA), said that this was an issue that she would be "following very closely to make certain Americans are dealt a fair hand, regardless of the outcome." She mentioned the arguments of both proponents and opponents of legalized Internet gambling.

Proponents argue that the prohibition on Internet gambling has merely driven gambling underground and offshore, that legalization would allow the government to provide greater consumer protection, and that the federal government would realize significant tax revenues.

Opponents argue that repealing the ban on Internet gambling will expose more Americans to serious problems such as compulsive gambling; it will increase fraud, money laundering, and organized crime; and it will harm state budgets because of the loss of revenue from state lotteries and other legal gambling activities.

Six witnesses were invited to testify at the hearing:

• Parry Aftab of FairPlayUSA wants an "online gambling policy solution that has three principal elements—strong law enforcement and strict regulation, consumer protection, and the rights of U.S. adult consumers to engage safely in legal pastimes."
• Ernest L. Stevens of the National Indian Gaming Association is opposed to liberalization of federal gambling laws because of the impact that might have on Indian gambling operations.
• Keith Whyte of the National Council on Problem Gambling focuses on the negative social consequences of gambling.
• Former senator Alfonse D'Amato represents the Poker Players Alliance. Along with supporting legislation to license Internet poker, he wants Congress to "finally clarify the laws governing Internet gambling and create

effective enforcement against whatever is illegal."

• Kurt Eggert, a law professor and director of the Adolescent Communication Institute, focused on consumer protection and regulation.

• Dan Romer of the Annenberg Public Policy Center believes that "by controlling online gambling the federal government could minimize the harm that this activity can inflict on the young and their families and could also make the use of these sites safer for them."

No one mentioned freedom or federalism. But they are the two most important things that relate to federal oversight of gambling.

Some feel that gambling is a bad habit, a vice, or a sin. Others believe gambling may be addictive, financially ruinous, and harmful to children and families. But these things are all irrelevant. As negative as any of these things may be, there is one thing that is more important: freedom. In a free society, consenting adults are free to engage in any voluntary activities that are peaceful without government supervision, licensing, or regulation as long as they don't infringe upon the freedom of anyone else to not participate. A free society can't have it any other way. It is simply not the business of government to mind everyone's business.

But even if someone still believes that because gambling is a bad habit, a vice, or a sin the federal government should prohibit or regulate it—and even if someone still believes that because gambling may be addictive, financially ruinous, and harmful to children and families the federal government should control or discourage it—they still have an insurmountable problem. The U.S. Constitution gives the federal government no authority whatsoever to pass laws and regulations that have anything to do with gambling.

As James Madison explained in *Federalist* no. 45,

> The powers delegated by the proposed Constitution to the federal government are few and defined. Those which are to remain in the State governments are numerous and indefinite. The former will be exercised principally on external objects, as war, peace, negotiation, and foreign commerce; with which last the power of taxation will, for the most part, be connected. The powers reserved to the several States will extend to all the objects which, in the ordinary course of affairs, concern the lives, liberties, and properties of the people, and the internal order, improvement, and prosperity of the State.

Our very simple federal system is not working as the Founders intended it, because the federal government has unconstitutionally usurped powers never intended for the national level, and it has made the states mere appendages of the central government.

Although he is a liberal who rarely meets a federal program he doesn't like, Maryland's Governor O'Malley was correct when he said in his letter to the supercommittee, "Historically, states have had the right to make their own decisions about whether to offer gambling and how to regulate the industry. These proposals would strip states of those rights."

The federal government has no authority to prohibit, license, regulate, control, or discourage gambling, online or otherwise. None whatsoever. The states have the sole authority to prohibit, license, regulate, control, or discourage any and all forms of gambling. Whether they should do so, is, of course, another issue.

Those who nevertheless still contend that we should have gambling laws at the federal level are contending in vain. Their argument is with the Founding Fathers, the framers of the Constitution, the Constitution itself, and federalism.

No committee in Congress needs to waste even five minutes on any hearings on gambling or the opinions of any witnesses about gambling. Freedom and federalism both demand that the federal government repeal all laws that relate in any way to gambling.

*****

REPUBLICANS JUST DON'T GET IT

Not without some controversy, the Democrats and Republicans have issued their new party platforms for 2012.

It was predictable, in the case of the Republicans, and surprising, in the case of the Democrats, that "civil liberties" are mentioned only one time in each platform. However, the term is not defined and no examples are given. The Democrats do have a section in their platform on civil rights, but it is focused mainly on abortion, same-sex marriage, and anti-discrimination legislation. In their discussion of the First Amendment, the Republicans focus mainly on religion. Both parties express concord with the Second Amendment. The Republicans give lip service to the Fourth Amendment. Both parties give credence to the drug war—one of the greatest violators of civil liberties that have ever existed.

The phrase "free speech" shows up only twice in the Republican platform and once in the Democratic platform. The Republicans don't address free speech as a basic human right; they focus mainly on political speech. In their defense of the Citizens United decision, they talk about the "free speech right to devote one's resources to whatever cause or candidate one supports." Then they claim to "oppose governmental censorship of speech through the so-called Fairness Doctrine or by government enforcement of speech codes, free speech zones, or other forms of 'political correctness' on campus." Free speech in the Democratic platform appears only in the context of the Internet: "President Obama is strongly committed to protecting an open Internet that fosters investment, innovation, creativity, consumer choice, and free speech, unfettered by censorship or undue violations of privacy." When it comes to the Internet, the Republicans again focus on the political: "We insist that there should be no regulation of political speech on the Internet."

Both parties have a section in their platform called "Internet Freedom." The Democratic section is quite clear: "The Obama administration has led the world to recognize and defend Internet freedom—the freedom of expression, assembly, and association online for people everywhere." The Republican section on Internet freedom focuses on such things as regulatory barriers, technology, and personal data—not on Internet freedom. For that we must go elsewhere in their platform:

> The Internet offers a communications system uniquely free from government intervention.Recognizing the vital role of social media in recent efforts to promote democracy, we support unrestricted access to the Internet throughout the world to advance the free marketplace of ideas.

But that focuses merely on the Internet as a medium of communication. To find out what Republicans really believe about Internet freedom, we must go to their section on "Making the Internet Family-Friendly." Just the title of this section is enough to inform the reader committed to an Internet "free from government intervention" that he is not going to like what he is about to read. The Republicans don't disappoint:

> We support the prohibition of gambling over the Internet and call for reversal of the Justice Department's decision distorting the formerly accepted meaning of the Wire Act that could open the door to Internet betting.

"The Wire Act" refers to the Interstate Wire Act of 1961 (18 U.S.C. §1084),which reads in part,

> Whoever being engaged in the business of betting or wagering knowingly uses a wire communication facility for the transmission in interstate or foreign commerce of bets or wagers or information assisting in the placing of bets or wagers on any sporting event or contest, or for the transmission of a wire communication which entitles the recipient to receive money or credit as a result of bets or wagers, or for information assisting in the placing of bets or wagers, shall be fined under this title or imprisoned not more than two years, or both.

In September 2011, Assistant Attorney General Virginia Seitz, in response to a query from officials of the New York State Division of the Lottery and the Office of the Governor of the State of Illinois, issued a "Memorandum Opinion" regarding the lawfulness of proposals by Illinois and New York to use the Internet and out-of-state transaction processors to sell lottery tickets to adults in their states. She concluded,

Given that the Wire Act does not reach interstate transmissions of wire communications that do not relate to a "sporting event or contest," and that the state-run lotteries proposed by New York and Illinois do not involve sporting events or contests, we conclude that the Wire Act does not prohibit the lotteries described in these proposals.

This ever-so-slight loosening of the screw that binds Americans' freedom to do anything that's peaceful as long as they don't violate other Americans' person or property is what Republicans are so upset about.

Republicans just don't get it.

First of all, Republicans don't get it from a constitutional perspective. "We are the party of the Constitution," they say in their platform. The Constitution is a "sacred document" and an "owner's manual," they say; it is the "greatest political document ever written."

The Constitution gives the federal government no authority whatsoever to pass legislation and issue regulations that have anything to do with gambling. As James Madison explained in Federalist No. 45, "The powers delegated by the proposed Constitution to the Federal Government, are few and defined. Those which are to remain in the State Governments are numerous and indefinite." The federal government has no right to prohibit, license, regulate, control, or discourage gambling—on the Internet or anywhere else. It is the states that have the sole authority to prohibit, license, regulate, control, or discourage any and all forms of gambling—on the Internet or anywhere else.

So since the Republicans maintain that "when the Constitution is evaded, transgressed, or ignored, so are the freedoms it guarantees," they should repudiate not only the gambling prohibition in their platform, but all federal gambling laws.

Republicans also don't get it from an economic perspective. "We are the party of maximum economic freedom," they say in their platform. "Republicans will pursue free market policies that are the surest way to boost employment and create job growth and economic prosperity for all," they add.

Casinos, poker rooms, bookies, Internet gambling sites, bingo halls, and state lotteries are all in the gambling business. They provide a service. They employ people. They stay in business by the voluntary actions of willing customers. There is no reason the free market should not include gambling establishments—online or otherwise. There is no reason the gambling industry should be governed by special government regulations.

But gambling is a vice and is not essential to society, counter gambling opponents. Yes, gambling is certainly both of these things. But vices are not crimes and there are plenty of services provided on the free market that are not "essential"—such as breast augmentation, nose jobs, and facelifts.

And finally, Republicans don't get it from a freedom perspective. "In a free society, the primary role of government is to protect the God-given, inalienable, inherent rights of its citizens, including the rights to life, liberty, and the pursuit of happiness," they say in their platform.

But if that is the case, then government has no business prohibiting people from engaging in peaceful behavior on or off the Internet. Whether such behavior is considered by some to be immoral or sinful or corrupting is irrelevant. It is a grave mistake to look to the state to enforce morality. And the costs associated with stopping peaceful activity always outweigh the benefits. The government should not be concerned with banning or regulating any activity that takes place between consenting adults or between a willing business and a willing customer.

Those who would seek to prohibit peaceful activity between consenting parties that does not aggress against the person or property of others are in opposition to the freedom philosophy, no matter how much they rail against socialism and liberalism and talk about their commitment to free markets and limited government. "The only freedom which deserves the name," said political philosopher John Stuart Mill, "is that of pursuing our own good in our own way, so long as we do not attempt to deprive others of theirs, or impede their efforts to obtain it." And one does not have to be a gambler to also recognize that it should be possible for voluntary activities to take place without being supervised, taxed, or regulated by the state.

The statement in the Republican Party platform supporting a prohibition on Internet gambling should come as no surprise to anyone who has read the rest of the Republicans' platform. Although they talk about freedom and federalism, they remain firmly committed to welfare, central planning, bloated military budgets, an interventionist foreign policy, the war on drugs, foreign aid, agricultural programs, and government intervention in health care and education.

*****

WHY IS GAMBLING ILLEGAL?

Every Wednesday and Saturday night at 10:59 p.m. five white balls are selected out of a drum containing 59 white balls, and one red ball is chosen out of a drum containing 35 red balls. The jackpot is won by matching all five white balls in any order and the red Powerball. Tickets cost $2.

After rolling more than 16 consecutive times without a winner, the Powerball jackpot shot up to $587.5 million, the second-largest in U.S. history, and the largest for Powerball, before two winning tickets with the numbers 5, 16, 22, 23, 29 and a Powerball of 6 were announced by the Multi-State Lottery Association, which has run the Powerball game since 1992.

The first winning ticket belonged to the Hill family of Dearborn, Missouri. They have already appeared at a press conference where they were handed an oversized check made out for their share: $293,750,000 (before taxes). Although the chances of any single ticket's winning the jackpot were 1 in 175 million (making it more likely that someone would die from a lightning strike or a bee sting than win), the Hills bought five tickets on the day of the Powerball drawing at the Trex Mart gas station in Dearborn, a town of 500 north of Kansas City. "Tickets sold at a rate of 130,000 a minute nationwide—about six times the volume from a week ago. That pushed the jackpot even higher," said Chuck Strutt, executive director of the Multi-State Lottery Association.

The other winning ticket was sold at a 4 Sons Food Store in Fountain Hills, a suburb of Phoenix, Arizona. The winner has come forward, but as of this writing his name has not been released.

About the same time the Powerball frenzy was taking place, the peaceful and voluntary actions of Americans who prefer another gambling medium were ended—thanks to the hypocritical and oppressive actions of the U.S. government.

The U.S. Commodity Futures Trading Commission (CFTC) filed a civil complaint in federal district court in Washington, D.C., on November 26 seeking an injunction against Intrade, a prediction market for non-sports-related events. Intrade is an exchange market that allows its customers to make predications (by buying and selling shares) on the yes or no outcome of real-world events: candidate x to win an election, actor x to win an Academy Award, contestant x to win on *American Idol.*

According to a CFTC press release, the complaint charges Intrade "with offering commodity option contracts to U.S. customers for trading, as well as soliciting, accepting, and confirming the execution of orders from U.S. customers, all in violation of the CFTC's ban on off-exchange options trading."

Said David Meister, the Director of the CFTC's Division of Enforcement,

> It is against the law to solicit U.S. persons to buy and sell commodity options, even if they are called "prediction" contracts, unless they are listed for trading and traded on a CFTC-registered exchange or unless legally exempt. The requirement for on-exchange trading is important for a number of reasons, including that it enables the CFTC to police market activity and protect market integrity. Today's action should make it clear that we will intervene in the "prediction" markets, wherever they may be based, when their U.S. activities violate the Commodity Exchange Act or the CFTC's regulations.

In its continuing litigation the CFTC seeks civil monetary penalties, disgorgement of ill-gotten gains, and permanent injunctions against further violations of federal commodities law, as charged, among other relief.

This is the same government agency that earlier this year rejected an application by the North American Derivatives Exchange to operate a market for contracts relating to the U.S. elections. The commission argued that political event contracts constitute "gaming" that is "contrary to the public interest."

Because of the CFTC complaint, Intrade issued this statement to its U.S. customers: "We are sorry to announce that due to legal and regulatory pressures, Intrade can no longer allow US residents to participate in our real-money prediction markets. Unfortunately this means that all US residents must begin the process of closing down their Intrade accounts."

With lotteries in more than 40 states and the District of Columbia, one would think that customers of Intrade would have no trouble finding another gambling option. But aside from state lotteries, Americans' gambling options are somewhat limited unless they live near, or are willing to travel to, Las Vegas, Atlantic City, or the Mississippi River. True, some states have casinos run by Indian tribes, some have horse or dog racing that one can wager on, and some have legalized slot machines or poker rooms in selected areas, but Nevada is the only state that has legalized casino-style gambling statewide.

All forms of gambling that have been legalized throughout the United States have one thing in common: they all exist only with government permission. It is the state governments that license and regulate casinos, pari-mutuel wagering, slot machines, and poker rooms. It is the state governments that maintain a monopoly on lotteries. In most areas of the country, private, unlicensed gambling is simply illegal.

For example, in my state of Florida: "Whoever plays or engages in any game at cards, keno, roulette, faro or other game of chance, at any place, by any device whatever, for money or other thing of value, shall be guilty of a misdemeanor of the second degree, punishable as provided in s. 775.082 or s. 775.083" [s. 849.08]. An exception is made for a penny-ante game of "poker, pinochle, bridge, rummy, canasta, hearts, dominoes, or mah-jongg in which the winnings of any player in a single round, hand, or game do not exceed $10 in value" [s. 849.085, 2, a].

And no one in Florida had better try to compete with the Florida Lottery, for it is unlawful in Florida to set up a lottery; dispose of property by a lottery; conduct any lottery drawing; assist in conducting a lottery; attempt to operate, conduct, or advertise a lottery; possess any lottery implement; sell or offer for sale any lottery ticket; possess any lottery ticket; assist in the sale of a lottery ticket; possess any lottery advertisement; or possess any "papers, records, instruments, or paraphernalia designed for use, either directly or indirectly, in, or in connection with, the violation of the laws of this state prohibiting lotteries" [s. 849.09, 1, a-k].

But why is that the case in Florida and elsewhere? Why are the peaceful, voluntary actions of consenting adults prohibited? Why is gambling illegal?

We are told by opponents of legalized gambling that gambling is psychologically addictive, that it leads to financial ruin, that it leads to compulsive gambling, that it harms families, that it leads to criminal activity to support one's gambling habit, and that it increases crime in areas where gambling venues are located. Religious people add that gambling is immoral, that it is a vice, or that is it a sin. Even economists weigh in on the subject, telling us how great the odds are against winning the lottery and that gambling is a type of regressive tax that hurts low-income people. Every time someone wins a substantial lottery jackpot, there are news stories about how bad it is to win such a large sum of money.

Those things may all be true, but none of them can legitimately be said to be a reason for gambling to be illegal.

Forty-three states and the District of Columbia have state-run lotteries. Forty-seven states allow charitable gambling such as bingo. Thirty-nine states permit pari-mutuel wagering. Nineteen states have legalized commercial casinos. Thirty states have Indian casinos. Only the states of Hawaii and Utah forbid all forms of gambling.

If gambling should be proscribed by governments because it is harmful, ruinous, crime-fostering, or immoral, then governments—to be consistent—should outlaw all forms of gambling and certainly not be running lotteries. How can the 48 states that allow certain forms of gambling justify any of their laws that make other forms of gambling a criminal activity?

The real reasons so many forms of gambling are illegal in so many states are that governments are grossly hypocritical and arbitrary when it comes to their gambling laws and governments see themselves as nanny states with their citizens as children who need to be protected from vice and their own stupidity.

In a genuinely free society (as opposed to a relatively free one), people have the freedom to make any wager or bet any amount of money they choose on sporting events, horse races, casino gambling, pari-mutuel wagering, lotteries, prediction markets, private poker games, or any other gambling activity.

That does not mean that gambling is good or that it has no negative consequences. There is a distinction between favoring a thing and favoring the legalization of a thing. It is perfectly consistent for someone to disdain some or all forms of gambling and yet fully support the legalization of all gambling enterprises and activities. The issue is one of freedom, not preference.

It goes without saying that there should be no federal or state laws that relate to gambling in any way. Not because the gambling industry provides people with jobs or the states with revenue, but for the simple reason that there should be no federal or state laws prohibiting any voluntary activity between consenting adults.

*****

SHOULD CHRISTIANS SUPPORT GAMBLING LAWS?

There is no disputing the fact that gambling can be addictive and financially ruinous. In some cases, compulsive gamblers might even neglect their family, ruin their physical and mental health, and turn to crime to support their habit.

But even if these problems are not widespread and there is relatively little chance they would ever happen, some people still oppose gambling because they see it as a wasteful, immoral vice or sin with horrible odds of winning that takes advantage of those least able to afford it.

So Christians should support gambling laws, right?

Of course not.

Some religious conservatives must not have gotten the memo.

The Southern Baptist Convention Ethics & Religious Liberty Commission, the National Association of Evangelicals, and Focus on the Family all recently spoke out in opposition to a bill that would ostensibly legalize online poker.

The Internet Gambling Prohibition, Poker Consumer Protection and Strengthening UIGEA Act of 2012, which was never actually introduced, was co-authored by Senate Majority Leader Harry Reid (D-Nev.) and Senator John Kyl (R-Ariz.). Time simply ran out to get the bill through Congress in 2012. "I am disappointed," said Reid, who served as chairman of the Nevada Gaming Commission from 1977 to 1981, but "remain committed to this issue and it will be a priority for us in the new Congress."

A draft of the bill did leak out in September, and can be seen here, as well as a summary of the bill here.

The Southern Baptist Convention's Ethics & Religious Liberty Commission "steadfastly opposes your efforts," wrote its president, Richard Land, to Senator Kyl in a December 5th letter. Said Land:

> We cannot support any effort that grants government sanction to any form of gambling.

> Your bill not only does that but also creates a regulatory mechanism that is certain to be used to introduce other forms of Internet gambling in the future.

> No amount of regulation or taxation could make such legalization a winning proposition for America.

We know all too well the destructive power of online gambling. It is ruinous not only to those who engage in the practice but also to their families and society as a whole. With its addictive lure, Internet gambling often leads to broken marriages, child neglect, and depleted finances, among other devastating consequences.

Land had previously written to Representative Joe Barton (R-Tex.) after he introduced a bill in the House to legalize online gambling.

"Pastors regularly see the destructive impact of gambling on families and children," said National Association of Evangelicals president Leith Anderson in a Dec. 11th statement. "Those problems will increase if gambling moves from buildings to home computers."

"This is being disguised as a protective bill, if you will, that would limit gambling, but in fact ... this is just a precursor bill" to opening the Internet to casino gambling a few years from now, said Chad Hills, gambling analyst for Focus on the Family, in a December 11th online interview.

The proposed Reid/Kyl bill would have legalized online poker in the sense that it reaffirmed the illegality of most online gambling in the United States and create a bureaucracy in the Treasury Department, the Office of Online Poker Oversight (OOPO), to assign licenses to online poker platforms and approve as "qualified bodies" to issue licenses states and Indian tribes. In other words, the bill would have further increased the federal government's regulatory oversight of the gambling industry.

But that's not all, one analysis of the bill said it was

> a self-serving piece of legislation that protects large Nevada-based casinos at the expense of consumer choice. The bill in effect criminalizes just about any other form of online wagering, while providing a tiny carve-out for online poker companies in a way that protects Nevada against competition from any other state in the nation.

The *Las Vegas Review-Journal* described the bill as "a priority for several Nevada casino companies seeking a lucrative new and national market for their brands and for poker players seeking legal and federally regulated online games accompanied by consumer protections."

But let's assume for a moment that the bill would have abolished all federal government restrictions and regulations relating to online gambling of any kind. Should Christians then have opposed the bill because it weakened gambling laws?

Of course not.

Note that I did not ask the question: "Should Christians support gambling?"

The nature of gambling and its negative effects are well known. And certainly every Christian is familiar with the biblical account of the Roman soldiers casting lots for Christ's garments after they crucified him (Matthew 27:25).

The decision to gamble or not to gamble should always be an individual decision, made on the basis of culture, morals, religion, risk aversion, and financial status, and in consultation with family, friends, church leaders, and economists.

The decision to gamble or not to gamble should never be a government decision.

The question is whether Christians—individually, or collective through the Southern Baptist Convention, the National Association of Evangelicals, or Focus on the Family—should support gambling laws.

There is a huge difference between opposition to gambling and opposition to gambling laws. It is the difference between paternalism and individualism, between statism and liberty, between the nanny state and a free society, and between compulsion and personal responsibility.

One can vehemently oppose all forms of gambling and yet at the same time just as stridently oppose all forms of gambling laws.

First of all, the Constitution nowhere authorizes the federal government regulate or prohibit any form of gambling. Just like the Constitution nowhere authorizes the federal government to regulate or prohibit any other vice, immoral activity, sin, or bad habit. Christians who support gambling laws, at least on the federal level, are anti-Constitution, anti-Founding Fathers, and anti-American; that is, they are opposed to everything they claim to revere and hold sacred.

Second, it is not the purpose of government at any level to prevent people from wasting their money, taking excessive risk, having bad habits, engaging in vice, acting immorally, or making bad decisions. It is a perversion of government to do so. Laws that regulate or prohibit gambling are impossible to reconcile with a limited government and a free society.

Third, in the words of the famed nineteenth-century classical-liberal political philosopher Lysander Spooner, vices are not crimes:

> Vices are those acts by which a man harms himself or his property. Crimes are those acts by which one man harms the person or property of another. Vices are simply the errors which a man makes in his search after his own happiness. Unlike crimes, they imply no malice toward others, and no interference with their persons or property.

But most importantly, from a theological perspective, there is no warrant in the New Testament for Christians to support gambling laws. There is no support in the New Testament for the idea that Christians should seek legislation to criminalize any victimless crimes. As I wrote in my article "Should Christians Support the War on Drugs?":

It is not the purpose of Christianity to change society as a whole outwardly; it is the purpose of Christianity to change men as individuals inwardly.

I believe that Christians have for the most part failed to fulfill their calling. Instead of making converts and instructing them in the biblical precepts of Christian living, they turn to the state to criminalize what they consider to be immoral behavior. Instead of changing people's minds about what is and what is not acceptable in society, they seek to use the state to change people's behavior. Instead of being an example to the world, they want to use the state to make the world conform to their example. Instead of educating themselves and other Christians about what is appropriate behavior, they rely on the state to make that determination. Instead of being the salt of the earth and the light of the world, they want the state to assume those roles. Instead of minding their own business, they mind everyone else's business.

I referenced above Leith Anderson of the National Association of Evangelicals. He opposed the legality of online gambling because "pastors regularly see the destructive impact of gambling on families and children." He believes that "those problems will increase if gambling moves from buildings to home computers." But if Anderson were just as concerned about the destructive impact of divorce on families and children and how divorce has increased among Christians over the years, then perhaps we could take him more seriously.

It is unfortunate that many Christians look to the state to enforce their moral code. One need not teach his children not to gamble when it is much more expedient to clamor for laws that make it illegal to do so.

*****

GAMBLING WITH FEDERALISM

The relation between the fifty states and the national government under the U.S. Constitution is a federal one in which power is divided and shared between the states and the national government.

Or at least it is supposed to be a federal relationship.

James Madison succinctly explained this simple federal system of government in *Federalist* No. 45:

> The powers delegated by the proposed Constitution to the Federal Government, are few and defined. Those which are to remain in the State Governments are numerous and indefinite. The former will be exercised principally on external objects, as war, peace, negotiation, and foreign commerce; with which last the power of taxation will, for the most part be connected. The powers reserved to the several States will extend to all the objects, which, in the ordinary course of affairs, concern the lives, liberties

and properties of the people; and the internal order, improvement, and prosperity of the State.

In contrast, the relationship between the states and their counties, cities, and towns is not a federal one. Those entities are not sovereign. Whatever power they exercise is granted or delegated by their state governments.

Article I, Section 8, of the Constitution spells out in eighteen paragraphs the "few and defined" powers granted to the national government. One paragraph each is devoted to commerce, naturalization and bankruptcies, post offices and post roads, copyrights and patents, federal courts, maritime crimes, and the governance of the District of Columbia. Four paragraphs concern money or taxes. Six concern the military or the militia. The list of powers delegated to the national government concludes with the power "to make all laws which shall be necessary and proper for carrying into execution the foregoing Powers."

It should be noted that there is no article that grants any powers to the states, because the states existed before the Constitution and retained their sovereignty when they ratified the Constitution.

The Bill of Rights that was added to the Constitution in 1791 protects the rights of the people. It grants to the national government no additional powers. In fact, the Ninth and Tenth Amendments of the Bill of Rights further protect rights and reinforce federalism:

> The enumeration in the Constitution, of certain rights, shall not be construed to deny or disparage others retained by the people.

> The powers not delegated to the United States by the Constitution, nor prohibited by it to the States, are reserved to the States respectively, or to the people.

Of the constitutional amendments that were added later (11-27), only two of them directly increased the power of the national government. The Eighteenth Amendment allowed the national government to prohibit the manufacture and sale of alcohol, but only until it was repealed by the Twenty-First Amendment. The Sixteenth Amendment allows Congress to levy an income tax without apportioning it among the states.

So, why the civics lesson?

I'm afraid that federal gambling laws have reared their ugly head again.

The Third U.S. Circuit Court of Appeals in Philadelphia recently ruled against a New Jersey law authorizing sports gambling in the state, upholding a lower court ruling that voided the state's repeal of some prohibitions against betting on games. The 2-1 ruling prevents New Jersey from joining just four other states (Nevada, Oregon, Montana, and Delaware) that are allowed by the federal government to have sports betting. Maryanne

Trump Barry, the sister of Republican presidential candidate Donald Trump and a judge on the court, voted with the majority. According to Geoff Freeman, president of the American Gaming Association, the casino industry's national trade organization, Americans bet "at least $140 billion on sports illegally each year."

The Restoration of America's Wire Act (RAWA) was recently introduced in the U.S. Senate by Republican presidential candidate Lindsey Graham. It is co-sponsored by another Republican presidential candidate, Marco Rubio. This legislation seeks to restore what opponents of online gambling believe to be the original and correct interpretation of the 1961 Federal Wire Act that specifically prohibited "betting or wagering" using "a wire communication facility for the transmission." The Federal Wire Act was reinterpreted by the Justice Department in 2011, which concluded that "interstate transmissions of wire communications that do not relate to a 'sporting event or contest' fall outside the reach of the Wire Act." The RAWA, as explained by former Republican congressman and presidential candidate Ron Paul, who opposes the legislation, "makes it a federal crime to gamble online." "It nullifies laws in three states allowing online gambling and it pre-empts ongoing debates in several states considering legalizing Internet gambling."

But in spite of each of these undertakings, the U.S. national government has been delegated by the Constitution no authority whatsoever to legislate, regulate, monitor, or dictate to the states anything related to gambling. There is nothing in the Constitution that relates in any way to gambling—or any other vice for that matter. Gambling was not unknown to the Framers of the Constitution. It has been around in various forms for thousands of years. The absence of any mention of gambling in the Constitution was therefore deliberate. None of the twenty-seven amendments to the Constitution relates in any way to gambling. During the Progressive Era, when the national government wanted to prohibit another vice—drinking alcohol—it proposed a constitutional amendment, which it sent to the states, that, if ratified, would give it the power to prohibit for beverage purposes "the manufacture, sale, or transportation of intoxicating liquors within, the importation thereof into, or the exportation thereof from the United States and all territory subject to the jurisdiction thereof." If the states had rejected the proposed constitutional amendment—instead of the requisite number of them ratifying it on January 16, 1919—the Prohibition Era would not have begun a year later on January 17, 1920.

That means that members of Congress who introduce, debate about, hold hearings on, and pass bills that relate in any way to gambling, just like rule-making bureaucrats in government agencies who issue gambling regulations, are woefully ignorant of basic middle-school civics. In our federal system of government, only the states can legislate and establish regulations concerning gambling. The states could choose to not do anything relating to gambling within their borders, make some basic rules for its operation, regulate it, control it, tax it, or ban it altogether. But whatever a state chose to do would have nothing to do with any action of the federal government.

No member of Congress, no federal official, no Democratic or Republican presidential candidate, and no liberal or conservative think tank is even questioning the legitimacy of the federal government's involving itself with restricting and regulating gambling—even though it is a gross violation of federalism and the Constitution.

To the libertarian, such questioning would be a good and necessary first step, but still a long way from a free society. Even though the states may have the power to legislate and establish regulations concerning gambling, it does not follow that it would be a good thing or a legitimate purpose of government for them to do so.

Casinos are illegal in most states. In states where they are legal they are heavily regulated. Most forms of public and private gambling are forbidden. Yet most states have state lotteries—which are just as much a form of gambling as playing slot machines, roulette, blackjack, or poker—and state residents are encouraged to "play the lottery." It is the height of absurdity for states, on the one hand, not just to permit a statewide lottery, but to actually run a lottery themselves and, on the other hand, to prohibit other forms of gambling. What governments don't like is unregulated gambling. It is strictly forbidden, but not because it is immoral, addictive, or ruinous. It is prohibited because the government doesn't get a cut of the action.

But even as the government permits and promotes gambling, it plays the role of a nanny state—with a great deal of support from religious groups and secular moralists—and demonizes gambling. And, as Ron Paul made clear in his opposition to the RAWA, "a 'conservative' nanny state is just as unconstitutional, and as dangerous to liberty, as a liberal one." "Those with moral objections to gambling," he explains, "have the right to try to persuade their fellow citizens to not gamble. What they do not have the right to do is use government force to stop people from engaging in activities, like gambling, that do not involve force or fraud."

In a libertarian society, that is, a free society, there would be no laws or regulations of any kind at any level of government—national, state, or local—concerning gambling. The decision to gamble—like the decision to abuse drugs or alcohol, partake in dangerous activities, smoke or chew tobacco, engage in risky behavior, or commit fornication or adultery—is a personal and individual decision and none of any government's business as long as one's conduct and interactions are peaceful, voluntary, and consensual.

*****

DUMB LAW, DUMBER PREACHER

The legislature of the state of Colorado recently passed, and the governor signed into law, a bill to repeal an antiquated state law that criminalized adultery. The only thing worse than such a dumb law is an even dumber preacher who bemoans its repeal.

Colorado House Bill 13-1166 repeals two sections of the Colorado Revised Statutes. Section 18-6-501, on adultery: "Any sexual intercourse by a married person other than with that person's spouse is adultery, which is prohibited," and section 18-7-208, on promoting sexual immorality:

Any person who, for pecuniary gain, furnishes or makes available to another person any facility, knowing that the same is to be used for or in aid of sexual intercourse between persons who are not husband and wife, or for or in aid of deviate sexual intercourse, or who advertises in any manner that he furnishes or is willing to furnish or make available any such facility for such purposes, commits promoting sexual immorality.

Although adultery was illegal, no criminal penalty was specified. However, promoting sexual immorality was a class 2 misdemeanor.

The bill was introduced on January 30 in the Colorado House and on March 13 in the Colorado Senate. It passed the House Judiciary Committee by a vote of 8-3 and the full House by a vote of 37-26. It passed the Senate Judiciary Committee by a vote of 3-2 and the full Senate by a vote of 23-10. It was signed into law by Governor John Hickenlooper on March 22. The bill takes effect on August 7.

Every "no" vote was a Republican vote. And only 4 Republicans out of 40 in the legislature voted in favor of the repeal bill. Republican Sen. Kevin Lundberg opposed the bill, arguing that the law is not archaic and that moral standards continue to be important.

I may not agree with anything else that Denver Democratic Rep. Daniel Kagan, an original supporter of the repeal bill, ever said or ever will say, but this comment he made about the bill is right on: "I see it as saying adultery is a matter between a spouse and his conscience and his God, but not his local sheriff."

Laws that criminalize adultery or "promoting sexual immorality" are dumb laws. There is no other way to describe them. As legal scholar Jonathan Turley said in 2011 when a similar attempt at repeal failed: "These laws harken back to an earlier period, where a majority of citizens claimed the right to impose their values and morals on their neighbors. The notion of a government policing immorality runs against the grain of our constitutional system. That is more often associated with countries like Iran, where morality police roam the streets." It is ridiculous to say, as Jessica Haverkate, director of Colorado Family Action, a political arm of Focus on the Family, did in 2011 that repealing the adultery law encourages "the moral decay of our society." Sorry, Jessica, but the morals of society have already decayed. And no one in Colorado who wanted to already decayed. And no one in Colorado who wanted to commit adultery was deterred by any dumb law against adultery. Laws that legislate morality are not what keep morality from decaying. If this were so, then no adultery would have taken place in Colorado during the last century.

The only thing dumber than a dumb law is a dumb preacher who defends it.

Dr. R. Albert Mohler appears to be an intelligent man. He is the president of the Southern Baptist Theological Seminary in Louisville, Kentucky. He holds a Th.M. and a Ph.D. (in systematic and historical theology) from the seminary where he is now the president. He also teaches at the seminary and edits its theological journal. Time calls him the "reigning intellectual of the evangelical movement in the U.S." The Chicago Tribune terms him "an articulate voice for conservative Christianity at large." Mohler is the author of several books, writes a popular blog, has a daily podcast, has appeared on national news programs, has been widely published, and has lectured at many prestigious institutions.

Back in March, when the Colorado legislature was considering the repeal of its adultery law, Mohler weighed in favor of keeping the law on the books. Explained Mohler:

> Throughout most of human history, morality and law were united and in agreement when it came to the reality of adultery and the larger context of sexual immorality. Laws criminalizing adultery were adopted because the society believed that marriage was central to its own existence and flourishing, and that adultery represented a dagger struck at the heart of the society, as well as the heart of marriage.

> Marriage was not considered merely a private arrangement. Every society regulates marriage, and most have adopted clear and punitive sanctions against adultery. But the moral and cultural revolutions of the past several decades have shifted the meaning of marriage from a public institution to a private contract.

Mohler criticizes the aforementioned Colorado legislator Daniel Kagan for saying:

> Adultery is a matter between a person and their spouse and their conscience and their minister, but not between a person and the full enforcement of the state of Colorado. Let's keep the police out of our bedrooms.

Although acknowledging that "the law in Colorado criminalizes adultery, but includes no penalty," Mohler likes the law because it "has been, at a bare minimum, a reminder of the public nature of marriage and the societal threat of adultery."

Some observations.

Governments at all levels—federal, state, and local—have too many laws. There are thousands of dumb and illegitimate laws that should be repealed by all levels of government. We should rejoice when any of these laws are repealed.

If a law is legitimate, then its purpose is never to make a statement or serve as a reminder of anything. The purpose of any legitimate law—those that criminalize aggression against one's person or property and protect people from the violence and fraud of others—is to punish genuine criminal activity. A law without a penalty for violating it is no law at all; it is merely a suggestion.

The fact that throughout human history rulers and government bureaucrats have been nanny statists and puritanical busybodies that wanted to unite law and their concept of morality is a historical fact, but it is certainly not the way things ought to be—not if we are to have a free society.

Laws that criminalize activities that voluntarily take place behind closed doors are unenforceable. An unenforceable law is no law at all. Again, it is merely a suggestion.

Every crime needs a victim, not a potential victim, a possible victim, or a supposed victim, but an actual victim who suffers actual harm or loss. This means that over 90 percent of all federal and state laws are bogus.

Moral crusades of the nanny state fail to distinguish between vices and crimes. As the 19th-century classical-liberal political philosopher Lysander Spooner explained it:

> Vices are those acts by which a man harms himself or his property. Crimes are those acts by which one man harms the person or property of another. Vices are simply the errors which a man makes in his search after his own happiness. Unlike crimes, they imply no malice toward others, and no interference with their persons or property.

> Unless this clear distinction between vices and crimes be made and recognized by the laws, there can be on earth no such thing as individual right, liberty, or property – no such things as the right of one man to the control of his own person and property, and the corresponding and coequal rights of another man to the control of his own person and property.

To be a crime, adds Spooner, there must exist criminal intent to invade the person or property of another. But vices are not engaged in with criminal intent. A man practices a vice "for his own happiness solely, and not from any malice toward others."

Another reason why the state should not have laws against adultery is that the state should not have anything to do with marriage in the first place. Marriage preceded the state, and doesn't need the state to oversee it.

And finally, there is no support in the New Testament for the idea that Christians should seek legislation that would criminalize immoral behavior. For Baptist Christians like myself and Mohler, the New Testament is our rule for faith and life. Christians are making a grave mistake when they look to the state to legislate morality. Why would they even think of looking to the state to enforce their moral code? The actions of the state are the greatest examples of immoral behavior that one could possibly think of. The state exists only by stealing and killing, and then lying about it. It is not the purpose of Christianity to use force or the threat of force to keep people from sinning. Christians who are quick to criticize Islamic countries for prescribing and proscribing all manner of behavior are very inconsistent when they support the same thing here. The Scripture is clear: "Marriage is honourable in all, and the bed undefiled: but whoremongers and adulterers God will judge" (Hebrews 13:4).

Let me be perfectly clear: I think adultery is always wrong. I believe it is immoral. I consider it to be a grave sin. But it is neither my business nor the business of government to keep people from bad habits, vice, or immoral activities that take place between consenting adults.

If Mohler wants adultery laws to be enforced he should volunteer to be the first to have cameras installed in his home, office, and car (with full NSA surveillance everywhere else), and be taxed to support the army of bureaucrats it will take to monitor the cameras to make sure he doesn't commit adultery.

Laws against adultery are not what deter people in Colorado or other states from committing adultery. Religion, morality, fear, reputation, and/or family might serve as deterrents, but not dumb laws.

I don't know if my state of Florida has an antiquated state law against adultery that is not enforced, but whether such a law exists or whether such a law is enforced has no bearing whatsoever on why I choose to be faithful to my wife.

*****

SHOULD ADULTERY AND FORNICATION BE CRIMINAL OFFENSES?

Like most Islamic states, some states in America use criminal penalties to police the morality of their citizens.

A recent attempt in Virginia to decriminalize adultery by reducing it from a criminal issue to a civil one has failed. According to the Code of Virginia, Title 18.2, "Crimes and Offenses Generally," Chapter 8, "Crimes Involving Morals And Decency," §18.2-365, "Adultery defined; penalty":

> Any person, being married, who voluntarily shall have sexual intercourse with any person not his or her spouse shall be guilty of adultery, punishable as a Class 4 misdemeanor.

A Class 4 misdemeanor is the lowest-level criminal offense in Virginia, and has a maximum punishment of a $250 fine.

Virginia senator Scott Surovell, a Democrat from Fairfax County, has been trying for years to get rid of his state's anachronistic adultery law. "Clearly, Virginia is outside the mainstream on this," he said. "The law is hardly ever enforced," he added, as well as raising this point about divorce proceedings: "Having the criminal law on the books complicates divorce proceedings because spouses suspected of adultery often invoke their Fifth Amendment shield against self-incrimination, fearing a criminal prosecution. Without an admission, adultery is hard to prove."

According to the Virginia Criminal Sentencing Commission, only eight people have been convicted of adultery statewide in the past 10 years.

In January, Senator Surovell offered a bill (SB174) "to amend and re-enact §18.2-365 of the Code of Virginia, relating to adultery; civil penalty." Here is his proposed revision:

> Any person, being married, who voluntarily has sexual intercourse with any person not his or her spouse is guilty of adultery, and is subject to a civil penalty of not more than $250, which shall be payable to the Literary Fund. Any law-enforcement officer may issue a summons for a violation of this section.

The bill failed after minimal debate in a Senate committee. Some notable Democrats even voted against it.

In recent years, thirteen states have repealed similar adultery statutes. Only about a dozen states still have laws on their books that regard adultery as a crime. Virginia may be for lovers, but Virginians better love just their own spouses lest they be deemed a criminal. And should any adulterous lovers in Virginia decide to move to Florida to cohabitate, they will be deemed criminals there as well.

According to Florida Statue 798.02 regarding "Lewd and lascivious behavior":

> If any man and woman, not being married to each other, lewdly and lasciviously associate and cohabit together, or if any man or woman, married or unmarried, engages in open and gross lewdness and lascivious behavior, they shall be guilty of a misdemeanor of the second degree, punishable as provided in s. 775.082 or s. 775.083.

Although bills to repeal this cohabitation ban died in both chambers of the Florida Legislature last spring, new bills have been introduced in the Florida House (HB4003) and Senate (SB498) to overturn the state's 1868 ban on cohabitation. "An act relating to the repeal of a prohibition on cohabitation; amending s. 798.02, F.S.; deleting provisions prohibiting cohabitation by unmarried men and women; providing an effective date," would delete the first provision on cohabitation while retaining the second provision on engaging in "open and gross lewdness and lascivious behavior." The revision would "take effect upon becoming a law."

Clearly, some legislators are reluctant to repeal such laws for fear of alienating their constituents. There must, therefore, be more than just a handful of people in America who favor such laws.

The question before us, then, is whether adultery and fornication should be criminal offenses.

Before proceeding I should say that, as a Bible-believing, theologically conservative Christian, I neither recommend nor condone adultery, fornication, open marriage, indecency, swinging, premarital sex, sodomy, lewdness, lasciviousness, uncleanness, shacking up, or cohabitation. I believe such things are wrong, immoral, unethical, sinful, bad, evil, wicked, depraved, and not a very good idea.

I hate to be so tedious and redundant, but if I am not (and in some cases even if I am) then some of my Christian brethren will smear me as a liberal, a moderate, a compromiser, a freethinker, a libertine, a sellout, and/or an antinomian who approves of these things. I approve of none of these things. I approve of holiness, decency, morality, wholesomeness, the sanctity of marriage, purity, modesty, discipline, chastity, and self-control.

Now that we have gotten that out of the way, we can look at the question: Should adultery and fornication be criminal offenses?

They shouldn't. Of course not. Absolutely not.

I want to briefly say ten things about this.

First of all, states have a tremendous number of old, archaic, outdated, anachronistic, obsolete, and antiquated laws that in most cases should never have been passed in the first place—including laws against adultery and fornication. States should be repealing these laws, not keeping them in place or passing similar ones.

Second, vices may be immoral, they may be bad habits, they may be foolish, and they may be sinful, but vices are not crimes. As the 19th-century classical-liberal political philosopher Lysander Spooner so eloquently explained it: "Vices are those acts by which a man harms himself or his property. Crimes are those acts by which one man harms the person or property of another. Vices are simply the errors which a man makes in his search after his own happiness. Unlike crimes, they imply no malice toward others, and no interference with their persons or property."

Third, is prosecuting and investigating acts of adultery or fornication really what we want the police doing? Law enforcement agencies and court systems are always clamoring for more money to enforce the laws and keep dangerous criminals off the streets. How much are taxpayers willing to fork over to the cops to arrest people for committing adultery or fornication? Real crimes that violate personal or property rights should be enforced to the fullest extent of the law. Prosecuting people for victimless crimes is a waste of time and money.

Fourth, as a practical matter, laws against adultery and fornication are almost impossible to enforce. And they have to potential to literally make millions of single adults criminals.

Fifth, the proper role of government is supposed to be to protect people's life, liberty, and property from the violence or fraud of others. The only legitimate purpose of government is to prosecute and punish those who initiate violence against others, commit fraud against them, or violate their property rights. It is simply not the business of government to keep people from vice, sin, bad habits, immoral practices or activities that take place between consenting adults.

Sixth, laws against adultery and fornication require a nanny state to enforce them. A nanny state must of necessity be a police state or else it has no teeth. This, of course, is inimical to individual liberty and personal privacy. Laws that prohibit and prosecute the non-crimes of adultery and fornication are impossible to reconcile with a limited government.

Seventh, laws that prohibit and prosecute the non-crimes of adultery and fornication are also impossible to reconcile with a free society. In a free society, behavior that some consider to be immoral, unsafe, addictive, unhealthy, risky, sinful, or destructive is neither the government's business nor the business of puritanical busybodies. In a free society, there is no such thing as nebulous crimes against nature, society, the family, the institution of marriage, or the state. Every crime would have a tangible and identifiable victim.

Eighth, Christian morality crusaders are woefully inconsistent. They would never call for all sins in the Bible to be crimes, just the ones they themselves don't commit, or at least no one knows about. What about the "seven deadly sins" of wrath, greed, sloth, pride, lust, envy, and gluttony—should they be crimes as well? Why not? If all sins were crimes, then everyone would sure be in trouble, including Christians.

Ninth, from a theological perspective, there is no warrant in the New Testament for Christians to support laws against adultery and fornication. This is because there is no support in the New Testament for the idea that Christians should seek legislation to criminalize any victimless crimes. It is not the purpose of Christianity to change society outwardly; it is the purpose of Christianity to change individuals inwardly.

And finally, religious people in particular make a grave mistake when they look to the state to enforce morality. The actions of the state are generally the greatest examples of immoral behavior that one could ever think of—and on a grand scale. It is not even the purpose of religion to use force or the threat of force to keep people from sinning. A government with the power to outlaw immoral practices is a government with the power to ban any practice.

I have deliberately been brief. This is because I am not saying anything that I haven't already said in more detail in my articles on victimless crimes, including my articles on gambling, and especially my many articles on the evils of the drug war.

There is a huge difference between opposition to adultery and fornication and opposition to laws against these things. Don't ever make the mistake of confounding the two.

*****

THE NEBULOUS CRIME OF TICKET SCALPING

Although the Olympics in Rio de Janeiro, Brazil, are over, for some people associated with the games, things are just beginning.

Athletes who won medals are now household names in their respective countries. Many were honored with parades. Some will receive lucrative endorsement deals. Others will appear in television commercials. And although U.S. athletes will have to pay taxes on the cash prizes that accompany their medals, the pride and sense of achievement felt by medal winners from every nation is certain to last a lifetime.

The incident in Brazil involving American Olympic swimmers is well known. One swimmer was charged with providing a false claim of a robbery and subsequently lost some endorsement deals. What may not be so well known is that an official with the Ireland's national Olympic committee—the Olympic Council of Ireland—was at the center of another incident in Brazil regarding ticket scalping.

Patrick Hickey, the president of the Olympic Council of Ireland—who is also a member of the International Olympic Committee's executive board, head of the European Olympic Committees, and vice president of the Association of National Olympic Committees—has been accused of plotting with at least nine others to sell tickets to the Olympics above their face value. It is alleged that Ireland's Olympic committee "helped transfer tickets to an unauthorized vendor who would set high fees and disguise the transaction as a hospitality package." Hickey was arrested and charged with "conspiracy, ticket scalping and ambush marketing and will be detained while the investigation continues." Hickey's arrest resulted from a police investigation in which more than 1,000 tickets were seized that were being sold at "inflated prices." Police said that "some Irish tickets for the Olympics' opening ceremony with a face value of $1,400 [each] were sold for $8,000 [each]."

But it is not just in Brazil where it is illegal to resell tickets for an amount higher than their face value. Ticket-scalping laws can be found in some areas of the United States as well.

Traditional ticket brokers, Internet ticket-resale sites, and individuals selling tickets outside of venues make up the secondary ticket market, which is more than a $5 billion-a-year industry with a forecasted annual growth rate above 10 percent. A helpful article in *Entertainment and Sports Lawyer* explains what is responsible for the secondary ticket market:

> The forces of supply and demand interact to help set the price on goods. In a perfect market situation, a good that is in limited supply, such as a ticket to a baseball game, would be sold by the supplier for the highest price that the market can stand. However, ticket suppliers (i.e., teams) routinely sell tickets for less than the highest price the market can stand. There are various reasons for this practice, including the desire to have consistent sellouts or develop a sustainable fan base. Because the tickets are sold for less than the market can bear, a situation of excess demand is created. The existence of the excess demand is responsible for the secondary ticket market.

Ticket sales in the secondary market can be discouraged only by allowing a ticket's original purchaser admission to a game or event. That can be easily implemented by requiring the ticket purchaser to present photo identification when the tickets are redeemed.

But ticket sales in the secondary market can also be prohibited or restricted by law. In many states there are no ticket-scalping laws whatsoever. However, some states only recently repealed their ticket-scalping laws. In other states and cities a ticket reseller must

• Be licensed.
• Pay an annual fee.
• Be a lawful ticket broker.
• Not sell tickets above face value without the event sponsor's permission.
• Not resell tickets for boxing matches.
• Not resell tickets to high-school, college, or charity events.
• Not resell tickets for more than face value in the vicinity of an event.
• Not resell tickets for more than a certain amount or percentage over face value.
• Not resell tickets for more than face value on the day preceding or the day of an event.
• Disclose the difference between face value and amount charged.

Some cities ban ticket scalping outright.

The nebulous crime of ticket scalping has got to be one of the most ridiculous examples of a peaceful, consensual action ever labeled as a crime.

Ticket scalpers, like all middlemen, perform a valuable service and should be welcomed and applauded instead of condemned and prosecuted. Ticket scalpers enable events to sell tickets more quickly and efficiently right up to the day of the event. Ticket scalpers enable those who uncertain whether they can attend an event the opportunity to purchase tickets at the last minute. Ticket scalpers transfer the risk of unsold tickets from the event organizer to themselves. They allow ticket purchasers who change their minds about attending an event to recoup all or a portion of their money. Ticket scalpers are entrepreneurs who provide a needed service.

What could possibly be wrong with an exchange of tickets for cash between a willing buyer and a willing seller, as long as their activity does not violate the property rights of the owner of the ground where they make their exchange?

Ticket scalping should not be a crime. Every crime needs a victim. Not a potential victim, not a possible victim, not a supposed victim, but an actual, direct, tangible victim with real harm and measurable damages.

That means that not only should ticket scalping not be a crime, but neither should

- Accepting money to have sex.
- Paying someone for sex.
- Gambling without government permission.
- Buying, selling, or using marijuana or some other drug.
- Serving your twenty-year-old child a glass of wine with Thanksgiving dinner.
- Not wearing a bicycle or motorcycle helmet.
- Raising prices too much (price gouging).
- Lowering prices too much (predatory pricing).
- Brewing too much beer at home or selling any of it.
- Paying a willing worker below the minimum wage.
- Charging an interest rate that is too high.
- Opening your car dealership on a Sunday.
- Refusing to bake a cake for a same-sex couple.
- Purchasing too much Sudafed to relieve a stuffy nose.
- Making more than six withdrawals per month from a savings account.
- Depositing large amounts of cash in a bank account.
- Taking a tube of toothpaste containing more than 3.4 ounces onto an airplane.
- Selling alcohol before a certain time on a Sunday.
- Having a garage sale without a permit.
- Practicing discrimination.
- Not wearing a seatbelt.
- Cutting hair without a license.
- Hiring an undocumented worker.
- Buying untaxed cigarettes on the black market.

Even if doing some of those things might be immoral, unethical, insensitive, addictive, dangerous, foolish, thoughtless, or mean, as long as those who freely and willingly participate in them are not harming or violating the personal or property rights of nonparticipants, they should not be crimes—as they are in some states or all states in what most Americans think is the "land of the free."

*****

THE LIBERTARIAN STICKING POINT

Why aren't more Americans libertarians? Why aren't more liberals becoming libertarians? They generally share the libertarian commitment to freedom of speech, civil liberties, personal freedom, privacy, and the Fourth Amendment, or at least they claim to do so. Why aren't more conservatives becoming libertarians? They generally share the libertarian commitment to the free market, limited government, free trade, property rights, and the Second Amendment, or at least they claim to do so.

Libertarianism

Libertarianism is the philosophy of nonaggression. Aggression is theft, fraud, the initiation of non-consensual violence, or the threat of nonconsensual violence. The initiation or threat of aggression against the person or property of others is always wrong. Aggression is justified only in defense of one's person or property or in retaliation against aggression toward those things, but is neither essential nor required. Violence is justified only against violence. No violence may be used against a nonaggressor. Nonaggression is the essence of libertarianism and the sole libertarian creed. One's lifestyle has nothing to do with it.

Libertarians believe that people should be free to live their life any way they desire, accumulate wealth, and engage in any economic activity they choose as long as their actions are peaceful, their associations are voluntary, their interactions are consensual, and they don't violate the personal or property rights of others. In a libertarian society, the only actions prohibited involve the initiation of violence against person (murder, rape, assault, et cetera) or property (robbery, embezzlement, arson, et cetera). Libertarianism respects personal privacy, financial privacy, free thought, individual responsibility, freedom of conscience, free exchange, free markets, and private property. Libertarianism celebrates individual liberty, personal freedom, peaceful activity, voluntary interaction, laissez faire, free enterprise, free assembly, free association, free speech, and free expression as long as they don't violate the personal or property rights of others.

Although many, if not most, Americans might say that they basic-ally agree with such a philosophy, they still hesitate to fully embrace libertarianism. Why is that? It turns out that once you narrow the conversation or focus on a specific issue, you find that these Americans are very selective about what they actually accept from the libertarian philosophy. Many of their claims to share certain libertarian commitments are hollow. And among liberals and conservatives—including even those who do share many libertarian commitments—there is universally a great sticking point to their full embrace of libertarianism.

The sticking point

The libertarian sticking point is the war on drugs. Now, this is not the only thing that liberals and conservatives find problematic about libertarianism. They sometimes falsely charge libertarians with being pacifists, idealists, isolationists, too individualistic, materialistic, libertines, hedonists, or irreligious. They sometimes mischaracterize libertarianism as being utopian, immoral, or impractical and reducing everything to economics, always supporting big business, having no compassion for the poor, rejecting tradition, celebrating alternative life-styles, and being unconcerned about social justice. But when it comes to specific issues, the drug war is universally the sticking point.

What is it that libertarians believe about drugs and the drug war that bothers liberals and conservatives so much about libertarianism? It can be summarized in two words: drug freedom. They mean that —

• The war on drugs should be ended immediately and completely.
• There should be no laws at any level of government for any reason regarding the buying, selling, growing, processing, transporting, manufacturing, advertising, using, or possessing of any drug for any reason.
• All government agencies devoted to fighting the war on drugs should be eliminated.
• All government bureaucrats who work for those agencies, from the drug czar on down to the janitors, should be permanently laid off.
• All government efforts to study and classify drugs and conduct surveys and issue reports on drug use should be ended.
• All government programs and advertising that seek to prevent drug abuse or warn about the dangers of drugs should be ended.
• All incarcerated nonviolent drug offenders should be pardoned and released from prison.
• There should be a free market in drugs without any government interference in the form of regulation, oversight, restrictions, taxing, rules, or licensing.

Why do libertarians say what seems to liberals and conservatives to be such radical things? Libertarians reason that—

Everyone should be free to live his live in any manner he chooses as long as his activities are nonviolent, nondisorderly, nondisruptive, non-threatening, and noncoercive.

Everyone should be free to pursue happiness in his own way even if his choices are deemed by others to be harmful, unhealthy, unsafe, immoral, unwise, stupid, destructive, or irresponsible.

Individuals, not government bureaucrats, should be free to decide what risks they are willing to take and what behaviors are in their own best interests.

Private organizations and individuals, not government programs and bureaucrats, are the solution to any problems resulting from drug abuse.

Buyers and sellers should be free to exchange with each other for mutual gain any product of their choosing.

Everyone should be free to engage in any economic enterprise or activity of his choosing without license, permission, restriction, interference, or regulation from government as long as he doesn't commit violence against others, violate their property rights, or defraud them in some way.

Once the government claims control over what a man can lawfully put into his mouth, nose, and bloodstream, there is no limit to its power.

Government attempts to protect people from bad habits, harmful substances, or vice lead to greater evils.

Every crime needs a tangible and identifiable victim, not a potential or possible victim. Drug use is the quintessential victimless crime.

A free society has to include the right of people to take risks, practice bad habits, partake of addictive conduct, engage in self-destructive behavior, exercise poor judgment, live an unhealthy lifestyle, participate in immoral activities, commit vice, and undertake dangerous actions—including the use and abuse of drugs.

Republican presidential candidate Ben Carson speaks for many Americans—liberal and conservative—when he says that he opposes the legalization of marijuana and wants to intensify the war on drugs. He is okay with a police state as long as it combats what he considers to be "hedonistic activity." Other Americans feel differently about marijuana—but just marijuana. Some Americans favor the decriminalization of marijuana with civil fines or mandatory drug treatment for possessors instead of arrest and jail. Some Americans favor the legalization of marijuana just for medical use. Some Americans also favor the legalization of marijuana for recreational use.

Americans who hold those three differing positions on the relaxing of marijuana prohibition laws nevertheless have three things in common. One, they support heavy government regulation of and restrictions on marijuana possession. Two, they don't extend their liberality to the so-called drug trafficking of marijuana. And three, they aren't interested in relaxing prohibition laws relating to other drugs such as LSD, crystal meth, cocaine, or heroin. In all three cases, those Americans still want a

Drug Enforcement Agency, still want a Controlled Substances Act, still want a drug war, and still want a nanny state. Why? Because using drugs is addictive, unhealthy, dangerous, or self-destructive. Because using drugs is immoral, sinful, a vice, or evil. Because using drugs may have societal costs, have unintended consequences, lead to crime to support one's drug habit, lead to financial ruin, lead to neglect of one's children, or lead to premature death.

The solution

There is a four-pronged solution to breaching the libertarian sticking point: the utilitarian, the practical, the constitutional, and the philosophical.

The first part of the solution to the libertarian sticking point is the utilitarian one. The war on drugs is a complete and total failure. It has utterly failed to prevent drug use; reduce drug abuse; end drug overdoses; reduce the demand for drugs; keep drugs out of the hands of addicts, prisoners, teenagers, and children; help drug addicts get treatment who want it; stop the violence associated with drug trafficking; and have any impact on the availability of most drugs in the United States.

Instead, the war on drugs has destroyed personal and financial privacy, negated personal responsibility and accountability, hindered legitimate pain management, hampered the treatment of debilitating diseases, turned doctors into criminals, unreasonably inconvenienced retail shopping, fostered violence, corrupted law enforcement, militarized the police, clogged the judicial system with non-crimes, turned America's inner cities into war zones, swelled prison populations with nonviolent offenders, made criminals out of hundreds of thousands of otherwise law-abiding Americans, eroded civil liberties, violated property rights, and weakened the Fourth Amendment.

The war on drugs has financial and human costs that far exceed any of its supposed benefits. It has wasted billions of taxpayer dollars even as it has ruined more lives than drugs themselves.

The second part of the solution to the libertarian sticking point is the practical one. There are plenty of other activities aside from drug use that Americans consider to be dangerous, but they don't want laws to prohibit them or federal agencies to enforce such laws. Things such as mountain climbing, cliff diving, skydiving, bungee jumping, boxing, pro wrestling, MMA fighting, auto racing, and using a chainsaw. There are plenty of other activities aside from drug use that Americans consider to be immoral but don't want laws to prohibit them or federal agencies to enforce such laws. Things such as adultery, fornication, topless dancing, living in a nudist colony, gambling, and viewing pornography. There are plenty of other activities aside from drug use that Americans consider to be unhealthy but don't want laws to prohibit them or federal agencies to enforce such laws. Things such as drinking energy drinks, eating junk food, drinking large sugar-laden soft drinks, consuming high-fructose corn syrup, eating food containing trans fats, smoking cigarettes, and drinking alcohol.

And regarding cigarettes and alcohol, everything bad that could be said regarding drug use could equally be said of tobacco and alcohol use. Tobacco use not only costs the U.S. economy billions of dollars every year in medical costs and lost productivity, but is the cause of hundreds of thousands of premature deaths every year from heart disease, stroke, cancer, and smoking-related diseases. Alcohol is also one of the leading causes of premature deaths in the United States. It is a regular factor in drownings, home accidents, suicides, pedestrian accidents, fires, violent crimes, divorces, boating accidents, child-abuse cases, sex crimes, and auto accidents. It is a contributing factor in many cases of cancer, mental illness, anemia, cardiovascular disease, dementia, cirrhosis, high blood pressure, and suppression of the immune system.

And then there is the fact that legal drugs—prescribed and administered by physicians—kill thousands every year by means of overdose or reactions with other drugs. Even over-the-counter drugs such as aspirin and Tylenol kill hundreds of Americans every year.

It certainly makes no sense for the government to wage war on "illegal" drugs when tobacco, alcohol, and prescription drugs kill far more people every year.

The third part of the solution to the libertarian sticking point is the constitutional one. That is because the Constitution nowhere authorizes the federal government to have a war on drugs. The Constitution nowhere authorizes the federal government to intrude itself into the personal eating, drinking, or smoking habits of Americans. The Constitution nowhere authorizes the federal government to have a drug czar, an Office of National Drug Control Policy, or a Drug Enforcement Administration. The Constitution nowhere authorizes the federal government to have a Controlled Substances Act, a Comprehensive Drug Abuse Prevention and Control Act, or a Combat Methamphetamine Epidemic Act. The Constitution nowhere authorizes the federal government to have a National Drug Control Strategy, a National Survey on Drug Use and Health, or a Domestic Cannabis Eradication/Suppression Program. The Constitution nowhere authorizes the federal government to restrict or oversee any harmful, unhealthy, or mood-altering substances that any American wants to consume. The Constitution nowhere authorizes the federal government to prohibit the buying, selling, growing, processing, transporting, manufacturing, advertising, bartering, trading, using, possessing, or "trafficking" of any drug for any reason. The Constitution nowhere authorizes the federal government to ban any substance.

When progressives in and out of the national government sought to institute alcohol prohibition after World War I, they knew they could do it on the national level only by amending the Constitution. That is why the Eighteenth Amendment to the Constitution was adopted in 1919. The Volstead Act to prohibit the "manufacture, sale, or transportation of intoxicating liquors" could not be passed by Congress until after the adoption of the Eighteenth Amendment.

The fourth part of the solution to the libertarian sticking point is the philosophical one. It is just simply not a legitimate purpose of government to wage war on drugs. It is not the purpose of government to study drugs, classify drugs, restrict drugs, prohibit drugs, or seek to prevent drug use. It is not the purpose of government to punish people for engaging in entirely peaceful, voluntary, and consensual actions that do not aggress against the person or property of others. It is not the purpose of government to prohibit, regulate, restrict, or otherwise control what a man desires to smoke, drink, inject, snort, sniff, inhale, swallow, or otherwise ingest into his mouth, nose, veins, or lungs. It is not the purpose of government to prevent people from practicing bad habits, partaking in risky behavior, performing addictive actions, or engaging in immoral activities. It is not the purpose of government to protect people from harmful substances, unhealthy practices, dangerous activities, or vice. It is not the purpose of government to control what people buy, sell, trade, manufacture, or distribute.

In a free society, the only possible legitimate functions of government are defense, judicial, and policing activities. Because libertarians consistently extend the nonaggression principle to acts of government, they believe there is no justification for any government action beyond keeping the peace; prosecuting, punishing, and exacting restitution from those who initiate violence against the person or property of others; and constraining those who would attempt to interfere with the peaceful actions of others. In a free society, government neither legislates morality nor prohibits actions that do not involve the initiation of violence against person or property. In a free society, government leaves alone those who don't initiate violence against the person or property of others so that they might pursue their own happiness, engage in commerce of their own choosing, and do what they want with their body and their property.

The war on drugs is incompatible with a free society. It is an assault on individual liberty, private property, limited government, and the free market. A philosophy of freedom and nonaggression has no sticking points.

*****

6

THE FREE MARKET

MINIMUM WAGE, MAXIMUM INTERVENTION

Many workers in my state of Florida received a pay raise this past May. No, Floridians did not suddenly become more productive and demand a salary increase because they are now more valuable to their employers. And no, Florida businesses did not suddenly become more profitable and decide to share their good fortune with their employees.

The reason many workers in Florida received a pay raise is that they voted for it. The new Section 24 in Article X of the Florida constitution annually and permanently raises the minimum wage in the state of Florida. It resulted from a constitutional amendment approved by Florida voters back on November 2, 2004. There are actually seven paragraphs (a–g) in Section 24 regarding the minimum-wage increase. Paragraph (c) contains the substance of the new requirement:

> Employers shall pay Employees Wages no less than the Minimum Wage for all hours worked in Florida. Six months after enactment, the Minimum Wage shall be established at an hourly rate of $6.15. On September 30th of that year and on each following September 30th, the state Agency for Workforce Innovation shall calculate an adjusted Minimum Wage rate by increasing the current Minimum Wage rate by the rate of inflation during the twelve months prior to each September 1st using the consumer price index for urban wage earners and clerical workers, CPI-W, or a successor index as calculated by the United States Department of Labor. Each adjusted Minimum Wage rate calculated shall be published and take effect on the following January 1st. For tipped Employees meeting eligibility requirements for the tip credit under the FLSA [Fair Labor Standards Act], Employers may credit towards satisfaction of the Minimum Wage tips up to the amount of the allowable FLSA tip credit in 2003.

What Florida voters saw on their ballots is this summary of the amendment:

> This amendment creates a Florida minimum wage covering all employees in the state covered by the federal minimum wage. The state minimum wage will start at $6.15 per hour six months after enactment, and thereafter be indexed to inflation each year. It provides for enforcement, including double damages for unpaid wages, attorney's fees, and fines by the state. It forbids retaliation against employees for exercising this right. The impact of this amendment on costs and revenues of state and local governments is expected to be minimal.

What is missing from this summary is the amendment's impact on the businesses that pay some of their employees the minimum wage as well as its impact on unskilled workers trying to find employment. One does not have to be an economist to see the detrimental effects of minimum-wage legislation. An increase in the minimum wage will increase a business's labor costs.

It doesn't matter if anyone thinks that businesses exploit their workers and should pay them all a higher wage because they can "afford it." It is an undeniable fact that their labor costs will go up. And if a business's costs increase, that business's profits will go down unless it can offset its increased costs by raising prices, lowering expenses, increasing productivity, or making use of some combination of the three. If a reduction in profit cannot be offset by any of these measures, then a business can go out of business, live with a lower profit margin, or stagnate because of a lack of funds to expand its operations. The minimum wage causes unemployment because it prices unskilled workers out of the market.

Florida voters probably also did not realize that up until the passage of this amendment, Florida had no minimum-wage law. In fact, the states of Alabama, Arizona, Louisiana, Mississippi, South Carolina, and Tennessee currently do not have a minimum-wage law. There are also two states with a minimum wage that is less than the federal minimum: Kansas ($2.65) and Ohio ($4.25).

This does not mean that employers in states with no minimum wage can pay their employees Third World wages. The federal minimum wage of $5.15 an hour applies to any employee in any state who is covered by the FLSA. And according to the U.S. Department of Labor,

> All employees of certain enterprises having workers engaged in interstate commerce, producing goods for interstate commerce, or handling, selling, or otherwise working on goods or materials that have been moved in or produced for such commerce by any person are covered by FLSA.

The FLSA basically applies to everyone in the United States because employees of firms that are not covered enterprises under FLSA still may be subject to its minimum-wage, overtime-pay, and child-labor provisions if they are individually engaged in interstate commerce or in the production of goods for interstate commerce or in any closely related process or occupation directly essential to such production. Such employees include those who work in communications or transportation; regularly use the mails, telephones, or telegraph for interstate communication or keep records of interstate transactions; handle, ship, or receive goods moving in interstate commerce; regularly cross state lines in the course of employment; or work for independent employers who contract to do clerical, custodial, maintenance, or other work for firms engaged in interstate commerce or in the production of goods for interstate commerce.

The reason Florida can raise its minimum wage is that the FLSA also permits states and cities to set their minimum wage higher than the federal minimum. In this case, the state minimum trumps the federal minimum. So, in addition to Florida, the following states have a minimum wage that is higher than the federal minimum: Alaska ($7.15), California ($6.75), Connecticut ($7.10), Delaware ($6.15), Hawaii ($6.25), Illinois ($6.50), Maine ($6.35), Massachusetts ($6.75), New York ($6.00), Oregon ($7.25), Rhode Island ($6.75), Vermont ($7.00), and Washington ($7.35). The rate in the District of Columbia ($6.60) is also above the federal minimum. And also like Florida, the District of Columbia and the states of Illinois, New York, Oregon, Vermont, and Washington just raised their minimum wage this year.

Increases in state minimum-wage rates are destined to continue. The new Florida minimum-wage law also contains an indexing provision. This means that Florida joins Oregon and Washington as the only states to index their minimum wage to inflation. The minimum wage is already scheduled to increase in New York to $6.75 in 2006 and $7.15 in 2007. New Jersey is increasing its minimum wage to $7.15 by October of 2006. Movements are also under way in Hawaii, Pennsylvania, New Hampshire, and Minnesota to boost their state's minimum wage.

Because of agitation by "living-wage" advocates such as the Association of Community Organizations for Reform Now (ACORN), some cities and counties have passed living-wage ordinances that raise the minimum wage within their jurisdiction. The city of Sonoma, California, recently mandated that "covered" employers pay a minimum of $11.70 an hour with health benefits or $13.20 without health benefits, indexed annually to the consumer price index. There are today about 125 cities and counties with living-wage ordinances.

Origins of the minimum wage

The minimum wage began as part of the Fair Labor Standards Act (FLSA) of 1938. Along with the Davis-Bacon Act and the National Labor Relations (Wagner) Act, the FLSA is one of the three major pieces of New Deal employment legislation that survive today. The original FLSA curtailed child labor, set the maximum work week at 44 hours, and established a minimum wage of 25 cents an hour.

That's right. There was no federal minimum wage in the United States until 1938. Since the turn of the century the states had sought to regulate child labor, the hours in the work day, and overtime pay, but in *Adkins v. Children's Hospital* (1923), the Supreme Court ruled that a minimum-wage law passed in the District of Columbia was "an unconstitutional interference with the freedom of contract included within the guaranties of the Due Process clause of the Fifth Amendment." The Court concluded that there was a fundamental difference between regulating hours and regulating the rate of pay. But a few years later, in the case of *West Coast Hotel v. Parrish* (1937), this ruling was overturned when the Court upheld a Washington state law setting a minimum wage for women. This prepared the way for Congress to pass a federal minimum wage law.

The work week was lowered to 40 hours in 1945, where it remains today, and the minimum wage has been raised 18 times, with the last increase being in 1997.

All arguments for the minimum wage come down to this: since no family can survive on an income lower than the minimum wage, it is the job of government to mandate a minimum wage to keep people out of poverty. No matter how elaborate the argument, this is the bottom line.

Even if that were a true statement it would still not be a valid argument for the minimum wage. If someone can't support a family on his salary, then he should not have a family until he has a higher salary. It is not the fault of business or society that an unskilled and uneducated worker decides to have a family and then finds out that he can't make ends meet. Moreover, why should the person who is giving him a job be forced to fund his excess expenses? Indeed, why should anyone be forced to do so?

The case against the minimum wage from an economic standpoint has been made many times. It increases the price of goods and services, since it raises employers' costs. It limits economic growth by increasing the cost of labor. And because it raises employment barriers for the unskilled and uneducated, it causes unemployment. As the Austrian economist Murray Rothbard (1926–1995) explains,

> In truth, there is only one way to regard a minimum wage law: it is compulsory unemployment, period. The law says: it is illegal, and therefore criminal, for anyone to hire anyone else below the level of X dollars an hour. This means, plainly and simply, that a large number of free and voluntary wage contracts are now outlawed and hence that there will be a large amount of unemployment. Remember that the minimum wage law provides no jobs; it only outlaws them; and outlawed jobs are the inevitable result.

If raising the minimum wage will truly lift people out of poverty and not lead to unemployment, then why raise it only a dollar or two? That still won't be enough for the typical family of four to make ends meet. Why not raise it to $12.50 an hour, as the Green Party advocated in its 2000 party platform? Why not just mandate that every employee is to be paid a minimum of $50 an hour? That would give everyone an income high enough that the government could end all transfer-payment programs. The trouble with a $50 per hour minimum wage is that the government could end all transfer payment programs but one—unemployment compensation. Massive unemployment would result from such a draconian increase in the minimum wage, as Rothbard again explains:

> It is obvious that the minimum wage advocates do not pursue their own logic, because if they push it to such heights, virtually the entire labor force will be disemployed. In short, *you can have as much unemployment as you want*, simply by pushing the legally minimum wage high enough.

But if raising the minimum wage is bad economics, why is there always agitation for its increase? The answer is that raising the minimum wage has everything to do with politics and nothing to do with economics. If the members of Congress really wanted to help the economy, they would adopt a laissez-faire approach to the economy instead of an interventionist one.

Naturally, those who are looking for an entry-level job, those who are currently making the minimum wage, and those who make more than the minimum wage but stand to benefit from its increase—as long as they can get a job, keep a job, or receive a wage increase that keeps up with an increase in prices—are happy to see any increase in the minimum wage regardless of the consequences. And so are the politicians in Congress, who are trying to pick up votes while they pander to the numerous "antipoverty" special-interest groups.

Other arguments against the minimum wage

In addition to the economic arguments, there are also philosophical and pragmatic arguments against the minimum wage.

First, all minimum-wage laws are based on the fallacy that selling one's labor on the market is something special compared with selling one's goods on the market. This Marxian fixation on the primacy of labor cannot overthrow the fact that the price of labor is ultimately determined by the forces of supply and demand, just like the price of anything else.

Second, if minimum-wage laws are needed to "protect" employees, then why aren't minimum prices needed to "protect" employers? If the government is going to establish a floor under which wages cannot fall, then why not a floor under which prices of goods cannot fall? Why doesn't the state just set minimum prices for everything? Unless one subscribes to the primacy-of-labor fallacy, this is the logical conclusion. This, of course, would be absurd. Can you imagine a store having to keep track of the minimum prices on a bar of soap, a pack of gum, a loaf of bread, and a can of peas—along with 50,000 other items?

Third, the making of minimum-wage laws by the government, whether federal, state, or local, means that the government must be able to determine the "correct" or "just" price for labor. But if the government can determine the "correct" or "just" price for labor, then it must also be able to determine the proper price of everything else. Allowing the state to intervene in the labor market merely opens the door for the state to intervene in every other market. Intervention begets more intervention.

Fourth, minimum-wage laws advance the notion that the government is responsible for our well-being and prosperity.

Fifth, all minimum-wage laws are based on the myth that businesses will exploit their workers without such laws. Supporters of the minimum wage act as though people would still be working for less than the original 25-cent-an-hour minimum wage without government intervention. But if businesses will exploit their workers without the minimum wage, then why do so many people make well above the minimum wage? Why can't businesses just force people to work for the minimum wage? The theory of the exploitation of labor is the foundation of Marxism and has no place in a capitalist society.

Sixth, minimum-wage laws are egalitarian because they foster the notion that everyone should be paid the same regardless of the employee's ability or the employer's benevolence.

Seventh, minimum-wage laws imply that everyone has a right to a "living wage." Everyone has the freedom to work or not work in whatever industry he chooses. Everyone also has the freedom to get or not get the necessary education or skills to obtain a good-paying job. But no one has the right to anything beyond what he and his employer agree to. If someone can't "make it" on the minimum wage, he has a variety of options: find a better job, take a second job, send a family member to work, get the necessary education or skills to obtain a good-paying job, or simply work hard and get promoted out of the minimum-wage job.

Sure, entry-level workers at McDonald's make the minimum wage, but McDonald's needs managers too, and it doesn't require a college degree. And who is more qualified to be a manager than someone who has worked his way up through the ranks? There is an imperative to work and strive to better one's self, but there is no right to a "living wage."

And finally, minimum-wage laws violate freedom of contract. They infringe the right of an employer and an employee to make whatever wage agreement they choose. This is what is done with most aspects of employment. According to the U.S. Department of Labor,

> While FLSA [the Fair Labor Standards Act] does set basic minimum wage and overtime pay standards and regulates the employment of minors, there are a number of employment practices which FLSA does not regulate. For example, FLSA does not require: vacation, holiday, severance, or sick pay; meal or rest periods, holidays off, or vacations; premium pay for weekend or holiday work; pay raises or fringe benefits; and a discharge notice, reason for discharge, or immediate payment of final wages to terminated employees. Also, FLSA does not limit the number of hours in a day or days in a week an employee may be required or scheduled to work, including overtime hours, if the employee is at least 16 years old.

The U.S. Department of Labor says about the things the FLSA doesn't require, "The above matters are for agreement between the employer and the employees or their authorized representatives." That statement says a mouthful, for it is exactly the way things ought to be—for every aspect of employment. There is no good reason that what the government says about these things ought not to apply to wages as well.

The solution is obviously to abolish all minimum-wage laws, whether federal, state, county, or city.

If you thought that the Republicans in Congress were conservatives who favored limited government intervention in the economy—think again. Republicans are not at all averse to raising the minimum wage—as long as their plan is adopted. A recent proposal by Senate Democrats to raise the minimum wage to $7.25 in three increments over 26 months garnered the support of only four Republicans.

But a Republican plan to increase the minimum wage to $6.25 over 18 months received the support of 38 Republicans. Sen. Rick Santorum (R-Pa.), the author of the Republican proposal, was quoted as saying, "I have not had any ideological problem with the minimum wage." This vote and this quotation show that the only difference between the Republicans and the Democrats when it comes to the minimum wage is the amount and the timing of its increase.

It is unfortunate that the party responsible for the minimum wage (the Congress) is also the only party that can abolish the minimum wage. Therefore, it is the members of Congress and their constituents who must be educated in the philosophy of liberty—a liberty that includes absolute freedom of contract when it comes to employment.

*****

PRICE DISCRIMINATION IS JUST AND FAIR

While on a recent cross-country flight, I looked around at the 200 or so other passengers on the plane and thought, not about the snacks we would be served (pretzels), the movie we would be shown (*Rise of the Planet of the Apes*), or whether the babies on the flight would cry the whole way (they did), but about economics and economic justice.

I wondered about the truth of the oft-repeated claim that no one on an airline flight pays the same amount for his ticket as anyone else and the question that is sometimes raised whether that practice is fair.

Airlines engage in a form of what is known as price discrimination. It is typically defined as selling the same product to different people for different prices on the basis of their willingness to pay and not for reasons associated with product costs.

This should not be confused with the price discrimination outlawed by antitrust legislation such as the Robinson-Patman Act of 1936 amendments to the Clayton Act of 1914. There the government attempted to protect small independent retailers and their independent suppliers from what was thought to be unfair competition from vertically integrated, multi-location chain stores. It was designed, according to the FTC and the Supreme Court, to assure, to the extent reasonably practicable, that businessmen at the same functional level would stand on equal competitive footing so far as price is concerned. But regardless, antitrust legislation is central planning and is therefore inimical to liberty and the free market, as I have shown here.

Other nonexamples are higher rates for life and auto insurance for males, and special discounts for employees or military personnel.

In order for real price discrimination to work, buyers must have differing abilities and the willingness to pay different prices for goods and services, and sellers must be able to recognize that and capitalize on it.

This is sometimes expressed by economists by the concept of price elasticity of demand; that is, the responsiveness of consumers of the quantity demanded of a good or service to a change in price. The demand for a good or service is inelastic when a change in price has a negligible effect on the quantity demanded; the demand for a good or service is elastic when a change in price has a significant effect on the quantity demanded. In order to charge a higher price to the group with a more inelastic demand and a lower price to the group with a more elastic demand, sellers must be able to prevent a consumer from the elastic group from purchasing a good or service at a low price and reselling it to a consumer from the inelastic group who is willing to pay a higher price.

In the case of airlines, they charge lower prices for consumers with elastic demand (generally pleasure travelers) and higher prices for consumers with inelastic demand (generally business travelers). One way they do it is by mandating advance-purchase or minimum-stay requirements that, in general, tourists can take advantage of and businessmen cant. The whole arrangement is enforced by making the discounted tickets nontransferable and nonrefundable and the expensive tickets just the opposite. Moreover, airlines in many cases charge different prices within each group, depending on how far in advance the ticket is purchased, the day of the week the ticket is purchased, the time of day the ticket is purchased, whether the ticket is refundable, whether the ticket is upgradeable, and the location where the ticket is purchased.

But is it true that no one on an airline flight pays the same amount as anyone else for his ticket? I think this has been overstated. There are plenty of reasons why the person sitting next to you on a flight may have paid a different amount.

Aside from the pleasure/business travel distinction and the resulting difference in the nature of the tickets (and hence their price), there are other factors to be considered as well. Sitting in first class, with its wider seats, beverage and meal perks, and proximity to the front of the airplane, is obviously worth more to most flyers and therefore commands a higher ticket price. The same could be said of sitting in an exit row with its increased legroom. It could also be argued that sitting near a lavatory, on the aisle, or next to a window might be worth more to some people.

But aside from those things, are all other seats of equal value? What many people forget is that since most airlines often fly multi-leg flights through a hub, such as Salt Lake City, Houston, or Atlanta, the person sitting next to you on a flight from Orlando to Los Angeles may in fact be going on to San Francisco (as I was) or to San Diego (as was the person next to me).

But suppose it is true. Suppose that every single person on every single airline flight pays a different price for no apparent reason other than his ability and willingness to pay. How can that be fair?

First all, price discrimination can actually be good for all parties. A columnist from *Forbes*, in an old, but still-relevant article, explains how that can be:

> Imagine that a ferryboat can be hired to cross a river at a cost of $200. Five customers are so eager to get across that they would pay up to $24 apiece. For another 15 the trip is worth only $8 max. What should the fare be? If its $8, revenues of $160 don't cover the costs. At any higher fare, revenues will be at most $120. The boat cant leave the dock. Now suppose there is some way to identify the prosperous five and get them to buy $22 tickets. Let the others board for $7. The passengers all pay less than the value of the journey to them; the ferryman makes a $15 profit. Everybody wins.

But second, and more important, there is nothing fairer than an exchange between a willing buyer and a willing seller. The free market allows buyers (who want to acquire goods at the lowest price possible) and sellers (who want to sell their goods at the highest price possible) to come together in harmony.

At a garage sale or flea market, the seller sets a price and then the buyer is expected to either pay the price or make an offer of a lower price. If a seller thinks he can get a price close to what he was originally asking from a particular buyer, he will continue haggling with him until he gets as much as he can; if not, the seller will either take less or stop negotiating. The fact that two identical items are sold at different prices to two different buyers is irrelevant. The fact that one buyer voluntarily pays a higher price to the same seller for an identical item is irrelevant.

No seller is legally or morally obligated to sell identical goods or services to different purchasers for the same price at any time. Similarly, no purchaser is legally or morally obligated to purchase identical goods or services from any sellers at any time for the same price. Furthermore, no seller is legally or morally obligated to tell any purchaser that he would have sold him a particular good or service for less. And no purchaser is legally or morally obligated to tell any seller that he would have paid more for a particular good or service.

People exchange goods in a market economy to their mutual advantage. Each party to an exchange values what he receives at least as much as what he exchanges for it. Both parties are of necessity better off after an exchange than they were before the exchange, or else they would never have made the exchange in the first place.

Government interference in the market cannot make the market fairer or more competitive; it can only distort or disrupt the market. Attempts to regulate markets by governments always have unintended consequences that are often worse than the problems that regulations were meant to cure. And besides, it is not the business of government to regulate how people conduct business.

*****

STATIST BAGGAGE ON THE AIRLINES

First it was the TSA; now its the airlines.

In addition to getting their bodies squeezed by the TSA, airline passengers are now getting their wallets squeezed by the airlines as well.

Some airlines have begun charging $5 for printing out your boarding pass at the airport. Even if you print from a self-service kiosk, you'll still pay a $1 printing fee. Some airlines are now charging a 10percent fee for infants traveling on international flights who are seated in your lap. One carrier, Ryanair, charges extra for babies on any flight, domestic or international. Some airlines have a fee of $40 for bringing a large carry-on onboard. The fee is only $20 if you indicate as much when you book your ticket. Some airlines are now charging extra for snacks. The last time I checked, JetBlue and US Airways were charging $7 for a blanket and pillow and American Airlines was charging $8. The extra fees were obviously not enough to help American, as it just filed for bankruptcy.

Obviously, to get around paying the fees, passengers could print their boarding passes at home, leave their infants with family members when flying overseas, travel only with small carry-on bags, eat before they board, forgo the blanket and pillow, or choose an airline that doesn't have the particular fee they don't want to pay.

But one practice that all airlines (except Southwest) have instituted, and maintained in spite of cries from the public that they are being gouged, is a fee for checked luggage. In a perfect illustration of the laws of supply and demand, as airlines imposed fees to check bags, more passengers began carrying their luggage onboard.

But the outrage of the flying public has only increased. According to

Steve Lott, spokesman for the airline industry group Air Transport Association, fewer than one in four passengers now pays a checked-luggage fee. That means not only that more carry-on bags must go through security checkpoints, further slowing down the security process, but that space for carry-on bags in airplane overhead bins is at a premium. Its no wonder that too much carry-on luggage toted by passengers recently emerged as the number-one complaint of air travelers.

Sen. MaryL. Landrieu (D-La.) aims to change all that. Like all statists in Congress the overwhelming majority in both parties she believes that the solution to any problem is government intervention. She has just introduced a bill (S.1913), the Basic Airline Services to Improve Customer Satisfaction Act, or BASICS Act, to forbid airlines to charge for the first checked bag.

In a press release, Landrieu maintains that airlines collected $3.9 billion in checked-baggage fees in 2008 and 2009. She asserts that her legislation will solve both the financial burden of paying a fee and the headache of trying to fit everything into a carry-on. Says the senator,

> When an airline advertises a flight, that is how much it should cost, plain and simple. Passengers should not be charged additional fees for checked or carry-on baggage, drinkable water or other reasonable requests. Air travel can be a stressful experience for many reasons, but unfair fees for basic amenities should not be one of them.... Passengers have been nickeled and dimed for far too long and something has to be done about it. Air carriers should be required to provide a minimum standard of service to their passengers or face additional fees that is what the Airline Passenger BASICS Act and the FAIR Act will do.

The FAIR Act would impose additional fees on airlines that do not comply.

The only redeeming thing about the bill is its brevity and simplicity. Section 1 gives the title of the bill and section 2 states just the following:

> Not later than 180 days after the date of the enactment of this Act, the Administrator of the Federal Aviation Administration shall prescribe regulations
>
> 1. to require an air carrier operating under part 121 of title 14, Code of Federal Regulations, to permit each passenger who has purchased a ticket for air transportation on the air carrier to, without paying a charge in addition to the price of the ticket
>   1. check one bag that is not considered overweight or oversized pursuant to the policy of the air carrier in effect on the day before the date of the enactment of this Act;
>   2. carry on to the aircraft one personal item and one carry-on bag that are not considered overweight or oversized pursuant to that policy; and
>   3. once the passenger boards the aircraft, have access to–

1. a seat;
2. potable water; and
3. bathroom facilities; and
2. to impose a civil penalty on an air carrier that fails to comply with the regulations prescribed under paragraph (1).

That is it. That is the entire bill. But a clear and concise bill is not necessarily a good bill.

First of all, Steve Lott points out that banning baggage fees would actually be less fair to customers, as it could result in higher ticket costs that all passengers would bear as opposed to just those who are checking bags. According to the Air Transport Association, airfare alone does not cover the operating cost of a flight. The price of jet fuel has risen from an average of a little more than $1 a gallon between 2001 and 2005 to more than $3 in 2011. According to Tony Tyler, the chief of the International Air Transport Association, Domestic and foreign carriers will transport about 7.6million people next year, but profits are projected at less than 1percent. The airline industry as a whole lost $25billion in the last decade. The lesson here is that things are not always as they seem and there are always unintended consequences whenever the government intervenes in the economy.

Second, banning airlines from charging fees for checked bags for whatever reason is a form of price controls like those instituted by Richard Nixon in 1971 and Venezuela's president, Hugo Chavez, in 2011. Nixon's temporary imposition of wage and price controls on August15, 1971, turned into more than two years of Soviet-style central planning in the United States with a cost-of-living council and pay boards and price commissions to approve requested price increases after a 90-day freeze. Invoking the ideals of Lenin, Chavez recently said that the Law for Fair Costs and Prices would prevent unscrupulous businesses from unjustly raising prices.

Although Nixon did it to institute a new economic policy (kind of like George W. Bush's saying he had to abandon free-market principles to save the free market), and Chavez to protect the people from capitalism, the result is the same: government central planning by bureaucrats.

Sometimes government price controls take other forms. Minimum-wage laws are a result of government bureaucrats setting a price floor below which the price of labor is forbidden by law to fall. Price-gouging laws are a result of government bureaucrats setting a price ceiling above which the price of goods is forbidden to rise.

But whether governments dictate that prices cant be raised, cant be lowered, or cant be changed at all, price controls are still a form of Soviet-style central planning.

Third, just as there is no right to a free drink with your meal at a restaurant or free use of bowling shoes when you go bowling, so there is no right to free checked luggage when you take an airline flight. Do I want to have to pay to check my luggage when I fly? Of course not. Who would? I don't want to have to pay for my flight either, but I do it if I want to board the plane. Just as I pay for dinner at a restaurant or for tickets at a theater, even though I would prefer to eat and watch for free.

Fourth, consumers have the power to persuade airlines to lower prices or eliminate fees without the heavy hand of government mandates and regulations. After major U.S. banks recently announced that they would begin charging their customers a monthly fee for using their debit cards, Americans in droves voiced their opposition and began transferring their money into local credit unions. The banks caved in and discontinued the fees.

Fifth, and most important, whether the airlines are gouging consumers, whether they are charging unfair fees, or whether the airlines can afford to not charge for checked bags is not the real issue. Where does Mary Landrieu or any other member of the Senate or House get the authority to tell businesses what services they can and cannot charge their customers for? Certainly not from the Constitution they have sworn to uphold. Congress is checking the Constitution at the door if it thinks it has the right to dictate such things. The BASICS Act is one more piece of statist baggage that further weighs down a free society.

*****

IS IT TIME TO RAISE THE MINIMUM WAGE?

During World War II, the Office of Price Administration (OPA), established by one of Franklin Roosevelt's executive orders in 1941, was given the power to ration the supply of certain goods and freeze prices on all goods except agricultural commodities. The OPA was abolished in 1946 and is generally defended today only as a wartime measure.

Richard Nixon's "temporary" imposition of wage and price controls in 1971, turned into more than two years of Soviet-style central planning in the United States with a cost-of-living council and pay boards and price commissions to approve requested price increases after a 90-day freeze. I don't know of anyone of any political persuasion who defends Nixon's actions today.

For some strange reason, the price of labor is viewed differently.

The federal minimum has been at $7.25 since 2009. It is the result of the Fair Minimum Wage Act of 2007, which raised the federal minimum wage in three steps from $5.15 per hour to $5.85 per hour on July 24, 2007, to $6.55 per hour on July 24, 2008, and finally to $7.25 per hour on July 24, 2009.

Three Democratic members of Congress think it's time to raise the minimum wage.

Reps. John Conyers Jr. of Michigan, Jesse Jackson Jr. of Illinois, and Dennis Kucinich of Ohio recently announced the introduction of the "Catching Up to 1968 Act of 2012" at a press conference in Washington, D.C. H.R. 5901, which was introduced in Congress by Jackson on June 6, currently has twenty co-sponsors. It would raise the federal minimum wage to $10 per hour effective "60 days after the date of enactment of the Catching Up to 1968 Act of 2012" and tie further increases every year "to the Consumer Price Index for all urban consumers for the preceding year."

The idea behind the bill's title is that at $10 an hour, the minimum wage would be about what it was in 1968, when adjusted for inflation.

"This legislation is long-overdue and sorely needed," said Conyers. "More than 30 million Americans would see their wages increased, which would provide an immediate boost to the economy."

Barack Obama hasn't yet endorsed the bill, although as president-elect he pledged to raise the minimum wage to $9.50 an hour by 2011 and index it to inflation.

Consumer advocate Ralph Nader, who was also on hand to announce the legislation at the press conference, likewise made some remarks:

> At a time when the issue of income inequality has been elevated in political discourse, it is surprising that a plight of millions of workers throughout the country hasn't been addressed....
>
> Nearly 23 million Americans are unemployed or underemployed. A single Wall Street executives' [sic] compensation of $15 million would pay the annual wages of over 700 workers working at a minimum wage of $10 per hour.
>
> It is way past time for Congress to wake up and enact a $10 minimum wage to catch up with 1968!

In an interview with *Democracy Now!* Nader said the minimum wage "is basically an issue that reflects the craven, cruel nature of the Republican Party on Capitol Hill, but it also reflects the caution, the cowardliness, the betrayal of the Democratic Party of its core constituency."

Does that mean that Republicans in Congress are opposed on principle to raising the minimum wage?

Not at all.

While campaigning in January, Republican presidential candidate Mitt Romney was asked about raising the minimum wage and replied, "My view has been to allow the minimum wage to rise with the CPI or with another index, so that it adjusts automatically over time."

One of his rivals at the time, former Pennsylvania senator Rick Santorum, said in 2005 in reply to criticism by Sen. Ted Kennedy, "I have not had any ideological problem with the minimum wage." Democrats and Republicans were at the time each pushing their own version of a plan to increase the minimum wage.

As mentioned previously, the last time Congress voted to raise the minimum wage was in 2007 with the passage of the Fair Minimum Wage Act. That was Title VIII of the U.S. Troop Readiness, Veterans' Care, Katrina Recovery, and Iraq Accountability Appropriations Act (H.R.2206) that was agreed to by a majority of Republicans in the House and Senate and signed into law by George W. Bush on May 25, 2007.

In a January 2007 interview with NPR, Senate Republican leader Mitch McConnell said about raising the minimum wage,

> Well, we've been willing to raise the minimum wage for quite some time. The problem is we haven't been able to do it in a bipartisan way. We offered a package when we were in the majority last Congress that raised [the] minimum wage as Senator Kennedy had suggested, but also modify the death tax, which is something the Republican majority cared a lot about.
>
> The president's indicated and we agree that the raising of the minimum wage is a good idea. We would like to, however, package that with some small businesses tax and regulatory relief to minimize the job loss that is the inevitable result of raising the minimum wage. But this is a deal that I think we ought to be able to make.

But it's not just Republicans in Congress. In an October 2010 poll conducted by the Public Religion Research Institute, a majority of Republican respondents favored raising the minimum wage. Even among those who identified themselves as belonging to the Tea Party, 47 percent approved of the increasing the federal minimum.

The only difference between Democrats and Republicans when it comes to raising the minimum wage is the timing and the amount.

The federal minimum wage began as part of the Fair Labor Standards Act of 1938, which also sets overtime pay standards and regulates the employment of minors. About twenty states and some cities have a higher minimum wage than the federal minimum. The state of Washington leads the states with a minimum wage of $9.04. Likewise, the city of San Francisco, with a minimum wage of $10.24.

Proponents of the minimum wage would have us believe that Americans would all be toiling in sweatshops for less than 25¢ an hour (the original federal minimum wage) were it not for the federal government's intervening to stop businesses from exploiting their workers.

But if that is the case, why is it that now, with a minimum wage in place, most workers make substantially more than the minimum? According to the Bureau of Labor Statistics (BLS), only about 5 percent of U.S. hourly-paid workers have wages at or below the prevailing federal minimum (there are some exemptions to the minimum-wage provisions of the law). That is down substantially from 15 percent of workers in 1981 who had wages at or below the legal minimum.

Oh, but the minimum wage is needed to combat poverty and income inequality. Since no family can survive on an income less than the minimum wage, it is needed to increase their standard of living. And without a minimum age, the poor will get poorer as the rich get richer.

But not only do relatively few workers earn the minimum wage, those who do, tend to be *temporarily* limited to certain segments of the economy. According to the BLS, the main characteristics of those earning the minimum wage are:

Minimum wage workers tend to be young. Although workers under age 25 represented only about one-fifth of hourly-paid workers, they made up about half of those paid the Federal minimum wage or less. Among employed teenagers paid by the hour, about 23 percent earned the minimum wage or less, compared with about 3 percent of workers age 25 and over.

Among hourly-paid workers age 16 and over, about 11 percent of those who had less than a high school diploma earned the Federal minimum wage or less, compared with about 5 percent of those who had a high school diploma (with no college) and about 2 percent of college graduates.

Part-time workers (persons who usually work less than 35 hours per week) were more likely than full-time workers to be paid the Federal minimum wage or less (about 13 percent versus about 2 percent).

The industry with the highest proportion of workers with hourly wages at or below the Federal minimum wage was leisure and hospitality (22 percent). About one-half of all workers paid at or below the Federal minimum wage were employed in this industry, primarily in restaurants and other food services. For many of these workers, tips and commissions supplement the hourly wages received.

From the standpoint of business, it has been argued that the minimum wage—even though it increases labor costs—is beneficial because it encourages efficiency, automation, and technological development—things that offset higher labor costs.

From the standpoint of the worker, it has been argued that the minimum wage increases the work ethic, encourages people to work rather than commit crimes and sell drugs, and directs workers to train for higher-skilled jobs.

From the standpoint of government, it has been argued that the minimum wage removes people from the welfare rolls and acts as an economic stimulus by giving low-income people more money in their pockets to spend. The added benefit, of course, is that the costs of those things are borne by businesses.

But if all of those claims are true, then why not raise the minimum wage to $20 per hour instead of $10 per hour. Wouldn't it basically eliminate poverty, give everyone a tremendous incentive to move into the labor force, and virtually compel businesses to be more efficient?

Even the most ardent supporters of the minimum wage would acknowledge that such an increase would cause unemployment as workers who are unproductive or unskilled were priced out of the labor market. So how do we know what the optimum minimum wage should be? The only answer is that it is up to government economists and bureaucrats to find the happy medium between subsistence living and unemployment. But what is that but Soviet-style central planning?

At issue is the proper role of government. Since when is it the job of government to encourage efficiency, automation, and technological development? Since when is it the job of government to increase the work ethic, encourage people to work, and direct workers' job training? Since when is it the job of government to provide welfare and stimulate the economy? And since when is it the job of government to combat poverty and income inequality?

Because government intervention is the antithesis of freedom, the other side of the coin is that the minimum wage is an assault on freedom. Establishing a minimum wage is nothing but forbidding workers from freely contracting with firms under mutually agreeable terms. What is so nonsensical about the minimum wage is that it prevents people from selling their labor for whatever amount they choose even while they are able to sell any of their goods for whatever amount they choose. But just as government should have no control overbuyer/sellerrelations, so government should have no control overemployer/employeerelations. Not in a free society.

No, it is not time to raise the minimum wage. But it is long past time to have freedom of contract in labor markets.

*****

WHY WE SHOULD NOT RAISE THE MINIMUM WAGE

The federal minimum wage has been $7.25 an hour since July 24, 2009. Although this is a long way from the first federal minimum wage of $0.25 an hour in the 1930s, it is not high enough according to some members of Congress, a group of over one hundred professional economists, President Obama, the executive director of the National Employment Law Project, and Juliette Fairley, who brings all this to our attention in her *MainStreet.com* article "Why We Should Raise the Minimum Wage."

According to the Bureau of Labor Statistics, only about 5 percent of U.S. hourly-paid workers have wages at or below the prevailing federal minimum (there are some exemptions to the minimum-wage provisions of the Fair Labor Standards Act). Minimum-wage workers tend to be people who are young, have never been married, are unskilled, have no more than a high-school education, work part-time, and work in the leisure and hospitality sectors of the economy.

Representative Alan Grayson (D-FL), who just so happens to represent my congressional district, introduced the "Catching Up to 1968 Act of 2013" (HR 1346) on March 21, 2013. It would "increase to $10.50 an hour (adjusted annually based on increases in the Consumer Price Index) the federal minimum wage for employees" and set "the federal minimum wage for tipped employees to be 70% of the federal minimum wage in effect for employees." The bill has 18 cosponsors.

Over one hundred economists from dozens of universities and research institutes have signed a petition in support of Rep. Grayson's bill. They argue,

> As is conveyed by the title of the bill itself, the real, inflation-adjusted, value of the federal minimum wage has fallen dramatically over time. In 1968, the real value of the minimum wage was $10.65, so that, in fact, an increase today to a $10.50 federal minimum would not even bring the minimum wage fully back to the 1968 standard. Moreover, since 1968, average U.S. labor productivity has risen by 135 percent. Thus, if, since 1968, the U.S. minimum wage had only just kept up with inflation and average labor productivity growth, the minimum wage today would be $25.00.

> In short, the "Catching Up to 1968 Act" will be an effective means of improving living standards for low-wage workers and their families and will help stabilize the economy.

These economists acknowledge that an increase in the minimum wage will cause businesses' costs to increase, but insist that the increased costs will be "modest" and "readily absorbed" through "minor increases in prices and productivity."

In his 2013 State of the Union Address, President Obama called for an increase in the federal minimum wage to $9 an hour, automatically adjusted each year for inflation. As president-elect, Obama pledged to raise the minimum wage to $9.50 an hour.

Christine Owens, the executive director of the National Employment Law Project, says it is "time to raise the federal minimum wage—raise it over time to $10.10 an hour, boost the guaranteed minimum wage rate for tipped workers, which has been stuck at $2.13 since 1991, and index the overall minimum wage to the cost of living."

In Juliette Fairley's *MainStreet.com* article about why we should raise the minimum wage, she points out that ten states raised the minimum wage at the beginning of this year: Arizona and Montana to $7.80, Colorado to $7.78, Florida to $7.79, Missouri to $7.35, Ohio to $7.85, Oregon to $8.95, Rhode Island to $7.75, Vermont to $8.60, and Washington to $9.19. The state of New York also recently enacted an increase in its minimum wage in three steps to $9 an hour by December 31, 2015. Nevertheless, Fairley still thinks it necessary that the federal government raise its minimum wage.

Almost without exception, liberals, progressives, and Democrats are always in favor of increases in the minimum wage on the federal, state, and local levels. This allows them to show how much they care for the poor at the expense of businesses that have to deal with the sudden increase in their labor costs. But if a minimum wage of $10.50 an hour, as in Rep. Grayson's bill, will keep some Americans out of poverty, then why don't these left-wing groups advocate a minimum wage of $20.50 and keep all Americans out of poverty? Perhaps even they realize that, as the Austrian economist Murray Rothbard said, "You can have as much unemployment as you want, simply by pushing the legally minimum wage high enough."

Republicans are inconsistent and hypocritical when it comes to the minimum wage. They are inconsistent because some of them support increasing the minimum wage, just not as much and as often as Democrats. They are hypocritical because those who are willing to increase the minimum wage talk about limited government and criticize increased government regulation of the economy—just like all the other Republicans who oppose increasing the minimum wage.

Conservatives make good economic arguments against raising the minimum wage: the minimum wage causes unemployment, because it increases a business's labor costs and prices unskilled workers out of the market. The problem with this and other arguments made by conservatives about the negative effects of raising the minimum wage is that they are usually countered by liberal economists—even using the same study or data concerning the effects of raising the minimum wage. This doesn't mean that the conservative economists are wrong; it just means that liberals who support raising the minimum wage can look to their own economists for support.

Constitutionalists are on firmer ground than traditional conservatives, because nowhere does the Constitution grant to the federal government the power to set a minimum wage or to regulate wages in any way, regardless of the economic consequences. In fact, FDR's National Industrial Recovery Act, which included the first federal minimum wage, was struck down by the Supreme Court in the 1933 case of *Schechter Poultry Corp. v. U.S.* It is true that in the 1941 case of *U.S. v. Darby Lumber Co.*, the Supreme Court upheld the Fair Labor Standards Act of 1938, which included a minimum-wage provision. But as the Supreme Court cannot rewrite the Constitution, it is still a fact that Congress has no constitutional authority to enact a minimum wage.

But there is just one problem: this prohibition only applies at the federal level. States are perfectly free to regulate wages in accordance with their constitutions. In fact, 19 states and Washington, DC, have minimum wages that are above the federal minimum. In addition to the 10 states mentioned above, which raised their minimum wages this year, the minimum wage is $7.40 in Michigan, $7.50 in Maine and New Hampshire, $7.75 in Arkansas, $8.00 in California and Massachusetts, and $8.25 in Connecticut, Washington D.C., Illinois, and Nevada. Additionally, some cities have their own minimum-wage laws, most notably Albuquerque ($8.50), San Jose ($10.00), and San Francisco ($10.55).

Libertarians have no problem with economic and constitutional arguments against raising or having a minimum wage, but they prefer a more philosophical, three-pronged approach to the issue.

(1) It is simply not the proper role of government to set a minimum wage or regulate the labor market—even if it meant keeping people out of poverty. In fact, governments at any level shouldn't even have labor departments.

(2) The minimum wage is an assault on freedom. It forbids employees from freely contracting with employers. It prevents people from selling their labor for whatever amount of payment they choose.

(3) The government establishing a minimum wage is nothing more than Soviet-style central planning. How is the optimal minimum wage determined? It is up to government economists and bureaucrats to find the happy medium between subsistence living and unemployment. But, as the Austrian economist Ludwig von Mises explained, "If one rejects laissez faire on account of man's fallibility and moral weakness, one must for the same reason also reject every kind of government action." Men do not suddenly become infallible when they act on behalf of government.

No, we should not raise the minimum wage. In a free society, it wouldn't even exist in the first place.

*****

GOVERNMENT MAXIMUMS AND MINIMUMS

The latest crisis that has some Americans calling for government intervention to fix the problem is subprime auto loans to the poor. The *New York Times* has had a series of articles on the subject. And NPR's *On Point* with Tom Ashbrook recently devoted a show to the topic.

The working poor with low credit scores who need transportation to get to work are increasingly taking out high-interest loans to purchase used cars. Thousands of these subprime auto loans are then bundled together and sold as securities to investors, including mutual funds, insurance companies, and hedge funds. The market for such securites has grown 302 percent, to $20.2 billion since 2010.

The demand for subprime auto securities has led to a rise in loans that contain falsified income or employment information. Justice Department examinations "are modeled on the federal investigation into the sale of mortgage-backed securities." Billions of dollars in settlements have been reached.

Related to this are title loans on existing cars that allow owners to borrow money against their cars. Aggressive advertising on radio, late-night television, and billboards in urban, predominantly low-income communities promises quick cash, but with the price of high interest rates. According to a survey by the Federal Deposit Insurance Corporation (FDIC), "More than 1.1 million households in the United States used auto title loans in 2013." A review of loan agreements by the *New York Times* found that "after factoring in various fees, the effective interest rates ranged from nearly 80 percent to over 500 percent." The lenders, of course, "argue that they are providing a source of credit for people who cannot obtain less-expensive loans from banks." High interest rates, they say, "are necessary to offset the risk that borrowers will stop paying their bills." Nevertheless, for some Americans, these loans sometimes result in repossessions, increased debt, and ruinous financial consequences.

The Federal Trade Commission (FTC)—for the first time—recently went after two car-title lenders on suspicions that they misled borrowers by failing to accurately disclose the terms and costs of the loans. Aggressive advertisements by First American Title Lending and Finance Select, both based in Georgia, pitched loans "with zero interest rates but failed to disclose that the interest rates on the loans jumped after an introductory period." A settlement deal between the lenders and the FTC requires the companies to "overhaul how they advertise and promote their loans" and "improve their disclosures about loan terms."

Now, although everyone is opposed to fraud and false advertising, critics of subprime and title loans for automobiles invariably call not only for more government oversight, but for government-decreed maximum interest rates depending on the type of loan. This is no different from laws that cap interest rates on credit cards from banks and payday loans from pawn shops. Price-gouging laws likewise fall into this category. And so does agitation for legal limits on CEO pay.

But it is not just government maximums that some Americans clamor for.

It has been a year now since a new minimum wage of $15 an hour took effect in the city of SeaTac, Washington, home of the Seattle-Tacoma International Airport. It was the result of a ballot initiative that won by just 77 votes.

Minimum wages also went up in nine states (Arizona, Colorado, Florida, Missouri, Montana, New Jersey, Ohio, Oregon, Washington) at the first of the year because of indexed increases in their state law. The minimum wage is scheduled to increase later this year in six states (Alaska, Delaware, Maryland, Minnesota, New York, West Virginia) and the District of Columbia. The federal minimum wage has been $7.25 an hour since July 24, 2009. However, states are allowed to set their own minimum wages. Twenty-nine states and the District of Columbia have a minimum wage higher than the federal minimum.

Four states (Alaska, Arkansas, Nebraska, South Dakota) approved minimum-wage increases through ballot measures in the 2014 general election while legislatures in ten states (Connecticut, Delaware, Hawaii, Maryland, Massachusetts, Michigan, Minnesota, Rhode Island, Vermont, West Virginia) and Washington, D.C., enacted increases during their 2014 sessions. As a consequence of this and previous legislation or initiatives, the minimum wage is already scheduled to increase next year in eleven states (Alaska, Arkansas, California, Connecticut, Hawaii, Maryland, Massachusetts, Michigan, Minnesota, Nebraska, Vermont).

Because only about a dozen states ban cities from setting their own minimum wage, some cities in addition to Washington's SeaTac have their own minimum wage. Seattle's minimum wage is scheduled to gradually increase to $15 an hour. New York City Mayor Bill de Blasio has called for a minimum-wage increase to $15 an hour by 2019. A recent poll "shows that 75% of Americans—including 53% of Republicans—support an increase in the federal minimum wage to $12.50 by 2020" and that "63% of Americans support an even greater increase in the minimum wage to $15.00 by 2020."

Other forms of government minimums include programs to guarantee certain margins to the dairy and sugar industries.

There are a myriad of reasons offered by the government and supporters of government intervention for the necessity of government to set maximums and minimums: to protect consumers, to fight income inequality, to level the playing field, to help the poor, to keep people out of poverty, to thwart people from making bad financial decisions, to prevent people from being taken advantage of, and so on.

There are a number of problems and inconsistencies with these government maximums and minimums.

First, why maximums on some products and services but not minimums? And why minimums on some products and services but not maximums? If there should be a maximum interest rate to protect borrowers then why not a minimum interest rate to ensure that lenders get a decent return?

Second, why just certain products and services? Why not a government maximum on the price of hotel rooms, haircuts, and dishwashers? Why not a government minimum on the price of bananas, newspapers, and CDs?

Third, there is a thin line between the government's setting maximum

prices and minimum prices and setting actual prices. In fact, once you accept that the government has the authority, knowledge, and competence to
establish maximum and minimum prices, no logical argument can be
made against the government's setting actual prices. Local governments
actually do this on taxis.

Fourth, government maximums and minimums are an assault on free
exchange, free trade, free contract, free markets, and a free society.

Fifth, government maximums and minimums are forms of Soviet-style
central planning and industrial policy.

Sixth, government maximums and minimums are arbitrary. They are
not based on some economic law or empirical study but are instead pulled
out of thin air or in response to agitation by a particular interest group.

And seventh, government maximums and minimums are political.
They are set at the whim of government bureaucrats, lawyers, economists,
regulators, and statisticians.

The free and unfettered interaction between employers and employees,
producers and consumers, buyers and sellers, borrowers and lenders, and
businesses and customers is always to be preferred to government intervention.

*****

THE ELUSIVE JUST PRICE

The annual meeting of the American Society of Clinical Oncology
(ASCO) was held in Chicago recently. The conference, which was attended by about 25,000 scientists and doctors concerned with the treatment of cancer, was heavily sponsored by the pharmaceutical industry.
Thus, it came as a big surprise when Dr. Leonard Saltz, chief of Gastroin-
testinal Oncology at Memorial Sloan Kettering Cancer Center in New
York, delivered a speech about the high price of cancer-treatment drugs.

It is unprecedented for plenary speeches "to substantially take on the
topic of drug costs," said Dr. Alan Venook, "a professor of medicine at the
University of California San Francisco who planned the meeting's scientific session and invited Dr. Saltz to speak." Discussing drug prices there
is "uncomfortable" because it could be seen as "biting the hand that feeds
you." He also remarked that doctors are "reluctant to antagonize the drug
industry because they need pharmaceutical firms to invest in developing
new medicines for patients."

Saltz has been vocal in the past about the high cost of cancer therapies,
and even managed to get one drug company to lower its price when his
center's team refused to use it. His remarks focused mainly on an experi-
mental melanoma treatment made by Bristol-Myers Squibb. He cited statistics showing that the median monthly price for new cancer drugs in the
United States had more than doubled in the last ten years, but that the

price increases didn't correspond to increases in the drugs' effectiveness.

In his talk, Saltz spoke specifically of ipilimumab and nivolumab, drugs that have "achieved dramatic results in the treatment of metastatic melanoma," which was thought to be "basically untreatable" just five years ago. Ipilimumab costs $157.46 per milligram—"about 4,000 times the cost of gold," he said.

There are many reasons why the prices of many drug have been deemed "too high."

The patent system. Patents are a grant of monopoly by the government. Patents allow companies to use the power of government to stifle competition and keep prices high for consumers.

The FDA approval process. It can take years for the FDA to approve a new drug. That imposes a great cost on drug companies that they will seek to recoup by charging "high" prices for drugs. There is no reason why an apolitical, voluntary, more efficient, market-based drug-approval process could not replace the FDA.

Government regulations. The government regulatory burden costs businesses billions of dollars every year. It drives up the costs of all products and services. Drug companies especially are saddled with burdensome government regulations.

Medicare. The government health-care system for the elderly known as Medicare is the single largest purchaser of drugs. And according to Saltz, Medicare is currently barred by law from negotiating prices directly with drug companies. Once the FDA approves a drug for a particular use, the Center for Medicare and Medicaid Services has to buy that drug at any price set by the drug manufacturer. Saltz also said that there is conflict of interest in the way doctors are paid. They currently receive a percentage of a drug's total sales price, which gives them an incentive to "make more money by using the most expensive drugs." Bushcare (The Medicare Prescription Drug, Improvement, and Modernization Act) and Obamacare (The Patient Protection and Affordable Care Act) have only made things worse.

The high drug use of Americans. There is seemingly a drug for every physical, emotional, and mental aliment nowadays. And—all the potential side effects on warning labels not withstanding—Americans are using them at record levels.

There is another reason why the prices of many drugs have been deemed to be not only too high, but excessive, unconscionable, exorbitant, prohibitive, unfair, or unjust.

While at the ASCO conference, Saltz took the time to speak by phone to Audie Cornish of NPR's *All Things Considered* regarding his concerns about the high price of cancer-treatment drugs. The first thing she asked him about was something he said in his speech regarding cancer-drug prices' not being related to the value of the drug. Here is exactly what he said: "Cancer-drug prices are not related to the value of the drug. Prices are based on what has come before and what the seller believes the market will bear."

As they should be.

Saltz spoke the truth about prices, even though he is not an economist, and even though he disagreed with what he was saying.

Elements of the medieval quest for the elusive just price, which gave rise to the misguided labor theory of value of Adam Smith, David Ricardo, and Karl Marx, are still with us. But as economists of the Austrian school have shown, value is subjective and subject to change. There is no such thing as intrinsic value. Price is independent of labor, expenses, cost, and risk. It is precisely because value is subjective that voluntary trades are always win-win situations.

That does not mean that prices are arbitrary. Prices, as economist Don Boudreaux recently explained,

(1) *reflect* underlying realities and, in doing so,
(2) *inform* producers and consumers about how best to coordinate their actions with each other and
(3) *give* incentives to countless producers and consumers to adjust their actions to each other in coordinating ways.

There is no such thing as the elusive "just" price." A just price is the market price. That means that in a free society there are a number of things that are true about a just price.

A just price is any price set by the lawful owner of a particular good or provider of a particular service.

A just price is any price based on supply and demand.

A just price is any price voluntarily agreed upon by buyer and seller.

A just price is any price that a buyer is willing to pay.

A just price is any price that a seller is willing to receive.

A just price does not exist independently of a transaction between buyer and seller.

A just price is any price not set under some arbitrary government maximum.

A just price is any price not set above some arbitrary government minimum.

A just price is not related to what a good costs to manufacture or a service costs to provide.

A just price is not related to what a good or service is "worth."

A just price includes any price that is raised in times of shortages and natural disasters.

A just price is any price not constrained by some government regulation.

A just price is both impossible and immoral for any government to calculate, institute, regulate, or control.

There is no such thing as price gouging, predatory pricing, or a price that is inherently unjust. A just price is the market price. In a free society, it couldn't be any other way.

*****

CAN A BUSINESS OVERCHARGE ITS CUSTOMERS?

How many times have we heard someone say that he was overcharged for something? The answer to the question of whether a business can overcharge its customers seems, on the surface, to be quite obvious. Yet, it is a question that has more than one answer.

At the end of last year, Whole Foods Market, a supermarket chain specializing in organic food, agreed to pay half a million dollars to New York City to settle allegations that it had overcharged its customers for prepackaged foods.

Also at the end of last year, Martin Shkreli, a former hedge-fund manager who went on to head three pharmaceutical companies, was arrested by the FBI after being indicted on charges of securities fraud and conspiracy. What is relevant here about the infamous Mr. Shkreli is that he was not arrested for what he did a few months prior, which some people would have liked to have seen him arrested for: buying the rights to a life-saving prescription drug and then overcharging for it.

Although both of those instances involve businesses that "overcharged" their customers, there is an important distinction between the two cases that should be maintained. Only in one case can a business legitimately be said to have overcharged its customers.

Fraudulent overcharging

Back in June of last year, the New York Department of Consumer Affairs (DCA) accused Whole Foods Market of overcharging New York City customers for some prepackaged foods by overstating the weight of the products being sold. According to the DCA, "Tests of 80 different prepackaged products bought in the company's nine New York stores showed that all were labeled with erroneous weights." Products mislabeled included vegetable platters, chicken tenders, and coconut shrimp.

The DCA accusation led the Whole Foods Market co-CEOs to apologize in an online video and pledge that the company would take steps to prevent overcharging its customers in the future, including increasing worker training. The company also vowed to give away any products that customers discovered were mispriced. Naturally, the bad publicity resulted in a drop in sales. And to make matters worse, the DCA fined Whole

Foods Market $1.5 million for all the violations it found. A lawyer for the company said it would fight the fines sought by the DCA because they were "excessive." It should be noted that the money collected would not be refunded to consumers but instead go into the city's budget.

A Whole Foods Market spokesman said that its $500,000 settlement with the DCA late last year was reached "in order to put this issue behind us so that we can continue to focus our attention on providing our New York City customers with the highest level of quality and service." The settlement was "in the best interest of the people of the City of New York and our stakeholders." The settlement also requires Whole Foods Market to provide extra training of its New York City employees who weigh and label products and conduct quarterly in-store audits to ensure that products are indeed accurately weighed and labeled. "Whether it's a bodega in the Bronx or a national grocery store in Manhattan, we believe every business needs to treat its customers fairly and, with this agreement, we hope Whole Foods Market will deliver on its promise to its customers to correct their mistakes," said DCA Commissioner Julie Menin.

That Whole Foods Market overcharged its customers has more to do with fraud than it has to do with price. If a package is supposed to contain x number of pieces of a product, said to contain x number of ounces of a product, or if a product is alleged to weigh x number of pounds and it doesn't, then it is labeled fraudulently. That could lead the purchaser of a product to be overcharged (if a package contains less product than it is supposed to) or undercharged (if a package contains more product than it is supposed to). That is true if a product is sold by number, volume, or weight, but is not the case if a product is sold by the unit. For example, roast beef, ham, and cheese might be sold at the deli counter for different amounts per pound, but also sold together for a fixed price on a platter. Charging consumers for a pound of meat or cheese while giving them less than a pound of meat or cheese is a genuine overcharge. However, no one could be overcharged for voluntarily purchasing a platter of meat and cheese sold by the unit no matter what the price was.

There are other ways that a business can fraudulently overcharge its customers. If an item rings up at a higher price than is marked on the package or that the store signage indicates, or if it simply rings up at a higher price than it is supposed to, that is a genuine overcharge. If the premium variety of a good has a higher price than the regular variety, but the package actually contains just the regular variety, then the customer is being overcharged when he pays the extra amount for the higher quality item but doesn't actually get what the package says he is getting. The same principle applies to a service. If a carpet cleaning service is supposed to clean the carpets throughout a house but omits to clean one room while still charging the customer for cleaning the whole house, then a fraudulent overcharge has taken place.

But some things that are considered to be overcharges are not overcharges at all.

False overcharging

Former hedge-fund manager Martin Shkreli founded the biotechnology company Retrophin Inc. in 2011. The company's board replaced him in 2014 and filed a $65 million lawsuit against him in 2015 over his use of company funds and "stock-trading irregularities and other violations of securities rules." Shkreli founded Turing Pharmaceuticals in February of 2015 with three drugs in development acquired from Retrophin. On August 10, Turing acquired the exclusive U.S. rights to Daraprim, the trade name of the drug pyrimethamine, from Impax Laboratories for $55 million. Pyrimethamine is used both as an anti-malarial drug and as a treatment for the parasitic disease toxoplasmosis. According to the Centers for Disease Control, toxoplasmosis is considered to be a leading cause of death attributed to foodborne illness in the United States. Pyrimethamine is often used in combination with two other drugs to treat HIV-positive patients with compromised immune systems. The drug is on the nineteenth edition of the World Health Organization's list of essential medicines. Daraprim has been available since 1953. The market for the drug is small, with only about eight thousand prescriptions filled a year. Although the patent on the drug has expired, no generic version is available in the United States, even though several companies do make and sell a generic version of Daraprim abroad.

After acquiring Daraprim from Impax, Retrophin raised the price of the drug from $13.50 per tablet to $750 per tablet—a 5,500 percent increase. According to a letter to Turing Pharmaceuticals from the Infectious Diseases Society of America (IDSA) and the HIV Medicine Association (HIVMA), "Under the current pricing structure, it is estimated that the annual cost of treatment for toxoplasmosis, for the pyrimethamine component alone, will be $336,000 for patients who weigh less than 60 kilograms and $634,500 for patients who weigh more than 60 kilograms. This cost is unjustifiable for the medically vulnerable patient population in need of this medication and unsustainable for the health care system." In the United Kingdom, Daraprim sells for less than a dollar a pill.

The Pharmaceutical Research and Manufacturers of America and other medical specialty and patient-related organizations joined the IDSA and the HIVMA in criticizing the overcharge. Presidential candidates Hillary Clinton, Bernie Sanders, and Donald Trump weighed in as well. Clinton termed the price hike "outrageous," and said that "price gouging like this in the specialty drug market is outrageous." Sanders talked about the "greed" of the drug makers, and said, "They can do it. They can get away with it. They can make outrageous sums of profits and money on this and that's what they're doing." He and Rep. Elijah Cummings introduced a bill in Congress aimed at curbing drug prices. Explained Sanders, "Our job in Congress is to say to these drug companies, 'You can't keep ripping off the American people. You can't force folks to be in a situation where they can't purchase the medicine they desperately need.' That's what we should be doing." Trump remarked about Shkreli, "That guy is nothing. He's zero. He's nothing. He ought to be ashamed of himself." At the time, Shkreli was dubbed "the most hated man in America." After the uproar over the Daraprim price increase, Shkreli promised to reduce the price by an unspecified amount, but then later said that he would not reduce the price after all. He pledged instead to negotiate volume discounts with hospitals.

So, did Retrophin overcharge its customers? Did Shkreli overcharge for Daraprim? At what level of price increase could purchasers of Retrophin be said to be overcharged? How much would the price of Daraprim have to rise for Retrophin to be overcharging its customers? By what percentage would the price of Daraprim have to increase for Retrophin to be overcharging its customers? Would it make any difference if Retrophin had competition and there were other companies that sold forms of pyrimethamine? Would it make any difference if Retrophin raised the prices of all of its drugs at the same time or by the same amount? Would it make any difference if one of Retrophin's competitors also began overcharging its customers? Would it make any difference if all of Retrophin's competitors increased the prices of any or all of their drugs? Would it make any difference if Retrophin wasn't a "lifesaving" drug? Would it make any difference if Daraprim were still protected by a patent? Would it make any difference if a generic version of Daraprim were available? Would it make any difference whether there were or weren't a shortage of Daraprim? Would it make any difference if health-insurance companies said they would still pay for Daraprim even with the price increase? Does it matter that Daraprim was available much more cheaply in other countries? Is there anything that could justify Daraprim's price increase?

But it's not just Retrophin and Daraprim that are at issue here. And it's not just the pharmaceutical industry. In the absence of fraud, can a business overcharge its customers? Any business, whether it sells products or performs services or both: gas stations, department stores, convenience stores, furniture stores, hardware stores, barber shops, auto-repair shops, pet stores, restaurants, landscapers, carpet cleaners, tanning salons, gyms, sporting-goods stores, bakeries, home-improvement warehouses, movie theaters, ice cream parlors. In the absence of fraud, is it possible for any of those places of business to overcharge its customers?

Fair and just prices

In the absence of fraud, deception, and coercion (but not necessarily in the absence of ignorance, laziness, or greed), and in the presence of a willing buyer and a willing seller, any price of a good or service is a fair and just price. A fair and just price is the market price. A fair and just price is any price voluntarily agreed to by a buyer and a seller that a buyer is willing to pay and a seller is willing to receive. It does not exist independently of a transaction between a buyer and a seller. As economists of the Austrian school maintain, value is subjective and subject to change. No good or service has intrinsic value. A fair and just price is not related to what a good or service is "worth." Because value is subjective, voluntary exchanges always result in win-win situations for both buyers and sellers.

Prices are independent of labor, expenses, cost, and risk. They are based on the laws of supply and demand. Fair and just prices are not related to what a good costs to manufacture or a service costs to provide. That does not mean that prices are arbitrary. Prices, as George Mason University economist Don Boudreaux has explained, "(1) reflect underlying realities and, in doing so, (2) inform producers and consumers about how best to coordinate their actions with each other, and (3) give incentives to countless producers and consumers to adjust their actions to each other in coordinating ways."

Fair and just prices are also prices that are not constrained by some arbitrary government maximum, minimum, or regulation. Laws against overcharging—price gouging or predatory pricing—violate the property rights of resource owners, they hinder the price system's signaling ability, they contribute to the misallocation of resources, and they cause shortages. A fair and just price is both impossible and immoral for any governmental body to calculate, suggest, institute, or regulate. It is impossible because government is not omniscient; it is immoral because government has no authority to intervene in the free market. And as the economist Ludwig von Mises pointed out, "Once price control is declared a task of government, an indefinite number of price ceilings must be fixed and many of them must, with changing conditions, be altered again and again."

The government doesn't need to monitor the prices that pharmaceutical companies charge for their drugs in order to make sure that Americans aren't overcharged. The government needs to get out of the business of regulating drugs, health insurance, hospitals, physicians, and medical care; eliminate Medicare and Medicaid; and let the free market work.

*****

PRICE GOUGHING AND PROPERTY RIGHTS

Price-gouging law has reared its ugly head in the wake of the flooding in Texas. This has totally overshadowed the alleged price gouging that occurred during the eclipse.

The price of solar eclipse safety glasses was as low in the months before the eclipse, but rose to as much as $150 for the identical product on the day of the eclipse. And it turns out that prices for these glasses were higher along the direct path of the eclipse. Naturally, some eclipse glasses vendors were accused of price gouging because they demanded unreasonably high payments by exploiting unusual market conditions.

Hundreds of complaints of price gouging were received by the office of Texas attorney general Ken Paxton in the aftermath of Hurricane Harvey. There were "reports of up to $99 for a case of water, hotels that are tripling or quadrupling their prices and fuel at $4 to $10 a gallon." "These are things you can't do in Texas," Paxton said. "There are significant penalties if you price gouge in a crisis like this." Indeed there are. Price gougers "can be hit with a $20,000 fine per occurrence, or up to $250,000 if the victim is someone age 65 or older."

By now the whole world has seen the picture of the case of water at a Best Buy store in Texas with a price tag of $42.96. "This was clearly a mistake in a single store," Best Buy spokesman Shane Kitzman said in a statement. "We feel terrible about this because, as a company we are focused on helping, not hurting people affected by this terrible event. We are deeply sorry that we gave anyone even the momentary impression that we were trying to take advantage of the situation."

In this Internet age, there is one thing that always follows stories about price gouging: articles by free-market economists and commentators about the economics of price gouging. This is not one of those articles.

This does not mean that these articles are wrong. To the contrary, they are right and needed. Here are statements from three such articles:

Prices should rise during emergencies. Price changes save lives. That's because prices aren't just money—they are information. Price changes tell suppliers what their customers want most, maybe chainsaws more than blankets, water more than flashlights. (John Stossel)

So-called price gougers face all the same challenges as anyone else, having to forego whatever income they otherwise would have earned if not for their disaster-relief project, and face the risk of losing future income because they took off from their jobs or put their own regular businesses on hold. These losses and risks must be compensated, which is another reason they sell products at a premium price, in addition to supply/demand realities. (Tom Mullen)

Because each 'gouging' price paid for any item is paid voluntarily by a consumer spending his or her own money – and because that consumer cannot conveniently find that item elsewhere at a lower price – the consumer clearly doesn't deem the price to be too high. That is, while the consumer would, as always, prefer to pay a lower than a higher price, the consumer prefers to pay the high price and actually get the item than to save money by going without the item. (Donald Boudreaux)

The economics of price gouging is simple. Price gouging is simply charging market prices for goods that are in high demand and short supply. Natural disasters don't negate economic laws.

And then there is the economic calculation problem. At what level of price increase does it become price gouging? A 100 percent increase? A 50 percent increase? A 20 percent increase? What about a 10 percent increase? Why or why not? All goods or just "essential" goods? For what period of time? How intense does a storm have to be in order to trigger price gouging laws? For the government to try and calculate how much prices should be allowed to rise on certain goods before, during, and after a natural disaster is pure Soviet-style central planning. Price-gouging laws are contrary the free market, free enterprise, and freedom itself.

There is another problem with price-gouging laws, and one that is often overshadowed by the economic arguments against them: property rights.

If I own a bottle of water it is my property. It belongs to me. No one has a claim on it. If I want to pour it out in down the drain, then that is my business, and not the concern of government. If I want to give it away, then that is my business, and not the concern of government. If I want to sell it for a high price to a willing buyer, then that is my business, and not the concern of government. If I want to keep it in my refrigerator until the end of time, then that is my business, and not the concern of government.

These things are true of every bottle of water I own. These things are true whether or not I own a business that regularly sells water. These things are true whether or not someone is dying of thirst. These things are true in the middle of a hurricane. These things are true even if you wish they weren't.

Price-gouging laws grossly violate property rights.

None of this means that raising prices on essential goods in the midst of a natural disaster is always moral, just, and right. But that is a matter of conscience, religion, and ethics, not law.

*****

BAN THE PUBLIC LIBRARY

Not everyone has the time or the inclination to read all the books on the *New York Times* bestseller list. But even those who have both may not be able to—if they're trying to find their favorite title at their local public library.

Fifty Shades of Grey, the first installment of an erotic, sadomasochistic trilogy by British author E.L. James (Erika Leonard, a wife and mother of two), contains sexually explicit descriptions of the relationship between the young, innocent heroine, Anastasia Steele, and Christian

Grey, a 27-year-old rich businessman. The book, which has sold more than three million copies, is sitting atop every major bestseller list in the country. However, it is no longer sitting on the shelves in the Brevard County Public Library system.

Brevard County, located on the east coast of central Florida—the so-called Space Coast—includes the major cities of Melbourne, Palm Bay, Cocoa, Cocoa Beach, and Titusville.

"It's quite simple—it doesn't meet our selection criteria," said Cathy Schweinsberg, library services director, who added, "Nobody asked us to take it off the shelves. But we bought some copies before we realized what it was. We looked at it, because it's been called 'mommy porn' and 'soft porn.' We don't collect porn."

But as the *Palm Beach Post* reports, copies of the sexually explicit *Complete Kama Sutra* and the erotic novels *Fear of Flying* and *Lolita*, as well as *Lady Chatterley's Lover, Tropic of Cancer,* and *Fanny Hill*—books that were once banned in the United States—are available through branch libraries in the Brevard County Library system.

Schweinsberg's explanation for why those other books are on library shelves but not *Fifty Shades of Grey* is that "those other books were written years ago and became classics because of the quality of the writing." *Fifty Shades of Grey* "is not a classic."

But even more perplexing about the library system's removal of this particular title when it carries other erotic titles is that it comes two years after the county's library system introduced a parental "opt-out" system that can prevent juveniles from checking out adult-oriented movies. A software alert tells librarians if a "flagged" child tries to check out any R-rated movies.

"I think it's worked well for the patrons who do care and are watchful of their children," said Schweinsberg. "I can't tell you how many have used it, but they have that option."

Although it seems as though that system could easily be extended to adult-oriented books as well, keeping *Fifty Shades of Grey* out of the hands of juveniles was not the reason given for removing the book from library shelves. It was to keep the book out of the hands of adults.

The reason that some library patrons in Brevard County—and communities everywhere that have public libraries—are disturbed about the banning of certain books is that everyone in the county pays taxes to fund public libraries, while it is left to an individual or small group of individuals at the library to decide whether a particular book is too violent, racist, sexist, homophobic, obscene, bigoted, erotic, sadistic, blasphemous, or pornographic to be placed on library shelves.

Meanwhile, other library patrons are pleased when "questionable" material is removed from shelves or never placed there to begin with. Even Mark Twain's novels *The Adventures of Tom Sawyer* (1876) and The *Adventures of Huckleberry Finn* (1884) have been banned by several libraries over the years.

The solution is a simple one. Instead of banning books, ban the public library.

First of all, in this digital age of the Internet and Amazon's Kindle, where even bookstores and traditional book publishing are on the decline, it makes no sense for taxpayers to continue to fund public libraries for the benefit of the few in the community who use them.

Second, modern public libraries have turned into video stores and Internet cafes. But if the market can provide movies at the theater, streaming over television, and in video stores, and if the market can provide Internet service in homes, WiFi in businesses, and Internet cafes, then the market can provide books as well.

But wait a minute. The market already does provide books. One can purchase books directly from the publisher, from Internet sites such as Amazon or Laissez-Faire Books, from book clubs such as the History Book Club or the Conservative Book Club, and in brick and mortar bookstores such as Barnes & Noble (which also has a web presence) or at a locally owned independent bookstore.

The objection, of course, is that books at the public library don't have to be purchased; they can be freely borrowed and read. And therein lies the problem. Why is someone entitled to read books at the expense of someone else?

Third, and most importantly, it is not the purpose of government to provide public libraries. Libertarians consistently maintain that if we are to have a government, its role should be strictly limited to the protection of life, liberty, and property from the violence and fraud of others. Period. That is the only justifiable purpose of government.

Yet, governments all over the United States on every level generate electricity, collect garbage, run liquor stores, operate bus services, build sports venues, *and provide public libraries*.

But let me be perfectly clear, it is *public* libraries that should be banned, not libraries. In a free society, corporations, civic groups, religious organizations, political parties, and philanthropists are free to open libraries—catering to select groups or the general public—where books could be sold, rented, lent, or only read on the premises.

And as far as banning books is concerned, in a free society, every library would have the liberty of allowing or prohibiting from its shelves any book for any reason. Just as parents might ban certain books from their home, businesses might ban certain books from the workplace, and doctors' offices might ban certain books from waiting rooms, so *private* libraries would do the same and be perfectly justified in doing so no matter what books they included or excluded.

The solution to the problem of "questionable" material in public libraries, as is usually the case, is getting government out of the picture and letting freedom and the free market reign.

*****

SICK ECONOMICS

Second only to their salary, all employees love and depend on their fringe benefits.

Fringe benefits can take the form of paid time-off for breaks, vacations, jury duty, personal reasons, maternity leave, or illness. They can be in the form of discounted or fully paid insurance for health, life, or disability. Participation in a pension or retirement program is a valuable benefit, especially when one's employer does most of the contributing. Depending on the employer, fringe benefits can also include stock options, company child-care, a severance package, uniforms, meals, a company car, and employee discounts. Even taking unpaid time-off is a fringe benefit if one can return to work at will with no loss of seniority.

With the exception of the Family and Medical Leave Act of 1993, which requires large employers to provide unpaid, job-protected leave for employees to take care of a new child or sick family member, the federal government does not concern itself with employee fringe benefits.

According to the U.S. Department of Labor's "Handy Reference Guide to the Fair Labor Standards Act" (FLSA),

> While the FLSA does set basic minimum wage and overtime pay standards and regulates the employment of minors, there are a number of employment practices which the FLSA does not regulate. For example, the FLSA does not require:
>
> 1. vacation, holiday, severance, or sick pay;
> 2. meal or rest periods, holidays off, or vacations;
> 3. premium pay for weekend or holiday work;
> 4. pay raises or fringe benefits; or
> 5. a discharge notice, reason for discharge, or immediate payment of final wages to terminated employees.

Then it says about the practices the FLSA doesn't require, "The above matters are for agreement between the employer and the employees or their authorized representatives."

Such is not the case, however, when it comes to state and local governments.

In my county in Florida, Orange County, there is circulating a petition to place on the November ballot an Earned Sick Time ordinance titled "A Proposal to Guarantee Earned Sick Time for Employees of Businesses in Orange County." The ballot summary reads,

Shall Orange County adopt an ordinance providing that employees of businesses in Orange County earn up to 56 hours of sick time each year unless the business provides more—with pay required only in businesses with 15 or more employees as defined—to seek medical care, recover from illness/injury, care for a family member as defined, or use when necessary during a public health emergency, with such ordinance enforceable in court?

The sponsor of this initiative petition is Citizens for a Greater Orange County, a coalition of progressive groups that is paying three shifts of workers to gather signatures by canvassing neighborhoods with lists of registered voters, by standing in front of shopping centers and bus stops, and by visiting community events and churches.

The petition drive, which was begun in May, needs 43,605 signatures from registered voters—the total of 7 percent of the registered voters in each of the county's six districts. Although county code gives petition drives a 180-day deadline, time is already running out for the Earned Sick Time petition.

Once the supervisor of elections verifies and reports to the Orange County Board of Commissioners that the requisite number of names has been submitted, the Board must then give notice and hold, within 30 days, a public hearing on the petition and vote on it. If it doesn't pass, a referendum would be held at the next election, which would be the upcoming election in November. The problem is that the ballots for the November election must be sent to the printer this month. No citizen initiative has ever made it on the ballot in Orange County.

Groups making up the coalition in support of the petition include Organize Now, Mi Familia Vota, Equality Florida, the NAACP, and the Federation of Congregations United to Serve. Liberal activists are hoping a sick-pay initiative on the November ballot will bring swing voters to the polls to vote for Democrats.

Opposed to the petition are the Florida Restaurant and Lodging Association, the Florida Retail Federation, the Employment Policies Institute, and the Central Florida Partnership.

Also opposing the measure is Orange County's Republican mayor,

Teresa Jacobs, who termed the sick-leave measure "well-intentioned" but "shortsighted," and said it would have "unintended negative consequences" at a time when the economy is still in tough shape. "I am a strong believer in a free market and businesses being able" to make this kind of decision, Jacobs said.

A coalition of Orange County business groups including the Greater Orlando Chamber of Commerce, the Central Florida Hotel and Lodging Association, and the Home Builders Association of Metro Orlando recently filed a lawsuit challenging a sick-time ballot initiative and asking the Orange Circuit Court for an injunction to stop it, contending that the ballot language is misleading.

Under the proposed sick-time ordinance, all businesses with 15 or more employees "shall provide for accrual of a minimum of one hour of paid sick time for every 37 hours worked by an employee," but not "more than 56 hours of paid sick time in a calendar year." The accrual of sick-time begins "at the commencement of employment." Employees "shall be entitled to use accrued paid sick time beginning on the 90th calendar day following commencement of their employment." Unused sick-time will carry over to the following year, but no more than 56 hours can be taken in a year. Employees who separate from their employer but are rehired within six months are entitled to "previously accrued paid sick time that had not been used." Covered employees include full-time, part-time, and temporary workers. Family members who can be cared for include domestic partners, grandparents and grandchildren, and "a designating person or support person as defined in Orange County Code."

Such an ordinance is said to be needed because

• many workers in the county will need limited time off from work each year to take care of the health needs of themselves or their families;
• when workers lack paid sick time, they risk losing income and jeopardizing their jobs, contributing to their financial insecurity;
• providing workers time off to attend to their own and their family's health care will have a positive effect on the public health of the county; and
• providing sick time is good for businesses, resulting in reduced worker turnover and reducing the competitive disadvantage that many employers face when they choose to provide sick time to their workers.

When reading the fine print that makes up the petition's 14 sections, it is clear that the proposed ordinance could function merely as a mandate for a seven-day vacation for workers in Orange County, courtesy of their employers.

That is because it is only "for sick time of more than 3 consecutive days" that "an employee may be required to provide reasonable documentation that the sick time has been used" for a covered purpose. Employers may not require that documentation signed by a health-care professional "explain the nature of the illness," and "disclosure of details of an employee's or an employee's family member's medical condition shall not be required as a condition of providing sick time." Moreover, "All persons are prohibited from retaliating or threatening retaliation against employees who request or use sick time." And "each employee has the right to bring a civil action if sick time as required by this Chapter is denied or the employee is retaliated against for requesting or taking sick time."

And even though the paid sick-leave part of the proposed ordinance doesn't apply to businesses with fewer than 15 employees, workers in businesses not entitled to paid sick-time are allowed to take, without threat of "retaliatory personnel action," up to 56 hours a year of sick-time without compensation. In other words, seven days off whenever they want them. And an agreement by a worker to waive his right to paid sick-leave "is void as against public policy."

It is not just paying the sick-leave that will cost employers if this ordinance is adopted. In section 7, "Records," it states that "employers shall maintain records documenting hours worked by employees and sick time taken by employees and shall retain such records for a period of five years."

But Orange County, Florida, is not alone. According to the National Partnership for Women & Families, a "nonprofit, nonpartisan advocacy group dedicated to promoting fairness in the workplace, access to quality health care and policies that help women and men meet the dual demands of work and family," paid-sick-day campaigns or legislation also exists in Arizona, California, Colorado, Hawaii, Illinois, Iowa, Maine, Massachusetts, Michigan, Minnesota, New Jersey, New York, North Carolina, Pennsylvania, Vermont, Washington, Wisconsin, and in the cities of Miami, New York, and Portland.

Mandates for paid sick-days are already in force in Connecticut; Washington, D.C.; Philadelphia; San Francisco; and Seattle. Before such legislation could be implemented in the city of Milwaukee, the Wisconsin state legislature passed a bill that prohibited local authorities from enacting such measures.

All such legislation is based on sick economics.

Mandates that force businesses to provide paid sick-leave or any other fringe benefit are all based on the anti-capitalistic notion that businesses are evil and are always looking for ways to exploit their workers. But if that is true then why do so many companies provide their employees with paid sick-leave and other fringe benefits without the government's mandating that they do so? The theory of the exploitation of labor is the foundation of Marxism and has no place in a capitalist society. Mandatory sick-leave ordinances are also predicated on the erroneous ideas that businesses, including restaurants and hotels, don't care if employees come to work sick and are just waiting to fire any employee who requests time-off because he or a family member is ill.

Smart businessmen won't take sick-leave mandates lying down. In the case of the proposed Orange County ordinance, small businesses can make sure they don't hire more than 14 people. Larger businesses that offer paid vacation-time can cut it by seven days to make up for the seven days of paid sick-leave that all of their employees would undoubtedly take under the earned-sick-time ordinance. It is economically ignorant to think that businesses should be required to provide paid sick-leave because they can "afford it." And it is economically foolish to think that businesses required to provide paid sick-leave will not look for ways to offset the cost of doing so.

Regardless of the reasons given by groups who support sick-pay initiatives and lawmakers who enact such legislation, and irrespective of the details of such initiatives, in the end they are all the same in that they are government mandates to employers to provide certain benefits to their employees—just like the mandate in the federal government's Affordable Care Act that business with 50 or more employees must provide health insurance to their employees or pay a fine. Government employment mandates are anathema to the ideals of limited government, free markets, freedom of contract, and a free society.

Backers of mandatory paid-sick-leave legislation always cite "the public health" as one of the justifications for government intervention in the workplace. But if public health is really the issue, then why not penalize or criminalize the act of coming to work while sick?

Here we also see the hypocrisy and sick economics of conservatives who oppose sick-leave and other fringe-benefit government mandates yet at the same time see no problem with the government-mandated minimum wage and overtime-pay requirements of the Fair Labor Standards Act. Every aspect of employment should be based on voluntary agreements between employers and employees.

Like laws establishing a minimum wage, laws mandating that businesses provide paid sick-leave mean that the government must be able to determine the "correct" or "just" number of hours of sick-leave per hours worked that employees should accrue. But that's not all. The omnipotent state must also determine all of the related smaller details, such as how much sick-leave can be taken each year, how much sick-leave should carry over to the next year, how many days of sick-leave can be taken without a doctor's note, what the valid reasons for sick-leave are, how soon after employment begins sick-leave should begin to accrue, how long an employee must work before he can use his accrued sick-leave, and how unused sick-leave should be accounted for upon retirement or severance from the company. All of that, of course, entails Soviet-style central planning.

Mandatory sick-leave ordinances likewise advance the notion that government is responsible for our well-being and prosperity, violate freedom of contract, and imply that there is a right to paid sick-leave.

If government can mandate that employers pay at least a minimum wage, pay overtime for more than 40 hours worked in a week, provide health insurance, comply with the Family and Medical Leave Act, and offer paid sick-leave, then it can also mandate that employers provide paid vacations, life insurance, a pension plan, child care, and any other fringe benefit it dictates. That is fascism.

Oh, and never look to Republicans to reverse the bad policies of Democrats. It has been almost 20 years since the Family and Medical mocrats. It has been almost 20 years since the Family and Medical Leave Act was passed. I am still waiting for the Republicans to repeal it.

*****

DON'T CALL FOR AN AMBULANCE

The two recent high-profile and highly deadly shootings in the United States have been the occasion of much dialogue about "gun control."

Liberals, predictably, have generally called for more and stricter gun-control laws. Conservatives, to their credit, have generally argued to the contrary (even though they have accepted decades of various federal gun-control laws that make a mockery of the Second Amendment).

But gun control is not the only issue related to the shootings that has come up. After any shooting—whether there are multiple victims or just one—there is one thing that is needed even more than the police: an ambulance.

After the shooting on a Sunday morning earlier this month at a Sikh temple in Oak Creek, Wisconsin, more than 60 paramedics and EMTs rushed to the scene in 22 fire trucks and ambulances.

But such was not the case after the midnight shooting last month at a theater in Aurora, Colorado, where some ambulances remained idle while police pleaded with dispatchers for more ambulances to come to the theater.

According to an account of events in the *San Francisco Examiner*, it took dispatchers more than 20 minutes into the crisis to ask the Cunningham Fire Protection District and other nearby agencies to send extra ambulances to the site of the shooting:

> On the police radio transmissions, officers said they lacked sufficient medical support for about 30 minutes after the 911 calls came flooding in around 12:39 a.m. and that medical teams didn't report getting inside the theater for about 24 minutes.

> Before the aid call went out to the other agencies, officers repeatedly implored dispatchers for more medical support and bemoaned the resources they had at their disposal. At one point, they also asked for an accounting of what resources were on the way. "To be honest with you, sir, I don't know an exact count of ambulances," one person said. They added that two more ambulances were getting dispatched then.

> About 15 minutes in, one officer asked whether he had permission to take victims with his car. "I have a whole bunch of people shot out here and no rescue," he said in a hurried tone. The response came immediately: "Yes, load them up, get them in cars and get them out of here."

At 18 and 20 minutes in, police coordinators repeated their calls for more medical assistance. At 27 minutes, an officer was still reporting that they were loading patients into the back of patrol cars. "Any ambos we could get would be nice," he said.

Thirty minutes into the chaos, an on-scene commander made a final, exasperated plea. He asked about Cunningham's resources and [about] another private company in the area—AMR.

"Anybody else that's in the area that we can contact?" he asked. "Maybe Cunningham? Somebody that we can get a hold of? AMR? Anybody?"

The response came back from a woman's voice that sounded equally worn. "We're working on finding additional transport rigs to assist us with transporting from the scene," she said.

Scot Phelps, professor of disaster science at the Emergency Management Academy in New York, says the ambulance system in the United States is a public-policy disaster. He was recently interviewed by Robin Young on PRI's *Here and Now* ("Getting the 4-1-1 on 9-1-1 Emergency Response").

According to Phelps, much of the country depends on a patchwork system holding ambulance services together: privately owned ambulances, publicly owned ambulances, and, increasingly, paramedics who arrive on the scene in fire trucks instead of more-costly ambulances.

The result is that many cities have failing emergency-reponse systems. Philadelphia has so few ambulances that police end up transporting as many as a third of shooting victims to the hospital in their squad cars. An ambulance in Detroit broke down in the middle of a gun battle last New Year's Eve.

"The problem is that the resources are not going to the ambulance system, whether it's a fire department system or a private system," Phelps said. "I'm not going to say we have too many fire trucks, but we certainly don't have enough ambulances, no matter who's operating the system." He argued that poor funding was the key factor that contributed to the low number of ambulances in some communities. "The fact that the private ambulance company has to rely to a large extent on billing Medicare and Medicaid means they're not going to staff a dozen ambulances just to have them standing by," Phelps said. He also believes ambulances should be reimbursed for the real cost of care they provide, instead of just for transporting a patient to the hospital.

Things obviously haven't changed since *USA Today* did a three-part story in 2005 on the state of emergency medical systems in the United States. Its 18-month investigation found fragmented, inconsistent, slow emergency medical systems in most of the nation's 50 largest cities; delays in providing emergency care caused by infighting and turf wars between fire departments and ambulance services; issues with firefighters' and paramedics' unions; and needless deaths because some cities fail to make basic, often inexpensive changes in the way they deploy ambulances, paramedics, and fire trucks.

The provision of ambulance services is another example of how government intervention at all levels has so permeated the health-care system in the United States.

Most people never think about having to be transported in an ambulance after an accident, a heart attack, or a shooting incident like the ones that recently occurred in Colorado and Wisconsin. Other than places such as Washington D.C., which estimates it saves only 4 percent of cardiac-arrest victims, Americans generally expect an ambulance to show up and take them to the hospital after they call for one or someone sees their plight and calls 911.

I suppose that few Americans have ever pondered who should provide ambulance services and who should pay for them.

No one would question the idea that anyone who makes a trip to an airport, a store, a movie theater, a theme park, or even a doctor's office should drive himself, persuade someone else to voluntarily transport him, or pay a friend, neighbor, or cabbie for the ride.

But let someone have a heart attack or gunshot wound, be unconscious or in agonizing pain, or be bleeding profusely or severely burned and that supposedly changes everything. Now the government is looked upon to provide emergency services to be paid for by the taxpayers.

But is it not true that it is not the fault of the person who has a heart attack, is shot, is unconscious, is in agonizing pain, is bleeding, or is burned that he needs an ambulance?

Yes, but that doesn't make it the fault of the taxpayers.

And from the fact that the current patchwork ambulance system is, in the words of Scot Phelps, "a public-policy disaster," it doesn't follow that the answer is more government intervention or control.

In a purely free-market system, private companies would compete for business by getting to sick customers promptly, getting them safely to the hospital, and providing them necessary medical care on the way. They would have every incentive to avoid delays, avoid accidents, and avoid poor-quality treatment.

Even with a real free market for ambulance services, there would certainly also exist voluntary ambulance services much like volunteer fire departments—just as they exist now. Just to give one example, the Hillsdale Volunteer Ambulance Service, which has been serving Hillsdale, New Jersey, residents since 1954, "provides emergency medical response to Hillsdale residents and surrounding communities on a mutual aid basis 24 hours a day, 365 days a year. In the last 12 months we have responded to well over 1,000 calls. We are always here for you, and we never charge for our services."

And there is no reason to think that a private ambulance service would require payment up front before they transported a dying man to the hospital. Emergency-room physicians want to make a living as much as you and I, but they don't let trauma victims die on a stretcher while they try to extort cash out of their grieving relatives. Ambulance services should simply be billed like any other medical procedure and be paid for out of pocket, through health insurance, or by charitable organizations that help the poor with medical expenses.

But privatizing all ambulance services is not enough. All aspects of medical care should be deregulated and released from government control. That includes medical licensing, medical devices, organ donations, medical insurance, medical records, medical research, clinical trials, hospital admissions, drugs, vaccinations, and medical schools.

And not only should Medicare and Medicaid, i.e., the taxpayers, not pay for ambulance services, those programs should not even exist in the first place.

Should, God forbid, you have an accident, a heart attack, or be involved in an "incident," I hope an ambulance arrives quickly to take you to the hospital. But don't call for an ambulance if you are expecting someone else to be forced to pay for it.

*****

GOVERNMENT IMPOSSIBLE

Restaurant: Impossible is a popular show on the Food Network. I don't watch much television. Not only do I have more writing projects in the works than I have time for, but the political shows on CNN, MSNBC, and Fox that I should be watching because I write about politics make me either mad or nauseated, and sometimes both. But I must confess that I enjoy taking a break from writing to watch *Restaurant: Impossible.*

In each episode of *Restaurant: Impossible*, Chef Robert Irvine faces the daunting task of "saving" a failing restaurant from impending failure—in just two days and with only $10,000.

On the first day, he conducts a thorough assessment of the restaurant. He observes the chefs, samples the food (and usually spits it out), talks to the owner and the employees, analyzes the menu, critiques the décor, inspects the kitchen, checks the freezer inventory, and consults with his design team on changes to be made to the restaurant's flooring, decorations, light fixtures, wall colors, tables, seating, and bar. Then everything is taken out of the restaurant—some of it after Chef Irvine takes a sledgehammer to it.

After the design team and its workers spend all night ripping up carpet, sanding, painting, building, and repairing and replacing various items, Irvine checks on their progress at the beginning of the second day. He revises the menu, retrains the staff, instructs the chefs, reorganizes the kitchen, gives further instruction to his design team, and eventually overcomes all the drama and the unforeseen obstacles that make the show interesting to watch. After some quick marketing in the local community, the restaurant has a grand re-opening in the evening. Tears flow when the owner sees the "new" restaurant spring from what looked impossible to fix.

For me, there is one part of the show that brings forth another emotion. That is when Irvine inspects the restaurant's kitchen and almost throws up. I myself feel nauseated when I see the roaches (dead and alive); the dead rats; the insect and rodent droppings; the mold in the ice machine; the undated, unrefrigerated, or rotten food; the grease; and the filth. It seems as though in every other show Irvine states that this is the worst restaurant kitchen he has ever seen.

Without fail, every time my wife and I are watching together and see a disgusting restaurant kitchen we turn to each other and say, "Where are the health inspectors?"

Just as the federal government has its agricultural inspectors, so every state, county, and city in the United States has health inspectors who make periodic inspections of restaurants. So how could any health inspector who had at least one good eye miss what seemed so obvious? Don't we rely on those inspections to keep restaurants clean and sanitary and to keep us from getting sick?

My state of Florida has a Department of Business and Professional Regulation. One of its many agencies is the Division of Hotels and Restaurants. It is responsible for licensing, inspecting, and regulating public-lodging and food-service establishments in Florida under Chapter 509 of the Florida Statutes. Its mission is to "protect the health and safety of the public by providing the industry with quality inspections and fair regulation." It also licenses and regulates elevators and escalators. Each of Florida's 67 counties is assigned to one of seven Bureau of Sanitation and Safety Inspections district offices.

According to its annual report, the Division of Hotels and Restaurants

• Was authorized 296 positions to provide program services and an operating budget of $19,249,720.
• Conducted a total of 162,953 public food-service and lodging-establishment inspections of the 85,148 licensed food-service and lodging establishments to ensure sanitation and safety standards.
• Performed more than 98 percent of the statutorily required inspections for public food-service and lodging establishments.
• Cited a total of 724,864 violations of sanitary standards in public food-service and lodging establishments.
• Logged 5,649 consumer complaints.

• Assessed $2,323,110 in fines and collected $2,101,251.

The Bureau of Sanitation and Safety Inspections is authorized to assess fines up to $1,000 per violation and to suspend or revoke an operator's license. In addition to routine safety and sanitation inspections, the bureau performs:

• Opening inspections for new establishments and changes of ownership.
• "Call-back" inspections on establishments cited for critical violations with a specified time period to verify the correction of deficiencies.
• Food-service inspections for alcoholic-beverage license applicants.
• Complaint investigations.
• Foodborne-illness investigations in coordination with the Florida Department of Health.

The Division of Hotels and Restaurants takes credit for the significant reduction in foodborne illness in Florida over the past 15 years: "Continued important reductions in foodborne illnesses indicate that Division of Hotels and Restaurants [sic] aggressive attention to science based policies and effective enforcement strategies is achieving positive results and improving public health and safety." "Protecting the public and preventing foodborne illness" is said to be "the driving force behind the division's food safety program."

There are a number of persistent and relentless myths concerning the importance of government health inspections, as opposed to leaving restaurant inspections up to the free market.

The first myth is that the federal government should have something to do with food safety. Although the federal government does not inspect restaurants, the annual report of the Florida Division of Hotels and Restaurants mentions that the agency participates in the U.S. Food and Drug Administration's voluntary "National Retail Food Regulatory Program Standards." It refers to "the FDA Food Code." It claims that the agency has "long been recognized by the Food and Drug Administration as a national leader in food safety." But since when does the U.S. Constitution authorize the federal government to have an FDA in the first place? The federal government has no authority to issue nutrition guidelines, make food pyramids, conduct agricultural research, promote or demonize certain foods, monitor school lunches, ban unpasteurized dairy products, regulate food production and labeling, stamp out obesity, or mandate that state governments meet certain food-safety requirements.

The second myth is that government licensing, regulation, and inspections are in the public interest and for the public good. Tell that to Julie Murphy of Portland, Oregon. The seven-year-old girl's lemonade stand was shut down because she had failed to obtain a $120 temporary restaurant license. Tell it to Diego Bartolome of Sacramento, California. The ten-year-old boy co-founded a salsa company that won him grocery-store accounts, a profile in the newspaper, and an appearance on television. That is, until an inspector from the state Department of Public Health noticed in a TV segment that the boy's salsa wasn't labeled properly and had possible temperature-control issues. The food police also forced the boy to get a $350 permit. Tell it to Bobby and Amanda Herring of Houston, Texas. The couple spent a year feeding the homeless with food that had been donated from area businesses and prepared in various kitchens by volunteers—until they were shut down by the city. "Anyone serving food for public consumption, whether for the homeless or for sale, must have a permit," said Kathy Barton, a spokeswoman for the Health and Human Services Department. To get the permit, food must be prepared in a certified kitchen by a certified food manager. And then there is the war on raw milk that is taking place in some states.

The third myth is that restaurants are clean and sanitary only because of government inspections. I suppose that is why the Florida Bureau of Sanitation and Safety Inspections "cited a total of 724,864 violations of sanitary standards in public food service and lodging establishments"? Oh, but without periodic government inspections there would be many more violations. That presupposes that absent government inspections every restaurant in the United States would have a disgusting kitchen like the failing restaurants on *Restaurant: Impossible*. It presupposes that restaurant customers would continue to patronize filthy and unsanitary restaurants. I beg to differ. The main reason that restaurants try to stay clean and sanitary and not make their customers sick is to keep their bills paid, their reputation intact, and their doors open so they don't become a candidate for *Restaurant: Impossible*. They not only want their customers to keep coming back; they also want to attract new customers. Proponents of the necessity of government health inspections would have us believe that it is just the risk of a few unannounced health inspections a year that stands between a good meal and getting food poisoning.

The fourth myth is that restaurants would never be inspected if government agencies were not required by statute to perform the inspections. Those who think this way must not be familiar with Underwriters Laboratories, or think it is an agency of the federal government. Underwriters Laboratories tests for safety thousands of products we use in our homes every day. No company is required to submit its products for testing, but look at the back of your computer monitor or the bottom of your toaster and you will see the symbol "UL" with a circle around it. Imagine what would happen to a restaurant if it became known that it refused to allow inspections. If the government doesn't oversee some occupation, some practice, some product, or some industry it doesn't follow that no one else will.

The fifth myth is that only government inspectors can do unbiased inspections. If it were left up to each restaurant to hire its own inspector, so it might be said, restaurant owners could just hire their friends or cronies to inspect their restaurants and give them high ratings. Another objection might be that private restaurant inspectors could take bribes from restaurant owners to provide favorable inspection reports or less-than-favorable reports on a restaurant's competitors. Or inspectors could simply give a restaurant a poor report because they were biased against it. But why is it that government inspectors are seen as so pure and so altruistic that they would never do any of those things? And why is it that people think no government inspector would ever say "good enough for government work" and fail to do a proper inspection of a restaurant?

The sixth myth is that restaurant inspections would never work if just left up to the free market. To the contrary, there is no telling how many restaurant-inspection services would exist on the free market, just like the home-inspection services that are in business today. There are already in existence websites and guides that relate to the quality of the food and service at restaurants. As it is now, there is no incentive for anything other than government health inspections. With a free market, there would undoubtedly also exist organizations to monitor health-inspection services, much like an accrediting agency.

The issue of government inspectors versus market inspectors comes down to the proper role of government—at all levels. Because the federal government is so monstrous, so corrupt, and so tyrannical, discussion of the appropriate nature and function of state and local governments often gets overshadowed by the ever-encroaching federal leviathan. But merely being in a state constitution doesn't make something right or even a good thing.

As is apparent from the condition of the restaurants on Restaurant: Impossible, it is impossible for government to keep make sure every restaurant is clean and sanitary and to make sure that everyone's meal at a restaurant is safe to eat. It is also impossible for government to improve on the free market.

*****

TAXI TYRANNY

One of the most prevalent and persistent myths about the American economy is that it is based on the free market, or laissez-faire capitalism. True, when compared with much of the rest of the world, the United States appears to have a *relatively* free economy. The truth, however, is that in some sectors of the American economy, government intervention is actually so substantial that it can be almost impossible to start and maintain a business.

In the 2012 edition of the *Index of Economic Freedom*, an annual report published by the Heritage Foundation and the Wall Street Journal that analyzes economic-policy developments in 184 countries, the United States is ranked tenth, behind Hong Kong, Singapore, Australia, New Zealand, Switzerland, Canada, Chile, Mauritius, and Ireland. Dead last among countries that are ranked is North Korea. The index grades and ranks countries on the basis of ten measures of economic freedom that evaluate the rule of law, the intrusiveness of government, regulatory efficiency, and the openness of markets. Although the scores of 75 economies improved, 90 countries lost economic freedom. The United States has been in the top ten since the first edition of the Index was published in 1995.

In the World Bank's 2012 edition of *Doing Business*, an annual report investigating the business climate in 183 countries that presents quantitative indicators on business regulation and the protection of property rights, the United States is ranked fourth, as it was last year, surpassed only by Singapore, Hong Kong, and New Zealand. Coming in last was the African nation of Chad. Covered in the study are regulations affecting 11 areas of the life of a business: starting a business, dealing with construction permits, getting electricity, registering property, getting credit, protecting investors, paying taxes, trading across borders, enforcing contracts, resolving insolvency, and employing workers. Many countries have made significant progress in streamlining the process of starting a business. For example, in South Korea, entrepreneurs starting a company in the past had to manually fill out more than 30 forms and visit six different agencies. Now they enter information once into an online system that automatically distributes it. Nevertheless, in some countries it can still take three months to start a business.

Tenth place out of 184 in economic freedom and fourth place out of 183 in business climate makes the United States, on paper, look like a free-enterprise paradise. Just don't talk about how economically free and business-friendly the United States is to those wanting to start a taxi service.

Licensing

In the United States it is almost impossible. Once in business, you are subject to so much government regulation that you don't have the economic freedom to set your own prices.

And don't think about trying to get around the law. Local governments don't think too highly of unauthorized taxi services—and neither do government-licensed taxi companies.

In Miami Gardens, Florida, a 78-year-old man was given two citations and his vehicle was impounded by the Miami-Dade County's Consumer Services Department after being entrapped by an undercover sting operation targeting people providing illegal taxi services. The man thought he was just helping a woman in need to get home from the grocery store; he said he never even discussed money until the woman insisted on it.

In Portland, Oregon, regulators waged an aggressive crackdown on car services known as livery drivers, independent drivers with a single car or limo. The city imposed a minimum fare of $50, even if a client is just going a few blocks in the downtown area. Livery vehicles must charge a minimum rate 35 percent higher than that charged by competing taxi companies for rides outside of the city. Livery drivers cannot park in front of hotels. And reservations for livery services must be placed at least an hour in advance of customer pickup. Two livery companies that offered a Groupon promotion for one-time limo or sedan rides for $32 were forced to cancel the promotion, refund the money collected, and pay a $500 fine for advertising services under the minimum fare. A Portland city official acknowledged to the Huffington Post that "the only real purpose of the regulations is to target small and independent businesses, while protecting the city's taxi monopolies."

In Houston, Texas, the drivers of a transport company using three electric vehicles and picking up passengers who tip rather than pay a metered fare were ticketed numerous times for offenses such as having no taxicab permit, no taxicab driver's license, and no fire extinguisher. Of course it was not just city officials who were concerned about this business. The Houston Yellow Cab Company complained to the city about the competing firm as well.

Licensed cab companies don't want to see new companies receive licenses. In Minneapolis, Minnesota, the city instituted reforms to raise the number of licensed taxis from 343, the limit in effect for years. The Minneapolis Taxicab Owners Association promptly sued the city, arguing that there was no demand for more taxis, that additional taxis would create more traffic congestion, and—the real reason—that a freer taxi market would hurt the resale value of taxi licenses, which could be sold for thousands of dollars. In a rare victory for freedom, the association lost.

Other cities don't care much for new cab companies either. Like many large cities, New York issues taxi medallions, an emblem of registration that artificially restricts the supply of taxis. The result is a textbook case of a government-created monopoly.

The natural result is the tendency toward higher prices and lower-quality service. In 2008 the New York City Taxi and Limousine Commission determined that the minimum bid price for each of the 43 available lots of two Minifleet (Corporate) Accessible Medallions to be auctioned off would be $700,000. One Individual Accessible Medallion was also made available for a minimum bid price of $189,000, and two Individual Alternative-Fuel Medallions went for $300,000. Because the medallions can be bought and sold, there is a profitable secondary market for them. In 2011 two New York taxi medallions sold for more than $1 million apiece, the highest recorded sale price since the medallion system began. These systems discriminate against anyone who is seeking to get into the taxi business but who lacks the necessary tens or in some cases hundreds of thousands of dollars.

Some cities even regulate the type of cab one can drive and how fares are collected.

The mayor of New York City has announced that the Nissan NV200 minivan will become the official taxi vehicle of the city beginning in 2013. All other models will be phased out over the following five years.

In Washington, D.C., cab drivers went on strike in 2008 to protest the mayor's decision to require that they use meters (as in other big cities) rather than a fare-zone system. The point here is not the superiority of one system over another but that it is government telling taxi companies how they must collect their fares.

I know of no major city in the United States that doesn't regulate taxi fares.

Micromanagement

Taxi companies begin and maintain their existence only at the whim of local governments. Consider Pensacola, Florida, where I lived for many years and whose city code for taxis I am familiar with.

No one is free to start a taxi business in Pensacola without the permission of the mayor:

> No taxicab vehicle permit shall be granted until the person applying for such permit has secured from the mayor that the public convenience and necessity warrants the operation of the additional taxicab or taxicabs for which taxicab vehicle permit is sought.

The cost of the permit is $50 annually, expiring on September 30. No company permits are granted "for operating less than five (5) vehicles." No company permits "may be sold, assigned, mortgaged, or otherwise transferred without the written consent of the mayor."

A vehicle permit must also be obtained for each taxicab used. However, "no taxicab vehicle permit shall be issued at any time to any person who has not attained the age of twenty-one (21) years" and "who is not a person of good moral character." Permits are $15 per vehicle per year. Each vehicle used as a taxi must be "thoroughly examined and inspected by the mayor and found to comply with such reasonable rules and regulations as may be prescribed by the mayor." Vehicles must then be inspected annually—after owners pay a fee of $10. The lettering on the side of each taxicab must be of a certain size and content.

Each taxi driver must obtain a license from the city. But first, the driver must be 21, pay a $10 fee, be photographed and fingerprinted, reveal much personal information, provide certificates of good character from three people, undergo a background investigation, already have a class "E" state license, and be approved by the chief of police and the mayor. Annual renewals are $6. Once on the job, drivers must "maintain a clean, neat, well-groomed appearance." Prohibited are T-shirts, tank tops, sandals, flip-flops, cut-offs, and short shorts.

Conducting business is highly regulated. The taxi driver's "daily manifest" must be "approved by the mayor." Drivers can't "solicit passengers for a taxicab except when standing immediately adjacent to the curb side thereof." Drivers can't be absent from their cabs for more than ten consecutive minutes. Drivers are prohibited from cruising "in search of passengers except in such areas and at such time as shall be designated by the Pensacola Police Department." Drivers can't "solicit business for any hotel, or … attempt to divert patronage from one hotel to another." No taxicab driver can "refuse or neglect to convey any orderly person or persons, upon request."

Rates are fixed by the city of Pensacola. No owner or operator of a taxi can "charge a greater or lesser sum for the use of a taxicab than in accordance with the following rates":

(1) Mileage rates. Two dollars ($2.00) for the first one-ninth (1/9) mile or fraction thereof; twenty-five cents ($0.25) for each additional one-ninth mile or fraction thereof; charge for additional passengers over the age of thirteen (13) years, fifty cents ($0.50) each;

(2) Waiting time. Eighteen dollars ($18.00) per hour;

(3) Airport trips—Minimum fare. Pickups from the airport, eleven dollars ($11.00) minimum per trip (limited to taxicab companies with valid permits to serve the airport). Fares over eleven dollars ($11.00) shall be calculated based upon the meter rate commencing at the airport pickup point.

No flat rates may be charged for any cab ride that starts within the city limits.

Consider for a moment what other industries would look like if they were as controlled by governments as taxi services are. Take, for example, the oranges that are grown all over central and south Florida. If the city and county governments in Florida's orange-growing regions forbade potential growers from planting orange trees on their property, made growers ask permission to plant a new orange tree, forced growers to pay a steep price for licenses to grow, pick, and sell oranges, and told growers the exact price to charge per orange, most people would think it was not only ludicrous, but totalitarian. But when governments treat taxi companies the same way, they get away with it in the name of "consumer protection."

Aside from the local governments that rake in millions of dollars from issuing taxi licenses and medallions and collecting taxes to fund consumer-services departments, regulatory agencies, and taxi and limousine commissions, there is only one group that benefits from the taxi tyranny that exists throughout the United States: existing taxi companies.

Whether it is driving taxis or selling oranges, it is ultimately a freedom issue: freedom to start a business, freedom to compete with existing businesses, freedom to hire workers of one's choosing, freedom to use the equipment of one's choosing, freedom to set prices and policies, and freedom from government laws that are anti–free enterprise, anti–free market, and anti-freedom.

*****

LEAVE SHOULD BE LEFT TO THE MARKET

Democrats, liberals, progressives, and the White House Summit on Working Families don't think the Family and Medical Leave Act goes far enough.

The Family and Medical Leave Act (FMLA) was passed in 1993 by the 103rd Congress—the only Congress with a Democratic majority that Bill Clinton had. The legislation (H.R.1) did, however, have some Republican support, including that from Sen. John McCain.

According to the U.S. Department of Labor, the FMLA "entitles eligible employees of covered employers to take unpaid, job-protected leave for specified family and medical reasons with continuation of group health insurance coverage under the same terms and conditions as if the employee had not taken leave." Covered employers include private companies with fifty or more employees and government agencies and public schools regardless of the number of employees.

Eligible employees are entitled to twelve workweeks of leave in a twelve-month period for:

• the birth of a child and to care for the newborn child within one year of birth;
• the placement with the employee of a child for adoption or foster care and to care for the newly placed child within one year of placement;
• to care for the employee's spouse, child, or parent who has a serious health condition;
• a serious health condition that makes the employee unable to perform the essential functions of his or her job;
• any qualifying exigency arising out of the fact that the employee's spouse, son, daughter, or parent is a covered military member on "covered active duty."

The leave is increased to twenty-six workweeks if necessary to care for a family member who is in the military and has a serious injury or illness. In light of the recent U.S. Supreme Court decision in the case of *United States v. Windsor*, which found unconstitutional Section 3 of the Defense of Marriage Act, the Labor Department's Wage and Hour Division has proposed to revise the definition of "spouse" in the FMLA to include "eligible employees in legal same-sex marriages."

The key thing to note about the FMLA is that the leave is unpaid.

Convened on June 23 in Washington, D.C., the White House Summit on Working Families was hosted jointly by the Center for American Progress (a progressive think tank), the U.S. Department of Labor, and the White House Council on Women and Girls. The summit convened "businesses, economists, labor leaders, legislators, advocates, the media, and ordinary citizens for a discussion on issues facing the entire spectrum of working families—from low-wage workers to corporate executives; from young parents to baby boomers caring for their own aging parents."

In addition to the subjects of the minimum wage, equal pay, job quality, job access, workplace flexibility, child care, and workplace discrimination, one of the topics addressed at the summit was paid leave:

> Many workers are unable to take the time they need to care for their families or themselves because they lack any form of paid time off. Strategies to provide different forms of paid leave—paid family and medical leave or paid sick days—can help both women and men, particularly those in low-wage jobs, take time off when necessary without leaving their jobs and putting their economic stability at risk.

The subject of paid leave was brought up by Barack Obama in a speech he delivered at the summit:

> The same goes with paid family leave. A lot of jobs do not offer it. So when a new baby arrives or an aging parent gets sick, workers have to make painful decisions about whether they can afford to be there when their families need them the most. Many women can't even get a paid day off to give birth. Now, that's a pretty low bar. You would think—that we should be able to take care of.

> For many hourly workers, taking just a few days off can mean losing their job. And even though unpaid family leave is available, if you can't pay the bills already the idea of taking a couple days off unpaid may mean you can't make the mortgage payment or the rent payment at the end of the month.

For several years now, Democrats, liberals, and progressives have been calling for the unpaid leave in the FMLA to be changed to paid leave. Since the passage of the FMLA, some states have enacted similar statutes that broaden its scope, including mandating that employers offer paid maternity and paternity leave. But according to the Labor Department's Bureau of Labor Statistics, only about 13 percent of full-time workers receive paid family leave.

Victoria Budson, a speaker at the summit who runs the Women and Public Policy Program at Harvard University, maintains that one of the dubious distinctions of the United States is that it is "the only industrialized nation in the world that has no mandatory paid leave." And, "You know, this is a real black eye for the United States," says Pamela Stone, a sociologist at Hunter College. Former House Speaker Rep. Nancy Pelosi (D-Calif.) recently wrote that California's mandatory paid family leave should be extended to the nation:

> Expanding paid family leave to all Americans is a central pillar of House Democrats' economic agenda for women and families.

> Paid leave is a keystone of an agenda built to empower all of America's women, along with raising the minimum wage, insisting on equal pay for equal work and providing affordable, quality child care.

"It's time to upgrade the Family and Medical Leave Act," says Nancy Kaufman, CEO of the National Council of Jewish Women. Like Nancy Pelosi, she is pushing the Family and Medical Insurance Leave Act, or FAMILY Act (H.R.3712), which was introduced in the U.S. House late last year. It mandates that employers provide qualified employees with a maximum of 12 weeks of paid leave at two-thirds of their salary. The FAMILY Act would be paid for by a 0.2 percent increase in both the employer and employee share of the FICA tax. The money would go into an independent trust fund within the Social Security Administration.

So, should family leave be paid or unpaid?

Democrats would generally say that family leave should be paid. They always oppose market solutions while favoring a paternalistic nanny state, government mandates, and government regulation of business. Republicans would generally say that family leave should be unpaid. However, that does not mean that they always favor market solutions and oppose a paternalistic nanny state, government mandates, or government regulation of business.

Although Republicans may say they are against government-mandated paid leave, they generally have no problem with government-mandated unpaid leave. They also generally don't have a problem with the Fair Labor Standards Act that instituted a minimum wage. But once it is accepted as a legitimate function of government to establish a minimum wage that employers must pay, no reasonable and logical argument can be made against the government's mandating that employers provide family leave or any other fringe benefit. Both the Family and Medical Leave Act and the Fair Labor Standards Act could have been repealed when the Republicans had a majority in the House and Senate for more than four years under the Republican president George W. Bush. That is, if the Republicans had any real philosophical objection to them.

Contrary to Democrats, Republicans, and most of their liberal and conservative cousins, libertarians say that the question of whether family leave *should* be paid or unpaid is one that has no answer. It is a question no different from asking whether Ford *should* offer Mustangs in lime green or whether Target *should* change the color of its logo from red to blue. The question of whether family leave *should* be paid or unpaid is one that only companies, businesses, and employers should be considering. Just like the questions of vacation pay, holiday pay, sick leave, jury-duty pay, paid time off, and any other fringe benefit.

What advocates of both paid and unpaid family leave are saying is that the federal government should be dictating the type and nature of fringe benefits that employers provide their employees.

But since when does the federal government have the authority to dictate those things? It is certainly an unconstitutional and illegitimate function of government to have anything to do with fringe benefits or employer-employee relations.

And what the governments of other countries do should have no bearing on U.S. government policies. After all, in some countries it is illegal for women to drive, it is illegal for anyone to be a homosexual, and blasphemy is punishable by death. Some countries have socialized medicine, and workweeks shorter than 40 hours, or are full-blown cradle-to-grave welfare states. Some countries have state-owned television and radio stations, speech restrictions, and press censorship.

To say that employers providing some form of family leave is a good and important thing for families is not saying anything. From the perspective of employees, of course it is. It is always good, from the perspective of employees, if they can be paid to not work or to stay home. Just like they think it is always good for them if they can be paid $50 an hour, have three months' paid vacation a year, and unlimited sick leave. But family leave, whether paid or unpaid, is not necessarily good for employers. Like any other fringe benefit they choose to offer, it comes with a price.

Leave should be left to the market.

To acquire and retain quality employees, most employers offer employees a variety of fringe benefits—vacation pay, sick leave, paid time off, holiday pay, jury-duty pay, child care, and discounts on food, merchandise, or services—none of which is mandated by the government. It should be no different with family leave. Whether an employer offers it, whether it is paid or unpaid, and what the length of it is, is a matter to be settled by agreement between the employer and employee.

There should be no government-mandated family leave any more than there should be any other government-mandated fringe benefits.

And of course, there should not be any White House Council on Women and Girls, Family and Medical Leave Act, Family and Medical Insurance Leave Act, Fair Labor Standards Act, Bureau of Labor Statistics, or even a Department of Labor in the first place.

*****

BUILD IT AND THEY WILL COME

The city of Los Angeles is the country's second-largest media market. Yet, the city has not had an NFL football team to call its own since the 1994 season, when the Rams and the Raiders each played their last games there. After beginning in Cleveland, the Rams called Los Angeles home from 1946 to 1994 before moving to St. Louis in 1995. The Raiders played in Oakland from the team's beginning in 1960 until 1981, relocated to Los Angeles from 1982 to 1994, and moved back to Oakland in 1995.

But the lack of a Los Angeles NFL franchise did not deter the City Council of Inglewood, California, a suburb of Los Angeles, from approving plans earlier this year to build the most expensive stadium in U.S. sports history near Los Angeles International Airport, the nation's fourth-busiest airport.

In January 2014, St. Louis Rams owner, real-estate titan, and sports mogul Stan Kroenke purchased, through a holding company, a 60-acre parcel of land in Inglewood just north of the old Hollywood Park Racetrack for about $100 million. After a year of speculation on what Kroenke's design for the site was (his wife is the daughter of Wal-Mart co-founder Bud Walton and he has developed plazas near Wal-Mart stores), a massive mixed-use development project was announced, including an 80,000-seat stadium, retail and office space, residential housing, a hotel, parks, playgrounds, and open space—all at a cost of $1.86 billion.

After receiving more than 20,000 signatures on a petition, the Inglewood City Council approved a re-zoning initiative by unanimous vote, thus clearing the way for developers to break ground later this year. "We need to do the will of the people and we need to do it tonight," said Inglewood's mayor, James Butts, before the vote.

The city of Inglewood is trying to lure the Rams back from St. Louis by approving the construction of a stadium with no guarantee from the Rams that the team will come back. And aside from that, NFL teams that want to move to a different city must have the permission of 24 of the league's 32 owners.

Build it and they will come.

Stadium economics

What is unusual about the new stadium is that it will be built entirely with private funds, except that the city will reimburse the developers for building streets and sidewalks if tax revenue from the project exceeds $25 million. That is not the case in Missouri, where politicians from the governor on down are desperately trying to keep the Rams in St. Louis.

According to the Federal Reserve Bank of St. Louis, "Between 1987 and 1999, 55 stadiums and arenas were refurbished or built in the United States at a cost of more than $8.7 billion." About 57 percent of this "was financed with taxpayer money." Pacific Standard magazine reported in 2013 that "over the past 20 years, 101 new sports facilities have opened in the United States—a 90-percent replacement rate—and almost all of them have received direct public funding."

That is what happened when the Rams moved from Los Angeles in 1995 after the city of St. Louis, St. Louis County, and the state of Missouri spent $280 million on what is now called the Edward Jones Dome to attract the team. Bonds for construction of the stadium and convention center are scheduled to be paid by all three entities through 2021. After a dispute between the Rams and the St. Louis Convention and Visitor Center over renovations to the stadium, arbitrators in February 2013 ruled in favor of the Rams' $700 million proposal to upgrade the stadium to the top tier of NFL stadiums, as required by the terms of the Rams' 30-year lease. Not doing so means that the Rams could either lease the stadium on a year-to-year basis beginning in 2015 or break the lease and move. The state of Missouri is now proposing to finance a $900 million new stadium for the Rams, $460 million to $535 million of which would be publicly financed.

The city of Inglewood wants the Rams because it projects that a football stadium would generate more than $800 million dollars a year in economic activity. St. Louis wants to keep the Rams for the same reason, and because of the hundreds of millions of dollars that it has already invested in the team.

There is just one problem with this: the negligible and sometimes negative economic impact of sports stadiums. Economists may disagree about a lot of things, but the economic impact of sports stadiums isn't one of them. Bloomberg Business reported in 2012 that "over the life of the $17 billion of exempt debt issued to build stadiums since 1986, the last of which matures in 2047, taxpayer subsidies to bondholders will total $4 billion." The Federal Reserve Bank of St. Louis concluded that "almost all economists and development specialists (at least those who work independently and not for a chamber of commerce or similar organization) conclude that the rate of return a city or metropolitan area receives for its investment is generally below that of alternative projects."

Michael Leeds, a sports economist at Temple University, says that sports stadiums have "no impact." He concluded after studying Chicago—a city with five major sports teams—that "if every sports team in Chicago were to suddenly disappear, the impact on the Chicago economy would be a fraction of 1 percent." Another sports economist, Victor Matheson, at the College of the Holy Cross, is dubious about the projected economic impact of sports stadiums: "A good rule of thumb that economists use is to take what stadium boosters are telling you and move that one decimal place to the left, and that's usually a good estimate of what you're going to get." University of Chicago economist Allen Sanderson even suggests that "it would be far preferable for the mayor of St. Louis to write a check to the Rams' owner for, say, $100 million and let it go at that, essentially a bribe to stay put and shut up."

In a paper for the National Association of Sports Economists, Dennis Coates and Brad Humphreys concluded that "sports subsidies cannot be justified on the grounds of local economic development, income growth, or job creation, those arguments most frequently used by subsidy advocates." The consensus of economists is that there is "no substantial evidence of increased jobs, income, or tax revenues for a community" associated with stadiums, arenas, or sports franchises. Economists universally mention several things that cause stadiums to be poor public investments. Sporting events can create such significant crowds and congestion that they can cause people to stop going to other area events. Sports fans do not spend additional money on entertainment after a stadium is built; they merely redirect the money they would have spent on movies, dining, or other entertainment options. Most of the jobs created by stadium-building projects are temporary jobs that are often low-paying or out-of-state contracting jobs that don't greatly contribute to the local economy.

Sound economic policy is not a hallmark of state and local governments any more than it is of the federal government. So why do states, counties, and cities continue to seek major league sports franchises at public expense? It could be for any number of reasons—prestige, tradition, bragging rights, civic pride, political self-interest—but sound economics has nothing to do with it.

Libertarian arguments

When writing about the economics of sports stadiums, economists discuss concepts such as market failure, marginal social benefits and costs, positive and negative externalities, opportunity cost, public goods, intangible economic benefits, allocation of resources, returns on investment, alternative use of resources, monopoly power, market distortion, regressive taxation, Pareto improvements, and Pareto-relevant externalities.

But one does not have to be an economist to understand why subsidizing sports stadiums is such a bad idea; one just has to be a libertarian. In

fact, most economists who write about the economic impact of sports stadiums miss the real point entirely. The libertarian arguments against governments' subsidizing sports stadiums have to do with fundamental issues
such as individual liberty, private property, the free market, limited government, and the free society. It doesn't matter if a municipality's spending millions, tens of millions, or hundreds of millions of dollars building a
stadium to keep or attract a major league sports team is a good investment,
has a high rate of return, creates or retains jobs, has positive externalities,
or has a positive economic impact.

Government entities' building or subsidizing the building of sports
stadiums is an immoral act and illegitimate function of government. It
fleeces taxpayers. It benefits the few (sports fans) at the expense of the
many (the taxpayers). Communities don't benefit by taxing working people so millionaires can pay ball teams for the privilege of sitting in luxury
boxes watching other millionaires play ball games. Owners of sports franchises are some of the richest people in America—why should tax money
be used to finance their business endeavors?

And that is what is usually lost in the debate about taxpayer-funded
sports stadiums: sports teams are businesses. Sports teams are in the entertainment business. Sporting events are entertainment. People attend football, baseball, basketball, and hockey games to be entertained—just as
they attend concerts, movies, amusement parks, and museums to be entertained. An entertainment business, like any other business, should not be
promoted, subsidized, supported, protected, or financed by government
any more than any other type of business; that is, it shouldn't be promoted,
subsidized, supported, protected, or financed by government at all. Any
government at any level.

Sports teams—like department stores, restaurants, and amusement
parks—should buy land, build facilities, advertise what they have to offer,
and hope that people will come. But they shouldn't expect any help from
taxpayers.

*****

FREE THE GAS PUMPS!

Aside from both being coastal states, New Jersey and Oregon have
little in common except for one infamous thing. Drivers vacationing or
passing through either state for the first time who have to stop to gas up
their cars are in for a rude awakening if they try to pump their own gas.
They will quickly find out from a gas station attendant that it is illegal to
pump your own gas in New Jersey and Oregon.

True, other states used to have the same prohibition. But restrictions on
self-service gas pumping were all lifted by the late 1970s. Thus, although
it is perfectly legal in "the land of the free" to pump your own gas in any

other of the 48 states and Washington, D.C., doing so in New Jersey or Oregon will still result in a fine. The prohibition in Oregon has been partially lifted, but doesn't take effect until the beginning of 2016.

Prohibitions

The prohibition in New Jersey goes back to the 1949 Retail Gasoline Dispensing Safety Act. According to the New Jersey Statutes,

No person shall dispense fuel at a gasoline station, unless the person is an attendant who has received instructions regarding the dispensing of fuel, had practical experience dispensing fuel under the direct supervision of an experienced operator for a period of not less than one full working day, and, upon examination at the end of that period, demonstrated his understanding of those instructions.

Riders of motorcycles are not exempt. Attendants "shall require a motorcyclist to dismount his or her motorcycle while gasoline is being dispensed into their vehicle." Violators are "liable for a penalty of not less than $50.00 and not more than $250.00 for a first offense and not more than $500.00 for each subsequent offense." The New Jersey Statutes justify the prohibition on self-service gas dispensing by appealing to "the public interest," "the common welfare," and "safety and convenience."

The prohibition in Oregon has been in place since 1951. According to the Oregon Revised Statutes (ORS),

An owner, operator or employee of a filling station, service station, garage or other dispensary where Class 1 flammable liquids, except aviation fuels, are dispensed at retail may not permit any person other than the owner, operator or employee to use or manipulate any pump, hose, pipe or other device for dispensing the liquids into the fuel tank of a motor vehicle or other retail container.

Unlike motorcyclists in New Jersey, motorcyclists in Oregon are exempt if they so request:

Upon the request of an operator of a motorcycle, the owner, operator or employee of a filling station, service station, garage or other dispensary where Class 1 flammable liquids are dispensed at retail shall set the fuel dispensing device and hand the discharge nozzle to the operator of the motorcycle.

The state fire marshal may impose on violators "a civil penalty not to exceed $500 for each violation of any provision of ORS 480.315 [policy] to 480.385 [civil penalty for gasoline dispensing law violations] or of any applicable rule adopted by the State Fire Marshal." The Oregon Statutes likewise justify the prohibition on self-service gas dispensing by appealing to "the public interest," "the public welfare," and "safety."

Bills were introduced in the New Jersey and Oregon legislatures this year to free, or partially free, the gas pumps even as public opinion polls still showed that a majority of residents in both states favored retaining the prohibition on self-service.

A bill was introduced in the New Jersey Senate to allow "voluntary" self-service but require gas stations to retain at least one full-service island. If a station discounted the price of self-service gas, it would still have to provide full service at the discounted rate to drivers with disabilities. But the senate president, Steve Sweeney, has indicated that the legislation will not pass as long as he is in charge. "We've been doing it the right way in New Jersey. We should not change," he said. An editorial in a New Jersey newspaper opines that "there is no compelling reason to eliminate full-service gas stations" and "every reason to maintain the convenience that motorists in the Garden State have come to treasure."

A bill to partially free the gas pumps in Oregon was introduced in February in the House, approved unanimously in April, amended by the senate, approved unanimously again in the House in June, and approved in the senate in June with only five negative votes. It was signed into law by the governor on June 22, but doesn't take effect until the beginning of 2016. The Oregonian reported that the chief sponsor of the bill, Rep. Cliff Bentz, "said several people drove hours from far-flung burgs around the state to testify in favor of the bill." They told stories "of drivers being forced to sleep in their cars or being stranded in an emergency because they couldn't purchase gas."

The relevant section of Oregon's HB 3011 reads:

> (2) Notwithstanding ORS 480.330 and 480.340, if a filling station, service station, garage or other dispensary where Class 1 flammable liquids are dispensed at retail is located in a low-population county, the owner or operator may, after
>
> 6 p.m. and before 6 a.m.:
>
> (a) Permit a person other than the owner, operator or employee to use or manipulate a device for dispensing liquids into the fuel tank of a motor vehicle or other retail container;
>
> (b) Permit the use of an installed coin-operated or self-service dispensing device for the liquids; and
>
> (c) Allow the use of an automatic nozzle to dispense the liquids without the owner, operator or employee being in the immediate vicinity of the tank or container being filled.

A "low-population county" is a county with a population "of not more than 40,000." This designation applies to more than half of Oregon's counties. Additionally, "If a county ceases to be a low-population county on or after the effective date of this 2015 Act, dispensaries located within the county may operate as described in subsection (2) of this section notwithstanding the change in county population."

Arguments

The arguments given by the states of New Jersey and Oregon in their statutes to prohibit the self-serve pumping of gas are both illogical and comical.

Safety is the biggest concern. Attendants are needed because gasoline is a flammable liquid and dispensing it is a fire hazard. Attendants are needed to make sure customers turn off their vehicles and refrain from smoking while refueling. Attendants are needed because cashiers inside a store are unable to maintain a clear view of the customers dispensing fuel. Attendants are needed because gasoline's toxic fumes make it a health hazard, especially to small children, pregnant women, and those with respiratory diseases. Attendants are needed because there is a risk that crime will take place when a driver leaves his vehicle to pay for his fuel. Attendants are needed because children are at risk when they are left in vehicles while the driver pays for his fuel purchase. Attendants are needed because there is a risk of personal injury to drivers from slipping on wet surfaces when they walk to the cashier to pay for their fuel. The ORS even says that the dangers of crime and slick surfaces "are enhanced because Oregon's weather is uniquely adverse, causing wet pavement and reduced visibility."

Another concern relates to the disabled—especially those who rely on a wheelchair, walker, cane, or crutches for mobility—the pregnant, the aged, and the infirm. The usual safety hazards are heightened. And pumping their own gas is a special burden and unreasonable discomfort. Oregon even invokes the Americans with Disabilities Act (Public Law 101-336), which "requires that equal access be provided to persons with disabilities at retail gasoline stations."

Another argument is that the use of self-service gas stations has diminished the availability of repair and maintenance services at gas stations. And because gas station attendants are not available to make maintenance checks, vehicle maintenance is neglected, which is dangerous to customers and other motorists, and leads to unneeded costly repairs that result from deferring maintenance.

And then there is the matter of employment. The ORS justifies Oregon's self-service prohibition by saying that "self-service dispensing at retail contributes to unemployment, particularly among young people."

The legislation in both New Jersey and Oregon maintains that the self-serve prohibition provides "increased safety and convenience without causing economic harm to the public in general." New Jersey adds that "the prohibition of customer self-service does not constitute a restraint of trade in derogation of the general public interest."

Answers

Not only are there plenty of substances just as dangerous as gasoline that anyone can purchase at his local hardware store, there are plenty of actions that people can undertake that are potentially much more dangerous than filling their car with gas. Consumers in New Jersey and Oregon can buy lye for their drains and weed killer for their lawns and use these hazardous chemicals themselves. Neither stores nor purchasers are required by state law to hire attendants to go to houses to pour lye into drains or apply weed killer to lawns. Residents of New Jersey and Oregon can freely use chainsaws, lawnmowers, and ladders even though thousands of Americans are injured every year while doing so.

All of the arguments about the bad things that could happen to a driver, his children, and his vehicle when he walks away from the gas pumps to pay for his gas seem rather ludicrous, since virtually all self-service gas stations are equipped with "pay at the pump" technology. And as mentioned above, Oregon just ended its prohibition on self-service between the hours of 6 p.m. and 6 a.m., effective the beginning of 2016. But if it is so hazardous for members of the general public to pump their own gas between the hours of 6 a.m. and 6 p.m. that an attendant must do it for them, then it is certainly just as hazardous between the hours of 6 p.m. and 6 a.m., when it is dark and cold.

The disabled and senior citizens who have trouble pumping their own gas are not disadvantaged and burdened in states that allow self-service gas. Some stations in those states do still provide full-service pumps. And every self-serve gas station that I have ever been to has a notice posted somewhere that you can honk your horn if you are handicapped and someone will come out of the store and pump your gas for you. But even if there are no store clerks available to provide assistance, all a handicapped individual at a gas station has to do is ask for help from the general public in pumping his gas just like he might ask someone to get something off the top shelf in a grocery store. There are no special clerks employed in grocery stores to get items off the top shelf for disabled and short people. The same principle applies in the case of senior citizens and pregnant women.

Refueling your vehicle and having it checked or fixed are two entirely different things. The fact that fifty years ago one could have them done at the same location has no relevance to whether self-serve gas should be prohibited. Shops that provide automobile repair and maintenance services are found in abundance throughout New Jersey and Oregon. Even if a station has only full-service gas, it doesn't follow that its attendants will be available to make maintenance checks on vehicles. That is not mandated by the governments of either New Jersey or Oregon. And there is nothing preventing a station that offers only self-service gas from having an auto-repair facility on the property.

If permitting self-service gas pumping contributes to unemployment, then allowing people to cook their own food, mow their own yards, and paint their own houses do likewise. To create more jobs, why don't the states of New Jersey and Oregon mandate that all of their residents hire cooks, landscapers, and painters? Why stop with gas station attendants? And why not ban ATMs and force banks to hire more tellers? Is it really in the public interest to force businesses to hire and pay the salaries and benefits of employees they don't need? In a free market without restraint of trade, gas stations in New Jersey and Oregon could hire attendants and reserve one or more gas pumps for full-service—and even charge more for it—if they felt there was a demand for it. But the decision to do so would be up to each individual business. And were it not for minimum-wage laws, teenagers could pump gas for tips at gas stations.

And of course, all of the arguments put forth by the states of New Jersey and Oregon—and any of their residents who are gas station attendants who don't want to lose their jobs, citizens who don't want to pump their own gas, or politicians who pander to both groups and argue likewise—are demolished by the fact that self-serve
dispensing of gasoline has been practiced without incident in the other 48 states and the District of Columbia for decades. Are there more fires at gas stations in all of the other states? Are all of the other states in violation of the Americans with Disabilities Act? Are cars really maintained less well in all of the other states? Are more children left unattended in cars in all of the other states? Is the weather better in all of the other states? Do more crimes take place at gas stations in all of the other states? Do more people suffer from respiratory ailments in all of the other states? Are more drivers injured at gas stations in all of the other states? The answer to all of those questions should be obvious.

Freedom

The prohibition on self-service gas pumping in New Jersey and Oregon is the ultimate in nanny-state paternalism. Here is what those laws are actually saying to the people and businesses of New Jersey and Oregon:

> You people are stupid. You are too stupid to pump your own gas without putting out your cigarette, breathing toxic gas fumes, causing a fire, leaving your children unattended, allowing your car to be vandalized, or slipping

and falling when you go to pay for your gas. You are so stupid that you cannot safely do what teenagers do without incident thousands of times a day in the other forty-eight states. But never fear, your state government will keep you safe by forbidding you to pump your own gas and by forcing gas stations to hire attendants to pump your gas for you.

You businesses are stupid. You are too stupid to make sure that when your customers pump their gas at your station they don't smoke, breathe toxic gas fumes, slip and fall, leave their children unattended, allow their car to be vandalized, and follow common-sense safety procedures so they don't start a fire and burn their car and your gas station to the ground. You are so stupid that you cannot safely run a gas station like thousands of other businesses do without incident in the other forty-eight states. But never fear, your state government will ensure that you keep your customers safe by forcing you to hire attendants to pump their gas, even though you will be unnecessarily paying employees to perform a service for customers that they may prefer to do for themselves.

The real issue, of course, is freedom. Freedom of gas stations to decide whether they want to have self-service, full service, or a combination of both types of gas pumps. Freedom of businesses to ensure the safety of their customers as they see fit. Freedom of businesses to hire just the employees they think they need. Freedom of consumers to pump their own gas if they choose to do so. Freedom of consumers to take care of their own children. Freedom of consumers to be treated like adults with basic common sense. Freedom from government paternalism. Freedom from a nanny state.

Free the gas pumps!

*****

THE FREE MARKET AT WORK

Even with all the government licensing, regulation, and oversight that American businesses are burdened with, the United States still has a relatively free market compared with most other countries. This is especially true on the consumer side.

One of the great weapons that consumers have is the boycott. Let's look at some high-profile boycotts and then see what it is that they have in common.

Back in 1997, an overwhelming majority of delegates to the Southern Baptist Convention's annual meeting voted to boycott the Walt Disney Company and its subsidiaries (which include ABC and ESPN) for Disney's "anti-Christian and anti-family direction." Many Southern Baptists object to Disney's policy of offering health benefits to same-sex partners of employees, "Gay Days" at theme parks, and the release by Disney and its subsidiaries of controversial books and movies. The vote was not binding on individual churches or members of the Southern Baptist Convention, the nation's largest Protestant denomination. The boycott was rescinded in 2005 after the Southern Baptist convention announced that it had "rightly and appropriately" challenged Disney and "communicated effectively our displeasure." However, the Southern Baptist Convention said it would continue to "monitor the products and policies" at Disney.

In 2012, Ron Johnson, the new CEO at retailer JC Penny, which, with more than a thousand department stores, operates in every state but Hawaii, directed the company to begin a new pricing approach. Store coupons, big sales, and huge mark-downs were eliminated and the policy of "everyday low prices" was instituted. But in April of 2013, Johnson was fired by JC Penny after only 17 months with the company. The new pricing strategy turned out to be a huge mistake, and resulted in a string of disappointing sales and earnings reports. No organized boycott was necessary because customers of JC Penny simply boycotted the policy change with their wallets. Although the traditional pricing approach was reinstated, the company is still struggling.

Also in 2012, the fast-food chain Chick-fil-A was subject to a boycott after it was revealed that the company's charitable endeavor, the Win-Shape Foundation, had donated millions of dollars to political organizations that defended traditional marriage and opposed same-sex marriage. Public statements opposing same-sex marriage by president and COO Dan Cathy didn't help the situation. LGBT activists called for a boycott of Chick-fil-A. Some city mayors expressed their desire to prevent the company from opening any restaurants in their cities. There were attempts by students at several colleges and universities to ban or remove Chick-fil-A restaurants from campuses. The boycott was embarrassingly ineffective. Chick-fil-A appreciation days were even held at some restaurants. In the end, the company released a statement stating, "Going forward, our intent is to leave the policy debate over same-sex marriage to the government and political arena."

And now, beginning just last month, Target, the nation's second-largest discount retailer (behind Walmart), which operates about 1,800 stores throughout the United States, is being boycotted for its new restroom policy. According to a company statement headlined "Continuing to Stand for Inclusivity,"

> We believe that everyone—every team member, every guest, and every community—deserves to be protected from discrimination, and treated equally. Consistent with this belief, Target supports the federal Equality Act, which provides protections to LGBT individuals, and opposes action that enables discrimination.

> In our stores, we demonstrate our commitment to an inclusive experience
> in many ways. Most relevant for the conversations currently underway, we
> welcome transgender team members and guests to use the restroom or fit-
> ting room facility that corresponds with their gender identity.

More than one million people have signed a petition promising to boycott
Target. The true number of American consumers boycotting Target is certainly much larger since many people will just simply stop shopping there
without formally signing a petition. It is not surprising, then, that the company's stock price has plummeted.

What do the official and unofficial boycotts of Disney, JC Penny,
Chick-fil-A, and Target over the issues of health benefits, product pricing,
same-sex marriage, and restroom use have in common?

They are all examples of the free market at work.

When an individual consumer (or group of consumers) determines that
some decision a company makes to institute a new policy, change a policy, raise a price, or promote some cause is not, for whatever reason, a
good decision, he (or they) must weigh the pros and cons of engaging in
commerce with said company and then ultimately decide whether to continue patronizing the company or to boycott it. Neither decision—that of
the company or that of the individual—should concern the government in
any way.

There are potentially thousands of decisions, large and small, that
businesses—from large corporations on down to small family-owned
business—make every day that don't make national news. Consumer reactions to all of those decisions—whether positive or negative—are likewise
examples of the free market at work.

There is, however, something peculiar about Americans and boycotts.
What is strange about boycotts is that most of the same people who support the right of an individual, a group, or a class to boycott a company or
place of business oppose the right of companies and businesses to boycott
serving or doing business with certain individuals, groups, or classes. The
fact that there is no right to live where you choose, be employed at a particular job, or obtain service from a place of business does not seem to
have entered their minds.

Nevertheless, it's not just the actions of consumers that show the free
market at work. Stockholders are concerned about company decisions that
might positively or negatively affect profits and stock prices. Advertising
agencies are concerned about good company decisions that might lead to
increased ad placement and bad decisions that might cause a reduction in
the necessity for their services. Manufacturers and vendors are concerned
about company decisions that might increase or decrease their business
with a particular company. Competitors are concerned about good company decisions that might take market share from them and bad decisions
that might increase their market share. Employees are concerned about

company decisions that they may have to help implement or will lead them to consider finding another job. And, of course, all parties are also concerned about positive and negative consumer reactions to changes in company policies.

The reactions of stockholders, advertising agencies, manufacturers and vendors, competitors, and employees to the decisions of their own or other companies are more examples of the free market at work.

The bottom line is simply this: the market is self-regulating. Americans don't need government to regulate businesses, impose industry standards, push Affirmative Action policies, decree minimum or maximum prices, require licensing for certain occupations, establish anti-discrimination laws, mandate that companies provide certain benefits, or oversee the market.

The free market works, and the freer the market the better it works.

*****

GOVERNMENT LICENSING OR PRIVATE CERTIFICATION?

Everyone understands the need for children to obtain permission from their parents before undertaking certain activities: sleeping over at a friend's house, viewing a particular movie, going on a field trip, participating in some sport, attending a particular party, staying up late, playing a particular video game, making a major purchase at a store, surfing the Internet, or having some medical procedure.

Whether the issue is safety, security, fiscal responsibility, liability, or morality, it is generally true that father and mother know best. Even when it is grandparents, older siblings, or other relatives that are the ones granting the permissions, it is still generally true that the families of the children know what is best for the children, not the children's friends, schoolmates, teachers, and neighbors.

But since government is not a parent, or even a babysitter, a caretaker, or a nanny, why is it that adults must get permission from it to open a business, engage in commerce, work in certain occupations, have a particular vocation, or provide a service to willing customers? In other words, why do Americans need permission from the government to work?

Since the war on poverty was declared as part of Lyndon Johnson's "Great Society," governments at all levels in the United States have spent trillions of dollars helping the poor. The government spends hundreds of billions of dollars every year providing a myriad of forms of welfare to low-income Americans. The vast majority of the programs have a means test; if a family's income were to increase above a certain amount, then the family would no longer be eligible to receive benefits from some or all of them. The government also spends many billions of dollars every year

on job-training programs. Some Americans are even paid by the government for not working in the form of unemployment compensation. So why
does government make it so difficult for some people to work?

Government licensing

Government makes it difficult for some people to work when it de-
crees that they obtain—sometimes at a great cost in time and money—an
occupational license. An occupational license is simply a certificate of
permission and approval from a government-sponsored board that a job-
seeker is required to obtain before he can begin working in a certain occupation. Such licenses are most commonly issued and regulated by state
governments, but government at the federal and local level also license
certain forms of work. An occupational license always involves paying a
fee and usually requires a certain level of education or completion of so
many hours of required training. Taking everything into account, the total
cost to obtain an occupational license, in dollars and time, can be considerable.

According to a study prepared by the Department of the Treasury Office of Economic Policy, the Council of Economic Advisers, and the Department of Labor, and published by the White House last year, occupational licensing has grown rapidly over the past few decades:

> More than one-quarter of U.S. workers now require a license to do their
> jobs, with most of these workers licensed by the States.

> The share of workers licensed at the State level has risen five-fold since the
> 1950s.

> About two-thirds of this change stems from an increase in the number of
> professions that require a license, with the remaining growth coming from
> changing composition of the workforce.

And as the study goes on to say, this share of workers "is higher when local and Federal licenses are included."

Although this White House report raises some concerns about the necessity and nature of some forms of occupational licensing, the common
thread woven throughout the report is that occupational licensing benefits
consumers by ensuring high-quality services and protecting them from the
potentially harmful actions of unskilled and untrained practitioners. Occupational licensing also offers workers "clear guidelines around professional development and training" and "may also help practitioners to pro-
fessionalize, encouraging individuals to invest in occupational skills and
creating career paths for licensed workers." At a recent Senate Judiciary
subcommittee hearing spearheaded by Sen. Mike Lee, a Republican, and

Sen. Amy Klobuchar, a Democrat, Jason Furman, the chairman of the Council of Economic Advisers, said that "licensing is usually justified on the grounds that it improves quality and protects safety."

The White House report estimates that "over 1,100 occupations are regulated in at least one State, but fewer than 60 are regulated in all 50 States." According to another study on occupational licensing by the Institute for Justice, the licensing burden in the states—in terms of education, experience, and examinations—ranges from an estimated average of 113 days in Pennsylvania to meet the requirements of the average licensed occupation to 724 days in Hawaii. The average fees range from $88 in Kansas to $505 in Nevada.

It is not just high-paid professionals such as doctors, lawyers, dentists, and accountants who are licensed. Lower-income occupations are licensed as well. Occupations such as barbers, auctioneers, child-care workers, animal breeders, manicurists, interior designers, skin-care specialists, upholsterers, shampooers, bill collectors, fire-alarm installers, midwives, make-up artists, crane operators, fishers, security guards, security-alarm installers, coaches, taxidermists, sign-language interpreters, locksmiths, bartenders, taxi drivers, funeral attendants, travel agents, and milk samplers.

Some occupations are licensed in all 50 states and the District of Columbia, such as cosmetologists, bus drivers, pest-control applicators, emergency-medical technicians, and vegetation-pesticide handlers. Other occupations are licensed only in one state, such as conveyor operators and forest workers (Connecticut), non-contractor pipe-layers and fire-sprinkler system testers (Wisconsin), and florists (Louisiana).

Along with occupational licensing come the government enforcement agencies and armies of government bureaucrats to make sure all the licensing rules and regulations are followed. Take Tennessee, for example. Tennessee is one of five states that licenses hair shampooers. To get a license requires a $140 fee, seventy days of training, and passing two exams. According to a recent report on occupational licensing by the Heritage Foundation (a conservative think tank), "The Tennessee Board of Cosmetology and Barber Examiners employs between 15 and 18 'field inspectors' hired to inspect barber and cosmetology schools and shops for proper sanitation and unlicensed activity. Under authority established by the board, its legal division has the power to issue consent orders for unlicensed activity."

According to a report an inspector filed with the state in April 2014, he entered a Memphis salon to conduct a "lawful inspection of the premises therein" and saw a manicurist running afoul of the law by shampooing a client's hair. You see, although the manicurist was a licensed manicurist, she was not a licensed shampooer. The manicurist was ordered to pay a $250 fine or face formal disciplinary charges and attend a hearing before an administrative law judge. That could result in a $1,000 fine and the loss of the manicurist's license.

The problems with licensing

The problems with occupational licensing can be classified as philosophical, empirical, logical, and rational.

First and foremost, occupational licensing needs to be recognized for what it is: government permission to work. But since when is it the proper role of government to forbid or permit people to exercise what should be their natural right to make a living? Since when is it the proper role of government to forbid or permit people to freely contract with other people to provide them services? Occupational licensing is an illegitimate purpose of government. It doesn't matter what the occupation is, or whether the licensing requirements are "reasonable" or "in the public interest." While the protection of the public's health, safety, and welfare is important, it is not the proper role of government to do it.

Second, occupational licensing results in higher prices for services, reduces employment opportunities and depresses wages for excluded workers, stifles entrepreneurship, limits competition, makes it difficult for immigrants to find work in fields where they might have valuable experience and training, makes entry to a particular field more difficult for those who might otherwise challenge the pricing practices of those currently in the field, and excludes otherwise qualified persons who have a criminal record, since in many states applicants can be denied a license if they have any kind of criminal conviction, regardless of the nature of the offense or how long ago it occurred. Occupational licensing also prevents licensed job-seekers from moving across state lines to seek better employment opportunities, since there is little interstate reciprocity when it comes to occupational licenses. It likewise includes working remotely or from home if it involves doing so from another state.

Third, the occupations necessitating a license and the requirements to obtain a license vary so widely from state to state that the whole process seems illogical. According to the aforementioned report on occupational licensing by the Institute for Justice, "The share of licensed workers varies widely state-by-state, ranging from a low of 12 percent in South Carolina to a high of 33 percent in Iowa. Most of these State differences are due to State policies, not differences in occupation mix across States." Five occupations are licensed only in one state. Five others are licensed only in two states. Two others are licensed only in three states. There are thirty-two occupations that only nine or fewer states license. Ten states require four months or more of training to be a manicurist, but Iowa requires only nine days and Alaska three days. It takes three years in Michigan to become a licensed security guard, but only eleven days in most other states.

And fourth, the difficulty of obtaining certain occupational licenses is irrational. It does not coincide with the public health, safety, and welfare risk that supposedly results from unlicensed practitioners. Take, for example, the occupation of emergency-medical technician (EMT). The actions of an EMT can affect people's lives, not just their hair or nails. Although every state and the District of Columbia require an individual to obtain a license to work as an EMT, the Institute for Justice reports that "66 occupations have greater average licensure burdens" than EMTs'. Education and training requirements to be an EMT vary from 140 days in Alaska to zero in Washington, D.C., and each location requires two exams, but the average amount of time required to become an EMT is only 33 days. Contrast that with the average amount of time needed to become a licensed cosmetologist: 372 days; a barber: 415 days; a security-alarm installer: 535 days; and an interior designer: 2,190 days.

Three other points

There are three other points about government licensing that need to be raised.

First of all, the vast majority of the government licensing in existence is on the state level. State governments can be just as evil, authoritarian, tyrannical, and harmful as the federal government, and even more so when it comes to being a nanny state. Merely because something is enshrined in a state constitution it doesn't follow that it is a legitimate purpose of government. And that includes local governments as well. Remember that it was the city of San Francisco that banned toy giveaways with children's meals at fast-food restaurants unless the meals met the city's strict nutritional standards and the city of New York that tried to ban large sugary drinks.

Secondly, although conservatives don't hesitate to point out what they consider to be the most egregious examples of government licensing requirements, they are very inconsistent when it comes to government regulation of business and the imposition of occupational licensing. For example, someone recently writing for the Heritage Foundation, although recognizing that "over the last 50 years, occupational licensing has grown substantially," nevertheless states, "Few disagree that those working in professions dealing with the public's health, safety, and welfare—doctors, pilots, lawyers—should be required to obtain a license." But at the aforementioned Senate Judiciary subcommittee hearing, Amy Klobuchar said basically the same thing, "Licensing is important when it protects the health and welfare of consumers or the safety of professionals." Conservatives have no problem with the government's licensing some occupations as long as it is "necessary" for public safety and the licensing requirements are "reasonable." But that is just what the nanny statists in the state legislatures say in defense of their actions when they enact new licensing laws or defend existing ones. Conservatives have no firm philosophical basis for accepting some occupational-licensing requirements and rejecting others. They are therefore inconsistent and untrustworthy when it comes to criticisms of occupational licensing. In the end, it is still government regulators, bureaucrats, and nanny statists who decide which occupations require a license and what the cost and requirements are for someone to obtain one.

And third, since the so-called Republican revolution, we have had more Republicans elected to office on the federal, state, and local level, and more Republican control over legislative bodies, than at any time in U.S. history since Reconstruction. Yet, we now have more government, more government debt, more government spending, more government regulations, and more government licensing at all levels of government than ever before. Not only do Republicans control the Congress, but the Republican majority in the U.S. House is the largest in recent memory. In twenty-three states, Republicans control both houses of the legislature and the governorship (including Nebraska, which has a unicameral, nonpartisan legislature, but is made up of mostly Republicans). In six other states, Republicans control the governorship. In eight other states, Republicans control both houses of the legislature. In eight other states, Republicans control one house of the legislature. According to Ballotpedia, on the state level there are 4,120 Republican lawmakers and only 3,059 Democrats ones. What does all that have to do with government business regulations and licensing requirements? It is Republicans who claim to be proponents of free markets, free enterprise, and capitalism, and in favor of fewer government regulations, more individual freedom, and less government overall. But as Mises Institute chairman Lew Rockwell has well said about the Republicans,

> Economic liberty is the utopia that they keep promising to bring us, pending the higher priority of blowing up foreign peoples, jailing political dissidents, crushing the left wing on campus, and routing the Democrats. Once all of this is done, they say, then they will get to the instituting of a free-market economic system. Of course, that day never arrives, and it is not supposed to. Capitalism serves the Republicans the way Communism served Stalin: a symbolic distraction to keep you hoping, voting, and coughing up money.

Clearly, Republicans merely want a government limited to one controlled by Republicans or else occupational-licensing requirements would be fewer and less onerous in the twenty-three states where Republicans control the legislature and the governorship.

Private certification

Proponents of occupational licensing would have us believe that without such government intervention in the economy, businesses would be full of untrained, incompetent, uneducated, unqualified, unscrupulous workers who would take advantage of consumers, rip them off, provide them with poor quality service, injure them, and possibly kill them.

Proponents of occupational licensing would have us believe that without licensing, barbers would give customers bad haircuts, cosmetologists would ruin their hair, fire-alarm installers would incorrectly wire fire alarms, bartenders would mix us the wrong drinks, coaches would never win a game, funeral attendants would not properly dress one's dead grandmother, EMTs would allow patients to die, travel agents would book travelers on wrong flights, accountants would prepare incorrect financial statements, security guards would allow burglars to break in, child-care workers would molest children, skin-care specialists would damage customers' skin, taxi drivers would drop passengers off on the wrong street, pest-control applicators would not be able to kill bugs, sign-language interpreters would tell deaf people the wrong thing, pharmacy technicians would give out the wrong drugs, taxidermists wouldn't stuff a dead pet properly, auctioneers would not be able to sell anything, and milk samplers would allow sour milk to be distributed.

Proponents of occupational licensing would have us believe that government protects consumers better than the free market, that government bureaucrats know better than business owners, and that government licensing is better than private certification.

Private certification—or licensing, endorsement, or accreditation—does work. Just consider the case of auto mechanics. I don't know of any state where auto mechanics and related occupations are subject to occupational licensing. But having worked as an auto mechanic in my younger days, I do know about ASE certification.

Founded in 1972, the National Institute for Automotive Service Excellence (ASE) is an independent nonprofit organization that works "to improve the quality of vehicle repair and service by testing and certifying automotive professionals." According to the organization's website, the ASE exists

> to protect the automotive service consumer, shop owner, and the automotive technician. We test and certify automotive professionals so that shop owners and service customers can better gauge a technician's level of expertise before contracting the technician's services. We certify the automotive technician professional so they can offer tangible proof of their technical knowledge. ASE Certification testing means peace of mind for auto service managers, customers.

To become certified, a mechanic must pass an exam written "in work-shops by a national panel of seasoned automotive industry professionals and executives, including working technicians, automobile manufacturers, aftermarket manufacturers, and educators." The 40-plus exams are "seg-mented by sub-specialty such as automobile, medium/heavy truck, truck equipment, school bus, collision repair, and more." Each exam is "de-signed to discern the automotive service technician's knowledge of job-related skills." The exams are not easy, "Only two out of every three test-takers pass on their first attempt." Moreover, there is the requirement of "two years of on the job training or one year of on the job training and a two-year degree in automotive repair to qualify for certification." To re-main certified, a retest is required every five years. More than 200,000 automotive technicians in the United States are ASE certified, along with 100,000 service consultants, collision-repair/refinish technicians, colli-sion-damage estimators, medium/heavy–truck technicians, engine machin-ists, parts specialists, and related occupations.

There is no legal requirement that auto mechanics be ASE-certified. Repair shops may or may not require that their technicians be ASE-certified. Customers may or may not insist that their vehicles are repaired by ASE-certified technicians. (Customers may or may not even know or care about ASE certification.) But it is the repair-shop owners and their customers who make the decisions, not the government.

There is absolutely no reason that all occupations could not be pri-vately certified just as auto and truck technicians are. Government licens-ing, aside from its many other problems, crowds out private certification and should be eliminated.

*****

FREE THE AIRPORTS!

According to the U.S. Department of Transportation's Bureau of Transportation Statistics (BTS), U.S. airlines and foreign airlines serving the United States carry about 900 million passengers per year systemwide on more than 9 million flights (domestic and international). The Federal Aviation Administration (FAA) projects that the total number of enplane-ments will grow to 1.2 billion by 2036. More than 400,000 Americans work in the airline industry. There are more than 5,100 public-use airports in the United States. The busiest airport in the United States (in terms of passenger count)—Atlanta's Hartsfield-Jackson—has more than 2,700 flights arrive and depart each day. More and more Americans are leaving the ranks of those who have never flown. And that is a good thing, since, on the basis of statistics of deaths per million miles traveled, it is much, much safer to fly than to drive a car or ride a motorcycle.

But in conjunction with the increasing number of airline flights and airline passengers and the decreasing number of crashes and fatalities associated with airline travel, airports remain under government control. Government at some level controls not only the security at airports, but the airports themselves.

The TSA

The Transportation Security Agency (TSA) was created by the Aviation and Transportation Security Act of 2001 that was passed with only minuscule opposition in the U.S. House of Representatives and signed into law by George W. Bush on November 19, 2001. It amended federal transportation law to make the TSA responsible for security in all modes of transportation, including:

(1) civil aviation security, and related research and development activities;

(2) security responsibilities over other modes of transportation that are exercised by DOT;

(3) day-to-day federal security screening operations for passenger air transportation and intrastate air transportation;

(4) policies, strategies, and plans for dealing with threats to transportation;

(5) domestic transportation during a national emergency (subject to the secretary of Transportation's control and direction), including aviation, rail, and other surface transportation, and maritime transportation, and port security; and

(6) management of security information, including notifying airport or airline security officers of the identity of individuals known to pose a risk of air piracy or terrorism or a threat to airline or passenger safety.

Although the TSA was originally part of the Department of Transportation (DOT), after the passage of the Homeland Security Act of 2002, the TSA was transferred to the new Department of Homeland Security (DHS) in 2003.

According to the TSA website, the agency's mission is to "protect the nation's transportation systems to ensure freedom of movement for people and commerce." Its vision is to "provide the most effective transportation security in the most efficient way as a high performing counterterrorism organization." Its core values are "integrity, innovation, and team spirit." Its work-force expectations are "hard work, professionalism, and integrity." The TSA employs about 55,000 people and has a budget of more than $7 billion a year.

The most common task of TSA Transportation Security Officers (TSO) is to screen passengers and baggage destined for commercial airline flights. Airports are allowed to opt out of federal-government-provided security under the TSA's Screening Partnership Program (SPP) and have private contractors provide their airport security. However, airports must apply to the TSA and be approved, the TSA is the entity that selects the contractors, and the contractors must still follow TSA procedures. There are currently 21 airports that have been approved to participate in the SPP, the largest one being the San Francisco International Airport.

The biggest complaint about the TSA is the long wait times to get through its security lines. At Chicago's O'Hare International Airport last year, two- to three-hour waits forced 450 passengers to miss their flights on American Airlines and the head of the TSA had to visit the Chicago airport and issue an apology.

In 2011, the U.S. Travel Association ("the national, non-profit organization representing all components of the travel industry") concluded a year-long project to formulate recommendations for travel-enhancing changes to the goals and performance of the TSA. A blue-ribbon panel that included a former secretary of the DHS and the CEO of American Airlines issued a report, "A Better Way," which made fourteen recommendations for reforming the TSA based on "the experience of security professionals, input from industry stakeholders, advice from privacy advocates and surveys of travelers." The U.S. Travel Association has just issued a new report—this time with fifteen recommendations in seven areas—that urges "the new administration and the new Congress to place a renewed focus on refining and enhancing the operations of the TSA."

"Transforming Security at Airports: An Update on Progress and a Plan for the Future of Aviation Security" offers "achievable steps Congress and the TSA can take right away to improve security and give travelers a better flying experience." The fifteen recommendations outlining how the TSA can improve include redirecting airline passenger fees to cover the cost of and improve TSA screening operations, expanding the TSA Pre-Check program to qualified travelers, ending repetitive security checks for bags that have already been screened, deploying modern staffing solutions, further utilizing canine screening units, and encouraging stakeholders to improve the checkpoint experience for travelers. On the basis of its research, the U.S. Travel Association believes that "travelers would take between two and three more trips per year if TSA hassles could be reduced without compromising security effectiveness—and these additional trips would add $85 billion in spending and 888,000 more jobs to our economy."

Other criticisms of the TSA focus on the agency's ineptitude, criminal activity, inefficiency, waste, sexual assaults, and abuses, which are all notorious and legion. In tests conducted by undercover teams at dozens of airports, TSA screeners failed to detect explosives and weapons a majority of the time. Hundreds of TSA personnel have been fired for stealing items from travelers' luggage. The millimeter wave scanners used to scan passengers have high false-positive rates, resulting in many unnecessary pat-downs. The TSA's Screening of Passengers by Observation Technique (SPOT), in which Behavior Detection Officers (BDO) observe passengers as they go through security checkpoints and look for behaviors that might indicate a higher security risk, was reviewed by the Government Accountability Office and found to be ineffective. Many passengers have reported that TSA screeners used pat-downs as a means to sexually assault them. TSA agents at the Phoenix Sky Harbor International Airport detained a 9-year old boy and his family, causing them to miss their flight and wait 15 hours for another one, because they mistook the boy's pacemaker for a bomb hidden in his chest.

Citing national-security concerns, the TSA has never in all the years of its existence provided any evidence that it has actually stopped a single terrorist from boarding an airplane. There is, in fact, no evidence that the TSA has prevented any more terrorist attacks than the private contractors who handled the airport security checkpoints before the Aviation and Transportation Security Act went into effect.

Government ownership and control

It is a given that governments own courthouses, election offices, military bases, police stations, jails, prisons, city halls, governors mansions, and capitol buildings. But as governments at all levels have strayed from their legitimate purpose, they have assumed ownership and control over many things that could be handled by the private sector.

One of those things is airports. In the United States, local governments own and operate the vast majority of airports, sometimes through public entities such as an airport authority. Such was not always the case. According to a recent Cato Institute Tax & Budget Bulletin, "Privatizing U.S. Airports," "In the early years of commercial aviation, numerous private airports operated alongside those established by state and local governments." Private airports once served major cities such as Miami, Los Angeles, and Philadelphia. The site of the Pentagon was once occupied by the private Washington-Hoover Airport. Unfortunately, many city governments were eager to own their own airports and the industry soon became dominated by government-owned facilities. From the very beginning, the U.S. military and the Post Office favored government-owned airports over private ones.

During the Great Depression, the federal government began providing aid to government-owned airports through New Deal programs. This led to a further crowding out of private airports around the country as federal funding of airport investment surpassed state and local funding. The federal government began to tax airline passengers after the passage of the Revenue Act of 1941. During World War II—in the name of national defense—Congress appropriated funds to construct and improve 250 government-owned airports while at the same time transferring unneeded military bases to state and local governments for public airport use.

After World War II—again, in the name of national defense—the Federal Airport Act of 1946 began regular federal aid to government-owned airports. Congress created the FAA in 1958, replacing previous agencies involved in air traffic control and airport development. In 1970, because of the passage of the Airport and Airway Development Act, all aviation taxes and fees were channeled into the new Airport and Airway Trust Fund (AATF) to be used for FAA operations, the provision of air traffic-control services, and grants-in-aid to airports. An additional source of funding for airports is the Passenger Facility Charge (PFC), first authorized by Congress in 1990. PFCs are imposed by local airports, but limited by the maximum charge set by Congress, currently $4.50 per passenger per flight segment. Smaller airports generally also rely on grants from state and local governments.

With federal funding comes federal control, and with federal control comes complexity, bureauc-racy, and politics resulting in increased costs, market distortions, and misallocation of resources. The primary grant program is the Airport Improvement Program (AIP). Established by the Airport and Airway Improvement Act of 1982, the AIP funds airport capital projects, such as runway expansions. According to the Cato study on privatizing U.S. airports, federal funding is "both through formula and discretionary grants under a complex set of rules and regulations" that are "determined by political and bureaucratic factors, not by marketplace demands, so the money is spent inefficiently."

According to a recent Heritage Foundation backgrounder report, "End of the Runway: Rethinking the Airport Improvement Program and the Federal Role in Airport Funding," "The current system of funneling passenger taxes through the federal government and back to airports via a politically directed mechanism makes little economic sense and has proved detrimental to airports and the aviation system." Funds end up being siphoned "from the airports that serve the most travelers and require the most investment to those that move the fewest." Because grants carry many federal requirements, "Airports must spend a large amount of time and resources navigating the large federal bureaucracy and conforming to various federal regulations, including those imposed on general airport practices, use of revenue, land acquisition, and providing opportunities for small businesses." Airports "must focus a great deal of resources simply complying with this mountain of federal regulations instead of running the airport as a business." PFC revenue can be used only for "FAA-approved projects that enhance safety, security, or capacity; reduce noise; or increase air carrier competition." Regulations concerning spending such as "Buy America" provisions, adherence to the Davis–Bacon Act, and the requirement that contractors use union labor drive up costs and "divert passenger tax revenues to favored special interests at the expense of much-needed airport improvements." The federal government has "limited airports' ability to achieve self-sufficiency and solidified their reliance on federal grants and other regulated means of revenues for capital funding."

It is interesting that government ownership of airports is an American phenomenon. According to the aforementioned Cato study, "The private sector plays a larger role in the aviation infrastructure of other countries than the United States. Hundreds of airports around the world have been partly or fully privatized. There are dozens of international companies that own and operate airports, finance airport privatization, or participate in projects to finance, build, and operate new airports and airport terminals." A recent study by the Airports Council International (ACI) found that 47 percent of airports in the 28 European Union (EU) countries were either "mostly" or "fully" private, including airports in London, Edinburgh, Glasgow, Lisbon, Venice, Rome, Naples, Antwerp, Budapest, Vienna, Brussels, and Zurich. And even government-owned airports are often structured as corporations with 51 percent ownership by the government and 49 percent by the private sector, such as Charles de Gaulle airport in Paris and the major airports in Spain. Privatization of some airports has occurred in Australia, New Zealand, Mexico, and Brazil.

The real issue

Clearly, as the Cato report concludes,

• Airports should be self-funded by revenues from passengers, airlines, concessions, and other sources.
• Federal subsidies should be phased out, and state and local governments should privatize their airports to improve efficiency, competitiveness, and passenger benefits.
• Privatization and increased competition would boost the performance of America's aviation infrastructure.
• Airlines, passengers, private-plane owners, and taxpayers would all benefit from a more entrepreneurial and commercial approach to airport operation.

Short of privatization, the federal government should "reduce or eliminate the income tax exemption for municipal bonds to put private airport financing on a level playing field with government financing," "phase out the AIP program (at least for medium and large commercial airports) to encourage greater self-funding of airport capital spending," and "eliminate the cap on PFCs to allow airports to fund operations through user charges on their own passengers."

The conclusions and suggestions of the Heritage report are similar.

Instead of continuing this top-down system, Congress should eliminate the AIP, reduce passenger ticket taxes, and reform federal regulations that prohibit airports from charging market prices for their services. These reforms would eradicate the inefficient and inequitable distribution of flier resources and would allow airports to fund capital improvements in a local, self-reliant, and free-market manner.

Airports "should be able to derive their own revenue and be self-sufficient just like any other business." Privatization "would increase efficiency and improve management."

And just as clearly, the need for "refining and enhancing the operations of the TSA" would be unnecessary if airport security were also privatized. Not to mention the need for stopping the ineptitude, criminal activity, inefficiency, waste, sexual assaults, and abuses of the TSA.

Yet, there is something missing from these reports on airport privatization, funding, and the TSA. The main reason, and ultimately the most important reason, that governments at any level should not own, operate, fund, finance, regulate, or provide security at airports is that it is not the proper role of government to do so. The only legitimate purpose of government—at any level—is to keep the peace; to prosecute, punish, and exact restitution from those who initiate violence against, commit fraud against, or otherwise violate the personal or property rights of others; to provide a forum for dispute resolution; and to constrain those who would attempt to interfere with people's peaceful actions. No government or government entity should own an airport any more than it should own a convenience store, a laundromat, or an auto repair shop.

It would "give travelers a better flying experience" if the TSA increased efficiency, shortened wait times, better respected privacy, eliminated unnecessary pat-downs, and didn't steal from or unnecessarily inconvenience travelers. But failing to do those things is not the reason the TSA should be abolished. The only security business the federal government should be in is national security. There is no reasonable or logical justification—and certainly no constitutional or philosophical one—for the federal government to provide security for non-federal entities. It is the owners of the airports who should not only provide security, but also make the rules and regulations for their security agents.

That does not mean that other government entities that own airports should necessarily provide security themselves. Local governments can be just as inefficient, just as bureaucratic, and just as burdensome as the federal government. But just as government entities that own airports regularly contract out concessions or maintenance, so could they hire a private contractor to take care of all their security needs (as most of them did before September 11) or provide or contract out general airport security and leave it up to the airlines to provide airline security or share responsibility for screening passengers with the airlines.

The main thing is to get federal TSA agents and regulations out of airports, not to make the agents friendlier and the regulations less burdensome to "give travelers a better flying experience." Although there is certainly nothing wrong with doing those things in the meantime, we should never lose sight of the ultimate goal of limiting the activities of the federal government to its constitutional functions.

Ideally, all airports should be owned by private concerns that make their own decisions about security—just like jewelry stores, amusement parks, and malls. Because building, operating, and maintaining airports and airplanes are very expensive undertakings, airports and airlines have tremendous incentives to keep undesirable people and products out of airports and off airline flights to protect the traveling public and preserve their multi-million-dollar investments. There is no reason that airports and airlines should not be treated the same as any other business that has to compete for customers and set its own policies and procedures.

Freeing the airports not only should be done, it can be done. It was done with the airlines, which were once under heavy government regulation. The federal Civil Aeronautics Board (CAB) regulated all domestic interstate airline flights, and actually set airline fares, routes, and schedules. Yet, the CAB was gradually abolished beginning in 1978 after the passage of the Airline Deregulation Act. Under deregulation, prices fell, airlines expanded their routes, airlines modernized their equipment, and the volume of air travel dramatically increased. The airlines today are not totally free, but they are certainly much freer than they were under the control of the CAB. They should be completely freed from the heavy hand of government along with the airports they fly in and out of.

It goes without saying that the AIP program should be ended, the AATF should be liquidated, the FAA should be eliminated, the TSA should be abolished, all government-owned airports should be sold to the highest bidder, all taxes on airline tickets should be repealed, and all government regulations concerning airports should be rescinded. The airports should be freed from government ownership and control, not just in the name of efficiency, competitiveness, and modernization, but because limiting government to its legitimate functions is simply the right thing to do.

*****

WHO SHOULD CONDUCT BACKGROUND CHECKS?

Taxi companies are not happy about having to compete with ride-share services such as Uber and Lyft. Taxi companies and taxi drivers are collectively "resisting an industry that they say threatens their livelihoods and the well-being of consumers."

In Los Angeles, the number of taxi trips arranged in advance has fallen by 42 percent, the total number of trips has plummeted by nearly 30 percent, drivers have seen their trips fall by as much as 40 percent, and the city has lost 586 drivers over the last three years.

In San Francisco—the corporate home of both Uber and Lyft—"the number of trips taken per taxi dropped by more than two-thirds over a two-year period."

Taxi drivers and taxi companies in cities in the United States and around the world have sometimes taken drastic measures to pressure government into stifling their competition. Taxi drivers have taken to the streets in protest of ride-sharing services. Taxi companies have taken Uber and Lyft to court. In Massachusetts, the state legislature implemented strict background checks that disqualified thousands of current Uber and Lyft drivers.

The regulations authorized by the Massachusetts legislature in 2016 for ride-hailing drivers are "some of the strictest in the nation." Drivers can be disqualified "if their records show license suspensions, driving infractions, or serious crimes such as sexual and violent offenses, among other charges." The new state system began checking the records of drivers in January after Uber and Lyft "signed an agreement to submit their drivers to the reviews a year before the law would have required." The state reviewed the criminal and driving records of nearly 71,000 drivers who had already passed background checks by Uber and Lyft and rejected 8,206 of them. The state looks back seven years for driving violations and less serious violent crimes, but looks back "for unlimited periods at other offenses, such as sex crimes, more serious violent crimes, and drunken driving that results in serious injury or death." The most common reasons for rejections were related to driver's-license status: "Many had suspended licenses or had not been driving long enough to qualify for the ride-hailing services." Hundreds were disqualified "for having serious crimes on their record, including violent or sexual offenses." Gov. Charlie Baker said that "public safety is a top priority" and that his administration looks forward "to future partnerships with Uber, Lyft, and others to grow this innovative industry and support more jobs and economic opportunities for all."

Cabdrivers argue that the new ride-share services "have an unfair advantage because, in most cases, they are allowed to operate free of the rules, regulations, and licensing requirements of traditional taxis."

But in a free society with a free market, taxi companies would be free of government rules, regulations, and licensing requirements. They would not be controlled or overseen by government in any way. There would be no taxi medallions. Anyone could start a taxi service. Any type of vehicle could be used. No taxicab would have to have a permit. Taxi drivers would not have to obtain a license. Taxi fares would not be set by the government. Vehicles used as taxis would not have special inspections. And taxi companies would have to compete with ride-share services.

The libertarian solution is not to have the government regulate companies such as Uber and Lyft more, but to have the government regulate taxi companies less so that both groups can compete on a level playing field.

The case of the state background checks of Uber and Lyft drivers in Massachusetts brings up an important issue that relates to any business.

Who should conduct background checks?

One cannot argue that the state of Massachusetts has the right to conduct additional background checks on Uber and Lyft drivers because the drivers are driving on state roads. No background checks are required for residents of Massachusetts or visitors from other states to drive on Massachusetts roads even though they might just as well have criminal records and might even have committed heinous crimes.

So, the background checks are apparently just a public-safety issue. That makes them legitimate, right? After all, "You can't be too safe," as Boston Police Commissioner William Evans said.

Really?

First of all, we know that the state background checks weren't just established because of public safety. The background checks were instituted "after tense negotiations that included lobbying by the taxi industry."

Second, outside Massachusetts, "The ride-hailing companies typically are the only entities that vet drivers; even states that have adopted regulations for the burgeoning industry generally rely on the companies."

Third, the government can do almost anything it wants in the name of "public safety." That is why we have laws concerning seatbelts, cell-phone use while driving, bicycle and motorcycle helmets, and car seats for children. But where does it all end? How many "public safety" laws are too many?

Fourth, many of the crimes that show up in state background checks are crimes in search of a victim. That is especially true in the case of drug crimes.

Fifth, if "public safety is a top priority" and "you can't be too safe," then why doesn't the state of Massachusetts perform background checks on all employment applicants to every company that does business with the public?

Sixth, the fact that some Uber drivers commit crimes is irrelevant. Plenty of doctors, lawyers, mechanics, accountants, clerks, welders, managers, engineers, laborers, carpenters, athletes, cashiers, and state government employees commit crimes. Uber drivers don't have a monopoly on criminal activity. Some parents commit child abuse. That doesn't mean that the state should perform background checks on all couples before they are permitted to have children.

Seventh, and most importantly, state government background checks imply that companies aren't interested in or can't be trusted to ensure the safety of their customers. That, of course, is ludicrous. Uber has said that "the company runs criminal background checks on all new drivers and rescreens them twice a year." Under the company's rules, "drivers can't join the service if they have had a felony conviction in the past seven years or a major driving violation, such as a suspended or revoked license or registration, in the past three years." Uber and Lyft have both pointed out that "they are limited by state law to checking just the last seven years of an applicant's history, which they said explains why so many drivers they had passed flunked the government's more thorough review." So here we have a case of the government creating a problem so it can offer a solution.

Who should conduct background checks? Any company that wants to. But the state should neither mandate them nor conduct them.

*****

FREE THE FIRE STATIONS!

Many boys, at one time or another when they are growing up, become enamored with firetrucks after taking a school field trip to their local fire station. Some of them will then insist that they want to be firemen when then grow up. They want such an occupation because of the excitement and the adventure they envision — and, of course, the chance to ride on one of the shiny red firetrucks. The pay and benefits of a firefighter are of no consequence to them at their young age. Although the interest in becoming a fireman usually wanes, some boys do in fact become firemen when they grow up, as a visit to one's local fire station will attest. In adulthood, however, pay and benefits no longer take a back seat to excitement and adventure. Mortgage and car payments have to be made, electric and water bills are due every month, and the kids are always needing new shoes.

Firefighting is not generally considered to be a high-paying job. According to annual reports by *Forbes*, *Business Insider*, and CNBC, using data drawn from places such as LinkedIn and the Bureau of Labor Statistics, the top-paying occupations in the United States are regularly said to be held by pharmacists, podiatrists, attorneys, engineers, dentists, physicians, surgeons, psychiatrists, orthodontists, anesthesiologists, radiologists, pathologists, and upper-level managers and directors.

According to Salary.com, the median annual firefighter salary, as of April 2017, is $44,770, with a range usually between $33,578 and $55,963. That does not include "bonus and benefit information and other factors that impact base pay." In states such as California, median salaries are generally higher. And even then, it depends on the city. For example, the median annual firefighter salary in Los Angeles is $49,490, with a range usually between $37,118 and $61,863. Again, that does not include

"bonus and benefit information and other factors that impact base pay."
Thanks to an abundance of overtime pay opportunities, some firefighters
in Los Angeles make significantly more.

Chief Donn

According to Transparent California, a watchdog project of the Nevada Policy Research Institute, a free-market think tank, there are thirty
employees of the Los Angeles Fire Department (LAFD) who made more
than $315,000 in base pay plus overtime last year. But three Los Angeles
firemen—Charles Ferrari, James Vlach, and Donn Thompson—each made
more than $300,000 just in overtime pay last year. Total pay and benefits
in 2016 were more than $483,000 for Ferrari and Vlach and more than
$439,000 for Thompson. But it is Thompson who may be the most well-
paid firefighter, not only in Los Angeles, but in the entire United States.

As reported on *Reason*'s "Hit and Run" blog, in a 1996 *Los Angeles
Times* story, Thompson was highlighted as a prime example of what the
newspaper called "paycheck generosity" at the LAFD. It turns out that
from 1993 through 1995, Thompson had made $219,649 in overtime pay
at a time when the LAFD was spending more than $58 million annually on
overtime pay. The newspaper reported that this "budget-wrenching"
amount far surpassed what fire departments in other big cities were paying. So well-known was the LAFD's reputation for paycheck generosity
that one Houston fire official commented, "We've all heard about what
they have going there. I don't know of any other department that has it
quite that lucrative." What the Los Angeles Times found just as surprising
as the amount of overtime pay was that most of the money spent was not
spent dealing with fires or other emergencies. Most of the overtime pay
was for firefighters to replace "those who are out because of vacations,
holidays, injuries, training, illnesses or personal leaves" or "to firefighters
on special assignments, such as in-house training and evaluation programs."

In 2009, it was reported by the *Los Angeles Daily News* that the
LAFD's overtime budget had "soared 60 percent over the last decade
while its ranks grew just 17 percent." The newspaper's analysis found that
Los Angeles firefighters averaged "six times more overtime than their
counterparts in Chicago, five times more than in Houston and two times
more than in San Diego." Fifty-six firefighters "earned at least $100,000
in overtime on top of their annual salaries." This 2009 newspaper article
also singled out Donn Thompson as the king of overtime earners. He had
pocketed $570,276 in overtime over the previous three years.

In 2016, the *San Diego Union-Tribune* featured Thompson in a story
about runaway overtime costs at California fire departments. According to
Transparent California, he received overtime pay of $286,536 in 2014 and

$286,733 in 2015. Thompson, a fireman for 34 years, said that he "never spent that much time at home," and "basically lived at the fire station."

Last year there were 439 LAFD employees who made more than $100,000 in overtime. Thompson pocketed $307,541 from California taxpayers. The LAFD spent more than 38 percent of its budget on overtime pay. In contrast, New York reported spending less than 20 percent, and other major fire departments reported even lower percentages.

Privatization

The millions of American workers who don't have any overtime opportunities, don't always work 40 hours in a week, live paycheck to paycheck, and struggle to make ends meet undoubtedly view the paychecks of these California firefighters to be obscene. Even doctors, lawyers, and managers who make six-figure incomes might be inclined to agree—especially when, according to the Bureau of Labor Statistics, the occupations of loggers, fishermen, roofers, garbage collectors, miners, truck drivers, construction laborers, electrical workers, pilots, and taxi drivers are much more dangerous than that of a firefighter.

When things such as the huge paychecks of LAFD firefighters are brought to light, there is always talk about the need to reform the system, reduce government bureaucracy, have more effective management, curtail the power of the unions that represent government workers, and make municipal governments more accountable to the taxpayers. Sometimes the privatization of fire departments is even suggested. This entails the shifting of functions and responsibilities from the public sector to the private sector. There are two forms of privatization that need to be distinguished: public-private partnerships and free-market competition.

In a public-private partnership, government entities contract out the provision of some service such as maintenance, facility management, or garbage collection. Study after study has documented the cost savings to municipalities achieved through this practice. Over the past few decades, more and more state and local governments have privatized certain "public services." Opening up the provision of a service to competitive bidding allows a government to secure the performance and cost-saving benefits that come with competition. Privatization allows government entities to control costs without sacrificing quality. In many cases, quality is even improved because companies want to ensure that their government contract is renewed. Yet, as pointed out in a Reason Foundation report, "Fire Protection Privatization: A Cost-Effective Approach to Public Safety," "For the most part, however, there has been no shift toward private contracting of fire service in cities with well-established municipal fire departments. The fire service is one of the most tradition-minded of all public services. It is also heavily unionized, and fire-fighters' unions have strongly resisted attempts to contract out existing fire department services to private firms."

There is, of course, one glaring problem with privatization by means of public-private partnerships: services are still publicly funded by tax dollars. Those using services the most might actually be paying the least or not at all. Some people end up paying for services that they never use. And no one has the option to change to a different service provider.

With free-market competition, no government at any level has anything to do with providing a "public service." No contracting, no funding, no oversight, no interference, no regulation, and no control. Many firms have a chance to provide services. Firms compete with one another for customers on the basis of price, quality, customer service, and the range of services offered. Prices for services are set freely by the forces of supply and demand. Customers choose what services they want to pay for. Prices are allowed to adjust according to economic conditions. New firms can freely enter the marketplace. Customers have a choice in what firm they want to purchase a service from. Firms that cannot compete or fail to meet the needs of their customers go out of business. No one firm has a monopoly on providing a service.

Fire stations need to be freed from government funding and control and be treated just like any other business. But high salaries, generous benefits, lots of overtime, and firefighter unions are not the reasons why. In fact, even with free-market competition, firefighters may earn high salaries, receive generous benefits, have lots of overtime, and belong to unions.

History, facts, and figures

As relayed by Annelise Graebner Anderson in an article in the *Journal of Libertarian Studies* ("The Development of Municipal Fire Departments in the United States"), "In 1852 not one city in the United States paid its firemen; they were all volunteers. By 1880 most of the cities with more than 10,000 people—and many with fewer—had municipally paid fire departments."

The first volunteer fire company was organized by Benjamin Franklin in Philadelphia in 1736. By 1752, Philadelphia had six volunteer fire companies and eight fire engines. Many leading citizens belonged to these fire companies, as was the case with social organizations. The fire companies were extremely competitive. Each fire was a contest to see whose engine would arrive first and pump water most efficiently. The volunteer companies, which were not profit-making enterprises, had several sources of financing: "contributions from grateful persons on whose property the company had put out a fire; donations from citizens; funds from benefits given by the volunteer firemen; contributions, dues, and fines of members; the city government; and the fire insurance companies." In time, however, "many cities gained considerable control

"many cities gained considerable control over the volunteer fire companies, and often paid the chief engineer whom the volunteers elected and
perhaps a few other full-time people." The country's first paid fire department was established in Cincinnati 1853. Within twenty years, Provi-
dence, St. Louis, New Orleans, Louisville, Chicago, Boston, Baltimore,
San Francisco, New York, Pittsburgh, and Philadelphia were all staffed by
career firefighters.

Anderson concludes that "the steam fire engine, the telegraph alarm
and potential insurance rate reductions resulting from lower losses probably led to a significant increase in the attractiveness of fire protection provided by a paid department." She asserts that "government activity in the
area of fire-fighting and in related areas was inimical to the development
of private enterprise." Gradually, "fire prevention and fire protection were
accepted as proper functions of a municipal government." And so they are
today.

According to the U.S. Fire Administration (an entity of FEMA),

• There are 27,211 fire departments listed with the National Fire Department Registry. That is about 91 percent of all U.S. fire departments.
• Registered fire departments represent approximately 50,908 fire stations
across the country.
• Ninety-six percent of the registered departments are local fire departments which include career, combination, and volunteer fire departments
and fire districts.
• Four percent of the registered departments are state and federal government fire departments, contract fire departments, private or industrial fire
brigades, and transportation authority or airport fire departments.

Of the registered fire departments, 9 percent are career (all firefighters are
career), 5 percent are mostly career (more than 50 percent of firefighters
are career), 16 percent are mostly volunteer (more than 50 percent of firefighters are volunteers), and 71 percent are volunteer (all firefighters are
volunteers).

It is a myth that volunteer fire departments don't receive tax money
and don't pay their firefighters anything. Some, of course, don't. But others are financially supported by local taxes in addition to fundraising, private donations, corporate donations, and federal grants. And some reimburse their firefighters for expenses, give them a small stipend, pay them
on a per-call basis, or provide free training and certification.

Private fire departments are few in number, but they do exist. According to a report by industry research firm IBISWorld,

The Private Firefighting Services industry includes privately operated companies that charge a subscription fee to homeowners and business owners
to provide fire prevention and suppression services. In addition, companies

companies provide fire-protection services to airports and industrial facilities on a contract basis or are employed by insurance companies or government agencies. Over the past five years, the number of private sector firefighters has grown at an average annual rate of 15.0% to an estimated 16,880 employees.

The Private Firefighting Services industry is expected to continue expanding, with industry revenue projected to rise through 2017. Continued state and local budget shortfalls are anticipated to lead to greater outsourcing to the private sector. Moreover, insurance companies offering private firefighting services to homeowners in the West and Southwest regions will be a continued source of growth for the industry over the coming five years.

The National Wildfire Suppression Association (NWSA) represents more than 150 private-sector contract companies in 16 states.

Observations

There is absolutely no reason why the provision of firefighting services cannot be handled by the free market.

First of all, according to the National Fire Protection Association (NFPA), of the 33,602,500 calls to fire departments for service in 2015, 2,533,500 were false alarms, 21,500,000 were for medical help, and only 1,345,000 were for actual fires. The provision of emergency services should be separate from the provision of firefighting services. And as Ryan McMaken of the Mises Institute points out, "An enormous number of firefighters could be replaced by paramedics—using much less-expensive vehicles—and no one would notice.

Second, although firefighting is an "essential service," that doesn't mean that it has to be supplied by government. Hospitals provide an essential service, but they are privately owned. Doctors provide an essential service, but they don't work for the government. In many large cities, taxi companies supply an essential service, but they are not owned by governments. The provision of food is certainly one of the most essential services throughout the United States since only a very small percentage of Americans are farmers. Yet the provision of food is entirely left up to grocery stores competing with one another for customers on the free market.

Third, the fact that 71 percent of all fire departments are already staffed entirely by volunteers clearly demonstrates that government firefighters do not need to staff fire stations.

Fourth, it would not be redundant to have more than one fire department in a city or town any more than it is redundant to have more than one gas station, restaurant, clothing store, strip mall, barbershop, grocery store, nail saloon, bar, or movie theater.

Fifth, competition among firms is necessary to ensure low-cost quality services for consumers. By nature, a government monopoly does just the opposite.

Sixth, it is because of government that Americans don't have private firefighting services, not because of market failure. Government interference always distorts the market.

Seventh, it is not the purpose of government to provide services. Libertarians alone consistently maintain that if we are to have a government, its role should be strictly limited to the protection of life, liberty, and property from the violence and fraud of others.

Eighth, if the government is to provide firefighting services, then where does it end? Once firefighting is accepted as a proper function of government, what logical argument can then be made against the government's providing pest-control services, lawn-mowing services, haircutting services, eye-exam services, house-painting services, accounting services, banking services, nanny services, insurance services, or travel-agent services?

Ninth, putting out fires is a job—just as digging ditches, mining coal, selling cars, editing magazines, mowing lawns, managing a company, truck driving, writing books, running a cash register, and waiting tables are jobs. There is nothing special about firefighting. Yet, government firefighters are regularly held up as heroes just for doing their jobs.

And tenth, to say that the private funding and private provision of firefighting services "just won't work" simply manifests the statist thinking and anti-market bias that is all too prevalent in American society. It "works" for a host of other services that Americans use every day and wouldn't begin to think that the government should provide.

The fire stations in the United States should be freed from government funding and control as a matter of principle. To focus only on firefighter salaries, benefits, overtime, and union membership is to miss the big picture—that of service provision in a free society. These things may be important from the standpoint of how taxpayer dollars are used, but they are not sufficient in and of themselves to prove that fire stations should be free. That is the same mistake conservatives make when they call for the elimination of some government funding, program, or agency because it has a liberal bias, funds pornographic art, is inefficient, performs abortions, has a lot of waste and fraud, or is too intrusive, instead of arguing that it shouldn't exist in the first place.

*****

7

THE FREE SOCIETY

TIME FOR A DRINK

While eating in a restaurant in the Atlanta airport recently, I noticed that the restaurant's bar was closed and—to make it perfectly clear—all the chairs had been turned over and placed on the bar.

Now, although I don't frequent bars in airports or anywhere else, I was nevertheless intrigued. "The bar doesn't open until 12:30 on Sundays," said my waiter. But, as I found out later, it isn't just this particular airport bar that didn't open until Sunday afternoon. In Georgia, no alcohol may be served in restaurants or bars until after 12:30 on Sundays.

In fact, until just recently, alcohol sales in retail stores on Sundays were prohibited by the Georgia legislature. On April 28, 2011, Nathan Deal, Georgia's governor, signed legislation allowing local communities the option of voting on whether to continue the Sunday alcohol-sales ban in their cities and counties or to eliminate it. Georgia's previous governor, Sonny Perdue, had always pledged to veto any measure ending the ban on Sunday sales, but he left office on January 10, 2011, constitutionally ineligible to seek a third consecutive term.

On November 8, 2011 (the first election date available under state law), about 120 of Georgia's almost 700 cities and counties held a referendum on the matter of Sunday alcohol sales. In more than 100 communities that voted, the Sunday restriction was lifted, in many cases by large margins. The effective date of the repeal varied from November to February. Sunday sales in Georgia's capital and largest city, Atlanta, began on January 1, 2012.

The cost of having a single-issue ballot kept many communities from having such a referendum. However, on March 6, voters in some Georgia communities had more than a Republican presidential nominee to vote on in the Super Tuesday elections. In 16 cities and counties, there also appeared on the ballot the Sunday alcohol-sales question. The measure passed everywhere it was voted on except in the city of Jeffersonville, where it failed by one vote.

But Georgia is not alone when it comes to states that restrict alcohol sales on Sundays. Unlike Nevada and Louisiana, where beer, wine, and liquor sales are legal 24 hours a day, seven days a week, most states (or cities and counties that have been given a local option) restrict alcohol sales in some way on Sundays. A distinction is usually made between alcohol consumed on-premises and alcohol purchased for consumption off-premises. In Indiana, Tennessee, Oklahoma, Minnesota, and Connecticut, the sale of alcohol is prohibited for consumption off-premises on Sunday. Most counties in Arkansas and Mississippi are the same way. In Colorado, the Sunday sales restriction wasn't lifted until 2008. Hard liquor cannot be sold for off-premise consumption on Sunday in Texas, Utah, North Carolina, or South Carolina. In Nebraska, there can be no on- or off-premises sales of hard liquor before noon on Sundays. No alcoholic beverages of any kind can be sold on- or off-premises before 1:00 p.m. on Sunday in West Virginia. Other states (and cities or counties) with Sunday restrictions generally have a later time on Sunday morning for alcohol sales (on- or off-premises) than during the other days of the week.

Why?

It can't possibly be because the states, counties, and municipalities are exercising what is commonly referred to as their police powers to protect the public's health, safety, and morals.

If there is something dangerous about drinking alcohol on Sunday morning before noon, then it is equally dangerous to drink alcohol before noon on any other day of the week. Yet most states with Sunday alcohol-sales restrictions generally allow the on-premises sale of alcohol the rest of the week sometime between the hours of 6:00 a.m. and 9:00 a.m. But what is so magical about 6:00 a.m.? Is there really any difference between letting someone be served a drink at 5:30 a.m. instead of 6:00 a.m.? Some states prohibit the sale of alcohol only between 2:00 a.m. and 6:00 a.m. Do they not care about the health, safety, and morals of their citizens the other 20 hours of the day?

States are doing a poor job if they are protecting their citizens from the dangers of alcohol only during certain hours and on certain days. Shouldn't all states at least follow the model of Kansas, Mississippi, and Tennessee? Those states are "dry" by default; individual counties must vote to become "wet." Thirty other states allow their counties to go dry only by public referendum, but at least they give their counties that option. Seventeen states preclude any of their counties from going dry.

Consistency was never the hallmark of government at any level. In Wisconsin, one can be served alcohol until 2:00 a.m. on Sunday through Thursday, but until 2:30 a.m. on Friday and Saturday, with no ending time at all on New Year's Day. That seems counterintuitive, since the government is extending alcohol sales during the times when people are more likely to abuse alcohol. And why is it that casinos all along the Mississippi River are permitted to be open 24/7 and give free alcohol to gambling patrons all hours of the day and night? Many convenience stores also sell pornography in addition to beer and wine. There are no time restrictions on the purchase of pornography. And there are no laws that forbid the purchase of pornography on Sundays.

There is really only one reason that state and local governments and voters in counties and cities support restricting alcohol sales on Sundays: they are puritanical busybodies clinging to Prohibition- or Colonial America-era blue laws.

It was generally religious preferences that led Georgians to vote against the November referendum on the matter of Sunday alcohol sales. In the city of Snellville, James Freedle voted against the referendum, saying, "I don't think it's appropriate to drink on Sunday." In the city of Forest Park, Mayor and Sunday School teacher Corine Deyton, who also said she voted no, commented, "If you can't do without alcohol one day a week, there's something bad wrong with you." In rural Elbert County, one of the few areas where the referendum failed to pass, church pianist Patsy Scarborough pointedly said, "This nation has a trend of turning away from good morals. Americans need to be in church on Sunday, not out buying alcohol." "Thanks for voting no to sell alcohol on Sunday," read a sign on an Elbert County local church after the referendum failed.

But it's not just alcohol sales on Sunday. In some states and counties it is still illegal on Sunday to hunt, hold horse races, sell cars, or open a store before noon.

Now, as a religious person myself who does attend church on Sunday and doesn't purchase alcohol on Sunday or any other day of the week, I am sympathetic to those Georgians' views of church attendance and alcohol. That does not mean, however, that I believe that people who, for whatever reason, don't attend church on Sunday should be punished by not allowing them to buy a six-pack of beer at 7-Eleven on Sunday morning before they go fishing.

Some religious people always focus on the negative. They don't drink, dance, smoke, chew, or go with girls who do—but then they want to spread the misery even if it means using the state to tell others how they should live. It reminds me of H.L. Mencken's famous definition of puritanism: "The haunting fear that someone, somewhere, may be happy."

The problem with alcohol prohibitionists—religious or otherwise—is that they, for whatever reason, have never accepted or been introduced to the philosophy of freedom. Restricting the sale of alcohol or any other product on Sunday is really a restriction on commerce, property, and freedom, things that Americans—religious or otherwise—say they hold dear.

In a free society, businesses make their own decisions as to the days and times when they will offer their products for sale, just as individual persons make their own decisions as to the day and time when, and place of business where, they will make purchases. In fact, a free society can't have it any other way.

No alcohol was consumed on Sunday during the writing of this article.

*****

WHY IS THE DRINKING AGE 21?

Last month, the parliament in Turkey passed legislation ostensibly designed to curb alcohol consumption among Turkish youth.

Retailers may not sell alcohol between 10 p.m. and 6 a.m. No alcohol may be sold within 100 meters of educational or religious centers. Educational and health institutions, sports clubs, and gas stations will be banned from selling alcohol. Although the advertising of alcohol is already illegal, the new law forces TV stations to blur images of alcoholic beverages shown on the screen. All liquor bottles must display warning signs about the dangers of consuming alcohol. There will also be stricter penalties for drunken driving.

"We don't want a generation walking around drunk night and day. We want a youth that is sharp and shrewd and full of knowledge," said Turkey's prime minister, Recep Tayyip Erdogan, in defense of the legislation. The Turkish president signed the legislation into law on June 10.

Yet even with those restrictions on alcohol sales, residents of Bridgewater, Connecticut, who want to purchase alcohol would have an easier time in Turkey than in their own town—the last remaining "dry" town in Connecticut. But Connecticut is not alone; thirty-two other states have laws that allow counties and local jurisdictions to prohibit the sale of alcohol. Three of those states—Kansas, Mississippi, and Tennessee—are "dry" by default; individual counties must vote to become "wet." More than half of the 75 counties in Arkansas are "dry." There are 35 municipalities in New Jersey that prohibit the retail sale of alcohol. The county in Tennessee where the Jack Daniel's distillery is located is a "dry" county!

Although every state in the Union has its own peculiar laws regarding the sale, possession, manufacturing, and consumption of alcohol, there is one thing that is uniform throughout the country—the drinking age of 21.

Why is the drinking age 21?

The United States is one of only three developed countries in the world with a nationwide drinking age over 18. The other two countries are Iceland and Japan, which both have a drinking age of 20.

The main problem with the United States' having a drinking age of 21 is that the age of majority is 18 (19 in Alabama and Nebraska), as it is throughout most of the world. That is the age when a person assumes the legal rights and responsibilities of an adult. Thus, anyone in the United States who has reached the age of 18 is legally eligible to vote, run for office, enter legally binding contracts, marry, engage in consensual sex with other adults, adopt children, join the military, be subject to the draft (when the draft is in force), purchase tobacco (except in Alabama, Alaska, New Jersey and Utah, where one must be 19), and purchase pornography; that is, everything under the sun except buy a beer.

Whether the age of majority should be higher, lower, or kept at age 18 is irrelevant. Whatever the age of majority, it makes absolutely no sense for it to be lower than the drinking age. In most countries, the age of majority coincides with the drinking age.

So why is the drinking age 21 in the United States?

Before Prohibition (1919), which prohibited only the manufacture, sale, and transportation of alcohol, not the drinking of it, only a handful of states even had a legal drinking age. After the repeal of Prohibition (1933), all of the states gradually established a minimum age to purchase alcohol. The most common age was 21. After the Twenty-Sixth Amendment to the Constitution was adopted in 1971, which prohibited the states from setting their voting age above 18, most states lowered their drinking ages, usually down to 18. From the late 1970s to the early 1980s, some states raised their drinking ages to 19, 20, or even 21. But by mid 1988, every state in the Union had raised its drinking age to 21.

Why is that? Why is the drinking age 21?

The answer is the National Minimum Drinking Age Act of 1984 (H.R.4616, P.L. 98-363), which mandated that the states raise their drinking ages to 21 or their federal highway funding would be cut by 10 percent beginning in fiscal year 1988.

On April 14, 1982, Ronald Reagan issued Executive Order 12358 establishing the Presidential Commission on Drunk Driving. The commission was composed of twenty-six members appointed by the president plus two members of Congress from each House. The functions of the commission were to:

(a) heighten public awareness of the seriousness of the drunk driving problem;

(b) persuade States and communities to attack the drunk driving problem in a more organized and systematic manner, including plans to eliminate bottlenecks in the arrest, trial and sentencing process that impair the effectiveness of many drunk driving laws;

(c) encourage State and local officials and organizations to accept and use the latest techniques and methods to solve the problem; and

(d) generate public support for increased enforcement of State and local drunk driving laws.

Although the commission was supposed to exist for one year, Reagan signed another executive order extending the term of the commission to December 31, 1983.

On December 13, 1982, "An Interim Report to the Nation from the President's Commission on Drunk Driving" was released. It recommended that "States should immediately adopt 21 years of age as the minimum legal drinking age for all alcoholic beverages." In a statement issued on April 5, 1983, Reagan noted this recommendation and informed the public that three states had already raised their legal drinking age. The commission's final report was issued in November of 1983 prefaced by a letter from Reagan stating that drunk driving was "a national menace, a national tragedy, and a national disgrace." The commission's eighth recommendation (out of 39), "Minimum Legal Purchasing Age," was not only that the states should raise their drinking age, but that

> legislation at the Federal level should be enacted providing that each State enact and/or maintain a law requiring 21 years as the minimum legal age for purchasing and possessing all alcoholic beverages. Such legislation should provide that the Secretary of the United States Department of Transportation disapprove any project under Section 106 of the Federal Aid Highway Act (Title 23, United States Code) for any State not having and enforcing such a law.

Reagan signed into law the National Minimum Drinking Age Act on July 17, 1984. It had been passed in the House by voice vote, passed in the Senate with an amendment by voice vote, and then agreed to in the House by unanimous consent; that is, it had no measurable opposition in either House of Congress. In an official statement, the president said he was convinced that the bill would "help persuade State legislators to act in the national interest to save our children's lives, by raising the drinking age to 21 across the country."

There have been some major criticisms leveled at this legislation:

1. That the exclusive interest in raising the drinking age marginalized the 38 other recommendations in the commission's final report.

2. That the majority of 18–20-year-olds choose to ignore the law and drink anyway, which meant that in many cases they drank unsafely and irresponsibly in clandestine locations to avoid prosecution.

3. That alcohol-related automobile accidents were already in decline before the adoption of the legislation.

4. That for alcohol-related fatalities not associated with automobiles, raising the drinking age to 21 has had no discernible effect on fatalities associated with alcohol.

5. That safer cars, higher awareness by drivers of all ages, greater utilization of a "designated driver," and more vigorous law enforcement are what had led to the decline of driving fatalities associated with alcohol.

There is another criticism of the National Minimum Age Act that has rarely been vocalized: it is incompatible with individual liberty and limited government—the things that Republicans in the Congress and the presidency at the time professed to believe.

First, it is not the federal government's business to prevent any legal adult of any age from purchasing alcohol. If a drinking age of 21 prevents highway deaths of those who are 18–20, then the same argument could be made that a drinking age of 25 would prevent highway deaths of those who are 18–24. But why stop there? If reducing highway deaths is the priority, and if merely raising the drinking age reduces highway deaths, then it follows that the government should just ban alcohol altogether—something that few Americans would be willing to accept no matter how many highway deaths it would be claimed to prevent. And second, it is not the federal government's business to dictate to the states. Under our constitutional system of federalism, it is actually the other way around.

Libertarians would go even further:

• It is not the proper role of the federal government to seek ways to reduce highway- alcohol-related fatalities.
• It is not the proper role of the federal government to discourage anyone from drinking alcohol.
• It is not the proper role of the federal government to set a minimum age to purchase, possess, or drink alcohol.
• It is not the proper role of the federal government to license businesses to sell alcohol.
• It is not the proper role of the federal government to have a Bureau of Alcohol, Tobacco, Firearms and Explosives.
• It is not the proper role of the federal government to give states highway funds.
• It is not the proper role of the federal government to have a Department of Transportation.

In a free society, it is the role of businesses, parents, friends, family, religious organizations, temperance unions, social-welfare groups, medical professionals, and others to instruct the young on the potential dangers and safe use of alcohol; that is, anyone but the government.

*****

PROHIBITION IS ALIVE AND WELL

The Eighteenth Amendment to the Constitution that instituted Prohibition was proposed by Congress in December 1917, ratified by the requisite number of states in January 1919, and took effect in January 1920.

The first and relevant section of the Amendment reads,

> After one year from the ratification of this article the manufacture, sale, or transportation of intoxicating liquors within, the importation thereof into, or the exportation thereof from the United States and all the territory subject to the jurisdiction thereof for beverage purposes is hereby prohibited.

The Eighteenth Amendment didn't ban the consumption or possession of alcohol, just its "manufacture, sale, or transportation." Nevertheless, it effectively curtailed the legal use of alcoholic beverages in the United States.

The "appropriate legislation" mentioned in section two of the Eighteenth Amendment that was passed by Congress (over President Wilson's veto) to formally institute Prohibition was the National Prohibition Act, also known as the Volstead Act. It stated that "no person shall on or after the date when the eighteenth amendment to the Constitution of the United States goes into effect, manufacture, sell, barter, transport, import, export, deliver, furnish or possess any intoxicating liquor except as authorized in this Act." It defined "intoxicating liquor" as any beverage containing more than 0.5 percent alcohol by volume, granted exceptions and exemptions for medical and religious purposes, and provided penalties for the law's violation. It also practically criminalized the possession of alcoholic beverages, because "the possession of liquors by any person not legally permitted under this title to possess liquor shall be prima facie evidence that such liquor is kept for the purpose of being sold, bartered, exchanged, given away, furnished, or otherwise disposed of in violation of the provisions of this title."

Although the Eighteenth Amendment was repealed by the Twenty-first Amendment (proposed, ratified, and effective all in 1933), prohibition is alive and well in the twenty-first century.

On the federal level, the unauthorized production of distilled spirits by individuals is still a crime. According to the Alcohol and Tobacco Tax and Trade Bureau (a division of the U.S. Treasury Department),

> There are numerous requirements that must be met that also make it impractical to produce spirits for personal or beverage use. Some of these requirements are filing an extensive application, filing a bond, providing adequate equipment to measure spirits, providing suitable tanks and pipelines, providing a separate building (other than a dwelling) and maintaining detailed records, and filing reports.

Although one may produce beer and wine at home, only an amount up to 100 gallons per calendar year (200 gallons if two or more adults reside in the home) is allowed without having to pay federal excise tax on it, and none of it may ever be sold.

Most alcoholic beverage laws in the United States are on the state and local level. They vary considerably by state, and within each state, by county and city.

In Louisiana, the sale of alcoholic beverages of any kind is permitted in supermarkets, drug stores, gas stations, and convenience stores. But things are quite different in most other states. In Pennsylvania, wine and distilled spirits may be purchased only in state-run liquor stores. Beer may be purchased at licensed beverage outlets, but not supermarkets. In Texas, breweries may not sell to-go beer to customers. In Utah, only beer containing 3.2 percent alcohol or less may be sold at grocery and convenience stores, restaurants must buy liquor from state stores at retail prices, no alcohol may be served in restaurants without the purchase of food, and sales of kegs of beer are prohibited. In Colorado, stores licensed to sell liquor are permitted to have just one location. Under a new law that initially takes effect next year, Colorado grocers will be permitted to sell alcoholic beverages at each of their stores in the state, but the law allows for an increase only to five locations immediately, twenty locations in 2032, and all locations in 2037.

The states of Kansas, Mississippi, and Tennessee are "dry" states: counties in those states must specifically authorize alcohol sales. Each of those states has dry counties. In Tennessee, that includes the county where the Jack Daniel's distillery is located. Only in seventeen states are local jurisdictions prohibited from enacting alcohol laws that conflict with state law. Many other states also contain some dry counties, cities, or towns— especially Alabama, Arkansas, Georgia, Kentucky, Pennsylvania, and Texas. In some of these areas, it is just the retail sale of distilled spirits that is prohibited. It has been estimated that about 18,000,000 people live in the 10 percent of the area of the United States that is dry.

Sunday sales of alcoholic beverages are heavily regulated in most states. In many states and counties, no alcoholic beverages of any kind can be sold before a certain time on Sunday. In some states and counties, no alcohol can be sold for off-premise consumption. In other states and counties, it is just distilled spirits that cannot be sold for off-premise consumption. Until only recently, some states banned alcohol sales on election day.

But even when it is generally acceptable for Americans to purchase and drink beer, wine, and liquor, the governments of all fifty states are united in prohibiting legal adults who have not reached the age of twenty-one from purchasing or drinking them. Even though it is perfectly legal for anyone in the United States who has reached the age of eighteen to vote, run for office, marry, adopt children, join the military, sign contracts, and purchase pornography, it is still illegal for those not yet twenty-one to sip a cocktail in a bar, order a glass of wine in a restaurant, or drink a beer while watching a football game in the privacy of their own home. The United States is one of only three developed countries in the world with a nationwide drinking age over 18. Why? Contrary to what many foreigners might think, the U.S. drinking age is not exactly the result of a federal law to that effect. Every state sets its own drinking age. However, the federal government has basically bribed the states into raising their drinking ages. The National Minimum Drinking Age Act of 1984, which was enacted with no measurable opposition in either House of Congress, mandated that the states raise their drinking ages to twenty-one or their federal highway funding would be cut.

There is neither rhyme nor reason to these laws. How can something be immoral or impious at one time, but perfectly acceptable a minute later? How can something be addictive or risky in one county, but perfectly fine across the county line? How can something be dangerous or unhealthy the day before someone turns twenty-one, but perfectly okay on his twenty-first birthday?

But even worse, prohibition laws are the backbone of the nanny state. A nanny state has a government that majors in micro-managing the behavior of its citizens.

Americans can sing all they want about living in "the land of the free," but it doesn't change the fact that a society where the government prohibits consenting adults from buying or selling alcoholic beverages or legal adults from consuming alcoholic beverages is an authoritarian society, not a free society.

It is an illegitimate function of government to discourage anyone from drinking alcoholic beverages, prohibit commerce in alcoholic beverages, make someone obtain a license to sell or serve alcoholic beverages, restrict when or where alcoholic beverages can be sold or consumed, or set a minimum age to purchase, possess, or drink alcoholic beverages.

All laws at the federal, state, and local levels that in any way concern alcoholic beverages in any form should be repealed, and repealed immediately. All such laws are inimical to liberty and property.

*****

LIQUOR SOCIALISM

As long as America has been a nation, governments at all levels have sought to tax, regulate, control, and even prohibit the manufacture, sale, and consumption of alcoholic beverages.

The most infamous example, of course, is the era of Prohibition.

The Eighteenth Amendment to the Constitution took effect in January 1920. It didn't ban outright the consumption or possession of alcohol, just its "manufacture, sale, or transportation." The National Prohibition Act (the Volstead Act), the "appropriate legislation" that formally instituted Prohibition, effectively criminalized the possession of alcoholic beverages, because "the possession of liquors by any person not legally permitted under this title to possess liquor shall be prima facie evidence that such liquor is kept for the purpose of being sold, bartered, exchanged, given away, furnished, or otherwise disposed of in violation of the provisions of this title."

Although the Eighteenth Amendment was repealed by the Twenty-first Amendment in 1933, the unauthorized production of distilled spirits by individuals is still a crime, the amount of beer and wine that one can produce at home is limited, Sunday sales of alcoholic beverages are heavily regulated, and there are hundreds of "dry" counties across the United States that prohibit the sale of alcoholic beverages.

One result of government intervention in the alcoholic-beverage market is the liquor store.

In Louisiana, the sale of alcoholic beverages of any kind is permitted in supermarkets, drug stores, gas stations, and convenience stores. But in most other states, distilled spirits can be purchased only at a liquor store.

In my state of Florida, Gov. Rick Scott recently vetoed a bill (SB 106) that would have allowed grocery stores, gas stations, and other retailers to sell liquor alongside the beer and wine they already sell. Currently, spirits must be sold in a stand-alone location or in an attached location that has its own entrance.

Independent liquor-store owners, the state's oldest and largest fine wine and spirits merchant (ABC Fine Wine & Spirits), and a major grocery chain (Publix Super Markets) that operates many liquor stores all opposed the legislation. The Florida Independent Spirits Association, an organization representing the privately owned, spirits-only retailers across the state, delivered more than 3,000 petitions to Governor Scott urging him to veto the bill. In a surprise move, Scott wrote in his veto message that although he has been committed from the day he took office "to eliminating regulations that impose duplicative and unnecessary requirements on Florida's citizens and businesses" and has "repealed almost 5,000 regulations to reduce unnecessary burdens on Floridians," he was vetoing the bill because of "concerns as to how this bill could affect many small businesses across Florida."

By Scott's reasoning, the best way for the state of Florida to help small businesses would be to mandate that each and every product currently sold in grocery and department stores must be sold in a separate store.

The truth, of course, is that the passage of the bill would positively affect Florida small businesses because it would allow them to begin selling a product that they have heretofore been prohibited from selling. It is just one type of small business (independent liquor stores) and large retailers that can afford to house separate liquor stores within their footprint that benefit from this bill's being squelched. Scott's veto is likewise anti-consumer, since it gives consumers fewer choices on store shelves and forces them to go to specific stores to purchase a certain commodity. Scott's veto is all about maintaining a government-granted privilege that benefits some businesses at the expense of others.

To see how ridiculous this protectionist scheme is just imagine that the state of Florida had mandated that meat must be sold only in meat stores, fruit must be sold only in fruit stores, and vegetables must be sold only in vegetable stores. Yes, there are butcher shops, fruit stands, and vegetable markets in Florida, but that doesn't mean that meat, fruits, and vegetables aren't also available in grocery stores. Even if Scott had signed SB 106 into law, that doesn't mean that there would be no more liquor stores in Florida.

Things are even worse in other states.

Seventeen states are "Alcoholic Beverage Control" states where the state has control over the wholesaling or retailing of some or all types of alcoholic beverages, especially distilled spirits.

Iowa, Maine, Michigan, Mississippi, Montana, Ohio, Oregon, Vermont, Wyoming, and West Virginia control alcohol on the wholesale level. Retail stores in those states are basically state-contracted liquor stores. There are not multiple suppliers from which stores may choose to purchase their liquor inventory.

In Alabama, Idaho, New Hampshire, North Carolina, Pennsylvania, Utah, and Virginia, the government owns and operates all of the liquor stores. Private liquor stores are not allowed. That is also the case in three counties in Maryland.

This is liquor socialism.

Although the governments in states with state-owned liquor stores don't own the means of production—that is, the state governments don't actually produce the alcohol that is sold—they effectively do, since it is the government that owns the liquor stores, decides where the liquor stores will be located, determines which brands and sizes will be offered for sale, sets the prices of the products, establishes what the operating hours of the store will be, and chooses who will be hired as employees. And of course, in conjunction with all of that, all other entities are prohibited from doing the same things. The government has an absolute monopoly on liquor sales. That is about as close to liquor socialism as one can get short of the government's actually distilling the spirits.

Imagine if the governments of each of the fifty states decided that they would have a monopoly on every good that was offered for sale: food, automobiles, paper products, computers, cosmetics, lumber, nails, coal, gasoline, natural gas, tires, plastics, appliances, clothing, shoes, hats, paint, office supplies, and so on. Imagine if those governments required a separate store dedicated to each good. Imagine if all manufacturers could sell their products only to the government, and not directly to stores or consumers.

Sounds absolutely ludicrous. And indeed it is. So why isn't a government monopoly on distilled spirits deemed to be just as ludicrous? And why stop there? All government efforts to tax, regulate, control, and prohibit the manufacture, sale, and consumption of alcoholic beverages should be viewed the same way.

*****

TOBACCO AND A FREE SOCIETY

Yet another successful lawsuit against a tobacco company, one that resulted in a jury's awarding the widow of a tobacco smoker more than $23 billion because of her husband's premature death, means that it is apropos to revisit the subject of tobacco and a free society.

A jury last month in Escambia County (Pensacola), Florida, after a four-week trial and a fifteen-hour deliberation, awarded Cynthia Robinson more than $16 million in compensatory damages and $23.6 billion in punitive damages after she sued tobacco company R.J. Reynolds on behalf of her late husband, Michael Johnson, 36, who died of lung cancer in 1996. He is reported to have been a chain smoker since age 13, and smoked until the day he died. His widow alleged that R.J. Reynolds had willfully concealed from her late husband the harmful effects and addictive nature of its product.

The case of *Cynthia Robinson v. R.J. Reynolds Tobacco Company* harkens back to the Florida class action case of *Engle v. Liggett Group Inc.* (2006). In that case, which actually began in 1994, a trial judge certified a nationwide class of people with smoking-related diseases and family members of deceased smokers. A jury then awarded $12.7 million in compensatory damages to three individual plaintiffs and $145 billion to the class. An appeals court later limited the scope of the class to Florida residents. The Florida Supreme Court then decertified the class, "but ruled that class members could file individual suits using the Engle jury's eight findings, including that smoking causes cancer, that nicotine is addictive, and that the tobacco companies sold defective and unreasonably dangerous cigarettes.

Robinson filed her individual lawsuit in 2008.

In 2013, the Florida Supreme Court re-approved its decision in *Engle*, making it easier for smokers or family members of deceased smokers to sue tobacco companies. In the case of *Philip Morris USA Inc. et al. v. Douglas et al.*, the high court ruled in favor of James Douglas, who sued Philip Morris USA Inc., R.J. Reynolds Tobacco Co., and Liggett Group LLC for being responsible for the death of his wife, Charlotte, 62, who died of chronic obstructive pulmonary disease and lung cancer in 2008. A jury had awarded him $5 million (later reduced to $2.5 million), but "the tobacco companies appealed, arguing that trial court erred in applying the phase I jury findings from *Engle*." The Florida Supreme Court then rejected the tobacco companies' argument that accepting as *res judicata* the eight phase I findings approved in *Engle* violated their due process rights, stating, "That certain elements of the *prima facie* case are established by the phase I findings does not violate the *Engle* defendants' due process rights because they were parties to and had notice and opportunity to be heard in the class action where those elements were decided."

The attorneys for Mrs. Robinson said that "the punitive damages are the largest of any individual case stemming from the original class action lawsuit." Yet one attorney, Willie Gary, insisted that "the lawsuit's goal was to stop tobacco companies from targeting children and young people with their advertising." Jeffery Raborn, R.J. Reynolds's vice president and assistant general counsel, called the damages "grossly excessive and impermissible under state and constitutional law." He also said that "this verdict goes far beyond the realm of reasonableness and fairness, and is completely inconsistent with the evidence presented."

According to the *Pensacola News Journal*, "Other Florida juries have hit tobacco companies with tens of millions of dollars in punitive damages in lawsuits stemming from the original class action lawsuit. Some large jury verdicts awarding tens of millions of dollars in damages to relatives of smokers have been upheld by appeals courts."

In June of this year, the U.S. Supreme Court rejected cigarette manufacturers' appeals in court judgments to Florida smokers. Thus, we can expect to see more and more of these lawsuits against the big tobacco companies.

In a free society, that would not be so.

In contrast to the legislative, litigious, nanny-state, regulatory society that exists in the United States today, a free society—which used to exist in this country—is a society based not only on individual liberty and freedom, but also on personal accountability and responsibility.

Tobacco has been cultivated and smoked in the United States since colonial times. James Bonsack revolutionized the tobacco industry when he invented the first cigarette-rolling machine in 1880. Although, according to the Centers for Disease Control and Prevention (CDC), "The percentage of adult Americans who smoke has declined since 1965 from 42.4% to 18.9% in 2011," more than a billion people worldwide are estimated to use tobacco in some form.

Smoking tobacco has been recognized as a health hazard since at least the mid twentieth century. The World Health Organization (WHO) considers tobacco use to be "the single most preventable cause of death in the world today." It estimates that tobacco use is responsible for "100 million deaths" during the twentieth century.

The CDC says about the health effects of tobacco,

Tobacco use is the single most preventable cause of disease, disability, and death in the United States. Each year, an estimated 443,000 people die prematurely from smoking or exposure to secondhand smoke, and another

8.6 million live with a serious illness caused by smoking.

Yet, continues the CDC, "despite these risks, approximately 46.6 million U.S. adults smoke cigarettes."

The United States was the first country to require health warnings on packs of cigarettes. The original warning label, appearing from 1966 to 1970, was "Caution: Cigarette Smoking May be Hazardous to Your Health." It was replaced from 1970 to 1985 with "Warning: The Surgeon General Has Determined that Cigarette Smoking is Dangerous to Your Health." Since 1985, cigarette packs have contained one of four surgeon-general's warnings:

• SURGEON GENERAL'S WARNING: Smoking Causes Lung Cancer, Heart Disease, Emphysema, And May Complicate Pregnancy.
• SURGEON GENERAL'S WARNING: Quitting Smoking Now Greatly Reduces Serious Risks to Your Health.
• SURGEON GENERAL'S WARNING: Smoking By Pregnant Women May Result in Fetal Injury, Premature Birth, And Low Birth Weight.
• SURGEON GENERAL'S WARNING: Cigarette Smoke Contains Carbon Monoxide.

Although the Family Smoking Prevention and Tobacco Control Act of 1999 (PL 111-31) gave the Food and Drug Administration (FDA) the legal authority to regulate tobacco, the attempt by the agency to replace the four familiar, small text warnings that currently appear on cigarette packages with nine new and larger graphic warning labels was overruled by a federal court. Cigarette advertising on television and radio has been banned since 1971.

But regardless of how hazardous tobacco is to one's health, regardless of how addictive smoking is, regardless of how tobacco companies have misled the public about their products, regardless of how governmental agencies and bureaucrats feel about tobacco, and regardless of how many Americans consider smoking to be a bad habit, a vice, or a sin, in a free society people are free to destroy their health, poison themselves, shorten their life, and engage in unpopular, bad, or sinful habits on their own property or the property of others with permission as long as they assume full responsibility for the consequences of their actions.

In a free society, it is not the business of government to require warning labels on cigarette packages; in a free society, it is not the business of government to require labels of any kind on any product.

In a free society, it is not the business of government to regulate the amount of nicotine in tobacco; in a free society, it is not the business of government to regulate the content of any substance.

In a free society, it is not the business of government to discourage or prevent anyone from smoking; in a free society, it is not the business of government to discourage or prevent anyone from engaging in any voluntary and peaceful activity.

In a free society, it is not the business of government to regulate the advertising of tobacco; in a free society, it is not the business of government to regulate the advertising of any product.

In a free society, it is not the business of government to institute smoking bans in bars or restaurants; in a free society, it is not the business of government to have anything to do with any voluntary and peaceful activity that occurs in any bar or restaurant.

In a free society, it is not the business of government to warn anyone about the dangers of smoking; in a free society, it is not the business of government to warn anyone about the dangers of any activity.

Tobacco use has a place in a free society. And so do anti-tobacco ads, smoking bans, the ostracism of smokers, and attempts to educate people about the dangers of smoking—but only if they are undertaken and paid for by individuals and organizations without government mandate, funding, oversight, or control.

*****

WORKPLACE SMOKING

While making a brief trip recently to a place of business in a local outdoor mall in central Florida, I noticed that a new sign had been posted on the information board in the middle of one of the sidewalks: "Smoking in Workplaces Is Prohibited by Law." The sign was gone the next week, replaced by an ad for a movie at the mall's theater, so I was glad that I had written down what was on it. Apparently, these signs change every so often, depending on how long organizations or places of business want to advertise something.

I remember that the smoking sign also contained a phone number for people to call for more information. And in small print at the bottom of the sign was the website address for Tobacco Free Florida (TFF). It turns out that TFF is not some private anti-smoking organization that was trying to draw attention to Florida smoking laws. TFF is a state agency designed "to protect the people of Florida from the dangers of tobacco."

TFF

According to the TFF website mentioned on the sign at the mall, "TTF is administered through the Florida Department of Health's Bureau of Tobacco Free Florida (BTFF), and funded by money derived from the state's tobacco settlement agreement with the major tobacco companies in 1997."

The state of Florida sued a number of tobacco companies in 1995 and eventually reached an $11.3 billion out-of-court settlement with them to compensate the state for the public-health costs caused by smoking-related illnesses. Florida's governor Lawton Chiles said the state won on three important battlegrounds: "protecting Florida's children, making tobacco pay for the damage it has cost our taxpayers, and for cigarette makers to finally tell the truth." Payments to the state by the tobacco companies under the settlement are made on April 30 and December 31 of each year and are based on the tobacco companies' national market share. Nonmonetary provisions of the settlement included the prohibition of billboard and transit advertisements of cigarettes and the removal of cigarette-vending machines from places accessible to children.

In 2006, the Florida Use of Tobacco Settlement Funds Amendment (amendment 4) appeared on the November election ballot—the result of a constitutional amendment initiative petition requiring 611,009 signatures (720,218 were obtained). More than 60 percent of Florida voters approved amending the Florida constitution to require the funding of statewide tobacco-education and -prevention programs with tobacco-settlement money. More than $5 million was spent on the media campaign focusing on the amendment's passage—all from one group: Floridians for Youth Tobacco Education.

The ballot title read, "Protect People, Especially Youth, from Addiction, Disease, and Other Health Hazards of Using Tobacco." The summary of the amendment on the ballot read,

> To protect people, especially youth, from addiction, disease, and other health hazards of using tobacco, the Legislature shall use some Tobacco Settlement money annually for a comprehensive statewide tobacco education and prevention program using Centers for Disease Control best practices. Specifies some program components, emphasizing youth, requiring one-third of total annual funding for advertising. Annual funding is 15% of 2005 Tobacco Settlement payments to Florida, adjusted annually for inflation. Provides definitions. Effective immediately.

The ballot language also contained this fiscal note:

> This amendment requires state government to appropriate approximately $57 million in 2007 for the Comprehensive Statewide Tobacco Education and Prevention Program. Thereafter, this amount will increase annually with inflation. This spending is expected to reduce tobacco consumption. As a result, some long-term savings to state and local government health and insurance programs are probable, but indeterminate. Also, minor revenue loss to state government is probable, but indeterminate.

TFF was launched in 2007 as a direct result of the passage of this constitutional amendment.

According to the Campaign for Tobacco-Free Kids, tobacco use is the leading cause of preventable disease in Florida, where each year more than 32,000 people die from smoking—more than die from "alcohol, AIDS, car crashes, illegal drugs, murders, and suicides combined." About 270,000 "kids now under 18 and alive in Florida who will ultimately die prematurely from smoking." The annual health-care costs in Florida directly caused by smoking are said to be $8.64 billion. The Medicaid costs are said to be $1.51 billion. Productivity losses are said to be $8.32 billion. Florida residents' state and federal tax burden from smoking-caused government expenditures is said to be $835 per household.

Following the principles established by the Centers for Disease Control and Prevention, TFF "reaches millions of Floridians through hard-hitting media campaigns, public relations, social media, evidence-based tobacco cessation services, grassroots initiatives, county-level grants that advance tobacco-free policies, a youth-led movement called Students Working Against Tobacco (SWAT), school-based interventions, and surveillance and evaluation to ensure effectiveness."

The BTFF-desired result for the TFF program is "to inspire Floridians to quit smoking and discourage youth from starting." The agency claims that TFF is working. TFF "awareness" is high throughout the state, and "shows a positive impact on smoking-related attitudes and behaviors." The smoking rate of adults in Florida is below the national average. The smoking rate for high-school students has decreased. Fewer high-school students are reporting living in a home where someone smokes. TFF "is saving lives and saving taxpayers millions of dollars."

But regardless of how unhealthy smoking is, regardless of how many people die from smoking-related diseases, and regardless of how successful Florida's TFF program is, some important questions must still be answered about the proper role of government:

1. Is it the proper role of government to educate people about the health risks of smoking?
2. Is it the proper role of government to persuade people to quit smoking?
3. Is it the proper role of government to help people to quit smoking?

From a libertarian perspective, the answer, of course, is a resounding "no" to all three questions. Libertarians see the purpose of government as being limited to the protection of people's lives, liberty, and property from the violence or fraud of others. The only legitimate purposes of government are to prosecute and punish those who initiate violence against others, commit fraud against them, or violate their property rights. Acts of government paternalism lead to a nanny state from which there is never an end. A nanny state is a perversion of government.

If it is the proper role of government to educate people about the health risks of smoking, then what about government's using tax money to educate people about the health risks of obesity? If it is the proper role of government to persuade people to quit smoking, then what about government's using tax money to persuade people to eat healthy foods? If it is the proper role of government to help people to quit smoking, then what about government's using tax money to help people to lose weight? And why should the government stop with obesity, healthy eating, and losing weight?

In a free society, private organizations would be free to educate people about the health risks of smoking, persuade people to quit smoking, and help people to quit smoking—as long as they were privately funded and not government funded. Once a nanny state is accepted in the name of the public interest, no logical argument can be made to limit its reach.

But what about the need for the state of Florida to be compensated for the public-health costs caused by smoking-related illnesses? That question also has a simple answer. There should be no public-health costs of any kind to begin with. There should be no Medicaid. Hospitals should not be forced to admit all comers. Smokers should be liable for their own medical expenses incurred as a result of their use of tobacco. Health- and life-insurance companies should be able to charge whatever they deem appropriate to insure smokers; and they should be able to refuse to issue any policies to them in the first place. Every member of society should be responsible for the consequences of his own actions. It is simply ludicrous to blame the tobacco companies for the premature deaths of smokers. And it should be noted that when Florida and the other states sued the tobacco companies, the money they were awarded included punitive damages, not just money to reimburse them for public-health spending.

Do states with anti-tobacco programs really want all of their residents to quit smoking? All states with anti-smoking programs face a dilemma. Cigarette excise taxes are a nice source of revenue for the states. Missouri has the lowest state tax on a pack of cigarettes at only 17 cents. The tax rates in Virginia (30 cents), Georgia (37 cents), and North Dakota (44 cents) are also fairly low. But the tax rate in most states is much higher, especially in the Northeast, where the tax on a pack of cigarettes is $3.90 in Connecticut, $3.51 in Massachusetts, $3.75 in Rhode Island, $4.35 in New York, and $3.08 in Vermont. And then there are local cigarette taxes, as in Chicago, where the combined state, county, and municipal taxes total $6.16 and in New York City, where smokers pay a total of $5.85 per pack. That is all in addition to the federal excise tax of $1.0066 on each pack of cigarettes. And then there is state sales tax on each pack sold.

It is one thing for the government to educate people about the health risks of smoking; it is one thing for the government to persuade people to quit smoking; it is one thing for the government to help people to quit smoking, but it is an entirely different matter for the government to ban smoking in workplaces. To do so is to go from a nanny state to an authoritarian state.

But that is exactly what the state of Florida did when it amended the Florida Clean Indoor Air Act (FCIAA).

FCIAA

The FCIAA was enacted by the Florida Legislature in 1995. Its stated purpose was "to protect the public health, comfort, and environment by creating areas in public places and at public meetings that are reasonably free from tobacco smoke by providing a uniform statewide maximum code." It decreed that "a person may not smoke in a public place or at a public meeting except in designated smoking areas." A "public place" was defined as an "enclosed, indoor area used by the general public." That included government buildings, public transportation and their associated terminals, elevators, hospitals, nursing homes, educational facilities, public-school buses, libraries, courtrooms, jury-waiting and jury-deliberation rooms, museums, theaters, auditoriums, arenas, recreational facilities, restaurants, retail stores, grocery stores, places of employment, health-care facilities, day-care centers, and common areas of retirement homes and condominiums.

In 2002, the Florida Prohibit Workplace Smoking Amendment (amendment 6) appeared on the November election ballot. Like the Florida Use of Tobacco Settlement Funds Amendment, it was the result of a constitutional amendment initiative petition. This time the initiative petition required 488,722 signatures (517,217 were obtained). The initiative was sponsored by Smoke-Free for Health, Inc. More than 70 percent of Florida voters approved amending the Florida constitution to prohibit smoking in more indoor workplace environments.

The ballot title read, "Protect People from the Health Hazards of Second-Hand Tobacco Smoke by Prohibiting Workplace Smoking." The summary of the amendment on the ballot read,

> To protect people from the health hazards of second-hand tobacco smoke, this amendment prohibits tobacco smoking in enclosed indoor workplaces. Allows exceptions for private residences except when they are being used to provide commercial child care, adult care or health care. Also allows exceptions for retail tobacco shops, designated smoking guest rooms at hotels and other public lodging establishments, and stand-alone bars. Provides definitions, and requires the legislature to promptly implement this amendment.

The text of the amendment defined "enclosed indoor workplace" as

> any place where one or more persons engages [sic] in work, and which place is predominantly or totally bounded on all sides and above by physical barriers, regardless of whether such barriers consist of or include un-

covered openings, screened or otherwise partially covered openings; or
open or closed windows, jalousies, doors, or the like.

It included as "work," without limitation, "any such service performed by
an employee, independent contractor, agent, partner, proprietor, manager,
officer, director, apprentice, trainee, associate, servant, volunteer, and the
like." The smoking prohibition became effective on July 1, 2003, and applied to all enclosed indoor workplaces "without regard to whether work
is occurring at any given time."

Now, there is no question that cigarette smoking is not only unhealthy,
but potentially deadly. According to the Centers for Disease Control and
Prevention,

• Cigarette smoking harms nearly every organ of the body, causes many
diseases, and reduces the health of smokers in general.
• Cigarette smoking causes more than 480,000 deaths each year in the
United States.
• More than 10 times as many U.S. citizens have died prematurely from
cigarette smoking as have died in all the wars fought by the United States
during its history.
• Cigarette smoking increases risk for death from all causes in men and
women.
• Smokers are more likely than nonsmokers to develop heart disease,
stroke, and lung cancer.
• Smoking causes diminished overall health, increased absenteeism from
work, and increased health-care utilization and cost.
• Cigarette smoking causes most cases of lung cancer.
• Smoking can cause cancer almost anywhere in the body.
• If nobody smoked, one of every three cancer deaths in the United States
would not happen.

Is there a cigarette smoker in America who doesn't realize that smoking is
unhealthy and potentially deadly? The danger of smoking was never the
issue.

It is one thing for the government to ban smoking in government
buildings and public; that is, government-owned and -operated, places
such as libraries, schools, buses, hospitals, transit systems, parks, museums, auditoriums, arenas, and recreational facilities; but it is an entirely
different matter for the government to ban smoking in restaurants, theaters, stores, workplaces, health-care facilities, nursing homes, day-care
centers, common areas of retirement homes and condominiums, and privately owned libraries, schools, buses, hospitals, transit systems, parks,
museums, auditoriums, arenas, and recreational facilities.

It is simply not the business of government to prohibit the use of what it deems to be unhealthy, addictive, or harmful substances. A government with the power to outlaw unhealthy, addictive, or harmful substances is a government with the power to ban any substance for the populace's "own good." The fact that a majority of people might favor banning some activity or a majority of voters indicate to a legislature that they want such a prohibition binding on others does not make the prohibition any less misguided, wrong, or authoritarian.

In a free society, all elements of the private sector individually decide on smoking policies. In a free society, it is entirely up to the owners of restaurants, transportation services, stores, shops, entertainment venues, recreation venues, and other places that do business with the general public to prohibit smoking, permit smoking, set up designated smoking areas, or otherwise regulate smoking on property or in vehicles they own. In a free society, it is likewise entirely up to the owners of offices, factories, plants, and other workplaces that don't do business with the general public to formulate their own smoking policies.

But it is not just decisions about smoking that should be left up to each individual business. The same principle applies to a whole host of things in the workplace that government at some level currently regulates or that many people would like to see government regulate.

Workplace sovereignty

In a free society, the workplace is sovereign. That means that the owners of the workplace—not the government—set policies relating to employees in the workplace and members of the public who enter the workplace to engage in commerce. If an employee (or potential employee) doesn't like a policy in the workplace he can suffer in silence, seek to have the offending policy changed, or find another place of employment. It is that simple. If someone from the general public doesn't like a policy in a particular workplace, he can likewise suffer in silence, seek to have the offending policy changed, or find another workplace to engage in commerce. It is that simple. It all comes down to the right of property owners to establish the rules for being on their property.

As it relates to employees, workplace sovereignty means that employers are free to mandate that certain uniforms be worn, whether facial hair is allowed, what hair styles are permitted, whether head coverings can be worn, and whether religious or other exemptions will be granted for any of those things. Workplace sovereignty means that questions of salary, health insurance, sick pay, family leave, and overtime pay are things to be negotiated between employer and employee—the government should have nothing to do with any of them or otherwise interfere with the employer/employee relationship. Workplace sovereignty also means that it is up to each employer whether employees are required, permitted, or forbidden to say "Merry Christmas" or "Happy Holidays."

As it relates to the general public, workplace sovereignty means that patrons of businesses may be required to dress a certain way as a condition of entering or engaging in commerce with a particular place of business. I am old enough to remember signs outside of stores reading, "No shirt, no shoes, no service." Workplace sovereignty means that patrons may be required to behave a certain way; for example, not using profanity. Workplace sovereignty also means that businesses have the right to refuse service to anyone for any reason or offer discounts to particular groups on any basis.

Workplace sovereignty works—in a free society where property rights are respected, freedom of association is observed, and the government stays out of the workplace.

*****

FIRST ALCOHOL, NOW TOBACCO

The United States is one of only three developed countries in the world with a nationwide drinking age over 18. The other two countries are Iceland and Japan, which both have a drinking age of 20.

The problem, of course, is that the age of majority—when a minor assumes the legal rights and responsibilities of an adult—is 18 in most states, 19 in two states (Alabama and Nebraska), and 21 in just two states (Colorado and Mississippi). There are generally exceptions for children who are married or have been legally emancipated. In most countries, the age of majority coincides with the drinking age.

So why is the drinking age 21 in the United States?

Before Prohibition (1919), only a handful of states had a drinking age. After the repeal of Prohibition (1933), all of the states gradually established a minimum drinking age, most commonly 21. After the Twenty-Sixth Amendment to the Constitution was adopted in 1971, which prohibited the states from setting their voting age above 18, most states lowered their drinking ages down to 18. But by 1988, every state in the Union had raised its drinking age to 21.

This happened because the National Minimum Drinking Age Act of 1984 (H.R.4616, P.L. 98-363) mandated that the states raise their drinking ages to 21 or their federal highway funding would be cut by 10 percent beginning in fiscal year 1988.

First alcohol, now tobacco.

Federal law requires states to have a minimum age of 18 for the purchase of tobacco products.

New Jersey governor Chris Christie signed 53 bills into law last month and vetoed 14 others. But one bill (S-359/A-2320) in particular will live in infamy because it raises the minimum age to purchase tobacco products in

New Jersey from 19 to 21. The bill passed the Democratic-controlled legislature by a vote of 53-16 in the Assembly and 23-14 in the Senate. Christie "vetoed a similar plan last year that was opposed by food retailers who feared the loss of potentially millions of dollars in revenue." The bill, which takes effect on January 1, 2018, also applies to e-cigarettes.

Said Governor Christie:

> By raising the minimum age to purchase tobacco products to 21, we are giving young people more time to develop a maturity and better understanding of how dangerous smoking can be and that it is better to not start smoking in the first place.

> My mother died from the effects of smoking, and no one should lose their life due to any addictive substance. Additionally, the less people who develop costly tobacco habits that can cause health problems, such as lung cancer, heart disease and developmental issues, the less strain there will be on our healthcare system.

This makes New Jersey the third state (after Hawaii and California) to raise its tobacco purchase age to 21. Similar bills are pending in Maine and Oregon. Hundreds of cities and counties also have a minimum purchase age of 21. In the states of Alabama, Alaska, and Utah, one must be 19 to purchase tobacco products.

The problem with a minimum age of 21 to purchase tobacco is the same problem with a minimum age of 21 to purchase alcohol: the age of majority is generally 18. This means that a legal adult in the United States who has not turned 21 can buy a gun, enter into binding contracts, vote, sue or be sued, serve on a jury, get a tattoo, marry, engage in consensual sex with other adults, donate plasma, get a credit card, change his name, open a bank account, adopt children, go to jail or prison, work at or go to a strip club, purchase lottery tickets, join the military, be subject to a military draft, purchase fireworks, rent a car or hotel room, and purchase pornography—but not buy a beer or, depending on where one lives, a pack of cigarettes.

And Americans think they live in a free society?

Because alcohol is banned in many Muslim countries and countries like Bhutan ban the sale, cultivation, and production of tobacco, Americans think they live in a free society when the truth is they live in a *relatively* free society.

Is tobacco unhealthy, deadly, and addictive? Of course it is. According to the Centers for Disease Control and Prevention (CDC):

• Cigarette smoking causes more than 480,000 deaths each year in the United States. This is nearly one in five deaths.
• Smoking causes more deaths each year than the following causes com-

bined: human immunodeficiency virus (HIV), illegal drug use, alcohol use, motor vehicle injuries, and firearm-related incidents.
• More than 10 times as many U.S. citizens have died prematurely from cigarette smoking than have died in all the wars fought by the United States.
• Smoking causes about 90% of all lung cancer deaths. More women die from lung cancer each year than from breast cancer.
• Smoking causes about 80% of all deaths from chronic obstructive pulmonary disease (COPD).
• Cigarette smoking increases risk for death from all causes in men and women.

But the dangers of tobacco use are not the issue. If the dangers were the issue, then the minimum age to purchase tobacco would be raised to 25 or 45 or 65. If the dangers were the issue, then every state in the Union would follow the lead of Bhutan.

It should also be noted that the minimum age to purchase tobacco is usually higher than the minimum age to possess or use tobacco. So, in general, any American 18 or older can legally smoke; he just can't buy a pack of cigarettes himself.

The issue here is the role of the state. Every state government, just like the federal government, thinks its mission is to protect its citizens from bad habits, vice, unhealthy actions, addictive behavior, and dangerous activity. In a word, to protect people from *themselves*. In a free society, any legal adult would be able to buy, sell, possess, and use any substance.

A nanny state is incompatible with a free society.

*****

NOAH'S ARK AND THE SANCTITY OF PRIVATE PROPERTY

The subject of a proposed religious theme park in Kentucky brings up an issue near and dear to the heart of libertarians: the sanctity of private property.

There is some controversy over the proposed construction of a $150 million Noah's Ark theme park on 800 acres near Interstate 75 in Kentucky. The theme park—to be called Ark Encounter—is a joint venture between Answers in Genesis and Ark Encounter LLC. The former group already opened a $27 million Creation museum in Petersburg, Kentucky, in 2007.

The proposed park, to be completed by 2014, will feature live animals, event venues, a children's play area, a replica of the biblical Tower of Babel, a 500-seat special effects theater, a reproduction of a first-century Middle Eastern village, an aviary, and a 500 by 75 foot wooden ark to replicate the biblical Noah's Ark. The project is expected to create more than 900 jobs, attract 1.6 million visitors in the park's first year, and have an economic impact of $214 million in the first year alone.

As expected, religious groups generally hailed the project even as other groups that focus on church-state issues had a problem with the project. Contrary to critics of the theme park who think the educational message of the park is "unscientific" and "embarrassing for the state" or that any jobs created would be "low-paying" and "transient," Rev. Barry Lynn, executive director of Americans United for the Separation of Church and State, seemed to raise two main arguments against the proposed park: First, Lynn pointed out that when Noah launched the Ark the first time, he was not looking for government funding. Second, he said that while the Constitution doesn't prevent someone from putting up a water park, it does prevent people from putting up a religious one, such as Noah's water park.

But both of Lynn's points are misguided.

Under Kentucky's Tourism Development Act, which exists to bring tourist attractions to Kentucky, up to 25 percent of the cost of an approved project can be recovered by developers via the state's refunding to them a portion of the sales tax paid by visitors on admission tickets, gift sales, and food. Up to ten percent of the tax incentives can be refunded per year for up to ten years. It is a common thing for states to use various tax incentive measures to lure new businesses to the state. The tax incentives here involve rebated sales tax money collected that would not even be available if Ark Encounter never opened its doors. No government funding will be used to construct the park. And not only will no money be taken from the state budget, the project will generate millions of dollars of government revenue in the form of increased federal payroll taxes, state sales taxes, and local real estate taxes. Like any for-profit business, Ark Encounter will be forced to be a tax collector for the state. And like any for-profit business, Ark Encounter is a legitimate candidate for Kentucky's tax incentives.

Libertarians would, of course, argue that states shouldn't collect sales tax (the states of Alaska, Delaware, Montana, New Hampshire, and Oregon have no general sales tax), force businesses to be tax collectors, or take money from people in the form of sales taxes (or any other kind of taxes) and redistribute it to private businesses—for any reason. But Rev. Lynn is not arguing against the sales tax incentives on libertarian grounds.

Lynn's second argument is a veiled reference to the establishment clause of the First Amendment. The principle of what he seems to be saying is true: governments shouldn't fund religious construction projects or business operations. But this has nothing to do with the First Amendment, which prohibits Congress from making a law respecting the establishment of religion. The reception by religious-oriented businesses of refunded sales tax collected is not establishing any religion. And neither does it violate the prevailing broad view of the federal courts on the First Amendment. Two groups that are not normally on the side of religion, the ACLU and American Atheists, agree. The ACLU of Kentucky said that so long as giving tax incentives to religious groups is nondiscriminatory, it does not violate the Establishment Clause of the Constitution. American Atheists stated that giving tax incentives to religious groups is only actionable when there is a demonstrable bias in the sort of religious groups who benefit.

From the perspective of libertarianism, the real issue is not one of religion, but whether governments should fund private construction projects or the operations of any business no matter how it obtains the money to do so. But not only should the government not do these things, it should not have its own construction projects or operate any business. The purpose of governments, should they exist at all, is to protect their citizens' life, liberty, and property from the violence or fraud of others. Governments shouldn't build sports venues, run liquor stores, pick up garbage, or operate a bus service. These goods and services should be left to the free market.

Whether Ark Encounter or any other business—secular or religious—should accept tax incentives *of this nature* is another matter.

First of all, there are always strings attached to deals like this and there is no exception here. Kentucky governor Steve Beshear insists that "Kentucky's contract with developers of the theme park will bar tax incentives if there is discrimination in hiring based on religion." Mike Zovath, Senior Vice President of Special Projects for Answers in Genesis, "pledged to be mindful of 'green' building standards and to use local contractors."

And second, there is the moral aspect since businesses that accept refunded sales tax collected can be said to be receiving stolen funds. However, some businesses may look at receiving a sales tax incentive as a return of money confiscated from the business in the form of state corporate income tax, unemployment tax, gross receipts tax, or franchise tax. Thus, they might accept state money up to the amount of the taxes they have paid.

So what does all of this have to do with private property? Plenty.

There are many principles to be noted here that relate to the sanctity of private property. In a truly free society, there are a number of things that a property owner should not be prevented from doing.

The owner of a piece of property should not be prevented by governments or anyone else from using his property as he sees fit. That means no zoning laws, building codes, eminent domain, or environmental regulations to strip someone of his property or limit its use.

The owner of a piece of property should not be prevented by governments or anyone else from constructing whatever he chooses on his property. That might mean building a home, a business, a monument, or a nature preserve.

The owner of a piece of property should not be prevented by governments or anyone else from promoting any religion with his property. That might be accomplished by putting up a church, a mosque, a synagogue, a Buddhist temple, or a statue of Darwin.

The owner of a piece of property should not be prevented by governments or anyone else from operating any business on his property. That might be a hospital, a bar, a retail store, or a theme park.

The owner of a piece of property should not be prevented by governments or anyone else from using whatever hiring practices they choose or making any compensation agreement with employees in the course of operating any business on his property. That might include low-paying jobs, transient jobs, immigrant workers, non-union labor, out-of-town and/or non-licensed contractors, and discrimination in hiring based on religion or any other criteria.

The owner of a piece of property should not be prevented by governments or anyone else from using his property for any educational mission. That might be promoting evolution or creation, free love or celibacy, or 'green' building standards.

The owner of a piece of property should not be prevented by governments or anyone else from using his property to promote something that people disagree with. That might mean something considered stupid, immoral, unscientific, or embarrassing to the state.

The owner of a piece of property should not be prevented by governments or anyone else from doing whatever he wants on his property. That might be erecting a cross or flag, burning a cross or flag, or creating or filling in a wetland.

Controversy over a Noah's Ark theme park—or the construction or operation of any other business—vanishes when the property rights of the park, its patrons, its critics, and the taxpayers are all respected.

*****

HANDICAPPED PARKING AND A FREE SOCIETY

Special parking permits that allow disabled motorists to park in spaces reserved for the handicapped are commonly issued in every state. But in the nation's most populous state—California—where more than two million of such permits have been issued, it was recently reported by the *Los Angeles Times* that 56,000 people that had a permit were deceased.

It turns out that the California Department of Motor Vehicles checks state death records only every two years.

So, were disabled parking placards still used after those holding them had died? Certainly they were. The California DMV even acknowledges that more than a third of the placards displayed in vehicles are used illegally.

In my state of Florida, disabled persons can apply for a "disabled person parking permit" on form HSMV 83039. Their disability must be certified by a licensed physician, chiropractor, physician assistant, or advanced registered nurse practitioner (under the protocol of a licensed physician). The disabled person must have a permanent disability that limits his ability to walk 200 feet without stopping to rest because of:

• Inability to walk without the use of or assistance from a brace, cane, crutch, prosthetic device, or other assistive device, or without assistance of another person.
• The need to permanently use a wheelchair.
• Restriction by lung disease to the extent that the person's forced (respiratory) expiratory volume for 1 second, when measured by spirometry, is less than one liter or the person's arterial oxygen is less than 60 mm/hg on room air at rest.
• Use of portable oxygen.
• Restriction by cardiac condition to the extent that the person's functional limitations are classified in severity as Class III or Class IV according to standards set by the American Heart Association.
• Severe limitation in a person's ability to walk because of an arthritic, neurological, or orthopedic condition.

If someone is legally blind, an optometrist can also certify his eligibility to obtain a permit.

The parking permit is free and good for four years. A temporary permit can be issued for $15. Making a false or misleading statement on the application can result in a penalty of "up to one year in jail or a fine of $1,000 or both."

But having a handicapped-parking permit is no good if there are no designated places to park one's vehicle in. Once again, the state of Florida comes to the rescue.

According to the Florida statutes regarding handicapped parking spaces (553.5041),

Each parking space must be no less than 12 feet wide. Parking access aisles must be part of an accessible route to the building of facility entrance. In accordance with ADAAG s. 4.6.3, access aisles must be placed adjacent to accessible parking spaces; however, two accessible parking spaces may share a common access aisle. The access aisle must be striped diagonally to designate it as a no-parking zone.

Each such parking space must be prominently outlined in blue paint and must be repainted when necessary, to be clearly distinguishable as a parking space designated for persons who have disabilities and must be posted with a permanent above-grade sign of a color and design approved by the Department of Transportation which is placed on or at a distance of 84 inches above the ground to the bottom of the sign and which bears the international symbol of accessibility meeting the requirements of ADAAG s. 4.30.7 and the caption "PARKING BY DISABLED PERMIT ONLY."

Additionally, regarding the signs parking spaces,

An approved Florida Department of Transportation (FDOT) sign is 12 inches wide by 18 inches high, designated FTO-25 in accordance with FDOT Design Standards 17355 sheet 3. Design requirements for this reflective sign are: 1 inch Series "C" letters on blue background with white legend and border on top, and a bottom portion of white background with black opaque legend and border.

FDOT standards require the blue outline to be a 6 inch wide blue stripe to be 2 inches inside of the standard 6 inch white stripe as shown in FDOT Design Standard 17346 sheet 10. This standard states "Use of pavement symbol in accessible parking spaces is optional, when used the symbol shall be 3 feet or 5 feet high and white in color." Blue pavement markings shall be tinted to match shade 15180 of Federal Standard 595a.

So how many handicapped parking spaces does a place of business need to provide? The state of Florida has determined that as well. Again, according to Florida statutes (553.5041), businesses with up to 100 parking spaces must have 1 handicapped parking space for each 25 regular spaces. For 101–200 parking spaces, 1 handicapped-parking space is required for each 50 regular spaces. For 201–500 parking spaces, 1 handicapped-parking space is required for each 100 regular spaces. For larger parking lots with between 501 and 1,000 spaces, 2 percent of the total must be reserved for the handicapped. For large parking lots with more than 1,000 spaces, the requirement is 20 handicapped parking spaces plus 1 for each 100 over 1,000.

Now, all of these rules and regulations would be a waste of time if the parking habits of motorists were not monitored. The Florida statutes regarding "handicapped parking enforcement" (316.1959) state that "the provisions of handicapped parking shall be enforced by state, county, and municipal authorities in their respective jurisdictions whether on public or private property in the same manner as is used to enforce other parking laws and ordinances by said agencies." Florida statute 316.008(4) provides for a fine of up to $250 for drivers who illegally park in designated handicapped-parking spaces.

I certainly have no problem with the premise of a business's designating a certain number of its parking spaces as reserved for the handicapped. And neither do I oppose standards for the color and size of parking spaces and signs. I would not even be against business owners' strictly enforcing handicapped parking. But all of that has less to do with sympathy for the disabled (which I certainly have) than it does with freedom.

The problem is governments' mandating a certain number of handicapped parking spaces and setting standards for their use, size, and color.

There are two issues here. The first is the ability of government to efficiently, equitably, and sensibly issue mandates and set standards for handicapped parking. The second is whether it is a legitimate function of government to issue mandates and set standards for handicapped parking.

Consider the issue of the number of spaces reserved for the handicapped. Here the government adopts the one-size-fits-all approach. We've all seen what appears to be an empty parking space on the other side of a parking lot. But upon driving to it, we find out that we are not able to park there even though it has been empty all day—it's a handicapped-parking space. And sometimes it seems as though the stores with the most handicapped-parking spaces have the fewest handicapped patrons. That is because the government requires a gym and a dance studio, where one is not very likely to run into a disabled person, to have the same number of handicapped-parking spaces per lot size as a Social Security office. Why is it that a Home Depot should have the same number of handicapped parking spaces as a hospital?

And regarding the size and color of parking spaces, signs, symbols, and lettering, standards could exist for those things on the free market.

The free market could also supply private agencies to certify those who are truly handicapped.

Businesses could police their own parking lots.

Opponents of liberty, antagonists of the free market, advocates of a nanny state, and other assorted statists would have everyone believe that without government intervention there would be few or no parking spaces reserved for the handicapped.

They are the same people who insist that the poor would go hungry without food stamps, children would be malnourished without the federal school-lunch program, the sick would die without Medicare and Medicaid, and old people would be living on the street without Social Security.

Nothing could be further from the truth. There is no reason to believe that handicapped parking would disappear if left up to the free market. To the contrary, some businesses might even reserve more of such parking spaces. Businesses that don't see very many disabled patrons might cut back the number of their handicapped parking spaces to a more reasonable number.

The free market is a wonderful thing. Without government handicapping the market, business owners would be free to cater to a diverse clientele, a select clientele, somewhere in between, or to no one in particular. In addition to handicapped parking, some businesses might want to provide special parking spaces for seniors, expectant mothers, people with small children, members of the clergy, military personnel, teachers, doctors, lawyers, plumbers, roofers, or those motorists willing to pay a fee to park close to a place of business.

The possibilities are endless, but only if parking is left to the free market instead of the government.

True, in a free society, the possibility would exist that business owners would not want to set aside a special parking spot for anyone, including the handicapped. But to have a truly free society, it would have to be their decision to make.

In the end, setting aside special parking spaces for the handicapped has nothing to do with someone's being disabled. It has to do with liberty, property, and a free society.

*****

ANYTHING THAT'S PEACEFUL MEANS ANYTHING THAT'S PEACEFUL

Leonard Read (1898–1983), opponent of Roosevelt's New Deal and founder of the Foundation for Economic Education, was one of the twentieth century's great champions of individual liberty, private property, the free market, and limited government. He counted among his friends and advisors such luminaries as Ludwig von Mises and Henry Hazlitt. Although he authored numerous collections of essays, Read's most enduring work has arguably been the 1964 book *Anything That's Peaceful.*

Read's one simple rule for society was that it should permit anything that's peaceful. Not only because the costs associated with stopping peaceful activity always outweigh the benefits, but also because it is immoral for individuals or government to prohibit anything but fraud and violence.

According to Read, the government should be strictly limited to "juridical and policing functions." The role of government is simply to "keep the peace." Explains Read, "Keeping the peace means no more than prohibiting persons from unpeaceful actions." Everything else should be left "to the free, unfettered market." When a government goes beyond this and prohibits peaceful actions, "such prohibitions themselves are, *prima facie*, unpeaceful."

Many people who claim to agree with Read and say they are for liberty, property, free markets, and limited government believe nothing of the kind. Those who call themselves conservatives may rail against socialism, liberalism, and government intervention, but they stop short of wholeheartedly embracing the freedom philosophy. Those who call themselves liberals may pride themselves on their commitment to tolerance and civil liberties, but they likewise reject real freedom. Both groups ultimately show by their actions that they are statists at heart. Just look, for example, at the wide bipartisan support for the war on drugs.

Read believed that "how much of a statist a person is can be judged by how far he would go in prohibiting peaceful actions." He maintained that "the difference between the socialist and the student of liberty is a difference of opinion as to what others should be prohibited from doing." This difference of opinion "highlights the essential difference between the collectivists—socialists, statists, interventionists, mercantilists, disturbers of the peace—and those of the peaceful, libertarian faith."

In my state of Florida, State Representative Ritch Workman, a Republican from the city of Melbourne, has filed a bill (4063) to make dwarf tossing in Florida legal once again. This bizarre competition, which once took place in Florida bars, consisted of bar patrons seeing how far they could throw dwarfs decked in protective gear. The practice was outlawed by the Florida legislature in 1989, when a law was passed that punished bars with $1,000 fines and the suspension or revoking of their liquor licenses if they sponsored a dwarf-tossing event.

Rep. Workman, who believes dwarf tossing to be "repulsive and stupid," nevertheless told the *Palm Beach Post* that he was on a quest to "seek and destroy unnecessary burdens on the freedom and liberties of people." "This is an example of Big Brother government," said Workman, who also focused on economic freedom: "All that it does is prevent some dwarfs from getting jobs they would be happy to get. In this economy, or any economy, why would we want to prevent people from getting gainful employment?" The bottom line, according to Workman, is that "it's none of the state's business if somebody wants to do this."

A statement released by the Little People of America, a nonprofit organization dedicated to advocacy and support for individuals with dwarfism, condemned the Florida bill because the practice of dwarf throwing is "undoubtedly unsafe and subjects the individual being tossed to serious medical harms. Even with padded gear on, dwarf tossing exposes the individual to permanent injuries to the spinal column or even death." "Far from participants, dwarf tossing treats people of short stature as a piece of equipment and encourages the general attitude that people with dwarfism are objects," said Gary Arnold, President of Little People of America. Leah Smith, the Vice President of Public Relations for Little People of America, added that "rather than limit the liberties of any citizen, the ban protects the health and welfare of the community."

Now, to some people, and perhaps even to most people, dwarf tossing may be repulsive; it may be stupid; it may be juvenile; it may be degrading to all little people; it may be unsafe, it may be dangerous; it may even be deadly. But—as long as it is practiced by adults on private property, is voluntarily undertaken by the dwarf, the bar owner, and the contestants, and is peaceful—there is no legitimate reason for government at any level to prohibit the practice. Rep. Workman is right: "It's none of the state's business if somebody wants to do this."

When Leonard Read wrote that society should permit anything that's peaceful, he meant anything that's peaceful. In a free society, that includes boxing, professional wrestling, mixed-martial-arts cage fighting, violent movies and video games, and anything else that some people find distasteful, including dwarf tossing.

Read admonished his readers to take stock of what they would prohibit others from doing to accurately find their own position "in the ideological line-up." But he also said that "this method can be used to determine anyone's position." Those who would seek to prohibit peaceful activity between consenting adults are in opposition to the freedom philosophy, no matter how much they talk about their commitment to liberty, free markets, and limited government.

It is understandable that the practice of dwarf tossing might offend people afflicted with dwarfism, and I am sympathetic toward them, but no one has the right to not be offended because of his stature—or his weight, deformity, handicap, disability, or nose shape. But I have no sympathy for the sensibilities of those offended by the practice of dwarf tossing—nanny statists, idealistic do-gooders, bureaucrats, regulators, politicians, and busybodies with nothing better to do than seek to prohibit peaceful activity.

*****

IN DEFENSE OF AFFIRMATIVE ACTION

In order to put together a "diverse" student body, it is standard practice for many colleges and universities to use race as a factor in admissions. An unintended consequence of this policy is that some students who otherwise qualify for admission are denied because of their race.

These race-factor admissions programs are invariably Affirmative Action programs like those that give special consideration to certain minorities in employment and contracting decisions.

Abigail Noel Fisher and Rachel Michalewicz allege that they were denied entrance to the University of Texas because they are white. After they were denied enrollment in the fall 2008 semester, Abigail went on to Louisiana State University, where she will graduate this spring; Rachel attended St. Edward's University in Austin (also the home of the University of Texas), graduated after three years, and is now a law student at Southern Methodist University.

But the girls did something in addition to attending other schools—they sued the University of Texas, challenging the constitutionality of its admissions process. Since then, U.S. District Court Judge Sam Sparks in Austin dismissed the lawsuit, a three-judge panel of the Fifth Circuit Court of Appeals in New Orleans affirmed the decision, and, in an *en banc* rehearing and by a 9-7 vote, the full Fifth Circuit refused to consider an appeal.

Opponents of Affirmative Action are hoping the Supreme Court will take up the case. A petition for a writ of certiorari was filed on September 15. Six amicus curiae briefs were then filed with the Court, which has asked the University of Texas to provide a reaction to the new challenge to its admission policy. (Rachel Michalewicz is no longer part of the case, since she has graduated from college already.)

On December 16, the Heritage Foundation and the Federalist Society co-sponsored a debate on the case featuring two advocates for each side, including the original counsel for the University of Texas in the case.

There hasn't been this much attention to a college admissions Affirmative Action case since *Gratz v. Bollinger* and *Grutter v. Bollinger*, both in 2003.

In *Gratz*, an undergraduate admissions policy at the University of Michigan with a point system awarding 20 points to members of "underrepresented groups" on the basis of race alone was struck down as unconstitutional by a vote of 6-3.

In *Grutter*, a preferential admissions policy at the University of Michigan Law School that was based on race and had no specific point system but admitted less-qualified minorities over more-qualified whites was ruled constitutional by a vote of 5-4 because "the Law School's race-conscious admissions program does not unduly harm nonminority applicants."

Both of those cases harken back to the first Supreme Court Affirmative Action case, *Regents of the University of California v. Bakke* (1978). In that case, Alan Bakke, a white man, was twice denied admission to the medical school at the University of California at Davis even though his qualifications exceeded those of any of the minority students admitted in the two years since his applications were rejected. Although the Supreme Court ruled, by a vote of 5-4, that the university's admission plan was unconstitutional and ordered that Bakke be admitted, it also ruled, by a vote of 5-4, that the use of race as a factor in admissions decisions in higher education was constitutional. In the words of Justice Lewis Powell, who cast the deciding vote in each case, "The judgment below is affirmed insofar as it orders respondent's admission to Davis and invalidates petitioner's special admissions program, but is reversed insofar as it prohibits petitioner from taking race into account as a factor in its future admissions decisions."

It is interesting that both California, in 1996, and Michigan, in 2006, had successful ballot initiatives that ended Affirmative Action in admissions to state universities and other public institutions, although the Michigan initiative was recently overturned by a federal court.

Affirmative Action had its beginnings not as a federal program, but as two words in a sentence. In 1961, John Kennedy, in Executive Order No. 10925, created the Committee on Equal Employment Opportunity to end discrimination in employment by the government and its contractors. Every federal contract was required to include this pledge:

> The Contractor will not discriminate against any employee or applicant for employment because of race, creed, color, or national origin. The Contractor will take affirmative action, to ensure that applicants are employed, and that employees are treated during employment, without regard to their race, creed, color, or national origin.

Applicants for positions would be judged without any consideration of their race, religion, or national origin.

The Civil Rights Act of 1964, in title VI, sec. 601, reinforced that idea:

> No person in the United States shall, on the ground of race, color, or national origin, be excluded from participation in, be denied the benefits of, or be subjected to discrimination under any program or activity receiving Federal financial assistance.

Lyndon Johnson, however, expanded that goal. In a 1965 commencement address at Howard University, he said,

> Thus it is not enough just to open the gates of opportunity. All our citizens must have the ability to walk through those gates. We seek not just freedom, but opportunity. We seek not just legal equity, but human ability; not just equality as a right and a theory, but equality as a fact and equality as a result.

He then issued Executive Order No. 11246, which laid the foundation for a federal program that would later develop into what is known as Affirmative Action:

> It is the policy of the Government of the United States to provide equal opportunity in Federal employment for all qualified persons, to prohibit discrimination in employment because of race, creed, color, or national origin, and to promote the full realization of equal employment opportunity through a positive, continuing program in each executive department and agency.

Under Richard Nixon, the Department of Labor in December 1971 issued Revised Order No. 4, requiring all contractors to develop "an acceptable affirmative action program," including "an analysis of areas within which the contractor is deficient in the utilization of minority groups and women, and further, goals and timetables to which the contractor's good faith efforts must be directed to correct the deficiencies."

So after beginning as two words in a pledge by federal contractors to employ people without regard to race, color, creed, or national origin, "affirmative action" morphed into a program enforced by the Equal Employment Opportunity Commission (EEOC). Headquartered in Washington, D.C., but also working through 53 field offices in every part of the country, the EEOC has 2,500 employees and a $367 million budget.

Affirmative Action is usually seen as a divisive issue, with liberals generally supporting it and conservatives generally opposing it, but such shouldn't be the case at all.

It is clear that government and public institutions have no business giving adverse or preferential treatment to anyone on the basis of race, color, religion, national origin, ethnic group, sex, age, et cetera. But that doesn't mean that affirmative action, quotas, discrimination, or preferential treatment based on those characteristics aren't viable options in a free society—as long as it is a matter of individual liberty and private property instead of government decree.

For the libertarian, the issue is not divisive at all, because, as Jacob Hornberger explains,

A person has the fundamental right to associate with anyone he chooses and on any basis he chooses. He might be the biggest bigot in the world, choosing only to associate with white supremacists, but that's what freedom is all about—the right to make whatever choices one wants in his life, so long as his conduct is peaceful—i.e., no murder, rape, theft, fraud, or other violent assaults against others.

In a free society, private schools, businesses, organizations, and individual persons would be free to practice or not practice affirmative action. In fact, it couldn't be otherwise and still be a free society.

If a private school wanted to grant preference in admissions to students of a particular race then so be it. If a parent or student thought the school was too white, too black, too Latino, or too Asian, then he could look for another school.

If a private business wanted to give discounts only to customers of a particular religion, then so be it. Customers of other religions could still continue to shop there or take their business elsewhere. (Strange that no one complains about the widespread prevalence of senior-citizen discounts, that is, age discrimination.)

If a private organization wanted to limit its membership to a specific sex, then so be it. No persons of either sex have the right to force any private organization to admit them.

If a person wanted to associate or not associate with people from particular ethnic groups, then so be it. It doesn't matter if it is illogical. It doesn't matter if it is based on false stereotypes. It doesn't matter what the reason, and it's no one's business what the reason is.

"Anything that's peaceful" means anything that's peaceful. That is the difference between a free society and one overseen, managed, or controlled by government bureaucrats at the EEOC and the myriad of other federal agencies that infringe upon liberty, property, and the freedom of association.

*****

IN DEFENSE OF CENSORSHIP

I was intrigued by the headline I saw in an evangelical magazine: "Google, iTunes, Facebook All Censor Christian Views."

The article turned out to be about the recent release at the National Press Club in Washington, D.C., of a report by the National Religious Broadcasters (NRB) on censorship by "new media" communications platforms.

The report is called *True Liberty in a New Media Age: An Examination of the Threat of Anti-Christian Censorship and Other Viewpoint Discrimination on New Media Platforms*. It was prepared after an 18-month analysis by The John Milton Project for Religious Free Speech, a project of the NRB under the direction of Sr. Vice President and General Counsel Craig L. Parshall.

The 47-page report contains a foreword by Frank Wright, president and CEO of the NRB, an executive summary by Craig Parshall, an introduction, five chapters, and eight brief appendices reproducing the pertinent content guidelines of the "new media" platforms under investigation.

According to the executive summary,

> The policies and practices of several major Internet-interactive "new media" communications platforms and service providers were examined and evaluated in order to determine the risk of those entities committing anti-Christian viewpoint censorship. The companies reviewed were: Apple and its iTunes App Store; Facebook; MySpace; Google; Twitter; and Internet Service Providers (ISPs) Comcast, AT&T, and Verizon. Our conclusion is that Christian ideas and other religious content face a clear and present danger of censorship on web-based communication platforms.

The report maintains that anti-Christian censorship has already been practiced by Apple, Google, Facebook, and Comcast. The claim is made about Apple that "of the 425,000 apps available on Apple's iPhone, the only ones censored by Apple for expressing otherwise lawful viewpoints have been apps with Christian content." Google is criticized for denying certain ads and self-censoring certain words on the China-based version of its search engine that the Chinese government didn't like. Facebook isn't specifically charged with any anti-Christian censorship, but it is faulted for removing "anti-gay" content. Comcast supposedly blocked the downloading of the Bible but "it is unknown whether Comcast's suspected blockage of these Bible downloads was viewpoint targeted or was simply a response to a large download that threatened traffic."

The current written polices of the "new media" are condemned for being vague and prohibiting content that is "hate speech," controversial, inflammatory, inappropriate, any-gay, or misleading. Only Twitter is praised for policies that would "pass First Amendment muster if they are analyzed according to free speech principles articulated by the Supreme Court." All of the other companies studied "have written policies in place that violate fundamental rules of free expression, as applied to religious free speech."

The report urges Apple, Facebook, MySpace, Google, Comcast, AT&T, and Verizon to do three things: modify their policies, renounce past censorship practices, and "affirm an intent to abide by a healthy view of the free speech rights of their users and customers."

If that doesn't work, then the report suggests three courses of action: legislation, regulation, and litigation.

Now, whether Apple, Google, and the other "new media" platforms singled out by the report have practiced, are practicing, or might practice anti-Christian censorship is irrelevant to the real issue. True, if any of those take place, it is understandable that Christians would object. Just as it is understandable that a Buddhist would not be happy with anti-Buddhist censorship, a Republican would object to anti-Republican censorship, and a Black would not be pleased with anti-Black censorship. But, even as a Christian myself, it is my contention that censorship by "new media" platforms not only doesn't pose a threat to free speech, it has nothing to do with the First Amendment and freedom of speech.

It is actually disingenuous to bring up the First Amendment, as is done throughout the report, because, as the report even acknowledges, "The First Amendment, like the other provisions of our Bill of Rights, does not reach private actions but only the actions of 'state actors.'" The First Amendment reads,

> Congress shall make no law respecting an establishment of religion, or prohibiting the free exercise thereof; or abridging the freedom of speech or of the press; or the right of the people peaceably to assemble and to petition the Government for a redress of grievances.

It is the government that is prohibited from abridging the freedom of speech, not any individual or private business. Historically, it is governments that have always been the enemies of free speech. It is governments that have sought to censor speech. It is governments around the world right now—including the U.S. government—that seek to censor the speech of their citizens.

Individuals and organizations censor speech everyday, and it is perfectly natural, reasonable, and accepted when they do so.

Christian churches censor anti-Christian viewpoints. Jewish synagogues censor anti-Jewish viewpoints. Muslim mosques censor anti-Muslim viewpoints. Atheist societies censor pro-God viewpoints. AA meetings censor calls to meet for drinks afterwards. Weight Watchers gatherings censor invitations to buffets. Pro-life groups censor pro-choice opinions. Tea Party get-togethers censor big-government rhetoric. A conservative conference censors the promotion of national health care in its lectures.

We all censor the speech of our children and visitors to our homes. And it has nothing to do with whether the censored speech is hateful, controversial, inflammatory, inappropriate, vulgar, or profane. A home of partisan Democrats might censor any visitor's praise of George W. Bush. Likewise, red-state conservatives might censor admiring opinions of President Obama expressed by visitors to their homes.

Even the NRB practices censorship. Does everyone have the freedom of speech to attend a board meeting of the NRB and express his views? Does anyone have the freedom of speech to utter obscenities in the lobby of the NRB headquarters?

If Apple prefers not to make available Christian apps, then Christians have several options. They can complain to Apple, boycott Apple, or start their own company to compete with Apple. If they don't like the terms of service of Facebook, MySpace, Google, Comcast, AT&T, or Verizon, then they can do likewise. They can do anything that's peaceful, which rules out legislation, regulation, and litigation.

Being able to censor what is said on one's property is a mark of a free and ordered society; not to be allowed to censor what is said on one's property is a mark of an authoritarian and lawless society.

The real issue is property. As economist George Reisman recently explained in writing about the Occupy Wall Street movement,

> A major lesson to be learned from the occupation is that hardly anyone nowadays understands the meaning of freedom of speech. Contrary to the prevailing view, freedom of speech is not the ability to say anything, anywhere, at any time. Actual freedom of speech is consistent withrespect for property rights. It presupposes that the speaker has the consent of the owners of any property he uses in speaking, such as the land, sound system, or lecture hall or radio or television studio that he uses.

> By the logic of the prevailing view of freedom of speech, protesters in the future will be able to storm into lecture halls and/or seize radio and television stations in order to deliver their message and then claim that their freedom of speech is violated when the police come to eject them, even

though the police in such cases would in fact be acting precisely in order to uphold the freedom of speech.

The prevailing view is totally incorrect. Actual freedom of speech, based on respect for property owners' rights to use their own property as they see fit, is the guarantor of rational communication.

As much as Christians may dislike what they see as anti-Christian censorship practiced by "new media" communications platforms, as much as they may dislike the "liberal bias" of social media companies, as much as they may dislike the "overbroad and vague" policies of Apple, as much as they may dislike the acceptable-use policies of Internet service providers, as much as they may dislike Google's advertising guidelines, and as much as they may dislike content restrictions imposed by MySpace, there is no "free speech obligation" that private entities must adhere to. In a free society, businesses of any type and companies large and small are free to cater to or not to cater to any group or cause they choose for any reason. That includes organizations such as the NRB, which would cry foul if it were not free to censor what was said on its property, posted on its website, or spoken at its meetings.

It doesn't matter whether "new media" platforms are censoring what is "right" and the NRB is censoring what is "wrong." Censorship, except when it is undertaken by government, is part and parcel of a free society.

*****

DISCOUNTS AND A FREE SOCIETY

We have all been there: a nice restaurant, a quiet evening, a companion of the opposite sex—only to have the experience shattered by loud, ill-mannered, or unruly kids.

From coast to coast, some restaurants have begun placing signs on their doors and menus saying things such as, "We love children, especially when they are tucked in chairs and well behaved," or "Kids must use indoor voices."

There are message boards, websites, and even petitions that promote child-free dining.

An online petition was once started in North Carolina to establish "child-free restaurants."

One "upscale casual" establishment near Pittsburgh, McDain's Restaurant, recently banned children under 6 strictly in response to customer complaints because the noisy children have become "too much of a bother for the other customers."

Even the usually family-friendly Disney has a no-child policy at its

Victoria and Albert's restaurant in the Grand Floridian Resort.

And it's not just restaurants. In 2011, Malaysia Airlines banned infants from the first-class sections of its Boeing 747 jumbo jets. Then last year it banned children under 12 from the upper-deck coach-class section of its Airbus A380s.

But one restaurant in Kingston in Washington state—an Italian restaurant named Sogno di Vino—instead of banning children, has taken to rewarding parents of well-behaved children. After a recent dinner of pizza and pasta, the King family—which includes three children ranging in age from 2 to 8—noticed a discount of four dollars on their check for "well behaved kids." "Our server came to our table and just really thanked us for having exceptionally behaved children," said Mrs. King. One of the family's friends posted an image of the receipt online where it went viral. The owner of the restaurant, Rob Scott, who said he fondly remembered the King family and its well-mannered children, said he "routinely offers complimentary desserts to customers with well-mannered children, but this was the first time he had actually typed the discount on the receipt." He further explained, "Sogno di Vino means 'to dream of wine' (in Italian); it doesn't mean Chuck E. Cheese. We love Chuck E. Cheese; they do a great job. That's why you go to Chuck E. Cheese, so the kids can play."

Although this is an unusual reason to receive a discount at a restaurant, other factors that result in discounts at restaurants and other places of business are quite common. Some restaurants offer senior-citizen discounts. Others allow children to eat free on certain nights. Many hotels offer discounts to members of AARP. Most companies give their employees discounts. Many bars have a ladies' night where ladies can drink for free. Some businesses have discounts for paying in cash. By far the most prevalent type of discount is the military discount. Business establishments of all kinds—from restaurants to storage facilities to theme parks—offer discounts to active-duty military personnel. Some sporting events even offer free admission to members of the military.

So it comes as a surprise that not everyone appreciates businesses' offering discounts—especially when the discounts concern religion.

A little more than a year ago, Prudhomme's Lost Cajun Kitchen in Columbia, Pennsylvania, began offering a 10 percent discount to diners who presented a church bulletin on Sundays. This upset a local atheist, John Wolff, who then filed a complaint in April 2012 with the Pennsylvania Human Relations Commission, alleging that the practice discriminates against him because he does not attend church. "I did this not out of spite, but out of a feeling against the prevailing self-righteousness that stems from religion, particularly in Lancaster County," said Wolff, a retired electrical engineer, who said he was considering eating at the restaurant but never did. He merely saw the discount offer on the restaurant's website.

Wolff also contacted the Freedom from Religion Foundation of Madison, Wisconsin, which sent a letter to the restaurant's owners telling them that the church-bulletin discount was "discriminatory" and "a serious civil rights concern" that violated both the federal Civil Rights Act and the Pennsylvania Human Relations Act.

Sharon Prudhomme, one of the co-owners of the restaurant, said she created the discount program to bring more traffic into the restaurant on what was traditionally a slow day. "I thought it would be nice to do something for Sunday dinners and encourage people to come in," said Prudhomme, who doesn't attend church herself. The church-bulletin discount was a marketing tool, not a religious outreach. "We're the kind of place where everybody can come," she said of the restaurant. In the past she has offered discounts to senior citizens, early-bird diners, shoppers at local businesses, and Columbia High School students. The restaurant currently offers a free meal on Tuesday evenings to children 12 and under who order from the kids' menu. Prudhomme has made it clear that she is not discriminating because diners don't actually have to attend church to get a bulletin. She said area religious leaders told her that anyone can walk into a church building and obtain a bulletin. She considered the investigation of the complaint against her to be "a waste, to actually give it merit." "I'm an American," she added, "This is an independent restaurant. I can do as I wish and I'm going to continue to offer the church-bulletin discount."

Well, it turns out that while Prudhomme is continuing to offer the church-bulletin discount, she can't exactly do as she wishes.

The Pennsylvania Human Relations Commission approved a Conciliation Agreement with the restaurant in September. According to the Terms of Settlement,

> Respondent will continue to give a discount for any bulletin from any group oriented around the subject of religious faith including publications from the Freedom From Religion Foundation as long as they maintain the Sunday discount program.

The restaurant's attorney commented that the complaint was "a frivolous thing." "It was really not in keeping with the really noble purposes behind the Pennsylvania Human Relations Act," he added. "I can't imagine that those who passed the act contemplated that somebody would try to use it in the future for something like this."

So what do discounts offered by restaurants have to do with a free society? Everything.

There are two sides of the coin to look at here. On the one side is what we can call moral freedom and on the other side is what we can label economic freedom.

Complaints about church-bulletin discounts have been made before. They are clearly the result of some religious bias, since no such complaints are ever made about senior-citizen discounts or military discounts. But there should be no difference in one's attitude toward discounts targeted to religious people. Complaining to some government agency about a company's peaceful and beneficial activity should be the last thing on anyone's mind.

As the twentieth century's great champion of individual liberty and a free society, Leonard Read, put it, government should not interfere with anything that's peaceful. Not only because the costs associated with stopping peaceful activity always outweigh the benefits, but also because it is immoral for governments to prohibit anything but fraud and violence. In a free society, individual persons and businesses have the natural right to favor or not favor the members of any particular group, class, organization, race, or religion by providing or prohibiting a discount or anything else that's peaceful.

The same principle applies when it comes to economic freedom. Contrary to popular opinion, the United States does not have a free-market or laissez-faire economic system where unbridled capitalism reigns supreme. That is a caricature of liberals and a pipe dream of conservatives. Government intervention in the economy—on both the federal and state levels—is the norm. In some sectors of the economy, government intervention is so strong and pervasive that one would think it was modeled after the central planning of the Soviet Union.

For example, about two-thirds of the milk in the United States is produced under the watchful eye of the federal government. The rest is produced under heavy state regulation. In Louisiana last month, the Department of Agriculture and Forestry forced a supermarket chain to stop its weekly promotion of "a gallon of skim, 1 percent, 2 percent or whole milk for $2.99 on Tuesdays, limiting the quantity to four per customer." It turns out that the Dairy Stabilization Board oversees milk prices in Louisiana. Retailers must mark up milk "no less than 6 percent of the invoice cost after adding freight charges." So, discount your milk too much and the bureaucrats from the Department of Agriculture and Forestry will send in the milk police.

But it's not just milk. If the government determines that the price of something is too high, then a firm is charged with the non-crime of price gouging. But if the government determines that the price of something has been discounted too much, then a firm is charged with the non-crime of "predatory pricing." But under the philosophy of "anything that's peaceful," what matters is not whether some government bureaucrat thinks a price is too low or too high, but whether there is a voluntary transaction between a willing buyer and a willing seller. Offering a discount to only one party does not aggress in any way against another party.

The ability to offer discounts on any product or service, at any time, and in any amount, to the general public, or just to certain persons on the basis of their age, sex, religion, or membership in some group is essential to any free society.

*****

RESTROOMS AND A FREE SOCIETY

We have all done it. While on a trip across the country with the family, we have all exited the Interstate and pulled into a McDonald's or some convenience store to use the restroom—and then driven away without making a purchase.

A woman in Tennessee will probably never do that again. She stopped at a restaurant in Erin, Tennessee, to use the restroom, and a few days later received in the mail the following handwritten note signed "Management":

> On Saturday Oct 27th you came into the Flood Zone. had to use the restroom said you had been to the turkey shoot. posted on our front door is a sign that states Restrooms Are for Flood Zone Customers Only. Not a Public restroom, On the inside of restroom is a sign that tells you there is a 5.00 Charge for non-Flood Zone Customers. you did not purchase Anything. So there for you were not a Customer. please send pymt to ...

The woman, Patricia Barnes, "said she didn't see the note until an employee approached her after she left the restroom." Said Barnes, "It was a little index card at the very bottom of the mirror. I didn't look in the mirror at all that day." "I don't feel it was a crime," she added. "I've been into plenty of restaurants here in this town and other towns, and, you know, other states."

Barnes was located by the restaurant after it asked the local sheriff to trace her vehicle license-plate number. But after going through all that trouble, the restaurant rebuffed the woman's attempt to pay the $5 restroom charge after she received the note in the mail and went back to the restaurant. A money order she then sent to the restaurant came back.

Celebrity chef Bobby Flay, himself a restaurant owner, called the incident "totally ridiculous." That members of the public come into your establishment only to use the restroom is "just part of doing business," he said. It also shows good will on the part of the owner. "There's plenty of people that come to the restaurant, use the bathroom, and leave, and that's the way it goes," Flay said.

It is not hard to find fault with the restaurant's restroom policy.

First of all, even though a business might occasionally have a problem with noncustomers who mess up its restrooms or delay the access of paying customers, things like that should be expected and just be considered a cost of doing business. After all, today's nonpaying restroom user might be tomorrow's paying customer.

Second, the negative publicity that a place of business could receive by trying to charge noncustomers who need to use the restroom surely outweighs any restroom fees the business would collect or any expense involved in maintaining clean restrooms in its place of business.

Third, go to any mall and you will find stores packed with prospective customers who may never make a purchase. And not only are stores full of browsers who don't buy anything, many shoppers enter stores with no intention of ever spending a dime. They might be just killing time. They might be just checking out the newest styles. They might be just hoping one day to have the money to buy a particular dress or pair of shoes or dreaming that they had it. Not only do those stores provide restrooms for potential patrons, they make available tens of thousands of dollars' worth of merchandise just for people to handle and look at.

And fourth, it is one thing for a business to post a sign on its front door saying that restrooms in the place of business are only for paying customers; it is one thing to put a sign in its restroom informing all who enter that there is a $5 charge for anyone who is not an actual customer of the business; it is one thing to try to collect a use fee from noncustomers as they exit the business's restroom; but to track someone down who used the restroom and to send a horribly written note in an attempt to collect $5 is just inviting media scrutiny and a viral Internet presence that could ultimately force a business to close because of all the potential customers that it alienated.

Even without incidents like this, many people would not have a problem with the government's making a law mandating that restaurants and other places of business have restrooms available for the general public. Others would argue that because restroom use is a necessity, businesses should be required to make their restrooms available to the general public. Some would say that because a place of business is open to the public, it becomes a public place like a state park or public library that provides restrooms for the public to use. A few would make the case that for places of business to not provide public restrooms is a public-health issue and therefore government intervention of some kind is warranted.

Others have come to the defense of the Flood Zone restaurant and its restroom policy, saying such things as:

• If restaurants don't let people sit down at a table without ordering something, why should they be expected to let people sit down on one of their commodes?
• No one opens a business to give away products and services.
• A place of business is not legally obligated to provide public restrooms.
• Since soap, paper towels, toilet paper, cleaning supplies, water, and labor cost businesses money, it is not unreasonable to limit its restrooms to paying customers.
• No one would allow a complete stranger to enter his home and use his

bathroom.

Although some who find fault with this restaurant's restroom policy would likewise think along these lines, libertarians and other advocates of a free society can both criticize the restaurant's policy as ludicrous and defend it as a business decision.

There is no right or wrong answer to the question of whether this particular restaurant should charge noncustomers a fee for using its restroom.

The libertarian looks at the bigger picture and envisions business practices in a free society.

In a free society, it would be entirely up to each business to decide whether it would charge noncustomers, or even customers, for the privilege of using one of its restrooms.

But that is because in a free society businesses would have the right to sell any good or service for any price they choose; raise or lower prices by any amount, at any time, and for any reason; and offer credit at any interest rate or terms.

Just as they would have the right to hire anyone from any country willing to be employed at any mutually agreed-upon wage-and-benefit package.

Just as they would have the right to fire anyone for any reason.

Just as they would have the right to discriminate against any potential employee for any reason.

Just as they would have the right to refuse to do business with any potential customer for any reason.

And just as they would have the right to provide as many or as few handicapped parking spaces as they choose to, or none at all.

But that also means that a business in a free society could not be too big to fail, could not use antitrust laws to tie up one of its competitors in expensive court proceedings, could not be the beneficiary of government eminent-domain proceedings, could not look to the government for a loan or bailout, could not help the government to craft regulations that would harm its competitors, and could not expect the government to place tariffs and quotas on imports to avoid having to compete on the world market.

Although businesses in a free society would be free from government regulation, they would not be free from the consequences of bad decisions, as restaurants such as the Flood Zone are finding out.

*****

DRESS CODES AND A FREE SOCIETY

At first glance, the idea of dress codes seems foreign to a free society. Actually, however, the case is just the opposite.

That truth was manifest most recently at, of all places, a press conference held at the Capitol Hill Club in Washington, D.C., to announce the inauguration of the Ron Paul Institute for Peace and Prosperity. As recounted by Executive Director Daniel McAdams,

> The front desk called nervously as we closed in on a half hour before the press conference start time yesterday. Two young men fully dressed in Ron Paul regalia, but unfortunately of the T-shirt-and-shorts variety, were desperate to get into the press conference announcing Ron Paul's new Institute for Peace and Prosperity. Unfortunately the venue had a dress code, and shorts and T-shirts were definitely out, Ron Paul fans or not. The young men were dejected, pleading with the front desk as I arrived downstairs.

According to the rules of the Capitol Hill Club,

> Members and guests are courteously requested to observe the following regulations regarding dress at the Club. Gentlemen will please wear coats and ties in the Main Dining Room. Coats with sport shirts will be acceptable throughout the other areas of the Club. Current trends dictate the acceptability of ladies' high-fashion attire.

The two young men were able to get proper attire and attend the press conference.

Now contrast that with what happened last year in Cocoa, Florida, a city on Florida's central east coast.

The Cocoa city council passed, by a 3-1 vote, a "saggy-pants" ordinance in October that was supposed to take effect on January 1, 2013. The ordinance sought to ban pants or skirts that expose underwear or skin more than 3 inches below the waistline. It was to be enforced on streets, sidewalks, and other designated city property. Police were to warn first-time offenders and give them a chance to pull up their pants (or skirts). Violation of the ordinance was to result in a fine of $25 for the first offense, $50 for the second, $75 for the third, and $100 for each time after that.

As to be expected, the ordinance was harshly criticized.

The president of the local NAACP, Alberta Wilson, termed it "nothing more than a vehicle for further harassment of young people." "I don't like the saggy pants any more than you do," she said, but added, "I respect people's Constitutional rights."

Other critics of the ordinance said it would give police the right to increase their stopping and frisking of people solely on the basis of their clothing, which could lead to racial profiling. Cocoa Police Chief Mark Klayman acknowledged that the new law would allow police broader power: "This would give the police officers the probable-cause stop. Just like if you stop a car with a tail light out, it can lead to other charges."

Amid concerns that the ordinance would entail costly legal battles to defend its enforcement, the Cocoa city council repealed the ordinance by a vote of 4-1 in December. Similar attempts have been made in other cities across the country.

The difference between the two dress codes should be obvious.

One is private; the other is public. One is voluntary; the other is mandatory. One has neutral consequences; the other has negative consequences. One is straightforward; the other is subject to manipulation. One is easy to enforce; the other is difficult to enforce. One results in exclusion; the other results in fines. One is compatible with a free society; the other is foreign to a free society.

"No Shirt, No Shoes, No Service"—I can remember seeing signs to this effect at the entrance to some business establishments. The ability of any place of business to have a dress code is a mark of a free society. In a free society, private-property rights are paramount. He who owns the property establishes the requirements for entry and restrictions on activities. That is true whether the property is a private residence or a place of business. It does not mean that property owners can aggress against their guests with impunity just because they make the rules. The "penalty" for violators of a home or business establishment's dress code is exclusion or refusal of service, not beatings, fines, or imprisonments. That is how the state operates. Refusing someone entrance to, or service on, your property is not aggression against him. In a free society there is no right to trespass on someone else's property.

Even in our only relatively free society, some clubs and restaurants have a dress code. But it is tolerated—even by those who profess to hold to the primacy of private property—only if society at large considers the dress code reasonable, logical, rational, or necessary, not because a business owner has the absolute freedom to decide who wears what in his place of business. But in a free society, a business owner has the right to require formal attire, no clothes at all, or anything in between. That is because in a free society all businesses have the right to refuse entrance or service to anyone on the basis not only of dress, but of height, weight, race, religion, gender, age, disability, sexual orientation, national origin, appearance, marital status, political party, or anything else. It doesn't matter whether the exclusion or denial seems logical or illogical, reasonable or unreasonable, rational or irrational, or necessary or unnecessary. In a free society, it couldn't be any other way.

The same goes for the employees in a place of business. In a free society, employers have the absolute right to dictate how employees should dress or not dress—whether or not it is considered reasonable, logical, rational, or necessary to the job. Just as there is no right to employment at a particular business, so there is no right of an employee to dress as he chooses. Not in a free society. That would forever settle the continual complaints and lawsuits concerning the rights of employees to wear religious or political jewelry or attire in the workplace.

But what about public property? What about public schools, parks, libraries, housing, stadiums, and other venues? There can be found at the beginning of every school year arguments about the pros and cons of requiring children to wear uniforms to public school. Libertarians take no sides in disputes of this nature. There is no right or wrong answer to the uniform question. In a private school it is up to the administration; parents who object can send their children to another school. In a free society there are no public schools. Just as there are no public parks, libraries, housing, stadiums, or other venues; they are all private.

A free society doesn't mean there are no rules, regulations, or standards of acceptable dress or conduct; it just means that government doesn't decree them.

*****

GAY SEX, RAW MILK, AND A FREE SOCIETY

Although gay sex and raw milk have nothing to do with each other, they have everything to do with individual liberty, private property, and a free society.

The governor or Montana recently signed into law a bill to strike unconstitutional language from a law on the books that criminalized sexual acts between two people of the same sex. However, he won't have a chance to sign into law a bill to allow the sale of raw milk in Montana because it failed to pass the legislature before it adjourned on April 24.

Under Montana law, deviant sexual conduct is a crime:

45-5-505. Deviate [sic] sexual conduct.

(1) A person who knowingly engages in deviate sexual relations or who causes another to engage in deviate sexual relations commits the offense of deviate sexual conduct.

(2) A person convicted of the offense of deviate sexual conduct shall be imprisoned in the state prison for any term not to exceed 10 years or be fined an amount not to exceed $50,000, or both.

The definition of "deviate sexual relations" initially meant "sexual contact or sexual intercourse between two persons of the same sex or any form of sexual intercourse with an animal." However, the "same sex" part of the law has been unenforceable since a 1997 Montana Supreme Court decision ruled that it was unconstitutional.

What the governor of Montana signed into law on April 18, 2013, was a bill (SB107) that included a provision to strike the "same sex" part of the definition and limit "deviate sexual relations" to just "any form of sexual intercourse with an animal." The bill passed the Montana Senate by a vote of 38-11 on February 20, 2013, and passed the House by a vote of 64-35 on April 10, 2013. The "no" votes were all by Republicans, who hold a 29-21 majority in the Montana Senate and a 61-39 majority in the House.

Current Montana law forbids selling milk in Montana that has not been pasteurized.

According to David Gumpert, author of The Raw Milk Revolution, about 20 states allow the sale of raw milk from the farm, 10 states allow the sale of raw milk at retail, and about 20 states don't allow the sale of raw milk at all.

A bill (HB574) to "establish a small herd exemption permit for certain producers of milk" passed the Montana House Agriculture Committee by a vote of 16-1 on March 21, 2013, and by the full House by a vote of 96-3 on March 26, 2013. The bill directed the Department of Livestock to issue "small herd exemption" permits to producers of raw milk or raw milk products for human consumption:

(a) if the person's dairy herd is:

(i) comprised of [sic] fewer than 15 lactating cows, 30 lactating goats, or 30 lactating sheep, except that the dairy herd may include other cows, goats, or sheep that are not lactating or are producing milk for purposes other than human consumption; and

(ii) registered with the department; and

(b) if the raw milk and raw milk products produced by the person's dairy herd are all produced and processed on the same premises.

Permit holders were to be exempted from the usual licensing, sanitation, quality, and labeling requirements for milk. Also, they could sell directly only to consumers and not for purposes of resale.

The bill was amended and passed by the Montana Senate Agriculture, Livestock and Irrigation Committee by a vote of 9-2 on April 11, 2013. The substantial changes made to the bill ended up killing it. As amended, the bill said "anyone selling raw milk would have to meet the 'Grade A' standards of larger dairies, that anyone buying milk from a smaller herd would have to own a share of the cow, goat or sheep, and that anyone harmed by consuming raw milk could not hold the state liable." Because of the liability exemption, a two-thirds vote was required for passage in the full Senate. So even though the vote for the bill on April 18, 2013, was 32-17, it still failed to pass.

The Montana Department of Livestock opposed the bill to allow the sale of raw milk. Christian Mackay, the executive director of the department, termed raw milk "a public-health risk, even with this kind of regulation." Naturally, Montana dairy farmers disagree and supported the original bill as passed by the House.

This dichotomy can be seen elsewhere.

The National Milk Producers Federation, which represents the big dairy companies, described raw milk as "a potentially dangerous product." However, small dairy farmers disagree and tout the safety and health benefits of raw milk.

The federal Food and Drug Administration, which banned the interstate sale of raw milk in 1987, maintains that there is "no meaningful difference in the nutritional values of pasteurized and unpasteurized milk" and that raw milk "can carry dangerous bacteria such as Salmonella, E. coli, and Listeria." Nevertheless, advocates of consuming raw milk disagree and have argued that unpasteurized milk is nearly as safe as pasteurized milk, has health benefits that outweigh its risks, is a significant factor in preventing allergies and asthma, and has more nutrients.

The real issue here is one of freedom, not health, safety, or nutrition. The merits and demerits of drinking raw milk are immaterial. Laws against the sale of raw milk are inconsistent with individual liberty, private property, and a free society.

As former Republican presidential candidate and member of Congress Ron Paul stated regarding the issue, "If we are not even free anymore to decide something as basic as what we wish to eat or drink, how much freedom do we really have left?"

Montana Republicans apparently agreed, since only three of them (out of 61) opposed the original bill to "establish a small herd exemption permit for certain producers of milk."

Yet when it came to sexual freedom, Montana Republicans cast aside their support for individual liberty, private property, and a free society because they viewed certain sex acts as immoral.

One representative said "he holds no ill will toward gay people, but he and other Republicans opposed the legislation and similar efforts along religious lines." Another representative said, "There is an enormous biblical principle here. There is a truth. I know that public opinion may be swaying with the time but the truth does not sway and so it was default to scripture."

The real issue here is one of freedom, not scripture, religion, or morality. Like the subject of consuming raw milk, the morality or immorality of certain sex acts is immaterial. And laws against the sexual practices of consenting adults in their own homes are likewise inconsistent with individual liberty, private property, and a free society. That a given act is a sin, a vice, or an immoral activity doesn't mean that it should be a crime.

But having no concept of a free society is not the only problem with Montana Republicans.

One, the part of the law on the books in Montana that criminalized sexual acts between two persons of the same sex was declared unconstitutional by the Montana Supreme Court in 1997 in response to a 1995 lawsuit. And then there was the U.S. Supreme Court case of *Lawrence v. Texas* (2003) that nullified state sodomy laws. Arguing against a bill that would remove unconstitutional language from a law is just political grandstanding by Republicans to appeal to their religious-right base.

Two, the scripture referred to by one of the Montana state representatives has a great deal more to say about fornication between members of the opposite sex than it does about fornication between members of the same sex. Is he or any Montana Republicans in favor of criminalizing sexual acts between consenting adults of the opposite sex? Why not?

Three, there are other things aside from "deviate sexual conduct" that are likewise immoral. Drunkenness, gluttony, and lying are sins in any religion. Why don't governments criminalize those activities? Why is it that sexual sins are always singled out?

And four, short of the state of Montana's putting cameras in the bedrooms of all its residents, laws criminalizing the activities of consenting adults on private property are utterly unenforceable.

Gay sex and raw milk—Montana Republicans just don't get their relation to a free society. Toleration is not approval; legal does not mean recommended; permissible does not mean wholesome; vices are not crimes.

*****

MILITARY DISCOUNTS AND A FREE SOCIETY

You see it on the signs, menus, websites, and advertisements of a wide variety of businesses: Military discount. All manner of businesses are now offering discounts of various percentages to military personnel. Some restaurants even give free meals on Veterans Day to patrons who show up in a military uniform or present their military ID.

This is a great thing, but it has nothing to do with the military.

I have ridiculed on a regular basis the various military discount schemes that are all-to-prevalent throughout the United States today. But I have done so from the standpoint of my opposition to the curse of military exceptionalism that pervades American society. However, from the perspective of private property, individual liberty, a free market, and a free society—things that I hold dear—the ability of a business to offer a discount to a select group is an example of one of the last vestiges of freedom that we have left in this increasingly totalitarian country.

Restaurants offer senior-citizen discounts. Hotels offer discounts to members of AARP. Bars have ladies' nights. Companies have employee discounts. Warehouse clubs offer discounts to members. Theme parks offer discounts to children. Companies offer discounts to customers who pay in cash, prepay, or pay within a specified period of time. Family members give relatives discounts on personal items they wish to sell. Stores extend discounts to customers with coupons. Businesses offer discounts for buying in bulk. And of course, there are the ubiquitous military discounts offered by just about every place of business.

Not everyone likes discounts, and especially when they concern religion.

There are atheists who have filed discrimination complaints against restaurants that offered discounts on Sunday meals to those who presented a church bulletin. I remember in the early 1990s when I lived in Pensacola, Florida, that there was a huge outcry when a gas station began offering a 10 percent discount on car repairs to Christians.

Military discounts and senior-citizen discounts and are what you call politically-correct discounts. Giving discounts to someone based on his religion or race is taboo in "the land of the free" because it is deemed discriminatory—as if discriminating against civilians and the young in favor of military personnel and the aged is somehow not discriminatory.

In a free society, any business would be perfectly free to offer discounts on any product or service, at any time, and in any amount, to any individual or group, and on any basis—including race, color, religion, religious denomination, political ideology, sex, sexual orientation, gender identity, national origin, age, pregnancy status, martial status, immigration status, disability, birthplace, ancestry, culture, appearance, or ethnicity.

If a Jewish Democrat business owner wants to offer discounts only to Jewish Democrats, then so be it. If a Christian Republican business owner wants to offer discounts only to Christian Republicans, then so be it. If a Protestant business owner wants to offer discounts only to his fellow Protestants, then so be it. If a Catholic business owner wants to offer discounts only to his fellow Catholics, then so be it. If a white business owner wants to offer discounts only to whites, then so be it. If a black business owner wants to offer discounts only to blacks, then so be it. If a transgendered atheist business owner wants to offer discounts only to LGBT individuals who are atheists, then so be it. If a business owner wants to offer discounts only to individuals who are not in the military, then so be it.

When people who think that offering discounts to veterans and military personnel is a good thing have a fit when someone even suggests that businesses should be able to offer discounts based on race or religion, this shows not only that they have a warped view of the military, but also that they have no concept of what a free society really is.

Businesses that offer military discounts may not be doing so because they actually admire the military; they may offer them for purely economic reasons—to sucker people who have a soft heart for the military into giving them their business. And businesses that offer military discounts may not be doing so because they actually believe in a free society; they may offer them while at the same time opposing the right of businesses to offer discounts based on other things.

But the ability of businesses to offer discounts to select groups is essential to any free society. As much as I oppose military exceptionalism, military recruiting practices, military appreciation days in churches, thanking the troops for their service, sporting events being turned into military worship services, national holidays being turned into military appreciation days, and almost everything the military does, I can still celebrate the existence of military discounts—and any other discount that businesses are allowed to offer in the tightly-controlled, heavily-regulated, mixed-market economy that passes for the free market in the United States.

*****

DOGS AND DINERS

Americans are dog lovers. In fact, many people love their dogs so much that they take them wherever they can. Some people would even take their dogs out to eat with them if they could.

If they live in California—now they can.

Gov. Jerry Brown has signed into law legislation that revises the California Health and Safety Code relating to outdoor dining facilities. The code currently prohibits live animals from being allowed in a food facility, except under specified conditions—e.g., dogs may be allowed when they are under the control of a uniformed law-enforcement officer or working as service animals accompanying a disabled person.

The new legislation (Assembly Bill No. 1965) authorizes "a food facility to allow a person to bring a pet dog in outdoor dining areas if specified conditions are satisfied." The bill allows California cities and counties to prohibit such conduct by ordinance.

The proposed legislation was introduced in the California State Assembly in February. It passed the Health Committee in March with only one "no" vote, the Local Government Committee in April with no "no" votes, the full Assembly in May with only one "no" vote, the Senate Health Committee in June with no "no" votes, and the full Senate in August with no "no" votes. It was approved by the governor on August 21.

The pertinent section of the legislation reads as follows:

(d) Pet dogs under the control of a person in an outdoor dining area if all of the following conditions are satisfied:

(1) The owner of the food facility elects to allow pet dogs in its outdoor

dining area.

(2) A separate outdoor entrance is present where pet dogs enter without going through the food establishment to reach the outdoor dining area and pet dogs are not allowed on chairs, benches, seats, or other fixtures.

(3) The outdoor dining area is not used for food or drink preparation or the storage of utensils. A food employee may refill a beverage glass in the outdoor dining area from a pitcher or other container.

(4) Food and water provided to pet dogs shall only be in single-use disposable containers.

(5) Food employees are prohibited from having direct contact with pet dogs while on duty. A food employee who does have that prohibited direct contact shall wash his or her hands as required by Section 113953.3.

(6) The outdoor dining area is maintained clean. Surfaces that have been contaminated by dog excrement or other bodily fluids shall be cleaned and sanitized.

(7) The pet dog is on a leash or confined in a pet carrier and is under the control of the pet dog owner.

(8) The food facility owner ensures compliance with local ordinances related to sidewalks, public nuisance, and sanitation.

(9) Other control measures approved by the enforcement agency.

Although it doesn't concern dogs, a potential ordinance in Lubbock, Texas, relates to the new legislation in California. Since about ten years ago, smoking inside enclosed public places and within 20 feet of them is prohibited in Lubbock, with exceptions for most bars, lounges, and sports grills. However, the West Texas Smoke Free Coalition wants the city to pass an ordinance that would make Lubbock businesses completely smoke-free.

And although it has nothing to do with any state law or city ordinance, an incident at a bar in Chesapeake, Virginia, likewise relates to dogs and diners. Customers at Big Woody's bar weren't comfortable with a woman who was breastfeeding her baby in the bar. When the manager went over to ask her to be more discreet, he noticed that she had drinks in front of her. Her tab was then closed down and she was asked to leave after things became confrontational. Breastfeeding "is a natural right that you're allowed to give your child," the woman said. She admitted to having a couple of sips of beer, but insisted that the shot of Fireball whiskey in front of her was for after she was done nursing her baby.

On the surface, the new law in California, the potential ordinance in

Texas, and the incident in Virginia don't look related in any way. On a deeper, more philosophical, level, however, they all concern the proper role of government, the use of private property, and the nature of a free society.

It should not have been necessary for the California legislature to pass a law to authorize "a food facility to allow a person to bring a pet dog in outdoor dining areas if specified conditions are satisfied." Doggy dining should have always been permitted at the discretion of the owner of the food facility.

Just as the city of Lubbock should not even consider banning smoking in bars, lounges, and sports grills that are within the city limits, and it should never have passed the ordinance that prohibited smoking inside enclosed public places and within 20 feet of them that it did pass ten years ago. Smoking should always be permitted at the discretion of the owners of the bars, restaurants, and stores in Lubbock.

And just as the bar in Virginia should have every right to refuse service to a woman who is breastfeeding—whether or not she is being discrete and whether or not she is drinking alcohol. There is no "natural right" to breastfeed one's child on someone else's property.

The domain of government regulation of dogs, smoking, and breastfeeding should be limited to public parks, post offices, public schools, courthouses, public libraries, city halls, public pools, and any other facility owned by government at some level. Now, whether governments *should* have any of those things is beyond the scope of this article (but see, for example, my articles on public libraries and schools). Be that as it may, it is an illegitimate purpose of government to regulate private businesses.

Business establishments that are open to the public are not "public places" or "public facilities" or "public accommodations." They are still private property with an owner or owners. It is market forces that should regulate whether dogs, smoking, breastfeeding, or consuming alcohol while nursing are permitted or prohibited in restaurants, bars, stores, and other places of business.

In a free society, business owners would have to weigh the costs—in terms of foot traffic, revenue, or profit—of allowing doggy dining, smoking, breastfeeding, or alcohol consumption in their place of business versus not allowing it.

That some or even a majority of people think that dogs in diners is unhealthy, smoking is hazardous to one's health, breastfeeding in public is rude, and nursing mothers' drinking alcohol is irresponsible is irrelevant. Those who feel that way can express their displeasure by not patronizing businesses that permit those things instead of looking to government to prohibit activities on private property that they don't approve of.

A free society, of course, is not just limited to the freedom of businesses to decide the above questions. There is a host of other actions that businesses may want to permit or prohibit in their establishments, but government intervention should not be the cause of any permission or prohibition. Not in a free society.

*****

SUNDAY SHOPPING

Just before Christmas, the country of Hungary joined other European countries such as Germany, Austria, and Switzerland in banning Sunday shopping.

Although the Hungarian Parliament passed the bill on December 16, it isn't scheduled to take effect until March 15 of this year. The legislation, which was supported by the prime minister but opposed by the economy minister, was promoted by its sponsoring lawmakers as insurance that shopping won't "shorten the time that families spend together." Prime Minister Viktor Orban said the bill "protects Sunday as a Christian day of rest." He also noted that the neighboring countries of Austria and Germany have similar Sunday-shopping restrictions. Very true. In fact, the German-speaking countries actually have the most limited shopping hours in Europe.

But like the Sunday-shopping bans in other European countries, the newly enacted one in Hungary is riddled with exceptions:

• Pharmacies, tobacconists, farmers' markets, and stores on military bases are permitted to operate on Sundays. Bakeries can also open between 5 m. and noon.
• Retail shops at airports, train stations, gas stations, and hospitals also are allowed to operate as late as 10 m. on Sundays.
• Shops with less than 2,150 square feet of retail space aren't covered by the law, provided that the Sunday work force consists of those who have at least a 20 percent stake in the business or who are immediate family members of the owners.
• The four Sundays preceding Christmas are exempt from the shopping ban, and all retailers will be allowed to open their doors once a year on a Sunday of their choosing.

Hungary's National Association of Entrepreneurs and Employers opposed the legislation, warning that its passage would lead to about 20,000 layoffs and citing an Economics Ministry report that about 20 percent of Hungarians do the bulk of their weekly shopping on Sunday.

Americans who are used to 24/7 shopping at Wal-Mart Supercenters and crowded malls on Sundays express amusement at these European Sunday-shopping laws. Other European economic and political interventions in the market are likewise subject to the scorn of Americans. France is famous for its 35-hour workweek. Belgian workers are entitled to a one-year "career break" during their working lifetime during which time the worker receives an allowance from the government. Belgians also receive 15 weeks' maternity leave, 10 days' paternity leave, and up to 3 months for parental leave. Danish workers average 33 hours a week and have a right to at least five weeks of paid vacation each year. In the Netherlands, four-day workweeks are the rule, not the exception. At 29 hours, the Dutch have the lowest average number of hours worked per week of any industrialized nation. Italian workers are entitled to at least four weeks of paid vacation each year. Socialized medicine is the norm in the countries of Europe. The hours that stores can be open for business each day of the week are also heavily regulated.

But Americans who laugh at and mock Europeans for their interventionism, their socialism, their business regulations, and their nanny statism while expressing pride in America's free enterprise system need to take a good, long look in the mirror. For example, Americans who want to shop on Sunday can generally do so—unless they want to buy alcohol or a car.

Most states (and cities and counties that are allowed a local option) restrict alcohol sales in some way on Sundays. In some states, and many counties, the sale of alcohol is prohibited for consumption off-premises on Sunday. In other states and counties it is just hard liquor that cannot be sold for off-premise consumption on Sunday. In many states, no alcoholic beverages of any kind can be sold before a certain time on Sunday. Alcohol consumption may be a vice, but in most states you can go to a strip club on Sunday as well as purchase tobacco and pornography.

It is illegal to buy a car on a Sunday in Colorado, Illinois, Indiana, Iowa, Louisiana, Maine, Minnesota, Missouri, New Jersey, Oklahoma, North Dakota, Pennsylvania, and Wisconsin. Maryland allows Sunday car sales in only three counties. Texas and Utah prohibit car sales over consecutive weekend days. In Michigan—the birthplace of the automobile—Sunday sales are restricted to counties with fewer than 130,000 people. Otherwise, according to Michigan state law,

> It shall be unlawful for any person, firm or corporation to engage in the business of buying, selling, trading or exchanging new, used or second-hand motor vehicles or offering to buy, sell, trade or exchange, or participate in the negotiation thereof, or attempt to buy, sell, trade or exchange any motor vehicle or interest therein, or of any written instrument pertaining thereto, on the first day of the week, commonly called Sunday.

There are four observations about these Sunday-shopping laws that come to mind.

1. The United States does not have a free market, does not have free-market capitalism, and does not have a free-enterprise system. The United

States has a relatively free market, a comparatively free market, a regulated free market.

2. Complaints, concerns, criticisms, and condemnations of the free market are misguided. Socialists, Democrats, liberals, and progressives who talk about market failures and the evils of corporations while blaming poverty and income inequality on laissez-faire capitalism and the unfettered free market are in reality opposing crony capitalism, a mixed-market economy, and the façade of the free market that exists in the United States.

3. State and local governments are just as regulatory and interventionist as the federal government. Sunday-shopping laws in the United States are state and local laws. Remember, it is local governments that regularly require permits for garage sales and ban plastic foam containers, plastic shopping bags, and "big gulp" drinks. Government intervention at any level is distortive and destructive.

4. To ban shopping or restrict the sale of alcohol or automobiles is to ban or restrict commerce, property, and freedom. The fact that these sales occur on a Sunday is irrelevant. Blue laws are the ultimate in victimless-crime legislation.

In a free economy, businesses determine whether they will offer family, paternity, maternity, or sick leave to their employees and how much they will offer them—not the government.

In a free economy, businesses determine how much vacation time to offer their employees—not the government.

In a free economy, businesses determine how many hours per week their employees should work—not the government.

In a free economy, businesses determine how many hours their employees must work before receiving overtime pay—not the government.

In a free economy, businesses determine what hours of the day and night they will be open—not the government.

In a free economy, businesses determine what days of the week they will be open or closed—not the government.

That does not mean that employees, families, unions, and other organizations have no say in the matter. It just means that those things are ultimately determined by businesses—not the government.

A free economy is an essential part of a free society.

*****

DRESS CODES, EMPLOYMENT, AND RELIGION

The U.S. Supreme Court heard oral arguments last month in a case relating to dress codes, employment, and religion. The case, *Equal Employment Opportunity Commission v. Abercrombie & Fitch Stores Inc.*, is a good point of departure for how these things relate to each other in a free

THE FREE SOCIETY

423

society. The High Court is expected to decide the case in the spring or early summer.

The case stems from an incident back in 2008. Samantha Elauf, a practicing Muslim teenager, applied for a Model position at the Abercrombie Kids store in the Woodland Hills Mall in Tulsa, Oklahoma. ("Model" is the company's word for sales-floor employees.) She wore a black hijab (a Muslim headscarf) to her job interview with the assistant manager, Ms. Cooke. A job offer was not extended to Ms. Elauf. A few days after the interview, she learned from a friend who worked at the store that she had not been hired because of her headscarf.

Abercrombie has a strict dress code for its employees. According to the decision of a U.S. Court of Appeals,

Abercrombie requires employees in its stores to comply with a "Look Policy." That policy is intended to promote and showcase the Abercrombie brand, which "exemplifies a classic East Coast collegiate style of clothing."

To Abercrombie, a Model who violates the Look Policy by wearing inconsistent clothing "inaccurately represents the brand, causes consumer confusion, fails to perform an essential function of the position, and ultimately damages the brand."

Employees must dress in clothing that is consistent with the kinds of clothing that Abercrombie sells in its stores. Notably, the policy prohibits employees from wearing black clothing and "caps."

Abercrombie contends that its Look Policy is critical to the health and vitality of its "preppy" and "casual" brand.

Elauf complained to the Equal Employment Opportunity Commission (EEOC), which filed a lawsuit against Abercrombie on September 17, 2009, alleging violations of Title VII of the Civil Rights Act of 1964, on the grounds that Abercrombie "refused to hire Ms. Elauf because she wears a hijab" and "failed to accommodate her religious beliefs by making an exception to the Look Policy." The EEOC sought injunctive relief, back pay, and damages. The jury in the U.S. District Court for the Northern District of Oklahoma case awarded the EEOC $20,000 in compensatory damages.

Title VII of the Civil Rights Act states that "it shall be an unlawful employment practice for an employer —

(1) to fail or refuse to hire or to discharge any individual, or otherwise to discriminate against any individual with respect to his compensation, terms, conditions, or privileges of employment, because of such individual's race, color, religion, sex, or national origin; or

(2) to limit, segregate, or classify his employees or applicants for employment in any way which would deprive or tend to deprive any individual of employment opportunities or otherwise adversely affect his status as an employee, because of such individual's race, color, religion, sex, or national origin."

Furthermore, "the term 'religion' includes all aspects of religious observance and practice, as well as belief, unless an employer demonstrates that he is unable to reasonably accommodate to an employee's or prospective employee's religious observance or practice without undue hardship on the conduct of the employer's business."

On appeal, the U.S. Court of Appeals for the Tenth Circuit in Denver, on October 1, 2013, reversed the decision of the district court and sided with Abercrombie.

But why?

Well, obviously the appeals court considered the decision of the district court to be wrong.

But why?

Were the three judges on the U.S. Court of Appeals for the Tenth Circuit concerned about property rights, freedom of association, government overreach, or the free society?

Not at all.

The Court basically ruled "that Abercrombie could not be held liable for violating anti-discrimination laws because it did not know, and Elauf had not told it, that she was wearing a headscarf for religious reasons."

According to the decision of the appeals court,

During the course of the interview, Ms. Elauf never informed Ms. Cooke that she was Muslim, never brought up the subject of her headscarf, and never indicated that she wore the headscarf for religious reasons and that she felt obliged to do so, and thus would need an accommodation to address the conflict between her religious practice and Abercrombie's clothing policy.

And "after offering a description of the dress requirements, Ms. Cooke asked Ms. Elauf at the end of the interview if she had any questions. Ms. Elauf did not ask any."

The decision of the appeals court was itself appealed and on October 2, 2014, the U.S. Supreme Court agreed to hear the case.

So, as Court reporter Lyle Denniston wrote about the oral argument,

Through much complexity, their opposing positions seemed to boil down to this: the government lawyer thought the employer should have the legal duty to spell out its policy so that the job applicant knows what is expected. The store's lawyer thought the employer should not guess at religion, and so the job applicant should have to tell it that she needed an accommodation for her religion.

In a free society, not only would a case like *EEOC v. Abercrombie* never be heard by the Supreme Court, no such case would ever be tried in any state or federal court. But that's not all.

In a free society, it would be solely at the discretion of corporations, companies, businesses, and employers generally whether or not they would be willing to provide a religious accommodation for dress codes or anything else.

In a free society, employers could institute any dress code of their choosing for employees.

In a free society, businesses could institute any dress code of their choosing for patrons.

In a free society, employers could require or prohibit any cultural, ethnic, religious, or political jewelry or attire.

In a free society, no one would be entitled to a particular job even if he is qualified for it.

In a free society, religion would not be treated as something exceptional, different, or special.

In a free society, there would be no right to know why one was not hired for a particular job.

In a free society, the Equal Employment Opportunity Commission would not exist.

In a free society, employers would be entirely free to question potential employees not only about their religion, but also about their sexual orientation, national origin, marital status, or political affiliation.

In a free society, religious discrimination in favor of or against an employee or potential employee would be perfectly legal.

In a free society, businesses would have the absolute right to refuse entrance, service, or employment to anyone not only on the basis of dress, but also because of hairstyle, tattoos, scars, facial hair, appearance, height, weight, gender, age, or disability.

In a free society, employers would not be forced to treat their employees wearing a hijab, yarmulke, scarf, or turban any differently from those wearing a Yankees ball cap.

In a free society, the government would not interfere in any way with the employer-employee relationship.

It all comes down to the question of property. It is property owners— residence owners and business owners—who establish the rules and requirements for entry, employment, service, interaction, transactions, and activity, not the government.

*****

EMPLOYMENT AND A FREE SOCIETY

The city of SeaTac, Washington, is the home of the Seattle-Tacoma International Airport. It is also home to the highest minimum wage in the country. SeaTac's minimum wage of $15 an hour took effect on January 1, 2014, the result of a ballot initiative. The minimum wage in the cities of San Francisco and Seattle is scheduled to gradually rise to $15 over the next few years.

The federal minimum wage has been $7.25 an hour since July 24, 2009. However, because states are allowed to set their own minimum wages, twenty-nine states and the District of Columbia have a minimum wage higher than the federal minimum. And because most states allow cities to set their own minimum wages, some cities have their own minimum wages that are higher than the minimum wages of their states.

Last month, thousands of fast-food workers from coast to coast—who typically make the minimum wage or just a little more—took to the streets in more than 200 cities to protest their low pay, with most demanding an increase in the minimum wage to $15 an hour. They were joined by labor activists, retail workers, home-care aides, adjunct professors, construction workers, child-care aides, and airport workers. They were even joined in Oakland by UC Berkeley Professor and former Secretary of Labor Robert Reich, who, in his impromptu speech, said, "It's not just a fight about higher wages," "it's a fight about morality, it's a fight about decency, it's a fight about dignity."

Workers in New York City started demonstrating at 6 a.m. "We demand the right to earn a living wage. We have a right to take care of our families just like the Trumps," said a local union president at a rally just outside the Trump Hotel. "I hope the workers get what they need to survive because the cost of everything keeps going up but the wages stay down," said a single mother who works a construction job. "I feel that corporations and institutions are taking in huge profits at the expense of low-wage workers," said a laid-off adjunct professor.

The demonstrations were organized by a group called Fight for $15. "We are winning," says the group, "but there's still a long way to go before every worker gets $15 an hour and union rights."

Strikes and demonstrations for a $15-an-hour wage have been going on for more than two years now after hundreds of fast-food workers walked off their jobs in New York City on November 29, 2012. In May 2014, more than 1,000 workers and supporters protested outside the McDonald's corporate headquarters in Oak Brook, Illinois, resulting in more than 100 arrests.

These strikes and demonstrations in support of a $15 an hour wage will only continue. McDonald's recent announcement that it will increase hourly wages for workers at company-owned stores (franchises account for 90 percent of McDonald's restaurants) has not placated the protests.

"This is too little to make a real difference, and covers only a fraction of workers," said a McDonald's worker from Charlotte, North Carolina. "We're going to keep fighting until we win $15 and union rights for all fast-food workers and our families," she added.

The hard truth, of course, is that workers at McDonalds, who have the quintessential McJob, aren't worth $15 an hour to their employers. If they quit their job today, they can be replaced before they clean out their locker or make it out the front door.

The elements that go into setting an employee's salary are much more numerous than most people realize: local, state, and federal laws; union contracts; competition for workers; the market; labor budgets; employee seniority; employee education; employee experience; employee value to employer; the employer portion of Social Security and Medicare taxes; unemployment taxes (which are borne completely by the employer); and benefits offered.

There are a number of things an employee *could* do to try and increase his pay: get more education, be more productive, stay with a company to build up seniority, work his way up the ladder, get into management, contribute to business growth, provide good customer service, have a good attitude, ask for a raise.

There are also some things an employee *should not* do if he wants to try and increase his pay: publicly complain about his pay rate; bad-mouth the company; go on strike; damage company property or reputation; run off business; anger customers; and participate in demonstrations, marches, and protests for a $15 an hour wage.

There are a number of things that could be said about employment in a free society.

In a free society, no one deserves a job, even if he is fully qualified for it.

In a free society, no one is entitled to a particular rate of pay.

In a free society, there is no local, state, or federal minimum wage.

In a free society, there is no such thing as a "living wage."

In a free society, there may not be a 40-hour work week.

In a free society, the availability and rate of overtime pay are set entirely by agreement between employers and employees.

In a free society, no one is "worth" a certain rate of pay.

In a free society, there are no government-mandated employee benefits.

In a free society, employees freely decide to take a job on the basis of the wage rate offered.

In a free society, socialistic-minded people can voluntarily pay a portion of their wages into an account to be distributed to workers who they think earn less money than they need to live on.

In a free society, union membership is voluntary.

In a free society, collective bargaining is voluntary.

In a free society, it is perfectly legal to fire Jews who refuse to work on Saturday and Christians who refuse to work on Sunday.

In a free society, it is entirely up to employers if they want to provide employees with a religious accommodation.

In a free society, employers have full control over the dress code of their employees.

In a free society, it is perfectly legal to fire workers who strike or otherwise refuse to work.

In a free society, it is perfectly legal for employers to fire employees at any time and for any reason.

In a free society, there are no government regulations to stifle businesses.

In a free society, employers can hire anyone they choose from any country without having to check his "papers."

In a free society, there is neither an employer nor employee share of payroll taxes.

In a free society, there are no unemployment taxes.

In a free society, unemployment insurance is private and voluntary.

In a free society, there is no income tax withheld from employee paychecks.

In a free society, employer discrimination against employees on the basis of race, religion, sexual orientation, sex, sexual identity, national origin, marital status, dress, tattoos, scars, facial hair, appearance, disability, age, height, weight, political affiliation, or anything else is perfectly legal.

In a free society, there is no Department of Labor.

In a free society, there is no National Labor Relations Board.

In a free society, there is no Equal Employment Opportunity Commission.

In a free society, there is no Family and Medical Leave Act.

In a free society, there is no government Bureau of Labor Statistics.

In a free society, no employee is entitled to pay equal to that of any other employee.

In a free society, employees may quit any job they don't like before or after they find another one.

In a free society, government would not interfere in any way with the employer-employee relationship.

It is a free society that Americans should be clamoring for.

*****

OVERTIME PAY AND A FREE SOCIETY

If there is only one thing that every American worker who gets paid by the hour knows about labor law aside from the minimum wage, it is that employers must pay time and a half for all hours worked over 40 hours. What many American hourly workers probably don't realize, however, is that some salaried workers are eligible for overtime pay as well.

This is all a result of the Fair Labor Standards Act (FLSA) of 1938 that introduced a national minimum wage, mandated time and a half for overtime in certain jobs, established a 40-hour work week, and prohibited most child labor.

Under current law, salaried workers who earn less than $455 per week are entitled to overtime pay for any hours over 40 that they work. Salaried workers who earn between $455 and $1,923 per week ($23,660 and $100,000 per year) are exempt from overtime regulations if they fall under the category of certain types of administrative, professional, and executive employees and meet certain guidelines. "Highly compensated employees," those performing office work and making an annual salary of $100,000 or more, are also exempt if they "customarily and regularly" perform "at least one of the duties of an exempt executive, administrative or professional employee." Other classes of workers who are exempt from overtime-pay requirements include certain outside salespeople and agricultural, live-in, computer, education, and transportation employees. Employees are not allowed to waive their right to overtime pay. Because independent contractors are not considered employees, they are not protected by the FLSA. These rules have been in place since August 2004.

The Obama administration wants to revise the overtime rules, including more than doubling the overtime exemption threshold to $50,400. Barack Obama raised the issue at the end of last month:

> We've got to keep making sure hard work is rewarded. Right now, too many Americans are working long days for less pay than they deserve. That's partly because we've failed to update overtime regulations for years—and an exemption meant for highly paid, white collar employees now leaves out workers making as little as $23,660 a year—no matter how many hours they work.

> This week, I'll head to Wisconsin to discuss my plan to extend overtime protections to nearly 5 million workers in 2016, covering all salaried workers making up to about $50,400 next year. That's good for workers who want fair pay, and it's good for business owners who are already paying their employees what they deserve—since those who are doing right by their employees are undercut by competitors who aren't.

> That's how America should do business. In this country, a hard day's work deserves a fair day's pay. That's at the heart of what it means to be middle class in America.

On July 6, the U.S. Department of Labor announced a proposed "rule that would extend overtime protections to nearly 5 million white collar workers within the first year of its implementation." The regulation "is a critical first step toward ensuring that hard-working Americans are compensated fairly and have a chance to get ahead." The Department's Wage and Hour Division has issued a fact sheet on the proposed rule that lists three key provisions:

The Notice of Proposed Rulemaking (NPRM) focuses primarily on updating the salary and compensation levels needed for white collar workers to be exempt. Specifically, the Department proposes to:

1. set the standard salary level at the 40th percentile of weekly earnings for full-time salaried workers ($921 per week, or $47,892 annually);

2. increase the total annual compensation requirement needed to exempt highly compensated employees (HCEs) to the annualized value of the 90th percentile of weekly earnings of full-time salaried workers ($122,148 annually); and

3. establish a mechanism for automatically updating the salary and compensation levels going forward to ensure that they will continue to provide a useful and effective test for exemption.

It should be pointed out that the Department "relied upon 2013 data in the development of the NPRM." The new proposed salary threshold of $970 a week, or $50,440 annually, mentioned by Obama would begin in 2016.

The Notice of Proposed Rulemaking concerning overtime pay was published on July 6, 2015, in the Federal Register (80 FR 38515). Interested parties are invited "to submit written comments on the proposed rule at www.regulations.gov on or before September 4, 2015."

The proposed rule is getting a lot of media attention. Liberals are generally claiming that the new overtime regulations will give millions of salaried workers a pay raise and create new jobs; conservatives are usually focusing on how this mandate will negatively impact employers through higher labor costs and employees through pay cuts, benefit cuts, or loss of flexibility in their schedule.

On NPR's *On Point* on July 1, someone from the conservative American Enterprise Institute was brought on the show to face off against the liberals and make the case against the proposed overtime rule. Not once did he say that it was not the proper role of government to dictate wage and hour standards. Not once did he make the moral case for no government intervention in the economy. Not once did he maintain that everything concerning the employer/employee relationship should be entirely left up to the free market. Not once did he explain the nature of a free society.

In a free society, an employee's overtime, just like his hour rate or salary, work schedule, work week, sick leave, lunch time, breaks, vacation pay, holiday pay, pension, life insurance, health insurance, family leave, severance pay, child care, and other fringe benefits would be determined solely by contract or agreement between an employee and his employer.

In a free society, there would be no Fair Labor Standards Act.

In a free society, there would be no U.S. Department of Labor.

In a free society, there would be no minimum-wage laws.

In a free society, there would be no government-imposed 40-hour work week.

In a free society, there would be no federal overtime-pay requirements.

In a free society, time off in lieu of overtime, or in addition to overtime, both of which are currently illegal for most occupations, would be options in the workplace.

In a free society, employees freely decide to take a job on the basis of the salary and benefits offered—including the availability and calculation of overtime pay.

In a free society, government would not interfere in any way with the employer-employee relationship.

Currently, some employers pay their employees double time in certain instances or offer increased pay for working nights and weekends. Neither of those things is required by the Fair Labor Standards Act. The same goes for vacation pay, sick pay, holiday pay, and severance pay. The Department of Labor says about these things, "These benefits are matters of agreement between an employer and an employee (or the employee's representative)." This is exactly how it should be when it comes to overtime pay. Why it isn't, is completely arbitrary on the part of the government.

*****

BEARDS AND A FREE SOCIETY

Although baseball season is over, one thing still remains: the New York Yankees' ban on players wearing beards.

The beard ban was instituted by the Yankees' principal owner. George Steinbrenner, in 1973. Long hair is not allowed either, but mustaches are permitted. Although Steinbrenner died in 2010, the policy remains in effect. The Yankees' manager, Joe Girardi, said he likes the policy because "the clean-cut look fits with the team's professional attitude." "It's who we are. It was Mr. Steinbrenner's rule, and I respect that," said Girardi. Some have speculated that the facial hair ban has cost the Yankees some star players. Former Yankee pitcher (2008–2014) David Robertson signed a four-year, $46 million deal with the Chicago White Sox before the 2015 season. One of the first things he did after going to Chicago was to grow a beard.

But it's not just the New York Yankees that don't allow its employees to wear beards. If you want to deliver packages for United Parcel Service (UPS), no facial hair is permitted other than a mustache.

The Publix supermarket chain in the Southeast does not allow its employees to have anything other than a mustache either.

Until just a few years ago, "cast members" at Disney theme parks were not allowed to sport any facial hair—even though Walt Disney had a mustache. The policy was changed in February of 2012.

I'm sure there are other companies that have similar facial hair policies. There are also some conservative Christian schools that forbid their male students to wear beards—or having shaved heads, mohawks, dreadlocks, long hair, goatees, long sideburns, or mustaches.

In most instances, the federal government permits private businesses (as opposed to the public sector) to have a "no-beard" policy. However, businesses must provide religious accommodations. The federal Equal Opportunity Employment Commission (EEOC) regulations, under the heading of "Religious Accommodation/Dress & Grooming Policies," state,

> Unless it would be an undue hardship on the employer's operation of its business, an employer must reasonably accommodate an employee's religious beliefs or practices. This applies not only to schedule changes or leave for religious observances, but also to such things as dress or grooming practices that an employee has for religious reasons. These might include, for example, wearing particular head coverings or other religious dress (such as a Jewish yarmulke or a Muslim headscarf), or wearing certain hairstyles or facial hair (such as Rastafarian dreadlocks or Sikh uncut hair and beard). It also includes an employee's observance of a religious prohibition against wearing certain garments (such as pants or miniskirts).

Employers must also allow employees to grow a beard if they have a verifiable medical reason for not shaving. Even so, employers can still have a "no-beard" policy if deemed necessary for workplace safety (like needing to wear a particular respirator).

Although Americans may question the motive of the New York Yankees in banning its players from sporting beards, they generally support the right of ball teams and businesses to institute "no-beard" policies no matter how illogical, irrational, or nonsensical they think the policies are.

In a free society, this is the way it should be, not just when it comes to facial hair, but to everything. The Yankees beard ban is therefore a great introduction to life, association, interaction, and conflict resolution in a free society. The implications of the Yankees' policy extend far out of the ballpark.

The prohibition on Yankees players' wearing beards should be viewed as just part and parcel of the requirements to play for the Yankees. To play for the Yankees (assuming you sign a contract with the team), you have to show up for practice, wear a clean Yankees uniform, show up for the games, hit above a certain percentage, make errors below a certain number, bat in so many runs, not strike out too many times, do what the manager tells you to do, not have long hair—and be clean shaven. If a member of the Yankees team doesn't like one or more the Yankees' policies he has only two options: conform or quit.

In a free society, a ball team's ability to select and regulate the appearance and behavior of its players would be absolute. If a team wanted to hire only players who were over a certain height, under a certain weight, between two specific ages, belonged or didn't belong to a particular political party, had a certain hair color, practiced or didn't practice a certain sexual orientation, belonged or didn't belong to a particular race, practiced or didn't practice a specific religion, or had or didn't have a certain marital status, then that would be up to each team. It may not be a wise thing to include or exclude a particular characteristic or practice, but that is irrelevant. Freedom includes the freedom make bad decisions. In a free society, there would be no government anti-discrimination laws or government-mandated exceptions or accommodations. Those would be up to each individual team. If a potential player doesn't like any of a team's stipulations, he has only two options: conform or play for a different team.

And the same is true throughout a free society.

In a free society, if an employer wants his employees to all be male, or all be female, or all be gay, or all be straight, or all be Catholic, or all be Protestant, or all be black, or all be white, then that should be his decision, not the government's.

In a free society, if a seller prefers a buyer to be a Yankees fan instead of a Cubs fan, then that should be his decision, not the government's.

In a free society, if a business owner prohibits his male workers from having dreadlocks and long sideburns, then that should be his decision, not the government's.

In a free society, if a business owner prohibits his female workers from wearing veils or burqas, then that should be his decision, not the government's.

In a free society, if a landlord prefers a renter to be Democrat instead of a Republican, then that should be his decision, not the government's.

In a free society, if an organization wants all of its members to have a beard, then that should be its decision, not the government's.

In a free society, if an individual prefers associating with and living near only people who are just like him in every way, then that should be his decision, not the government's.

In a free society, it couldn't be any other way.

The question for Americans is whether or not they want to live in a free society. Not just a society that gives them the freedom to do what they want to do, but a free society for all Americans as long as they engage in peaceful, voluntary activity.

The question is simply this: Should individuals decide or should government decide? Should individuals decide whom they sell to, buy from, trade with, associate with, hire, fire, rent to, or lease to, or should the government decide? Should individuals decide what they eat, drink, or smoke, or should the government decide? Should individuals who own businesses decide what standards of dress, appearance, and conduct are appropriate in the workplace, or should the government decide?

In a free society, it is each individual who makes the decisions how he will live his life, interact with others, engage in commerce, or operate a business; in any other kind of society, the government makes the decisions for each individual.

*****

UNIONS AND STRIKES IN A FREE SOCIETY

The labor-union membership rate of American workers has been declining for years. Labor-union strikes have concomitantly decreased as well. Unions have historically been associated with violence, corruption, anti-capitalistic propaganda, Democratic politics—and strikes.

Unions

According to the Bureau of Labor Statistics, in 2014, union membership fell to 11.1 percent, down 0.2 percent from 2013, although the number of workers belonging to unions held steady at about 14.6 million. By contrast, in 1983, "the first year for which comparable union data are available, the union membership rate was 20.1 percent, and there were 17.7 million union workers." Public-sector workers have a union membership rate (35.7 percent) more than five times that of private-sector workers (6.6 percent). Workers in education, training, library occupations, and protective-service occupations had the highest unionization rate (35.3 percent). The states of New York and North Carolina continue to have the highest (24.6 percent) and lowest (1.9 percent) union participation rates.

Unions are nothing more than labor cartels that restrict the supply of workers in a company or industry to drive up the existing workers' wages or benefits. The cost of higher wages and benefits either lowers profits, is passed on to consumers through higher prices, or both. In general, labor unions benefit their members at the expense of consumers and workers who are denied job opportunities.

The power of labor unions lies in collective bargaining, the power of unions to negotiate with management on behalf of an entire work force.

All discussions about compensation, benefits, performance, promotions, or working conditions must occur only between the union and the employer. Directly negotiating with unionized employees is prohibited by law and enforced by government. If negotiations between the union and management fail and union demands are not met, unions use the tactics of strikes, picketing, and hindering replacement workers from entering the workplace or performing their jobs in order to force companies to give in to union demands.

Unions oppose free trade, outsourcing, immigrant workers, automation, and competition, since a cartel can get away with charging higher prices—in this case wage rates—only as long as it retains its monopoly power.

Strikes

Although strikes are not as commonplace in America as they used to be, the longest strike in recent history occurred this past summer in Tucson, Arizona.

In 1905, the Tucson Rapid Transit Company assumed operations of and electrified the town's horse-drawn streetcars. The streetcar lines were converted to buses by the 1930s. In 1969, the City of Tucson assumed control of Tucson Rapid Transit's struggling transportation system. Public transit flourished when new buses were added and service improved. In 1975, the public transportation system was renamed Sun Tran. Today, Sun Tran operates about 250 buses on 40 routes to destinations in and around Tucson, and makes about 20 million passenger trips annually.

On August 6, after negotiations between the Teamsters Union and Sun Tran broke down, around 530 bus drivers, mechanics, and other Sun Tran workers went on strike. The striking workers were represented by Teamsters Local 104, which demanded a 75-cent hourly wage increase this year, $1-per-hour increases in the next two years, $1.58-per-hour increases to pension contributions this year, and $1 increases in each of the next two years. Top pay for drivers is $19.22 an hour; for mechanics, it is $22.66 an hour.

Naturally, transportation through- out the city was crippled during the work stoppage, as only limited weekday service on a few routes was available, with even more limited Saturday service. Tucson Mayor Jonathan Rothschild issued a statement encouraging both parties to restart negotiations because the strike was "hurting the community." But he said that he and the City Council could not by law intervene in the negotiations. The strike went on for 42 days until Teamsters Local 104 and Sun Tran management firm Professional Transit Management signed a two-year contract that is good until June 30, 2017. Sun Tran workers previously went on strike for one week in 1997, two weeks in 2001, and one week in 2010.

A free society

In a free society, there would be no government monopoly on transportation. Ideally, there would be no city or county bus, trolley, streetcar, subway, or train service—it would all be privately owned, financed, and operated. But even in the event that cities or counties still had public transit systems, there would be no prohibitions, restrictions, regulations, or licensing to hinder private transit systems from competing with public ones.

The problem is simply that Americans do not live in a free society. They live in a relatively free society. Compared with North Korea, Cuba, Venezuela, Egypt, and Saudi Arabia—yes, it appears that Americans live in a freedom paradise. But compare living in the United States with living in the United Kingdom, Western Europe, Canada, New Zealand, or Australia and the freedom gap narrows considerably or disappears.

Americans sing on the Fourth of July that they are proud to be Americans "where at least I know I'm free." But they are free only if they don't possess a plant the government doesn't approve of, don't brew too much beer at home, don't hire someone for less than the minimum wage, don't set the wrong prices on their products, don't have a garage sale, and don't work as raisin farmers.

Get caught in possession of too much of a plant the government doesn't approve of and you might end up in jail; get caught too many times and you might go to prison for life.

It used to be illegal on the federal level to brew beer at home. That changed in 1979. However, it is a federal crime for an individual to brew more than 100 gallons of beer at home. A household with two or more adults can brew up to 200 gallons. None of the home-brewed beer can be sold. There are also state laws relating to that as well.

Minimum-wage laws violate the freedom of contract between employers and employees, and especially young, unskilled minority employees. In addition to worrying about the federal minimum wage, many states and cities have a higher minimum that employers need to be cognizant of.

If you own a business and you charge too much, the government accuses you of price gouging. Charge the same as your competitors and the government will accuse you of collusion. Charge too little and the government will accuse you of predatory pricing.

In many communities across the United States, one cannot have a garage sale without first getting a government permit.

Writer James Bovard in these pages a few months ago pointed out that the U.S. Agriculture Department's Raisin Administrative Committee in one year "prohibited producers from selling 47 percent of their raisin harvest in order to drive up raisin prices as part of a 'reserve' scheme" and in the next year "decreed that producers must forfeit 30 percent of their harvest to the Raisin Committee."

There is no labor freedom in the United States either. The Wagner Act of 1935 forces employers to bargain collectively "in good faith" with any union the National Labor Relations Board decides has been chosen by a majority of an arbitrarily defined "bargaining unit." In some states you are required to either join the union at your workplace or pay union dues. In other states you can be forced to have a union represent you, but not to pay union dues. Employees who strike over "unfair labor practices" cannot be fired or permanently replaced. Any replacement workers who are hired must be let go when the strike is over. Employers must provide unions with organizing space and cannot discriminate against union organizers or members. Union contracts make firing underperforming workers difficult. And federal anti-trust laws exempt labor unions.

There are a number of things that could be said regarding unions and strikes in a free society.

In a free society, any or all striking workers could legally be fired and never rehired.

In a free society, "scabs" could freely be hired to temporarily or permanently replace striking workers.

In a free society, acts of violence, trespassing, or vandalism committed by strikers would be criminal and subject to prosecution.

In a free society, there would be no National Labor Relations Board.

In a free society, there would be no Department of Labor.

In a free society, there would be no Bureau of Labor Statistics.

In a free society, there would be no government labor economists.

In a free society, there would be no Wagner, Norris-LaGuardia, or Railway Labor Acts.

In a free society, union membership would be voluntary.

In a free society, no one could be forced to pay union dues while not a member of a union.

In a free society, workers could agree as a condition of employment to join a union.

In a free society, workers could agree as a condition of employment not to join a union.

In a free society, individual workers not belonging to a union could go on strike.

In a free society, businesses could refuse to collectively bargain with unions.

In a free society, companies would still be responsible to maintain safe work environments.

In a free society, increased pay and benefits would depend on individual productively, seniority, or overall value to the company, not membership in a union.

In a free society, workers at a company might be organized into several different unions.

In a free society, employers could prohibit the dissemination of information concerning union membership when such dissemination occurred on an employer's property.

In a free society, businesses could forbid their workers to form or join unions.

In a free society, work- places might contain a mixture of unionized and nonunionized employees.

In a free society, employers could collectively bargain with some or all employees without going through a union.

In a free society, the relationship between management and unions wouldn't necessarily be antagonistic, as it is now.

In a free society, the government would not interfere in any way with the employer-employee relationship.

There is nothing inherently wrong with labor unions or collective bargaining. As long as like-minded people want to join together into groups, there will be unions of some kind—even in a free society. And it might be easier and cheaper for a company to engage in collective bargaining with all or a portion of its employees. The difference is that in a free society everything concerning unions and their relation to employers, management, and employees would be voluntary, peaceful, and noncoercive.

In a free society, the union's chief weapon—the strike—might still exist as well. But it is mistaken to think that all workers who strike—that is, refuse to work—would just summarily be fired. They certainly might be fired—and blacklisted, and denied severance pay, and deemed ineligible for re-employment. But a company might very well give in to the demands of striking workers if it calculates that the cost of training new workers to replace them exceeded the cost of acceding to the strikers' demands. But again, in a free society, strikes would be voluntary, peaceful, and noncoercive—or they would not be allowed to take place.

The widely disseminated union propaganda that without unions American workers would labor in unsafe working conditions, for long hours, at subsistence wages, and receive no benefits is ludicrous. The 89 percent of American workers who are not members of a labor union certainly don't all toil in dangerous sweatshops for seven days a week at minimum wage with no time off. Union propaganda certainly doesn't apply to companies such as Netflix, which now allows its employees to take unlimited paid parental leave during the first year after a child is born or adopted, with full salaries and benefits. And just because a company has unionized employees, it doesn't necessarily follow that it pays them high or even above-average wages. Most of the workers at Disney theme parks in Florida are represented by unions, but starting pay is still less than $10 an hour.

Labor unions could conceivably still exist in a free society, and strikes might very likely still take place by workers in and out of unions. The difference in a free society would be that unions and strikers would receive no special government protection, promotion, patronage, or privilege.

*****

BIBLES, HOTELS, CHRISTIANS, AND ATHEISTS

The Gideons International wants to place copies of the Bible in all hotel rooms. Most hotels have complied with the request. Many Americans like the idea. Other Americans don't care one way or the other. Some Americans want the Bibles removed.

In a free society, the questions of whether the Gideons should or shouldn't make such a request, whether hotels should or shouldn't acquiesce, whether Americans should or shouldn't like the idea, whether Americans should or shouldn't care one way or another, and whether Americans should or shouldn't seek to have Bibles removed from hotel rooms are questions that have no answers. Nevertheless, the current controversy between Christians and atheists over Bibles in hotel rooms still serves as an introduction to how conflict in a free society can be resolved without interference by government.

The Gideons International, founded in 1899, and headquartered in Nashville, Tennessee, focuses on "distributing complete Bibles, New Testaments, or portions thereof," in more than 90 languages, to individuals and for placement in "selected public locations where large numbers of people" may be "searching for answers." Bibles are freely distributed to students, prisoners, and police, fire, medical, and military personnel. Bibles are also freely placed in hospitals, convalescent homes, medical offices, prisons, jails, domestic-violence shelters, motels, and hotels. With a current membership of more than 300,000, The Gideons International has distributed more than 2 billion Scripture portions around the globe since its founding, including more than 88 million in 2014.

The American Hotel & Lodging Association (AH&LA), serving the hospitality industry for more than a century, and headquartered in Washington, D.C., is "the sole national association representing all segments of the 1.9 million-employee U.S. lodging industry, including hotel owners, REITs, chains, franchisees, management companies, independent properties, state hotel associations, and industry suppliers." The AH&LA claims to be "the voice of the nearly $163 billion lodging industry" and "the primary resource for timely hospitality news, statistics, and expert comment." Representing approximately 16,000 members, the AH&LA provides "focused advocacy, communications support, and educational resources for an industry of more than 53,000 properties generating $176 billion in annual sales from 5 million guestrooms."

The Freedom from Religion Foundation (FFRF), incorporated in 1978, and headquartered in Madison, Wisconsin, is a "national membership association of approximately 20,000 freethinkers: atheists, agnostics and skeptics of any pedigree." The organization's purpose is to "promote the constitutional principle of separation of state and church, and to educate the public on matters relating to nontheism." It "works as an umbrella for those who are free from religion and are committed to the cherished principle of separation of state and church." The Foundation and its staff attorneys "act on countless violations of separation of state and church on behalf of members and the public including: Prayers in public schools, payment of funds for religious purposes, government funding of pervasively sectarian institutions, and the ongoing campaign against civil rights for women, gays and lesbians led by churches."

The co-presidents of the FFRF recently sent a letter to the president and CEO of the AH&LA urging the organization to "offer bible-free rooms, just as establishments now offer smoke-free rooms" and say "NO to the Gideons" and their attempts to exploit "hotels and motels to proselytize a captive audience." Because "today almost one in four adult U.S. citizens" identifies as nonreligious, many hotel guests are "freethinkers—atheists, agnostics, skeptics or Nones—who are offended to be charged high fees only to be proselytized in the privacy of their own bedrooms," and because the majority of international guests are not Christians, FFRF believes "it's simply bad business to promote divisive religious teachings to a diverse clientele." And besides, "Those who must read the bible every day will surely take precautions to travel with their own copies."

But, of course, the FFRF has another issue with the Bible in hotel rooms. The organization maintains, among other things, that the Bible "makes gruesome bedtime reading," has harmed "millions of men, women and children" by "bible teachings and primitive beliefs," and "preaches women's inferiority and submissiveness." The letter concludes with an admonition to the hotel industry to follow the lead of one American hotel chain that has "removed religious materials from rooms, but offers such materials to guests upon request" and one British hotel chain that removed Bibles from its rooms "in order not to discriminate against any religion."

The FFRF letter was followed by a press release stating that a similar letter was sent to the fifteen hotel companies that "are responsible for more than 33,000 hotels in the U.S. and more than 4.1 million rooms internationally." The press release mainly quotes from the original letter, but adds that Gideon Bibles "in a bedstand drawer" are like a harmful "invasive species." Because the FFRF is "an organization whose members embrace reason and science," it "would prefer placement of Charles Darwin's 'On the Origin of Species' to the invasive Gideons."

Naturally, Christians—and especially conservative and evangelical Christians—are upset with the FFRF's attempt to pressure hotels to say "NO to the Gideons." They see it as part of the FFRF's larger goal of removing all references to God from the Pledge of Allegiance, U.S. currency, government buildings and monuments, and public places. They also point out that some "freethinkers" have even defaced hotel Bibles with FFRF stickers reading, "Warning! Literal belief in this book may endanger your health and life."

There are several reasons why hotel owners might want to retain Bibles in their hotel rooms regardless of what the FFRF thinks or what the AH&LA recommends: tradition, religion, business.

One, it is a long-standing American tradition that they may not want to break with. They may not care one way or another whether hotel rooms have Bibles, but they may not want to do anything that might give some people the impression that they are un-American or irreligious.

Two, for some hotel owners who are devout Christians, it might be a religious conviction. In cases like these, one might also find other religious literature in the hotel rooms to supplement the Bible. What people think about the Bible and other religious literature, or how their placement in hotel rooms affects business, is irrelevant to such owners.

And three, they might view it as good for business even though they personally are "freethinkers" themselves. They may think that Christians who stay at their hotels and find a Bible in the dresser drawer are more likely to return the next time they travel. They may think that the absence of a Bible will have the opposite effect. Or they may simply reason that the publicity resulting from the removal of Bibles from their hotel rooms will anger more Christians than the number of atheists it would delight.

Should hotels have Bibles in their rooms? That is entirely up to hotel owners. Just as it is entirely up to hotel owners whether their rooms contain hair dryers and coffee makers. Just as it is entirely up to hotel owners whether the televisions in their rooms have HBO or Showtime. Just as it is entirely up to hotel owners whether copies of the Muslim *Koran*, Marx's *Kapital*, Darwin's *On the Origin of Species*, Smith's *Wealth of Nations*, the *New York Times*, the Democratic Party Platform, *MAD* magazine, or nothing will be placed in hotel rooms. Rooms in the Mormon-owned Marriott hotel chain generally contain a copy of the *Book of Mormon* alongside the Bible.

In a free society, individuals (and groups of individuals who unite to support some common cause) who *don't* want hotels to place Bibles or literature in their rooms, *don't* want hotels to offer pornographic pay-per-view movies, or *don't* want some other practice of a hotel are free to make requests, write letters, send emails, issue press releases, organize boycotts, present petitions, or otherwise attempt to pressure hotels *not* to take a particular course of action—as long as their conduct is peaceful. And likewise for individuals and groups who *want* hotels to take a particular course of action. Again, as long as their conduct is peaceful.

But it's not just hotels. In a free society, any individual or group who objects to the product or practice of some business can likewise make requests, write letters, send emails, issue press releases, organize boycotts, present petitions, or otherwise attempt to pressure a particular business or industry not to take a particular course of action—as long as their conduct is peaceful.

A free society does not mean a society without conflict. It simply means a society where someone cannot pressure the government to violate the rights of someone else.

*****

SERVICE DOGS AND A FREE SOCIETY

I can remember when I was a kid that some stores would have a notice posted on the front door or window that dogs were not allowed in the store except for guide dogs leading the blind. Like any kid, I thought it would be a cool thing to be able to see one of these dogs, but I don't remember having ever seen one.

I have noticed in recent years the proliferation, not of guide dogs leading the blind, but of service dogs accompanying what appear to be perfectly healthy people. Now, if you have some disability or handicap and feel you need one of these service dogs to help you cope, get around, live a relatively normal life, etc., then I mean no offense.

But not only am I seeing these dogs everywhere, I have noticed that people shopping with one or more of their friends or family members still have their service dogs with them. I have even seen a husband and wife together each with their own service dog.

I admit it: I am not a dog person. I don't own a dog, don't like to pet dogs, don't like to hear my neighbor's dog barking, don't like to sit next to someone with a dog on an airplane, and certainly don't like to see dogs in stores while I am shopping.

However, I believe in personal freedom and a free society. If someone wants to own a dog, then fine. If someone wants to take his dog on a cross-country trip in his car, then fine. If someone wants to spend thousands of dollars getting his dog's hip replaced, then fine. If someone wants to treat his dog better than his children, then fine. If someone wants to give his dog an elaborate funeral and burial, then fine.

The issue of service dogs is a good a way as any to look at life in a free society.

I should begin by saying that Americans don't live in a free society, although most of them think they do. True, we live in a relatively free society. Americans are relatively free compared to the citizens of North Korea, Cuba, Myanmar, Nepal, Saudi Arabia, and Venezuela. But this doesn't mean that we live in a free society. Not when you need a permit to have a garage sale, not when you need a salt-water fishing license, not when you can go to jail for purchasing too much Sudafed to relieve your stuffy nose, not when you need a license to cut hair, not when you can be arrested for reselling a concert ticket, not when the government reads your e-mails and listens to your phone calls.

A free society is a libertarian society, a free-market society, a private property society.

It is not a society where chaos reigns and everyone just does what he pleases. It is not a "war of all against all" where life is "nasty, brutish, and short." A free society is a society where property rights are supreme and respected.

In a free society, dog lovers, dog haters, and everyone in between— including those who rely on service dogs—can get along just fine. It is what we have now that results in conflict.

Just this month, at a Whole Foods store in Texas, a man claims he was humiliated after he and his service dog were kicked out of the store. The police were called when the man supposedly refused to leave the store. According to a spokesperson for Whole Foods, the company

> has a "no pets" policy, but welcomes service animals and complies with all applicable ADA guidelines. We immediately contacted our local store once notified of the situation and learned the customer informed our store team that the dog was a "search and rescue" animal. Since our policy only per-mits service animals to accompany shoppers, the customer's dog was not allowed inside our store. We've reached out to the customer directly to see if there was a misunderstanding.

The Americans with Disabilities Act (ADA) has standards that relate to service dogs. The U.S. Department of Justice, Civil Rights Division, Disability Rights Section, asks and answers 37 questions in its "Fre-quently Asked Questions about Service Animals and the ADA." Evi-dently, a person can bring a service dog with him through a salad bar or other self-service food line, not be restricted to "pet-friendly" rooms in hotels, bring more than one service animal into a public place, bring a ser-vice dog with him in an ambulance, and file a complaint with the Justice Department as well as a private lawsuit in federal court if they feel they have been discriminated against for having a service dog.

In a free society, it is property owners who decide whether they will allow guide dogs leading the blind to enter their property—not the gov-ernment.

In a free society, it is property owners who decide whether they will allow service dogs to enter their property—not the government.

In a free society, it is property owners who decide whether they will allow any other dogs to enter their property—not the government.

It doesn't matter if someone suffers from some mental or physical aliment, impairment, disability, or handicap: Even if someone is blind or an injured war veteran, there is no natural right for anyone to bring a dog with him on someone else's property—or breastfeed a child, use profanity, wear a shirt with an offensive message, smoke a cigarette, or be scantily clad.

Not in a free society.

This is because—in a free society based on respect for property rights— no one has a natural right to enter anyone else's property even if he is childless, has impeccable manners, is modestly dressed, doesn't smoke, and doesn't have a dog with him.

This is what people don't get. But freedom of association, discrimination, and partiality are part and parcel of a free society. And it doesn't just apply to individuals. In a free society, business, which are owned by individuals or groups of individuals, would have the same property rights as individuals—including the rights to refuse service and establish a dress code and standards of conduct for employees and customers that are on their property.

The domain of government regulation of service dogs and anything else should be strictly limited to public; that is, government property, like parks, schools, libraries, and pools that are owned and operated by the government. Business establishments open to the public are not "public places" or "public facilities" or "public accommodations." They are still private property. It is an illegitimate purpose of government to regulate private businesses.

But it should be pointed out that even a business owner who hates all manner of dogs—guide, service, or otherwise—might not choose to prohibit them in his stores. In fact, he might advertise that all dogs are welcome in his stores.

This is the beauty of the free market. In a free society, business owners would have to weigh the costs and benefits of allowing or not allowing in their places of business guide dogs for the blind, service dogs for the disabled, and dogs in general.

What characterizes a free society? In a free society, individuals and businesses make their own decisions based on customs, traditions, preferences, and the market. In an authoritarian society, the government makes the decisions based on lobbying, complaints, and the caprice of bureaucrats—and enforces its decisions with badges and guns.

By the way, I still don't think I have ever seen a guide dog leading the blind.

*****

DO AMERICANS LIVE IN A FREE SOCIETY?

Whenever I hear someone say that U.S. troops fighting overseas somewhere, anywhere—it doesn't matter where—are defending our freedoms, it makes me want to vomit, and for two reasons.

The troops aren't defending anything. They are engaging in offense: intervening, violating, invading, occupying, killing, maiming, destroying, and making widows and orphans. This I have written about scores of times.

But there is another reason hearing that the troops are defending our freedoms makes me nauseated. The troops couldn't possibly be defending our freedoms because we don't live in a free society. What are these freedoms that the troops are defending? It seems as though the more the U.S. military intervenes in other countries the more freedoms that Americans lose.

Although we don't live in a free society, most Americans think they do. They sing that they are proud to be an American "where at least I know I'm free." They sing the national anthem and roar when it comes to the line about America being "the land of the free."

Oh sure, Americans are free compared with the citizens of North Korea, Sudan, Myanmar, Yemen, Saudi Arabia, and Venezuela, but there are 190 other countries in the world. The terrible truth is, we live in a *relatively* free society when compared with people in many other countries. The American people are *relatively* free when compared with people in Thailand, Egypt, the Republic of the Congo, Turkmenistan, Cuba, Nepal, Vietnam, and Pakistan.

But this doesn't mean that the United States is the freest country in the world, although most Americans would say that it is.

Even when it comes to economic freedom—where you would expect the United States to come out on top—America is not even in the top ten. The latest edition of The Index of Economic Freedom, compiled by The Heritage Foundation and The Wall Street Journal to measure the degree of economic freedom in the world's countries, ranks the United States number 11 in economic freedom—behind Ireland and Estonia. According to the Fraser Institute's Economic Freedom of the World, which aims to identify how closely the institutions and policies of a country correspond with a limited government ideal, the United States ranks even lower at number 16—just above Romania.

And when you look at things other than economic freedom, the United States drops even further. In the Freedom of the Press report published by Freedom House, the United States ranks below countries like Estonia, Costa Rica, Barbados, Canada, and New Zealand, as well as most of the countries in Western Europe. In the Press Freedom Index compiled by Reporters Without Borders, the United States is ranked number 41—behind countries like Cyprus, Iceland, Ireland, Belgium, Latvia, Uruguay, and Ghana.

So, when someone says that Americans live in a free society, you have to ask: compared to what?

Do Americans live in a free society when they need to get a permit to have a garage sale?

Do Americans live in a free society when the government listens to their phone calls?

Do Americans live in a free society when police issue tickets to motorists for not wearing seatbelts?

Do Americans live in a free society when they need a salt-water fishing license?

Do Americans live in a free society when the United States is the only developed country in the world with a drinking age of 21?

Do Americans live in a free society when they can go to jail for purchasing too much Sudafed to relieve their stuffy nose?

Do Americans live in a free society when they have to be scanned, groped, and forced to throw out tubes of toothpaste over 3.4 ounces before they can board an airplane?

Do Americans live in a free society when police can break down your door in the middle of the night and drag you out of bed if you are suspected of having illegal drugs in your home?

Do Americans live in a free society when beer brewed at home cannot be sold and the amount of beer one can brew is restricted?

Do Americans live in a free society when the government regulates the size of the holes in Swiss cheese?

Do Americans live in a free society when it is illegal to resell a concert ticket?

Do Americans live in a free society when the government reads their e-mails?

Do Americans live in a free society when they are limited to six withdrawals from their savings accounts per month?

Do Americans live in a free society when police drive around in unmarked older vehicles to ensnare unsuspecting motorists?

Do Americans live in a free society when in many states, no alcoholic beverages of any kind can be sold before a certain time on Sunday?

Do Americans live in a free society when the government regulates the amount of water that toilets are allowed to flush?

Do Americans live in a free society when the United States has one of the highest per-capita prison populations in the world?

Do Americans live in a free society when the Supreme Court has said that police can "strip-search individuals who have been arrested for any crime before admitting the individuals to jail, even if there is no reason to suspect that the individual is carrying contraband."

Do Americans live in a free society when in many states it is illegal for car dealers to be open on Sunday?

Do Americans live in a free society when police can perform forcible DNA, urine, and blood extractions?

Do Americans live in a free society when there are a myriad of federal and state laws that restrict, regulate, or prohibit gambling?

Do Americans live in a free society when they need a license to cut someone's hair?

Do Americans live in a free society when the government seizes more assets from Americans than the amount of money taken in burglaries?

Do Americans live in a free society when they collectively spend more in taxes than they do on food, clothing, and housing combined?

Do Americans live in a free society when they can be locked in a cage for possessing too much of a plant the government doesn't approve of?

And then, to add insult to injury, we also live in a nanny state. We have a government full of politicians, bureaucrats, and regulators, and a society full of statists, authoritarians, and busybodies, who all want to use the force of government to impose their values, hinder personal freedom, remake society in their own image, restrict economic activity, compel people to associate with people they may not want to associate with, and limit the size of soft drinks you can purchase at a convenience store.

Yet, most Americans think that because they can find fifty varieties of salad dressing at the grocery store, choose from among a hundred types of wine at the liquor store, select a television channel from over 1,000 choices, download any movie or song they want from the Internet, and sit at home for hours playing the latest video game that they live in a free society. They are oblivious to the extent of government encroachment on their freedoms. They are complacent when it comes to government edicts. And they are ignorant as to what a free society really means.

Wake up, and don't be one of them. And don't settle for less than a genuinely free society.

*****

IS THERE A CONSTITUTIONAL RIGHT TO BIRTH CONTROL?

The junior senator from New Jersey, Democrat Cory Booker, recently introduced a bill "to establish certain duties for pharmacies to ensure provision of Food and Drug Administration-approved contraception, and for other purposes." An offhand remark by one of the bill's co-sponsors is an ideal segue to the question of the role of government in relation to private, peaceful activity.

The Access to Birth Control Act (S.2960) finds, among other things, that there have been reports of pharmacists who refuse to fill prescriptions for contraceptives in twenty-three states and the District of Columbia, even though "access to legal contraception is a protected fundamental right in the United States and should not be impeded by one individual's personal beliefs."

The bill therefore mandates that "a pharmacy that receives Food and Drug Administration-approved drugs or devices in interstate commerce" shall provide upon request of a customer a contraceptive that is in stock "without delay." If a customer requests a contraceptive that is out of stock, the pharmacy must "immediately" inform the customer and "without delay" either (depending on customer preference) refer the customer to another pharmacy that stocks the contraceptive or "obtain the contraceptive under the pharmacy's standard procedure for expedited ordering of medication and notify the customer when the contraceptive arrives."

Pharmacies must also ensure that their employees do not harass customers requesting contraception, obstruct the delivery of services relating to a request for contraception, deceive customers about the availability of contraception, breach medical confidentiality with respect to a request for contraception, or refuse to fill a prescription for contraception.

A pharmacy found in violation is liable for a civil penalty "not exceeding $1,000 per day of violation," but "not to exceed $100,000 for all violations adjudicated in a single proceeding."

The bill is co-sponsored by seventeen Democratic senators and presidential candidate Bernie Sanders, an Independent.

One of the bill's co-sponsors, Sen. Timothy Kaine of Virginia, told a local television station that he's co-sponsoring the bill because "if it's a constitutional right, you should be entitled to seek this kind of medical care and not have arbitrary barriers put in your way."

There are so many questions that this bill raises that I almost don't know where to begin.

Why does the Food and Drug Administration alone have the right to approve drugs or devices?

Where does the Constitution authorize the federal government to have a Food and Drug Administration?

Why is a doctor's prescription needed to purchase approved drugs or devices?

Why must drugs or devices be purchased only at pharmacies?

Will this bill lead to the government's mandating that certain contraceptives be stocked by pharmacies?

Is there a right to be served by a particular business?

Why must pharmacists be licensed?

If a bill mentions "interstate commerce" to appear constitutional, does that make it so?

Where does the Constitution authorize the federal government to have anything to do with birth control?

Where does the Constitution authorize the federal government to have anything to do with medical care?

What business is it of the government to establish certain duties for pharmacies and pharmacists?

Is there a constitutional right to birth control?

It is that last question that I want to focus on.

Of course there is no constitutional right to birth control. How could there be? The Constitution not only doesn't mention any form of birth-control device, it likewise doesn't contain any reference to medical care, pharmacies, pharmacists, physicians, sex, drugs, or even rock and roll.

However, that does not mean that Americans don't have the right to manufacture, buy, sell, or use birth control. Merely because a right is not explicitly mentioned in the Constitution, it doesn't follow that it doesn't exist. The Constitution doesn't grant rights; the Constitution guarantees rights. Rights that the government gives, the government can take away. The Constitution specifically guarantees certain natural rights, imposes limits on the government's power, and explicitly declares that all powers not delegated to the federal government by the Constitution are reserved to the states or the people. That the government does not now follow its own Constitution is true but irrelevant.

Americans have the natural right to manufacture, buy, sell, or use birth control—just as they have the natural right to manufacture, buy, sell, or use any product in a peaceable manner that doesn't threaten or injure someone else. They don't have the natural right to purchase birth control at taxpayer expense. They also don't have the natural right to purchase birth control from someone who doesn't want to sell it to them. If a pharmacist—for some religious reason (or any reason)—doesn't want to fill a particular prescription for contraception, then that is between him and the pharmacy that employs him. It is not the role of government to adjudicate such disputes.

Although Americans have the legal right to birth control, such was not always the case. There were once laws in the United States against the mailing, sale, and use of birth-control devices. In 1961, the state of Connecticut still had such a law. It was challenged when the Planned Parenthood League of Connecticut Executive Director Estelle Griswold and a physician opened a birth-control clinic on November 1, 1961. They were both arrested, tried, found guilty, and fined $100. The conviction was upheld by the Connecticut Appeals and Supreme Courts. The U.S. Supreme Court, in the case of *Griswold v. Connecticut* (1965), declared the Connecticut law unconstitutional, but not on the basis of individual liberty, personal freedom, or private property. The Court declared that the right to contraception (for married couples at least) was based on the right to privacy, which existed because "specific guarantees in the Bill of Rights have penumbras, formed by emanations from those guarantees that help give them life and substance."

This newfound government right to privacy was, of course, very arbitrary, as it still is. The government doesn't care about Americans' personal privacy. Can you distill spirits in the privacy of your own home? Of course not. Can you sell beer or wine that you make in the privacy of your own home? Of course not. Can you have sex for money in the privacy of your own home? Of course not. Can you snort cocaine in the privacy of your own home? Of course not. Can you operate a blackjack game in the privacy of your own home? Of course not. The government doesn't care about Americans' financial privacy either. Try depositing or withdrawing more than $10,000 and your bank must report the transaction to the federal government.

In a free society, private, peaceful activity—even if some consider it to be immoral—is not the business of government. It doesn't matter whether the activity relates to birth control, pornography, prostitution, drug use, deviant sexual practices, gambling, or making and selling alcohol. It is simply not the proper role of government to concern itself with private, peaceful activity that takes place between consenting adults.

Is there a constitutional right to birth control? Of course not. But there is a natural right for willing buyers and willing sellers to exchange any lawfully acquired merchandise for cash without any government interference. There is also a natural right to engage in any peaceful activity on one's property or in the privacy of one's home. There is in a free society. And the Constitution has nothing to do with it.

*****

THE RIGHT TO HIRE AND FIRE

Do businesses have the right to hire whomever they want for a particular job? Most Americans would agree that they certainly do. But when you ask the same people whether businesses have the right to not hire whomever they don't want for a particular job, most of them will say that it depends on the reason someone is not hired. And the same thing is true if you ask the typical American whether businesses have the right to fire whomever they want from a particular job. Most of them will say that it depends on the reason someone is fired.

If you really want to complicate matters when it comes to hiring and firing, just introduce the subject of religion. What role, if any, can or should religion have in the hiring and firing process? Obviously, if someone is interviewing for a position as a minister of some sort, then everyone expects, and everyone accepts, that a Catholic church will hire only a Catholic, a Unitarian church will hire only a Unitarian, a Jewish synagogue will hire only a Jew, an Islamic mosque will hire only a Muslim, and an evangelical church will hire only an evangelical. But other than that, most Americans would say that a person's religious beliefs and practices should never have anything to do with whether someone is hired or fired, while some Americans would continue to say that a person's religious beliefs and practices might have something to do with whether someone is hired or fired.

In a free society, is it possible to be illegally not hired? Is it possible to be unjustly not hired? The first question must always and everywhere be answered in the negative. And of the second question it can only be said, Perhaps in certain situations. However, in a free society, things are not the same when it comes to firing. Is it possible to be illegally fired? Is it possible to be unjustly fired? This time, of both questions it can only be said, Perhaps in certain situations. The other question to be considered is how religion affects the legality and justness of hiring and firing. The short answer is, in a free society, it doesn't.

Much of this runs contrary to the thinking of most Americans, and especially those focused on anti-discrimination laws and religious exemptions instead of freedom and property rights. But first, let's look at some recent firings that did take place and some hirings that didn't.

Firings

A number of high-profile firings have taken place over the past year—many related to religion in some way.

ESPN baseball analyst Curt Schilling was fired in April of this year after commenting in a Facebook post in support of a North Carolina law that bars transgender people from using bathrooms and locker rooms that do not correspond to their birth sex. "ESPN is an inclusive company," said the network in a statement. "Curt Schilling has been advised that his conduct was unacceptable and his employment with ESPN has been terminated."

Also in April of this year, the presiding bishop of the Episcopal Church, Michael Curry, fired two top executives for failing "to live up to the church's standards of personal conduct in their relationships with employees." The deputy chief operating officer and the director of public engagement and mission communications were accused of misconduct and put on administrative leave late last year. The exact complaints against the two men have not been made public.

In February of this year, the University of Missouri board of curators voted 4-2 to fire communications professor Melissa Click for failing to meet the standards expected of faculty members after she was captured on video in a confrontation with a police officer and a student journalist during a campus protest last year over racial issues. She was charged with misdemeanor assault after the skirmish, and had been suspended with pay from the school since January 27. In a statement, Click said she apologized for her behavior but would not apologize for her "support of black students who experience racism at the University of Missouri." Click claims that she was fired without due process when the university's board of curators "overstepped their authority." She has appealed her firing and is now getting support from the American Association for University Professors.

Late last year, Wheaton College, an evangelical liberal arts college of about 3,000 students about an hour west of Chicago, placed on leave one of its political-science professors. Associate Professor Larycia Hawkins was put on paid administrative leave "in order to give more time to explore theological implications of her recent public statements concerning Christianity and Islam." Hawkins had posted on Facebook a statement to the effect that Christians and Muslims worship the same God. She first came to her employer's attention after she wore a hijab (a Muslim veil) as an act of solidarity with Muslims, although the college maintains that her suspension "resulted from theological statements that seemed inconsistent with Wheaton College's doctrinal convictions, and is in no way related to her race, gender, or commitment to wear a hijab during Advent." Following an impasse between the professor and the administration, a "Notice of Recommendation to Initiate Termination-for-Cause Proceedings" was given to Hawkins in January. In February, the college and the professor "found a mutual place of resolution and reconciliation" and "reached a confidential agreement under which they will part ways."

Also late last year, about 150 Muslim workers were fired from their jobs at a Colorado meat-packing plant after staging a walkout after a dispute over the accommodation of prayer in the workplace. Cargill Meat Solutions says it "makes every reasonable attempt to provide religious accommodation to all employees based on our ability to do so without disruption to our beef-processing business." Since 2009, the company has had two "reflection rooms" for prayer at its Fort Morgan plant. The plant employs about 2,000 people, including more than 400 immigrants from Somalia. During a shift on a Friday, eleven employees requested to go to prayer together. After being told that they needed to go in smaller groups, all of the employees went to prayer together, but ten resigned at the end of the shift. On the following Monday, approximately 200 employees refused to show up for work, apparently fearing that the company wasn't allowing some workers to take prayer breaks. Cargill said it fired the workers, after "multiple attempts were made to discuss the situation with local Somali employees and union representatives" without a successful resolution. According to company policy, "Employees that do not show up for work, or call in, for three consecutive days were at risk of termination of their employment."

Hirings

But it's not just firings that have made national news over the past year. Late last year, the Massachusetts Superior Court ruled against a Roman Catholic school in the state that had withdrawn an offer of employment to a man when he identified another man as his husband.

Fontbonne Academy is an all-girls' preparatory high school in Milton,

Massachusetts, sponsored by the Congregation of the Sisters of Saint Joseph of Boston. The school's stated mission is "the education of young women rooted in gospel values and the teachings of the Catholic Church." After Matthew Barrett was hired as the food- service director at the school, he listed his "husband" as an emergency contact person on a "new employee" form. But because hiring someone in a same-sex relationship was deemed to be inconsistent with both the teachings of the Catholic Church and the school's policy that all employees be role models for the students, his employment offer was rescinded. With the help of Boston-based GLBTQ Legal Advocates & Defenders (GLAD), Barrett filed a complaint with the Massachusetts Commission Against Discrimination. The case ended up in Massachusetts Superior Court in May 2014. There, Justice Douglas Wilkins ruled in *Barrett v. Fontbonne Academy* that the school had illegally discriminated against Barrett on the basis of his sexual orientation and gender.

After the decision, Barrett's attorney issued a press release stating, "Religiously affiliated organizations do not get a free pass to discriminate against gay and lesbian people. When Fontbonne fired Matt from a job that has nothing to do with religion, and simply because he is married, they came down on the wrong side of the law." However, the executive director of the Catholic Action League, C.J. Doyle, remarked that "religious freedom consists not merely of the right of worship, but of the right of religious institutions to govern their internal affairs free of state interference." He also commented that the judge's ruling "would compel Catholic institutions to hire those who reject and despise Catholic teaching, fatally impairing the constitutionally protected right of those institutions to carry on their mission. This is precisely the sort of 'excessive entanglement' of government with religion decried and prohibited by the U.S. Supreme Court."

Earlier, there was the case of the Muslim girl who claimed that she wasn't hired for a job at an Abercrombie & Fitch store because she wore a hijab to her job interview. She complained to the Equal Employment Opportunity Commission (EEOC), which filed a lawsuit against Abercrombie. After winning her case at the federal district court level and then losing at the U.S. Court of Appeals, she won an 8-1 U.S. Supreme Court decision against Abercrombie & Fitch in 2015—seven years after she initially applied for the job.

Hiring

As it stands now in contemporary society, if someone from the ever-growing list of protected classes (women, minorities, veterans, handicapped, ex cons, pregnant, elderly, LGBT, et cetera) is not selected for a particular job, ultimately denied employment at some point in the hiring process, or is not interviewed for a job that he has applied for in the first place, he can allege that he was illegally discriminated against and file a complaint against his potential employer with a state or federal "equal-opportunity" agency or commission.

But in a free society, no one could illegally not be hired, ever. That is because no one has the right to any particular job no matter how qualified he is. It doesn't matter how much experience someone has, how much talent he has, how much education he has, how much seniority he has, how much skill he has, how many recommendations he has, or how much knowledge he has—he still doesn't have the right to be offered a particular job. It doesn't matter how healthy he is, how little pay he is willing to work for, how honest he is, how hard a worker he is, how punctual he is, or how much of an asset he would be in some position—he still doesn't have the right to work for a particular company.

That means that, in a free society, business owners, and their agents, have the absolute right of discrimination in hiring. In a free society, employment discrimination must be permissible for any reason: race, creed, color, religion, national origin, ancestry, sexual identity, health, disability, height, weight, sex, age, pregnancy, marital status, sexual orientation, political ideology, ability, experience, education, socio-economic status, criminal record, hair color, facial hair, et cetera. And in a free society, discrimination must be permissible on any basis—including stereotypes, prejudice, hate, "sexism," xenophobia, "homophobism," bigotry, or racism—no matter how insensitive, unfair, erroneous, illogical, irrational, nonsensical, or unreasonable the basis is, or is perceived to be.

And as it relates to religion, in a free society, religious institutions would not need to be granted certain exemptions to allow them to practice discrimination in hiring for positions in which religion is an integral part of the position—like a church minister or a seminary professor. Just as any other business or organization, they would be permitted to discriminate on the basis of religion or anything else for any position—from president on down to janitor—on any basis and for any reason. At least in a free society they would.

But discrimination can work both ways.

While government agencies and public institutions have no business hiring on the basis of some Affirmative Action guidelines—that is, giving preferential treatment to someone on the basis of his race, color, national origin, or ethnic group—it doesn't follow that preferential treatment in hiring on the basis of those or any other criteria couldn't be practiced in a free society by the private sector. If a private entity—from a large corporation on down to a small family business—wanted to hire only people of a particular race, religion, age, or sexual orientation—and discriminate against all others—in a free society it would be perfectly free to do so.

The case of Matthew Barrett, the man in a same-sex relationship who was denied employment by a religious institution, is a simple one. In a free society, the school that interviewed him and offered him a position could ultimately not hire him for any reason or no particular reason. The religious orientation of the school and the sexual orientation of the applicant are irrelevant.

How, then, could someone be unjustly not hired? The only possible way is for some agent of a business owner to disregard any hiring guidelines he is given to follow. Suppose, for example, that a business owner wants an ethnically diverse work force because he reasons that it might be better for business, believes that there is strength in diversity, or thinks it makes a great public-relations statement. But suppose also that the business owner's personnel manager whom he has entrusted to actually do the hiring for the business is a closet racist and disregards the business owner's instructions and hires only applicants who look and sound just like him. Then it might be said that an otherwise qualified applicant was unjustly not hired. But, since no one is entitled to any particular job, in a free society there would be no legal recourse available to the applicant. The disconnect between a business owner's wishes and a personnel manager's practices is an internal company matter. It would be entirely up to the business owner to make sure his wishes are carried out. A personnel manager who does not follow company hiring guidelines could simply be fired. Or could he?

Firing

Just as there is no right to become employed in a particular job, so there is no right to stay employed in a particular job. Yet, the question of firing is somewhat different from that of hiring.

No one objects to someone's being fired "for cause": theft, embezzlement, financial mismanagement, serious violation of some company policy, et cetera. And it is also reasonable that any position at a private company—from a large corporation on down to a small family business—held by any employee—from president on down to janitor—could be protected in some way by a union or employment contract, a tenure or seniority system, certain policies and procedures, or simply an agreement of some kind. Such things are true now, and would be equally true in a free society. But barring any of those situations, the right of an employer to fire an employee is absolute, even without "cause." At least in a free society it would be.

That means that, in a free society, employers would have the right to discriminate against current employees just as they do against potential employees. Employment discrimination would be permissible on any basis and for any reason. Only those whose job is protected in some way would have any legal recourse if they were fired. Only they could be illegally fired.

Now, once someone is employed, it is much less likely that he would be fired because of his race, sex, age, or some other physical characteristic. If an employer had some objection to the way an applicant looked, he would simply not hire him in the first place. But as ridiculous as it sounds, and as uncomfortable to employees as it might be, in a free society, a business owner could conceivably fire one of his employees after waking up one day and deciding to rid his work force of those with red hair or green eyes or tattoos. (It sounds no more ridiculous than that a business might have to enact a quota system and hire personnel on the basis of race or sex to avoid harassment by federal and state anti-discrimination bureaucrats and regulators.) The issues of religion, sexual orientation, health, and other matters that may not be outwardly apparent, would be more likely to cause an employee to lose his job at some point after the hiring process. So again, in a free society, a business owner could conceivably fire one of his employees after waking up one day and deciding to rid his work force of smokers or homosexuals or Presbyterians.

The case of the recent high-profile firing of ESPN baseball analyst Curt Schilling, who some people thought offended transgender persons, is likewise a simple one. Even though Schilling was sacrificed to appease the gods of political correctness, in a free society, businesses have the right to make such sacrifices.

How, then, could someone be unjustly fired? Again, the only possible way is for some agent of a business owner to disregard any firing guidelines he is given to follow. And again, since no one is entitled to any particular job, in a free society there would be no legal recourse available to the employee. It is entirely an internal company matter. All illegal firings are unjust, but not all unjust firings are illegal.

In conclusion, because no one has the right to any particular job, a free society must include the right of employers to hire and fire employees at will, without any interference from the government.

*****

THE FREEDOM TO TRAVEL

One of surest ways to identify a totalitarian state is when a government prevents its citizens from leaving.

The most infamous example of this tyranny is, of course, the Berlin Wall built by communist East Germany to keep its people from fleeing to West Germany. The Berlin Wall was built in 1961 and torn down in 1989. In the meantime, thousands of Germans risked their lives to breech the wall and flee to the West. Over a hundred never made it because they were killed by East German border guards who followed orders to shoot their fellow citizens who were attempting to flee the oppressive communist state.

Even now the repressive governments of some countries require special exit visas for foreigners, guest workers, and visitors. Others go out of their way to do what they can to strongly discourage or prevent their own citizens from leaving. Such is the case in communist North Korea—"the Democratic People's Republic of Korea"—and the communist island "paradise" of Cuba.

Americans look with disdain on the government of any country that has emigration controls—every government but their own.

Until just recently, Americans who wanted to travel to Cuba were prevented from doing so without first establishing that they fit into one of twelve travel categories approved by the U.S. government (e.g., family visits, journalistic activities, professional research and meetings, educational activities, public performances, humanitarian projects, religious activities) and then booking a costly charter flight to the island from Miami or Fort Lauderdale because no regular commercial flights were allowed. Diplomatic relations between the United States and Cuba were severed in 1961 and not reestablished until 2015. In February of 2016, the United States and Cuba signed a deal to restore commercial airline service between the two countries. The first flight occurred on August 31, 2016, when JetBlue flight 387 flew from Fort Lauderdale to Santa Clara. Just recently, almost while the dead body of Fidel Castro was still warm, the first commercial flight from the United States to Havana in more than 55 years landed in Cuba's capital. There are still travel categories, travel restrictions, and spending limits, but several airlines are now making regularly scheduled flights between a number of cities in the United States and several cities in Cuba even as travel to Cuba for tourist activities remains prohibited by law.

This is an outrage. It was an outrage in 1961 when the United States broke diplomatic relations with Cuba and then imposed an embargo, and it is an outrage now even though diplomatic relations have been restored.

Now, before continuing, let me be perfectly clear. Fidel Castro was a bad guy. After his death, President Obama spoke of "the countless ways in which Fidel Castro altered the course of individual lives, families, and of the Cuban nation." Castro certainly did alter the course of these things— but, as Obama neglected to say, it was to the detriment of individual lives, families, and the Cuban nation.

The U.S. State Department says about Cuba:

> Cuba is an authoritarian state that routinely employs repressive methods against internal dissent and monitors and responds to perceived threats to authority. These methods may include physical and electronic surveillance, as well as detention and interrogation of both Cuban citizens and foreign visitors. Human rights conditions in Cuba remain poor, as the Cuban government limits fundamental freedoms, including freedom of expression and

peaceful assembly.

Recent descriptions of Castro and life in Cuba can be found here, here, and here:

> Under Castro's control, all forms of political dissent were severely punished. Those who dared to speak out became political prisoners and were sent away to horrific prisons, some never to be heard from again. Journalists who were caught attempting to report the truth were dismissed as "mercenaries" working for the United States government and were tried in secret tribunals.

> In the cities, the people live in squalor of communal apartments literally falling apart as they have not been properly maintained since 1959. In many old high rises that I have visited, elevators and indoor plumbing was gone and the buildings were surrounded by primitive outhouses.

> Castro was one of the most tyrannical dictators in the world. After taking power in 1959, he refused to permit democratic elections, suppressed dissent, censored the news, and controlled travel. And, of course, Castro was a communist or socialist. As president, he imposed a socialist economic system on the island, which entailed the nationalization of all private property. Most everyone became an employee of the state.

But as bad as Castro was, that still doesn't justify the U.S. government restricting the freedom of Americans to travel to Cuba.

In a free society, any American would have the right to travel to any country by any means for any reason for any period of time and spend any amount of his money while he is there.

It doesn't matter if the country is ruled by a brutal dictator. It doesn't matter what the leaders or the people of the country think of America, Americans, or the American government. It doesn't matter how the government of the country oppresses its people. It doesn't matter if the country has little chance of becoming more democratic in the near future. It doesn't matter if the country forbids its citizens from traveling to the United States. It doesn't matter how tyrannical the country's government is. It doesn't matter if the country is communist. It doesn't matter if the country is a police state. It doesn't matter if the country punishes dissent. It doesn't matter if the country has jails full of political prisoners. It doesn't matter if the country commits massive human rights violations. It doesn't matter if the country supports terrorism around the globe. It doesn't matter if every other country in the world prohibits its citizens from traveling to that country.

Now, I don't know why any American would want to go to a country characterized by some of these things, but that is not the point. The point is that Americans in the "land of the free" should have the freedom to travel—anywhere. It is individual Americans and American businesses that should have the liberty to decide whether they want to visit, do business with, or do business in Cuba.

The trouble is, Americans don't live in a free society, although most Americans think they do. Americans live in a relatively free society, as I explained here. Just because there is no wall to keep Americans in, and just because Americans are free to travel to most countries in the world, doesn't mean that they have the freedom to travel—not if they have to jump through a maze of hoops to get to a country 90 miles away from Miami.

I would be remiss if I failed to mention two things related to the freedom to travel.

With freedom comes responsibility. Americans who travel to a country with an authoritarian government travel at their own risk. They can't expect the U.S. government to send in the Marines should they get in trouble.

I am speaking only about emigration, not immigration. The freedom to travel doesn't mean the freedom to trespass.

Instead of worrying about violations of freedom around the globe and wanting the U.S. government to "do something" about them, Americans should demand freedom from their government to travel to any country they wish, for business or pleasure.

*****

TRUMP SENDS PROPERTY RIGHTS UP IN FLAMES

Alongside of Catholicism and Protestantism, the primary religion in the United States is not Islam or Judaism but the American civic religion. The Pledge of Allegiance is the creed of this religion and the American flag is its chief symbol.

In the American civic religion, the worst sin that an American can commit is to refuse to pledge allegiance to the flag or to desecrate it. Federal law contains numerous provisions regarding the use, handling, display, and disposal of the flag.

After some college students recently burned American flags on their campuses, President-elect Donald Trump tweeted, "Nobody should be allowed to burn the American flag—if they do, there must be consequences—perhaps loss of citizenship or year in jail!"

Outrageous statements like that from Trump are commonplace and can ordinarily be ignored. But this one is different. The main problem with Trump's flag-burning statement is that many Americans—especially many flag-waving conservatives—no doubt agree with him that nobody should be allowed to burn the American flag.

There are a number of problems with Trump's statement regarding flag-burning, and one in particular that is not being addressed.

First of all, the government cannot strip from a natural-born American citizen his citizenship just because he commits a crime. In the case of *Trop v. Dulles* (1958), the U.S. Supreme Court ruled that citizenship is not a license that expires upon misbehavior. Citizenship can only be voluntarily renounced. I note also that mass murderers and those who try to assassinate presidents are not stripped of their citizenship. It is nonsensical that they could retain their citizenship while flag-burners are stripped of theirs. But that is not the only thing that is nonsensical. What would happen to an American who is stripped of his citizenship? Would he be deported for being an illegal alien? Where would he be sent? What if no country would take him? Could he stay in the United States if he was issued a green card or a visa?

Second, in some cases, the government considers it perfectly proper to burn an American flag. According to U.S.C., Title 36, Chapter 10, §176(k), "The flag, when it is in such condition that it is no longer a fitting emblem for display, should be destroyed in a dignified way, preferably by burning."

Third, flag-burning (unless it violates someone's rights while it is being done)—like gambling, prostitution, ticket-scalping, and not wearing a seatbelt or helmet—is a crime in search of a victim. Every real crime needs a tangible victim with measurable damages. The only thing harmed by burning a flag other than a piece of cloth is someone's sensibilities.

Fourth, the Supreme Court already decided the flag-burning issue more than twenty-five years ago. Criminal penalties for acts of flag desecration were once contained in state and federal law. They were struck down in the case of *Texas v. Johnson* (1989). In 1984, Gregory Johnson burned an American flag in front of the Dallas City Hall in protest of Reagan administration policies. He was tried and convicted under a Texas law against flag desecration, sentenced to one year in jail, and fined $2,000. The Texas Court of Criminal Appeals reversed the conviction and the state of Texas appealed to the Supreme Court, which ruled in Johnson's favor. The Court ruled that flag-burning was symbolic speech protected under the First Amendment. Congress responded by passing the Flag Protection Act of 1989, which stated that "whoever knowingly mutilates, defaces, physically defiles, burns, maintains on the floor or ground, or tramples upon any flag of the United States shall be fined under this title or imprisoned for not more than one year, or both." The Flag Protection Act was then struck down by the Supreme Court in the case of *United States v. Eichman* (1990). Shawn Eichman and others burned an American flag on the steps of the U.S. Capitol after the Flag Protection Act took effect. Although charges against Eichman and the others were dismissed by a federal district judge, U.S. attorneys appealed to the Supreme Court, which ruled in Eichman's favor. The Flag Protection Act was declared unconstitutional because "its asserted interest is related to the suppression of free expression and concerned with the content of such expression."

Since that time, Congress has come close to passing a proposed amendment to the Constitution to circumvent the Supreme Court and criminalize flag-burning. A resolution for such an amendment was actually passed several times in the House, but always failed in the Senate. It should be noted that this is a bipartisan issue—on both sides. In 2003, Republican House member Ron Paul opposed a flag-burning amendment on the House floor. In 2005, Democrat Hillary Clinton, who was then a senator from New York, co-sponsored a bill, as an alternative to a constitutional amendment, to ban flag-burning in some situations.

Fifth, and most important, laws to prohibit flag-burning violate property rights. In spite of the rulings of the Supreme Court, flag-burning has nothing to do speech, expression, the First Amendment, or even flags, and everything to do with property.

In a free society, anyone can burn anything he owns on his own property. But, for the sake of argument, and because of Trump's controversial remarks about flag-burning, we can use the example of a flag.

In a free society—

• It is lawful for anyone to burn his own flag on his own property.
• It is lawful for anyone to burn his own flag on someone else's property with permission.
• It is lawful for anyone to burn someone else's flag with permission on his own property.
• It is lawful for anyone to burn someone else's flag with permission on someone else's property with permission.
• It is not lawful for anyone to steal a flag from a government entity, business, or individual.
• It is not lawful for anyone to trespass on someone else's property in order to steal, transport, or burn a flag.
• It is not lawful for anyone to commit arson.
• It is not lawful for anyone to burn a flag he owns on public property if in so doing he violates zoning, permitting, pollution, or burning laws.

Whether anyone thinks that burning a flag is desecration, abominable, or unpatriotic is irrelevant. Whatever message that the flag-burner wants to send is irrelevant. Whoever is offended by the sight of a flag's being burned is irrelevant.

Laws against flag-burning are ultimately an attack on property rights. And as former congressman Ron Paul reminds us,

Freedom of speech and freedom of expression depend on property. We do not have freedom of expression of our religion in other people's churches;

it is honored and respected because we respect the ownership of the property. The property conveys the right of free expression, as a newspaper would or a radio station. Once Congress limits property rights, for any cause, no matter how noble, it limits freedom.

Trump is sending property rights up in flames.

*****

PARKING SPACES AND PROPERTY RIGHTS

What do parking spaces have to do with property rights?
Everything.
The Islamic Society of Basking Ridge, "dedicated to providing Islamic religious, educational, cultural and social services to Muslims living or working in Somerset Hills and the surrounding areas," last year sued Bernards Township, New Jersey, several months after its application to build a mosque was denied after more than three years and thirty-nine public hearings.
The stated issue was parking spaces.
The township argued that it was "completely appropriate to insist a mosque provide more off-street parking than a comparably sized church or synagogue because of its unique worship times and traditions."
The Islamic Society's attorney argued that "parking requirements were the tool municipalities used to thwart construction of mosques."
Early this year, a federal court ruled in favor of the Islamic Society. U.S. District Judge Michael Shipp stated that "Bernards Township violated the Religious Land Use and Institutional Persons Act by applying a different standard to Muslims." He found that the township's planning board had "unbridled and unconstitutional discretion" because of its vague parking requirements.
Most liberals no doubt applaud the judge's decision because they look to the federal government to stamp out discrimination in every sphere.
Many conservatives no doubt applaud the efforts of any city to prevent Muslims from building a mosque—by any means, legitimate or otherwise.
Libertarians, whatever their religion, personal feelings about Islam, or concern about the construction of mosques in their communities, see an entirely different and much more important issue here: property rights.
The question that only libertarians are asking is a simple one: who should decide how many parking spaces someone has on his own property?
In a free society, the owner or owners of a business or organization decide how many parking spaces they will provide for themselves, patrons, and guests. Although this principle is a simple one, it serves as the foundation of a free society. In a free society, property owners not only

decide how many parking spaces they will provide, but the nature of the parking spaces. It is the property owner who should determine how many parking spaces, if any, should be reserved for the handicapped, pregnant women, parents with young children, employees, the elderly, the sick, veterans, or valet parking. It is the property owner who should determine how wide the parking spaces are. It is the property owner who should determine the color and dimensions of the lines around the parking spaces—or even if there are to be any lines. It is the property owner who should determine whether parking bumpers should be installed, what color they will be, and what material they will be made out of. This doesn't mean that there couldn't be privately established standards and guidelines for these things. It just means that, ultimately, in a free society, it is property owners who should decide these things—not the government.

This fundamental principle extends far beyond parking spaces.

In a free society, property owners decide whom they allow to enter their property.

In a free society, property owners decide whom they will prohibit from entering their property.

In a free society, business owners decide whom they will serve.

In a free society, employers owners decide whom they will hire.

In a free society, employers owners decide whom they will fire.

In a free society, property owners decide whom they will sell or rent to.

In a free society, business owners decide the dress code and standard of conduct for customers.

In a free society, employers owners decide if employees are allowed to wear head coverings or have facial hair.

In a free society, organizations decide whom they will hire as leaders.

In a free society, organizations decide whom they will admit as members.

In a free society, organizations decide whom they will exclude as members.

In a free society, businesses decide what their prices will be—even after a flood or a storm.

In a free society, businesses decide what products they will sell.

In a free society, businesses decide to whom they will offer their products for sale.

In a free society, businesses decide what interest rates they will charge.

In a free society, employers decide the minimum rate of pay they will offer.

In a free society, employers decide the rate of overtime pay they will offer, if any.

In a free society, employers decide whether they will offer health insurance.

In a free society, property owners decide what speech is allowed on their property.

In a free society, property owners decide whether guns are allowed on their property.

In a free society, businesses decide if they will have a smoking section.

In a free society, businesses decide if they will be open on Sunday.

In a free society, businesses decide their operating hours.

In a free society, businesses decide at what time they will begin serving alcohol on Sundays.

In an authoritarian society, the government decides these things.

A free society is a society based on respect for property rights.

*****

WHY SHOULD SOMEONE DIE WAITING FOR A KIDNEY?

The war on drugs is insidious. A kidney patient in Maine has been taken off a transplant wait list for using medical marijuana, even though both the medical and recreational use of marijuana is legal in Maine.

Garry Godfrey has Alport Syndrome, a hereditary disease which causes renal failure at a young age. He suffers from debilitating pain, nausea, and anxiety, which he treats with medical marijuana. "I've tried so many pharmaceuticals and none of them worked, but the medical cannabis does," he said. "It helps me function. It helps me take care of my kids." "You should not be discriminated against for the type of medicine you choose," he added.

Godfrey was put on Maine Medical Center's kidney transplant list in 2003. In 2010, Maine Medical Center adopted a new policy that "prohibits transplant candidates from using marijuana, due to the risk of an invasive fungal infection known as Aspergillosis." Godfrey says he was informed of the new policy and taken off the transplant list.

The hospital says that "once off marijuana, patients can requalify and get put back on the hospital's wait list." State lawmakers are considering a bill that would prohibit Maine hospitals from "rejecting transplant patients solely for using medical marijuana." Godfrey even testified in support of the bill, which is now in committee.

It is a shame that using marijuana—even for medical reasons—may ruin your life. It is an outrage that it may cost you your life. Not, of course, because of the marijuana, but because of society's reaction to the use of marijuana.

Let's assume for a moment that the risk of infection is the sole reason that the hospital took Garry Godfrey off its kidney transplant list. Since I am not a physician, I will not comment on the risk of fungal infections or whether the hospital is telling the whole truth about marijuana. But let's assume that the risk of infection is extremely high and it is really a bad idea for a kidney transplant patient to use marijuana. And let's further assume that marijuana is not only perfectly legal, but has no stigma associated with its use.

Under these circumstances, what could possibly be wrong with this situation?

Plenty, and it has nothing to do with marijuana.

Mr. Godfrey has been waiting for a kidney since 2003. Why? Why can't he just buy one from a willing donor or the family of a deceased individual? Because the federal government won't let him. Why can't some philanthropist just buy one from a willing donor or the family of a deceased individual? Again, because the federal government won't let him.

In 1984, Congress passed the National Organ Transplant Act (NOTA) to outlaw the sale of body organs and established the Organ Procurement and Transplantation Network (OPTN) to facilitate the procurement of such organs. The program is administered by the United Network for Organ Sharing (UNOS), a non-profit organization.

According to the NOTA: "It shall be unlawful for any person to knowingly acquire, receive, or otherwise transfer any human organ for valuable consideration for use in human transplantation if the transfer affects interstate commerce." The penalty is a fine of $50,000 or up to five years in prison, or both. The Senate Report accompanying NOTA stated that "human body parts should not be viewed as commodities."

There are three things that need to be said about this.

First of all, overseeing the procurement of bodily organs is an unconstitutional and illegitimate function of government that could be handled entirely and more efficiently by the private sector on the free market.

Second, as Judge Napolitano wrote in *It Is Dangerous to Be Right When the Government Is Wrong: The Case for Personal Freedom*: "By preventing the buying and selling of organs, the government is making it extremely difficult to find sufficient organ donors because there are zero incentives to donate."

Third, and most important, do you own your own body? If there is anything that the poorest man owns it is his own body. Anyone should be able to do what he wants with his own body as long as his activities are peaceful, his interactions are consensual, his associations are voluntary, and he doesn't violate the personal or property rights of anyone else. And if you own your own body, then you certainly also own the organs in your body.

If you can't use the medicine you want without the government's permission, then you don't own your own body, the government does. If you can't ingest any substances you want without the government's permission, then you don't own your own body, the government does. If you can't sell any part of your own body without the government's permission, then you don't own your body, the government does. If you can't do what you wish with your own body without the government's permission, then you don't own your own body, the government does.

In a free society, your body belongs to you—not the government. But Americans don't live in a free society, do they?

*****

THERE IS NO RIGHT TO BREAST-FEED

A Virginia woman did what she normally did when her 19-month-old baby was agitated—she breast-fed her. Trouble is, she did it in church, and she did it uncovered. Now she feels like her "rights as a mom have been violated" because the church objected. Is there a right to breast-feed in a church? Is there a right to breast-feed in public? Is there a right to breast-feed anywhere? Is there a right to breast-feed uncovered? Is there an absolute right to breast-feed?

No.

The Summit Church in Springfield, Virginia, does not allow breast-feeding without a cover because it could make men, teenagers or new churchgoers "uncomfortable." Duh.

When a woman breast-fed her baby in the middle of a church service, she was asked to go to a private room. She declined. She was also told by a woman that the sermon was being live-streamed and that she would not want her to be seen breast-feeding.

The woman then fled the church, "embarrassed and in shock." The next day, she posted on Facebook a video of her breast-feeding her child, "telling viewers what happened and urging women to stand up for breast-feeding." "Breast-feeding is normal," she said. "I have breast-fed in a few different countries. I have breast-fed all over the place," she said. "No one has ever said anything to me."

Now the woman and her attorney "are pressing church leaders to issue a statement and reverse their policy."

Turns out that in Virginia a law was passed in 2015 protecting a woman's right to breast-feed in public. Identical bills were introduced in Virginia's Republican-controlled House (HB 1499) and Senate (SB 1427) "relating to the right to breastfeed in public places." The bills passed without any opposition whatsoever. The governor signed this in law on March 10, 2005, and it became effective on July 1, 2005. The law adds to Title 32.1 of the Code of Virginia "a chapter numbered 17, consisting of a section numbered 32.1-370, as follows":

CHAPTER 17.
BREASTFEEDING.
§ 32.1-370. Right to breastfeed.

> A mother may breastfeed in any place where the mother is lawfully present, including any location where she would otherwise be allowed on property that is owned, leased, or controlled by the Commonwealth in accordance with § 2.2-1147.1.

Before passage of this law, Virginia law guaranteed mothers the right to breast-feed on state-owned property or any public place without violating the state's indecent exposure law.A mother may breastfeed in any place where the mother is lawfully present, including any location where she would otherwise be allowed on property that is owned, leased, or controlled by the Commonwealth in accordance with § 2.2-1147.1.

The church said it "was not aware of the law and would look into it."

A similar incident recently happened in North Carolina. There a judge told a women in his courtroom who was breast-feeding her son:

> Ma'am, you need to cover up. For you not to realize that is absolutely ridiculous. Step outside, and cover up right now. Stand up, and go, now.

> To nurse the child in the courtroom is just absolutely inappropriate. Now step outside and button up, or whatever you need to do to button up.

Yet, under North Carolina law: "A woman may breast feed in any public or private location where she is otherwise authorized to be, irrespective of whether the nipple of the mother's breast is uncovered during or incidental to the breast feeding."

These laws (like most laws) should never have been passed because there is no right to breast-feed.

Some observations—

Let me say first of all that I consider breastfeeding to be in the best interests of the baby and the mother. Here are 101 reasons why.

Second, like the woman who breast-fed her baby in church, I believe that "breast-feeding is normal." However, urination, defecation, and intercourse are normal, but that doesn't mean that people should be able to do these things in public as long as they clean up their mess.

Third, because I am a man with red blood in my veins, I prefer that I don't, and that my sons don't, see women breast-feeding anywhere uncovered.

Fourth, I have never understood the desire of some women to use breast-feeding as a means to expose themselves.

Fifth, the issue here concerns breast-feeding on private property. Libertarians can argue all day long about what conduct is permissible on public property and at the end of the day never reach a consensus. I am not stepping into that quagmire. I will say that, ideally, all land should be privately owned. In the meantime, public property should be reduced as much as possible. This is something that all libertarians can agree on.

Sixth, no one, including government, has the right to tell anyone what they must allow people to do on their own property.

Seventh, restaurants, stores, and churches are not public property.

And eighth, if government *can* tell you that you must allow women to breast-feed on your property, then what *can't* government tell you that you must allow people to do on your property?

There is no right to breast-feed. There is a right to do what you want on your own property. And there is a right to do what you want on someone's else's property as long as you have permission. That goes for breast-feeding, swearing, smoking, drinking, and wearing a red shirt.

But it works both ways. If you are on someone's property and you see a woman breast-feeding her child uncovered, you have several options: avert your eyes, stare, move to another location on the property, ask her to stop or cover up, or leave the property. You don't have the option to pressure the government to make her stop breast-feeding anymore than she has the option to pressure the government to grant her the right to breast-feed. At least not in a free society.

****